PUBLIC Management:

A Research Handbook

PUBLIC Management:

A Research Handbook

The Author/Editor

Sung Min Park

Daeyoung Moonhwasa Publising Company
Seoul, Republic of korea

PUBLIC Management:

A Research Handbook

The Author/Editor

Sung Min Park

ISBN 978-89-7644-452-3
Published By Chun Hwan Leem
Daeyoung Moonhwasa Publishing Co.
172-2 Chungpa-dong 1-ga, Yongsan-gu, Seoul 140-869, KOREA

TEL (02) 716-3883, (02) 714-3062
FAX (02) 703-3839
Published on 31 July 2013

***Price* KR₩33,000**

About the Author/Editor

Sung Min Park (sm28386@skku.edu) is currently an associate professor in the Department of Public Administration & Graduate School of Governance at Sungkyunkwan University (SKKU). He has also served as assistant professor in the Greenspun School of Environmental and Public Affairs (SEPA) at the University of Nevada in Las Vegas. Park conducts research on management and human resource management in the public sector, focusing on leadership; values and motivations; organizational culture and structure; organizational behavior and performance; human resource development; IT management; and human resource information systems in the public, private, and nonprofit sectors. His academic work appears in *American Review of Public Administration; Review of Public Personnel Administration; International Public Management Journal; Public Personnel Management; International Review of Administrative Sciences; Public Management Review; International Journal of Human Resource Management; and International Review of Public Administration.*

In 2005, Sung Min Park received Sage *Publications' Best Doctoral Conference Paper Award* presented by the Public and Nonprofit Division of the Academy of Management. In 2006, *Bill Collins Award* for the outstanding doctoral student paper was presented to him at the 2006 Southeastern Conference for Public Administration. In 2008, he received the 2007 *Review of Public Personnel Administration (ROPPA) Best Article Award,* conferred jointly by the American Society for Public Administration and Sage Publications. In the same year, he also received the 2007 *Academy of Management (AOM) PNP Division Best Dissertation Award.* In 2013, when he returned to Korea, he received the SKKU-Fellowship (Young Fellow) Award for Excellence in Research and Teaching, conferred by Sungkyunkwan University. Until now, Park has served as a director of the Global MPA Program in the Graduate School of Governance at SKKU and has worked as a managing editor of *Korean Social Science Journal.* He is also serving as a guest reviewer/referee of a wide range of internationally renowned ISI indexed journals. He received his B.A. degree from Yonsei University in 1997 (from the Department of Political Science and International Studies) and his M.I.A. degree from Columbia University in 2002 (from the School of International and Public Affairs). He continued his formal education until 2007 when he received his Ph.D. degree from the University of Georgia (from the Department of Public Administration and Policy in the School of Public and International Affairs).

Preface

This book has been conceptualized as a broad overview of the critical issues, theoretical and practical, involved in public organizations and trends pertaining to their management. The emphasis is on the implication of these issues at both the "micro" (i.e., internal issues) and "macro" (i.e., external issues concerning relations and strategy) levels in an organization. This book also discusses important aspects of effective management in public organizations. Specifically, it looks at various aspects of theories on public organization, management, research and practices, regarding (1) organizational environment; (2) public-private distinctions; (3) structure, design, and technology; (4) leadership, culture, and motivation; and (5) effectiveness of goals.

All articles in the book discuss the theoretical, conceptual, and methodological considerations that are appropriate to each topic; they also provide a critique of existing work on the respective topics. Additionally, they delineate the implications of future theory and research, and reflect on the implications of policy and practice at the individual, organizational, and societal levels. Specifically, this is a research handbook that includes literature on interdisciplinary research pertaining to management of public organizations, and covers several academic disciplines such as psychology, leadership studies, organizational theory/behavior, public values/ethics, and NGO studies. Moreover, it has a multilevel approach, addressing issues from the individual, managerial, organizational, and socio-cultural perspectives. Acknowledging the global and universal nature of issues related to public management, the editor has included research articles from several countries (Korea, China, Indonesia, and the US) and ensured that both the "East and West" have been represented in the book.

Based upon Dr. Rainey's "A framework for Organizational Analysis" (Rainey, 2009, p. 19-23), the 16 empirical studies in this book have been broadly conceptualized, categorized, and arranged according to 8 key themes: (1) Auspices: Public, Nonpublic, and so on; (2) Environments; (3) Leadership; (4) Culture; (5) Structures; (6) Processes; (7) People; and (8) Organizational Performance and Effectiveness. At the end of each section, relevant cases studies have been included in order to give readers access to the key managerial issues in virtual circumstances, and they are followed by a set of discussion questions. The case studies prompt discussion on a number of topics, including but not limited to the administrative environments, authority and structures, managing for effectiveness, leadership and culture, and the relationship between government and nonprofit organizations. For example, the case study in Section 7 has been introduced to illustrate the human element of motivation in public and nonprofit sectors. Some case studies introduce students to the nature and complexities of the management of public organizations and provide an opportunity to explore the competencies required for their effective management. The discussion questions that follow the case studies are linked to the topics illustrated in each chapter. These case studies and questions can be used in class to prompt discussions on key themes or assigned to students as homework. In the Appendix, a different set of public agency websites have been included to guide and facilitate class activities, for example, developing group application project papers and presentations. This book is expected to serve as a useful reference source for academics and researchers, a guide for public managers, policy makers, and practitioners, and as a teaching resource for undergraduate and graduate courses.

Acknowledgements

It requires a somewhat herculean effort to bring together this many expert coauthors from around the world and mesh them between two covers. To bring a book of this magnitude to fruition has required a team of authors committed to the effort of seeing this book come to life. I would like to express my heartfelt thanks to my coauthors who contributed to each of the chapters: Dr. Hal G. Rainey (UGA), Dr. Jessica Word (UNLV), Dr. M. Ernita Joaquin (SFU), Dr. Miao (ZJU), Dr. Hyung Jun Park (SKKU), Seona Kim (SKKU), Min Young Kim (SKKU), and the others. A doctoral student in the Graduate School of Governance at Sungkyunkwan University provided invaluable assistance with this edition. I am thankful to Seona Kim (Ph.D. candidate), my coauthor for Chapter 16, whose academic and editorial work was a major contributor to the accuracy and success of this volume. Her energy, initiative, and creativity are really appreciable. I also owe my gratitude to Chun Hwan Leem (CEO) and other representatives of Daeyoung Moonhwasa Publishing Company who have helped and supported the work on this edition. By the same token, it was a pleasure to work with a Marketing Director like Jae Hoon Jung, who provided us with a lot of information on publishing processes.

Sung Min Park
July 2013
Sungkyunkwan University
Seoul, Korea

Contents

Introduction

The purpose of this handbook is to provide essential knowledge on public management research to readers. It comprises 8 sections, 16 chapters, and an Appendix. **Section 1** distinguishes between public and nonprofit organizations. By probing what makes public and nonprofit agencies distinctive, the two chapters in this section lay the foundation for the book. The topic of *Chapter 1* is the "Intrinsic and Extrinsic Motivation for Public and Nonprofit Managers." The chapter is organized around the following: (1) what the main motivational dimensions and constructs of managers in public and nonprofit sectors are; (2) how these different types of work motivations are related to each other; and (3) what the differences between these sectors are in terms of the level of intrinsic and extrinsic work motivation. *Chapter 2* provides an overview of human resource management in the nonprofit sector and examines (1) job choice motivation, (2) intrinsic and extrinsic motivation, and (3) demographic and organizational factors affecting individuals working in the nonprofit sector. More specifically, drawing upon previous research on career motivation and volunteering, this chapter develops and tests several hypotheses based on (1) the role of individual factors, managerial attributes, and organizational influences in shaping the job choice motivation of nonprofit managers, and (2) the consequences of job choice motivation in terms of the social and professional activities pursued by nonprofit managers outside of work.

Section 2 zooms in on organizational surroundings and the environmental contingencies of public organizations, particularly the philosophical, ideological, and technological environments of public organizations. *Chapter 3* suggests that New Public Management (NPM) and post-NPM reform values are critical environmental factors, which might actually have an enormous influence on the work of public employees. Identifying the configuration of reform values in the federal bureaucracy over a period spanning the last several years, this chapter examines how the values of NPM and its humanist (post-NPM) counterpart have been ingrained in US federal agencies. Similarly, *Chapter 4* discusses the importance of ICT-based environments, focusing on how the adoption of Electronic Human Resource Management (e-HRM) would affect the level of e-HRM acceptance, and how it could create HRM values (i.e., the strategic role of the HRM and HRM service quality) in the public sector.

Two chapters in **Section 3** provide an overview of the leadership theories, practices, and implications relating to other positive job attitudes such as Public Sector Management (PSM), job satisfaction, and organizational trust, etc. Confirming a distinct factor structure for the main variables, such as leadership and PSM, *Chapter 5* affirms how leadership and other contextual factors affect the emotional dimensions and job attitudes of over 6,900 federal employees. This study suggests research and practical implications for future leadership and motivation research in the public sector. From an organizational behavior perspective, *Chapter 6* explores the important nexus between affective and cognitive trust outcomes and the leadership-motivation interface. Utilizing large data sets from the Merit Principles Survey (MPS) and the Best Places to Work (BPTW) survey, as well as drawing upon the scholarly works of several disciplines, this study develops an antecedent-trust model, and analyzes the different antecedents of organizational trust in the public sector in terms of a hierarchical and multi-level ordering structure.

Section 4 deals with the topic of organizational culture and other related issues. The authors posit that certain types of organizational cultures have either positive or negative outcomes vis-à-vis either the effectiveness of the organization or for individual employees within the organization. *Chapter 7*, titled "Determinants of Positive Job Attitude and Behavior in the Asian Work Context: Evidence from Korean Central Government Agencies," discusses the nature of Asian public management/administration in relation to dominant Western models, and analyzes the most crucial features. More specifically, it examines whether hierarchical, centralized, and formalized structures associated with Confucian societies are able to nurture positive job attitudes and behaviors of public employees, as anticipated in Western texts. Similarly, *Chapter 8*, against the backdrop of Chinese organizational culture (e.g., guanxi, Confucianism, collectivism, and Chinese communism), investigates relationships between three types of leadership—servant leadership, ethical leadership, and participative leadership—mediators, and organizational outcomes in the Chinese public sector.

The chapters comprising **Section 5** broadly examine issues related to organizational structures, contexts, systems, and processes in public and nonprofit sectors. Regardless of the types of governing structures, as the authors propose in these chapters, organizations function as informal and formal institutions (or systems) that influence and shape job-related attitudes and administrative behaviors. Especially in the public and nonprofit sectors, the influence of organizational institutions—for example, culture, norms, rules, regulations, and structure—cannot be emphasized enough as key factors in understanding these attitudes and behaviors. In *Chapter 9*, the authors analyze the impact of personal, managerial, and institutional factors (e.g., hierarchical culture, job tenure, and red tape) on the job involvement of public and nonprofit managers. *Chapter 10* concentrates on structural issues that could burgeon from the peculiar Korean public personnel administration system, that is, a rank-based combination of the career civil service and position classification systems. This study also addresses the important consideration of an organizational context, such as PSM and Person-Organization (P-O) fit, for understanding trust and accountability in Korean central government agencies.

Section 6 covers organizational processes and communications in general. For example, drawing on the self-determination theory (SDT) approach, the authors posit in *Chapter 11* that social communication processes (i.e., organizational communication and mentoring socialization) function as important organizational mediators (i.e., intervening to affect the impact of motivations on outcomes) or moderators (i.e., affecting the effect of the mediating), which facilitates the internalization process of extrinsic motivation. Using a broader theoretical perspective (i.e., the principal-agent approach), *Chapter 12* illustrates the overall effects of four different personnel reform systems on the attitudes of public employees. As the author explains, the connection between personnel reform systems and attitudinal outcomes, such as job satisfaction and turnover intentions, are irrefutable. To this end, the author proposes research implications and practical caveats to readers.

Section 7 reviews two empirical studies within the public sector on "how to motivate people" and "how a set of different incentives would work to enhance organizational effectiveness." More specifically, in *Chapter 13* the authors test and measure: (a) The dimensionality of the three commitment constructs, (b) how and to what extent antecedent variables affect the three different commitment variables—affective, normative, and continuance—and (c) how these three commitment values influence several outcome variables differently. *Chapter 14* examines the relationship between the antecedents and consequences of acceptance by employees of performance appraisal systems (APAS) in the public sector. Positioning APAS as a key variable in the proposed research model, the authors investigate factors that potentially affect employee acceptability of performance appraisal systems, hypothesizing that APAS is influenced by the effects of mission congruency, adequacy of rewards, and organizational justice as perceived by employees. In addition, APAS increases job satisfaction and trust in supervisors among employees. Implications of the findings for both public management theory and practice are also highlighted in the chapter.

Section 8, the last section of this handbook, mainly investigates the configuration of organizational performance and effectiveness in the public sector. *Chapter 15* explores how effectiveness and performance values are distributed across government agencies based on three well-known assessment instruments used during the Bush administration: the Office of Management and Budget (OMB) management scorecard, the Performance Assessment Rating Tool (PART), and the Best Places to Work (BPTW) survey. A cluster analysis of the scores from these assessment tools allows us to examine the topography of the agencies in terms of the relationship between the tools and the context of performance, namely the type of mission carried out by the agencies. Finally, the purpose of *Chapter 16* is to probe the main determinants of organizational effectiveness indicators, namely, job satisfaction (JS) and turnover intention (TI), in the public sector as identified in the relevant literature: goal congruence, intrinsic and extrinsic work motivation, and interpersonal trust. Drawing on Simon's two-factor theory, as well as employing a systematic conceptual and empirical model, the authors analyze two dimensions of TI among public employees (i.e., conflictual TI and developmental TI) to identify important antecedents and mediating conditions, in other words the pull factors and push factors of TI.

At the end of this handbook, an **Appendix** lists the websites of major government offices and public institutions in Korea. I hope that readers will find something of interest and will use this appendix to obtain additional information, contacts, and to track emerging issues and policy changes in the public sector.

Reference

Rainey, H. G. (2009). *Understanding and managing public organizations.* San Francisco, CA: Jossey-Bass.

Framework

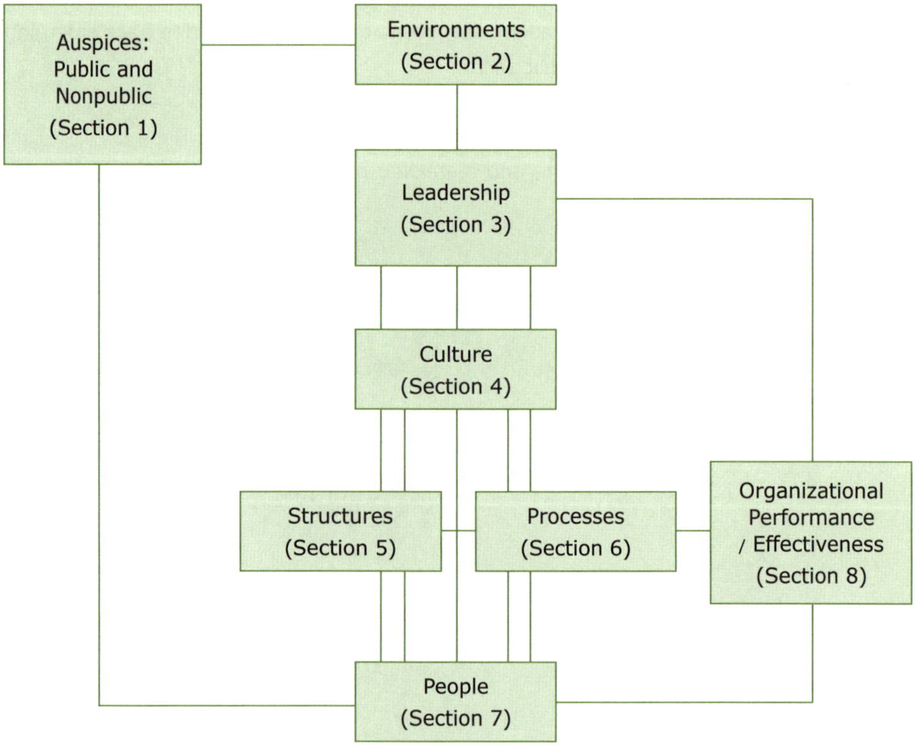
Auspices:
Public and
Nonpublic
(Section 1)
Environments
(Section 2)
Leadership
(Section 3)
Culture
(Section 4)
Structures
(Section 5)
Processes
(Section 6)
Organizational
Performance
/ Effectiveness
(Section 8)
People
(Section 7)

Section 1

Auspices
: Public and Nonpublic

- **Driven to Service**
  : Intrinsic and Extrinsic Motivation for Public and Nonprofit Managers

- **Serving the Mission**
  : Organizational Antecedents and Social Consequences of Job Choice Motivation in the Nonprofit Sector

Section 1

Auspices
(Public and Nonpublic)

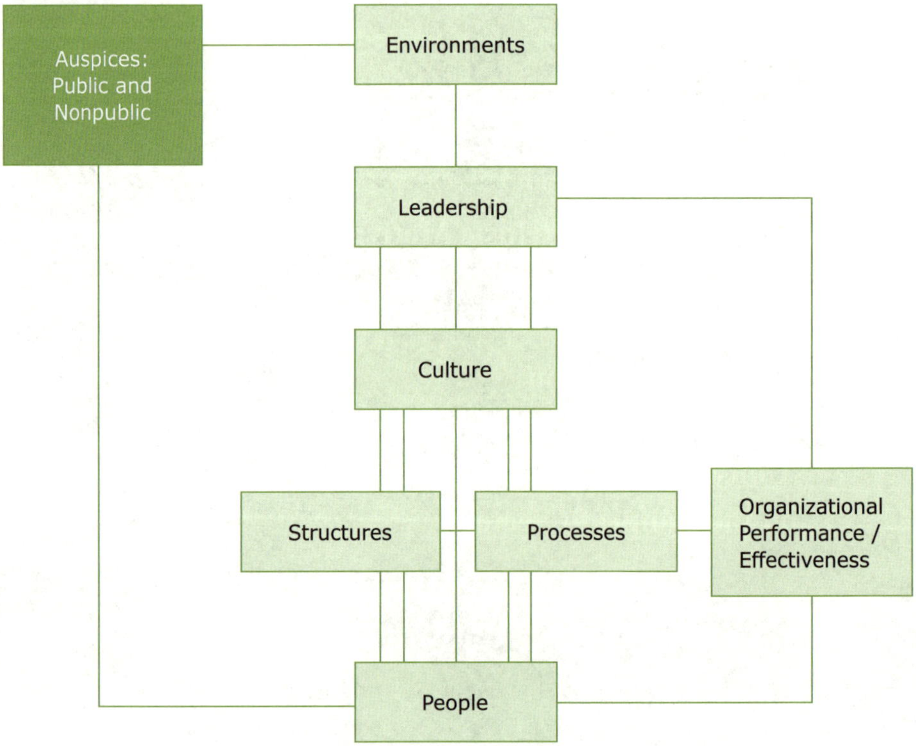

Chapter 1

Driven to Service
: Intrinsic and Extrinsic Motivation for Public and Nonprofit Managers

Summary

This research draws upon a survey of nonprofit and state government managers to examine the role service motivation plays in both sectors. The research addresses three main research questions: 1) What are the main motivational dimensions and constructs of managers in the public and nonprofit sectors? 2) How are these different types of work motivations related to each other? and 3) What differences exist between these sectors in terms of level of intrinsic and extrinsic work motivation? Our findings suggest there are four different motivational constructs and in many ways public and nonprofit managers are similar in terms of the importance of intrinsic rather than extrinsic motivation. While the mean level of extrinsic motivation in the public sector is statistically higher than in the nonprofit sector, certain types of extrinsic motivation such as advancement motivation and WLB motivation are highly correlated with intrinsic motivation in both the public and nonprofit sectors. Finally, directions for future research and practical implications are also discussed.

Keyword

- □ Intrinsic Motivation
- □ Extrinsic Motivation
- □ Public Human Resource Management
- □ Nonprofit Management
- □ Organizational Behavior

Sung Min Park Associate Professor, Sungkyunkwan University
Jessica Word Associate Professor, University of Nevada, Las Vegas

Introduction

In recent years, public service has been broadened to include not only those working directly for government but also other forms of employment serving the community. This has been reflected in the public administration literature through an increased interest in governance rather than government and discussion of complex interrelationships between nonprofits and governments (Brinkerhoff & Brinkerhoff, 2002). Increasingly individuals wishing to serve their communities, choose between the public and nonprofit sectors or move between the sectors over the span of their careers. Traditionally, public administration literature has thought of public service in terms of work for or with a governmental agency (Perry & Wise, 1990). But more recent literature suggests the transfer of service delivery from the public to the nonprofit and for-profit sectors means those serving the public may be employed in a variety of organizations not traditionally examined in public administration literature. The broadening of the term "public service" has implications for how public and nonprofit managers deliver services and how these two linked sectors create communities.

This research seeks to address the motivational relationships and differences between public and nonprofit sector employees in an effort to explore the similarities and differences between the sectors and aid managers in understanding ways to better motivate employees. It has been well established that individuals choosing to work in the public sector are differently motivated than those working in the for-profit sector (Brewer, 2003; Fredrickson & Hart, 1985; Houston, 2006; Wittmer, 1991). However, little empirical research has examined the motivation of those working in the nonprofit sector or the possibility that they may be similarly motivated to their public sector counterparts. Anecdotal and limited descriptive evidence indicate nonprofit employees are in some ways similar to their public sector counterparts and might be motivated by a sense of duty to their communities and a desire to help others (Houston, 2006; Light, 2002; Mann, 2006). It is important to examine this possibility and reveal any possible differences in terms of motivation between managers in these two sectors which might help policy makers find more effective means to deliver public services by taking advantage of motivational differences. This research employs data collected as part of the National Administrative Studies Project III (NASP III) to identify the nature of motivation and confirm the differences between motivational constructs and the consequences of motivation between the two sectors. The primary focus of this paper is to expand our understanding of the differences between the public and nonprofit sector workforces in terms of motivation and examine any underlying differences between the two.

A review of public service motivation literature and existing research concerning the motivation of nonprofit sector workers was conducted in three phases. In Phase 1, drawing on organizational behavior (OB) and human resource management (HRM) perspectives, as well as employing two different factor solution analyses, we explore and confirm whether motivational types and constructs of public and nonprofit managers in the workplace are different and distinct. In phase 2, using correlation analysis, we measure the strength and direction of the relationships between intrinsic and extrinsic motivations. In Phase 3, on the basis of the results from Phases 1 and 2, we also test for statistically significant differences in motivation types between public and nonprofit managers. Specifically, we investigate whether nonprofit managers are more intrinsically and affectively motivated than those individuals working in public agencies. Finally, theoretical and practical implications for comparative motivation research in the public and nonprofit sectors are discussed.

Conceptualization of Work Motivation in Public and Nonprofit Organizations

Motivation is "an umbrella concept that captures the psychological forces that direct, energize, and maintain action (Grant, 2008)." Motivating employees to be both positive and effective in performing their work remains a crucial challenge for managers, and selecting, retaining, and managing highly motivated people are primary human resource (HR) functions. In the public sector, as Robert Behn (1995) suggested, one of the "big questions" of public human resource management is how to enhance employees' work motivation to increase job and organizational performance and effectiveness at the micro-level as well as ultimately pursuing social purposes at the macro-level (Behn, 1995). From a managerial standpoint, employee's and manager's work motivation is one of the determining factors of an organization's development and success. That is, work motivation is directly linked to an employee's perceptions and behaviors, which in turn reflects how well the manager oversees an organization's employees. Public managers and supervisors set the example when it comes to employee motivation. Once a supervisor or personnel manager is motivated to do a good job, their behaviors tend to transfer over to the employees they manage. Public managers and supervisors play the role of leader when it comes to employee motivation. PSM can be effectively managed and enhanced by incorporating PSM into the public sector management systems (Paarlberg, Perry & Hondeghem, 2008).

Reviews of the literature reveal there are different kinds of work motivation; two of these being the main determinants of human behavior in organizations—intrinsic motivation and extrinsic motivation. Especially from the public HR management perspective, public service motivation (PSM) is characterized as a reliance on intrinsic rewards (e.g., sense of accomplishment, reputation for serving the public interest, or duty of a public employee) over extrinsic rewards (e.g., a pay raise, opportunity for advancement, or job security)

(Crewson, 1997; Park & Rainey, 2007). Research has consistently demonstrated that due to recruitment, self-selection, and the process of socialization, public-sector employees are less likely to be interested in extrinsic rewards and more likely to value intrinsic rewards than private sector employees. Public employees tend to be more affectively committed (i.e., committed to the organization's culture and values) and highly motivated by a concern for the community and a desire to serve the public interest or intrinsic values, although some are also motivated extrinsically (Crewson, 1997; Houston, 2000; 2006).

Theoretical Perspectives

Self-Determination Theory (SDT)

Deci & Ryan's self-determination theory (SDT) provides a well-established theoretical framework for understanding an individual's motivation in public and nonprofit organizational settings. SDT suggests intrinsic motivation can be either crowded-in or crowded-out by some specific organizational conditions and social-environmental factors such as rewards and disciplines, work environment and culture, and organizational communication (Deci & Ryan, 2004; Frey, 1997). That is, certain external factors can facilitate or undermine the effects of intrinsic motivation on individuals or organizational outcomes. SDT focuses on "the degree to which human behaviors are volitional or self-determined—the degree to which people endorse their actions at the highest level of reflection and engage in the actions with a full sense of choice (Ryan & Deci, 2000)." SDT posits three different categories of work motivation; 1) amotivation (i.e., inability or unwillingness to participate in normal social situation), 2) extrinsic motivation, and 3) intrinsic motivation.

Within SDT, intrinsic motivation is seen as "the motivational instantiation of the proactive, growth-oriented nature of human beings which is the basis for learning and development (Vansteenkiste, Lens, & Deci, 2006)." Intrinsically motivated employees are more likely to pursue "enjoyment, interest, satisfaction of curiosity, self-expression, or personal challenge" in the work while extrinsically motivated employees seek to obtain "some goals that is apart from the work itself (Amabile, 1993)." Ryan and Deci (2004) also describe the different forms of extrinsic motivation in terms of a continuum, claiming that there are four types of extrinsic motivation, which range from 1) external regulation, 2) introjected regulation, 3) identified regulation or identification, 4) and integrated regulation or integration (from least autonomous to most autonomous motivation), all of which could be differently affected by external and contextual factors (Ryan & Deci, 2004). The third and fourth types of extrinsic motivation (identification and integration) possess a full range of "autonomous" regulations and "internal" (perceived) locus of causality with high degrees of autonomy (see Figure 1). Thus, these types of extrinsic motivation are regarded as autonomous types of motivation, whose characteristics are very similar to intrinsic motivation. Individuals motivated by extrinsic autonomous motivation are expected to be fully internalized and highly self-determined much like individuals motivated intrinsically (Vandenabeele, 2007).

Work motivation of the public and nonprofit employees, in this regard, can be dominantly influenced by an autonomous type of identity regulation based upon internalized public service values (Deci & Ryan, 2004). To differing degrees, within a SDT framework, the social environment (e.g., a job content, job context, and work climate) and individual differences (e.g., autonomous causality orientation) influence work motivation, as well as the organizational behavioral outcomes (e.g., performance, organizational trust and commitment, and job satisfaction) (Frey, 1997). Each of these three categories provides a different idea as to how employees can become self-motivated. This process allows managers to encourage employees to reach within themselves and decide how to adequately handle a work situation, based on their own values, ideas, and perceptions. Overall, SDT should be a valuable overarching research framework to explore the different types of work motivation in the public and nonpublic sectors.

Figure 1. A Self-Determination Theory (SDT) Framework: Intrinsic and Extrinsic Motivation Continuum (Ryan & Deci, 2000)

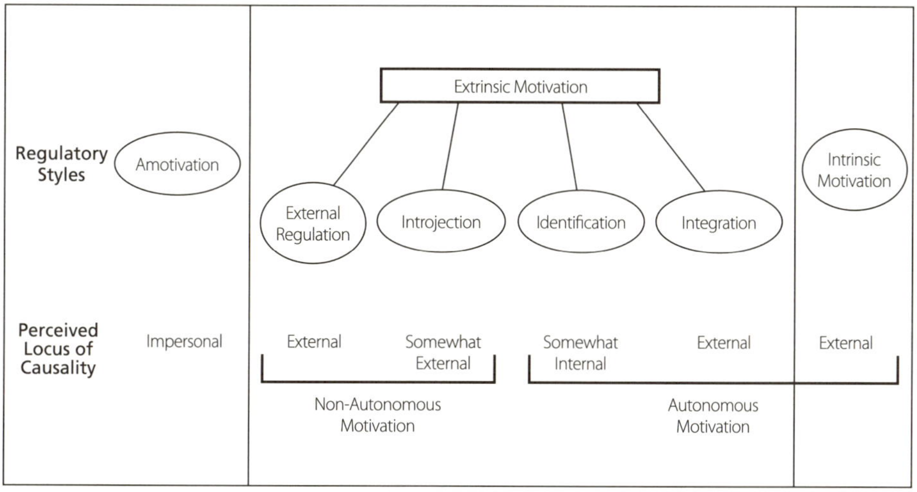

Source: Adapted from Ryan & Deci (2000, p. 61).

Work Motivation in the Public Service

Public service motivation (PSM) is regarded as a specific sub-type of intrinsic work motivation in the public sector, which may "transcend" the public sector (Perry & Hondeghem, 2008). PSM was introduced broadly to the public administration literature in the 1990's and has largely been supported as a unique set of motivational characteristics existing in the public sector (Coursey, 2007). PSM, composed of affective, normative, and rational motives, is an intrinsic, altruistic, and prosocial value set which is closely related to several managerial and organizational outcomes in the public sector (Perry & Wise, 1990). That is, PSM is the "belief, values, and attitudes that go beyond self-interest and organizational interest, that concern the interest of a larger political entity and that motivate individuals to act accordingly whenever appropriate (Vandenabeele, 2009)." PSM studies empirically analyzed the value categories of work motivation in the public sector and found there are two qualitatively and quantitatively different motivational constructs—e.g., intrinsically- or public service-oriented motivation (PSOM) and extrinsically-oriented motivation (EOM). Public service employees are motivated less by extrinsic motivators and more concerned with intrinsic factors, in comparison to private sector employees and managers (Horton & Hondeghem, 2006). PSM and intrinsic motivation, in this regard, theoretically and empirically share common values and orientations especially within the public and nonprofit organizational contexts.

Prior to formal definition of public service motivation many early public administration scholars argued public sector employees were unique in terms of their concern for the public good and their motivation to serve their communities. The empirical research exploring PSM has supported these assertions especially in comparison to for-profit employees that appear to be motivated more by extrinsic rewards (Boyne, 2002; Houston, 2000; Wright, 2001). Prior to the introduction of PSM, rational choice models assumed public employees would simply seek to maximize their own utility by shirking or padding agency budgets but these models failed to explain why public employees achieve. The introduction of PSM has led to a greater emphasis on non-economic rewards of public service. This strain of research has significantly added to our understanding about what makes the public sector unique and how those unique qualities are shaped by public employees. Recent research also found public sector employees are also more engaged in their communities and this engagement leads to other types of prosocial behavior such as volunteering, voting, and blood donation (Houston, 2006). Previous studies also suggest that the current emphases on running government like a business and market based incentive structures might actually backfire and cause a loss of motivation for those with high PSM (Kellough & Lu, 1993).

Since public service motivation mainly describes the intrinsic motivation of public sector workers, it has largely left other types of motivational issues unexplored. We propose that other service motives are also important to understanding public sector employees.

Motivation of public sector employees encompasses other types of work motivation that are not encompassed by the PSM concept or intrinsic motivation (Perry & Hondeghem, 2008). Some public employees are more likely to be extrinsically motivated than others—they are motivated to choose their job as well as committed to their work because of other work conditions such as job security or public sector retirement/benefit plans, monetary compensation, or family-friendly policies. While all these factors are akin to external incentives and rewards, some of these factors may provide employees internalized values especially when the types of motivation are identified regulation or integrated regulation(Ryan & Deci, 2004; 2005).

Work Motivation in the Nonprofit Service

Theories surrounding the motivation of the public sector workforce were introduced at a time when government was still responsible for most direct public service delivery. However, "New Public Management" created an emphasis on "steering rather than rowing" that has dramatically altered the way in which governments deliver services. The traditional model of public services being delivered by government employees protected by civil service provisions only applies to modern public administration in very limited settings. Delivery of many public services is now done through contracts carried out by either for-profit or nonprofit organizations that share some but not all of the characteristics of traditional public service. More recent examinations of public service motivation have tended to include nonprofit human service workers and managers in examinations of PSM without exploring possible underlying differences between the sectors (Lyons, Duxbury & Higgins, 2006).

Paul Light (2002) argues the era of new public management and the increased use of contracting to deliver public goods has created a new multi-sectoral approach to "public service (Light, 2002)." Since, one of the aims of public service motivation literature is to understand what motivates public sector workers to choose their jobs and to find better ways to motivate this workforce; we seek to extend this research to understand what shapes nonprofit sector motivation (NPSM) and compare this to traditional public service. The delivery of public services by nonprofit organizations makes extension of this line of research an important topic to explore for both public and nonprofit managers so that they may find better ways to attract talented employees to the nonprofit sector and better methods to motivate these employees.

Similar to claims made regarding the public sector workforce, theoretical and anecdotal arguments have long persisted that the nonprofit sector labor force is different from the general labor force in important ways. Early theories explaining the existence of nonprofit organizations and motivations for starting such organizations propose individuals starting nonprofit organizations are motivated by the mission, or the work itself rather than the desire for financial rewards (Santora & Sarros, 2001). Additional research has found this leads some managers to choose one sector over another on the basis of personal goals and personality type (Weisbrod, 1988).

Many models of employee motivation rely heavily upon the use of market based incentive systems to promote employee motivation (Moynihan & Pandey, 2007a). The focus on market based incentives includes such tactics as improving pay or pay for performance to motivate employees to achieve in the workforce. Market based incentive structures mainly rely upon extrinsic or tangible benefits. The findings surrounding nonprofit motivation indicate a motivational model contrary to some market based incentive models (Mann, 2006). These theories also suggest that nonprofit employees' performance, like public employee performance, will be negatively impacted by market based incentive structures that crowd out intrinsic motivation.

Many nonprofit theorists have posited prosocial behaviors play a role in motivation of nonprofit employees and often use this to explain long-standing pay gaps that persist especially at the managerial level in the nonprofit sector (Leete, 2001; 2006). The relationship between pay and prosocial behavior was largely put forth in the donative labor hypothesis. The donative labor hypothesis suggests nonprofit employees accept lower wages than their for-profit counterparts due to the intrinsic rewards received from working for an idealistic or moral goal (Frank, 1996). This theory proposes nonprofit sector organizations produce different goods or different qualities of goods than similar organizations found in the for-profit sector. For example, an aid worker may be willing to accept lower pay because they believe their work is important and they find working to help those in need to be rewarding in ways that are more important than money.

The idea that nonprofit employees are motivated by intrinsic rewards has also been supported by recent empirical research (Leete, 2001). A survey examining work related attitudes of public, nonprofit and for-profit workers found significant differences between the responses of workers in different sectors (Light, 2002). In particular, nonprofit employees were much more likely to indicate they came to work because of the nature of their job and the common good than either public or private employees. This supports the idea that nonprofit employees are significantly motivated by a desire to serve the public interest. This interest in service to others is potentially one of the most unique aspects of work in the nonprofit sector. This finding is further supported by research by Lyons, Duxbury, and Higgins (2006) which found nonprofit sector workers were much more likely than either public or for-profit employees to value work that contributed to society (Lyons, Duxbury & Higgins, 2006).

Nonprofit employees were also less likely than public and private sector employees to believe their jobs were a dead-end (Gazely, 2009). This implies the type of work offered by nonprofit organizations may create intrinsic rewards and personal development that individuals may be unable to receive through employment in the other sectors. Additional research has suggested mission attachment helps enhance employee retention in the sector (Brown & Yoshioka, 2003). This has significant implications as this line of research continues to develop for nonprofit managers wishing to retain their employees with limited financial resources. Another unique aspect of the nonprofit sector, which might impact employee motivation, is the relatively small size of many nonprofit organizations. The sector as a whole, is made up of very small organizations often having few employees and tends to be much more flexible and less bureaucratic(Ban, Drahnak-Faller & Towers, 2003). However, a significant number (24%) of nonprofit sector employees expressed frustration with a limited ability to advance within their organization (Light, 2002).

Recent research conducted by Word and Park (2009) comparing the job involvement of public and nonprofit mangers found there are distinct characteristics of nonprofit managers and the work they perform. Their research found nonprofit managers were more involved in their jobs (Word and Park, 2009). Additionally, Feeney and Bozeman (2009) found nonprofit managers worked longer hours than their public sector counterparts in part because of cultural differences between the sectors (Feeney & Bozeman, 2009). However, these findings are somewhat counter-intuitive since economic theories point out workers in both sectors lack ownership or profit incentives (Kim & Mahoney, 2005). This leaves us to wonder what motivates nonprofit managers to work longer hours and display higher levels of job involvement.

Our study uses a broadly inductive approach to probe our main research questions. Drawing on theoretical perspectives of SDT, PSM, and nonprofit service motivation (NPSM), we empirically analyzed work motivation of public and nonprofit managers. First, employing exploratory and confirmatory factor solutions, this study examines motivational constructs and dimensions in the public and nonprofit sectors. We also probe which types of motivation (e.g., intrinsic and extrinsic motivation) are more salient for public and nonprofit managers.

> **Research Question 1** (Work motivation in the public sector): Is work motivation in the public service composed of sub-dimensional motivation constructs—i.e., different types of intrinsic and extrinsic motivations? Are these latent constructs conceptually and empirically separate and distinct?

> **Research Question 2** (Work motivation in the nonprofit sector): Is work motivation in the nonprofit service is composed of sub-dimensional motivation constructs—i.e., different types of intrinsic and extrinsic motivations? Are these latent constructs conceptually and empirically separate and distinct?

As previously discussed, the Deci and Ryan's SDT proposes a continuum of motivations, including amotivation, four types of extrinsic motivation, and intrinsic motivation. Among those types of extrinsic motivation, two forms of extrinsic motivation, i.e., identification and integration, are very similar to intrinsic motivation in light of regulatory styles and locus of causality (Deci & Ryan, 2004). Based on the SDT framework and the correlate procedure, we test the bivariate relationships among different types of intrinsic and extrinsic motivations—e.g., we investigate to what extent certain types of extrinsic motivation are associated with intrinsic motivation. We expect certain advanced types of extrinsic motivation such as identification and integration values in the SDT framework are significantly related to intrinsic motivation because those types of extrinsic motivation could share some qualities and characteristics with intrinsic motivation.

> **Research Question 3** (The relationship among intrinsic and extrinsic work motivations): Are there significant relationships among intrinsic and extrinsic work motivation of public and nonprofit managers?

Third, using the mean difference tests, we also propose a research question concerning whether there are significant theoretical and statistical differences in the level of work motivation among public and nonprofit managers.

> **Research Question 4** (Differences in work motivations across the sectors): Are there significant differences in the level of work motivations between public and nonprofit managers?

Data and Sample

This study utilizes data from the NASP-III survey that collected data from managers working in public (N = 790) and nonprofit (N = 430) agencies in the states of Illinois and Georgia. Each agency was represented by a number of respondents, with no serious unevenness in responses from different agencies (Details available from the authors).[1] The sample was a representative sample of state public and nonprofit managers, including 61 public agencies and 305 nonprofit organizations in these two states. The overall response rate was 39.0% (42.5% for the public sector sample and 33.0% from the nonprofit sector sample). Regarding missing data adjustments, rather than using the listwise deletion method, we employed the expectation-maximization (EM) algorithm method to preserve effective sample size. This method can increase statistical power of the regression model and reduce possible non-response bias in parameter estimates (Roth, 1994).

Most of the constructs used in this study were measured using a 4-point Likert scale (i.e., 1= not important, 2= somewhat unimportant, 3= somewhat important, 4=

very important). The survey instrument measured the managers' perceptions regarding various organizational issues such as work motivation, mentoring and communication, career histories, hiring practices, and organizational cultures and structures, in addition to investigating numerous individual, managerial, and organizational attributes—e.g., job responsibility, supervisory status, job tenure, and organizational size and age. To probe and confirm the constructs and dimensions of job choice and work motivations in the public and nonprofit sectors, we analyzed 16 survey items included in the NASP III. Table 1 provides the descriptive statistics of work motives and other demographic information for public and nonprofit managers.

Table 1. Descriptive Statistics: Work Motivation for Public and Nonprofit Managers

Variables: Managers' Work Motivation	Public Managers					Nonprofit Managers				
	Valid N	Mean	SD	Min	Max	Valid N	Mean	SD	Min	Max
Intrinsic Motivation	780	**3.14**	.69	1.00	4.00	418	**3.22**	.72	1.00	4.00
Monetary Motivation	773	2.29	.64	1.00	4.00					
Security Motivation	780	3.06	.67	1.00	4.00	418	2.91	.78	1.00	4.00
Advancement Motivation	778	3.10	.68	1.00	4.00	416	3.01	.73	1.00	4.00
WLB Motivation						416	2.60	.84	1.00	4.00

Data Analysis and Methods

We employed four different statistical methods in three phases. First, to operationalize observed motivation variables, exploratory factor analysis (EFA) was employed. Second, through a confirmatory factor analysis (CFA) model, we estimated the latent constructs of different types of motivation in the public and nonprofit sectors. Third, using correlation analysis, we statistically examined the relationship among intrinsic and extrinsic motivation of public and nonprofit managers. Finally, we used independent samples t-test to see whether there are statistically significant differences in the levels of public and nonprofit managers' different types of work motivation (e.g., intrinsic and extrinsic motivations). In a CFA model, the maximum likelihood (ML) method was employed. From multivariate normality tests, severe non-normality patterns are not observed and we can expect that the ML method in CFA would be more unbiased, consistent, and efficient, especially when the population distribution for the endogenous variables is multivariate normal (Kline, 2005). Also, the covariance matrix was used as input to the LISREL 8.72 version to examine the measurement model of CFA.

Findings and Results

Phase 1-1: Exploratory Factor Analysis (EFA) Model

As discussed in the previous section, multiple motivational values are identifiable in the public and nonprofit sectors. In order to examine the factor structures of work motivation values, an EFA was employed on the 16 items initially developed to infer the latent dimensionality (see the Appendix for the motivation items included). In this study, the principal axis factoring (PAF) extraction method was used since the purpose of this study is to identify whether these latent constructs or factors of the instrument underlie the variables or subscales.[2]

Determination of Number of Factors and Rotation Techniques

To determine the number of factors to extract, several rules such as the scree plot, Kaiser's eigenvalues greater than 1 rule, Velicer's MAP test, and parallel analysis were generated from raw data. The results suggested four different motivational factors should be retained for public and nonprofit managers. Among several rotation methods, an oblique direct oblimin rotation method was chosen because of the assumption that the underlying constructs of NPM and normative values in this study would be mutually interconnected and correlated. This rotation technique is used to produce factors with the smallest number of cross-loadings from a parameter called delta.[3] Tables 2 (motivations in the public sector) and 3 (motivations in the nonprofit sector) illustrate the communalities after rotation and results of rotation such as the percent of variance accounted for by each factor and eigenvalues of the four-factor solution in the public and nonprofit sectors (the communalities of variables, e.g., the table of factor pattern matrix, are available from the authors). The percentage of variance accounted for by these factors is 55.49% (for public managers) and 58.65% (nonprofit managers) of the total variance. In order to ensure internal consistency, a reliability test using Cronbach's Alpha scores was employed. The results indicated that the scores of the subscales have a relatively high degree of internal consistency (all above .7) on each of the factors for public and nonprofit managers.

Table 2. Total Variance Explained *After* Rotation (Motivation in Public Agencies)

Factor	Initial Eigenvalues			Extraction Sums of Squared Loadings			Rotation Sums of Squared Loadings (a)		
	Total	% of Variance	Cumulative %	Total	% of Variance	Cumulative %	Total	% of Variance	Cumulative %
1	4.53	28.36	28.36	4.00	25.00	25.00	2.59		
2	1.82	11.39	39.75	1.24	7.76	32.77	1.79		
3	1.40	8.80	48.56	.892	5.57	38.34	2.64		
4	1.10	6.93	55.49	.55	3.43	41.78	2.492		

Table 3. Total Variance Explained *After* Rotation (Motivation in Nonprofit Agencies)

Factor	Initial Eigenvalues			Extraction Sums of Squared Loadings			Rotation Sums of Squared Loadings (a)		
	Total	% of Variance	Cumulative %	Total	% of Variance	Cumulative %	Total	% of Variance	Cumulative %
1	3.71	23.21	23.21	3.20	20.00	20.00	2.60		
2	1.54	9.68	32.89	1.06	6.67	26.67	1.84		
3	1.32	8.28	50.65	.77	4.86	37.07	1.65		
4	1.27	7.99	58.65	.66	4.18	41.25	1.07		

Interpretation of Factors: Public Managers

Tables 2 and 3 suggest the four-factor solution extracted distinctive factor loadings in the public sector model. As is customary, each of the factors were interpreted and named in terms of their highest loadings, focusing mainly on those equal to or greater than .50.

The items on factor 1 reflect intrinsic job choice motives of public sector managers who are greatly motivated by an ability to serve the public and the public interest and attracted by the overall quality and reputation of the public agency. This factor was named "intrinsic motivation," and accounted for 28.36% of the variance. The second factor (accounting for 11.39% of the variance) reflected monetary motives such as salary, cost of living in the region, and employment opportunities for spouse or partner. This factor is labeled "monetary motivation." Factor 3, accounting for 8.80% of the total variance, addressed security motives for public managers. They are motivated to choose their job since the public organization provides public managers a higher level of job security while guaranteeing better retirement and benefit plans. This factor is named "security motivation." Finally, the items on factor 4 accounted for 6.93% of the variance and included such motives as advancement, training and career development, and job responsibility. This factor is named "advancement motivation." In order to confirm these results using CFA, each factor is operationalized into four observable variables.

Interpretation of Factors: Nonprofit Managers

There are four motivational factor dimensions in the nonprofit sector model. The items on factor 1 reflect values of intrinsic and public service-oriented incentive and motives for nonprofit managers. These individuals are likely to be more motivated by the organizational reputation or ability to serve the public and public interest than by other incentives. This factor was named "intrinsic motivation," and it accounted for 23.21% of the variance. The second factor accounted for 9.68% of the variance; this factor represents how nonprofit managers value their work environments and family-friendly policies in nonprofit agencies such as telework/telecommuting, flexible work schedules (e.g., compressed workweeks), and other employee assistance programs. Some of nonprofit managers were motivated to choose their job because of the desire for less bureaucratic red tape or the desire for a low conflict work environment in the nonprofit organization. We labeled this factor as "work-life balance (WLB) motivation." Factor 3, accounting for 8.28% of the variance, addressed the motives for career advancement within their organization. Those nonprofit managers are significantly motivated by opportunities for advancement or increased responsibility. This factor is named "advancement motivation." Lastly, factor 4, which explains 7.99% of the total variance for nonprofit managers' motives, includes such motive items as job security, pension or retirement plan, and medical or insurance benefits. This factor is named "job security motivation." In order to confirm these results using CFA, each factor is operationalized into four observable variables.

Phase 1-2: Testing the Measurement Model: Confirmatory Factor Analysis (CFA)

To test Research Questions 1 and 2 (i.e., to confirm latent constructs of work motivation in the public and nonprofit sectors), we employed a second-order CFA model of 1) work motivation in the public sectors and 2) work motivation in the nonprofit sectors. LISREL was used to generate and obtain factor scores for each sub-dimension. Drawing upon 1) the previous empirical research such as Deci & Ryan (1980) and Bozeman &

Murdock (2007) and 2) EFA results shown in step 1, we developed work motivation scales in public and nonprofit sectors based on relevant survey items (see Appendix) (Bozeman & Murdock, 2007; Deci & Ryan, 1980).

First, the results indicate the four motivation latent constructs (first-order factors) in the public and nonprofit sectors are significantly salient and distinct— 1) intrinsic motivation, monetary motivation, security motivation, and advancement motivation in public agencies and 2) intrinsic motivation, worklife balance (WLB) motivation, advancement motivation, and security motivation in nonprofit agencies (see Figures 2 and 3). Second order factors (i.e., motivations in public and nonprofit agencies) are significantly and positively explained by these four first order factors. The results of CFI, NNFI, NFI, IFI, RFI, RMSEA, and SRMR values in both of the models suggest the models of public and nonprofit agencies can be considered a very good fit for the data. However, the values of chi-square in these CFA models (232.44; 243.67) are significant and reject the null hypothesis ($p< 0.05$) and this result might be viewed as disconfirmatory evidence. Conversely, the chi-square statistic is very sensitive to sample size and model complexity; the probability of rejecting a hypothesized model increases as N increases.

Second, the results of R^2 and standardized factor loadings in the public and nonprofit models suggest intrinsic motivation (the factor loading is .79) is most salient among public managers. In a similar vein, intrinsic motivation is also most significant (the factor loading is .82) among nonprofit managers. That is, in Georgia and Illinois, public and nonprofit managers are more prone to be motivated by such intrinsic motives as nonmonetary recognitions, feelings of pride or responsibility to serve the public than other types of job choice motives (e.g., security motivation or monetary motivation). This research also revealed monetary motivation as the second largest factor (the factor loading is .72) in the public sector while WLB motivation is the second most important motive (the factor loading is .76) in the nonprofit sector. The finding indicates that monetary reward systems are more valued than other extrinsic compensations by public managers and implies policies promoting work friendly environments attract nonprofit employees to choose their job.

Third, the values of R^2 on each latent motivation variable are moderate to high, confirming that the amount of variance in the indicators is well measured and explained by a number of latent factors. Third, from the t-tests (the critical value is ± 2), we found that all indicators (11 items of the public sector model and 11 items of the nonprofit sector model) have significant factor loadings on each of four first-order factors—that is, all factor loadings (parameter values) of these four latent variables of each model are positive and significantly different from 0, which shows good evidence of reliable and valid measures of motivation constructs in both of the sectors. The overall results of CFA indicate the factor loadings support the use of these items as indicators of the underlying motivational constructs.

Figure 2. CFA Model: Motivation in the Public Sector

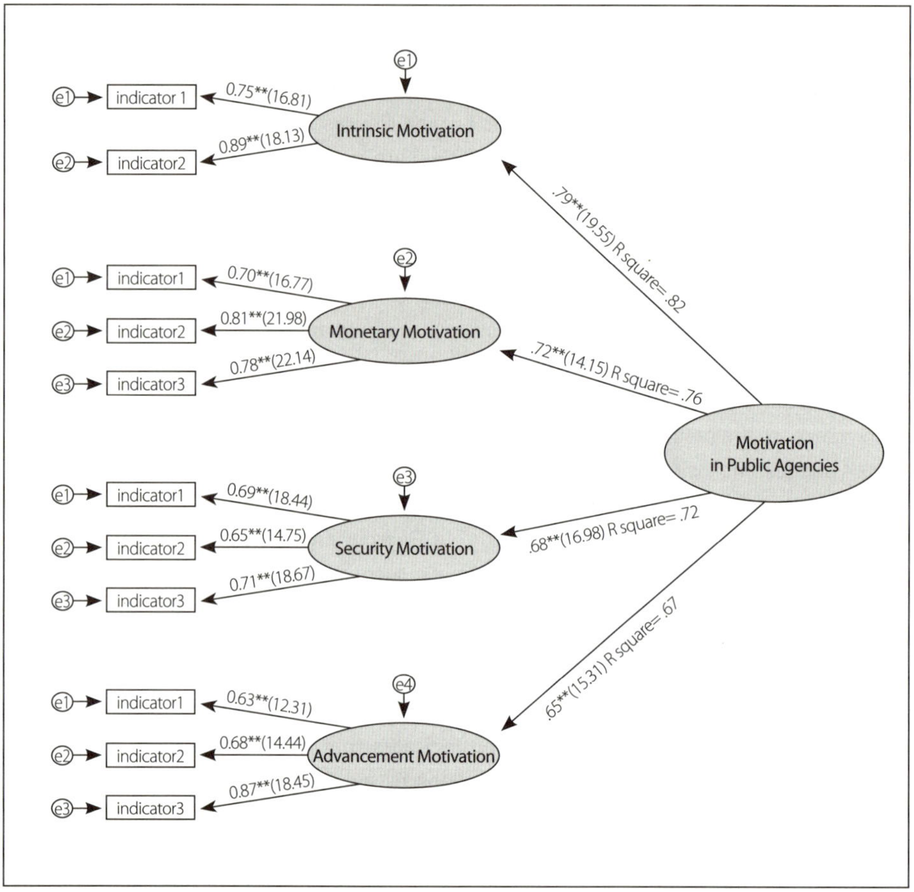

Overall Fit Indexes of the CFA Model

Model 1	df	Chi-Square	CFI	NNFI	NFI	IFI	RFI	RMSEA	SRMR
Suggested Cut-off Valu es			>.95	>.95	>.95	>.95	>.95	<.08	<.08
A Measurement Model	212	232.44	.98	.96	.97	.98	.96	.058	.067

[a]Based on the WLS (ADF) method, all coefficients of the factor loadings (lambda-Ys and gammas) in this CFA model are standardized (t-statistics are in parentheses).

Figure 3. CFA Model: Motivation in the Nonprofit Sector

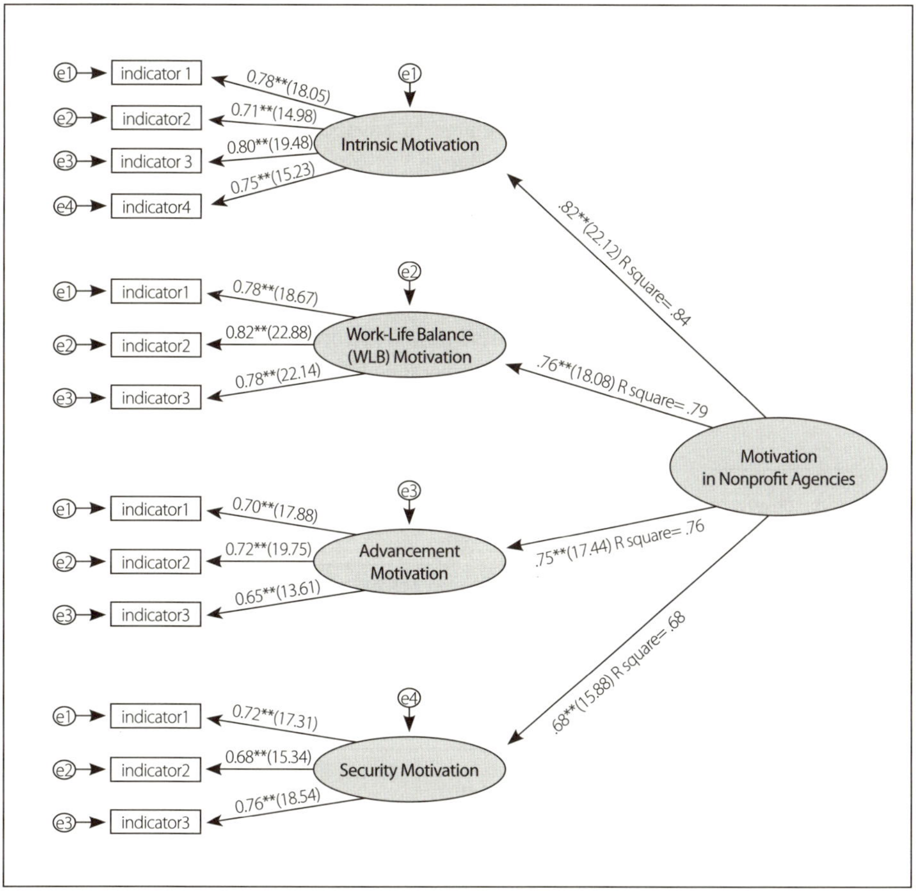

Overall Fit Indexes of the CFA Model

Model 1	df	Chi-Square	CFI	NNFI	NFI	IFI	RFI	RMSEA	SRMR
Suggested Cut-off Valu es			>.95	>.95	>.95	>.95	>.95	<.08	<.08
A Measurement Model	268	243.67	.96	.97	.99	.98	.96	.06	.067

[a]Based on the WLS (ADF) method, all coefficients of the factor loadings (lambda-Ys and gammas) in this CFA model are standardized (t-statistics are in parentheses).

Phase 2: Correlation Analysis

In the second phase of our analysis, we examined the relationships between intrinsic motivation and three types of extrinsic motivation in public and nonprofit sector. From a zero-order correlation matrix of intrinsic and extrinsic motivation variables, most of the variables are statistically significant and the correlation coefficients are moderately high overall. First, according to the correlation coefficients in the public sector model (Table 5), intrinsic motivation is most significantly related to advancement motivation (r= .418**), suggesting advancement motivation could be an "advanced" type of extrinsic motivation which shares many characteristics with intrinsic motivation in the public sector. Second, in the nonprofit model, we found that the correlation between intrinsic motivation and WLB motivation is high and statistically significant (r= .174**). That is, family and work conflict issues in nonprofit agencies are more intrinsic issues rather than extrinsic. Although the correlation matrix shows all variables are somewhat strongly correlated with each other, the variance-inflation factor less than 3 and tolerance levels larger than .20 for this model indicate there is no critical multi-collinearity problem among these variables.

Table 4. Zero-Order Correlations: Motivation in the Public Sector

Variables	1	2	3	4
1. Intrinsic Motivation	1.00	.174**	.193**	**.418****
2. Monetary Motivation	.174**	1.00	.300**	.181**
3. Security Motivation	.193**	.300**	1.00	.304**
4. Advancement Motivation	.418**	.181**	.304**	1.00

**. Correlation is significant at the 0.01 level (two-tailed).
*. Correlation is significant at the 0.05-level (two-tailed).
The numbers in parentheses are Cronbach's Alpha values.
N= 777

Table 5. Zero-Order Correlations: Motivation in the Nonprofit Sector

Variables	1	2	3	4
1. Intrinsic Motivation	1.00	**.174****	.137**	.173**
2. Monetary Motivation	.174**	1.00	.284**	.379**
3. Advancement Motivation	.137**	.284**	1.00	.362**
4. Security Motivation	.173**	.379**	.362**	1.00

**. Correlation is significant at the 0.01 level (two-tailed).
*. Correlation is significant at the 0.05-level (two-tailed).
The numbers in parentheses are Cronbach's Alpha values.
N= 353

Phase 3: Independent Samples t Test

In the third phase of our analysis, we test for statistically significant differences in work motivation between the two sectors, we used an independent samples *t* test method by dividing the sample on the basis of the two groups—public (Group 1) and nonprofit (Group 2) sectors. Drawing upon EFA and CFA results, we statistically compare the sample means of intrinsic and extrinsic motivation of public and nonprofit managers. Extrinsic motivation in the public sector includes monetary motivation, security motivation, and advancement motivation whereas WLB motivation, advancement motivation, and security motivation are included as nonprofit sector extrinsic motivation. First, Table 6 of Group Statistics shows descriptive information about the means of intrinsic and extrinsic motivation for state and nonprofit managers. We can see that the mean level of nonprofit managers' intrinsic motivation (3.22) is slightly higher than that of state managers' intrinsic motivation (3.14) but the difference is not statistically significant. The mean level of public (state) managers' extrinsic motivation (2.83), on the contrary, is shown to be higher than that of nonprofit managers' extrinsic motivation (2.65).

The results of the independent samples t-test in Table 7 which evaluates the mean difference of intrinsic motivation between two sectors indicate that the mean level of intrinsic motivation in these two sectors are not statistically significantly different ($t= -1.80; p > .05$). This implies public and nonprofit managers are similarly motivated by intrinsic factors regardless of the sectors where they work. On the other hand, Table 8 illustrates the t-tests of extrinsic motivation among public and nonprofit managers are statistically significant ($p < .05$). The mean levels of public managers' motivation for extrinsic factors such as security, advancement, and salary is greater than those of nonprofit managers, and the difference is statistically significant—in sum, public managers are more highly motivated by thes extrinsic factors than nonprofit managers.

Table 6. Group Statistics

		N	Mean	Std. Deviation	Std. Error Mean
Intrinsic Motivation	Public (State) Managers	780	**3.14**	.69	.024
	Nonprofit Managers	418	**3.22**	.72	.035
Extrinsic Motivation	Public (State) Managers	763	**2.83**	.51	.018
	Nonprofit Managers	404	**2.65**	.49	.024

Table 7. Independent Samples T Test: Intrinsic Motivation in the Public and Nonprofit Sectors

		Levene's Test for Quality of Variance		t-test for Equality of Means				
		F	Sig.	t	df	Sig. (2-tailed)	Mean Difference	Std. Error Difference
Intrinsic Motivation	Equal Variance Assumed	1.08	.299	-1.80	1196	.071	-.076	.042
	Equal Variance Not Assumed			-1.78	819.87	.075	-.076	.043

Intrinsic motivation among public managers: Group 1
Intrinsic motivation among nonprofit managers: Group 2
Mean difference: Group 1-Group 2

Table 8. Independent Samples T Test: Extrinsic Motivation in the Public and Nonprofit Sectors

		Levene's Test for Quality of Variance		t-test for Equality of Means				
		F	Sig.	t	df	Sig. (2-tailed)	Mean Difference	Std. Error Difference
Extrinsic Motivation	Equal Variance Assumed	.183	.669	5.73	1165	.00	.178	.031
	Equal Variance Not Assumed			5.76	834.28	.00	.178	.030

Intrinsic motivation among public managers: Group 1
Intrinsic motivation among nonprofit managers: Group 2
Mean difference: Group 1-Group 2

Discussion and Implications

The need to propose and create better management strategies in both the public and nonprofit sectors is one of the most pressing issues in public administration today. The contracting out of public services to the for-profit and nonprofit sectors makes understanding motivation across the sectors a critical issue for public administration researchers as we seek to be good stewards of resources and explore ways to improve the quality of services. Given the existence of significant differences between the two sectors, our results suggest several important implications for the management of both public and nonprofit organizations especially in terms of the type and shape of benefits and training programs, which might be the most effective in enhancing outcomes for both individuals and their organizations. This study assessed the constructs, relationships, and mean levels of motivation in public and nonprofit sectors while analyzing the different types of work motivations in the two sectors. The results indicate a number of managerial implications for public and nonprofit managers.

Public and nonprofit employees are both significantly motivated by intrinsic factors. The factors most significantly related to motivation in both sectors included the overall reputation of the organization, ability to serve the public, and a desire for less bureaucratic red tape. The strong ties of both public and nonprofit managers to intrinsic motivating factors sheds light on the theoretical similarities between the two sectors and suggest the workforces of these sectors are in many ways similar even though the organizational contexts are somewhat unique. In part, it is likely that what draws public and nonprofit employees to their jobs is their motivation to work in respected organizations and while serving their communities.

The results of EFA and CFA models in this study show that public and nonprofit managers are motivated differently at work—nonprofit managers are more motivated by work environments that allow for a balance between work and family than public managers. Public managers are more inspired by monetary motivation than nonprofit managers. However, managers in both of the sectors are motivated by intrinsic factors as well as security and advancement motivators. In the future, these findings urge us to analyze and compare these different types of work motivators across the sectors within broader organizational contexts.

However, some significant differences were observed in other attributes for the two sectors in terms of motivation. Interestingly, public managers experienced higher mean levels of motivation in the areas of security, advancement and salary than nonprofit managers (See table 1). All of these motivational characteristics are more related to extrinsic reward structures than might have been indicated through earlier comparisons with the for-profit sector workers. So if we think of intrinsic vs. extrinsic motivation as a continuum across the different sectors, nonprofit managers were the least motivated by extrinsic rewards and for-profit employees the least influence by intrinsic rewards with public managers in between. Public managers appear to be balancing their need for both intrinsic and extrinsic rewards. In contrast, nonprofit managers appear to be balancing their need for intrinsic rewards with family concerns as expressed by the importance of WLB motivation to nonprofit managers.

The results of mean-difference tests (independent samples t-tests) reveal, while nonprofit managers are more intrinsically motivated than public managers, the mean levels of intrinsic motivation were not significantly different across the public and nonprofit sector managers. This suggests intrinsic motives similarly influence managers regardless of sector. This is somewhat surprising based upon the findings of Word and Park (2009), which found nonprofit employees on average were more involved in their job than public employees. However, we confirm the mean levels of extrinsic motivation were statistically different in these two sectors—nonprofit managers are less attracted by extrinsic factors, which is fairly consistent with the previous findings (Word & Park, 2009).

Additionally, nonprofit managers were much more motivated by benefits that helped them achieve a work life balance, i.e., WLB motivation. The emphasis on work life balance includes flexible organizational practices such as family-friendly policies, alternative work schedules, telecommunications, and employment opportunities for spouse or partner. The strong relationship between these policies and motivation in the nonprofit sector may be due to several characteristics of nonprofit sector organizations themselves and the unique characteristics of the nonprofit workforce. Nonprofit organizations often have very limited budgets which force nonprofits to more widely adopt alternative methods to attract and retain talented workers, such as flexible schedules and family friendly work environments. This may have led to workers, valuing this type of environment, to select the nonprofit sector over other sectors because of these benefits. Another possible explanation is the overwhelming number of women working in the nonprofit sector as a whole (Leete, 2006). The nonprofit sector in comparison to both government and the for-profit sector have a much larger percentage of female workers. It is likely the role women play in this sector enhances the ties between work life balance policies and motivation for nonprofit sector employees.

The correlation analyses found intrinsic and advancement motivation are significantly and positively associated with each other in the public sector. That is, as the level of intrinsic motivation increases, the level of advancement motivation also increases. In nonprofit agencies, intrinsic motivation and WLB motivation are positively and significantly related to each other. Those findings imply advancement and WLB motivation might share similar motivational constructs or patterns with intrinsic motivation. According to SDT, it might also indicate those types of extrinsic motivation are more advanced and could be easily transformed into intrinsic motivation once some contextual factors are introduced.

SDT contends an employee needs a sense of self-control to experience intrinsic motivation. Essentially, one needs to feel that one is choosing to engage in the activity, based on internalized motives and values. Deci and Ryan further contend that a person with predominantly extrinsic motivation for a task can move toward intrinsic motivation(Deci & Ryan, 2004). If the individual experiences more control over the task and her or his actions in relation to it, the person is more likely to internalize the task goals and values. The individual will be more likely to experience intrinsic motivation for task performance—that she or he is doing it for his or her own interests, fulfillment, and values, rather than for salary or some other extrinsic incentives. Following this reasoning, advancement and WLB motives should have characteristics which might enhance their sense of control, support, and engagement. Those managers reporting advancement and WLB motivations drove their job choice will possibly move more toward intrinsic motivation and positive perceptions of the organization in the future.

Overall, our findings support the assertion that nonprofit and public sector workers are similar in many respects. These two sectors share a similar concern with service that enriches communities and civil society. The importance of intrinsic motivation to public and nonprofit managers suggests there are unique qualities workers in these sectors possess and their choice to work in these sectors is a reflection not just of their desire to earn a living but also to find value in their work. The importance that both public and nonprofit managers place upon working in an organization that is respected has interesting implications for the practice and training of new public and nonprofit managers. This finding implies we need not just attend to running our organizations efficiently but also to the effectiveness and ethical nature of operations. Public and nonprofit organizations, unlike businesses, are run in very public arenas that often draw attention to the mistakes and misdeeds committed by individuals and organizations in these sectors. The importance of reputation to the motivation of public and nonprofit employees suggests ethical breaches by organizations or individuals representing them could not just affect the reputation of organization but the motivations and morale of its workforce. This suggests the need for training in ethics to prevent such situations as well as the need for training in public relations to limit the damage inflicted upon organizations once an event has occurred.

Our findings also imply these distinctions between the sectors have unique implications for policy and practice in both the nonprofit and public sectors. Both the public and nonprofit sectors need to emphasize the importance of their service missions to continue to attract employees who will value the unique rewards offered by working in these sectors. However, the public sector needs to think about ways to capitalize on the distinctive desire of public employees for advancement as a reward for public service. Nonprofit organizations, in contrast, need to continue to think about creative ways to be flexible especially as they take on contracts with the public sector which may make these strategies more difficult as restrictions and regulations are increased by governmental contracting requirements.

Notes

1. Skewness can show whether the item's distribution deviates from the symmetry distribution. We can argue that skewness values outside the range of ±2 would be problematic because this is a serious level of skew. Kurtosis measures the degree to which the area in a distribution is in the middle and the tails of a distribution. As a rule of thumb, the range of ±2 is often considered as a significant departure from normality (Pedhazur, 1997). In this research, most items show a relatively stable and similar amount of variance. The results of Kolmogorov-Smirnov and Shapiro normality tests suggest that items in this study do differentiate responses fairly well. In terms of individual normality, most items have a high positive kurtosis value, which means that most respondents have selected the same response option. Most variables of skewness or kurtosis are all between $-2 < s(k) < 2$, and we can argue that these variables are approximately normally distributed. Relative multivariate kurtosis (1.155< 2.0) also indicates approximate multivariate normality.
2. Principal components analysis (PCA) is usually used to determine how many components we really need to capture the different kinds of information in the variables or when we need to get the PCs and use them instead of the variables. For the EFA model in this study, principal axis factoring (PAF) analysis is used which is one of the common factor analysis (CFA) methods to reveal the number and identity of the latent constructs and factors. In CFA, we assume that not all of the variance and covariance of the variables is accounted by the factors and therefore, this method is a linear combination of only the common variance—not the unique variance factors.
3. Oblique direct oblimin rotation is a generalization of orthogonal rotation that can be estimated as a more realistic and accurate way to present the results of this research. In this study, the delta value that controls the degree of correlation among the factors was set to be 0, which is expected to maintain a moderate degree of factor correlation.

References

Amabile, T. A. (1993). Motivational synergy: Toward new conceptualizations of intrinsic and extrinsic motivation in the workplace. *Human Resource Management Review, 3*(3), 185-201.

Ban, C., Drahnak-Faller, A., & Towers, M. (2003). Human resource challenges in human service and community development organizations: Recruitment and retention of professional staff. *Review of Public Personnel Administration, 23*(2), 133-153.

Behn, R. (1995). *The bog questions of public management. Public Administration Review, 55*(4), 313-324.

Boyne, G. A. (2002). Public and private management: What's the difference?. *Journal of Management Studies, 16*(1), 67-88.

Bozeman, B., & Murdock, A. (2007). Public managers' religiosity: Impacts on work attitudes and perceptions of co-workers. *International Public Management Journal, 10*(3), 287- 306.

Brewer, G. A. (2003). Building social capital: Civic attitudes and behavior of public servants. *Journal of Public Administration Research and Theory, 13*(1), 5-25.

Brinkerhoff, J. M., & Brinkerhoff, D. W. (2002). Government-nonprofit relations in a comparative perspective: Evolution, themes, and new directions. *Public Administration and Development, 22*(1), 3-18.

Brown, W. A., & Yoshioka, C. F. (2003). Mission attachment and satisfaction as factors in employee retention. *Nonprofit Management and Leadership, 14*(1), 5-18.

Coursey, D. H., & Pandey, S. K. (2007). Public service motivation measurement: Testing an abridged version of Perry's proposed scale. *Administration & Society, 39*, 547-568.

Crewson, P. E. (1997). Public service motivation: Building empirical evidence of incidence and effect. *Journal of Public Administration Research and Theory, 4,* 499-518.

Deci, E. L., & Ryan, R. M. (1980). The empirical exploration of intrinsic motivational processes. In L. Berkowitz (Ed.), *Advances in experimental social psychology* (Vol. 10, pp. 39-80). New York: Academic Press.

Deci, E. L., & Ryan, R. M. (2004). *Handbook of self-determination research.* Rochester: University of Rochester press.

Feeney, M. K., & Bozeman, B. (2009). Staying Late: Comparing work hours in public and nonprofit sectors. *The American Review of Public Administration, 39*(5), 459-477.

Frank, R. (1996). What price the high moral ground?. *Southern Economic Journal, 63*(1), 1-17.

Fredrickson, H. G., & Hart, D. K. (1985). The public service and the patriotism of benevolence. *Public Administration Review, 45*(5), 547-553.

Frey, B. S. (1997). On the relationship between intrinsic and extrinsic work motivation. *International Journal of Industrial Organization, 15,* 427-439.

Gagné, M., & Deci, E. L. (2005). Self-determination theory and work motivation. *Journal of Organizational Behavior, 26,* 331-362.

Gazely, B. (2009). Personnel recruitment and retention in the nonprofit sector: The 21st century challenge. In S. W. Hays, R. C. Kearney & J. D. Cogburn (Eds.), *Public personnel administration: Problems and prospects.* Uppers Saddle River, NJ: Prentice Hall.

Grant, A. M. (2008). Employees without a cause: The motivational effects of prosocial impact in public service. *International Public Management Journal, 11*(1), 48-66.

Horton, S., & Hondeghem, A. (2006). Public service motivation and commitment. *Public Policy and Administration, 21*(1), 1-12.

Houston, D. J. (2000). Public service motivation: A multivariate test. *Journal of Public Administration Research and Theory, 10*(4), 713-727.

Houston, D. J. (2006). "Walking the walk" of public service motivation: Public employees and charitable gifts of time, blood, and money. *Journal of Public Administration and Theory, 16*(1), 67-86.

Kellough, J. E., & Lu, H. (1993). The paradox of merit pay in the public sector: Persistence of a problematic procedure. *Review of Public Personnel Administration, 13*(2), 45-64.

Kim, J., & Mahoney, J. T. (2005). Property rights theory, transaction costs theory, and agency theory: An organizational economics approach to strategic management. *Managerial and Decision Economics, 26*(4), 223-242.

Kline, R. B. (2005). *Principles and practices of structural equation modeling.* New York: Guilford.

Leete, L. (2001). Whiter the nonprofit wage differential? Estimates from the 1990 Census. *Journal of Labor Economics, 19*(1), 136-170.

Leete, L. (2006). Work in the nonprofit sector. In W. W. Powell & R. Steinberg (Eds.), *The nonprofit sector: A research handbook* (pp. 159-179). New Haven, CT: Yale University Press.

Light, P. C. (2002). The Content of their character: The State of the nonprofit Workforce. *The Nonprofit Quarterly, 9*(3), 6-16.

Lyons, S. T., Duxbury, L. E., & Higgins, C. A. (2006). A Comparison of the values and commitment of private sector, public sector, and parapublic sector employees. *Public Administration Review, 66*(4), 605-618.

Mann, G. A. (2006). A motive to serve: Public service motivation in human resource management and the role of PSM in the nonprofit sector. *Public Personnel Management, 25*(1), 33-48.

Moynihan, D. P., & Pandey, S. J. (2007). The role of organizations in fostering public service motivation. *Public Administration Review, 67*(1), 40-53.

Paarlberg, L. E., Perry, J. L., & Hondeghem, A. (2008). From theory to practice: Strategies for applying public service motivation. In J. L. Perry & A. Hondeghem (Eds.), *Motivation in public management: The call of public service* (pp. 268-293). Oxford University Press.

Park, S. M., & Rainey, H. G. (2007). Antecedents, mediators, and consequences of affective, normative, and continuance commitment: Empirical tests of commitment effects in federal agencies. *Review of Public Personnel Administration, 27*(3), 197-226.

Park, S. M., & Rainey, H. G. (2008). Leadership and public service motivation in U.S. federal agencies. *International Public Management Journal, 11*(1), 109-142.

Perry, J. L., & Hondeghem, A. (2008). Editors' introduction. In J. L. Perry & A. Hondeghem

(Eds.), *Motivation in public management: The call of public service* (pp. 1-14). Oxford University Press.

Perry, J. L., & Wise, L. R. (1990). The motivational bases of public service. *Public Administration Review, 50*(3), 367-373.

Roth, P. L. (1994). Missing data: A conceptual review for applied psychologists. *Personnel Psychology, 47,* 537-560.

Ryan, R. M., & Deci, E. L. (2000). Self-determination theory and the facilitation of intrinsic motivation, social development, and well-being. *American Psychologist, 55*(1), 68-78.

Ryan, R. M., & Deci, E. L. (2004). An overview of self-determination theory: An organismic-dialectic perspective. In E. L. Deci and R. M. Ryan (Eds.), *Handbook of self-determination research.* Rochester: University of Rochester Press.

Santora, J. C., & Sarros, J. C. (2001). CEO tenure in nonprofit community based organizations: A multiple case study. *Career Development International, 6*(1), 56-60.

Vandenabeele, W. (2007). Towards a public administration theory of public service motivation: An institutional approach. *Public Management Review, 9*(4), 545-556.

Vandenabeele, W. (2009). The mediating effect of job satisfaction and organizational commitment on self-reported performance: More robust evidence of the PSM performance relationship. *International Review of Administrative Sciences, 75*(1), 11-34.

Vansteenkiste, M., Lens, W., & Deci, E. (2006). Intrinsic versus extrinsic goal contents in self-determination theory: Another look at the quality of academic motivation. *Educational Psychologist, 4*(1), 19-31.

Weisbrod, B. A. (1988). *The nonprofit economy.* Cambridge, MA: Harvard University Press.

Word, J., & Park, S. M. (2009). Working across the divide: Job involvement in the public and nonprofit sectors. *Review of Public Personnel Administration, 29*(2), 103-133.

Wright, B. E. (2001). Public sector work motivation: A review of current literature and a revised conceptual model. *Journal of Public Administration Research and Theory, 10*(4), 559-586.

Appendix

Construction of Indices Selected Representative Survey Items

Intrinsic and Extrinsic Motivation in the Public Sector

1) Intrinsic Motivation Scale (Deci & Ryan, 1985) (two items)
a. Overall quality and reputation of this organization
b. Ability to serve the public and the public interest

2) Monetary Motivation Scale (three items)
a. Salary
b. Relatively low cost of living in the region
c. Employment opportunities for spouse or partner

3) Security Motivation Scale (Bozeman & Murdock, 2007) (three items)
a. Job security
b. The organization's pension or retirement plan
c. Benefits (medical, insurance)

4) Advancement Motivation Scale (Bozeman & Murdock, 2007) (three items)
a. Opportunity for advancement within the organization's hierarchy
b. Opportunity for training and career development
c. Desire for increased responsibility

Intrinsic and Extrinsic Motivation in the Nonprofit Sector

1) Intrinsic Motivation Scale (two items)
a. Overall quality and reputation of this organization
b. Ability to serve the public and the public interest

2) Work-Life Balance (WLB) Motivation Scale (three items)
a. "Family friendly" policies (e.g. flexible work hours, parental leave)
b. Desire for less bureaucratic red tape
c. Desire for a low conflict work environment

3) Advancement Motivation Scale (Bozeman & Murdock, 2007) (three items)

a. Opportunity for advancement within the organization's hierarchy
b. Opportunity for training and career development
c. Desire for increased responsibility

4) Security Motivation Scale (Bozeman & Murdock, 2007) (three items)

a. Job security
b. The organization's pension or retirement plan
c. Benefits (medical, insurance)

Chapter 2

Serving the Mission
: Organizational Antecedents and Social Consequences of Job Choice Motivation in the Nonprofit Sector

Summary

Competition for employee talent is important to the success of any organization, including those in the nonprofit sector. This research examines the motivational and demographic characteristics of nonprofit managers in order to gain a better understanding of these managers that may ultimately inform both practice and theory. This research examines 1) job choice motivation, 2) intrinsic and extrinsic motivation, and 3) demographic and organizational factors affecting individuals working for the nonprofit sector. Subsequently, our model proposes that job choice motivation comprises intrinsic motivation and three types of extrinsic motivation, and examines the organizational antecedents and social outcomes of motivation to work in the nonprofit sector. The findings suggest that individuals who work in the nonprofit sector are intrinsically motivated in terms of job choice. Furthermore, personal characteristics such as gender, age, ethnicity, type of job, and level of education impact both job choice motivation and the level of intrinsic motivation.

Keyword

- □ Human Resource Management
- □ Public Service Motivation
- □ Public Sector Motivation
- □ Job Choice Motivation
- □ Community Involvement

Sung Min Park Associate Professor, Sungkyunkwan University
Jessica Word Associate Professor, University of Nevada, Las Vegas

Introduction

In recent years, public service has been broadened to include not only those working directly for government but also other forms of employment that serve the community. This has manifested in an increasing interest in governance rather than government (Brinkerhoff and Brinkerhoff, 2002) and complex interrelationships between nonprofits and governments. The argument that the motivation of the public sector workforce was introduced at a time when government was still responsible for direct service delivery, but "new public management" created an emphasis on "steering rather than rowing" that has dramatically altered the nature and shape of public service today. The traditional model of public service being delivered to citizens by government employees protected by civil service provisions only applies to modern public administration in very limited settings. Most delivery of public services is now done through contracts carried out by either for-profit or nonprofit organizations that share some but not all of the characteristics of traditional public service. In fact, more recent examinations of public service motivation have tended to include nonprofit human service workers and managers in examinations of public service motivation without exploring possible underlying differences between the sectors (Lyons, Duxbury, and Higgins, 2006).

The motivation and choice of career path of individuals in the public and for-profit sectors have been well explored (Rainey and Steinbauer, 1999; Park and Rainey, 2007; Perry and Wise, 1990; Boyne, 2002; Wright, 2001). However, very few studies have examined the motivation of nonprofit employees to choose a career serving the community. This research seeks to determine the factors influencing the decision of managers to work in the nonprofit sector and how these choices are impacted by intrinsic and extrinsic motivation of individuals. The findings of this research will allow for a deeper understanding of what makes the nonprofit sector and its employees unique. Additionally, we examine the impact of job choice motivation on social, community, and professional outcomes.

Recent research conducted by Word and Park (2009) suggests that employment within the public and nonprofit sectors is somewhat unique. Their research found that nonprofit managers are more involved in their jobs than public sector managers. Additionally, Feeney and Bozeman (2008) found that nonprofit managers work longer hours than their public sector counterparts due to cultural differences between the sectors. These findings, however, are somewhat counterintuitive, since theories based on economic rationality (e.g., rational choice, new public management, and principal-agent theories) suggest workers in both sectors lack ownership or profit incentive (Kim and Mahoney, 2005) and therefore face lower power incentive to make efforts beyond their required job duties. This leaves us wondering what drives nonprofit managers to work longer hours and display higher levels of job involvement than their public sector counterparts. Previous research suggests that important organizational factors, including incentives, motivation, rules and regulations, strategies, processes, and the working environments in public organizations, might be strikingly different from those in both for-profit and nonprofit agencies and result in the observed differences in job involvement and work habits (Rainey and Bozeman, 2000; Rainey, 2009).

Job choice motivation research has primarily focused on the constructs, determinants, and outcomes of employee motivation in the public or private sector (Baldwin 1984, 1987; Crewson, 1997; Emmert and Taher 1992; Houston 2006; Park and Rainey, 2008; Posner and Schmidt 1982; Rainey 1979, 1983; Wright 2008). This research project extends the existing research to incorporate nonprofit managers. The current study employs data collected as part of the National Administrative Studies Project (NASP III) in order to identify the nature and the antecedents of job choice motivation in the nonprofit sector and the resulting social outcomes for communities. First, we present a theoretical model that guides our inquiry into what motivates individuals to choose a job in the nonprofit sector. We examine the concept of nonprofit job choice motivation by introducing intrinsic and extrinsic motivation in the nonprofit sector with three exploratory research questions. Second, drawing upon previous research on career motivation and volunteering, we develop and test several hypotheses based on 1) the role of individual factors, managerial attributes, and organizational influences in shaping the job choice motivation of nonprofit managers; and 2) the consequences of job choice motivation in terms of social and professional activities pursued by nonprofit managers outside of work. Finally, we discuss the implications of our findings for both nonprofit theory and practice.

Theoretical Perspectives

Human Resource Management in the Nonprofit Sector

In the popular media, nonprofit employees are generally portrayed as either heroic, underpaid, and overworked saints trying to save the world, or villainously overpaid CEOs at prominent nonprofit organizations taking advantage of charitable causes for personal benefit. Indeed, these two extremes of hero and villain leave much to be examined concerning the nature of nonprofit employees and their choice of career path. While the academic literature is rich with examinations of employment in the other sectors, research centered on nonprofit human resources (HR) has mainly focused on issues related to incentives and compensation and volunteer management practices (Ben-Ner, Ren and Paulson 2011; Ruhm and Boroski 2003; Leete 2006: Steinberg 2006; Brudney 1999; Young 1984).

The tendency for nonprofit management research to focus on issues other than human resource management (HRM) is not surprising given the small size and relative informality of many nonprofits. Most nonprofit organizations are very small and lack formal HR departments or functions (Ban, Drahnak-Faller, and Towers 2003). It is possible this lack of formality has been somewhat responsible for the shortage of research concerning the unique aspects and issues surrounding nonprofit HR management and the motivation of nonprofit employees.

A deeper examination of employee motivations in nonprofits will provide a clearer understanding of the professional and organizational changes that have impacted nonprofit organizations. One of the major issues influencing the development of the nonprofit sector is the increased professionalization of the workforce (Leete, 2006), and the emergence of distinct educational and training programs for individuals seeking a job in a nonprofit organization (Mirabella and Wish, 2000; Dimaggio and Anheier, 1990). The nonprofit sector of today is more professionalized and formal than the nonprofit sector of the past (Salamon, 1987). Sixty-nine percent of all nonprofit employees have some education at the college level or greater, compared to 45.6 percent of for-profit employees (Leete, 2006). As the nonprofit sector has become more professionalized and specialized in terms of training, development, and identity, the need to understand HR issues and employee motivation has become vital to improve both employee management and organizational strategies.

Job Choice Motivation in the Nonprofit Sector

When choosing a career, individuals are driven and motivated by different factors, for example, financial success, prestige, individual recognition, or the desire to positively affect communities. Individuals, when given options, make career choices that align with their own needs, values, and motivations. Prior research concerning the motivation of public sector employees has found that job choices are often driven by the desire to serve the community, as well as other more tangible benefits (Rainey and Steinbauer, 1999; Crewson, 1997; Park and Rainey, 2007; Boyne, 2002; Wright, 2001). In the public sector, many organizational researchers and practitioners have pointed out the importance of employees' job choice motivation in the linear processes of recruitment, attraction, selection, and retention. These experts emphasize a need to understand what types of individuals seek out particular jobs and why those jobs are attractive, in order to better manage these processes, which is vital for the success of an organization as well as an important function of HRM (Leisink and Steijin, 2008; Lewis and Frank 2002).

In general, while work motivation refers to a person's desire to work hard and work well, and to the arousal, direction, and persistence of effort in the work setting, job choice motivation refers to the motives, forces, or pre-conditions that initiate and affect job choice (Ritz and Waldner, 2011). Job choice motivation is generally formalized prior to actually being employed in an organization. For this reason, job choice motivation should be conceptually and empirically differentiated from work motivation.[1] Prospective employees are expected to consider and choose jobs on the basis of various factors, including personal preferences, perceptions, organizational-social values, demographic background, previous work experience, and expectations concerning intrinsic or extrinsic rewards.

Matching organizational and employee characteristics is crucial for the success of organizations. The Person-Environment (P-E) fit model has been presented and used as a basic theoretical framework to explicate the link between employee values and job choice (Cable and Judge, 1996; Chatman, 1991). The P-E fit model is defined as "the compatibility between an individual and work environment that occurs when their characteristics are well matched" (Kristof-Brown et al., 2005: 281). From a supplementary or complementary point of view, the model, being composed of four conceptual domains—person-job, person-organization, person-group, and personsupervisor—implies that a fit between person and organization could be achieved either by attracting applicants with appropriate characteristics or by affecting the applicants once they are employed (Kristof-Brown et al., 2005: 315–16). Specifically, person-job fit is defined as value congruence at the individual level, and person-organization fit is defined as mission/strategy congruence at the organizational level. Conceptually, these definitions have a close relationship with job choice motivation as important job-entry antecedents (Leisink and Steijin, 2008). For example, research has found that individuals whose primary value orientations are consistent with public service (e.g., self-sacrifice, social equity, public interest, and civic responsibility) are more likely to accept jobs in organizations that emphasize prosocial and altruistic values, and to actively serve the goals and missions of such organizations (Judge and Bretz, 1992; Wright and Pandey, 2008).

While a number of influential extrinsic motivators that might induce job applicants to want to work in the public sector (such as opportunities for training and development, traditional job security, pension systems, and work-life balance policies) have been defined as public sector motivation, public service motivation (PSM) can be described as "individuals' pro-social (or intrinsic) motivation to do good for others and society through the delivery of public services" (Perry and Hondeghem, 2008: 3), "the motivational force that induces individuals to perform meaningful ... public, community, and social service" (Brewer and Selden, 1998: 417) and "the beliefs, values and attitudes that go beyond self-interest and organizational interest, that concern the interest of a larger political entity and that motivate individuals to act accordingly whenever appropriate" (Vandenabeele, 2007: 547). The literature concerning PSM is generally supportive of the P-E fit model, assuming that "the greater an individual's PSM, the more likely the individual will be to seek membership in a public organization" (Perry and Wise 1990: 370). Recent work (Coursey et al., 2011, Word and Park, 2009), has suggested that PSM is not restricted to organizations that are legally identified as public but is also relevant to organizations that have a public service mission. Potential employees are attracted to work or mission that values public service and personally motivates their work. Such a proposition could be similarly applied in the nonprofit sector, where the personal values of employees influence their job choice motivation and job decisions. An employee's job choice reflects his or her beliefs, attitudes, behaviors, and social activities (Park and Word, 2012).

> **Research Question 1:** Is job choice motivation in the nonprofit sector composed of sub-dimensional motivation constructs and concepts, i.e., different types of prosocial motivation, intrinsic, or extrinsic motivation? Are these latent constructs of motives conceptually and empirically distinct?
>
> **Research Question 2:** What is the impact of demographic, managerial, and organizational factors on nonprofit job choice motivation?
>
> **Research Question 3:** What is the impact of job choice motivation on community level outcomes, e.g., social and professional activities?

Intrinsic Job Choice Motivation

Intrinsic motivation is often associated with the concepts of altruism, spiritual recognition, social and job responsibility, prosocial behavior, and public service motivation. Previous research and theories concerning the origins of the nonprofit sector suggest nonprofit employees and managers are motivated by intrinsic rewards to serve their communities (Leete, 2001; Mann, 2006; Santora and Sarros, 2001; Weisbrod, 1988). Philanthropy and volunteerism are cited as unique aspects of nonprofit organizations in the face of increasingly blurred sectoral boundaries. Nonprofit organizations with a social mission or which rely on volunteers for service delivery have a "long history, deep traditions, and cultures, steeped in voluntaristic values" (Ott, 2001: 289). These values shape the culture and experiences of individuals working in the sector in both paid and unpaid positions.

A recent study examining the choice of sector by MPA and MBA graduates demonstrated the importance of values to the nonprofit sector. Tschirhart et al. (2008) found the nonprofit sector attracted graduates who were least interested in a high salary when compared to public and for-profit workers. Individuals choosing a nonprofit career placed the most importance on helping others. These findings demonstrate the importance of intrinsic motivation to nonprofit employees.

Extrinsic Job Choice Motivation

Many models of employee motivation assume market-based incentives are among the most important incentives to induce employee achievement. Market-based incentive structures rely mainly on extrinsic or tangible benefits. Extrinsic motivation refers to a desire to work for benefits such as pay, rewards, and recognition. Research suggests extrinsic rewards can crowd out, or undermine, intrinsic motivation (Deci et al, 2001). However, a recent examination of motivation among human service workers suggests that the relationship between intrinsic motivation and extrinsic reward may be more complex than commonly understood. Travis (2007) suggests extrinsic rewards are important for human service workers because extrinsic rewards are seen as tangible indications of the value of their work.

Work-Life Balance (WLB) Motivation

Work-life balance (WLB) is a key human capital strategy in organizations (Ezra and Deckman, 1996). Many organizations seek to assist employees in balancing the demands of work and family. A study of federal employees suggests that some employees are more concerned with WLB, including issues of conflict between the two, than other HRM values and systems (Park & Joaquin, 2012).[2] Compressed work weeks or flexible work hours can lead to a domino effect of positive outcomes in the areas of employee attendance, absenteeism and turnover, job satisfaction, worker savings, environmental changes, and more.[3] While scholars have examined the use of "flex time" in government, very few have examined these issues in the nonprofit sector. An examination of differences in HR practices between public and nonprofit drug treatment centers in the United Kingdom found nonprofit organizations are more likely to offer flexibility as a benefit to workers (Parry, Kelliher, Mills and Tyson, 2005). Similarly, in the United States, surveys of executives in the nonprofit sector revealed nonprofit employees place a higher premium on non-monetary aspects of their job, including fringe benefits (Leete 2001; Ban, Drahnak-Faller and Towers 2003). The importance of WLB rewards may reflect the importance of policies and practices intended to aid workers in coping with family and personal needs outside work.

Job Security Motivation

Frederick Herzberg's two-factor theory of work motivation suggests that work motivation contains two separate and independent components, which can be called hygiene factors (dissatisfiers) and intrinsic factors (motivators). Hygiene factors include job security, working conditions, salary, and interpersonal relations. According to the theory, these factors usually do not lead to higher levels of motivation, though the absence of adequate levels of pay or job security can lead to dissatisfaction. For this reason, we are examining the role that job security plays in job choice motivation.

Advancement Motivation

In contrast, the motivating factors of Herzberg's two-factor theory do have the potential to increase worker satisfaction and motivation. Motivators are mainly related to the nature of the work itself, such as performing interesting and important work, having meaningful job responsibilities, and opportunities for advancement. Many of the satisfiers, or motivating factors, are associated with advancement or recognition from an individual's employer or peers.

While "advancement" or "promotion" in organizations is generally regarded as an extrinsic reward or recognition, Herzberg's theory categorizes achievement and advancement/growth or career development as higher-level motivators, which, by definition, involve what employees actually do on the job.[4] A study of nonprofits by Devaro and Brookshire (2007) suggests that advancement in a nonprofit organization is a mode of better matching individuals with different skills and abilities to jobs for which they are best suited. The study also finds that advancement opportunities are less common for nonprofit workers because of the relatively small size of the organizations.

> **Hypothesis 1:** Job choice motivation in the nonprofit sector is composed of sub-dimensional motivation constructs, i.e., intrinsic and extrinsic job choice motivation.

Antecedents of Job Choice Motivation

The attraction-selection-attrition model (Schneider, 1987) suggests that individuals choosing a job are very likely to search for an organizational environment that matches their personal characteristics or experience, with a view to maximizing the fit between individual and environment (Ritz, 2011). For example, at the attraction-selection stage, individuals' previous work and sector experience and sector/organizational preference would be critical predictors of job choice.

Previous Sector Job Experience

Individuals now hold many jobs over the span of a career. It is likely an individual's previous work and sector experience influence their socialization, as well as the importance they place on salary and other benefits as motivational factors. Research conducted by Tschirhart et al. (2008) found graduates of MBA and MPA programs favor a particular sector and tend to remain within that sector over their career. This suggests that previous job or sector experience shapes the attitude of employees toward work and the community.

Boardman, Bozeman, and Ponomariov (2010) also found previous work experience has an impact on job satisfaction and job involvement for individuals who switched from the private to the public sector. They found that individuals who had previously worked in the private sector were more involved in their jobs than those who had no private sector experience. Similarly, Word and Park (2009) found that nonprofit sector employees demonstrate a higher level of job involvement than their public sector counterparts. Job involvement has been found to be related to intrinsic motivation (Cook et al., 1981). The higher level of job involvement characterizing those who have switched sectors suggests that individuals who leave for-profit and public organizations to join the nonprofit workforce are more intrinsically motivated than those who have only worked in the nonprofit sector.

Hypothesis 2a: Intrinsic job choice motivation will be significantly and positively associated with previous private and public sector job experience of nonprofit managers.

Hypothesis 2b: Extrinsic job choice motivation will be significantly and negatively associated with previous private and public sector job experience of nonprofit managers.

Types of Nonprofit Organizations

Hansmann (1987) suggests that different types of nonprofit organization arise to meet different needs of the market. The typology of nonprofit organizations can be determined by examining their sources of income and the ways in which they are controlled. The typology separates donative nonprofits (nonprofits that receive a substantial portion of their income from donations) from commercial nonprofits (nonprofits deriving their income primarily from sales of goods or services). This model also distinguishes nonprofits by their mode of control. Nonprofits that elect a board of directors are classified as mutual nonprofits. Nonprofits in which the board is self-perpetuating are classified as entrepreneurial nonprofits. Hansmann's model delineates four types of nonprofit: 1) donative-mutual, 2) donative-entrepreneurial, 3) commercial-mutual, and 4) commercial-entrepreneurial.

We expect that individuals working for donative nonprofits will have a stronger service orientation. Individuals working for organizations that provide selective or mutual benefits or that are in direct competition with commercial businesses will be less likely to have a strong orientation toward nonprofit service motivation.

Hypothesis 2c: Intrinsic job choice motivation will be more positively associated with nonprofit organizations that are donative-entrepreneurial (public charities) than will extrinsic job choice motivation.

Hypothesis 2d: Intrinsic job choice motivation will be less positively associated with nonprofit organizations that provide more selective benefits (commercial-entrepreneurial and donative-mutual) than will extrinsic job choice motivation.

Social and Community Outcomes of Job Choice Motivation

Previous research found that public workers with higher levels of PSM were more likely to participate in activities which promote community and enhance civic engagement, including volunteering and voting (Houston, 2006). We hypothesize that these behaviors are primarily related to the intrinsic motivations of public sector workers, rather than extrinsic or market-oriented motivations. Individuals who seek a career serving the community have been found to be more involved in activities such as voting, donating, and volunteering for charities. We anticipate the relationship between intrinsic motivation and civic and volunteer activities will be similar to the relationship reported for public sector employees, if not stronger, for nonprofit employees.

Especially from a socialization process perspective, we posit that social and community activities could be valid and reliable indicators showing how nonprofit organizations "transmit a public institutional logic and seeding PSM in the individual" and how the agencies "implement an individual's sense of public service and inculcate public service-related virtues and norms" (Brewer, 2008: 149). The relationship between motivation and the outcome of job choice motivation may be stronger partially because many nonprofit employees work on a daily basis with volunteers, and they see the importance of this type of activity directly. Research concerning volunteer retention finds that individuals are more likely to continue actively volunteering for an organization if they believe the work they are doing is challenging and provides opportunities for growth (Jamison, 2003). These findings suggest that individuals who work in the nonprofit sector might be more strongly motivated to volunteer than others because of their unique understanding of the importance of volunteering.

Different types of nonprofit organization serve different purposes (Hansmann 1987). Donative-entrepreneurial nonprofit organizations largely exist to serve broadly defined public interests, and primarily achieve those ends through donations or government subsidies. Donative-mutual nonprofit organizations mainly benefit dues-paying members, but can also benefit more broadly defined public and societal interests. In contrast, commercial-entrepreneurial and commercial-mutual nonprofits tend to provide goods and services on a fee-for-service basis, and the benefits are meant to accrue only for those paying for the

Figure 1. Antecedents and Consequences of Job Choice Motivation

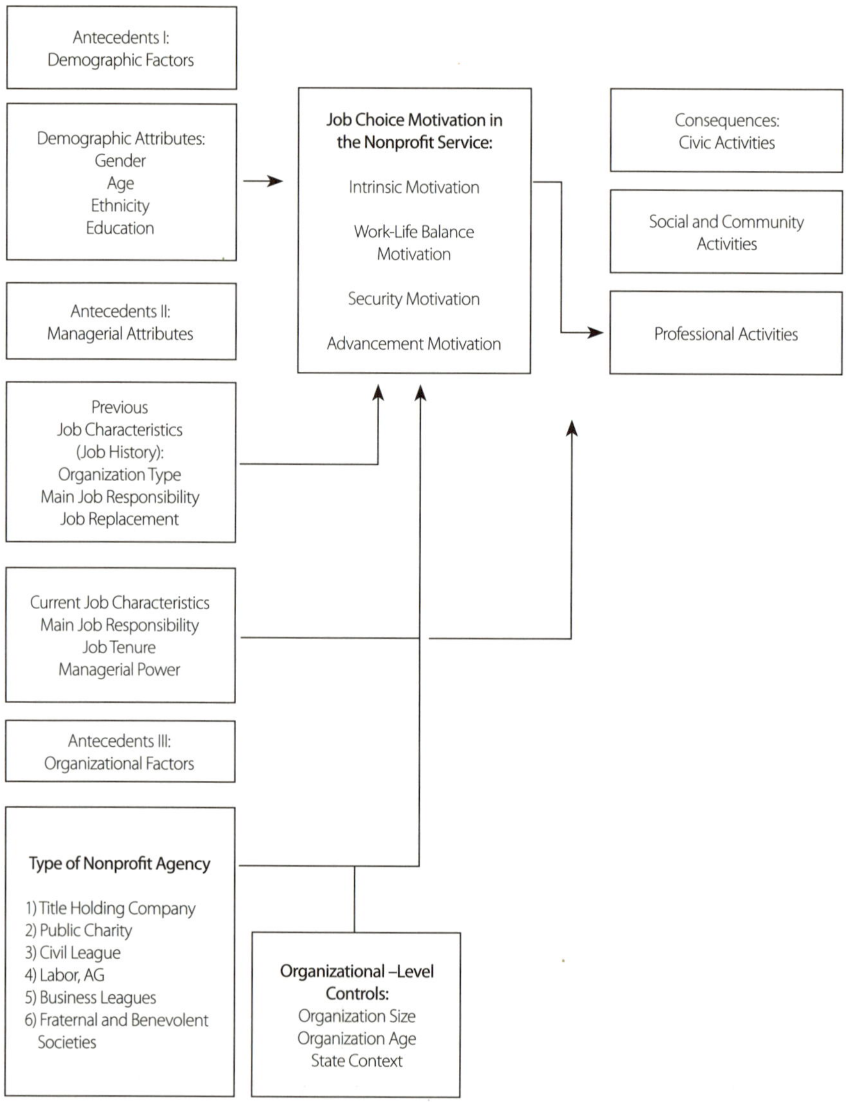

Note: Arrows denote the direct and controlling impacts on work motivation in the nonprofit sector and civic activities.

services, similar to the way in which for-profit businesses deliver goods and services to paying customers. The more narrow interests served by commercial nonprofit organizations are similar to small businesses, and the organizations have a more closed-linked market-based incentive structure than nonprofit organizations that are entrepreneurial in nature. Therefore, we predict that individuals employed by commercial and donative-mutual nonprofits will be more likely to engage in professional activities based on individual goals and rewards, rather than service to the community more broadly. In contrast, we predict that organizations serving less selective interests will be associated with individuals engaging in social and community activities that benefit a common good. Overall, we hypothesize that 1) intrinsic and extrinsic job choice motivation and 2) different types of nonprofit agency have different relationships with social and professional activities. Figure 1 summarizes the model probing the antecedents and consequences of job choice motivation in nonprofit organizations.

Hypothesis 3a: Intrinsic job choice motivation will be more positively and significantly associated with social and community activities than will extrinsic job choice motivation.

Hypothesis 3b: Intrinsic job choice motivation will be more positively and significantly associated with professional activities than will extrinsic job choice motivation.

Hypothesis 3c: Nonprofit organizations that are donative-entrepreneurial (public charities) will be positively and significantly associated with social and community activities.

Hypothesis 3d: Nonprofit organizations that are more entrepreneurial in nature (donative-mutual and commercial-entrepreneurial or -mutual) will be positively and significantly associated with professional activities.

Data and Methods

Data Sources and Sample

This study utilizes data from the NASP-III survey. The survey instrument measured mid- and upper-level managers' perceptions of various organizational issues, including work motivation, mentoring and communication, career histories, hiring practices, and organizational cultures and structures. The survey was distributed to managers (N = 430) working in nonprofits in the states of Illinois and Georgia.[5] Each organization was represented by a number of respondents, with no serious unevenness in responses from different organizations (details about descriptive statistics [Table 1] are available from the authors upon request).[6] The sample included 305 nonprofit organizations in two states, with 107 (25%) of the respondents from Georgia and 323 (75%) from Illinois. However, the organizations represented in the sample included more membership and professional associations than does the overall nonprofit sector. This over-representation of these types of organizations in part limits the generalizability of these findings, but it also allows us to more thoroughly understand this unique subset of organizations that serve the predominantly narrow interests of their members. The overall response rate was 33.0 percent. Regarding missing data adjustments, we employed the expectationmaximization (EM) algorithm method to preserve the effective sample size. This method can increase the statistical power of the regression model and reduce possible nonresponse bias in parameter estimates (Roth, 1994).

Measures of Antecedent Variables

We included three different levels of antecedent variables relative to the outcome variables—demographic factors, managerial factors, and organizational attributes. Four variables were used to examine demographic attributes of nonprofit managers: gender, age, ethnicity, and education. Gender (female = 0) and ethnicity (non-white = 1) were coded as dummy variables. Age and education factors were recoded as ordinal-level variables with four and three categories, respectively.

Previous and current job characteristics in nonprofit agencies were included as managerial attributes. Previous job characteristics (based on the preceding jobs of respondents) were 1) previous organization type, such as public (government), private company, or nonprofit organization, 2) main job responsibility, including managerial, professional, and technical positions, and 3) job replacement from promotion, lateral and upward move, or first job

Current job characteristics also included 1) current job responsibility, 2) job tenure, and 3) managerial authority (total number of employees supervised).

As key organizational factors, first following Hansmann's typology of nonprofit firms, we included three types of nonprofit organization: 1) donative-mutual, 2) donative-entrepreneurial, and 3) commercial-entrepreneurial. Public charity organizations were coded as donative-entreprenuerial agencies, whereas organizations such as civic leagues and fraternal and benevolent societies were coded as donative-mutual agencies. Examples of organizations coded as commercial-entrepreneurial/mutual included title holding companies and labor and business league organizations. Second, organizational-level controls, such as organizational size and age, and state context (Georgia = 1) were included. Organizational size and age variables were log-transformed to correct for skewness in the distribution of these variables.

Measures of Nonprofit Job Choice Motivation

Nonprofit job choice motivation variables were measured on a four-point Likert scale (1 = not important, 2 = somewhat unimportant, 3 = somewhat important, and 4 = very important), with specific statements concerning job choice motives in nonprofit agencies (see Appendix). In the NASP-III questionnaire, nonprofit managers were asked to respond to 16 survey items, regarding the factors motivating them to accept their current job. In order to obtain the underlying latent motivational dimensions from the items, we performed confirmatory factor analysis (CFA) to operationalize variables and to confirm latent constructs of nonprofit job choice motivation. Based on CFA, four nonprofit job choice motivation scales were developed from relevant survey items: 1) intrinsic motivation, 2) work-life balance (WLB) motivation, 3) security motivation, and 4) advancement motivation. The results of CFA indicated the factor loadings supported the use of these items as indicators of the four underlying constructs.

Measures of Outcome Variables: Civic Activities

In this study, 1) social and community activities and 2) professional activities were included as outcome variables. Social and community activities (nine items) were measured by asking nonprofit managers to indicate whether they were currently a member of certain organizations, such as religious organizations, political party, youth support groups, or charity/community service groups. Professional activities (eight items) were measured based on the number of memberships indicated for organizations such as professional societies, labor unions, health-related organizations, or historical associations. Using these survey responses, we developed two ordinal-level outcome variables (an 8-point scale for social and community activities and a 9-point scale for professional activities).

Statistical Analyses

A hierarchical regression model was employed to reduce effective multicollinearity problems among multiplicative and interaction terms, which often occur in organizational behavior and social science studies (Cohen and Cohen, 1983; Simons and Peterson, 2000).[7] In this research, we employed three statistical analysis procedures. First, we explored and estimated the latent constructs of different types of job choice motivation in the nonprofit sector using CFA.[8] Second, based on a multivariate hierarchical regression procedure, we tested the relationships between different types of antecedent hypothesized to affect nonprofit job choice motivation. Third, based on three hierarchical statistical steps, we analyzed the relationships among antecedents and social outcomes.

Findings and Results

The Effects of Organizational Antecedents on Job Choice Motivation

Table 2 provides the results of hierarchical multivariate regression analyses examining the impacts of individual, managerial, and organizational factors on the job choice motivations of nonprofit managers (intrinsic motivation): WLB motivation, security motivation, and advancement motivation. The different equations (steps 1, 2, and 3) were regressed on four motivation variables in order to examine changes in total variance affected by each step of factors (R^2 and F-value changes). The empirical findings of the antecedent model are summarized in Table 2.

In step 1, we probed the impact of demographic attributes on job choice motivation (R^2 ranged from 0.012 to 0.102). First, we found that gender is significantly and negatively associated with all types of motivation. The findings indicate that female nonprofit managers are likely to possess a higher level of nonprofit job choice motivation than male nonprofit managers, regardless of the type of motivation. For example, regarding the impact on intrinsic motivation, male managers reported, on average, 0.321 less intrinsic motivation than female managers in the nonprofit sector. Second, the results reveal that the age of nonprofit managers is negatively and significantly related to three types of motivation, except for intrinsic motivation, which indicates that as nonprofit managers get older, they are less concerned with security or advancement issues. Rather, they are more intrinsically motivated to choose and to stay in their job.

In step 2, the results indicate nonprofit managers who moved from the public to the nonprofit sector are more intrinsically motivated ($b = 0.374$, $p < 0.10$), and less interested in security ($b = -0.392$, $p < 0.05$) and advancement ($b = -0.297$, $p < 0.10$). This finding suggests that nonprofit workers who previously worked in the public sector are more intrinsically motivated than other nonprofit managers, which implies that the managers who made a career transition within a particular NPO category would not perceive the importance of intrinsic rewards, as they did not make a sector change and hence still have similar value/mission/motivational constructs in the new working environment. However, managers who transitioned from the public sector might more seriously recognize the importance of intrinsic values, motives, and rewards, as they perceive that there is a meaningful difference between intrinsic motives and values in the public sector (i.e., PSM) and intrinsic motives and values in the nonprofit sector (i.e., NPSM). Hence, the sector change from public agency to NGO might have a significant and positive impact on intrinsic job choice motivation within NGOs, so-called NPSM. This finding further suggests that a well-established and defined culture or structure of intrinsic rewards matters in selecting, hiring, and retaining highly qualified managers in nonprofits.[9]

Second, the results show that the managers whose previous job was obtained via promotion to a higher position from within the same organization are more likely to have a high level of advancement motivation (b = 0.393, $p < 0.05$). In contrast, WLB motivation is significantly high (b = 0.489, $p < 0.05$) if their previous job was a first job. These findings suggest that previous job and work experience are critical factors affecting current work motivation for nonprofit managers. Overall, the results of step 1 and step 2 partially support the hypothesis that nonprofit job choice motivation is significantly associated with previous private and public sector job experience. [Partially supports hypotheses 2a and 2b]

Finally, in step 3, we investigated the relationships between organizational and agency attributes (e.g., type of nonprofit agency) and four types of job choice motivation (R^2 ranged from 0.142 to 0.155). As expected, the results indicate that donativeentrepreneurial nonprofits (public charities) are positively and significantly associated with intrinsic motivation (b = 0.287, $p < 0.05$), while they are negatively and significantly related to security motivation, one type of extrinsic motivation (b = -0.195, $p < 0.05$). That is, nonprofit managers who are working in public charity agencies are prone to intrinsic motivation and tend to be less extrinsically motivated, especially in the area of job security.

Second, the results demonstrate that managers working for commercial-entrepreneurial organizations are less intrinsically motivated (b = -0.143, $p < 0.05$), but are more likely to perceive a high level of security motivation in their workplace (b = 0.095, $p < 0.10$). Overall, the findings from step 3 fully support the hypotheses suggesting intrinsic motivation will be more positively associated with nonprofit organizations that are donative-entrepreneurial (public charities), whereas intrinsic motivation will be less positively associated with nonprofit organizations that are more commercial. [Supports hypotheses 2c and 2d]

Table 2. Results of Hierarchical Multivariate Regression Analysis: Antecedents of Nonprofit Job Choice Motivation

	Dependent Variables			
	Model 1: Short-Term Consequences Job Choice Motivation in the Nonprofit Sector			
Antecedent Variables	Intrinsic Motivation (N=415)	WLB Motivation (N=414)	Security Motivation (N=418)	Advancement Motivation (N=416)
Step 1: Individual-Level Controls	Coefficient (SE)	Coefficient (SE)	Coefficient (SE)	Coefficient (SE)
Gender (female: 0)	**-.321***** (.119)	**-.225**** (.116)	**-.236**** (.116)	**-.236**** (.118)
Age	.003 (.006)	**-.018***** (.006)	**-.016***** (.006)	**-.018***** (.006)
Ethnicity (non-white: 1)	-.044 (.264)	**.486*** (.277)	**.466*** (.261)	.006 (.263)
Level of Education	.004 (.089)	**-.237***** (.088)	**-.267***** (.088)	-.122 (.088)
Partial F Value	1.872	7.564***	7.942***	4,956***
R^2	.012	.099	.102	066
Step 2: Managerial Attributes (Previous Sector Job Experience)				
1. Organizational Type (Previous)				
Public Agencies to NPO	**.374*** (.207)	.094 (.206)	**-.392**** (.206)	**-.297*** (.174)
Private Companies to NPO	.029 (.144)	.030 (.143)	-.062 (.144)	**-.333**** (.142)
Nonprofit Organizations to NPO	.042 (.119)	.088 (.118)	.109 (.118)	-.097 (.118)
2. Main Responsibility (Previous)				
Job Responsibility: Manager	-.288 (.201)	.296 (.199)	.147 (.196)	.021 (.194)
Job Responsibility: Professional	**-.550**** (.226)	.288 (.225)	-.036 (.223)	-.169 (.220)
Job Responsibility: Technical	**-.659*** (.337)	.406 (.335)	.141 (.335)	.009 (.332)
3. Managerial-Level Controls: Job Replacement (Previous)				
Promotion	.313 (.221)	.005 (.219)	.075 (.216)	**.393**** (.203)
Lateral Move	.201 (.221)	.089 (.219)	.110 (.217)	.052 (.214)
Upward Move	.144 (.206)	.231 (.204)	.171 (.200)	.084 (.199)
First Job	.162 (.414)	**.489**** (.197)	.219 (.411)	-.127 (.407)
Partial F Value	7.664***	2.359***	2.706***	2.654***
R^2	.131	.126	.139	.137
ΔR^2	.119	.027	.037	.071
Step 3: Organizational Attributes				
1. Type of Nonprofit Agency				
Donative-Entrepreneurial Agencies: Public Charity	**.287**** (.120)	-.074 (.119)	**-.195**** (.101)	-.038 (.117)

Donative-Mutual Agencies: Civil League; Fraternal and Benevolent Societies	-.047 (.498)	-.201 (.493)	-.157 (.494)	**-.977**** (.489)
Commercial-Entrepreneurial/Mutual Agencies: Title Holding Companies; -Labor, AG; Business Leagues	**.143** (.059)**	.018 (.057)	**.095*** (.574)	0.32 (.059)
2. Agency-Level Controls				
Organization Size (natural log)	.000 (.000)	.000 (.000)	.000 (.000)	.000 (.000)
Organization Age (natural log)	.001 (.002)	.001 (.002)	**-.003*** (.002)	.000 (.002)
State Context (Georgia: 1)	**.300**** (.146)	**.406**** (.146)	**-.278**** (.144)	.164 (.144)
Partial F Value	7.311***	2.475***	2.771***	2.290***
R^2	.153	.154	.155	.142
ΔR^2	.034	.028	.016	.005

***p < 0.01: significant at the 0.01 level
**p < 0.05: significant at the 0.05 level
*p < 0.10: significant at the 0.10 level
Critical values (two-tailed test) are 1.96 for p < 0.05 and 1.65 for p < 0.10 (t-statistics are in parentheses).

The Effects of Job Choice Motivation on Social and Community Outcomes

Table 3 presents the results of the analysis of the effects of job choice motivation on social outcomes, including 1) social and community activities and 2) professional activities. Gender effects at step 1 show that male managers are more likely to contribute to social and community activities (b = 0.516, $p < 0.01$) than female managers. However, there is no relationship between gender and professional activities, which implies that the higher contributions of male managers to social and community activities is a function of there being more opportunities and preference for male managers to be involved with political, religious, and community issues than for female managers. At the managerial level in step 2 ($R^2 = 0.094$ for social and community activities; $R^2 = 0.044$ for professional activities), intrinsic motivation in nonprofit agencies, which is one of the key variables in this study, is positively and significantly associated with both outcome variables (b = 0.232, $p < 0.05$; b = 0.043, $p < 0.10$, respectively). The significant relationship between the outcome variables suggests that intrinsically motivated managers are more involved with social and professional activities than managers who are motivated by extrinsic or other hygiene factors, such as security or advancement motivation. In addition, we found security motivation to be negatively related to social and community activities. In other words, the more managers are concerned with their job security, the less likely they are to spend time on social activities. One explanation for this relationship is that managers might work extra hours and might have substantial additional job obligations to ensure job security and advancement at the expense of having time for social activities.

In analysis at the organizational level (step 3), we examined the relationships among type of nonprofit agency and social and professional activities (R^2 = 0.135 for social and community activities; R^2 = 0.079 for professional activities). These results indicate that nonprofit managers from commercial-mutual agencies are significantly involved with social and community activities (b = 0.117, $p < 0.05$). The findings also show that commercial-entrepreneurial nonprofit managers are more likely to contribute to professional activities (b = 0.139, $p < 0.05$), but nonprofit managers at donative-entrepreneurial (public charity) agencies are less concerned with professional activities (b= -0.097, $p < 0.05$). The overall findings from the model partially support our initial hypotheses predicting that intrinsic motivation will be more positively and significantly associated than extrinsic motivation with social, community, and professional activities, and that nonprofit managers working at different types of nonprofit agencies will have different preferences for social and professional activities. [Partially supports hypotheses 3a, 3b, 3c, and 3d]

Table 3. Results of Hierarchical Multivariate Regression Analysis: Consequences of Nonprofit Job Choice Motivation

	Dependent Variables	
	Model 2: Long-Term Consequences Personal Civic Activities	
Antecedent Variables	Social and Community Activities	Professional Activities
Step 1: Individual-Level Controls	Coefficient (SE)	Coefficient (SE)
Gender (female: 0)	**.516****** (.170)	-.034 (.041)
Age	.009 (.009)	.002 (.002)
Ethnicity (non-white: 1)	.026 (.401)	-.009 (.096)
Level of Education	.025 (.190)	.032 (.031)
Partial F Value	3.283**	.640
R^2	.05	.010
Step 2: Managerial Attributes (Current Job Characteristics)		
1. Managerial-Level Controls: Main Responsibility (Current)		
Job Responsibility: Manager	-.632 (.483)	.131 (.116)
Job Responsibility: Professional	-.628 (.536)	.090 (.129)
Job Responsibility: Technical	**-1.736*** (1.051)	.100 (.253)
Job Tenure	.003 (.014)	.001 (.003)
Managerial Authority (Supervisory Status)	.000 (.001)	.000 (.000)
2. Managerial-Level Controls: Job Replacement (Current)		

Promotion	.056 (.233)	.041 (.056)
Lateral Move	-.020 (.509)	.149 (.122)
Upward Move	.155 (.226)	**.086*** (.044)
First Job	-.141 (1.337)	.048 (.322)
3. Job Choice Motivation in the Nonprofit Sector		
Intrinsic Motivation	**.232*** (.096)**	**.043* (.024)**
WLB Motivation	-.015 (.096)	.013 (.023)
Security Motivation	**-.169* (.093)**	-.029 (.022)
Advancement Motivation	-.063 (.099)	.002 (.024)
Partial F Value	2.431*	.637
R^2	.094	.044
ΔR^2	.044	.034
Step 3: Organizational Attributes		
1. Type of Nonprofit Agency		
Donative-Entrepreneurial Agencies: Public Charity	.066 (.178)	**-.097**** (.043)
Donative-Mutual Agencies: Civil League; Fraternal and Benevolent Societies	**.117**** (.062)	-.116 (.165)
Commercial-Entrepreneurial/Mutual Agencies: Title Holding Companies; -Labor, AG; Business Leagues	-.082 (.062)	**.139**** (.064)
2. Agency-Level Controls		
Organization Size (natural log)	.000 (.000)	.000 (.000)
Organization Age (natural log)	-.003 (.003)	.000 (.001)
State Context (Georgia: 1)	**.433** (.220)**	.032 (.053)
Partial F Value	2.498**	.783
R^2	.135	.079
ΔR^2	.041	.035

***p < 0.01: significant at the 0.01-level
**p < 0.05: significant at the 0.05-level
*p < 0.10: significant at the 0.10-level
Critical values (two-tailed test) are 1.96 for p < 0.05 and 1.65 for p < 0.10 (t-statistics are in parentheses).

Discussion and Implications

Light (2002) suggests that one of the most important qualities of the nonprofit sector is the ability to motivate and attract a workforce through the appeal of serving one's community. In this regard, HR management is one of the most pressing management concerns for professional organizations in all sectors. Essentially, we anticipated that the core HR management functions such as planning, classification, recruitment, selection, compensation, benefits, performance evaluation and assessment, training, development, discipline, termination, and EEO would play crucial roles in enhancing NGO managers' job choice motivation per se. For example, objective and sustainable employee appraisal systems, effectively adopted employee-friendly policies/diversity management policies, or well-designed and implemented human resource development policies would eventually contribute to boosting the job choice motivation of nonprofit managers in a meaningful way. The findings of this research support the idea that intrinsic motivation is an important aspect of job choice motivation for individuals in the nonprofit workforce. In addition, this research found that other characteristics, including policies that enhance WLB, advancement, and job security, are important to understand the motivations of the nonprofit workforce and their choice to work in the sector. This research also found that these different motivational aspects have consequences for communities, and that not all types of nonprofit agencyies attract similarly motivated individuals, or lead to equivalent community outcomes.

As the nonprofit sector has developed, researchers and scholars have tended to focus on public charities, since they make up the largest portion of the sector. However, many different types of organization populate the nonprofit sector, and our research reveals the differences that exist between the type of nonprofit organization and the factors that motivate individuals to choose nonprofit jobs across the sector. Our study used Hansmann's typology to examine the differences in employee motivation between more charitable organizations and organizations that tend to serve more narrow or market-based interests.

First, employees working for donative-entrepreneurial nonprofit organizations tended to be more intrinsically motivated and less concerned about job security. This finding suggests that employees in this part of the sector are especially drawn to intrinsic values commonly associated with service and volunteerism. In contrast, employees working for commercial-entrepreneurial nonprofits are less intrinsically motivated and more motivated by issues related to job security. This suggests organizations that tend to compete more directly with businesses, or serve more narrowly defined interests, have employees who are differently motivated than their public charity counterparts.

Additionally, our findings suggest that different types of nonprofit organization have different impacts on the communities they serve. Mutual nonprofits, such as civic leagues and fraternal orders, have a strong positive relationship with involvement in social and community activities. This is not surprising, since community involvement is exactly the type of activity that many of these organizations have been created to promote. Additionally, commercial-entrepreneurial agencies tend to increase participation in professional activities, and decrease participation in social and community activities. Again, the strong relationship between professional activity and commercial-entrepreneurial agencies is tied to the core mission of many of these organizations, which were created to serve the promotion of a particular business or profession. However, the negative relationship between employment in these agencies and social and community activities suggests that one type of activity may crowd out the other. Finally, employment in donative-entrepreneurial nonprofits tends to decrease participation in professional activities. This might be due to the lack of a strong professional identity for individuals in the nonprofit sector, which includes individuals from many different professions.

One of the more surprising findings of our research is the significant impact that gender has on motivation and its consequences. Being male has a strong negative effect on all four motivational constructs: intrinsic, work-life balance, security, and advancement. The negative relationship between being male and expressing a strong commitment to work-life balance policies is likely due to the role that women play in society outside of the office. Although gender roles have changed, significant evidence suggests that women still perform more unpaid domestic labor (Kroska, 2004; Lee and Waite, 2005) and place a stronger emphasis on family (Mennino, Rubin and Brayfield, 2005).

The findings regarding advancement, security, and intrinsic motivation are more surprising. Bright's (2005) examination of public service motivation does find that women, in general, are more likely to value public service. In light of our findings about intrinsic motivation, the tendency of women to value public service more than men seems to hold true for the nonprofit sector. The tendency for men in the nonprofit sector to value advancement less than women may say more about the characteristics of women in the nonprofit sector than it does about men. Women may see the sector, which tends to be heavily female, as supportive of their desire to advance, whereas in other sectors, the expression of the desire to advance might be muted due to social pressures for women not to compete.

One of the more interesting findings is related to employees who had previously worked in the public sector. These employees demonstrated higher levels of intrinsic motivation and were less interested in security and advancement. This suggests that moving to the nonprofit sector is a choice based on the desire of these individuals to serve others. Similarly, those moving from the for-profit to the nonprofit sector placed a lower emphasis on advancement. This finding supports the assertion that workers in the nonprofit sector are unique in their valuation of service to others (Light, 2002; Benz, 2005; Rose-Ackerman, 1996). Another interesting difference in terms of intrinsic motivation is the negative relationship between professional and technical job responsibilities. This finding suggests that individuals in professional or technical positions in nonprofit organizations may have different motivations, which are more closely related to their profession than to values of public or community service.

The positive relationship between intrinsic motivation and all aspects of civic engagement suggests that intrinsic motivation has a positive influence not only on individuals, but also on the communities they serve. This finding supports the notion that nonprofit organizations embody and encourage community building and civic activities (LeRoux, 2007; Berry and Arons, 2003). The link between nonprofit employment and community outcomes also suggests that nonprofits not only support and encourage engagement in those they serve, but also in their own employees. In this regard, nonprofit agencies should consider innovative managerial strategies for effectively developing key nonprofit HR functions to attract and retain the right employees (e.g., the functions of selecting and hiring, and training and development). Additionally, strategies aimed at maintaining optimal levels of employee morale and engagement could ultimately contribute to the enhancement of the intrinsic motivation of employees, as well as to increasing their involvement in social and professional activities to benefit their community.

The important contributions of this study should be acknowledged in light of certain limitations. This study relied on a cross-sectional design. Thus, conclusions regarding causal connections between individual-level and organization-level factors and community-level outcomes (e.g., social and professional activities) of NGO managers should be made with great caution. First, the cross-sectional design does not offer a clear cause-and-effect relationship between the variables examined in the present study. We need more qualitative studies to shed light on what happens in the nonprofit sector. Though we can make a number of observations here based on quantitative data, it would be greatly useful to take a closer look at the causal mechanism to know more about the roles of crucial variables such as job choice motivation, job characteristics, and various types of civic activity. Second, the individual-level analysis of self-reported data cannot avoid common method bias. Based on Harman's single-factor test, we found that common method variance is not a huge concern in this study, but future researchers should collect panel data from multiple sources, at multiple locations to reduce the potential bias. Future research is needed to investigate more fully the motivations of nonprofit employees. Future research may include the application of a similar scale to public service motivation, or the creation of a new model entirely. Further development and testing of motivational models for the nonprofit sector will enhance the ability of nonprofit managers to understand how to better manage and motivate their workforce, and ultimately, to more effectively carry out their mission. Additionally, improvements in our understanding of motivation in the nonprofit sector will enhance our understanding of what makes the sector unique and what types of management strategy (e.g., either from a supplementary or complementary perspective) are appropriate to achieve a best fit between person and organization in the nonprofit sector.

Notes

1. Upon a reviewer's request, we highlighted the different constructs between job choice motivation and work motivation based upon the measurement scales that are popularly used in the field of HRM.

1) Job Motivation Scale (Patchen, Pelz, and Allen, 1965)

This questionnaire, one of the few direct measures of job motivation, poses the following questions:

- On most days on your job, how often does time seem to drag for you?
- Some people are completely involved in their job—hey are absorbed in it night and day. For other people, their job is simply one of several interests. How involved do you feel in your job?
- How often do you do some extra work for your job that isn't really required of you?
- Would you say that you work harder, less hard, or about the same as other people doing your type of work at [name of organization]?

2) Work Motivation Scale (Wright, 2004)

- I put forth my best effort to get the job done regardless of the difficulties.
- I am willing to start work early or stay late to finish a job.
- It has been hard for me to get very involved in my current job. (Reversed)
- I do extra work for my job that isn' really expected of me.
- Time seems to drag while I am on the job. (Reversed)

2. Regarding the WFP issues, Hoyman & Duer (2004) discuss the shift from traditional familyfriendly policies (FFP) to the worker-friendly policies that are currently preferred. They present a fourfold typology of systematic criteria to measure the effectiveness of the different worker-friendly policies. The four worker-friendly policies consist of the following: 1) old family/personal type of policies, 2) removing impediments to work, 3) training and education, and 4) non-traditional incentives.
3. Compressed workweeks (CW) or flexible work hours are non-traditional, flexible work schedules that can be used to supplement, complement, transform, or replace the traditional 40-hour work week. In CW, the worker attends a shorter number of days within the workweek, but works a longer workday, e.g., a 4-day-week, 10-hour-day schedule.
4. Career development (CD) can be defined as an ongoing process by which individuals progress through a series of stages, each characterized by a relatively unique set of issues, themes and tasks. CD is usually divided into two steps: 1) Career Planning,

which assesses individuals' skills and abilities in order to establish a realistic career plan, and 2) Career Management, which focuses on taking necessary steps to achieve that established plan.

5. Hierarchical linear modeling (HLM) explicitly explains the nested nature of data, and simultaneously estimates the impact of factors at different levels on individual-level outcomes while maintaining appropriate levels of analysis for predictors (Raudenbush et al., 2000). One of the rationales for using the HLM method is that ordinary least squares (OLS) modeling does not take into account the interdependence of individual-level observations (N=430) nested within higher-level (i.e., agency-level) nonprofit agencies (N=305). As a hierarchical ordering structure is evident in nonprofit agencies, first, this study employed ANCOVA and the intercepts- and slopes-as-outcomes models, which provide unique intercept and slope estimates for each nonprofit agency. However, the results from their hierarchical regression models are not significantly different to those from the ANCOVA and the intercepts- and slopes-as-outcomes models of HLM. Some of the local nonprofit organizations at level 2 (agency-level) included in the sample are:
Nonprofit organizations based in Georgia (Total N: 92 local NPOs)
Nonprofit organizations based in Illinois (Total N: 213 local NPOs)

Local Nonprofit Agency Name	STATE
Accreditation Review Commission on Education for the Physician Assistants	GA
AGC - Georgia Branch	GA
Alston & Bird	GA
American Academy of Pediatrics Georgia Chapter	GA
American Academy of Religion	GA
American Apparel Producers Network	GA
American Association of Occupational Health Nurses Inc	GA
American Association of Physician Specialists Inc	GA
Association for Clinical Pastoral Education	GA
Association of Black Cardiologists	GA
Association of Energy Engineers	GA
Association of Rheumatology Health Professionals	GA
Association Services Group	GA
Atlanta Convention & Visitors Bureau	GA
Atlanta Enterprise Center	GA
Bobby Dodd Institute	GA
Council of Administrators of Special Education Inc.	GA
Decision Sciences Institute	GA
Delta Air Lines	GA
Elberton Granite Association	GA
Georgia Association of Educational Leaders	GA
Georgia Association of Homes & Services for Children	GA
Georgia Association of Realtors	GA
Georgia Council on Substance Abuse	GA
Georgia Society of Association Executives	GA
Georgia Tech Alumni Association	GA
Georgia Tennis Association	GA
Georgia Trial Lawyers Association	GA
Georgia Utility Contractors Association	GA
Georgia Water & Pollution Control Association Inc	GA

Georgia World Congress Center	GA
Greater Atlanta Home Builders Association	GA
Greater Columbus Home Builders Association	GA
Hyatt Regency Atlanta	GA
Independent Insurance Agents of Georgia Inc	GA
Institute for Professionals in Taxation	GA
Institute of Industrial Engineers	GA
International Group of Accounting Firms	GA
Jekyll Island Club Hotel	GA
Jones & Kolb Certified Public Accountants	GA
Marriott Bay Point Resort Village	GA
My Brothaz HOME	GA
Professional Photographers of America Inc	GA
Professional Pricing Society	GA
Radisson Riverfront Hotel Augusta	GA
Rechargeable Battery Recycling Corporation	GA
SACS	GA
Savannah Area Convention & Visitors Bureau	GA
Savannah International Trade & Convention Center	GA
South Eastern Fabricare Association	GA
Southeastern Electric Exchange	GA
Southern Cable Telecommunications Association	GA
Southern Crop Production Association	GA
State & Territorial Injury Prevention Directors Association	GA
State Bar of Georgia	GA
Tech Association of the Pulp & Paper Industry	GA
The One Joshua Group LLC	GA
US Poultry & Egg Association	GA
Utilities Protection Center Inc	GA
Wood Component Manufacturers Association	GA
Academy of General Dentistry National Office	GA
Accreditation Association for Ambulatory Health Care	IL
Air Movement & Control Association International Inc	IL
All AmericaSelections	IL
Allerton Crowne Plaza Chicago	IL
Ambassadors International Inc	IL
AMC-Association Management Center	IL
American Academy of Cosmetic Surgery	IL
American Academy of Dermatology	IL
American Dietetic Association	IL
American Farm Bureau Foundation for Agriculture	IL
American Health Info Management Association	IL
American Hospital Association	IL
American Hospital Association Certification Center	IL
American Institute of Architects - Illinois	IL
American Institute of Architects Chicago Chapter	IL
American Library Association	IL
American Massage Therapy Association	IL
American Medical Association	IL
American Nuclear Society	IL
American Oil Chemists Society	IL
American Orthopedic Association	IL
American Orthopedic Society for Sports Medicine	IL
American Osteopathic Association	IL
American Planning Association Chicago Office	IL
American Rental Association	IL
American Society for Clinical Pathology	IL
American Society for Gastrointestinal Endoscopy	IL
American Society for Healthcare Central Service Professionals	IL

American Society for Surgery of the Hand	IL
American Society of Anesthesiologists	IL
Casket & Funeral Supply Association of America	IL
CCIM Institute	IL
Champaign County Convention & Visitors Bureau	IL
Chicago Bar Association	IL
Chicago Convention & Tourism Bureau	IL
Chicago Dental Society	IL
Chicagoland Chamber of Commerce	IL
Child Care Association of Illinois	IL
Children Affected by Aids Foundation	IL
College of American Pathologists	IL
Conference Services Inc	IL
Cook Witter Inc	IL
Corcoran Expositions Inc	IL
Council of Residential Specialists	IL
Crowne Plaza Metro	IL
Dairy Management Inc	IL
Dental Assisting National Board	IL
Depression & Bipolar Support Alliance	IL
Desmond & Ahern, LTD	IL
DuPage County Farm Bureau	IL
HAB Assoc Inc	IL
Healthcare Financial Management Association	IL
Healthcare Financial Management Association	IL
Healthcare Info & Management Systems Society	IL
Home Sweet Home Ministries Inc	IL
Illinois Agricultural Association Foundation	IL
Illinois Agricultural Association Winnebago County	IL
Illinois Association of Health, Physical Education, Recreation & Dance	IL
Illinois Association of Mutual Insurance Companies	IL
Illinois Association of Park Districts	IL
Illinois Association of Realtors	IL
Illinois Association of School Administrators	IL
Illinois Association of School Boards	IL
Illinois Association of School Business Officials	IL
Illinois Bankers Association	IL
Illinois Certified Public Accountants Society	IL
Illinois Funeral Directors Association	IL
Illinois Health Care Association	IL
Illinois Movers & Warehousemen' Association	IL
Illinois Municipal League	IL
Illinois Optometric Association	IL
Library & Info Technology Association	IL
Manufacturers Representatives Educational Research Foundation	IL
Material Handling Equipment Distributors Association	IL
McLean County Chamber of Commerce	IL
Mechanical Contractors Association of Chicago	IL
Metals Service Center Institute	IL
Mid America International Agriculture Trade Council	IL
Midwest Association of Golf Course Superintendents	IL
National PTA	IL
National Roofing Contractors Association	IL
Radiological Society of North American Inc	IL
Real Estate Buyers Agent Council	IL
Refrigeration Service Engineers Society	IL
Rotary International	IL
RSM McGladrey Inc - Schaumburg	IL
Sheraton Chicago Hotel & Towers	IL

Society of Women Engineers	IL
Springfield Illinois Convention & Visitors Bureau	IL
The Center for Association Growth	IL
The Council of State Governments	IL
The Sanford Org Inc	IL
The Sherwood Group Inc	IL
The Stolberg Group	IL
Training Systems Inc	IL
Turnaround Management Association	IL
Urban & Regional Info Systems Association	IL
Urban Libraries Council	IL
US Business & Industry Council	IL
USA Council of Serra International	IL
W T B Assoc Inc	IL
West 40 Intermediate Service Center	IL
Wheeling Prospect Heights Area Chamber of Commerce & Industry	IL
Window & Door Manufacturers Association	IL

6. Skewness indicates whether the item's distribution deviates from the symmetry distribution. Kurtosis measures the degree to which the area in a distribution is in the middle and the tails of a distribution. As a rule of thumb, the range of ±2 is often considered a significant departure from normality (Pedhazur, 1997). In this research, most items show a relatively stable and similar amount of variance. In terms of individual normality, most items have a high positive kurtosis value, which means that most respondents have selected the same response option. Most variables of skewness or kurtosis are between $-2 < s(k) < 2$, and we can argue that these variables are approximately normally distributed.
7. At the initial stage, we employed both OLS regression and ordered logit regression techniques, and found that most results show similarity. For example, in terms of the effects of job choice motivation on social and community outcomes, ordered logit regression results reveal that intrinsic motivation is also positively and significantly associated with both outcome variables ($b = 0.436$, $p < 0.05$; $b = 0.091$, $p < 0.10$, respectively), whereas other types of job choice motivation show relatively weak or negative relationships with the variables. In this regard, for ease of interpretation, we focus on the OLS regression outputs in the text.
8. In the CFA model, the maximum likelihood (ML) method was employed. Severe nonnormality patterns were not observed on multivariate normality tests, and therefore the ML method in CFA was deemed more unbiased, consistent, and efficient for this analysis, especially because the population distribution for the endogenous variables was multivariate normal (Kline, 2005). Also, the covariance matrix was used as input to LISREL 8.72 in order to examine the 4-factor measurement model of CFA. The CFA results reported are shown below.

Motivation in the Nonprofit Sector

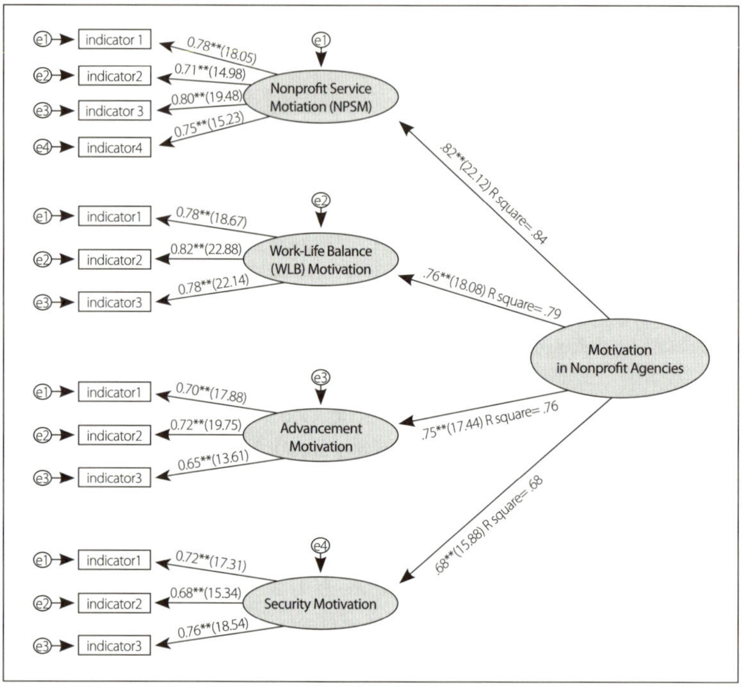

Overall Fit Indexes of the CFA Model

Model 1	df	Chi-Square	CFI	NNFI	NFI	IFI	RFI	RMSEA	SRMR
Suggested Cut-off Valu es			>.95	>.95	>.95	>.95	>.95	<.08	<.08
A Measurement Model	268	243.67	.96	.97	.99	.98	.96	.06	.067

9. One of the plausible explanations for "why previous sector job experience in a public agency shows a positive impact on intrinsic job choice motivation, while previous sector job experience in NPO is not likely to increase intrinsic job choice motivation" might come from Deci and Ryan's SDT, which provides a valuable comprehensive research framework to explore the different types of job choice motivation in the nonprofit sector. That is, SDT suggests that there is a higher level of extrinsic motivation called "identification and integration," and these types of extrinsic motivation are regarded as autonomous types of motivation, whose characteristics are very similar to intrinsic motivation. Those categorizations imply that PSM or public service-based job choice motivation might be similar to autonomous types of motivation, whereas intrinsic (job choice) motivation itself might share some similarities with nonprofit sector motivation (NPSM) or nonprofit sector job choice motivation.

References

Ban, C., Drahnak-Faller, A., & Towers, M. (2003). Human resource challenges in human service and community development organizations: Recruitment and retention of professional staff. *Review of Personnel Administration, 23*(2), 133-153.

Berry, J. M., & Arons, D. F. (2003). *A voice for nonprofits.* Washington, DC: Brookings Institution.

Boardman, C., Bozeman, B., & Ponomariov, B. (2010). Private sector imprinting: An examination of the impacts of private sector job experience on public managers' work attitudes. *Public Administration Review, 70*(1), 50-59.

Boyne, G. A. (2002). Public and private management: What's the difference?. *Journal of Management Studies, 16*(1), 67-88.

Brewer, G. A. (2008). Employee and organizational performance. In J. L. Perry & A. Hondeghem (Eds.), *Motivation in public management: The call of public service* (pp. 136-156). New York: Oxford University Press.

Brewer, G. A., & Selden, S. C. (1998). Whistle blowers in the federal civil service: New evidence of the public service ethic. *Journal of Public Administration Research and Theory, 8,* 413-439.

Bright, L. (2005). Public employees with high levels of service motivation: Who are they, where are they, and what do they want?. *Review of Public Personnel Administration, 25*(2), 138-154.

Brinkerhoff, J. M., & Brinkerhoff, D. W. (2002). Government-nonprofit relations in a comparative perspective: Evolution, themes, and new directions. *Public Administration and Development, 22*(1), 3-18.

Cohen, J., & Cohen, P. (1983). *Applied multiple regression/correlation analysis for the behavioral sciences* (2nd ed.). Hillsdale, NJ: Erlbaum.

Cook, J. D., Hepworth, S. J., Wall, T. D., & Warr, P. B. (1981). *The experience of work: A compendium and review of 249 measures and their use.* London: Academic Press.

Crewson, P. E. (1997). Public service motivation: Building empirical evidence of incidence and effect. *Journal of Public Administration Research and Theory, 7*(4), 499-518.

Deci, E. L., Ryan, R. M., & Koestner, R. (2001). The pervasive negative effects of rewards on intrinsic motivation: Response to Cameron. *Review of Education Research, 71*(1), 43-51.

Devaro, J., & Brookshire, D. (2007). Promotions and incentives in nonprofit and for profit organizations. *Industrial and Labor Relations Review, 60*(3), 311-339.

DiMaggio, P. J., & Anheier, H. K. (1990). The sociology of nonprofit organizations and sectors. *Annual Reviews of Sociology, 16*(1), 137-159.

Feeney, M. K., & Bozeman, B. (2008). Staying late: Comparing work hours in the public and nonprofit sectors. *American Review of Public Administration, 39*(5), 459-77.

Hansmann, H. (1987). Economic theories of nonprofit organization. In W. W. Powell (Ed.), *The nonprofit sector: A research handbook.* New Haven: Yale University Press.

Hogue, M., DuBois, C. L., & Fox-Cardamone, L. (2010). Gender differences in pay expectations: The roles of job intention and self-view. *Psychology of Women Quarterly, 34*(2), 215-227.

Houston, D. J. (2006). "Walking the walk" of public service motivation: Public employees and charitable gifts of time, blood, and money. *Journal of Public Administration and Research Theory, 16,* 67-86.

Jamison, I. B. (2003). Turnover and retention among volunteer human service agencies. *Review of Public Personnel Administration, 23*(2), 114-132.

Kim, J., & Mahoney, J. T. (2005). Property rights theory, transaction costs theory, and agency theory: An organizational economics approach to strategic management. *Managerial and Decision Economics, 26*(4), 223-242.

Kline, R. B. (2005). *Principles and practices of structural equation modeling.* NY: Guilford.

Kroska, A. (2004). Divisions of domestic work: Revising and expanding the theoretical explanations. *Journal of Family Issues, 25*(7), 900-932.

Lee, Y., & Waite, L. J. (2005). Husbands' and wives' time spent on housework: A comparison of measures. *Journal of Marriage and Family, 67*(2), 328-336.

Leete, L. (2001). Whiter the nonprofit wage differential? Estimates from the 1990 Census. *Journal of Labor Economics, 19*(1), 136-170.

Leete, L. (2006). Work in the nonprofit sector. In W. W. Powell & R. Steinberg (Eds.), *The nonprofit sector: A research handbook* (pp. 159-179). New Haven, CT: Yale University Press.

LeRoux, K. (2007). Nonprofits as civic intermediaries: The role of community-based organizations in promoting political participation. *Urban Affairs Review, 42*(3), 410-422.

Light, P. C. (2002). The content of their character: The state of the nonprofit workforce. *The Nonprofit Quarterly, 9*(3), 6-16.

Lyons, S. T., Duxbury, L. E., & Higgins, C. A. (2006). A Comparison of the values and commitment of private sector, public sector, and parapublic sector employees. *Public Administration Review, 66*(4), 605-618.

Mann, G. A. (2006). A motive to serve: Public service motivation in human resource management and the role of PSM in the nonprofit sector. *Public Personnel Management, 25*(1), 33-48.

Mennino, S. F., Rubin, B. A., & Brayfield, A. (2005). Home-to-job and job-to-home spillover: The impact of company policies and workplace culture. *Sociological Quarterly, 46*(1), 107-135.

Mirabella, R. M., & Wish, N. B. (2000). The "best place" debate: A comparison of graduate education programs for nonprofit managers. *Public Administration Review, 60*(3). 219-229.

Ott, J. S. (2001). *The nature of the nonprofit sector.* Boulder, CO: Westview Press.

Park, S. M., & Joaquin, M. E. (2012). Of alternating waves and shifting shores: The configuration of reform values in the U.S. federal bureaucracy. *International Review of Administrative Sciences, 78*(3), 514-536.

Park, S. M., & Rainey, H. G. (2007). Antecedents, mediators, and consequences of affective, normative, and continuance commitment: Empirical tests of commitment effects in federal agencies. *Review of Public Personnel Administration, 27*(3), 197-226.

Park, S. M., & Word, J. (2012). Driven to service: Intrinsic and extrinsic motivation for public and nonprofit managers. *Public Personnel Management, 41*(4), 681-710.

Parry, E., Kelliher, C., Mills, T., & Tyson, S. (2005). Comparing HRM in the voluntary and public sectors. *Personnel Review, 34*(5), 588-602.

Perry, J. L., & Hondeghem, A. (2008). *Motivation in public management: The call of public service.* New York: Oxford University Press.

Perry, J. L., & Wise, L. R. (1990). The motivational basis of public service. *Public Administration Review, 50*(3), 367-373.

Pinder, C. G. (1998). *Work motivation in organizational behavior.* Upper Saddle River, NJ: Prentice-Hall.

Rainey, H. G. (2009). *Understanding and managing public organizations.* San Francisco: Jossey-Bass.

Rainey, H. G., & Bozeman, B. (2000). Comparing public and private organizations: Empirical research and the power of the a priori. *Journal of Public Administration Research and Theory, 10*(2), 447-469.

Rainey, H. G., & Steinbauer, P. (1999) Galloping elephants: Developing elements of a theory of effective government organizations. *Journal of Public Administration Research and Theory, 9*(1), 1-32.

Ritz, A. (2011). Attraction to public policy making: A qualitative inquiry into improvements in PSM measurement. *Public Administration, 89*(3), 1128-1147.

Ritz, A., & Waldner, C. (2011). Competing for future leaders: A study of attractiveness of public sector organizations to potential job applicants. *Review of Public Personnel Administration, 31*(3), 291-316.

Roth, P. L. (1994). Missing data: A conceptual review for applied psychologists. *Personnel Psychology, 47,* 537-560.

Salamon, L. M. (1987). Of market failure, voluntary failure, and third-party government: Toward a theory of government-nonprofit relations in the modern welfare state. *Journal of Voluntary Action Research, 16,* 29-49.

Santora, J. C., & Sarros, J. C. (2001). CEO tenure in nonprofit community based organizations: A multiple case study. *Career Development International, 6*(1), 56-60.

Schneider, B. (1987). The people make the place. *Personnel Psychology, 40,* 437-453.

Simons, T. L., & Peterson, R. S. (2000). Task conflict and relationship conflict in top management teams: The pivotal role of intragroup trust. *Journal of Applied Psychology, 85,* 102-111.

Su, X., & Bozeman, B. (2009). Dynamics of sector switching: Hazard models predicting changes from private sector jobs to public and nonprofit sector jobs. *Public Administration Review, 69*(6), 1106-1114.

Travis, D. J. (2007). Is doing good enough? A path analytic model of intrinsic satisfaction among human service workers. *Journal of Workplace Behavioral Health, 22*(1), 13-32.

Tschirhart, M., Reed, K. K., Freeman, S. J., & Anker, A. L. 2008. Is the grass greener? Sector shifting and choice of sector by MPA and MBA graduates. *Nonprofit and Voluntary Sector Quarterly, 37*(4), 668-688.

Vandenabeele, W. (2007). Towards a theory of public service motivation: An institutional approach. *Public Management Review, 9,* 545-556.

Weisbrod, B. A. (1988). *The nonprofit economy.* Cambridge, MA: Harvard University Press.

Word, J., & Park, S. M. (2009). Working across the divide: Job involvement in the public and nonprofit sectors. *Review of Public Personnel Administration, 29*(2), 103-133.

Wright, B. E. (2001). Public-sector work motivation: A review of the current literature and a revised conceptual model. *Public Administration Review, 11*(4), 559-586.

Appendix

Construction of Indices[a]
Selected Representative Survey Items

Antecedent Variables:

Individual Attributes

- Gender (female: 0)
- Age
- Ethnicity (non-white: 1)
- Level of Education

Managerial Attributes

- Previous Job Characteristics

- Organizational Type: Private, Public, Nonprofit
- Main Responsibility: Manager, Professional, Technical
- Job Replacement: Promotion, Lateral and Upward Move, First Job
• Current Job Characteristics
- Main Responsibility: Manager, Professional, Technical
- Job Replacement: Promotion, Lateral and Upward Move, First Job

Organizational Factors

• Type of Nonprofit Agency
- Donative-Entrepreneurial Agencies: Public Charity
- Donative-Mutual: Civil League, Fraternal and Benevolent Societies
- Commercial-Entrepreneurial/Mutual Agencies: Title Holding Companies, Labor, AG, Business Leagues

• Organization Size
• Organization Age
• State Context

Motivation Variables:

Respondents were asked to respond to the following statements (1 = not important, 2 = somewhat unimportant, 3 = somewhat important, 4 = very important): Please indicate the extent to which the factors below were important in making your decision to take a job at your current organization.

• Opportunity for advancement within the organization's hierarchy
• Opportunity for training and career development
• Job security
• Organization's reputation for opportunities for women or minorities
• Overall quality and reputation of this organization
• The organization's pension or retirement plan
• Desire for less bureaucratic red tape
• Desire for a low conflict work environment
• Desire for increased responsibility
• Benefits (medical, insurance)
• "Family friendly" policies (e.g., flexible work hours, parental leave)
• Salary

- Ability to serve the public and the public interest
- Few, if any, alternative job offers
- Relatively low cost of living in the region
- Employment opportunities for spouse or partner

Outcome Variables: Civic and Political Activities

Social (Political) and Community Activities (9 items)

- Church, synagogue, mosque, or religious organizations
- Political club or political party committees
- Service organizations such as Rotary or Lions
- Youth support groups
- Neighborhood or homeowners associations
- PTA, PTO, or school support groups
- Group sports team or clubs
- Charity/community service
- Arts (music, museums, art, dance)

Professional Activities (8 items)

- Professional societies, trade or business associations, or labor unions
- History Associations
- Animal related organizations
- Health related organizations
- Environmental organizations
- Book clubs
- Public Safety
- Board member

[a] A complete listing of items and variables used in this study is available from the authors. (Also, details about descriptive statistics [Table 1] are available from the authors upon request.)

Case Study

Where should government-NGO relations go next?

You-kyung Suh

It is no secret that civil society in Korea emerged directly from a series of social movements for democratization in the 1980s and subsequent civic movements in the 1990s.

In particular, the 1987 pro-democracy uprising by middle-class citizens, which sociologists often compare to the May 1968 incident in Paris, brought about an accommodating social milieu for progressive political ideals on top of strong enthusiasm for a plebian democracy.

The major actors - students, workers, environmentalists, pacifists, women - of the 1987 citizen uprising comprised the backbone of Korean civil society. Most of them found new roles as members of civil society or the NGO sector.

Nevertheless, their political significance was not lightly valued by civilian governments, who felt that they owed the reinstated democratic republic to those former revolutionaries. Political parties, too, turned to their practical experience and wisdom to set policy agenda.

In limited cases, political parties even officially nominated some of them to stand for local seats in the general elections. A few female activists were able to place themselves high on the party proportional representation candidate lists and eventually entered the National Assembly.

As such, the NGO sector served not only as a policy provider but as a recruiting pool for national politics, and acted like a surrogate political party.

To be sure, it appears that government-NGO relations have been gradually evolving over the successive four civilian governments in the past two decades. Under the Roh Tae-woo administration, relations between the government and NGOs began to take shape in an initially fragile form against the backdrop of the 1987 citizen uprising for a plebiscite democracy.
Under the Kim Young-sam administration, relations developed in a more meaningful way.

A significant number of seats on various government advisory committees and decision-making processes were reserved for the representatives of the NGO sector. In this way, the government and the NGO sector actually were able to set up a kind of policy partnership. It was a most drastic step taken by the then "civilian government."

The Kim Dae-jung administration made a much more substantive contribution to the NGO sector than its predecessors. Above all, it underwent a thorough revision of the Law to Support Nonprofit Civil Organizations, putting aside some 15 trillion won ($16.8 billion) annually for the purpose of financing the projects to be proposed by the NGOs. In addition, some of the able NGO activists started to move over to some government posts. In this regard, government-NGO relations shifted from a policy partnership to an administrative cooptation.

This fashion continued under the incumbent Roh Moo-hyun administration. The appointment of Prime Minister Han Myeong-sook, which was followed by other women aides with specific work experience in the NGO sector, apparently spoke itself for the intimacy of the government-NGO relation. On the other hand, however, the 15 trillion won support fund was cut down to 10 trillion won in 2004 and from 2007 it will not be given to some NGOs involved in violent and illegal protests against government policies such as the recent FTA with the United States.

It is commonly known that the Korean NGO sector presently faces three difficulties: its much lessened political influence, lowered social recognition and ever-declining membership. As we know, the political influence and social recognition of the NGOs reached a peak with the vast success of the 2000 Civil Action for the General Elections campaign against some corrupt and unqualified candidates on their "fatwa" list. Yet this campaign was fined by the Supreme Court for being illegal and its sequel at the 2004 general election campaign period was not so successful in attracting public attention as its predecessor had done.

Another factor which apparently damaged its political influence as a radical policy agenda setter was the emergence of the Democratic Labor Party. It entered the National Assembly with 10 seats after the 2004 general election.

Its policy area largely coincides with that of the NGO sector and the latter no longer could monopolize such radical political agenda as social justice. In short, the official appearance of a leftist political party had a negative effect on the NGO sector`s policy-providing function. This technically means the end of its political period.
As for diminishing social reputation, there have been several factors arisen from the sector

itself. Some shameful stories concerning sexual harassment, public money embezzlement, and forced goods purchase for donations contributed a great deal to eroding the dimensions of its integrity and work ethics. Obviously, less volunteer workers and less dues money are available for the NGOs now than several years ago because of their tarnished reputation. What remains to be done? How can we save the NGO sector from its present dire situation?

Let's face the fact that the NGOs are not charity organizations, that the NGO people are not voluntary workers regardless of our prejudice about them, and that they are breadwinners like everybody else working in other sectors. Nevertheless it is generally an impoverished, underqualified, and strikingly feminized economic sector in Korea. There are reasons for this.

First, a regular civic organization`s full-time worker (or "gansa" in Korean) gets paid more or less 1 million won per month, only half of the initial salary of a college graduate who has just joined the mainstream economic sector in Korea.

Considering the notoriously dear costs of living in Seoul, this 1 million won monthly salary is not a sufficient amount at all for an average spending adult person to manage to survive a month. It becomes even harder for the person if he (or she) has a family to support financially. As a result, impoverishment has become a byword for the NGOs.

Second, as the income level of the NGO sector is very low, ordinary commonsensical college graduates do not choose the sector as their first choice of employment. Hence the applicants for the sector tend to be with less qualifications, experience, and ability than those who have already gone into the mainstream economic sector. More women than men are likely to go into the sector for the same reason - the low levels of income. Thus, it is only natural that the rate of turnovers be very high.

This, however, does not mean to dishonor those respectable people who in spite of the financial inconveniences have decided to go into the NGO sector in the first place and stayed there since with a strong personal commitment to their work.

Even for those who wish to work in the NGO sector, however, their preference is clear to the extent that those who with better qualifications and more abilities mostly opt for some major NGOs such as the People Solidarity for Participatory Democracy, the Coalition for Economic Justice, the Korean Federation for Environmental Movement, or the Women21 (KWAU).
All this brings me to my last point. Believe it or not, the NGO sector has been depoliticized

little by little in order to adapt to the changing conditions in Korea`s notional political configurations during the past 20 years. In this connection a gradual shift in government-NGO relations has been observed.

A most striking feature of the recent change in these relations is the government`s willingness to back away from any policy partnership with the NGO sector in the political dimension but to contract out social welfare services to the NGO sector. Many unemployed people, young and old, around us have already started applying for such temporary social workers` positions offered by the NGOs, who have made some sub-contractual arrangements with the government.

What worries me about these newly developed government-NGO relations is a possible situation in which the NGOs become permanently dependent upon government funding and in turn give up their organization`s objectives and independence for the sake of the government contract. What I really fear is a situation in which "the British disease" in the last century comes over here and affects Korean folks in this century.

From this same point of view, the annual 10 trillion won support fund could also be seen in this light. The way this government money is allotted seems not to have been adopted with a long-term view. In my opinion, under the present arrangements, the 10 trillion won is just wasted away each year with various one-time events proposed by the NGOs.

In conclusion, what I want to suggest here is that this bulky support fund be systematically invested in building the socio-economic infrastructure for the NGO sector economy and in improving the life conditions of its workers, not by giving away lottery-type project money, but by taking some substantive institutional measures.

It needs urgent attention because the impoverished, underqualified, feminized NGO sector is on the risk of selling its revolutionary spirit to make this world a better place to live in, not to mention its independence. I do not want to see "the British disease" take hold on our soil.

Source: The Korea Herald (2007.05.22)

Questions for Discussion

1. What makes public management (PM) "public", that is, what differentiates PM from approaches in the private or nonprofit sectors? What is meant by the "blurring" of the sectors? In what ways does this occur? What are some major problems and approaches to analyzing the distinction between public and private organizations?

2. Consider a local public department with which you have recently interacted. List and discuss the nature of services they provide. What groups do they serve? Do you consider the department effective or ineffective? Explain. To what standards should they be held? Explain.

3. What do you think is the best way to manage NGO employees and managers to get those people more driven to services and missions of NGO?

Section 2

Environments

- Of Alternating Waves and Shifting Shores
  : The Configuration of Reform Values
  in the US Federal Bureaucracy

- Analyzing Value Creation of Electronic Human
  Resource Management (E-HRM)
  : An Indonesian Case

Section 2

Environments

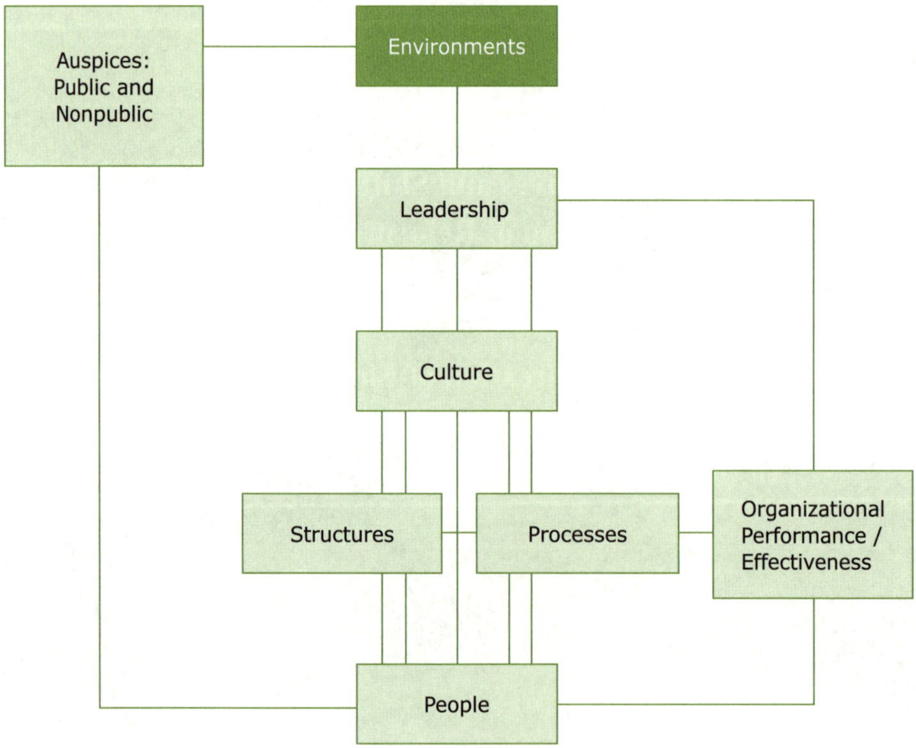

Chapter 3

Of Alternating Waves and Shifting Shores

: The Configuration of Reform Values in the US Federal Bureaucracy

Summary

Scholars have noted that United States federal government reforms come in waves (Barley and Kunda, 1992; Kettl, 2002; Light, 1998), often accompanied by values that alternate between rational and normative conceptions of public administration and service. The idea of alternation also suggests the importance of time in gauging the effect of new reforms when previous reforms have accumulated from the past (see Pollitt, 2008). Time is a necessary variable in implementing reforms; time is crucial to know if reform values have taken hold. Extending Paul Light's (1998) reform waves metaphor, we investigate here whether two predominant management philosophies have influenced and reconfigured the shoreline of values found among federal agencies over a particular period of time. Using empirical methods, we examine how the values of New Public Management and its humanist (post-NPM) counterpart have settled and taken hold among US federal agencies. We followed three lines of inquiry: determining the existence of reform values in the bureaucracy, examining the prevalence of different sets of values, and investigating whether 'crowding out' of values occurred, that is, whether there was a detectable shift in the distribution of values as a new wave came on top of others. Our analysis yields evidence for the predominance of certain NPM and post-NPM values and indicates that bureaucracy concurrently holds what may be regarded as competing values side-by-side. Implications for research and future reforms are suggested in the final section of the article.

Keyword

- □ Bureaucratic Values
- □ Federal Agencies
- □ New Public Management
- □ Public Management
- □ Waves of Reform

Sung Min Park Associate Professor, Sungkyunkwan University
M. Ernita Joaquin Associate Professor, San Francisco State University

Points for Practitioners

Practicing public administration requires constantly navigating reform pressures that espouse different, sometimes opposing, value sets. NPM and post-NPM reforms differed in their emphasis on applying rationalistic and humanistic values to the work of government. Based on federal workforce surveys, NPM values appeared ascendant from the reinvention period till the end of the Bush administration, when a more humanist outlook began to emerge. Bureaucratic values are dynamic and change could go faster with network structures. Following previous research, this study suggests that a 'layering' of reform occurs; the strongest values are held intact even as newer philosophies of organization and management are introduced. Results suggest that government professionals can adhere to differing values, but further study is required to see how those values actually influence their work.

Introduction

The last few decades have seen several initiatives to reform the US federal bureaucracy. Scholars recognize that certain types of reform have a tendency to alternate or overlap, although there are slightly different approaches to anticipating what will occur next. Paul Light (1998) typologized US federal management reforms using a tides metaphor, with four types washing ashore alternatingly – scientific management of government offices, a war on wasteful spending, a watchful eye through checks and balances, and liberation management in the executive branch. The tides connote an ebb and flow, guaranteeing the comeback of previous reforms and inevitable depositing of some sediments behind. Other scholars have argued that, in order to objectively assess the current reforms as well as to accurately predict the future directions, we need to look back at what has happened over time and to recognize what theoretical approaches could be well applicable to explain 'the temporal dimension' of specific public policies (Pollitt, 2008: 30).[1] For example, drawing upon a sequential perspective, the path dependency framework explains why some specific policies are more durable and stable than others, 'despite the changing environments around them' (2008: 42) whereas theories of cycles or alternations suggest that tides of governmental changes and mechanisms could be observed and identified in different fashions (see Pollitt, 2008).

While reforms often tack the 'new' label upon their names, they sometimes resemble a pendulum with discernible interplay between more efficiency-driven initiatives and initiatives that prize values other than efficiency in public service performance. Barley and Kunda (1992: 392) suggest that, 'rather than having progressed steadily from coercive to rational and then to normative conceptions of control', American managerial ideology has been conceptualized in waves that have alternated between normative and rational rhetoric (p. 363). Of late, this has been observed in the shift from corporatist, New Public Management (NPM)-based values to a more normative, post-NPM emphasis on value-laden, knowledgebased, and team-based ethical management (Christensen and Lægreid, 2008).

NPM reforms emphasize individualism, production (productivity and performance), rationality, and materialism (Fox and Miller, 1995). The administration of George W. Bush (2001–08) carried out a managerialist agenda with a theme that aligned with NPM. 'The Bush administration was enamored of practices believed to be common in the private sector where managers typically have greater discretion than their counterparts in the public services in recruitment, selection, management, and retention of employees' (Kellough et al., 2010: 417). In contrast, post-NPM reforms pursue the antithesis of logical positivism and the post-rationality-based social science approaches, sharing common perspectives with organizational humanism, postmodern public administration, organizational development values, and even the old notion of New Public Administration (Denhardt and Denhardt, 2003; Frederickson and Smith, 2003). These approaches reveal the limitations of rational and public choice models (see Argyris, 1973; Barley and Kunda, 1992), expose the internal contradictions of NPM (Fox, 1996), and seek ways to 'enlarge the area of discretion . . . to increase individual freedom' and 'create an open problem-solving climate through the organization' (Denhardt and Denhardt, 2003: 37; Golembiewski, 1967: 305).

The many reform initiatives since the 1980s – privatization, the National Public Review, the President's Management Agenda, cutback management, and performance and human capital assessment – prompt us to explore the configuration of values in the federal bureaucracy today. Over time, there is a strong likelihood that previous waves of presidential-driven reforms had lingering influence even as newer ones were implemented. What exactly would it look like if the configuration of values were to be mapped with a visual model? Is there evidence that NPM's strict, market-based values have taken hold? If so, to what extent? Can we also find evidence of so-called post-NPM values, even though NPM reforms have been executed? This last point acknowledges what Pollitt (2008) observed of time as a neglected but subtly influential variable in assessing the clout of past management initiatives. We speak here of alternation but note the possibility that previous decisions have lasting impact even when newer reforms come about. Light (1998) had remarked that 'sediment' build-up from multiple waves of bureaucratic tinkering. Could we sift through these sediments and identify distinctions?

Focusing on the years of the Bush administration, this article investigates salient values among federal agencies in the United States, as reflected by employee surveys from the period. We establish whether a sort of 'crowding out' occurred, meaning whether some values predominated over others. We also determine whether a shift in values happened over time. This investigation is significant in practical and conceptual ways. Practically, in light of ceaseless attempts to 'improve' the US bureaucracy: is there evidence that some principles have been cherished more than others, or have been more lastingly influential? As more fluid governance arrangements emerge, public administrators need to understand what salient values have taken hold at any point among bureaucratic agencies. In turn, this may subsequently help us determine whether newer structures and governance arrangements align with, or support, existing values. In theoretical terms, this study contributes a bit to the debate on how accurate it is to speak of distinctly NPM or post-NPM reform philosophies. Some scholars have questioned whether or not NPM and post-NPM represented coherent agendas (Goldfinch and Wallis, 2010), and if 'reforms' that carried their banners were actually semantic games that hid little substance beyond the rhetoric (Pollitt, 2001). To the extent that we test, in our research methodology, certain values as 'NPM' and others as 'post-NPM', we essentially gear toward two distinctive sets of values. And while we do not directly investigate the coherence issue – that NPM and post-NPM agendas in different places mean different things due to institutional variations (Goldfinch, 2006; Goldfinch and Wallis, 2010) – the results of our analysis that both sets are identifiable in the US federal bureaucracy allows for an interpretation of a 'layering' of reforms (Thelen, 2003), rather than an outright replacement or alternation.

Interplay of Reform Values

Stone (1997) defines and compares two different models of society – the so-called polis and market models. The polis model, which is based on the political community and anti-rational-analytic rationales, can be a useful framework for thinking about government reform, especially when a rationality based, market model might not provide significant, real-life implications for employees. Two influential philosophies behind many federal management reforms are New Public Management (NPM) and post-NPM principles, which have a more humanist bent relative to NPM's more economic approach to public service and management of bureaucracy. Paralleling the tension between the polis and market society, this section briefly compares the tenets of each reform philosophy.

New Public Management

Since the 1980s, NPM reforms have emphasized the values of individualism and economic rationality. NPM is known for systems and cultures of productivity improvement, reinvention, process re-engineering, entrepreneurial leadership, privatization, and performance measurement (Fox and Miller, 1995; Kelly, 1998; Lane and Woodard, 2001; Osborne, 2006; Pollitt, 1995). NPM offers a shift in 'how we think about the role of public administrators, the nature of the profession, and how and why we do what we do' (Denhardt and Denhardt, 2000: 550). It sees 'citizens as consumers, taxpayers, and customers', and 'leads people to evaluate government according to what each individual receives rather than what the community as a whole receives' (King and Stivers, 1998: 57). The key managerial components of NPM varied from place to place; they boiled down to five according to Hays and Kearney (1997) and to Pollitt (1995), eight. At its core, we can distill NPM reform values into three sets: (1) performance and results-oriented values (or managerialism and debureaucratization), (2) market and customer-oriented values (downsizing, privatization, and decentralization), and (3) goal and strategy-oriented values (strategic and workforce planning management).

NPM's most recent incarnation occurred with the Bush administration's (2001–08) human resources reforms that plugged partially into a strategy pursued since the presidency of Ronald Reagan (Milakovich, 1988). Broad reflections on the civil service legacy of George W. Bush (see for instance, Campbell et al., 2007; Durant et al., 2010b; Maranto et al., 2009) mostly acknowledge his political, ideological, and technical resolve to shape the bureaucracy after conservative values.

At the heart of Bush's big government conservatism (Durant et al., 2010a) were the President's Management Agenda (PMA), the Program Assessment Rating Tool (PART), and the personnel management system overhaul of both the Defense (DOD) and Homeland Security (DHS) departments. Guided by market-based values, the PMA, for example, focused on improving five management areas: (1) strategic management of human capital, (2) competitive sourcing of government services, (3) financial performance improvement, (4) electronic government, and (5) budget and performance integration (US Office of Management and Budget, 2004), with competitive sourcing meeting the most resistance from federal employees (Joaquin, 2009). The Program Assessment Rating Tool (PART), launched in 2003, tried to build upon the earlier Government Performance and Results Act (GPRA). PART evaluated nearly a thousand federal programs on the basis of (1) program purpose and design, (2) strategic planning, (3) program management, (4) program results, and (5) overall rating scores. As the White House intended it, PART was an opportunity to examine agency factors related to performance, findings that would, in turn, inform the budgetary process, linking tax dollars to program improvements or results.

In addition to the PMA and PART, far-reaching changes were also carried out at the DHS and DOD (e.g. the Max HR and Human Capital Operational Plan in the DHS and the National Security Personnel System in the DOD). The DHS initiatives were intended to create a system that would be flexible, contemporary, and grounded in principles of merit and fitness, equal pay for equal work, and equal employment opportunities. The ascendancy of management rights was considered of paramount importance due to national security concerns, thus enabling management to retain maximum flexibility pertaining to hiring, pay, discipline, job classifications, and labor relations (see Ryan, 2003: 101–106). The DOD's National Security Personnel System also shaped a new HR system. It proposed a merit-pay system, an occupational classification, an objective performance appraisal system, as well as labor relations, adverse actions, and employee appeals systems (see Risher and Fay, 2007: 10). The Bush administration's confrontational and ideological approach to implementing these reforms (Kellough et al., 2010), however, met union backlash and forced management to modify some of these proposals with a more incremental HR system (Riccucci and Thompson, 2008; Thompson, 2010; Underhill and Oman, 2007). Still, NPM philosophy was fundamental in the proposed reforms, which some authors observed to be distinguished clearly from traditional principles of public administration (Battaglio and Condrey, 2006; Condrey, 2005).[2]

Criticism of NPM includes its neglect of 'the creation and development of an intense relationship of the individual with the larger issues of community, constitutional government, democratic values, and public service' (Perry, 1996: 7). The market model for society also modified selection processes and incentive systems, adversely affecting the attitudes and performance of employees (Moynihan, 2008a). Many critics have noted the lack of convincing evidence that government agencies are inherently less effective than private firms in performing public services (Boyne, 1998; Lowery, 1998; Savas, 2000; Sclar, 2000). The case of the Internal Revenue Service during the late 1990s also showed that the implementation of a radical performance measurement system did not bring about a more positive organizational culture, or a more productive workforce (Thompson, 2006). NPM is also said to undermine democratic and constitutional values, as well as the 'public ethos' that provides civil service with a constitutive role in the traditional American governance system (Berry et al., 1999; Thompson, 2001).

Beyond Efficiency: Post-NPM Values

In reaction to the NPM philosophy, newer conceptions of public management arose that shared perspectives with organizational humanism, postmodern public administration, organizational development values, and even the old notion of New Public Administration (Denhardt and Denhardt, 2003; Frederickson and Smith, 2003). Post-NPM approaches point out the limitations of rational and public choice models (see Argyris, 1973; Barley and Kunda, 1992), expose the internal contradictions of the NPM movement in public agencies (Fox, 1996), and seek ways to 'enlarge the area of discretion . . . to increase individual freedom' and to 'create an open problem-solving climate through the organization' (Denhardt and Denhardt, 2003: 37; Golembiewski, 1967: 305).

Current normative approaches trace their foundations to the work of Chester Barnard (1938), and later, of Douglas McGregor (1960), and organizational humanists (Roethlisberger and Dickson, 1939). In the late 1960s, the normative approach informed the thinking of the New Public Administration (NPA). Frederickson (1996) argued that unlike NPM, NPA espoused the importance of humanistic and democratic administration, professionalism, and most importantly, social equity. After NPA, Denhardt and Denhardt (2000, 2003) conceptualized the New Public Service (NPS), a movement emphasizing democratic governance and civic engagement. The model recognizes public servants not just as employees who crave the security and structure of a bureaucratic job (as typified by the old public administration), or as participants in a market (as they would be considered under New Public Management), but as people whose motivations and rewards are beyond the material or the monetary (Perry and Wise, 1990). Moore's (1995) and Bozeman's (2007) conception of 'public values', defined as 'the desires and perceptions of individuals . . . citizen's aspirations, expressed through representative government' (Moore, 1995: 52) and as 'the content-specific preferences of individuals concerning, on the one hand, the rights, obligations, and benefits to which citizens are entitled and, on the other hand, the obligations expected of citizens and their designated representatives' (Bozeman, 2007: 14), recognize that public goods and services are provided to fulfill public values. In a similar vein, discourse theory, which supports the postmodern participatory and humanistic approach to public administrative reforms, suggests that the role of the public administrator is to act as a facilitator of discourse and communications outside the confines of institutional settings, and to prioritize equality among social groups, humanization of the workplace, intrinsic job involvement, empowerment, and expanded political and social participation (Box, 2002; Wise, 2002). In addition, the tenet of social equity further embraces distributive justice, equal opportunities for employment, fair treatment, and the value of diversity, while prohibiting discrimination in the workplace. Finally, democratization values include employee empowerment, greater employee participation, and cooperative management practices (Wise, 2002).

These newer perspectives raise expectations for better quality of work life in organizations, and other broad social changes (Ingelhart, 1997; Ingraham and Jones, 1999). They provide an alternative framework for viewing management reform in public agencies. In light of recent attempts to evaluate the Bush administration's impact on federal human resources management (Kellough et al., 2010), it is useful to take a look at the configuration of values during those years in order to see what the findings suggest about future reforms. Reform, by definition, will never cease from executive or legislative action. Future forms of governance might require that bureaucracy overcome the rigid dichotomy between values of efficiency, and more normative values, in order to effectively address new problems in public administration.

Research Questions

Based on the preceding literature review, this study aimed to identify the configuration of reform values in the federal bureaucracy over a period spanning the last several years. We structured the research questions as follows:

Question 1: What management reform values (pertaining either to NPM or post-NPM) are salient in the US federal bureaucracy? Can we identify those values?

Question 2: Is a particular set of reform values more predominant than other sets? Is there a crowding out of certain values by one set of values over others?

Question 3: Can a trend be detected in changing values over a certain period of time, resulting from differing reform philosophies?

We aimed to capture value presence and dynamics over time. Based on the descriptive literature of NPM-oriented and post-NPM values, we developed Figure 1 to guide us in discovering and analyzing values from the results of federal agency surveys.

Figure 1. A Conceptual Framework for NPM and Normative Reform Values

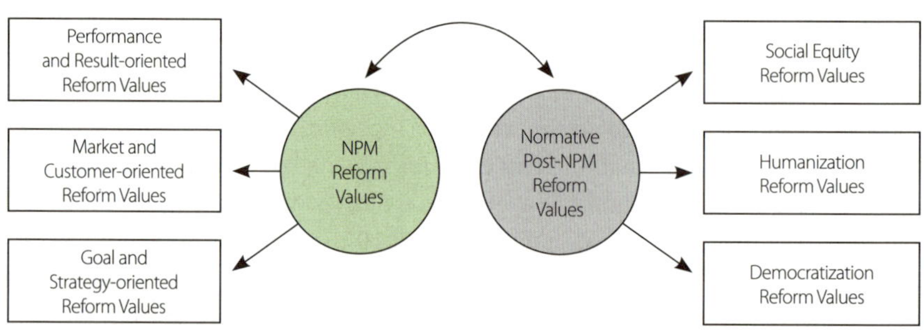

Methodology

The unit of analysis is the United States federal bureaucracy as represented by agencies whose employees participated in the Federal Human Capital Survey (FHCS). Administered by the Office of Personnel Management in 2002, 2004, and 2006, the FHCS project consisted of surveys that contained 71 common questions between the 2004 and 2006 surveys, and 59 common questions between the 2002 and 2006 surveys. The largest federal-level survey of its kind, the 2006 sample covered 390,657 full-time permanent civilian employees from 29 agencies and 59 small/independent agencies (88 agencies in total). The response rate was approximately 57 percent (almost 221,479 responses). The original questionnaire contained 84 questions on employee job satisfaction and work attitudes, leadership, knowledge and diversity management, performance culture, and other personnel and managerial reform issues.

This study required three phases of data analysis to answer our research questions. Our methods consisted of (1) exploratory factor analysis, (2) confirmatory factor analysis, and (3) latent growth curve modeling to operationalize variables, reveal and confirm latent constructs and important factors, and investigate a growth process in federal agencies using structural equation modeling (SEM). SEM is a useful tool for testing interrelationships among variables in a multivariate setting and assessing the relative strengths of each variable (Jöreskog, and Sörbom, 1996).

To construct the factor structures base, the three sets (years) of FHCS data were collapsed into a single database using the means of the scores. The surveys used a 5-point Likert scale to measure agreement on given survey statements. This study used 14 questions to measure the factorial structure of NPM reform values, and 21 questions for post-NPM values (see Appendix). From there, the instrument revealed various sub-factors for NPM and post-NPM reform values, following in particular the taxonomy of reform values proposed by Wise (2002).

We screened the data for outliers and extreme non-normal distribution patterns. See Table 1 for the means and standard deviations for all variables. No problematic case of skewness was noted, and all values exhibited a high value of kurtosis (more than absolute 2.0). Missing data were excluded by the listwise deletion function, and the final survey sample amounted to 74,505 valid sample numbers. Since SEM is subject to problems based on missing data, we performed additional missing data analysis using the expectation maximization method. In addition, from KMO Measure of Sampling Adequacy results, the adequacy value was 0.970, indicating that the matrix for this dataset is highly acceptable. In other words, the variables in the matrix may share common factors at a high level.[3]

Results and Discussion

Identifying Existing Values

First, in order to establish the structure of reform values present in the bureaucracy, exploratory factor analysis was employed on the items initially developed. The method of principal axis factoring extraction was used. To determine the number of factors to extract, the scree plot, Kaiser's rule of eigenvalues greater than 1, Velicer's MAP test, and parallel analysis were generated from raw data. The results suggested that six factors should be retained.

Under the assumption that these bureaucratic value constructs would be interrelated, an oblique direct oblimin rotation method was used to produce factors with the smallest number of cross-loadings from a parameter called delta. Table 2 shows the results of rotation. The percentage of variance accounted for by these six factors was 53.153 percent. To ensure internal consistency, we employed Cronbach's alpha scores, which showed that the scores of the subscales had a relatively high degree of internal consistency (all above 0.7) on each of the six factors.

Based on this analysis, we detected evidence to answer our first research question: multiple reform values do exist and are identifiable in the federal bureaucracy during recent years. NPM as well as post-NPM values are held. These results suggest that the six-factor solution extracted six distinctive values according to those having the highest factor loadings (equal to or greater than 0.50). These are market values, work–life balance values, performance values, social equity values, knowledge management values, and democratization. These loadings fit our assumption that an array of values, which are aligned with different philosophies, can be found in the federal bureaucracy. Their distribution is as follows:

Factor 1 – values based on the missions and objectives of federal agencies, customer service, and service improvement; dubbed *Market and Strategy-oriented values*; accounted for 39.99 percent of variance.

Table 1. Descriptive Statistics (FHCS 2002, 2004, and 2006) (Item Mean, Standard Deviation, and Sample Size)

Items	N	Minimum	Maximum	Mean	Std. Deviation
NPM value 1	97,080	1	5	3.12	1.254

NPM value 2	98,528	1	5	3.29	1.209
NPM value 3	98,097	1	5	3.21	1.212
NPM value 4	98,405	1	5	3.30	1.162
NPM value 5	98,133	1	5	3.19	1.166
NPM value 6	99,657	1	5	2.83	1.168
NPM value 7	94,546	1	5	2.75	1.181
NPM value 8	100,159	1	5	4.00	.816
NPM value 9	97,085	1	5	3.61	1.057
NPM value 10	96,645	1	5	3.74	.982
NPM value 11	98,172	1	5	3.57	1.068
NPM value 12	100,089	1	5	4.27	.791
NPM value 13	96,800	1	5	3.44	1.105
NPM value 14	98,816	1	5	3.69	1.217
Normative value 15	95,531	1	5	3.69	.965
Normative value 16	96,881	1	5	3.73	.977
Normative value 17	98,093	1	5	3.76	.976
Normative value 18	92,839	1	5	3.3147	1.137
Normative value 19	99,639	1	5	3.0625	1.197
Normative value 20	95,689	1	5	3.3399	1.214
Normative value 21	93,012	1	5	3.5266	1.121
Normative value 22	97,629	1	5	3.67	1.065
Normative value 23	99,485	1	5	3.24	1.098
Normative value 24	100,420	1	5	3.54	1.025
Normative value 25	100,210	1	5	3.83	.979
Normative value 26	98,949	1	5	3.37	1.140
Normative value 27	100,571	1	5	4.00	.868
Normative value 28	100,571	1	5	3.56	1.033
Normative value 29	100,571	1	5	3.78	.896
Normative value 30	100,571	1	5	2.99	.967
Normative value 31	100,571	1	5	3.65	1.089
Normative value 32	100,571	1	5	2.95	.607
Normative value 33	100,571	1	5	3.25	.721
Normative value 34	100,571	1	5	3.26	.841
Normative value 35	100,571	1	5	3.02	.544
Effective sample size	74,505				
(Valid N)					

Table 2. Total Variance Explained *After* Rotation

Factor	Initial Eigen Values			Extraction Sums of Squared Loadings			Rotation Sums of Squared Loadings (a)
	Total	% of Variance	Cumulative %	Total	% of Variance	Cumulative %	Total
1	13.999	39.996	39.996	13.580	38.801	38.801	10.231
2	2.344	6.698	46.694	1.770	5.056	43.857	4.711
3	1.428	4.079	50.773	1.078	3.079	46.936	10.474
4	1.256	3.589	54.362	.849	2.426	49.362	10.035
5	1.217	3.478	57.840	.764	2.183	51.544	7.793
6	1.031	2.945	60.785	.563	1.608	53.153	7.297

*A Factor Pattern Matrix table, which indicates six-factor dimensions, is available from the authors upon request.

Factor 2 – reflected values of work-life balance in the bureaucracy; dubbed *Work-Life Balance values;* accounted for 6.69 percent of variance.

Factor 3 – values related to performance management, award programs, accountability for results, and merit systems; dubbed *Performance and Results-oriented values;* accounted for 4.07 percent of variance.

Factor 4 – related to values of representative bureaucracy, diversity management and culture, and organizational fairness and procedural justice; dubbed *Social Equity values;* accounted for 3.58 percent of variance.

Factor 5 – reflected values of learning and training, information and knowledge for job performance; dubbed *Knowledge Management-based values;* accounted for 3.47 percent of variance.

Factor 6 – represented values of empowerment, knowledge sharing, and cooperative communication; dubbed *Democratization values;*[4] accounted for 2.94 percent of variance.

Distinguishing Outstanding NPM and Post-NPM Values

We tried to determine which values predominate among these values. Confirmatory factor analysis of the type typically used to test the factor structure of an instrument was conducted. Overall fit indices and modification indices were used to identify a best-fit model. We added an error covariance among several indicators and respecified the model for the sake of decreasing the chi-square value. Then we tested and retested all alternative models. In our second-order CFA model, the two sets of reform values of NPM and post-NPM (second-order factors) in federal agencies were explained by six different reform values (first-order factors), indicating that NPM and post-NPM reform values are salient, distinct, and positively correlated (the covariance coefficient is 0.88). Several goodness-of-fit indices indicate that the entire model fits well (see Figure 2). The chi-square value was 1434.06 ($p<.05$).

Figure 2. The Results of the NPM and Normative Reform Value Structures (A Pooled Cross-Sectional Model)

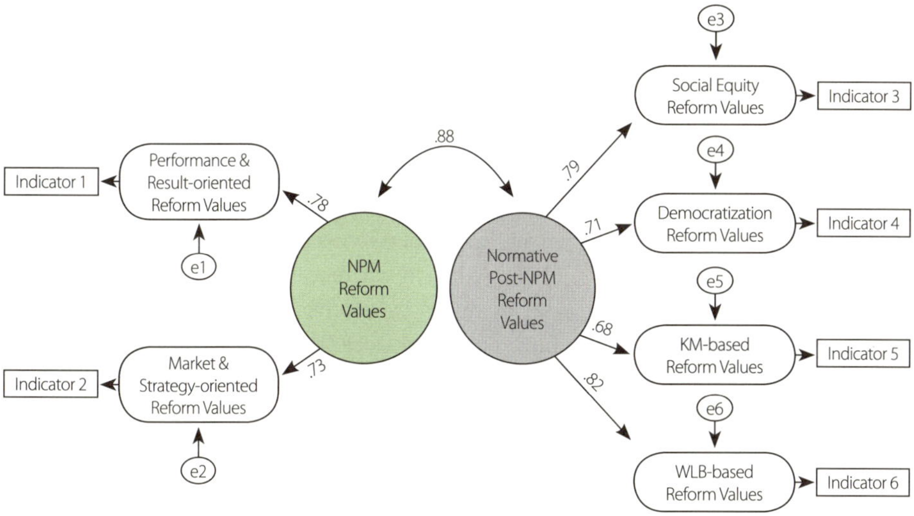

Using a Second-Order Confirmatory Factor Analysis (CFA)[a]

Overall Fit Indices of the CFA Model

Model 1	df	Chi-Square	CFI	NNFI	NFI	IFI	RFI	RMSEA	SRMR
Suggested Cut-off Values			>.95	>.95	>.95	>.95	>.95	<.08	<.08
A Measurement Model	598	1434.06	.97	.98	.97	.97	.955	.064	.058

[a]Based on the WLS (ADF) method, all coefficients of the factor loadings (lambda-Ys and gammas) in this CFA model are standardized.

The results show moderate to high R^2 for each of the first-order factors (from 0.68 to 0.82). Two reform values stand out among agencies in terms of factor loadings: (1) performance and results-oriented reform values (R^2=0.78) on the NPM side, and (2) work-life balance values (R^2=0.82) on the post-NPM side. These values predominate among reform values in federal agencies, partially answering our second research question. Thus, an NPM value that emphasizes performance and cultures of accountability, together with a post-NPM value that focuses on employee discretion and flexibility, could be outstanding components of any future reform initiatives. This might indicate that agencies already found ways to balance the conflicting objectives and goals of reform (Lasseter, 2002). It also supports the view that post-NPM reforms were not diametrically opposite NPM ones; in fact the latter are an adaptation of the former (Christensen and Lægreid, 2007; Hood and Peters, 2004).

T-tests (the critical value is ±2) indicated that all six first-order factors had significant loadings. The second-order factor analysis confirmed that NPM and post-NPM values are distinct, co-variant, and significantly related to each latent first-order factor. This means that differing managerial reform features are blended and preserved in bureaucracies, while remaining distinctive and salient among federal employees, as previous studies predicted (e.g. see Barley and Kunda, 1992; Denhardt and Denhardt, 2003; Kaufman, 1969; Wise, 2002). The interplay and alternation of reforms do produce layers of sediments on the bureaucratic shore (Light, 1998). Although our results do not provide evidence of the complete crowding out of one set of values by another, analysis implies that values from clashing philosophical camps have dually influenced the bureaucracy and may have complemented one another's strengths. To stretch this to a logical conclusion, one might say that reforms leave a legacy of their best and strongest features, while weaknesses and gaps are filled by succeeding reform movements.

Detecting a Shift in Bureaucratic Values

Next, owing to the influence of time in assessing the impact of any reform (Pollitt, 2008), longitudinal analysis was used to address our third research question, if and how bureaucratic values shifted during the period under study, and, if possible, pinpointing when a shift occurred. In latent growth curve modeling, intercept and slope terms are treated as latent variables (factors). This method allowed us to obtain an estimate of the initial level of main outcome variables and the rate of change over time, and to link these parameters of growth to time-varying and timeinvariant variables. The maximum likelihood method was used. The covariance matrix was used as input to LISREL 8.72 in order to evaluate the measurement model and full structural model.

The slope (linear change) and intercept (initial status) parameters were measured at

Figure 3. The Results of the NPM and Normative Reform Value Structures (A Pooled Cross-Sectional Time-Series Model): Using a Latent Growth Model (LGM)[a]

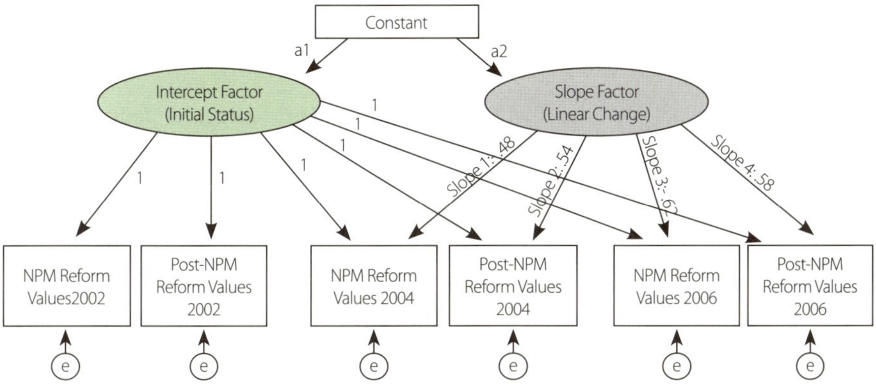

Overall Fit Indices of the Latent Growth Curve Model

Model 1	df	Chi-Square	CFI	NNFI	NFI	IFI	RFI	RMSEA	SRMR
Suggested Cut-off Values			>.95	>.95	>.95	>.95	>.95	<.08	<.08
A Measurement Model	466	103.55	.96	.96	.96	.965	.955	.07	.06

[a]The intercept and slope are defined as latent variables. Variables representing all 3 time points have loadings of 1 on the intercept factor.
This sets the initial status in equations for each time point as the same.
The parameters a1 and a2 represent the slope and intercept means.

Figure 4. Mean Score Profiles for Two Reform Values in Federal Agencies

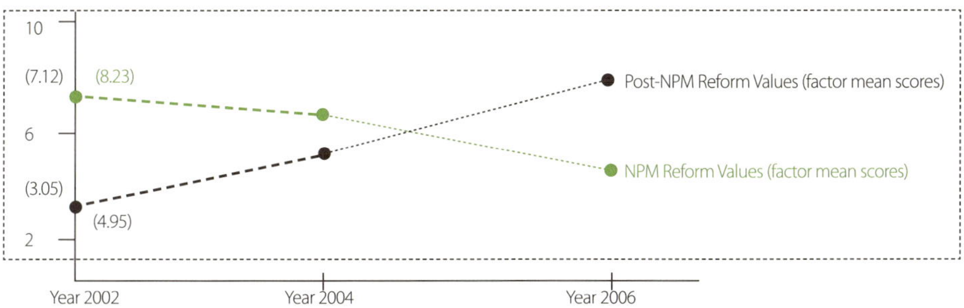

each of the three time points: the years 2002, 2004, and 2006. The resulting NNFI (0.960), NFI (0.960), IFI (0.965), RFI (0.955), RMSEA (0.07), and SRMR (0.06) values suggest that this model fits well. The coefficients for intercept and slope were fixed in the equations. The only parameters estimated were the error variances, which showed that the amount of variability in the three time points is not explained by the intercept and slope parameters. The error variances in NPM and post-NPM at time 1 (year 2002), time 2 (year 2004), and time 3 (year 2006) were 0.15, 0.04, and 0.58, respectively. None of these variances was statistically significant.

The results indicate that the levels of NPM reform values in federal agencies diminished over time (negative slope), whereas post-NPM values constantly increased (positive slope) during the same period (see Figure 3). While one set of values emphasizing democratization, equity, and other normative principles was ascendant in the bureaucracy, it was accompanied by a decline in the more rationalistic, efficiency-driven set of values. At what point did this occur? When we consider the period under study, NPM-based values were more influential in 2002 (after the reinventing government movement peaked) and more prominent in federal agencies. Reforms introduced by the Bush administration carried those values forward. As Figure 4 illustrates, however, the growth trajectories of the reforms show that after 2002, NPM values marginally but continuously decreased as more normative initiatives gained popularity at the federal level. Regardless, NPM reform values are still principal pillars of current public management reform philosophies. Can we expect that these two schools of reform values will be in constant flux, depending on political and socioeconomic contingencies? Or does this trend mean that with new forms of governance taking hold, public administration is returning to its traditional and long-cherished normative principles before embarking on less conventional arrangements?

Conclusions

Between 2002 and 2006, the United States federal bureaucracy was inundated with NPM-inspired executive orders, directives, and congressional actions. In this study, we have tried to determine the prevalence of certain values by means of analyzing the results of three consecutive surveys of employee perceptions about their agencies. Most observers frequently distinguish NPM from post-NPM management reform initiatives according to the extent to which each prioritizes market-type values. As reforms constantly arise from executive or legislative actions, new forms of governance might require that bureaucracy overcome the rigid dichotomy between the value of efficiency and more normative values, to effectively address evolving problems in public administration. As the findings reveal, bureaucracy, in fact, is well able to blend what the literature often portrays as two extremely differing agendas. We focus our conclusions here on two major concerns: the values that we found to be important from the surveys, and what that suggests about the tireless bouts of 'reforms' visited upon the federal bureaucracy. The values that we found to be predominant suggest that diversity management in relation to social equity is crucial in the near future. A labor force with many different characteristics will invariably impact organizational performance. Also, organizational justice, and the way this is perceived by employees, might be related to attitudes about work and the activities of employees and should therefore be explored.

From a human capital perspective, the findings from the knowledge management construct imply that basic human resources development initiatives that many authors have emphasized (Swanson and Holton, 2001; Werner and DeSimone, 2009) will remain integral to the goal of a humanized, democratized, and equitable bureaucracy. The direct participation of employees in strategic management, and developmental cultures focusing on people, flexibility, and adaptability may contribute to a high level of motivation, and enhance the level of effective and normative commitment of employees.

That agencies value policies of work-life balance behooves us to ask about the stress felt by agencies due to the relentless criticism of bureaucracy that accompanied NPM. Policies of work-life balance might have mitigated some of the pressures from being cast as inept, free-riding bureaucrats compared to their private sector counterparts, policies that help generate positive employee perceptions of their work and the citizens they serve (Ezra and Deckman, 1996; Facer and Wadsworth, 2008; Saltztstein et al., 2001). As Frederickson (1996) noted, to expect civil servants to be loyal to their work, the bureaucracy must also be loyal to them, and safeguard certain values and principles on behalf of the employees. Moynihan (2008b) echoed this injunction when he noted that governments must link performance measures to intrinsic values. The pre-eminence of work-life balance values at the same level as performance values must be seen as a good thing. These principles should inform future efforts, although classical organizational principles have already indicated that performance rationality should be tempered with incentives that value the human worker.

These results suggest the importance of finding connections between the normative values and the core characteristics of agencies and employees representing those values (see Rainey et al., 2008). For example, when taken as an individual attribute, public service motivation (PSM) is usually associated with serving the public good or public interest (Perry and Wise, 1990). PSM is expected to influence certain values (e.g. rational/extrinsic and normative/intrinsic values), behaviors (e.g. prosocial behaviors and institutionally grounded behaviors), and cultures (e.g. group or developmental culture) in public organizations (Park and Rainey, 2012). It is necessary to determine whether variations in conceptions and patterns of motivation relate to public values at the individual level, as well as to making meaningful differences in organizations.

What of the interplay of reforms and the values embedded in them? We detected evidence for the concurrent existence of various reform values from different decades in the United States, for one. Two, certain reform values were more emphasized by agencies than others, and some were more ascendant than others. The former dips into the discussion of the appropriateness of discussing how mutually exclusive the post-NPM agenda is from NPM. The results indicate a blending of values, implying the kind of 'layering' that Thelen (2003) argued occurred with decades of reform mindedness. Past policy initiatives might give way to new ones, but, as values go, they could not completely be replaced, or they could influence new ones in ways that new reformers might not easily detect (see Pollitt, 2008). Bureaucracy can be an adaptive organism; NPM and post-NPM reforms, like their predecessors, are thrown into the mix and the emerging picture would caution us from declaring that NPM is dead.

The results reveal that some values were ascendant at some point in time. Ebb and flow are present. Again, ascendance is not total crowding out. Methodologically speaking, it can be argued that the factor analysis model is formative and heuristic, rather than reflective, because the model was not specified in advance. We acknowledge this limitation. Nonetheless, the results indicate that despite, or with, the ebb and flow, the shoreline might indeed be shifting (Kettl, 1997, 2002) – bureaucracy changes each and every time a reform is instituted in ways that NPM or post-NPM categorization cannot contain – and the pendulum of more, and then less, normative value of public administration may have to be transcended in order for bureaucracy to be more capable of meeting twentyfirst-century challenges. Despite its limits, this study is necessary in conducting further inquires. For instance, which predictors significantly influence any shift in values? And, does a shift correspond to better results, whichever standards (normative or rationalistic) are used? Our study does not address whether changing values reflect changing party control (from Republicans to Democrats), or rather, fundamental value changes separate from partisan control. The existing literature is replete with accounts of what not to do. It is acknowledged that a 'one-size-fitsall' reform strategy or policy never works. Non-incremental approaches do not work (Mazmanian and Sabatier, 1989). Careful planning does not work for dramatic reforms (Maranto, 2002: 188). Because the work of governments is complex and increasingly complicated as time passes, any reform efforts should also be able to guide public administrators in a way that enables effective action and efficient use of resources. A focus on exclusive, sectoral goals (cost-cutting) needs to be qualified in the eyes of managers, their program evaluators, the politicians, and the public so that everyone recognizes that efficiency can only be met within limits. As some authors have noted (e.g. see Rainey and Steinbauer, 1999), there may be no crisis in a bureaucracy, but crisis will sometimes be manufactured so that reforms can be launched. In the same vein, bureaucracy may be as efficient as it can be, but problems will arise when we evaluate efficiency in non-logical ways.

From the results of this study, we know that bureaucracy encompasses normative and managerialist values, despite the clashing tenets at the rhetorical level (see Pollitt, 2001) or about the substance of reform. Weaknesses in individual pieces of reform, the passage of time, politics, and complications of the dilemma of public administration may have led agencies to adopt these conflicting values side-by-side. We are not certain, but data suggest that the best elements of reforms tend to rise to the top, and leave lasting legacies for employees and agencies, even when an empirical approach is not able to test how, in practice, those values have taken hold or are reflected in agency actions. But what does this imply for future initiatives in public administration? Public management reform has been, and will continue to be, a difficult task if differing reform values are conceived as being mutually exclusive. The challenges of reforming public bureaucracies are increasingly complex and wide-ranging, because governments must simultaneously recognize political leadership and management oversights, they must encompass and balance the competing and contradictory values of citizens, and they must fairly evaluate the performance of their agencies (Breul, 2007). The findings herein impel us to examine the norms that arise with network arrangements and other forms of governance structures, for example, the New Public Governance (see Osborne, 2006). Can network governance accommodate these values, or eschew them for something completely new? Having become accustomed to evaluating bureaucratic improvements in terms of efficiency or democratization, would we uphold these same values when assessing reforms that might fundamentally change bureaucracy to structures of hollow networks? Would the multi-sector service, currently comprising traditional civil servants, contractors, grantees and/or partners, find these same values meaningful? We do not know the answers to these questions. As bureaucracy evolves, however, it is worthwhile to remember historical configurations of values, before everything changes again.

Notes

This article was supported by SEOK CHUN Research Fund, Sungkyunkwan University, 2010.

1. Pollitt (2008) points out that there are six main approaches or frameworks (so-called timeships) by which we can explore to theorize the importance of time dimension: (1) Traditional historical approaches; (2) The path dependency framework; (3) Theories of cycles or alternations in administrative fashion; (4) Sociological studies of time and management; (5) The organizational ecology/organizational evolution perspective; (6) The analysis of the cognitive processes and biases of decision makers.
2. For example, Condrey (2005) identifies and classifies four models of Human Resource Management Service Delivery: the traditional model, the reform model, the strategic model, and the privatization model. The traditional model is depicted as a centralized, merit-based system with top-down management and uniform enforcement of rules, policies and procedures, where the role of HR managers is to be the 'enforcers of merit'. On the other hand, NPPM principles may include the other three models which mainly focus on such values as decentralization, multi-directional communication and collaboration, and contract-out systems based on a strategy, effectiveness, and the efficiency management model.
3. The Kaiser-Meyer-Olkin (KMO) values greater than 0.9 are regarded as superb; 0.8–0.9 are meritorious, 0.7–0.8 are middling, 0.5–0.7 are mediocre, and less than 0.5 are unacceptable. In addition, Bartlett's test of sphericity determines whether the correlation matrix is an identity matrix. H0: R=I (the variables are completely uncorrelated with each other); in this case, we can reject the null hypothesis because the chi-square (595) is 1478131.365, $p<.0001$. So we can conclude that the variables are not completely uncorrelated with each other and there is a meaningful relationship among the variables. Both methods suggest that the correlation matrix is amenable to factor analysis.
4. Wise (2002) suggests that democratization values include democratic accountability, employee empowerment, greater employee participation, and cooperative management practices. Some examples of organizational democratization values are: 'effort to advance access to leadership to more social groups, including mentoring; participative decision-making styles; use of work teams and leaderless teams' (2002: 558).

References

Argyris, C. (1973). Some limits of rational man organization theory. *Public Administration*

Review, 33(3), 253-267.

Barley, S. R., & Kunda, G. (1992). Design and devotion: Surges of rational and normative ideologies of control in managerial discourse. *Administrative Science Quarterly, 37,* 363-399.

Barnard, C. (1938). *The function of the executive.* Cambridge, MA: Harvard University Press.

Battaglio, R. P., & Condrey, S. E. (2006). Civil service reform: Examining state and local government cases. *Review of Public Personnel Administration, 26*(2), 118-138.

Berry, F. S., Chackerian, R., & Wechsler, B. (1999). Reinventing government: Lessons from a state capital. In H. G. Frederickson & J. M. Johnston (Eds.), *Public management reform and innovation: Research, theory, and application* (pp. 329-353). Tuscaloosa: University of Alabama Press.

Box, R. C. (2002). Pragmatic discourse and administrative legitimacy. *American Review of Public Administration, 32*(1), 20-39.

Boyne, G. A. (1998). Bureaucratic theory meets reality: Public choice and service contracting in US local government. *Public Administration Review, 58*(6), 474-483.

Bozeman, B. (2007). *Public values and public interest: Counterbalancing economic individualism.* Washington, DC: Georgetown University Press.

Breul, J. D. (2007). Three Bush administration management reform initiatives: The President's management agenda, freedom to management legislative proposal, and the program assessment rating tool. *Public Administration Review, 67*(1), 21-26.

Campbell, C., Rockman, B. A., & Rudalevige, A. (2007). *The George W. Bush legacy.* Washington, DC: CQ Press.

Christensen, T., & Lægreid, P. (2007). The whole-of-government approach to public sector reform. *Public Administration Review, 67*(6), 1059-1066.

Christensen, T., & Lægreid, P. (2008). NPM and beyond: Structure, culture and demography. *International Review of Administrative Sciences, 74*(1), 7-23.

Condrey, S. E. (2005). Toward strategic human resource management. In S. E. Condrey (Ed.), *Handbook of human resource management* (2nd ed., pp. 1-14). San Francisco, CA: Jossey-Bass.

Denhardt, R. B., & Denhardt, J. V. (2000). The new public service: Serving rather than steering. *Public Administration Review, 60,* 549-559.

Denhardt, R. B., & Denhardt, J. V. (2003). *The new public service: Serving, not steering.* New York: M.E. Sharpe.

Durant, R. F., Stazyk, E. C., & Resh, W. (2010). Faithful infidelity: 'Political time', George W. Bush, and the paradox of 'big government conservatism'. *Review of Public Personnel Administration, 30*(4), 379-403.

Durant, R. F., Stazyk, E. C., & Resh, W. (2010). Introduction: Symposium on HRM, 'big government conservatism', and the personnel legacy of George W. Bush. *Review of*

Public Personnel Administration, 30(4), 372-378.

Ezra, M., & Deckman, M. (1996). Balancing work and family responsibilities: Flextime and child care in the federal government. *Public Administration Review, 56*(2), 174-179.

Facer, R. L., & Wadsworth, L. L. (2008). Alternative work schedules and work–family balance: A research note. *Review of Public Personnel Administration, 28,* 166-177.

Fox, C. J. (1996). Reinventing government as postmodern symbolic politics. *Public Administration Review, 56*(3), 256-262.

Fox, C. J., & Miller, H. T. (1995). *Postmodern public administration: Toward discourse.* Thousand Oaks, CA: Sage Publications.

Frederickson, H. G. (1996). Comparing the reinventing government movement with the new public administration. *Public Administrative Review, 56*(3), 263-269.

Frederickson, H. G., & Smith, K. B. (2003). *The public administration theory primer.* Boulder, CO: Westview Press.

Goldfinch, S. (2006). Rituals of reform, policy transfer, and the national university corporation reforms of Japan. *Governance, 19*(4), 585-604.

Goldfinch, S., & Wallis, J. (2010). Two myths of convergence in public management reform. *Public Administration, 88*(4), 1099-1115.

Golembiewski, R. T. (1967). *Men, management, and morality.* New York: McGraw-Hill.

Hays, S. W., & Kearney, R. C. (1997). Riding the crest of a wave: The National Performance Review and public management reform. *International Journal of Public Administration, 20*(1), 11-40.

Hood, C., & Peters, G. (2004). The middle aging of New Public Management: Into the age of paradox?. *Journal of Public Administration Research and Theory, 14*(3), 267-282.

Ingelhart, R. (1997). *Modernization and Postmodernization.* Princeton, NJ: Princeton University Press.

Ingraham, P. W., & Jones, V. D. (1999). The pain of organizational change: Managing reinvention. In H. G. Frederickson & J. M. Johnston (Eds.), *Public management reform and innovation: Research, theory, and application* (pp. 211-229). Tuscaloosa: University of Alabama Press.

Joaquin, M. E. (2009). Bureaucratic adaptation and the politics of multiple principals in policy implementation. *American Review of Public Administration, 39*(3), 246-268.

Jöreskog, K. G., & Sörbom, D. (1996). *LISREL 8 User's Reference Guide.* Chicago, IL: Scientific Software International.

Kaufman, H. (1969). Administrative decentralization and political power. *Public Administration Review, 29*(1), 3-15.

Kellough, J. E., Nigro, L. G., & Brewer, G. A. (2010). Civil service reform under George W. Bush: Ideology, politics, and public personnel administration. *Review of Public Personnel Administration, 30*(4), 404-422.

Kelly, R. M. (1998). An inclusive democratic polity, representative bureaucracies, and the new public management. *Public Administration Review, 58,* 201-208.

Kettl, D. F. (1997). The global revolution in public management. *Journal of Policy Analysis and Management, 16*(3), 446-442.

Kettl, D. F. (2002). *The transformation of governance: Public administration for twenty-first century America.* Baltimore, MD: The Johns Hopkins University Press.

King, C. S., & Stivers, C. (1998). *Government is us: Public administration in an anti-government era.* Thousand Oaks, CA: Sage Publications.

Lane, L. M., & Woodard, C. A. (2001). Merit without the system. In S. E. Condrey & R. Maranto (Eds.), *Radical reform of the civil service* (pp. 127-149). Lanham, MD: Lexington Books.

Lasseter, R. W. (2002). Georgia's merit system reform 1996-2001: An operating agency's perspective. *Review of Public Personnel Administration, 22,* 125-132.

Light, P. C. (1998). *The tides of reform: Making government work, 1945-1995.* New Haven, CT: Yale University Press.

Lowery, D. (1998). Consumer sovereignty and quasi-market failure. *Journal of Public Administration Research and Theory, 8*(2), 137-172.

Maranto, R. (2002). Praising civil service but not bureaucracy. *Review of Public Personnel Administration, 22,* 175-192.

Maranto, R., Lansford, T., & Johnson, J (Eds.). (2009). *Judging Bush.* Stanford, CA: Stanford University Press.

Mazmanian, D., & Sabatier, P. (1989). *Implementation and public policy: With a new postscript.* Lanham, MD: University Press of America.

McGregor, D. (1960). *The human side of enterprise.* New York: McGraw-Hill.

Milakovich, G. T. (1988). *With the stroke of a pen: Executive orders and presidential power.* Princeton, NJ: Princeton University Press.

Moore, M. (1995). *Creating public value: Strategic management in government.* Cambridge, MA: Harvard University Press.

Moynihan, D. P. (2008a). The normative model in decline? Public service motivation in the age of governance. In J. L. Perry & A. Hondeghem (Eds.), *Motivation in public management: The call of public service* (pp. 247-267). Oxford: Oxford University Press.

Moynihan, D. P. (2008b). *The dynamics of performance management: Constructing information and reform.* Washington, DC: Georgetown University Press.

Osborne, S. P. (2006). The new public governance?. *Public Management Review, 8*(3), 377-387.

Park, S. M., & Rainey, H. G. (2012). Work motivation and social communication among public managers. *The International Journal of Human Resource Management, 23*(13). 2630-2660.

Perry, J. L. (1996). Measuring public service motivation: An assessment of construct reliability and validity. *Journal of Public Administration Research and Theory, 6,* 5-22.

Perry, J. L., & Wise, L. R. (1990). The motivational bases of public service. *Public Administration Review, 50*(3), 367-373.

Pollitt, C. (1995). Justification by works or by faith? Evaluating the new public management. *Evaluation, 1*(2), 133-154.

Pollitt, C. (2001). Convergence: The useful myth?. *Public Administration, 79*(4), 933-947.

Pollitt, C. (2008). *Time, policy, management: Governing with the past.* Oxford: Oxford University Press.

Rainey, H. G., & Steinbauer, P. (1999). Galloping elephants: Developing elements of a theory of effective government organizations. *Journal of Public Administration Research and Theory, 1,* 1-32.

Rainey, H. G., Koehler, M., & Jung, C. (2008). Public values and public service motivation: How do public values relate to patterns of public service motivation? *A paper proposed for the workshop on public values and public interest: Normative questions in the evaluation and development of the public sector.* University of Georgia, Athens, GA.

Riccucci, N. M., & Thompson, F. J. (2008). The new public management, homeland security, and the politics of civil service reform. *Public Administration Review, 68*(5), 877-890.

Risher, H., & Fay, C. H. (2007). *Managing for better performance: Enhancing federal performance management practices.* IBM Center for the Business of Government (Human Capital Management Series).

Roethlisberger, F. J., & Dickson, W. J. (1939). *Management and the worker.* Cambridge, MA: Harvard University Press.

Ryan, R. W. (2003). The department of homeland security challenges the federal civil service system: Professional lessons from a department's emergence. *Public Administration & Management: An Interactive Journal, 8*(3), 101-115.

Saltzstein, A. L., Ting, Y., & Saltzstein, G. H. (2001). Work-family balance and job satisfaction: The impact of family-friendly policies on attitudes of federal government employees. *Public Administration Review, 61*(4), 452-467.

Savas, E. S. (2000). *Privatization and public-private partnership.* New York: Chatham.

Sclar, E. (2000). *You don't always get what you pay for: The economics of privatization.* Ithaca, NY: Cornell University Press.

Stone, D. (1997). *Policy paradox: The art of political decision making.* New York: W.W. Norton & Co.

Swanson, R. A., & Holton, E. F. (2001). *Foundations of human resource development.* San Francisco, CA: Berrett-Koehler.

Thelen, K. (2003). How institutions evolve. In J. Mahoney & D. Rueschmeyer (Eds.), *Comparative historical analysis in the social sciences* (pp. 208-241). Cambridge: Cambridge University Press.

Thompson, J. R. (2001). The civil service under Clinton. *Review of Public Personnel*

Administration, 21, 87-113.

Thompson, J. R. (2006). The federal civil service: The demise of an institution. *Public Administration Review, 66*(4), 496-503.

Thompson, J. R. (2010). Toward 'flexible uniformity'? Civil service reform, 'big government conservatism', and the promise of the intelligence community model. *Review of Public Personnel Administration, 30*(4), 423-444.

Underhill, J., & Oman, R. (2007). A critical review of the sweeping federal civil service changes: The case of the Departments of Homeland Security and Defense. *Review of Public Personnel Administration, 27*(4), 401-420.

US Office of Management and Budget. (2004). *Competitive sourcing: Report on competitive sourcing results fiscal year 2003.* Washington, DC: Author.

Werner, J. M., & DeSimone, R. L. (2009). *Human resource development* (5th ed.), Mason, OH: Mason.

Wise, L. R. (2002). Public management reform: Competing drivers of changes. *Public Administration Review, 62,* 555-567.

Appendix

Construction of index variables: selected representative survey items

New Public Management (NPM) Reform Values

1. Performance and Results-oriented Reform Values Scale (Cronbach's alpha=0.913)
   - Selections for promotions in my work unit are based on merit.
   - Awards in my work unit depend on how well employees perform their jobs.
   - High-performing employees in my work unit are recognized or rewarded on a timely basis.
   - Employees are rewarded for providing high quality products and services to customers.
   - I am held accountable for achieving results.
   - In my work unit, steps are taken to deal with a poor performer who cannot or will not improve.

2. Market and Strategy-oriented Reform Values Scale (Cronbach's alpha=0.821)
   - In my work unit HRM strategies are targeted to achieve my agency's missions and objectives.
   - Managers review and evaluate the organization's progress toward meeting its goals and

objectives.

- Products and services in my work unit are improved based on customer/public input.
- I believe my organization can perform its function as effectively as any private sector provider.

Normative Post-NPM Reform Values

1. Social Equity Reform Values Scale (Cronbach's alpha=0.892)
   - Supervisors/leaders in my work unit are committed to a workforce representative of all segments of society.
   - Policies and programs promote diversity in the workplace.
   - Managers/supervisors/team leaders work well with employees of different backgrounds.
   - Complaints, disputes, or grievances are resolved fairly in my work unit.
   - Arbitrary action, personal favoritism and coercion for partisan political purposes are not tolerated.

2. Knowledge Management (KM)-based Reform Values Scale (Cronbach's alpha=0.828)
   - Employees have electronic access to learning and training programs readily available at their desk.
   - I receive the training I need to perform my job.
   - I am given a real opportunity to improve my skills in my organization.
   - I have enough information to do my job well.

3. Work-Life Balance (WLB)-based Reform Values Scale (Cronbach's alpha=0.730)
   How important are the following WLB programs to you?
   - Telework/telecommuting
   - Alternative work schedule
   - Childcare subsidies
   - Employee assistance programs
   - My supervisor supports my need to balance work and family issues

4. Democratization Reform Values Scale (Cronbach's alpha=0.770)
   - Employees have a feeling of personal empowerment and ownership of work processes.
   - Employees in my work unit share their knowledge with each other.
   - Managers promote communication among different work units.

Note: All Cronbach scores are standardized based on the standardized items. A complete listing of items in the indices is available from the authors.

Chapter 4

Analyzing Value Creation of Electronic Human Resource Management (E-HRM)

: An Indonesian Case

Summary

The advancement of ICT coupled by an ever increasing demand to the HRM function to be more efficient, effective, and capable of supporting strategic goals of every business function have led to the adoption of Electronic Human Resource Management (e-HRM). This study aims at providing insight and empirical evidence on the success enabler of e-HRM acceptance and e-HRM value creation in public sector. The study confirmed that Perceived Usefulness is found to be a strong predictor of e-HRM usage. On the other hand the study does not provide any evidence that Perceived Ease of Use is a critical factor of e-HRM usage as it is stated on the Technology Acceptance Model (TAM). The relationship between these user acceptance factors and technology usage are not affected by the existence of Transformational Leadership. From the organization factor, Human Resource Management Strength has a positive influence on the e-HRM usage. In the creation of HRM value, we found e-HRM usage as a strong predictor of Perceived HR Service Quality, but not in the creation of strategic role of HRM function. Furthermore, the study indicates HRM Strength as an important direct predictor of the creation of HRM values. This suggests the importance of policy clarity and consistency. In order for ensuring e-HRM to be used in a more strategic way, core business of organization, HRM strategy, and IT management should be clearly aligned and integrated.

Keyword

□ e-HRM □ Value Creation □ Technology Acceptance Model □ Leadership
□ Perceived Usefulness □ Perceived Ease of Use □ Service Quality

Eri Wahyudi M.P.A., Sungkyunkwan University
Sung Min Park Associate Professor, Sungkyunkwan University

Introduction

Problem Definition

The advancement of information and communication technologies (ICT) is altering the way of life and work, including practice in business and government. It is believed that ICT development drives business processes and strategies of change. In human resource management (HRM) for example, organizations have finally realized the growing importance of using ICT in leveraging their HRM functions. Moreover, an increasing demand for the HRM function to be more efficient, effective, and capable of supporting strategic goals of every business function has led to the adoption of electronic human resource management (e-HRM) in organizations. e-HRM has been considered as a means for an organization to innovate itself, both in private and public, in response to demands and changes in the business.

Ruel (2007) defined e-HRM as a way of implementing HRM strategies, policies, and practices in organizations through the conscious and directed support of, and/or the full use of, web technology-based channels. e-HRM has a wide range of uses and may support particular HR activities such as recruitment and selection, performance management, compensation and benefits, training and development, health and safety, employee relations, retention, policies on work–life balance (Enshur et. al., 2002), and managing employee information across the entire employment cycle (Parry, Tyson 2011).

The use of e-HRM is a common practice today in many organizations, profit and non-profit, and is expected to create value for them. Consequently, academic interest in e-HRM has increased in an attempt to investigate the value creation of e-HRM. Lepak and Snell (1998) suggested that e-HRM investment goals include transformation of the HRM function to a strategic business partner. Strohmeier (2007) found that research on e-HRM has shown that it alleviates the administrative burden and produces increased accuracy of results and quality of HR activities. Similarly, Ruel et al. (2006) suggested the following four goals: cost reduction, improving HR services, improving strategic orientation, and global orientation. However, despite the great potential for HR functions to create value beyond administrative outcomes, in practice many organizations use e-HRM more for an 'automating' approach that focuses primarily on administrative efficiency rather than supporting strategic "human capital management" processes (Foster, 2010). Foster (2010) stated that the annual CedarCrestone (2009) HR study indicates that while process-based administrative tools are used by over 90 percent of organizations, strategic HR technology tools have a much lower organizational penetration rate, typically at the 30-40 percent level (Foster, 2010).

Adoption of information technology in the HR system will change the relationship between employees and the HR Department, and the dependency and interaction between employees and computers may increase. Therefore, the e-HRM implementation process must take into account the challenges of both change management and technology acceptance. Incorporation of the Technology Acceptance Model (Davis et.al. 1989) into recent e-HRM studies has resulted in the notion that the use of e-HRM by targeted employees is highly determined by the level of usefulness and ease of use of the technology (Ruta, 2005).

However, studies that attempt to find empirical evidence for the success enabler of e-HRM acceptance and a possible HRM outcome created by the usage of e-HRM in a single model are relatively scarce. The majority of previous studies have focused on only the value creation side or the acceptance side. Furthermore, studies on e-HRM usually focus on the private sector as their object. This study aimed to close this gap by investigating the success enabler of e-HRM adoption and e-HRM value creation in the public sector using an integrated model.

Research Questions

This research study attempts to answer the following research questions:

1. What are the key success enablers in the adoption of e-HRM?
2. To what extent does usage of e-HRM applications predict HRM value creation?
3. Does a direct leadership environment, considered to be a contextual factor, have a moderation effect on the relationship between user acceptance factors and e-HRM usage?

Literature Review

E-HRM and Value Creation

The growing literature on the topic of e-HRM and value creation has discussed a range of broad goals for e-HRM introduction (Ruel et al., 2004; Marler, 2009), including cost and efficiency savings, strategic aims, and improvements in client services (Parry, Tyson, 2011). e-HRM has been defined as "an umbrella term covering all possible integration mechanisms and contents between HRM and information technologies, aiming at creating value within and across organizations for targeted employees and management" (Bondarouk & Ruel, 2009, p.507). Ruel and Kaap (2012) stated that e-HRM, as a relatively new technology-driven phenomena, has raised questions regarding value creation (Currie & Parikh, 2006), most importantly whether e-HRM creates value and how value created by e-HRM can be measured.

According to Porter (1985), value creation occurs when organizations are developing new ways of doings things and using new methods. e-HRM provides a new approach to managing human resources. It changes the nature of HRM procedures, HRM practice, and HR policy by utilizing the advantages of information technology. This new approach may allow organizations to secure benefits or competitive advantages when such technology is successfully implemented. Following Haksever et al.'s (2004) definition of value as "the capacity of a good, service, or activity to satisfy a need or provide a benefit to a person or a legal entity," we consider those potential benefits of e-HRM to the employee or organization as "value," which can be created through successful implementation of e-HRM.

Research by Ruel and Van der Kaap (2012) confirmed that e-HRM usage significantly contributes to the creation of efficiency, in term of effectiveness, and HR service quality in an organization. Contextual factors facilitating e-HRM usage, such as data quality, HRM policy, and HR technology competencies, were found to be positively related to HRM value creation. For their study, Rule and Van der Kaap developed a questionnaire to collect data. Explorative factor analysis (via PAC) was used to identify the three dimensions of the dependent variable, HRM value creation. Explorative factor analysis (via PAC) was also used to identify the four dimensions of the context variable of HRM facilitation. The researchers tested their hypotheses using hierarchical regression analysis on 151 valid questionnaires.

Parry's (2011) research from a large-scale survey across 12 countries showed that e-HRM helps HR to increase its value by becoming more strategic, but found no evidence of cost savings due to reductions in HR headcount. This finding suggests that organizations are using e-HRM in order to redeploy HR practitioners from transactional work to more strategic and value-added activities. Her investigation is based upon cross-sectional data, targeted at the senior HR manager in each firm, as these professionals are presumed to be knowledgeable about the characteristics of their workforce and the existence of HRM practices within their organizations.

By means of a questionnaire, as well as through face-to-face interviews with HR professionals, line managers, and non-managerial employees in the Belgian public service, Bondarouk and Ruel (2012) were also successful in finding two generally acclaimed strategic advantages of e-HRM: changing the role of HR toward that of a business partner and increasing the time available for strategic HR issues.

However, Marler and Fisher (2012) found that there is very limited systematic empirical evidence concerning whether e-HRM is related to strategic outcomes, particularly organizational performance. Using integrative synthesis to examine 40 studies in peer-reviewed e-HRM literature published over the last 12 years, they suggested that e-HRM is not implemented to achieve typical strategic outcomes (e.g. competitive positioning or performance), but primarily to improve employee welfare such as increased HR services and better communication.

Transformational Leadership

In e-government initiatives, strong leadership with vision and strategies is considered to be an important success factor that enables values and ideas to be shared by all stakeholders, goals and objectives to be achieved, and strategies to be implemented (OECD, 2003). Leadership refers to the ability to "influence processes involving determination of the group's or organization's objectives, motivating task behavior in pursuit of these objectives, and influencing group maintenance and culture" (Yukl, 1989; Park, 2011). Leadership in the public sector is an important aspect of the work environment for employees (e.g., Oldham & Cummings, 1996; Scott & Bruce, 1994; Park, 2011). Wart (2003) has summarized that effective leadership within an organization provides beneficial outcomes such as higher-quality and more efficient goods and services, a sense of cohesiveness, personal development, and higher levels of satisfaction among those conducting the work, an overarching sense of direction and vision, an alignment with the environment, a healthy mechanism for innovation and creativity, and a resource for invigorating the organizational culture.

A new paradigm of leadership has begun to capture attention. Leadership is conceived to be transactional and/or transformational (Burns, 1978; Bass, 1985). Evidence has accumulated that transformational leadership can move followers to exceed expected performance. According to Conger (1999), research shows "the advantages of the transformational leadership style over the more traditional forms . . . in terms of achieving organizational goals" (pp. 145–179). Transformational leaders motivate others to do more than they originally intended and often even more than they thought possible. They set more challenging expectations and typically achieve better performance.

Factor studies including those by Bass (1985) and Avolio and Howell (1992) have identified the four main components of transformational leadership.[1] Park and Rainey (2008) also stated that transformational leadership can have a direct relationship with organizational performance and an effect on individual and work-group performance through its effects on subordinates' satisfaction with their leader, a sense of empowerment, and related responses (Howell and Avolio 1993; Hater and Bass 1988; Podsakoff 1996).

E-HRM and Strategic Human Resource Management

In recent years, the internet has revolutionized the way individuals in organizations access information. In addition to channels such as business-to-business and business-to-consumer, the internet has permitted human resource management to implement HR processes where business-to-employee (B2E) solutions are possible (Harris, Phifer, & Berg, 2002). Since more of the administrative tasks are available on HR portals, HR professionals are expected to have more time to engage in strategic HR activities (Ruta, 2005). Huselid et al. (1997) noted that there is broad agreement that strategic HRM involves the development and implementation of policies and practices that ensure human capital contributes to the organization's achievement of its goals (which are aligned with its business strategy).

The current e-HRM literature distinguishes three types of e-HRM: operational e-HRM, relational e-HRM, and transformational e-HRM (Ruël, Bondarouk, and Velde, 2007). Within all the types of HRM, choices have to be made in terms of which HRM activities will be offered face-to-face and which will be offered through web-based HR (i.e. e-enabled). For the operational type of HRM, this issue amounts to a choice between asking employees to keep their own personal data up-to-date through an HR website or having an administrative force in place to do this for them. In terms of relational HRM, there is a choice between supporting recruitment and selection through a web-based application or using a paper-based approach (advertisements, paper-based application forms and letters, etc.). Finally, in terms of transformational HRM, there is a choice between creating a change-ready workforce through an integrated set of web-based tools that enables the workforce to develop in line with the company's strategic choices and using paper-based materials. Transformational impact redefines the focus of HR by emphasizing the strategic focus of HR (Snell, Stueber, and Lepak, 2002).

Research Design

Research Model

Based on the literature review, we developed our research model, seen in figure 1.

Figure 1. Research Model

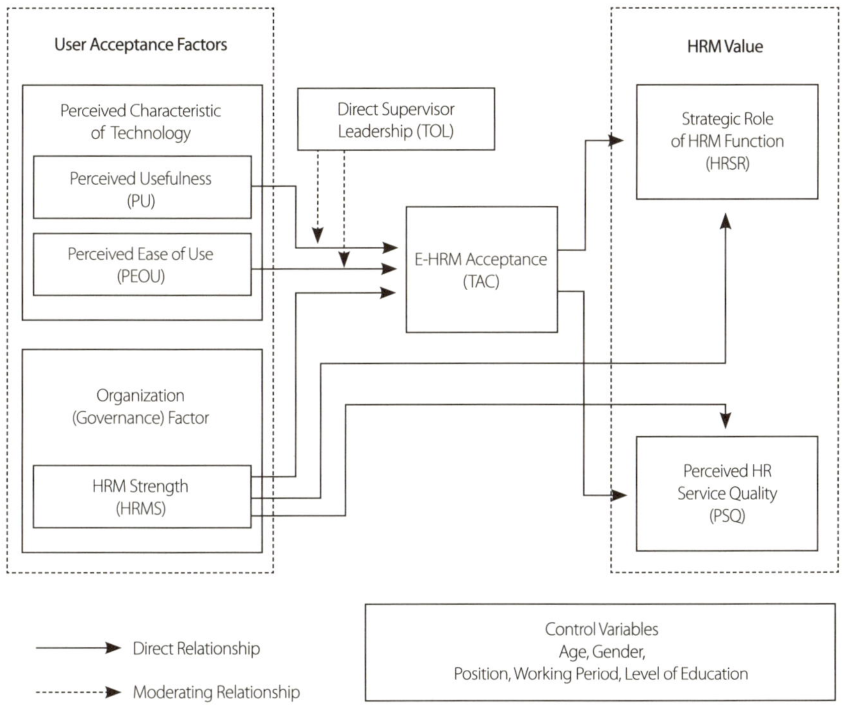

This study conducted an inquiry to find empirical evidence as to what extent the implementation of e-HRM provides specific HRM-related value to an organization. For this purpose, we included two important values, HR service quality and strategic role of HRM function. Within this framework, we also investigated the factors that influence the acceptance of e-HRM. We looked into two important factors from the Technology Acceptance Model, including perceived usefulness and perceived ease of use toward e-HRM, and conducted a statistical test to determine whether they play a significant role in enabling e-HRM acceptance within an organization.

Research also takes specific and related organizational factors into account to determine their impact on technology acceptance. We proposed that HRM strength, as an important organizational (governance) practice, has an influence on the acceptance of e-HRM and HRM value creation. As a certain type of leadership may have an impact on employee empowerment, this study conducted an inquiry into whether the relationship between individual perceptions of e-HRM (perceived usefulness and perceive ease of use) and e-HRM acceptance is also influenced by characteristics of a direct leadership environment. We treated direct leadership environment, measured by the existence of transformational leadership, as a contextual factor that may influence the relationship between individual perception on technology (e-HRM) and technology (e-HRM) acceptance. We predicted that the absence of transformational leadership as a moderating variable would reflect that the user acceptance factors are a crucial predictor of the acceptance of e-HRM.

Research Variables

Independent Variables: User Acceptance Factors

It has been noted that users' attitudes toward and acceptance of a new information system have a critical impact on successful information system adoption (Davis, 1989; Venkatesh and Davis, 1996; Succi and Walter, 1999). If users are not willing to accept the information system, it will not bring its full benefits to the organization (Davis, 1993; Davis and Venkatesh, 1996). We utilized constructs from the Technology Acceptance Model (TAM) to explain factors contributing to the acceptance of new technology.

According to the theory, information system acceptance involving actual system use is determined by perceived usefulness (PU) and perceived ease of use (PEOU), which first influence intention to use, and then influence behavior. PU refers to the prospective user's subjective likelihood that the use of a certain system will increase his or her performance. PEOU is defined as the degree to which the prospective user expects the potential system to be free of effort (Davis et al., 1989).

Hypothesis 1: Perceived usefulness has a positive effect on the acceptance of an e-HRM system.

Hypothesis 2: Perceived ease of use has a positive effect on the acceptance of an e-HRM system.

Managerial actions can help to manage change and develop successful IT implementation plans (Leonard-Barton & Deschamps, 1988; Ruta, 2005). Besides IT, HRM system strength is an important contributor to the success of e-HRM. An HRM system is the overall set of HR practices in a company. The HR practices in a company can be seen as communication from employer to employee (Bowen and Ostroff, 2004). Through HR practices, employees develop skills, knowledge, and motivation to contribute to the firm's strategy. Thus, through the HRM system, the perceptions, attitudes and behaviors of employees are influenced (Bowen and Ostroff, 2000). Therefore, we considered a strong HRM system to be a value-creating factor.

To achieve a strong HRM system, employees have to work in accordance with the strategy of the organization. The emphasis is on improving the communication of the HR practices to the employees. The content of the HR practices is a matter of secondary importance for achieving a strong HRM system. To achieve a strategic orientation of employees, the HR practices should communicate unambiguous messages to employees about what is appropriate behavior. Two main criteria for measuring HRM strength are distinctiveness and consistency.[2] The stronger the HRM system, the clearer and more unambiguous the message that organizations send to their employees about desired appropriate behavior. In order for an organization to improve its strategic orientation, it should send clear and unambiguous messages about desired appropriate behavior. Thus, it can be said that the strength of an HRM system determines the success of e-HRM.

Hypothesis 3: A strong HRM system has a positive effect on e-HRM acceptance.

Mediating Variable: e-HRM Acceptance

According to Ruta (2005), literature on the management of information systems describes the success of IT implementation mostly through IT system usage (Davis et al., 1989; Igbaria, Zinatelli, Cragg, & Cavaye, 1997; Straub, Limayem, & Karahanna-Evaristo, 1995; Thompson et al., 1991) and user satisfaction (Baroudi, Olson, & Ives, 1986; Gelderman, 1998; Kim, Suh, & Lee, 1998; Taylor & Todd, 1995b). Discussing both measures, Al-Gahtani and King (1999) pointed out that system usage is a more precise measure of IT acceptance. Moreover, Igbaria et al. (1997) also defined system usage as the primary indicator of IT acceptance and said, "System usage has a notable practical value for managers interested in evaluating the impact of information technology." For these reasons, in this study, success of HR portal acceptance was measured by the degree of usage.

Frequency of use is one of the most common metrics of usage exploited in IS research (Straub et al., 1995). It makes no sense to implement a system that is not used by end-users. Users should notice the need for e-HRM in their daily activities and use the system intensively. In this research, we also include appropriation of use as one of the measurements of technology acceptance. According to Orlikowski (1996), as cited by Ruel and Kaap (2012), appropriation is the "continuous, progressive, and mutual adjustments, accommodations, and improvisations between the technology and the users." The implementation of an e-HRM system involves the process of appropriation. When implementing a new system or practice in an organization, management should be concerned with internalizing this system with the employees. Management has to teach them how they should use it. Also, there should be a condition where employees are able to execute the applications in line with the purposes of the organization (Ruel and Kaap, 2012).

Dependent Variables: HRM Value Creation

HRM value creation consists of two main dependent variables: strategic HRM roles and perceived HR service quality. One of the goals of organizations making steps toward e-HRM is to improve the strategic orientation of HRM (Lepak and Snell, 1998). As Kavanagh et al. (1990) states, HR departments will be more involved in strategic planning processes if they are able to provide adequate, accurate, and fast information through the use of information technology. A related change for HR departments is that with appropriate use of information technology, they can improve their client focus. That is, the HR group is expected to focus on providing services to internal stakeholders, e.g., employees, line managers, and senior management, often by serving as an internal consultant (Kavanagh et al., 1990).

Hypothesis 4: The usage of an e-HRM system will increase the strategic role of the HRM Department.

The implementation of e-HRM can create value for an organization by improving the service level of the HRM department. Parasuraman et al. (1985) defined service quality as a comparison of expectations of the HRM services an organization offers to its employees with the performance of these services. Service quality involves not only the outcome of the e-HRM system but also the way the service is delivered. Service quality is an important value-creating factor because there are different kinds of gaps that exist between the perceptions of executives regarding service quality and the perceptions of the actual users. To ensure good quality, service quality should exceed customer expectations of the service.

Hypothesis 5: The usage of an e-HRM system will increase perceived HRM service quality.

We also looked into how the HRM governance practice in an organization contributes directly to the creation of HRM values. For this purpose, we developed relevant hypotheses as follows:

Hypothesis 6: A strong HRM system will significantly shift HRM function to have a more strategic role.

Hypothesis 7: A strong HRM system will have a significant positive impact on perceived HR service quality.

To test whether the usage of e-HRM has a mediating role on the value creation of human resource management, we developed the following hypothesis:

Hypothesis 8: The usage of e-HRM mediates the relationship between user acceptance factors and HRM value.

Moderating Variables: Contextual Factors

Contingency theory is widely used in IS and HRM research and as a result has been applied in e-HRM studies as well. In most cases, contingency theory researchers suggest that outcome variables such as organizational performance depend on the "best fit" with independent variables such as individual characteristics and organizational characteristics. These independent variables are referred to as context variables in many of the studies. It is not uncommon for aspects of the organizational context of information systems (IS) research, and more specifically IS usage, to be taken into consideration (e.g. Ein-Dor and Segev, 1978; Franz and Robey, 1986). When introducing an IT application such as an HR portal, it is necessary to take into account the general context for change, considering there will be a new application for users and that it will modify the relationship between employee and organization. According to Strohmeier (2007), contextual factors are obviously of relevance for e-HRM. For instance, on the individual level, computer availability or attitudes of peer groups may constitute relevant contextual factors, while the organizational level may be affected by contextual factors like culture or legal conditions.

The contextual factor that may affect user acceptance in this study is the existence of transformational leadership (TOL). As described by Ruta (2005), the behavior of the leader is extremely critical to communicating the need for change (Kotter, 1995). The leader has to demonstrate strong sponsorship of the project (Zmud, 1984) because when people see their bosses fail to remain involved in the innovation introduced, they stop making an effort to use the innovation. Armenakis, Harris, and Field (1999) identified seven influence strategies: (a) persuasive communication, (b) active participation by those affected, (c) human resource management practices, (d) symbolic activities, (e) diffusion practices, (f) management of internal and external information, and (g) formal activities that demonstrate support for change initiatives. These collective efforts are expected to produce an effective e-HRM implementation plan geared toward increasing employee usage.

Hypothesis 9: Transformational leadership has a moderating effect on the relationship between user acceptance factors and the acceptance of an e-HRM system.

The conceptualization of all constructs is written in Table 1 to provide a clear understanding of each construct being measured within the framework. Each concept is taken from a corresponding theory in the literature review, such as the Technology Acceptance Model (TAM), Leadership, and Human Resource Management.

Table 1. Conceptualization of Variables

No	Concepts	Definition
1	Perceived Usefulness (Davis, 1989)	The degree to which a person believes that this system can improve his or her job performance. Usefulness can result in increased productivity of HR-related activities and a faster working process.
2	Perceived Ease of Use (Davis, 1989)	The degree to which targeted users expect the IS not to involve effort.
3	Leadership (Yukl, 1989; Park, 2011)	The ability to "influence processes involving determination of the group's or organization's objectives, motivating task behavior in pursuit of these objectives, and influencing group maintenance and culture."
4	HRM Distinctiveness (Delmotte et.al, 2007)	Features of HRM that allow a situation to stand out in the environment and to capture attention and interest.
5	HRM Consistency (Delmotte et.al, 2007; Bowen & Ostroff, 2004)	Establishment of an effect over time and modalities regardless of the form of interactions. The consistency of an HRM system is high when it is consistent over time, people, and context. Consistency of HRM messages and the e-HRM system reassures the employees that the HRM practices will work in line with the main goals of the organization as well as with the personal goals of the employees.
6	Actual Usage Frequency (Straub et. al., 1995)	The amount of actual usage of the system. The more the system will be used, the greater the success probability.
7	Appropriation (Beaudry and Pinsonneault, 2005)	The continuous, progressive, and mutual adjustments, accommodations, and improvisations between the technology and the users.
8	HR Roles (Ulrich and Brockbank, 2005)	A set of norms and expectations that govern the behavior of HRM professionals and define their responsibilities and the content of the HRM work to be done.
9	Service Quality (Parasuraman et al., 1985)	The expectations that arise for HRM services an organization offers to its employees when they are used.

Research Methodology

Scope of the Study

The study was carried out in the Ministry of Finance, specifically at the Directorate General of Tax Services. We selected the Indonesian Taxation Authority to test the proposed model because since 2006, it has begun to implement an e-HRM application called SIKKA (Sistem Informasi Kepegawaian, Keuangan, dan Aktiva – Integrated Human Resource,

Finance, and Asset Information System). Taking into account the period of application implementation, this case allowed us to see whether this business process innovation brings significant improvement or added value to the organization and to examine the success factors of e-HRM implementation. For these reasons, the Directorate General of Tax Services was the most appropriate subject for this study.

Method of Analysis

The proposed model was tested to find empirical evidence for the proposed arguments. In order to test the model, this study employed quantitative analysis of employee perception and organizational characteristics related to the success enablers of e-HRM acceptance and value creation of e-HRM. Qualitative analysis through interviews was used for providing in-depth discussion of research findings.

Data for quantitative analysis was collected through questionnaires and recapped and analyzed using structural equation modeling. Exploratory and confirmatory factor analysis were employed to ensure high reliability on measurement and estimates. Testing for mediating effects was conducted through partial regression.

Sampling Plan

The target population of this study included all employees working in the Directorate General of Tax Services under the Ministry of Finance of the Republic of Indonesia. Employee was considered as the unit of analysis in this study. Since structural equation modeling was utilized, a sample consisting of 300 respondents was the minimum size that we aimed to obtain. The sample for quantitative analysis was obtained through a simple random sampling method. For qualitative analysis, purposive sampling was utilized, selecting only three to five key persons (holding at least a manager position) who were involved in human resource and information technology management in the headquarters of the Directorate General of Tax Services.

Research Instrument

The questionnaire was designed to ascertain employees' perceptions on success factors and the outcome of IT innovations and implementation on human resource management.[3] Existing scales were used to measure most of the variables to generate reliable measurement.

Table 2. Variables, Source of Scale, and Sample Item per Scale

No.	Variable	Sample of Measurement Item	Source of Scale
1	Perceived Usefulness	I find e-HRM helpful for dealing with my HR-related activities.	Venkatesh et al., 2003
2	Perceived Ease of Use	Interacting with e-HRM requires a lot of mental effort.	Venkatesh et al., 2003
3	HRM Distinctiveness	I am regularly informed about the initiatives taken by the HR Department.	Delmotte et al., 2007
		The HR activities in my organization are easy to understand.	Delmotte et al., 2007
4.	HRM Consistency	There is a clear fit between HR promises and deliverables.	Delmotte et al., 2007
5	Actual Usage Frequency	I use Employee Self Service in my day-to-day work.	Ruel and Kaap, 2012
6	Appropriation	I use Employee Self Service in accordance with the manual.	Ruel and Kaap, 2012
7	Strategic HRM Roles	HR professionals partner with line mangers to help them reach their goals.	Loijen, 2008
8	Perceived HR Service Quality	The HR department provides its services at the time it promises to do so.	Parasuraman et al., 1985
		Since the introduction of e-HRM, HR services minimize error administration.	Parasuraman et al., 1985
9	Transformational Leadership	Managers would try to help a poor performer improve.	Park and Rainey, 2008

Empirical Analysis

Data Collection

As mentioned before, questionnaires were sent to the employees of the Directorate of Tax under the Ministry of Finance of the Republic of Indonesia randomly to obtain primary data for analysis. In the end, we managed to collect 356 respondents. The final sample included in the analysis was 306 respondents since 50 samples were removed due to incomplete filling. Data was collected from civil servants from different genders, positions, ages, work experience, and e-HRM interaction experience to provide a representative data sample from the population.

Descriptive Statistics

Respondents' Demography Univariate Analysis

Among the 306 respondents who participated in the survey, 78% respondents were male and the rest (22%) were female. The participants of this survey were part of different age ranges: 8% of respondents were 20 - 25 years old, 67% were 26 - 30 years old, 19% were 31 - 35 years old, 5% were 36 - 40 years old, and 1% were 41 - 45 years old. Given the sample size, respondents were also classified based on their level of education. Among the respondents, 38% had a high school diploma, 58% had a bachelor's degree, and 4% had a master's degree. For work experience, we divided our sample into three categories: 33% of respondents had 1-5 years' experience, 50% had 6-10 years' experience, and 17% had 10-15 years' experience.

Figure 2 shows the e-HRM interaction experience frequency distribution of respondents. Fifty percent of respondents had 1-3 years of interaction with e-HRM, 43% respondents had more experience with e-HRM, ranging from 4-6 years interaction. Six percent of respondents had more than 6 years interaction experience, and only 1% of respondents had less than 1 year of experience using e-HRM.

Figure 2. Respondents' e-HRM Interaction Experience Frequency Distribution

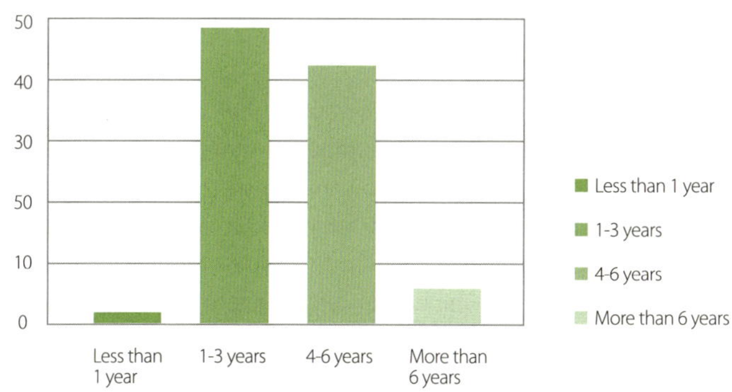

Multivariate Descriptive Statistic Analysis of Survey Responses

Descriptive statistics of the survey responses including mean, standard deviation, maximum, and minimum values of all variables included in this research are presented in Table 3. For multivariate analysis purposes, we first generated composite data of each latent variable. The value of each latent variable for each observation was obtained by taking the average value of all the factors associated with certain latent variables.

All variables had minimum values ranging from 1.00 to 2.00, whereas their maximum values were all the same at 5.00. Perceived usefulness (PU) had the biggest mean, valued at 4.0467 with a standard deviation of 0.69956. On the other hand, the smallest mean was for human resource management strength (HRMS), a variable that only generated a value of 2.9433 with a standard deviation of 0.83827.

Table 3. Minimum, Maximum, Mean, and Standard Deviation of Variables

	N	Minimum	Maximum	Mean	Std. Deviation
PU	100	2.00	5.00	4.0467	.69956
PEOU	100	1.67	5.00	3.8900	.65999
HRMS	100	1.00	5.00	2.9433	.83827
TAC	100	1.00	5.00	3.8450	.67306
HRSR	100	1.00	5.00	3.1833	.82249
PSQ	100	2.00	5.00	3.6775	.68746
Valid N (listwise)	100				

Factor Analysis

We used factor analysis to identify a small number of factors that explained most of the variance observed in a much larger number of manifest variables. Factor analysis helped us to search for such joint variations in response to unobserved latent variables. We conducted two types of factor analysis, including exploratory factor analysis (EFA) and confirmatory factor analysis. EFA is used to identify complex interrelationships among items and group items that are part of unified concepts, where the researcher makes no "a priori" assumptions about relationships among factors. Meanwhile, CFA, a more complex approach, tests whether the items are associated with specific factors and uses structural equation modeling to test a measurement model in which loading on the factors allows for evaluation of relationships between observed variables and unobserved variables.

Exploratory Factor Analysis

From the exploratory factor analysis output, first we looked at the determinant value to see whether the data had a multicollinearity problem. A determinant value of 0.005, which is greater than the 0.001, reflects that respondents' response data does not have any multicollinearity problems.

Table 4. Correlation Matrix[a]

		pou1	pou2	pou3	pe1	pe2	pe3	hrmd1	hrmd2	hrmd3	hrc1	hrc2
Correlation	pou1	1.000	.644	.674	.308	.087	.137	.328	.209	.211	.113	.003
	pou2	.644	1.000	.727	.232	.135	.133	.352	.333	.214	.294	.087
	pou3	.674	.727	1.000	.334	.198	.189	.398	.319	.287	.276	.012
	pe1	.308	.232	.334	1.000	.655	.582	.286	.270	.400	.275	-.082
	pe2	.087	.135	.198	.655	1.000	.506	.216	.219	.254	.283	-.027
	pe3	.137	.133	.189	.582	.506	.1000	.309	.260	.322	.289	.014
	hrmd1	.328	.352	.398	.286	.216	.309	1.000	.642	.576	.673	.279
	hrmd2	.209	.333	.319	.270	.219	.260	.642	1.000	.646	.569	.194
	hrmd3	.211	.214	.287	.400	.254	.322	.576	.646	1.000	.587	.104
	hrc1	.113	.294	.276	.275	.283	.289	.673	.569	.587	1.000	.353
	hrc2	.003	.087	.012	-.087	-.027	.014	.279	.194	.104	.353	1.000
Sig. (1-tailed)	pou1		.000	.000	.001	.194	.088	.000	.019	.017	.131	.487
	pou2	.000		.000	.010	.090	.093	.000	.000	.016	.001	.194
	pou3	.000	.000		.000	.024	.030	.000	.001	.002	.003	.454
	pe1	.001	.010	.000		.000	.000	.002	.003	.000	.003	.209
	pe2	.194	.090	.024	.000		.000	.015	.014	.005	.002	.395
	pe3	.088	.093	.030	.000	.000		.001	.004	.001	.002	.447
	hrmd1	.000	.000	.000	.002	.051	.001		.000	.000	.000	.002
	hrmd2	.019	.000	.001	.003	.014	.004	.000		.000	.000	.026
	hrmd3	.017	.016	.002	.000	.005	.001	.000	.000		.000	.153
	hrc1	.131	.001	.003	.003	.002	.002	.000	.000	.000		.000
	hrc2	.487	.194	.454	.209	.395	.447	.002	.026	.153	.000	

[a]. Determinant = .005

Prior to the extraction of the factors, several tests were used to assess the suitability of the respondent data for factor analysis. These tests included Kaiser-Meyer-Olkin (KMO) Measure of Sampling Adequacy and Bartlett's Test of Sphericity. Our results included a KMO value of 0.796 (above 0.5), which meant that the data in our sample was adequate and appropriate for factor analysis. It also indicated that the pattern of correlation was relatively compact and thus factor analysis should yield distinct and reliable factors.[4]

Confirmatory Factor Analysis

Based on our EFA results, we conducted confirmatory factor analysis (CFA), which enabled us to test whether the data fit the hypothesized measurement model. Figure 3 shows the CFA model. From the model fit output, the results of chi-square/df, TLI, NFI, IFI, CFI, RMSEA, and SRMR showed that the entire model is within acceptable levels. For example, the comparative fit index (CFI) was 0.988 (greater than 0.90 is acceptable) and the root mean square error approximation (RMSEA) was 0.041 (less than 0.08 is acceptable). This reflected that the models of user acceptance factors could be considered a very good fit for the observed data.

Figure 3. Confirmatory Factor Analysis of User Acceptance Factors

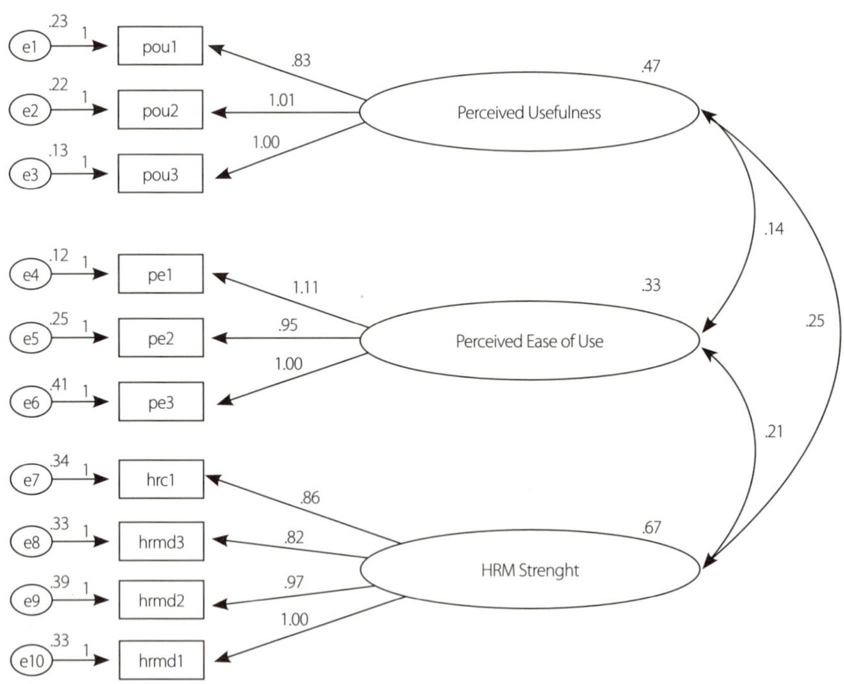

Table 5. Overall Fit Indexes from CFA Output

Model (Valid N = 100)	df	Chi-Square	Chi-Square/ df	TLI	NFI	IFI	CFI	RMSEA	SRMR
Suggested cut-off values			<3	>0.90	>0.90	>0.90	>0.90	<0.08	<0.08
Proposed Model Score	32	37.387	1.168	0.983	0.925	0.988	0.988	0.041	0.03

The analysis results showed that all observable variables measuring these three latent constructs had significant factor loadings (the standardized parameter estimates) on the factors based on the t-test (significantly different from 0).

Table 6. Regression Weights from CFA Output

			Estimate	S.E.	C.R.	P	Label
hrmd1	←	HRMS	1.000				
hrmd2	←	HRMS	.966	.117	8.262	***	par_1
hrmd3	←	HRMS	.818	.103	7.952	***	par_2
pou3	←	PU	1.000				
pou2	←	PU	1.012	.111	9.151	***	par_3
pou1	←	PU	.826	.098	8.456	***	par_4
pe3	←	PEOU	1.000				
pe2	←	PEOU	.950	.154	6.168	***	par_5
pe2	←	PEOU	1.112	.175	6.343	***	par_6
hrc1	←	HRMS	.861	.106	8.104	***	par_7

***significant at the 0.001-level

Structural Equation Modeling

Model Fit Testing

Several goodness-of-fit indices indicated that the hypothesized structural equation model accurately explained the data. From seven model-fit indexes, the chi-square value produced significant results, which was not consistent with a good model fit. However, the values of TLI, IFI, and CFI exceeded those that pointed to a good model fit overall (see table 7). In addition, RMSEA and SRMR were 0.068 and 0.043, suggesting a relatively well-fitting model (a cut-off value is 0.08). We added an error covariance among several indicators and did respecification of the model to get a lower value of the chi-square, following some possible modification index (MI) suggestions. For example, we added error covariance between e1 and e4 of the latent variable HRM strength. In the end, we found that our model provides a good explanation of the dependent variables. Figure 4 and Table 7 show the proposed model in SEM and the assessment of model fit, respectively.

Figure 4. Structural Path Estimates

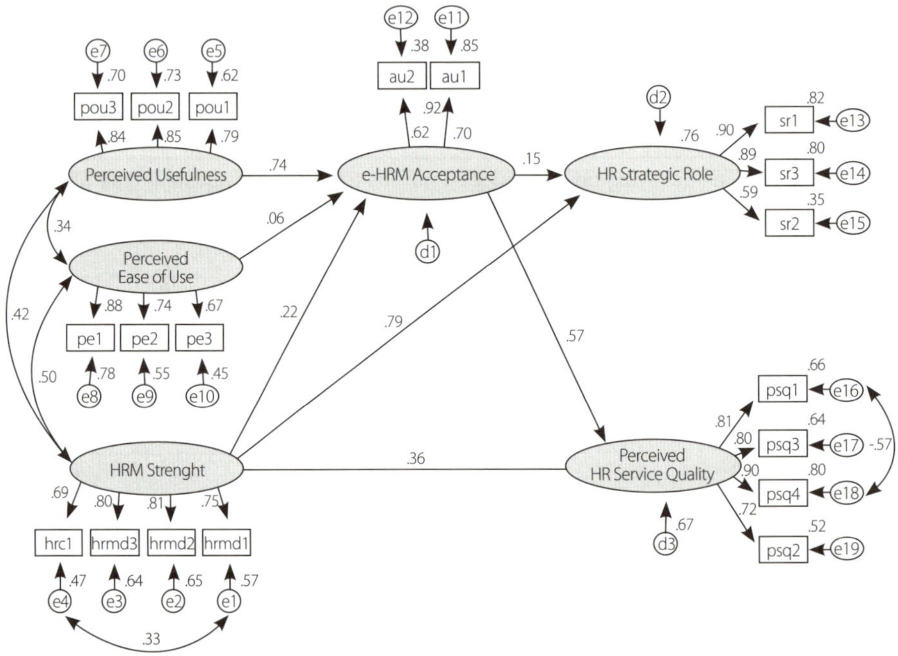

Table 7. Overall Fit Indexes from SEM Analysis

Model (Valid N = 100)	df	Chi-Square	Chi-Square/ df	TLI	NFI	IFI	CFI	RMSEA	SRMR
Suggested cut-off values			<3	>0.90	>0.90	>0.90	>0.90	<0.08	<0.08
Proposed Model Score	140	203.582	1.454	0.931	0.843	0.945	0.943	0.068	0.043

The mediator variable TAC has an R-squared value of 0.703, which means it is estimated that the predictors of TAC explain 70.3% of its variance. In other words, the error variance of TAC is approximately 29.7% of the variance of TAC itself. On the other hand, PSQ and HRSR have R-squared values of 0.674 and 0.761, respectively, reflecting that the model provides a good explanation of perceived service quality and strategic role of human resource management function.

Research Hypotheses Testing

Hypotheses testing was conducted based on regression output generated by AMOS software from SEM analysis. Table 8 summarizes the regression estimates by which we decided whether proposed relationships among variables in the research model were significant or not.

Table 8. Regression Estimates

Directionality between variables in SEM	Unstandardized Estimates	Standardized Estimates	S.E.	t-value	p-value
TAC ← PU	0.496	0.744	0.096	5.159	0.000***
TAC ← PEOU	-0.050	-0.063	0.078	-0.637	0.524
TAC ← HRMS	0.128	0.223	0.063	2.043	0.041**
HRSR ← TAC	0.303	0.152	0.183	1.652	0.099
HRSR ← HRMS	0.897	0.785	0.136	6.619	0.000***
PSQ ← HRMS	0.350	0.364	0.096	3.631	0.000***
PSQ ← TAC	0.092	0.574	0.208	4.626	0.000***

*** significant at the 0.001-level (two tailed)
** significant at the 0.05-level (two tailed)

First, we prove whether user acceptance factors are statistically supported in predicting e-HRM acceptance. From Table 8, we can observe that perceived usefulness (PU) directly, significantly, and positively influences e-HRM acceptance (TAC) with a coefficient regression value of 0.496 at the 0.001-level of significance. This means that Hypothesis 1 is supported by the observed data. On the other hand, we find that perceived ease of use (PEOU) is not a predictor of e-HRM acceptance (TAC). Observed data only generates a coefficient regression value of -0.050 (very weak relationship) and a p-value of 0.524 (bigger than 0.05), which causes a failure in rejecting the null hypothesis of Hypothesis 2.

Hypothesis 3 posits that a strong HRM system has a positive effect on e-HRM acceptance. From Table 8, we can conclude that this hypothesis is supported. The regression weight for Human Resource Management Strength (HRMS) in the prediction of e-HRM acceptance (TAC) is significantly different from zero at the 0.05 level (two-tailed). Given the regression coefficient of 0.128 with a p-value of 0.041, it reflects a positive and significant relationship.

Moving to value creation from acceptance of e-HRM, Hypothesis 4 posits that the usage of an e-HRM system will increase the strategic role of an HRM Department. Regression analysis output shows that the relationship between TAC and Strategic Role of Human Resource Management Function (HRSR) has a p-value of 0.099, meaning that we should not have rejected the null hypothesis of Hypothesis 4. Hence, we can conclude that the usage of e-HRM is not followed by an increase in the strategic role of the human resource management function of an organization. As hypothesized, e-HRM Acceptance (TAC) has a significant positive effect on Perceived HR Service Quality (PSQ) at 0.001-level. Regression analysis produces a high slope coefficient on TAC over PSQ, which amounts to 0.962. This finding supports Hypothesis 5.

To see how the HRM governance practice in an organization contributes directly to the creation of HRM values, we check into the relationship between HRMS and HRSR and the relationship between HRMS and PSQ. Regression analysis confirms Hypothesis 6, that a strong HRM system will significantly shift HRM function to have more strategic role. The regression coefficient for this relationship is 0.897 (significant at 0.001-level). We also find that Hypothesis 7 is supported. Table 8 confirms that HRMS has a direct, positive, and significant influence on PSQ with slope coefficients of 0.350 (significant at 0.001-level). Table 9 summarizes the direct effect, indirect effect, and total effect among variables in the model.

Table 9. Direct, Indirect, and Total Effect

Model	Standardized Estimates			
	HRMS	PEOU	PU	TAC
Direct				
TAC	0.223 (0.106)	-0.063 (0.564)	0.744 (0.002)	-
PSQ	0.364 (0.011)	-	-	0.574 (0.003)
HRSR	0.785 (0.004)	-	-	0.152 (0.191)
Indirect				
TAC	-	-	-	
PSQ	0.128 (0.080)	-0.036 (0.518)	0.427 (0.002)**	-
HRSR	0.034 (0.106)	-0.010 (0.294)	0.113 (0.178)	-
Total				

TAC	0.223 (0.106)	-0.063 (0.564)	0.744 (0.002)	-
PSQ	0.492 (0.003)	-0.036 (0.518)	0.427 (0.002)	0.574 (0.003)
HRSR	0.819 (0.004)	-0.010 (0.294)	0.113 (0.178)	0.152 (0.191)

Numbers in bracket are p-values
**Mediation relationship is significant using two tailed t-test with bootstrapping at 0.05

We also conducted the Sobel test using bootstrapping to confirm whether there is a significant mediation role of TAC on the value creation of HRM. Since PEOU and HRSR do not have a significant relationship with TAC, the mediation test is only applied to the relationship between PU→TAC→PSQ and HRMS→TAC→PSQ. From the t-test, we confirm that TAC is a significant mediator of PU on PSQ with an indirect effect of 0.427 (standardized estimates) and a significant p-value at 0.002 (less than 0.05). On the other hand, TAC does not have a significant mediation role on the relationship between HRMS→TAC→PSQ since the indirect effect of this relationship is only 0.128 with a p-value of 0.08. This finding means that Hypothesis 8 is supported for the relationship between PU→TAC→PSQ, depicting the role of TAC on mediating PU and PSQ.

Moderating Test

We examine the moderation effect of transformational leadership on the relationship between user acceptance factors and e-HRM usage using a separate (partial) test outside SEM analysis, regression with SPSS. On other words, we attempt to confirm whether the strength and/or direction of the relationship between user acceptance factors and e-HRM usage is influenced by the existence of transformational leadership of the employee's supervisor. Instead of a mediation effect, we seek a moderation effect, although a hypothesized causal relationship is weak or not found empirically (Baron and Kenny 1986; Chaplin 1991; Frazier et al. 2004). Thus, we test the moderation effect both on the relationship between PU and TAC and between PEOU and TAC.

The proposed regression equation for the moderating relationship is as follows:

1) $TAC = a + b1PU + b2TOL + b3|PU - TOL| + \varepsilon$

2) $TAC = a + b1PEOU + b2TOL + b3|PEOU - TOL| + \varepsilon$

To minimize multicollinearity in moderation testing, we first transform the data of the independent variable, mediator variable, and interaction term into mean-centered variables. Several authors (i.e., Aiken & West, 1991; Cohen, 1978; Cronbach, 1987) have shown that if the first-order variables are mean-centered (i.e., transformed from a raw-score scaling to a deviation-score scaling by subtracting the variable mean from all observations), the resulting product term will be minimally correlated or uncorrelated with the first-order variables if the variables are more or less bivariate normal.

Moderation Test of TOL on PU-TAC

The model has an R-squared value of 0.487, which means that 48.7% variance of the TAC is explained by the predictors included in the proposed model. With an F-value of 30.337, significant at 0.05-level, depicting the predictors of TAC included in the model has significant and simultaneous influence on TAC. From the regression output, MOD_PUTOLTAC, the interaction effect only has -0.051 of regression coefficients with a p-value of 0.308 (p-value larger than 0.05) suggesting that TOL does not have any significant moderating effect on the relationship between PU and TAC. From the plots analysis on figure 5, we can see that the slope does not change according to the level of transformational leadership. Hence, we can conclude that that leadership environment does not influence the strength or direction of the relationship between PU and TAC.

Moderation Test of TOL on PEOU-TAC

The second test of the moderating effect of transformational leadership is conducted on the relationship between PEOU and TAC. Regression results show that the model produces an R-squared value of 0.487. With an F-value of 13.663, significant at the 0.05-level, depicting the predictors of TAC included in the model has significant and simultaneous influence on the TAC. Regression analysis shows regression coefficients of interaction effect only -0.058 with a p-value of 0.216 (p-value larger than 0.05), suggesting that TOL also does not have any significant influence on the relationship strength or direction between PEOU and TAC. From this result, we can conclude that Hypothesis 9 is not supported.

Figure 5. Plot for Moderating Effect

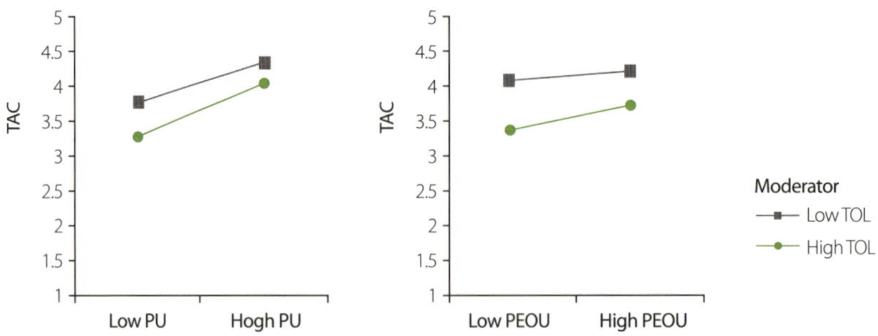

Discussion

The research findings suggest that perceived usefulness (PU) has a direct and significant relationship with e-HRM usage. This finding is consistent with the previous studies conducted by Maier et al. (2012), Davis (1993), Dulcic et al. (2012), Pikkarainen et al. (2004), and Lederer et al. (2000) on new technology acceptance such as e-HRM. The finding refers to the fact that employees use e-HRM for the benefits it provides in dealing with HR-related activities. On the other hand, this study does not fully support the Technology Acceptance Model argument since we find that perceived ease of use (PEOU) is less important than it was expected to be as a critical factor for e-HRM acceptance. This finding is consistent with a study on e-HRM implementation by Loijen (2008), which found that usefulness has a positive significant relation with usage, while easiness has no significant relation with usage. This finding is also confirmed by research by Pikkarainen et.al. (2004).[5]

Boundarouk and Ruel (2008) stated that HRM practices have the potential to support targeted employees of an introduced software application. HRM system strength should influence organizational effectiveness through individual behavior (Bowen and Ostroff, 2004). This is the reason we take HRM strength into account as one of the predictors of e-HRM acceptance in our model, which is measured by HRM distinctiveness and HRM consistency. According to Kwon (2012), policy clarity and policy consistency are very important to e-government policy success. Based on the regression results, human resource management strength (HRMS) has a positive influence on e-HRM usage with a β value of 0.128 and p-value of 0.041 (significant at the 0.05-level). This result confirmed Loijen's (2008) finding that HRM system strength has a positive significant effect on the usage of a system.

We found that e-HRM usage (TAC) has a significant positive effect on perceived HR service quality (PSQ) with direct effect of 0.574. The Sobel test also confirms that TAC fully mediates PU to the PSQ with an indirect effect of 0.472 (significant at the 0.05-level). This finding means that after the technology of e-HRM is accepted by the employee with his or her consideration of e-HRM benefits, the perceived HR service quality (PSQ) will become higher. This finding is consistent with previous studies. For example, Strohmeier (2007) found that research on e-HRM so far has shown that it alleviates the administrative burden and improves the accuracy of results and quality of HR activities. It leads to better information responsiveness and more information autonomy. Boundarouk and Ruel (2009) also confirmed that e-HRM usage produces a higher service quality consisting of a decrease in information errors, improvement in tracking and control of HR actions, service delivery improvement, and an increase in transaction speed.

Here we also find that HRMS has a significant and positive effect on the creation of perceived HR service quality. However, the direct effect of e-HRM usage (TAC) on PSQ is higher than the direct effect of HRMS on PSQ. Statistical output confirms that the direct effect of TAC on PSQ is 0.574 with a p-value of 0.003, whereas the direct effect of HRMS on PSQ is only 0.364 with a p-value of 0.011. This finding suggests that the usage of e-HRM has a critical role in providing HR service quality to the user (employee). Nevertheless, based on the Sobel test we conducted, TAC was not proven to significantly mediate the relationship between HRMS and PSQ.

One of the important inquiries of this study was to examine whether e-HRM is able to provide a higher strategic role of the HRM function. According to Caldwell (2003), the implementation and use of new systems such as an HRIS enable a transformation of HR from a largely administrative role to one of a strategic partner, change agent, or employee champion in organizations. Research studies by Strohmeier (2007) and Boundarouk and Ruel (2009) also found that e-HRM implementation can increase the strategic role of an HR Department. However, we could not find any significant relationship between e-HRM usage (TAC) and a strategic role shift of HRM function (HRSR). This finding is consistent with what most researchers find to be the primary goal of e-HRM, i.e. improving HR's administrative efficiency or achieving cost reductions (Ruël et al., 2004). This role entails supporting the execution of the business or HR strategy, rather than e-HRM explicitly having a pivotal role in such a strategy. The possibility of e-HRM adoption is triggered by the availability of HRIS technology instead of specific strategic HR deliverables and business drivers (Schalk et.al., 2012). When the decision to introduce e-HRM is made mainly to establish additional infrastructure in the absence of strong relations with the business, the strategic value of e-HRM is not likely to be achieved.

However, based on the interview with one of the key people who was involved in the establishment of the system, we found that the e-HRM application was built in order to provide a reliable web-based system that could support not only the HR Department to automate their administration process but also to support the core business of the Directorate of Tax. Previous systems of HRIS existed, but no longer matched the needs of the organization. Previous HRIS systems were not connected to the performance appraisal system, did not conform to the business flow of the organization, and did not provide employee self-service and online data retrieval for decision support system. Features of the newly developed e-HRM system were designed in accordance with the workflow and business process characteristics of the organization. Both a top-down and bottom-up approach were used. The top-down approach applied to the development of the main architecture, infrastructure, and enforcement. The bottom-up approach was used for the involvement of all employees in building the database and verification of the data. Here, we found one success factor of e-HRM usage that was not included in the model: employee participation. According to Barki and Hartwick (1994), users who participate in the development of the system are likely to develop beliefs that a new system is good, important, and personally relevant. Thus, they will form a positive attitude toward the system, which leads to a greater usage probability of the system (Hartwick and Barki, 1994). The more employees are involved in the implementation process, the greater the probability that they will have a positive attitude, and thus the greater probability of success.

Based on the interview, continuous development of the system is being done by considering the suggestions and propositions from the employees to provide a system that can really fulfill the needs of the employees and the organization as a whole. But the intention and the implementation in reality could be different. As noted by Tansley and Newell (2007), the strategic intent for e-HRM may be present, but there are many complications in system development and implementation that may stand. They studied two different development teams to examine factors that could help these teams realize the intended goals of e-HRM. They found that leadership competencies were very important, such as the ability to bring together individuals from different role perspectives (e.g., IT and HR). Project leaders in this context must be able to identify, manage and dispel political issues that have potential to derail the project. The role of HR practitioners is also critical to the creation of e-HRM strategic value. Many HR professionals still see e-HRM as merely an administrative tool, and its role in the development of strategic HR practice is often disregarded (Foster, 2009).[6]

This study also confirmed that the creation of strategic value of e-HRM is significantly influenced by human resource management strength (HRMS). The governance practice of HR, consisting of policy clarity (distinctiveness) and consistency, plays a critical role in the creation of a strategic role for the HR function. This assertion suggests that when an organization intends to create absolute value in its HRM, the implementation of e-HRM is not enough. It should be complemented and supported by policy clarity and consistency. Without good governance practices, implementation of such technology cannot provide strategic value to the organization. Instead, it will just serve as a tool of automation and cost reduction in administrative areas.[7]

Conclusion and Implicaions

Conclusion

This research examines a couple core questions of e-HRM implementation: to what extent does the usage of e-HRM applications explain HR value creation? What are key success enablers of e-HRM implementation? Furthermore, this study investigates an innovative question as well: should direct leadership from an employee's supervisor be considered a contextual factor having a moderating effect on the relationship between user acceptance factors and e-HRM usage?

From an organizational perspective, human resource management strength (HRMS) has a positive influence on e-HRM usage. In the creation of HRM value, we find e-HRM usage (TAC) to be a strong predictor of perceived HR service quality (PSQ). However, this study shows that e-HRM usage does not make the HRM function more strategic. Somehow, previous studies support this finding. From the Sobel test, we confirm that e-HRM usage also fully mediates the relationship between PU and PSQ. The study also indicates that HRM strength is an important direct predictor of the creation of HRM values in organization, both for PSQ and HRSR. It suggests that an organization should have its attention on its governance practices, especially in HRM policy clarity and consistency in order to create HRM value in the organization. Furthermore, we find that HRM strength (HRMS) is a strong predictor of the strategic role of HRM function (HRSR). However, we are unable to generate evidence that e-HRM usage impacts the strategic role of HRM function.[8]

Theoretical Implications

This study has several theoretical implications for e-HRM research, as it makes contributions to the existing theories. First, this study adds to the evidence that e-HRM usage provides creation of HRM value within an organization. Second, our research indicates that that perceived ease of use (PEOU) is less likely to be a critical factor in the acceptance of e-HRM than it was proposed in the Technology Acceptance Model (TAM) by Davis (1989). This finding is in line with other TAM studies that found that PEOU has less of an impact on technology acceptance than PU (Pikkarainen et.al., 2004; Yousafzai et.al., 2012; Venkatesh, 1999). This finding might lead to the argument that despite level of ease in using a certain new technology, people tend to rely on their perceived usefulness in accepting or using new technology, including e-HRM. Another relationship could be developed for PEOU, which may contribute to the acceptance of e-HRM indirectly through PU. As it was stated by Venkatesh (1999, p. 332), considering time and experience, the effect of PEOU has been found to be indirect and will operate through PU.

Third, the TAM is strengthened by the finding that there is no significant influence of the leadership environment of the employee, which may confound the direct relationship between user acceptance factors (PU and EOU) and e-HRM usage and acceptance (TAC). The absence of a moderation effect suggests that PU is a strong predictor in the usage of e-HRM. Fourth, in investigating the value creation of HRM, the involvement of organizational factors such as policy consistency and/or policy clarity is beneficial in confirming the real power of e-HRM usage and predicting the creation of HRM value. This finding suggests that e-HRM usage (TAC) provides stronger prediction power of perceived quality of HR service (PSQ) compared to the direct effect of HRM strength (HRMS) on the perceived quality of HR service (PSQ). Furthermore HRMS provides an explanation for why e-HRM usage fails to make a significant contribution to the role shift of the HRM function to be more strategic (HRSR). Based on our finding, this outcome variable is significantly explained by HRMS through a direct relationship. This argument is in line with Foster's (2009) study, which indicated that many HR professionals still see e-HRM as merely an administrative tool and that its role in the development of strategic HR practice is often neglected.

Policy Implications and Recommendations

This study has some implications for practice, and it provides an insight for the organization to find the right strategy in order to get the maximum benefit from the adoption and implementation of e-HRM.

E-HRM as Strategic Role Enabler

According to Bell, Lee, and Yeung (2006), e-HRM frees up time of HR professionals that was previously spent on administrative tasks and can now be spent on strategic tasks. As the findings of this study indicate, e-HRM implementation is not perceived as a key trigger to change the HRM function to be more strategic. One of the key points that should be noted is how to utilize e-HRM and exploit strategic potential from it. The fact that HR personnel are known to use e-HRM only as a tool for automation of their routine tasks could be the reason that e-HRM cannot contribute to the strategic role of the HRM function (Ngai and Wat, 2006). In order to ensure that e-HRM is used in a more strategic way, the core business strategy of the organization, the HRM strategy, and IT management should be clearly aligned and integrated.

Strong leadership to move the HRM function paradigm from administrative to strategic is important. The mindsets and behaviors of HR personnel, line managers, and employees concerning e-HRM need to be changed. For this purpose, facilitation of education in the field of strategic human resource management (SHRM) will be essential. Cooperation between the HRM division and the functional division should also be strengthened in order to ensure that the HRM division supports the functional division's strategic goals through e-HRM. Another precondition for e-HRM to be successfully utilized for more than just administrative purposes is that strategic considerations are taken into account in the decision-making process around the implementation of e-HRM. Use of e-HRM for services with "strategic added values" such as learning, career development, connection to the business process and model, and facilitating work-related dialogues between managers and employees through virtual collaboration, will most likely put the e-HRM system in a position to enable the HRM function to be more strategic.

Policy Clarity, Consistency, and e-HRM Content Aspect

Given our research finding that suggests perceived usefulness as a strong predictor of e-HRM acceptance, a profound amount of attention should be paid to ensure that the organization members have a clear idea about the reasoning behind the online HR tools. The philosophy underlying the usefulness of the technology should be internalized and incorporated into the day-to-day business process. When employees can be assured of these aspects, then acceptance for the solution and creation of its value can be accomplished. Another important aspect is that e-HRM should not run as a "too technology-driven" solution. It should aim to incorporate the real needs of line managers, employees, and HR departments. As the results of this study support Kwon's (2012) argument regarding the importance of policy clarity, consistency, and content aspects of e-government solutions for e-policy success, organizations should also ensure that the implementation route map is clear and understandable.

Limitations and Further Research

The study has a few limitations that should be considered when making critical decisions. The limitations of the research derive, first of all, from the fact that the sample of respondents was very small in the SEM analysis. We only managed to collect responses from 306 individuals. This condition might lead to potential impairment on the reliability and accuracy of the estimates. Second, the sample only included employees in one specific organization and therefore may not be representative for another type of organization. Third, the respondents were dominated by young employees and males, which might reduce the generalizability of the results to the general population. Moreover, the data collected regarding the independent and dependent variables all come from the respondents who participated in our study using the same questionnaire, which creates a single source bias. Mixed method research would be a way to overcome these biases. Another limitation is that we collected all empirical data at one time during the implementation, when the system went live. Hence, we do not know how the perceptions of HR service quality and the role of HR functions may have differed prior to the implementation of e-HRM.

For future research, we encourage researchers to utilize another method to investigate the influence of contextual factors using hierarchical linear modeling. Furthermore, we suggest that other factors beyond the most commonly included contextual factors in other research fields within organization and management studies may help to explain value creation of e-HRM. Suggestions for such variables are: implementation approach, change management, communication, user involvement and commitment, structure (unit, department, group), culture (organization and group), and project management.

Notes

1. The four main components of transformational leadership are:
   1) Charismatic leadership or idealized influence. Transformational leaders behave in ways that result in their being role models for their followers. The leaders are admired, respected, and trusted.
   2) Inspirational motivation. Transformational leaders behave in ways that motivate and inspire those around them by providing meaning and challenge to their followers' work. The leaders get followers involved in envisioning attractive future states. The leaders create clearly communicated expectations that followers want to meet, and they demonstrate their commitment to the goals and shared vision.
   3) Intellectual stimulation. Transformational leaders stimulate their followers' efforts to be innovative and creative by questioning assumptions, curbing problems, and approaching old situations in new ways. Creativity is encouraged. New ideas and creative problem solutions are solicited from followers, who are included in the process of addressing problems and finding solutions.
   4) Individualized consideration. Transformational leaders pay special attention to each individual's needs for achievement and growth by acting as coach or mentor. Followers and colleagues are developed to successively higher levels of potential. Individualized consideration is practiced as follows: new learning opportunities are created along with a supportive climate and individual differences in terms of needs and desires are recognized.
2. An HRM system is distinctive when its effect is highly observable for the employees. This situation is achieved when the HR practices in the system are visible, understandable, relevant, and have a legitimacy of authority (Bowen and Ostroff, 2004). The consistency of an HRM system is high when the HRM system is consistent over time, people, and context. This means that employees should receive the same reaction to their behavior, that the intention behind the operation of the system and the actual functioning of the system should be the same, and that the HRM message itself should be consistent (Bowen and Ostroff, 2004).
3. The responses were measured using a five-point Likert-type rating scale. We measured responses as follows: Strongly Agree (SA) = 5; Agree (A) = 4; Neutral (N)=3; Disagree (D) = 2; Strongly Disagree (SD) = 1. The items in the questionnaire were ordered per variable. This helped the respondent place the question within a specific subject and helped to decrease the time needed to complete the questionnaire.
4. Bartlett's Test measure evaluates the null hypothesis that the original correlation matrix is an identity matrix. Therefore, we wanted this test to be significant. The result showed that Bartlett's Test was significant, which meant that the variables would meet the

assumption to load together properly. In the end, each question was categorized to each factor with a corresponding factor loading value after rotation. Using varimax as a rotation method, we had factor 1 with 4 questions related to HRM Strength (HRMS), factor 2 with 3 questions related to perceived usefulness (PU), and factor 3 with 3 questions related to perceived ease of use (PEOU).

5. This study on the acceptance of an online banking system in Finland found that perceived ease of use (PEOU) is not a critical factor in the acceptance of new technology. They argue that their finding is in line with other TAM studies that assert that PEOU has less of an impact on technology acceptance than PU. This relationship is explained by the fact that as users learn about PEOU, its impact becomes instrumental. In other words, PEOU impinges on acceptance through PU (Pikkarainen et.al., 2004). Meta-analysis of TAM conducted by Yousafzai et.al. (2012, p.230) confirmed the same finding of this research. Yousafzai et.al. (2012) stated that most of the TAM studies have not found a direct linkage between PEOU and usage, leading to PEOU's being treated as something of a "step-child" (Venkatesh, 1999, p. 254). With time and experience, the effect was found to become indirect, operating through PU (p.332). This finding might lead to the argument that despite a consideration of their effort on the ease of using certain new technology, people tend to rely on their perceptions of usefulness in accepting or using new technology, including e-HRM.
6. In the case of the Directorate of Tax, the unsuccessful efforts of e-HRM usage in providing a more strategic role for the HRM function might have been caused by the intervention of the higher authority to develop the unified e-performance application for the whole organization of the Ministry of Finance. Before, the e-HRM system was developed exclusively by the Directorate of Tax to fulfill the needs of that organization. Nevertheless, the higher authority wanted to develop a new e-HRM system focused on e-performance, which had to be applied by all organizations under the Ministry of Finance. This decision caused some features on the current e-HRM in the Directorate of Tax to be abolished, which led to a system that was no longer integrated. Therefore, the e-HRM systems no longer fit well with the needs and characteristics of the Directorate of Tax, hence reducing its ability to support the strategic practice of the HRM function.
7. According to Yousafzai (2007), although TAM has been proven to be a robust model with highly predictive validity, results from a variety of studies suggest that in some circumstances, the model does not provide a complete understanding of the phenomenon studied. More specifically, in some cases, the predictive efficacy of an independent variable and/or the form of relationship may vary systematically as a function of some other variable(s). Therefore, we attempt to inquire into whether the relationship between perceived usefulness and perceived ease of use in e-HRM usage is influenced by the direct leadership environment of the employee. The moderation test of this relationship produces insignificant results. These results suggest that perceived usefulness is really

an essential factor in the acceptance of e-HRM. Hence, in the development of an e-HRM system, an organization needs to pay a lot of attention to the content and the real benefits of the system to the end user.

8. Through qualitative analysis of the interviews we conducted, we find that at the initial stage, e-HRM applications are intended to support core business strategies of the Directorate of Tax. The organization wanted to develop such a web-based integrated HRM system in accordance with the workflow and business process characteristics of the organization. But then after six years of implementation, some interventions from the higher authority were pushed, impacting a substantial change to the system, which led to the use of a "double system." This situation could be one reason that e-HRM failed to shift the HRM function to be more strategic.

References

Armenakis, A. A., Harris, S. G., & Field, H. S. (1999). Making change permanent: Institutionalizing change interventions. In W. A. Pasmore & R. W. Woodman (Eds.), *Research in organizational development and change* (vol 12, pp. 97-128). Stamford, CT: JAI Press.

Bondarouk, T., & Ruel, H. (2012). The strategic value of E-HRM: Result from exploratory study in a governmental organization. *The International Journal of Human Resource Management,* 1-24.

Bondarouk, T., Ruel, H., & Van der Heijden, B. (2009). E-HRM effectiveness in public sector organization: A multi-stakeholder perspective. *The International Journal of Human Resource Management, 20*(3), 578-590.

Bell, B. S., Lee, S., & Yeung, S. K. (2006). The impact of e-HR on professional competence in HRM: Implications for the development of HR professionals. *Human Resource Management, 45*(3), 295-308.

Bowen, D.E., & Ostroff, C. (2004). Understanding HRM-firm performance linkages: The role of the "strength"of the HRM system. *Academy of Management Review, 29*(2), 203-221.

Buckley, P., Minnette, K., Joy, D., & Michaelis, J. (2004). The use of an automated employment recruiting and screening system for temporary professional employees: A case study. *Human Resource Management, 43*(2-3), 233-241.

Currie, W., & Parikh, M. (2006). Value creation in web services: an integrative model. *Journal of Strategic Information Systems, 15*, 153-174.

Dillon, A. (2001). User acceptance of information technology. In W. Karwowski (Ed). *Encyclopedia of human factors and ergonomics.* London: Taylor and Francis. *Taken from: http://www.ischool.utexas.edu/~adillon/BookChapters/Dillon-acceptance.htm*

Enshur, E., Nielson, T., & Grant-Vallone, E. (2002). Tales from the hiring line: Effects of the internet technology on HR processes. *Organizational Dynamics, 31*(3), 224-244.

Foster, S. (2010). Creating HR value through technology. *Strategic Direction, 26*(8), 3-5. Gardner, S. D., Lepak. D. P., & Barthol, K. M. (2003). Virtual HR: The impact of information technology on the human resource professional. *Journal of Vocational Behavior, 63*(2), 159-179.

Haksever, C., Chaganti, R., & Cook, R. G. (2004). A model of value creation: strategic view. *Journal of Business Ethics, 49*(3), 291-305.

Harris, K., Phifer, G., & Berg, T. (2002). *Business to employee: The road map to strategy.* Stamford, CT: Gartner Group.

Huselid, M. A., Jackson, S. E., & Schuler, R. S. (1997). Technical and strategic human resource management effectiveness as determinants of firm performance. *Academy of Management Journal, 40*, 171-188.

Karunasena, K., Deng, H., & Singh, M. (2011). Measuring the public value of e-government: a case study from Sri Lanka. *Transforming Government: People, Process and Policy, 5*(1), 81-99.

Kavanagh, M. J., Gueutal, H. G., & Tannenbaum, S. I. (1990). *Human resource information systems: Development and application.* Boston (Mass.): PWS-Kent publishing company.

Kets de Vries, M. F. R. (2006). *The leadership mystique.* London: FT Prentice Hall.

Kwon, Gi-Heon. (2012). *전자 정부론.* 박영사.

Lepak, D., Smith, K., & Taylor, M. (2007). Value creation and value capture: A multilevel perspective. *Academy of Management Review, 32,* 180-194.

Lepak, D., & Snell, S. (1998). Virtual, HR: Strategic human resource management in the 21st century, *Human Resource Management Review, 8*(3), 215-234.

Loijen, Y, (2008). *Electronic HRM: From implementation to value creation: Quantitative analysis of the factors and consequences of e-HRM. Thesis.*

Maier, C., et al. (2012). *Analyzing the impact of HRIS implementations on HR personnel's job satisfaction and turnover intention.* J. Strateg. Inform. Syst.

Ngai, E. W. T., & Wat, F. K. T. (2006). Human resource information systems: A review and empirical analysis. *Personnel Review, 35*(3), 297-314.

Overman, S. (1992). Reaching for the 21st Century. *HR Magazine, 37,* 61-63.

Park, S. M. & Rainey, H. G. (2008). Leadership and public service motivation in U.S. federal agencies. *International Public Management Journal, 11*(1), 109-142.

Parry, E., & Tyson, S. (2010). Desired goals and actual outcomes of e-HRM. *Human Resource Management Journal, 21*(3), 335-354.

Parry, E. (2011). An examination of e-HRM as a means to increase the value of the HR function. *The International Journal of Human Resource Management, 22,* 1146-1162.

Panayotopoulou, L., Vakola, M., & Galanaki, E. (2007). E-HR Adoption and the Role of HRM: Evidence from Greece. *Personal Review, 36*(2), 277-294.

Rotchanakitumnuai, S. (2008). Measuring e-government service value with the E-GOVSQUAL-RISK model. *Business Process Management Journal, 14*(5), 724-737.

Ruel, H., & Van der Kaap, H. (2012). E-HRM usage and value creation: Does a facilitating Context Matter?. *German Journal of Research in Human Resource Management, 26*(3), 260-281.

Ruël, H., Bondarouk, T., & Van der Velde, M. (2007). The contribution of e-HRM to HRM effectiveness: Results from a quantitative study in a Dutch Ministry. *Employee Relations, 29*(3), 280-291.

Ruta, C. D. (2005). The application of change management theory to HR portal implementation in subsidiaries of multinational corporations. *Human Resource Management Journal, 44*(1), 35-53.

Sareen, P., & Subramanian, V. (2012). E-HRM: A strategic review. *International Journal of Human Resource Studies, 2*(3), 119-127.

Shilpa, V. (2011). The implications of implementing electronic-human resource management (E-HRM) systems in companies. *Journal of Information Systems and Communication, 2*(1), 10-29.

Snell, S. A., Stueber, D., & Lepak, D. P. (2002). Virtual HR departments: Getting out of the middle. *Center for Advanced Human Resource Studies (Working Paper Seriese), 71,* 1-29.

Straub, D., Limayem, M., & Karahanna-Evaisto, E. (1995). Measuring system usage: Implications for IS theory testing. *Management Science, 41*(8), 1328-1342.

Strohmeier, S. (2007). Research in e-HRM: Review and implications. *Human Resource Management Review, 17,* 19-37.

Tansley, C., & Newell, S. (2007). A knowledge-based view of agenda-formation in the development of human resource information systems. *Management Learning, 38*(1). 95-119.

Tero, P., Kari, P., Heikki, K., & Seppo, P. (2004). Consumer acceptance of online banking: an extension of the technology acceptance model, *Internet Research, 14*(3), 224-235.

Venkatesh, V., Morris, M. G., Davis, G. B., & Davis, F. D. (2003). User acceptance of information technology: Toward a unified view, *MIS Quarterly, 27*(3), 425-478.

Yousafzai, S. Y., Foxall, G. R., & Pallister, J. G. (2007). Technology acceptance: a meta-analysis of the TAM: Part 1, *Journal of Modelling in Management, 2*(3), 251-280.

Case Study

Government Innovation Makes Big Strides

Keun Namkoong

It is well known that government innovation has been ubiquitous in many countries since the 1980s. In Korea, the 1997 financial crisis and the ensuing economic recession instigated the reform programs of the Kim Dae-jung administration (1998-2003). The Kim administration sought to create "a small and efficient but better serving government," the ultimate goals of which were to raise Korea`s national competitiveness.

To achieve these aims the Kim Dae-jung administration introduced extensive reforms embracing the entire public sector including the central government, local governments, state owned enterprises, and government-affiliated agencies. The Kim administration followed the Anglo-American model of a new public management (NPM) reform strategy which concentrated on reducing the size of the public sector and streamlining the bureaucracy through privatization and downsizing.

The Kim administration achieved substantial efficiency gains by reducing the range of activities in which the government is involved, by lowering staff levels, and by reducing operating costs. However, it has been suggested that these reforms have not resulted in a better serving government.

The Kim administration also sought innovation of operating systems through an open recruitment system; greater autonomy for ministries in personnel, organization, budget affairs, and performance-oriented management; and to design a customer-oriented administrative service system using advanced information technologies.

The government innovation of the Roh Moo-hyun administration inherits elements of the previous Kim Dae-jung administration`s pursuit of an "efficient and better serving government." But it has several differences from the past. The direction of the innovation distinguishes itself. In the past, the "small government" with minimized government intervention was the main idea. But the Roh administration is emphasizing the active role of the government. In essence, the Roh administration adopted a participatory model of governing rather than the previously sought market model or the new public management model.

In this context, the Roh administration called itself the "Participatory Government." It views the civil service as the main partner of the innovation. In other words, it has chosen the strategy to encourage participation from middle and low level public workers. The Roh administration vigorously sought expert and citizen participation in the process of government innovation. In fact, the creation of the Roh government had been based on the power of popular participation. Popular participation continues to play a pivotal role in the operation of the Roh administration, as it did during its birth.

Framework for innovation A prominent feature of the Roh administration`s government innovation is the fact that a presidential committee was set up for the sole purpose of taking charge of government innovation and decentralization. The previous Kim Dae-jung administration had instead relied on an official government organization in the Ministry of Planning and Budget.

Although an official organization has the merit of having legal binding powers to enforce proposed plans, it inherently lacks creativity which is an essential element of the innovative process.

On the other hand, ad hoc advisory commissions of the past, comprising only outside specialists, lacked legal binding powers. The "Presidential Committee on Government Innovation and Decentralization (PCGID)" consisted of both outside specialists and government officials. It was established in April 2003 shortly after the inauguration of the Roh administration.

The composition of PCGID members has the merits of the creativity of the private sector and the binding powers of a government organization. Many civilian professionals and civic organization representatives have been participating in agenda setting and the policy formation stages.

By August 2003, the innovation road-map was developed based on the opinions of academics and civilian professionals participating in the presidential committee.

According to the road-map, government innovation envisioned a "transparent and competent government" which is to be achieved through improved efficiency, services, transparency, decentralization, and people-centeredness. The road-map provided 150 specific reform tasks in 23 areas covering general administration, personnel management, electronic government operation, finance and tax systems, and decentralization.

Major progress in the past 3 years During the past three years, the Roh administration has been actively striving to legislate and implement each item of the road-map agenda.

Consensus was also reached through substantive discussions and the participation of civilian professionals and government agencies in the course of promoting the road-map.

According to the PCGID, as of December 2005, 98 out of 150 specific road-map tasks, or 65.3 percent are already in the implementation stages, 36 or 24 percent are in the policy adoption stages, and the remaining 16 or 10.7 percent are still in the policy formulation stages. This means that most of the reform tasks have been legislated or are in the process of legislation. Major achievements of the past three years are summarized below.

Autonomy and decentralization: The Roh administration has actively pursued autonomy and decentralization. Authority is being delegated down the hierarchy from higher to lower institutions, and from central to local governments. The Roh administration is convinced that autonomy and decentralization, deconcentration, private-public partnership, and the networked society drives everyone to their utmost potential while simultaneously increasing the government`s capabilities.

Programs that have already been legislated or are in the legislative process include: introduction of the municipal police system (auxiliary to the National Police) for crime prevention, control of food products and law enforcement with community participation; consolidation of the educational autonomy system with local governments; the establishment of the Jeju Special Administrative District as an innovative model of a decentralized government; a total personnel cost system to allow autonomy in organizing government agencies and workforce; the "top-down" system that expands autonomy in the budget allocation of government agencies; and the devolution of the national administrative agencies which transfers functions and tasks to local agencies.

Reform of the evaluation and audit system: Evaluation and audit allow organizations to recognize problems of their own as the process of innovation progresses. In other words, the establishment of an evaluation and audit system ultimately increases an organization`s problem identification and problem-solving capacities.

Moreover, providing incentives to members according to an evaluation of their own performance will increase their determination to carry out innovation and also strengthen organizational competitiveness. In this context, a Digital Budget and Accounting system which allocates resources and evaluates policies will be introduced soon.

The Digital Budget and Accounting system is being developed in partnership with the World Bank. Meanwhile, the National Evaluation Infrastructure has been thoroughly reviewed, and a comprehensive system of performance and policy evaluation will be introduced.

Enhancing transparency: Transparency paves the way for a "clean administration," brings to light problems that had been veiled for a long time, and increases opportunities for innovation.

For this, a government achievements management system is being introduced to secure records, public access, and the responsibility for policy formation.

An electronic information system will be introduced, giving access to all public information except national secrets and privacy-related information. The Digital Budget and Accounting system can also be used for enhancing transparency.

On March 9, 2005, some 40 influential persons from the public, political and business sectors and the civil society signed the Korea Pact on Anti-Corruption and Transparency that includes the anti-corruption agendas of Korean society.

The formulation of the K-Pact was a collaborative effort for controlling corruption. The K-Pact, which is a kind of social convention, is different in nature from the anti-corruption campaigns of the past administrations. While most of the past campaigns were attempts by those in powerful positions, this one represents efforts by social leaders to make the nation more transparent and cleaner.

Due to these efforts of innovation, the overall transparency level in Korea has improved remarkably during the past few years. Korea's scoring in the Transparency International's Corruption Perceptions Index was 5.0 out of perfect 10 in 2005, ranked 40th out of 159 countries. This represents considerable progress compared to the 2003 scoring of 4.3.

Openness of government operation: The Korean government continues to reform the previously closed public service system by recruiting competent personnel and professionals from outside. Expansion of the open recruitment system will increase the competitiveness of the public sector. In this regard, the Roh administration is expanding the open recruitment system introduced by the Kim Dae-jung administration, with diverse and open recruitment systems.

Along this line, the Senior Civil Service (SCS) system will be introduced in July 2006 for strategic and systematic management and training of senior civil servants.

Professionalism and efficiency: Increasing the professionalism and efficiency of civil servants will lead to a further improvement of the government's capability. This will enhance the quality of government policies.

For this, a career development plan for civil servants has been introduced, preventing the frequent job rotation practices of the past. The Roh administration has also established systematic procedures for improving the quality of policies and work performance.

The government also promotes a paperless administration through continued digitalization of administrative services and the streamlining of internal business processes.

Education, training and learning organizations: Education and training among civil servants are important factors in elevating the capacity of innovation and government competitiveness.

For this, the government has already innovated the civil servant training system and training institutes. A Knowledge Management System was also introduced to create and share knowledge between members of the Ministries and Agencies.

Future tasks The legislative efforts are almost complete, but for the government innovation to be successful, implementation studies are required for a certain period. Studies show that the process can easily be delayed and distorted without proper monitoring and evaluation. The experience of other countries has shown that government innovation is a long-term process that requires continuous attention over a number of years in order to achieve the changes in behavior and culture of civil servants needed to serve better government.

Innovation is not an end in itself. As President Roh Moo-hyun said, "Government innovation is the basis for market competitiveness, and ultimately the foundation of national competitiveness." Innovation activities must enable Korean society to meet the new challenges of globalization in the rapidly developing information era.

Source: The Korea Herald (2006.02.20)

Questions for Discussion

1. Using a nonprofit entity and a public agency as examples, prepare a memo describing the general environmental conditions of both organizations. Describe the technological, legal, political, economic, ecological, and cultural conditions.

2. Chose a public agency or department and describe the ways in which societal values and institutions influence its operation. Describe a change in rules or policy that has occurred where you work or at the university. Where did the impetus for change come from? How did the organization respond to pressures for change?

3. How can information systems and IT be used for internal coordination and external coordination? What are intranets, and what is knowledge management? How does IT influence organization design and service quality?

4. Consider any government agency with which you have interacted. What laws, rules, and regulations are relevant to the particular services they provide? Describe the political environment of the agency. How might the department and its structure, tasks, and clientele change if the political environment changes? How does the economic environment affect the department? What job competencies should be required of the employees? What type of training should they have?

Section 3

Leadership

- Leadership and Public Service Motivation in U.S. Federal Agencies
- Toward the Trusted Public Organization : Untangling the Leadership, Motivation, and Trust Relationship in U.S. Federal Agencies

Section 3

Leadership

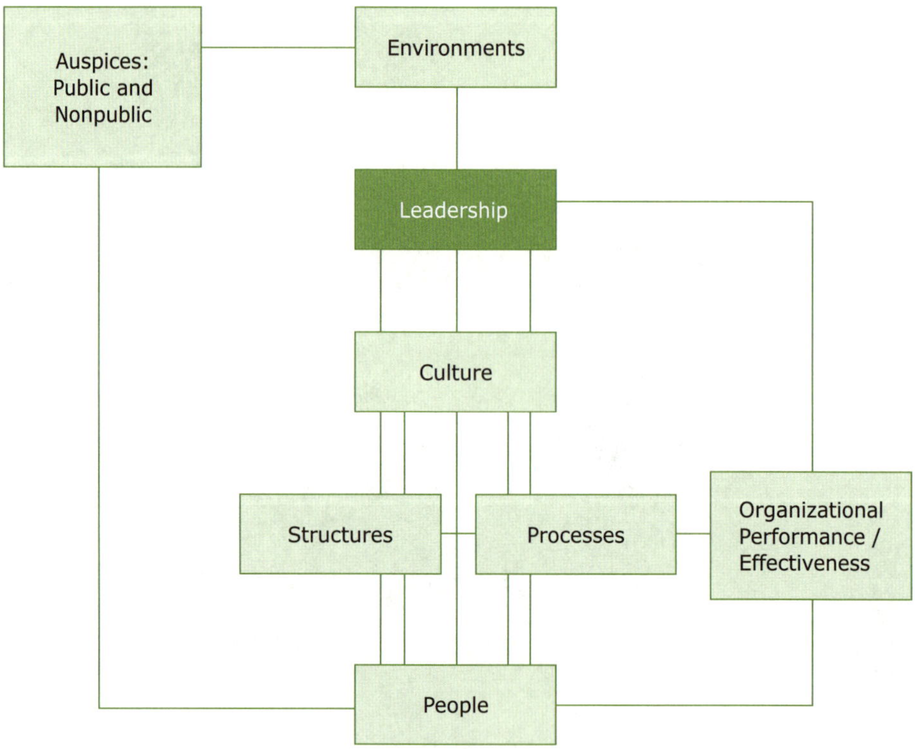

Chapter 5

Leadership and Public Service Motivation in U.S. Federal Agencies

Summary

This analysis of over 6,900 federal employees' responses to the Merit Principles Survey 2000 examines the influences of leadership and motivational variables, and especially public service motivation, on the "outcome" variables job satisfaction, perceived performance, quality of work, and turnover intentions. CFA confirms a factor structure for transformation-oriented leadership (TOL), public service-oriented motivation (PSOM), transaction-oriented leadership (TSOL), and extrinsically oriented motivation (EOM). Multivariate regression analysis shows that TOL and PSOM, as well as interaction effects of TOL-TSOL and TOL-PSOM, have strong relations to the outcome variables. SEM analysis examines direct and indirect effects of the main variables. Overall, the results indicate that TOL and PSOM have more positive relations to the outcome variables than do TSOL and EOM. The combination of high TOL and high PSOM has the strongest positive, and hence desirable, relation with organizational outcomes. Among this very large sample of federal employees, those who perceived their leader as displaying TOL (i.e., leadership that is encouraging, supportive, informative, and that emphasizes high standards) also expressed higher levels of PSOM and higher levels of job satisfaction, perceived performance and work quality, and lower turnover intentions. The SEM analysis further indicates that TOL has these effects by way of empowerment, goal clarification, and PSOM, and is distinct from TSOL (transaction-oriented) leadership, which shows no such relationships.

Keyword

□ Leadership □ Public Service Motivation □ Transformational Leadership
□ Transactional Leadership □ Extrinsic Motivation

Sung Min Park Associate Professor, Sungkyunkwan University
Hal G. Rainey Alumni Foundation Distinguished Professor, The University of Georgia

Introduction

One of the important research issues and practical challenges in human resource management and organizational behavior in government is to increase employees' motivation, commitment, and job satisfaction, as well as to decrease turnover intentions, thereby increasing government agencies' performance. Although several researchers (e.g., see Alonso and Lewis 2001; Houston 2000; Naff and Crum 1999; Perry 1996; Perry and Wise 1990) have found significant relationships among variables such as Public Service Motivation (PSM), leadership, organizational commitment, job satisfaction, and performance, there remains a need for more research to assess the linkage between antecedents, mediators, and consequences in public organizations. For example, while many organizational experts (e.g., Tett and Meyer 1993) have argued that job satisfaction is an important antecedent of turnover intentions, researchers have reported little evidence about this relationship in the public sector.

This study analyzes organizational leadership and work motivation in federal agencies, and tests the hypotheses that these main predictors and other contingent factors relate to job satisfaction, performance, quality of work, and turnover intentions.[1] First, this article reviews the theory of transformational and transactional leadership, and the theory of public service motivation (PSM). Second, this study probes the dimensions and latent constructs of the two leadership styles—transformationoriented leadership (TOL) and transaction-oriented leadership (TSOL)—as well as both public service-oriented motivation (PSOM) and extrinsically oriented motivation (EOM) using confirmatory factor analysis (CFA). Third, using multivariate regression and a structural equation model (SEM), we empirically test and measure 1) how and to what extent the specific leadership styles (i.e., TOL and TSOL) and motivation styles (i.e., PSOM and EOM) affect outcome variables directly and indirectly (Hypotheses 1a, 1b, 2a, and 2b); 2) how interaction effects between leadership and motivation influence organizational consequences (Hypotheses 1c, 2c, 2d, and 2e); and 3) how different types of endogenous organizational outcomes are associated with one another in the SEM (Hypothesis 3). Finally, this study suggests research and practical implications for future leadership and motivation research in the public sector. Among this very large sample of federal employees, those who perceived their leader as displaying transformation-oriented leadership (TOL, i.e., leadership that is encouraging, supportive, informative, and that emphasizes high standards) also expressed higher levels of public service-oriented motivation (PSOM) and higher levels of job satisfaction, perceived performance and work quality, and lower turnover intentions. The SEM analysis further indicates that TOL has these effects by way of empowerment and PSOM, and that TSOL (transaction-oriented) leadership shows no such relationships.

Theories of Transformational and Transactional Leadership

Organizational leaders must strive to maximize the performance and job satisfaction of their subordinates in order to achieve organizational goals (e.g., see Yukl 2002; Zacharatos, Barling, and Kelloway 2000; Jung 2001). Indeed, leadership can be defined as "a process whereby an individual influences a group of individuals" to attain common goals . . . by mobilizing and motivating the workforce (Northouse 2004, 3). Effective leadership provides "cohesiveness, personal development, and higher levels of satisfaction," and gives a sense of "direction and vision, an alignment with the environment, a healthy mechanism for innovation and creativity, and a resource for invigorating the organizational culture" (Van Wart 2003, 214). Increasingly prominent in leadership research are the concepts of transformational and transactional leadership. According to Conger (1999), research shows "the advantages of the transformational leadership style over the more traditional forms . . . in terms of achieving organizational goals" (pp. 145–179).

Transformational Leadership

Bass and Avolio (1994; 1997) characterized transformational leadership as composed of four unique but interrelated behavioral sub-dimensions: inspirational motivation (communicating an appealing vision, using symbols to focus subordinate effort, and modeling appropriate behaviors), intellectual stimulation (increasing follower awareness of problems and influencing followers to view problems from a new perspective; promoting creativity and innovation), idealized influence (arousing strong follower emotions and identification with the leader), and individualized consideration (providing support, encouragement, and coaching and mentoring to followers). Research has found that leaders who show these four behaviors are able to "realign their followers' values and norms, promote both personal and organizational changes, and help followers to perform beyond their initial performance expectations specified in the implicit or explicit exchange agreement" (e.g., Jung and Avolio 2000, 951; Jung et al. 2003).

Transformational leaders also empower followers and make them less dependent on the leader by delegating significant authority to individuals, developing follower skills and self-confidence, creating self-managed teams, providing direct access to sensitive information, eliminating unnecessary control, and building a strong team and employee empowerment culture (Barling et al. 1996; Bass 1985a). Such leaders provide ideological and cognitive frameworks that connect followers' identities to the collective identity of their organization, thereby increasing followers' intrinsic motivation (rather than just providing extrinsic motivation) to perform their job (Bass 1985b). By providing intellectual stimulation (Bass and Avolio 1997), transformational leadership provides and enhances "exploratory thinking and creativity by encouraging critical thinking, rationality, and rethinking of ideas by group members" (Sosik, Avolio, and Kahai 1998, 112-113). It stimulates their followers to think about old problems in new ways and encourages them to challenge their own values, traditions, and beliefs (Hater and Bass 1988). It helps to develop followers' commitment to long-term goals, missions, and vision and to shift their focus from shortterm objectives to long-term and fundamental solutions and objectives.

Hence, transformational leadership can have a direct relationship with organizational performance, as well as affecting individual and work-group performance through its effects on subordinates' satisfaction with their leader, sense of empowerment, and related responses (Howell and Avolio 1993; Hater and Bass 1988; Podsakoff 1996). It has consistently been linked to a number of positive outcomes across samples and cultures (e.g., Bass 1997; Howell and Avolio 1993), leading some scholars to view transformational leadership as an unbounded, parsimonious, and universal theory (Bass 1997; Bass and Avolio 1994). By articulating an important vision and mission for the organization, transformational leaders increase followers' understanding of the importance and values associated with desired outcomes, get them to perform above and beyond expectations, and provide them with higher levels of intrinsic and altruistic motivation (e.g., public service motivation) to work for collective and community goals rather than to pursue self-interest or extrinsic rewards (Conger and Kanungo 1998; Whittington et al. 2004). However, until now, few studies in government agencies have examined the influence processes that account for the positive relationship between the transformational leader's behavior and public employees' job behaviors.

Transactional Leadership

Transactional leadership behaviors include 1) contingent reward leadership, 2) passive management by exception, and 3) active management by exception (see Bass 1998; Bass and Avolio 1994; 1997). Contingent reward behavior refers to "clarification of the work which is required to obtain rewards and the use of incentives and contingent rewards to influence motivation" (Antonakis and House 2002, 9-11; Yukl 2002). Contingent reward leadership can motivate subordinates, but with less positive impact on motivation than that of transformational leadership (Antonakis and House 2002; Bass and Avolio 1997). Passive management by exception includes use of contingent punishments and other corrective action in response to deviations from performance standards. Active management by exception involves correcting mistakes and enforcing rules and regulations; the leader watches subordinates' misbehaviors and actively provides corrective action to avoid routine mistakes (Bass and Avolio 1990; Yukl 2002). The active and passive management-by-exception styles are similar, but differ in that passive management leaders wait until employees' attitudinal or behavioral deviations happen before intervening. The transactional leadership style appeals to subordinates' self-interest and uses extrinsic reward systems; an exchange relationship between leaders and subordinates provides followers with rewards such as wages and promotions for complying with a leader's wishes and orders. Contingent reward involves rewarding followers for attaining specified performance levels.

In transactional contingent reinforcement (reward or punishment), the individual receives a reward from the leader for successful enactment of the role as agreed upon with the leader. For punishment, the leader corrects, threatens, or disciplines the subordinate for failing to achieve a specific standard of performance. Transactional leadership, in sum, concentrates on task accomplishment, rather than on developing followers. The primary influence process involves "instrumental compliance and contingent sanctioning behavior" (Bass and Avolio 1990; Kohn 1993; Podsakoff, Todor, and Skov 1982, 811–812). Antonakis and House (2002) suggest that leaders should show transformational behaviors most often, then contingent reward leadership, then active management by exception, and then passive management by exception. They argue that this hierarchical leadership framework can be traced from a meta-analysis by Lowe et al. (1996), which confirmed that transformational leadership more strongly affects outcome variables than does transactional leadership.

Transformational-Transactional Leadership Distinctions

Transformational and transactional leadership styles have substantive differences. Transformational leaders are more internally and intrinsically directed, whereas transactional leaders are more externally and extrinsically oriented (Howell and Avolio 1993). The transactional leader works "within the rules of the organizational culture" whereas the transformational leader "redefines or changes them based on their vision of a more satisfactory alternative future state" (Bass 1985a; Avolio and Bass 1995, 203). Although the two forms of leadership have been identified and contrasted for decades, theorists have moved toward integrating them (Moynihan and Ingraham 2004; Van Wart 2003).[2] These leadership behaviors share common elements such as providing clarity of desired outcomes, recognizing accomplishments, and rewarding high performance. Effective leaders use a combination of both types of leadership by increasing followers' intrinsic motivation (e.g., PSM in the public sector) as well as by adopting varying degrees of transactional interaction with subordinates (Rafferty and Griffin 2004; Rainey 2003).[3]

Transformation-Oriented Leadership (TOL) and Transaction-Oriented Leadership (TSOL)

The Merit Systems Protection Board (MSPB) survey provides opportunities to analyze federal employee attitudes with a large dataset. The survey, however, like other large federal surveys, does not use the same constructs and measures for such concepts as Transformational Leadership and Public Service Motivation (PSM) as those used by researchers who have developed those concepts (i.e., Bass and Avolio 1994; Perry 1996). To emphasize the distinction between our measures based on the MSPB data and the more highly developed ones, we use the constructs of transformation-oriented leadership (TOL) and transaction-oriented leadership (TSOL) as the main variables in this study (Park and Rainey 2007). While these concepts are not identical with the more developed ones, they provide valuable evidence about very similar matters from a large sample of federal employees. In pursuit of such evidence we analyzed the dimensions and latent constructs of the two styles, then we hypothesized that TOL and TSOL will influence directly and indirectly several "outcome" variables through mediators and moderators. We began with the following research question and hypotheses:

Research Question 1: In federal agencies, are the latent constructs of TOL and TSOL conceptually distinct? In a measurement model, do these two latent variables (i.e., endogenous variables) have a positive causal effect on the relevant observable variables (i.e., exogenous variables)?

Hypothesis 1a: In federal agencies, TOL has a strong positive relationship with job satisfaction, perceived performance and quality of work, and will decrease turnover intentions. TOL is positively associated with these organizational outcomes in direct and indirect ways through intrinsic rewards.

Hypothesis 1b: In federal agencies, TSOL alone does not affect job satisfaction, perceived performance and quality of work, and turnover intentions as strongly as TOL does. TSOL is positively but marginally associated with these organizational outcomes in direct and indirect ways through extrinsic rewards.

Hypothesis 1c: In federal agencies, TOL interacts with TSOL to predict organizational outcomes; that is, TOL positively moderates the relationship between TSOL and job satisfaction, and perceived performance and quality of work whereas TOL negatively moderates the relationship between TSOL and turnover intentions.

Theory of Work Motivation in Public Organizations

Motivating employees remains a crucial challenge for public managers (Mann 2006, 35). Work motivation can be categorized into two distinct types based on different reward systems within applied organizational settings: intrinsic and extrinsic motivation. Intrinsic motivation refers to "behaviors for which there is no apparent reward except the activity itself " whereas extrinsic motivation refers to "behaviors in which an external controlling variable (such as explicit reward, incentive, or threat) can be readily identified" (Cameron and Pierce 2002, 12).[4] Intrinsic and extrinsic motivation can have different relationships with behavioral and attitudinal outcomes. The positive effects of intrinsic motivations have long been recognized; that is, intrinsic motivation can enhance job performance and satisfaction (Herzberg 1968; McGregor 1960). Cognitive evaluation theorists further argue that, in general, extrinsic sources of motivation (e.g., extrinsic reward systems or feedback) can be detrimental to employees' intrinsic and internal motivation, especially when those extrinsic sources are perceived as controlling rather than as informative. (For further discussion of the different cognitive evaluation theory perspectives on motivation, see Cameron, Banko, and Pierce 2001; Eisenberger and Cameron 1996; Deci, Koestner, and Ryan 1999; Deci and Ryan 1985; Ryan and Deci 1996). On the other hand, from a social learning theory perspective, extrinsic incentives such as monetary rewards are supposed to increase the level of self-efficacy and self-motivation (e.g., see Bandura 1986).

Recently, self-determination theory (SDT) has analyzed social-contextual conditions that facilitate or hinder self-motivation within organizations (Ryan and Deci 2000). Deci and Ryan (1985) introduced the self-determination continuum that categorizes motivational states as moving from amotivation, to extrinsic motivation, to self-determined or autonomous motivation. These states relate to the different forms of extrinsic motivation—i.e., external regulation, introjected regulation, identified regulation, and integrated regulation. As an individual moves towards internalizing the external regulations and incentives and integrating them with his or her own values, the person moves toward more autonomous and intrinsic motivation (Ryan and Deci 2000). More autonomy in work provides better conditions for intrinsic motivation. SDT thus proposes that organizational factors such as autonomy in work climates and managerial systems enhance intrinsic motivation, resulting in more positive outcomes (Ryan and Connell 1989). Where individuals have more autonomy as opposed to external regulation, they have more opportunities to derive personal fulfillment and satisfaction from the work itself. Ryan and Deci (2002, 12) add, however, that external influence in the form of positive performance feedback can enhance intrinsic motivation. The results we report below provide an example of such dynamics, since they indicate that transformational leadership (TOL) enhances employee empowerment, and that TOL and empowerment both enhance public service oriented motivation (PSOM), which can be conceived as an intrinsic motivation. In turn, PSOM relates positively to job satisfaction, perceived organizational performance and to a lower level of intent to turnover.

As this example suggests, the SDT analysis of intrinsic motivation, which emphasizes autonomous work and internalized motives, can apply to public service motivation (PSM). (Perry and Wise 1990, 367–368) define PSM as "an individual's predisposition to respond to motives grounded primarily or uniquely in public institutions and organizations." Research on PSM indicates that many public employees espouse a public service motive that has the character of an intrinsic motive. Publicsector employees express less interest in extrinsic rewards than intrinsic rewards, as compared to employees in private business organizations (Crewson 1997; Houston 2000; 2005). Jurkiewicz et al. (1998) found that public and private sector employees pursue different values in their jobs (e.g., commitment to the public interest versus self interest maximization). Romzek (1985) detected a strong positive relationship between recognition for public service and organizational involvement among federal, state, and local government employees. Similarly, others report evidence that public service motivation causes individuals to self-select into public sector work (e.g., Perry 1997; Perry and Porter 1982; Yaeger, Rabin and Vocino 1982). Perry and Wise (1990) postulated that public service motivation (PSM) includes three interrelated components: rational, norm-based, and affective factors. They suggested that, although pay and benefits might inspire some people to choose and excel in government jobs, public employees often place more value on participation in policy formulation and the opportunity to serve altruistic goals such as the public interest (Alonso and Lewis 2001; Perry and Wise 1990, 368).[5] They suggested that public agencies emphasize "normative and affectual incentives" rather than "utilitarian reward systems" (Perry and Wise 1990, 371).

Recent PSM studies have reported evidence about the importance of PSM and its positive effects: 1) Wright (2007) reports evidence that a government organization's public service mission enhances PSM; 2) analyses of differences in work motivation between public and private employees continue to indicate lower levels of extrinsic motivation among public employees, and higher levels of PSM (e.g., Buelens and Broeck 2007; Houston 2005); 3) meta-analyses and reviews of previous research suggest many considerations common to governmental and private sector organizations, but also stress the relevance of PSM (see Perry, Mesch, and Paarlberg 2006); 4) one study reports evidence that higher PSM relates to lower perceived levels of "red tape," suggesting that PSM leads to stronger determination to overcome obstacles to delivering public services (Scott and Pandey 2005); 5) another recent study indicates that public service-oriented motivation (PSOM) enhances organizational commitment, and especially affective and normative bases of commitment (Park and Rainey 2007); and 6) another recent study reports evidence that individual and organizational factors, such as professional identification and educational level, relate to higher levels of PSM (Moynihan and Pandey 2007). Space constraints preclude a detailed review of each study, but these recent analyses support the hypotheses stated and tested in the present study.

Of course, as Gabris and Simo (1995) and others observe, public employees differ in their levels of PSM. This leads, in our analysis, to dichotomizing respondents into those that espouse high levels of PSM, and another group who espouses high levels of extrinsic motivation. From a theoretical perspective, the logic of dichotomizing work motivation in public organizations into two distinct constructs is akin to Frederick Herzberg's (1968) motivation-hygiene theory, which suggests that job motivation or satisfaction involves two independent dimensions, intrinsic factors (motivators) and hygiene factors.[6] The hygiene factors—extrinsic incentives such as pay, job security, and physical working conditions—have external effects on the job and cause dissatisfaction when they are not present, but they do not significantly heighten employees' positive job attitudes even when they are present. On the other hand, the intrinsic factors positively motivate employees because of their association with the need for self-actualization—the ultimate intrinsic drive (Miner 2005). Consequently, Herzberg suggests that "because motivators are the real sources of stimulation and motivation for employees, managers must avoid the negative techniques of controlling and directing employees," which may undermine perceptions of autonomy and intrinsic motivation, and "should instead design work to provide for the individual growth, achievement, recognition, and other elements people need, which are represented by the motivators" (Rainey 2003, 253). This association between autonomy and intrinsic motivation is consistent with the self determination theory (SDT) perspective described earlier.

In order to measure two similarly distinct motivation constructs, this research utilized questions from the federal survey about rewards that most motivate the respondents.[7] We operationalized public service-oriented motivation (PSOM) (intrinsic and altruistic motives) and extrinsically oriented motivation (EOM) (extrinsic and monetary motives) as two distinct variables.We expected that PSOMwill function as amotivator, whereas EOM works as a hygiene factor. First, we hypothesized that PSOM and EOM will directly and indirectly influence the four dependent variables. Perry and Wise (1990) postulated that employees with higher degrees of PSM would be more positive about working for the government. Naff and Crum (1999) found a positive relationship between PSM and federal employees' job satisfaction and performance. These and findings cited earlier suggest the following research question and hypotheses:

Research Question 2: In federal agencies, are the latent constructs of PSOM and EOM conceptually separate and distinct? In a measurement model, do these two latent variables (i.e., endogenous variables) have a positive effect on the exogenous variables?

Hypothesis 2a: In federal agencies, PSOM has a positive relationship with job satisfaction, and perceived performance, and quality of work, and an inverse relationship with turnover intentions.

Hypothesis 2b: In federal agencies, EOM has less impact on job satisfaction, perceived performance, and quality of work, and turnover intentions than does PSOM.

We further hypothesized that PSOM positively moderates the relationships between TOL, TSOL, and job satisfaction, and perceived performance and quality of work, whereas PSOM will negatively moderate the relationships between TOL, TSOL, and turnover intentions. That is, if employees are positively influenced by TOL and TSOL, then higher levels of PSOMwill relate to more positive job attitudes and perceived organizational performance and effectiveness (Kennedy and Anderson 2002).[8] It is also hypothesized that EOM will yield weaker positive outcomes than PSOM, and will moderate the relationships between TOL, TSOL, and four organizational outcomes, but with less positive effects.

Hypothesis 2c: In federal agencies, employees' PSOM interacts with TOL to predict the four organizational outcomes; that is, federal employees' PSOM increases the positive effects of TOL on job satisfaction, perceived performance, and quality of work, whereas it will increase the negative effects of TOL on turnover intentions.

Hypothesis 2d: In federal agencies, employees' EOM interacts with TOL to predict the four organizational outcomes; that is, federal employees' EOM will marginally increase the positive effects of TOL on job satisfaction, perceived performance, and quality of work, whereas it will marginally increase the negative effects of TOL on turnover intentions.

Hypothesis 2e: In federal agencies, employees' PSOM interacts with TSOL to predict four organizational outcomes; that is, federal employees' PSOM will increase the positive effects of TSOL on job satisfaction, perceived performance, and quality of work, whereas it will increase the negative effects of TSOL on turnover intentions.

Mediators, Moderators, and Consequences of Leadership and Work Motivation

Mediators and Moderators

We analyze moderating (i.e., exogenous) and mediating variables that may have effects on the outcome (i.e., endogenous) variables, including: 1) empowerment, 2) procedural equity perceptions, 3) goal clarity, 4) objective performance appraisal systems, 5) effects of downsizing (RIF), 6) reliance on contingent personnel, and 7) managerial flexibility.[9] We include in the analysis, as demographic and agency control variables, gender, education level, job experience, and pay grade (current GS level), as well as 22 agency-based dummy variables (the dummy variable of "other agencies" was left out of the model as a reference group).[10]

Organizational Consequences

Employees more satisfied with their jobs are more likely to engage in collaborative effort and accept organizational goals in ways that enhance performance (Ostroff 1992). For years, while some authors have regularly pointed out that job satisfaction shows no consistent relationship to individual performance (Petty, McGee, and Cavender 1984; Rainey 2003), other analyses conclude that it strongly influences job performance (e.g., Waters, Roach, and Waters 1976) and relates to other problems such as "burnout" (Cherniss 1980; Maslach 1983). The controversial evidence indicates the importance of further analysis of job satisfaction in government.

Job satisfaction influences employees' turnover intentions (for example, Angle and Perry 1981; Bedeian and Armenakis 1981). Turnover intentions "mediate the relationship between affective variables (e.g., motivation, commitment, or job satisfaction) and actual turnover" (Hellman 1997, 677–678; Tett and Mayer 1993). Turnover of desirable employees in public agencies is detrimental due to replacement costs and work disruption.

In addition to job satisfaction, perceived performance, perceived quality of work, and turnover intentions are included as organizational "outcomes" or consequences. The relevant empirical literature (e.g., see Hellman 1997; Judge et al. 2001) suggests that these factors are closely and significantly correlated with each other, so we hypothesize that job satisfaction will affect perceived performance and quality of work, and turnover intentions in federal agencies.[11]

> **Hypothesis 3:** In federal agencies, the more satisfied the federal employees are, the higher the perceived performance and the quality of work and the lower their turnover intentions

Instrumentation and Measurement

Data and Instrumentation

The sample includes 22 agencies and over 6,900 federal employees' responses to the Merit Principles Survey 2000, conducted by the U.S. Merit Systems Protection Board (MSPB). The survey sample was stratified by agencies (*n* was 750 surveys per agency). To generalize to the government-wide population, data were weighted by the STRATWGT variable.

Missing Data Adjustments

Although listwise or pairwise deletion is the common technique for handling missing observations, this approach sacrifices a large amount of data by eliminating all cases with any missing data (Roth 1994). Instead of the listwise deletion method, in order to keep as much data as possible, we analyzed the incomplete data with the Expectation-Maximization (EM) method.[12] EM produces a new covariance matrix based on imputed values that are used in the OLS, CFA, and SEM models. These methods can increase the statistical power of the models as well as minimize possible bias in parameter estimates (Roth 1994; Enders and Bandalos 2001).

Measurement of the Four Main Variables[13]

To confirm latent constructs from the survey questions, we used a composite factor score index of the multiple item measures,[14] and principal component (PC) analysis and the varimax rotation technique to obtain factor extraction.[15] These methods enable us to extract communalities from different variables and then to combine them into new variables.[16]

1) TOL and TSOL: Leadership behaviors were separated into transformationoriented leadership (TOL) and transaction-oriented leadership (TSOL) clusters, measured by 14 questionnaire items as shown in the Appendix. Based on Bass and Avolio's (1995; 1997) questionnaire instruments, the TOL factor index includes the components of 1) Individualized Consideration, 2) Idealized Influence, 3) Inspirational Motivation, and 4) Intellectual Stimulation, whereas the TSOL factor index has the components of 1) Active Management, 2) Passive Management, and 3) Contingent Reward Management.

2) PSOM and EOM: PSOM concerns motives for public service, whereas EOM is related to the extrinsic rewards and self-interest or rational motives (Moynihan and Pandey 2007). These two motivation variables were measured by dummy variable scales, not by an ordinal Likert Scale. Using a categorical factor analysis method(i.e., a polychromic-based, PC, solution), we dichotomized the motivation construct into PSOM as a motivator and EOM as a hygiene factor.[17] In this solution, "there is no assumption of continuous normally distributed observed data" and the PC represents "relationships between the variables at the latent level, and it is these latent correlations that are of interest to reproduce" (Finney and Distefano 2006, 284–285).[18] Eleven survey items were used to measure the two types of work motivation. The results of factor analyses (i.e., EFA and CFA) indicate that the factor loadings support the use of these items as indicators of the underlying motivational constructs. The first factor indicates federal employees' preferences for intrinsic rewards as major job-related motivators—PSOM (motivators), while the second factor reveals preferences for extrinsic and materialistic rewards, or EOM (hygiene factors).

Measurement of the Interaction Effects

To confirm the multiplicative and joint effects among the main variables, four interaction terms are operationalized and measured: 1) TOL-PSOM, 2) TOL-EOM, 3) TSOL-PSOM, and 4) TOL-TSOL. By adding interaction terms we can statistically incorporate the additional joint effects of the four main antecedents.

Measurement of Mediating, Moderating, and Outcome Variables

Using factor analysis (i.e., EFA factor scores), we operationalized seven mediating and moderating variables. Also, to control spurious statistical effects, a set of demographic and agency-dummy variables were included.[19] As organizational consequences, four outcome variables were operationalized from the survey items: The first variable, "job satisfaction," includes six items that all converged on one factor. The second outcome variable, "job performance," was measured by three 10-point scale items. The third variable, "quality of work," was measured by a factor analysis collapsing four survey items into one factor. The fourth outcome variable, "turnover intentions," was measured using a factor analysis that placed five items into one factor index (see the Appendix).[20]

The Statistical Modeling: CFA, OLS Regression, and SEM

We employed three statistical methods. First (phase 1), through a CFA model, we estimated the latent constructs of TOL and TSOL, and PSOMand EOM. Second, we employed OLS multivariate regression to examine the relationships among the main independent variables, mediating and moderating variables, and outcome variables (phase 2). Third, in order to measure the total, direct, indirect, and spurious effects in this model, we employed a full structural equation model (SEM) (phase 3); using LISREL 8.72 and PRELIS 2.72, we can assess the empirical evidence that each type of organizational leadership and work motivation, as well as the mediating and moderating factors, directly and indirectly affect the outcome variables (Joreskog and Sorbom 1996). In the CFA and SEM models the maximum likelihood (ML) method was used because most of the ML-based estimates can be less biased than the GLS or ADF estimates.[21] Also, the covariance matrix was used to examine secondorder measurement models (i.e., CFA) and the structural equation model (SEM).

Findings and Results

Phase 1: Test of a Confirmatory Factor Analysis (CFA) Model

To test Research Questions 1 and 2, we first employed a second-order CFA model of TOL and TSOL that indicates that both of the two latent organizational leadership constructs are significantly salient and distinct (see Figure 1). An organizational leadership composite construct (a second order factor) is significantly and positively explained by TOL and TSOL (first order factors). Second, the CFA model of work motivation suggests that the latent factor of PSOM(the factor loading is .65) is more salient than that of EOM (the factor loading is .34). Moreover, the latent constructs of organizational leadership and work motivation (second order factors) are positively related to each other (r = .55). Third, all observable variables measuring these six latent constructs have significant factor loadings (the standardized parameter estimates) on the factors based on t-test (significantly different from 0).

The values of R^2 on each variable are moderate to high (from 0.34 to 0.64), showing that the the amount of variance in the indicators is relatively well measured and explained by latent factors. Regarding the model fit of the four-factor measurement model, several goodness-of-fit indices (see Figure 1) show that the fit of the entire model is within acceptable levels. For example, the comparative fit index (CFI) is .96 (greater than .90

is acceptable) and the root mean square error approximation (RMSEA) is .045 (less than .08 is acceptable). This proposed model of leadership and motivation in federal agencies is a good fit to the data, supporting the construct validity of a second-order measurement model.[22]

Figure 1. Second-Order Confirmatory Factor Analysis (CFA)[a]

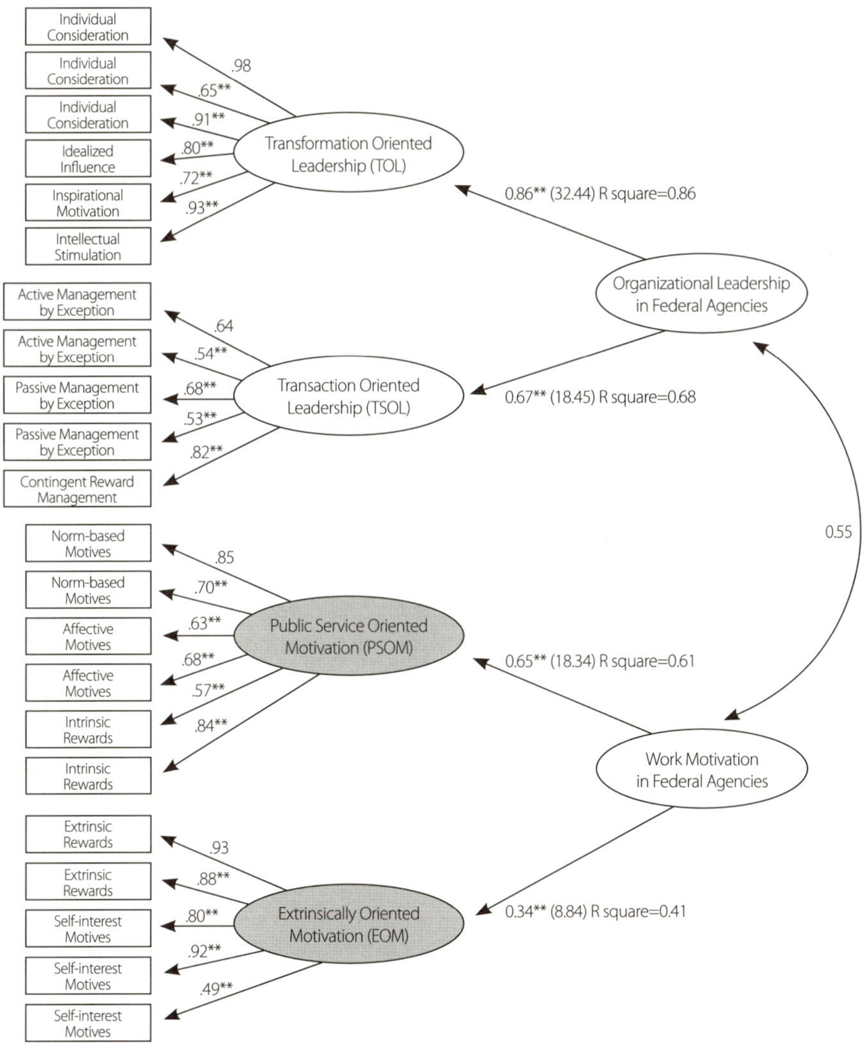

Overall fit Indexes of the Confirmatory Factor Analysis (CFA) Model

Model (Valid N= 6957)	df	Chi-Square	Chi-Square/df	RFI	NFI	GFI	CFI	RMSEA	SRMR
Suggested cut-off values			<3	>.90	>.90	>.90	>.90	<.08	<.08
A Model of Leadership & Motivation in Federal Agencies	203	1590.73	7.79	.92	.950	.940	.96	.045	.03

[a]Based on the ML method, standardized coefficients of the factor loadings (lambda-Ys and gammas) and a covariance estimate are presented in a second-order CFA model.

Phase 2: Correlations and Multiple Regression Results

We examined the correlation relationship between the four main variables, controls (i.e., mediators and moderators), and outcome variables. As shown in Table 1, the job satisfaction and performance variables are positively and significantly correlated with public service-oriented motivation (PSOM), transformation-oriented leadership (TOL) and transaction-oriented leadership (TSOL), but are not significantly associated with extrinsically-oriented motivation (EOM). Although both TOL and TSOL are significantly correlated with job satisfaction, performance, and quality of work, TOL shows a much more positive relation to job satisfaction and perceived performance than TSOL. PSOM is also more significantly correlated with job satisfaction, performance, quality of work, and turnover intentions than is EOM.[23]

Next, with OLS multivariate regression (see Table 2), we examined relationships between antecedent variables—including several interactive variables and control variables—and the outcome variables. Even though we did not find a significant relationship between the independent variables and turnover intentions, there were marginally significant effects from TOL and PSOM (i.e., $p < .10$). The weak relationship can be explained by indirect impacts—via several intermediating variables—on turnover intentions.[24] Other than turnover intentions, significant relationships among the variables were found, as described below.

First, both TOL and TSOL have statistically significant effects on job satisfaction, performance, and quality of work (except for the relationship between TSOL and job satisfaction, which is marginally significant). This means that not only transformational style leaders but also transactional style leaders increase their followers' job satisfaction and perceived organizational performance. The results, however, indicate that TOL is much more effective than TSOL in increasing these outcomes [Confirmed Hypotheses 1a and 1b].

Second, PSOM is positively and significantly related to the job satisfaction, performance, and quality of work. On the other hand, EOM is negatively or marginally related to job satisfaction, performance, and quality of work. These results support the interpretation that PSOM plays a role as an intrinsic motivator, whereas EOM works as a hygiene factor, as Herzberg's two-factor theory suggested. From these findings, we can infer that transformational leadership skills and intrinsic rewarding systems prove more effective in enhancing the level of the dependent variables [Confirmed Hypotheses 2a and 2b].

Third, four interaction terms show the regression for determining whether four main variables would interact with one another (e.g., PSOM's effects on performance depend on the particular level of TSOL); most notably, interaction variables of TOL-PSOM and TOL-TSOL show significant relationships with all three outcome variables. The regression results suggest that, when TOL is accompanied with PSOM, the corresponding coefficients for the variables are positive and statistically significant, indicating that there are positive acceleration effects on job satisfaction (31.2% more), performance (18.5% more), and quality of work (16.1% more) than when TOL exists alone. In other words, the positive relationships among job satisfaction, performance, quality of work, and TOL become more pronounced as the level of PSOM increases. In a similar vein, when TOL and TSOL are combined, an additional 28.8%, 12.2%, and 38.3% in positive moderation effects increase for job satisfaction, performance and quality of work, respectively. These results imply that when supervisors or managers in federal agencies demonstrate both transformational and transactional behaviors, and when employees with a high level of public service orientation have transformation-oriented leaders, we can expect more positive organizational outcomes. Finally, by examining the effects of the controls, we found that additional variables are significantly associated with the outcome variables[25] [Partially Confirmed Hypotheses 1c, 2c, 2d, 2e, and 2f].

Phase 3: Test of the Structural Equation Model (SEM)

In the third phase of this study, we examined the full structural equation model (SEM). The SEM shows results similar to the OLS analysis, with an alternative analytical method. More importantly, it provides evidence that elaborates the relations among TOL, TSOL, and PSOM. The SEM indicates that TOL relates to PSOM directly and by way of empowerment. PSOM relates to job satisfaction and turnover intentions, and through job satisfaction influences perceived performance and work quality. TSOL shows no such relations, and mainly relates to extrinsic motives (EOM), which influences job satisfaction and turnover intentions, but less strongly than does PSOM. The results also further indicate the beneficial effects of perceived procedural equity (fairness) and objective (i.e., fair and effective) performance appraisals. These findings are consistent with self-determination theory (SDT) and Herzberg's analysis, as discussed earlier.

Several goodness-of-fit indices indicate that the hypothesized structural equation model accurately explains the data. Of the seven model-fit indexes, the chi-square value is not consistent with a good model fit. However, RMSEA and SRMR are .018 and .04, indicating a relatively a well-fitting model (a cut-off value is .08). Moreover, the values of RFI, NFI, GFI, and CFI also exceed those that point to a good model fit overall (see Figure 2). In addition, following some of the modification index (MI) suggestions, we added an error covariance among several indicators and respecified the model for the sake of decreasing the chi-square value of this model.[26] Second, from Figure 2 and Table 3, we can observe that TOL directly, significantly, and positively influences PSOM (B = .36**; t = 27.51). Moreover, as hypothesized above, TOL indirectly and significantly affects job satisfaction, performance, quality of work, and turnover intentions. TSOL is directly and positively related to EOM (B = .09**; t = 4.59). TSOL also indirectly affects the four outcome variables, but the standardized effects are far less than those of TOL, indicating that TOL affects four outcome variables more significantly than TSOL does. These findings are also consistent with the results ofOLS regression [Confirmed Hypotheses 1a and 1b].

Third, as hypothesized, PSOM significantly and directly influences job satisfaction (B = .37**; t = 34.37) and turnover intentions (B = -.16**; t = -9.67) and indirectly affects performance and quality of work. On the other hand, EOM has only marginal effects, at most, on job satisfaction (B = .008; t = .72), turnover intentions (B = .001; t = .41), and other outcome variables. Fourth, as moderators and mediators, goal clarity, empowerment, procedural equity perceptions, and objective performance appraisal systems are directly and indirectly related to TOL, PSOM, and the outcome variables. For example, the variable of procedural equity perceptions is positively and significantly associated with PSOM (B = .17**; t = 16.21) and with job satisfaction (B = .22**; t = 18.55). Fifth, in the relationship among the four outcome variables, we also confirmed our hypotheses that job satisfaction positively and significantly influences performance (B = .40**; t = 34.23) and quality of work (B = .45**; t = 37.25), whereas job satisfaction affects turnover intentions negatively (B = -.30**, t = -15.33). Finally, in terms of R2 values, substantial amounts of the variance in PSOM (.51), empowerment (.44), and goal clarity (.43) were explained. The explained variances for job satisfaction, performance, and quality of work were more modest [Confirmed Hypotheses 2a, 2b, and 3].

Table 1. Zero-Order Bivariate Correlations and Reliabilities (N= 6918)

Variable	1	2	3	4	5	6	7	8
1. TOL Mean: 2.87 SD: 1.21	(.935)							
2. TSOL Mean: 2.95 SD: 1.26	.546**	(.770)						
3. PSOM Mean: 2.76 SD: .61	.483**	.272**	(.775)					
4. EOM Mean: 3.09 SD: .62	–.032**	–.001	–.084**	(.712)				
5. Empowerment	.667**	.325**	.454**	.011	(.812)			
6. Procedural Equity Perceptions	.608**	.277*	.355**	–.022	.597**	(.845)		
7. Objective Performance Appraisal Systems	.670**	.403**	.437**	–.076	.561**	.399**	(.816)	
8. Managerial Flexibility	.294**	.018	.096**	–.006	.261**	.252*	.477**	(.725)
9. Goal Clarity	.559**	.302**	.371**	–.034	.688**	.341**	.571**	.367**
10. Effects of Downsizing(RIF)	–.107**	–.037**	–.072**	.013	–.128**	–.075**	–.141**	–.012
11. Reliance on Contingent Personnel	.018	.070	–.010	.008	.000	–.002	–.037**	–.074**
12. Job Tenure	.002	–.077*	.025*	.108**	–.028*	.024	–.005	.040
13. Current Pay (GS) Level	–.038*	–.111*	.097**	.148**	–.163*	–.185*	–.055**	.118*
14. Gender (female: 1)	.032**	.048**	.010	.026*	.025*	–.016	.020	–.028*
15. Education Level	–.17**	–.067**	–.014	–.018	–.072**	–.063**	–.033**	0.063**
16. Job Satisfaction	.710**	.300**	.489**	.016	.721**	.652**	.683**	.419**
17. Performance	.382**	.223**	.191**	–.035	.413**	.289**	.354**	.263**
18. Quality of Work	.396 **	.268**	.208**	–.032*	.451**	.378**	.415**	.282**
19. Turnover Intentions	–.248**	–.139**	–.112**	–.014	–.334**	–.250**	–.231**	–.042

The numbers in parentheses are Cronbach's Alpha values.
Correlation is significant at the 0.05-level (two-tailed).
Correlation is significant at the 0.01 level (two-tailed).

Table 1 – continued

9	10	11	12	13	14	15	16	17	18	19
(.716)										
–.124**	(.703)									
–.014	–.090*	(.705)								
–.010	–.104**	–.006								
–.048**	.022	–.191**	.192**							
–.044**	.061**	–.012	–.026*	–.277**						
–.007	.015	–.006	–.116**	.538**	–.181**					
.588**	–.196**	–.028	.046*	–.091**	–.038**	.018	(.779)			
.418**	–.051**	–.017	–.003	.096**	–.126**	.101**	.405**	(.769)		
.420**	–.081**	.044	–.038*	.026	–.067**	.045**	.449**	.617**	(.773)	
–.202**	.110**	–.053	.047*	.167**	–.026*	.093**	–.281**	–.095**	–.160**	(.758)

Table 2. OLS Multiple Regression (Antecedents, Controls, and Outcomes)

Outcome Variables	Job Satisfaction		Performance	
Main Variables:	Un-standardized Coefficients (B)	Standardized Coefficients (β)	Un-standardized Coefficients (B)	Standardized Coefficients (β)
TOL	**.575** (6.987)**	.531	**.283** (3.394)**	.335
TSOL	**.166* (1.844)**	.154	**.182** (2.333)**	.212
PSOM	**.262** (2.450)**	.208	**.129** (2.207)**	.182
EOM	**.118* (1.779)**	–.089	–.001 (–.024)	–.001
Interaction between TOL and TSOL	**.288** (2.772)**	.184	**.122** (2.283)**	.165
Interaction between TOL and PSOM	**.312** (3.731)**	.221	**.185** (2.495)**	.250
Interaction between TSOL and PSOM	.083 (1.058)	.068	–.030 (–.410)	–.030
Interaction between TOL and EOM	.063 (.656)	.051	.023 (.323)	.024
Controls:	Unstandardized Coefficients (B)		Unstandardized Coefficients (B)	
Empowerment	**.143* (1.677)**		**.350** (4.033)**	
Procedural Equity Perceptions	**.135** (1.994)**		–.101 (–1.233)	
Job Flexibility	.226** (3.968)		.069 (1.184)	
Goal Clarity	–.082 (–.987)		–.066 (–.785)	
Effects of Downsizing (RIF)	.018 (.298)		–.046 (–.817)	
Reliance on Contingent Personnel	–.047 (–.827)		–.055 (–1.002)	
Objective Performance Appraisal System	**.206** (3.040)**		**.182** (2.359)**	
Gender (Female:1)	**–.314** (–2.147)**		–.136 (–.928)	
Education Level	–.043 (–.066)		–.036 (–.857)	
Job Tenure	.001 (.031)		.031 (.927)	
Current Pay Grades	–.015 (–.521)		.027 (1.094)	
Adjusted R^2	**.625**		**.565**	
Standard Error	.636		.536	
F Statistics	8.347 (.000)		6.939 (.000)	
N of Cases[a]	5911		5872	

[a]Missing variables were recalculated and adjusted by the EM algorithm.
- Critical values are 1.96 for $P < .05$ and 1.65 for $P < .10$ (t-statistics are in parentheses).
- 22 Agency-Dummies (reference group: Other Agencies) were included as control variables in the

$P < .10$: significant at .10-level.
$P < .05$: significant at 0.05-level.

Table 2 – continued

Outcome Variables	Quality of Work		Turnover Intentions	
Main Variables:	Un-standardized Coefficients (B)	Standardized Coefficients (β)	Un-standardized Coefficients (B)	Standardized Coefficients (β)
TOL	**.371** (3.413)**	.409	**–.355* (–1.733)**	–.387
TSOL	**.146** (2.083)**	.155	–.219 (–1.401)	–.173
PSOM	**.159** (2.333)**	.175	**–.358** (–1.761)**	–.388
EOM	**–.121* (–1.801)**	–.120	–.060 (–.361)	–.046
Interaction between TOL and TSOL	**.383** (2.921)**	.290	.024 (.268)	.042
Interaction between TOL and PSOM	**.161** (2.464)**	.189	**–.365 (.832)**	–.117
Interaction between TSOL and PSOM	–.003 (–.038)	–.003	.187 (.852)	.134
Interaction between TOL and EOM	.021 (.220)	.021	–.062 (–.251)	–.048
Controls:	Unstandardized Coefficients (B)		Unstandardized Coefficients (B)	
Empowerment	–.006 (–.053)		**–.571** (–2.992)**	
Procedural Equity Perceptions	**.166* (1.754)**		–.646 (–.159)	
Job Flexibility	**.124* (1.837)**		.041 (.114)	
Goal Clarity	–.027 (–.278)		.348 (1.137)	
Effects of Downsizing (RIF)	–.033 (–.520)		.165 (1.239)	
Reliance on Contingent Personnel	**–.204** (–2.053)**		.033 (.069)	
Objective Performance Appraisal System	**.235** (2.634)**		.618 (1.393)	
Gender (Female:1)	**–.341** (– 1.982)**		–.102 (–.241)	
Education Level	**–.094* (–1.914)**		.231 (1.173)	
Job Tenure	**–.087** (–2.042)**		–.021 (–.268)	
Current Pay Grades	**.052* (1.858)**		**.224** (2.502)**	
Adjusted R^2	**.539**		**.479**	
Standard Error	.590		.743	
F Statistics	6.105 (.000)		4.247 (.000)	
N of Cases[a]	5282		2281	

OLS model. A listing of federal agencies is available from the authors.

Figure 2. Leadership and PSM Structural Equation Model (SEM)

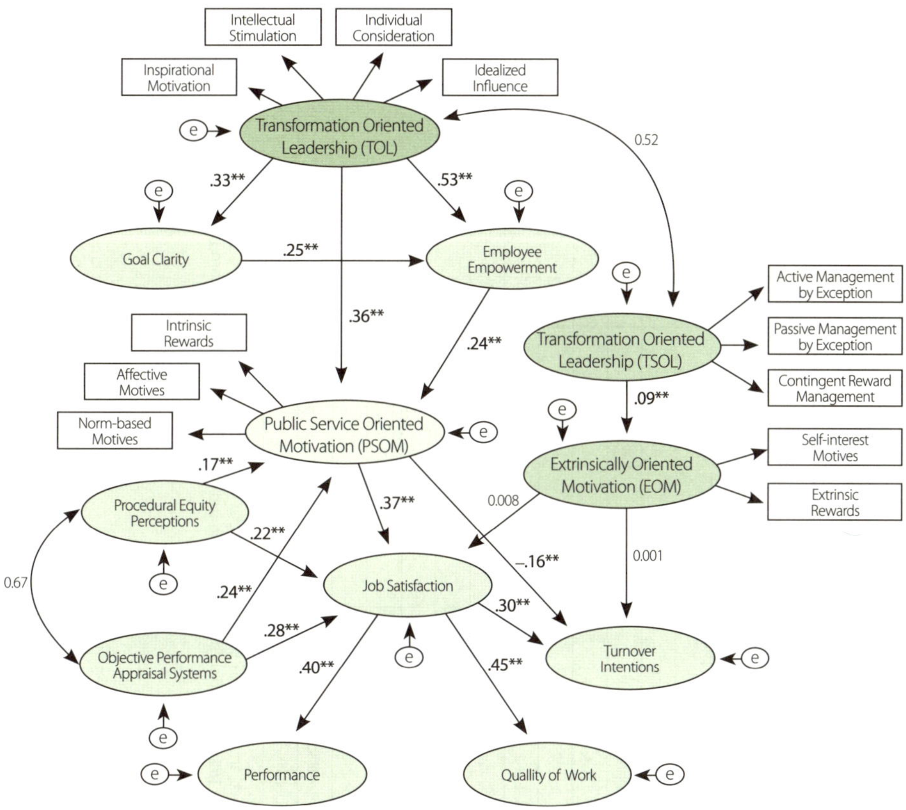

Notes : The structural path estimates are presented as unstandardized regression weights (B).
*Path coefficienrs are statistically significant at p<.05.
**Path coefficienrs are statistically significant at p <.01.

Overall Fit Indexes of the CFA Model

Model 1	df	Chi-Square	Chi-Square /df	RFI	NFI	GFI	CFI	RMSEA	SRMR
Suggested cut-off values			<3	>0.90	>0.90	>0.90	>0.90	<0.08	<0.08
Model of Leadership and Motivation in Federal Agencies	235	3050.11	12.98	.95	.92	.92	.94	.018	.04

[a]Total effective sample size (N=6,957) of the SEM model is imputed based on the EM method.

Table 3. Unstandardized and Standardized Total Effects[a]

Directionality between Variables in SEM			Unstandardized Estimate (B)	Standardized Estimate (β)	S.E.	t Statistic	R^2	P-Value
Goal Clarity	←	TOL	.33**	.45	.007	42.20	.43	.00
Empowerment	←	TOL	.53**	.64	.01	55.05	.44	.00
Empowerment	←	Goal Clarity	.25**	.19	.01	19.39		.00
PSOM	←	TOL	.36**	.51	.01	27.51	.51	.00
PSOM	←	Empowerment	.24**	.24	.01	18.07		.00
PSOM	←	Procedural Equity Perceptions	.17**	.14	.01	16.21		.00
PSOM	←	Objective Appraisal Systems	.24**	.19	.01	19.76		.00
EOM	←	TSOL	.09**	.02	.02	4.59	.08	.00
Job Satisfaction	←	PSOM	.37**	.38	.01	34.37		.00
Job Satisfaction	←	EOM	.008	.01	.01	.72	.15	> .05
Job Satisfaction	←	Procedural Equity Perceptions	.22**	.20	.01	18.55		.00
Job Satisfaction	←	Objective Appraisal Systems	.28**	.25	.01	21.87		.00
Turnover Intentions	←	PSOM	−.16**	−.15	.015	−9.67		.00
Turnover Intentions	←	EOM	.001	.01	.004	.41	.12	> .05
Turnover Intentions	←	Job Satisfaction	−.30**	−.27	.02	−15.33		.00
Perceived Performance	←	Job Satisfaction	.40**	.38	.01	34.23	.18	.00
Perceived Quality of Work	←	Job Satisfaction	.45**	.38	.01	37.25	.26	.00

[a]Total effects can be calculated by summing up direct, indirect, and spurious effects.
•Not all total effects were included in this table. The full information about total and indirect effects is available from the authors.
**Values are significant at $p < .01$ and $p < .05$ (one-tailed).

Discussion

This analysis of a large survey of federal employees finds beneficial effects when the respondents perceive their leaders as transformation-oriented (TOL)—where the leader informs the respondent, supports her or his development and personal welfare, emphasizes high standards, and helps poor performers improve. The analysis also finds beneficial effects of public service-oriented motivation (PSOM). Both TOL and PSOM show strong positive relations to job satisfaction, and perceived performance and work quality, and negative relations to intent to turnover. Transactionoriented leadership (TSOL) shows similar beneficial relations with the dependent variables, but weaker ones. Analysis of interactions among the variables indicates support for Bass's (1985) contention that transformational leaders also display transactional leadership behaviors; the interaction of TOL and TSOL enhances positive effects on the dependent variables (with the exception of turnover intent). The interaction of TOL and PSOM also enhances positive results on the dependent variables.

The OLS regression analysis and the structural equation model provide further evidence about relations among the variables and about the roles of empowerment, goal clarity, perceived procedural equity (fairness) and objective (i.e., merit-based and communication enhancing) performance appraisal systems. The SEM, in particular, suggests that TOL relates positively to PSOM and to empowerment (with an additional indirect effect on empowerment through goal clarity). That is, TOL fosters PSOM via empowerment in federal agencies. Our finding about the TOL-empowerment-PSOM relationship is also consistent with the findings of an inverse relationship between red tape and PSM (see Moynihan and Pandey 2007) in that red tape would severely attenuate or eliminate the culture of TOL and empowerment in the public sector. Empowerment relates positively to PSOM, and PSOM relates positively to job satisfaction and to lower turnover intentions; job satisfaction then relates positively to perceived performance and quality of work, and relates to lower turnover intentions. We conceive PSOM as an intrinsic motivation and interpret these results as consistent with the perspective of self-determination theory (SDT), that contends that external regulation can reduce intrinsic satisfaction, and greater autonomy (in the present study, due to TOL, empowerment, procedural fairness, and merit-based, communicative performance appraisals) can increase it. They are also consistent with the conclusion in SDT that external influence in the form of supportive and positive feedback can enhance intrinsic motivation. Moreover, they are consistent with Herzberg's emphasis on autonomy as conducive to "motivators" that are predominantly intrinsic. These observations raise the ongoing theoretical challenge of further developing theory about public service motivation as an intrinsic incentive, and how it relates to leadership behaviors, autonomy, and empowerment.

Reliance on an employee attitude survey raises concerns about mono-method bias, positive response bias, and subjective measures of the variables, especially the dependent variables. Countering these concerns are the very large, anonymous nature of the survey, which reduce the likelihood, remote in any case, that federal employees can be cowed or duped into providing invalid positive responses. In this and other surveys, federal employees have responded negatively or critically about important matters. Countering concerns about subjective measures are reports of appreciable correlations between subjective and objective performance measures (e.g., see Brewer 2006, 36–37; Walker and Boyne 2006; Wall et al. 2004). Moreover, the pattern of positive responses about TOL and PSOM were by no means preordained. We need to take seriously the evidence provided here, that many federal employees in the stereotypically constraining federal "bureaucracy" perceive their leaders as transformation-oriented, as conceived here. In response to such leadership, they feel empowered and express public service oriented motivation and these responses relate strongly to positive responses on job satisfaction, perceived performance, and turnover intentions. Federal employees frequently express concerns about their pay and promotion systems (as emphasized in EOM), and they could have more heavily emphasized those concerns as influences on their job satisfaction, on perceived performance and on work quality. More research with different methods and more objective outcome measures will clearly be valuable, but the results reported here provide important evidence to confirm, extend, or refute in further studies.

Practical and policy implications include the value of encouraging and training leaders in the behaviors indicated in the TOL measure used here, and in empowering. The results underscore the value of fair, communicative personnel practices that can enhance and reward PSOM. For decades, reform efforts have emphasized pay for performance, and more recently pay-banding, in spite of mixed or disappointing results of such reforms (Alonso and Lewis 2001; Kellough and Lu 1993; Lewis 1991). As analysts have pointed out (e.g., Lyons, Duxbury, and Higgins 2006, 605; Barzelay 2001) reforms in the New Public Management movement in many nations have often emphasized organizational efficiency and effectiveness based on economic rationales that depict managers and employees as heavily dependent on their narrow material self-interests and seeking "to maximize their personal utility." The pursuit of efficiency and effectiveness should and will continue, as should the pursuit of effective pay and incentive systems. The evidence reported here, however, emphasizes the importance of continuing to develop ways to avoid letting such emphases crowd out concerns with encouraging, recognizing, and rewarding distinctive motives and incentives in the public service— public service motivation (Bright 2005, 151; Houston 2005, 81). The evidence further suggests means to do so, through such approaches as transformational leadership behaviors, communication-enhancing performance appraisal systems, clear goals and missions, and empowerment.

Notes

1. The original version of this essay was awarded the Sage Publications Best Doctoral Student Conference Paper from the Public and Non-Profit (PNP) Division at the 2005 Annual Conference of the Academy of Management, August 5–10, in Honolulu, Hawaii.
2. For instance, Bass and his colleagues have revealed that the more effective leaders are both transformational and transactional (Hater and Bass 1988), and transformational and transactional forms of leadership are distinct but not mutually exclusive processes (Bass 1985a).
3. In the public sector, we can hypothesize that these two leadership types are sometimes combined and overlapped, which engenders interaction effects—the effect of transformational leadership on outcome variables is different, depending on the effect of transactional leadership. Based on this rationale, an interaction variable of TOL-TSOL was included in this study.
4. In this study, it is assumed that the relationship between these two types of work motivation is independent, additive (i.e., non-spurious), or even interactive. For instance, a lot of empirical evidence suggests that extrinsic or monetary incentives undermine intrinsic motivation either marginally or markedly, depending on other moderating organizational factors.
5. More broadly, PSM can be characterized as a reliance on intrinsic rewards (i.e., sense of accomplishment and of fulfilling a duty as a public employee) over extrinsic rewards (i.e., a pay raise, a promotion, job security, and pay for performance ratings) (Crewson 1997).
6. For example, according to Herzberg, the opposite of job satisfaction is not dissatisfaction but rather a simple lack of satisfaction; also, the opposite meaning of dissatisfaction is not satisfaction but rather no satisfaction.
7. Some of these were about more intrinsic, altruistic, and public service-oriented rewards, while others asked about extrinsic and more self-interested rewards such as a pay raise and a promotion. Many of these items asked respondents to choose three of these categorical items that will most motivate them.
8. For example, we can think of the situation where many employees are not only motivated by publicness itself, but also inspired by transformation-oriented leaders, which could have more positive and significant effects on job satisfaction and performance. Following this rationale, a TOL-PSOM interaction variable was added in this research.
9. Empowerment means giving employees the authority, skills, and self-control to perform their tasks. Although empowerment and managerial flexibility have similar constructs in their items, they are distinctive in that empowerment is more of a behavior-oriented

variable whereas managerial flexibility is more related to the organizational structure and design issues. Based on this rationale, we separated these two variables, and factor loadings also statistically supported our distinctions between the two variables.

10. These variables were included to control and moderate the leadership and work motivation effects among federal employees, leading to more rigorous and accurate research findings. Moreover, by including these variables, we can observe whether the different types of leadership and work motivation will show the direct and indirect effects on outcome variables through these mediators in a structural equation model (SEM). In SEM, procedural equity perceptions and objective performance appraisal systems are included as moderators whereas goal clarity and empowerment function as mediators.
11. In this study "performance and quality of work" were operationalized by perceptual and subjective measures (rather than using objective ones) based on federal survey data. Previous empirical studies suggested that "there is evidence of a high correlation between perceptual and objective measures at the organizational level" and found that "measures of perceived organizational performance were correlated positively to objective measures of organizational performance" (e.g., see Kim 2005, 250).
12. The EM method utilizes an iterative method to impute missing values. This method consists of two steps and the process is iterated until the difference between the reproduced covariance matrices obtained by two adjacent iterations falls below some prespecified criterion (Little and Rubin 1987).
13. Using the VIF and R^2 test, we checked the multicollinearity in the independent and interactive variables. The tolerance level is about .3 and VIF value is less than 3, showing that no serious problems were found in this model, which could be due to using factor scores in regression analysis. Generally, using factor scores as explanatory variables is supposed to reduce multicollinearity problems.
14. One of the assumptions of factor analysis is interval data; however, Kim and Muller (1978) suggest that ordinal data can be used if it is regarded that the ordinal categories to the data do not seriously distort the underlying metric scaling. In the same vein, they argue that use of dummy variable data can also be allowed if the underlying metric correlations between the variables are thought to be moderate (.7) or lower. In this study, all these conditions are met.
15. After obtaining factor scores and, subsequently, new variables, we tested the reliability, or the internal consistency, using Cronbach's alpha. All the scales have an Alpha value of .7 or above.
16. The formula for factor scores is $F_{jk} = PW_{ji}Z_{ik}$ (F = individual factor scores; W = weighted values; Z = the standardized variables). We can have three advantages by using factor scores in regression. First, we can reduce or eliminate multicollinearity because the variables causing the multicollinearity will combine to form a factor. Second, using the factor index, we can make interval variables instead of ordinal or nominal variables

because all ordinal level data can be transformed into interval data that have factor scores rather than 5-level Likert scales. Third, we can reduce the number of variables by making new variables.

17. In measuring these constructs of motivation, eight dichotomous variables were used, which might cause potential problems of nonlinearity and nonnormality—both nonnormality and nonlinearity will generally result in underestimation of the relationship among variables. In other words, variable communalities, percentage of variance accounted for, and factor loadings will be lower than continuous and normally distributed data. As one solution to this problem, a polychroic-based solution was used in this model. Polychoric correlations (PC), ranging from - 1.0 to 1.0, were developed for ordinal or dichotomous data.
18. Theoretically, polychromic correlations should yield higher correlations among categorized variables, as they disattenuate for the effects of categorization. They should also result in higher communalities, percentage of variance accounted for, and factor loadings. Moreover, polychromic-based analysis yields a much clearer solution, with clear separation between the two factors.
19. Education level, job experience, and current pay grade are important as control variables especially for turnover intentions because turnover intentions could naturally occur without any effect. We can expect that these moderators can reduce the internal validity threat, called history effect.
20. Please contact the authors for a detailed explanation of the rationale for this turnover intention measure.
21. In ML estimation, the weight matrix is the inverse of the reproduced covariance matrix. The ML method is generally both scale free and scale invariant. It also assumes multivariate normality and, hence, non-normality would influence the significant test and the chi-square value. From multivariate normality tests, severe non-normality patterns are not observed and we can expect that this method would be more unbiased, consistent, and efficient, especially when the population distribution for the endogenous variables is multivariate normal (Kline 2005).
22. However, of the seven tests, the maximum likelihood chi-square test was inconsistent with a good model fit ($\mathcal{X}^2$ = 1590.73; $p < .01$). This particular fit index, which assesses the discrepancy between the sample covariance matrix and the implied covariance matrix based on the hypothesized model, is sensitive to sample size, with larger samples increasing the chi square and decreasing the likelihood of achieving a good model fit (James, Mulaik, and Brett 1982). Consequently, with large samples, virtually all models would be rejected as statistically untenable regardless of a good model fit (Kemery, Bedeian, Mossholder, and Touliatos 1985).
23. We also conducted an independent samples test to determine if there is a mean difference in four outcomes for PSOM, EOM, TOL, and TSOL. The results indicate that

the mean level of four outcome variables is significantly different at .05 level for PSOM and EOM (e.g., in job satisfaction, t = 2.447, p = .015) and TOL and TSOL (e.g., in job satisfaction, t = 3.543, p = .008). Based on these results, we rejected H0 states and confirmed that the impacts of PSOM, EOM, TOL, and TSOL on outcome variables are statistically different.

24. In this regard, one of the rationales for adopting a structural equation model (SEM) in this research is to examine the indirect and spurious effects among antecedent variables and outcome variables, (e.g., turnover intentions), which cannot be measured by the OLS regression method.
25. For example, the "empowerment" variable gives a significant effect on performance and turnover intentions. Also, the effect of "objective performance appraisal systems" is highly and positively related to job satisfaction, performance, and quality of work.
26. Modification indexes (MI) show the amount by which the chi-square value would decrease if the suggested paths or error covariances were added to the model. In order to drop out chi-square values, we added a set of error covariance among indicators of latent variables (e.g., public service motivated-job satisfaction and empowerment-job satisfaction) as MI suggested.

References

Alonso, P., & Lewis, G. B. (2001). Public service motivation and job performance: Evidence from the federal sector. *American Review of Public Administration, 31,* 363-380.

Angle, H. L., & Perry, J. L. (1981). An empirical assessment of organizational commitment and organizational effectiveness. *Administrative Science Quarterly, 26,* 1-14.

Antonakis, J., & House, R. J. (2002). The full range leadership theory: The way forward. In B. J. Avolio & F. J. Yammarino (Eds.), *Transformational and charismatic leadership: The road ahead* (pp. 3-33). Kidlington, Oxford: Elsevier Science.

Avolio, B. J., & Bass, B. M. (1995). Individual consideration viewed at multiple levels of analysis: A multi-level framework for examining the diffusion of transformational leadership. *The Leadership Quarterly, 6,* 199-218.

Bandura, A. (1986). *Social foundations of thought and action: A social cognitive theory.* Upper Saddle River, NJ: Prentice Hall.

Barling, J., Weber, T., & Kelloway, E. K. (1996). Effects of transformational leadership training on attitudinal and fiscal outcomes: A field experiment. *Journal of Applied Psychology, 81,* 827-832.

Barzelay, M. (2001). *The new public management: Improving research and policy dialogue.* Berkeley: University of California Press.

Bass, B. M. (1985a). *Leadership and performance beyond expectations.* New York: The Free Press.

Bass, B. M. (1985b). Leadership: Good, better, best. *Organizational Dynamics, 13*(3), 26-40.

Bass, B. M. (1998). *Transformational leadership: Individual, military, and educational impact.* Mahwah, NJ: Erlbaum.

Bass, B. M., & Avolio, B. J. (1990). The implications of transactional and transformational leadership for individual, team, and organizational development. In R. W. Woodman & W. A. Pasmore (Eds.), *Research in Organizational Change and Development 4* (pp. 231-272). Greenwich, CT: JAI Press.

Bass, B. M., & Avolio, B. J. (1994). *Improving organizational effectiveness through transformational leadership.* Thousand Oaks: Sage Publications.

Bass, B. M., & Avolio, B. J. (1997). *Full range leadership development: Manual for the multifactor leadership questionnaire.* Palo Alto, CA: Mindgarden.

Bedeian, A. G., & Armenakis, A. A. (1981). A multivariate analysis of the determinants of job turnover. *Journal of Applied Psychology, 67,* 350-360.

Brewer, G. A. (2006). All measures of performance are subjective: More evidence on U.S. federal agencies. In G. A. Boyne, K. J. Meier, L. J. O'toole, Jr., & R. M. Walker (Eds.), *Public service performance: Perspectives on measurement and management* (pp. 35-54). Cambridge, UK: Cambridge University Press.

Bright, L. (2005). Public employees with high levels of public service motivation. *Review of Public Personnel Administration, 25*(2), 138-154.

Buelens, M., & Broeck, H. V. D. (2007). An analysis of differences in work motivation between public and private sector organizations. *Public Administrative Review, 67*(1), 65-74.

Cameron, J., & Pierce, W. D. (2002). *Rewards and intrinsic motivation: Resolving the controversy.* Westport, CT: Bergin and Garvey.

Cameron, J., Banko, K. M., & Pierce, W. D. (2001). Pervasive negative effects of rewards on intrinsic motivation: The myth continues. *The Behavior Analyst, 24,* 1-44.

Cherniss, C. (1980). *Staff burnout: Job stress in human services.* Thousand Oaks, CA: Sage Publications.

Conger, J. A. (1999). Charismatic and transformational leadership in organizations: An insider's perspective on these developing streams of research. *The Leadership Quarterly, 10*(2), 145-169.

Conger, J. A., & Kanungo, R. N. (1998). *Charismatic leadership in organizations.* Thousand Oaks, CA: Sage Publications.

Crewson, P. E. (1997). Public service motivation: Building empirical evidence of incidence and effect. *Journal of Public Administration Research and Theory, 4,* 499-518.

Deci, E. L. (1971). Effects of externally mediated rewards on intrinsic motivation. *Journal of Personality and Social Psychology, 18,* 105-115.

Deci, E. L., & Ryan, R. M. (1985). *Intrinsic motivation and self-determination in human behavior.* New York: Plenum Press.

Deci, E. L., Koestner, R., & Ryan, R. M. (1999). A meta-analytic review of experiments examining the effects of extrinsic rewards on intrinsic motivation. *Psychological Bulletin, 125,* 627-668.

Eisenberger, R., & Cameron, J. (1996). The detrimental effects of reward: Myth or reality?. *American Psychologist, 51,* 1153-1166.

Enders, C. K., & Bandalos, D. L. (2001). The relative performance of full information maximum likelihood estimation for missing data in structural equation models. *Structural Equation Modeling. 8*(3). 430-457.

Finney, S. J., & Distefano, C. (2006). Non-normal and categorical data in structural equation models. In G. R. Hancock & R. O. Mueller (Eds.), *A second course in structural equation modeling* (pp. 269-314). Greenwich, CT: Information Age.

Frederickson, H. G., & Hark, D. K. (1985). The public service and the patriotism of benevolence. *Public Administration Review, 45*(5), 547-553.

Gabris, G. T., & Simo, G. (1995). Public sector motivation as an independent variable affecting career decisions. *Public Personnel Management, 24*(1), 33-51.

Goodwin, V. L., Wofford, J. C., & Whittington, J. L. (2001). A theoretical and empirical extension to the transformational leadership construct. *Journal of Organizational Behavior, 22,* 759-774.

Hater, J. J., & Bass, B. M. (1988). Superior's evaluations and subordinates' perceptions of transformational and transactional leadership. *Journal of Applied Psychology, 73,* 695-702.

Hellman, C. M. (1997). Job satisfaction and intent to leave. *The Journal of Social Psychology, 137*(6), 677-689.

Herzberg, F. (1968). One more time: How do you motivate employees?. *Harvard Business Review, 46,* 53-62.

Houston, D. J. (2000). Public-service motivation: A multivariate test. *Journal of Public Administration Research and Theory, 10,* 713-727.

Houston, D. J. (2005). Walking the walk of public service motivation: Public employees and charitable gifts of time, blood, and money. *Journal of Public Administration Research and Theory, 16,* 67-86.

Howell, J. M., & Avolio, B. J. (1993). Transformational leadership, transactional leadership, locus of control and support for innovation: Key predictors of consolidated-business-unit performance. *Journal of Applied Psychology. 78.* 891-902.

James, L. R., Mulaik, S. A., & Brett, J. M. (1982). *Causal analysis: Assumptions, models, and data.* Beverly Hills, CA: Sage.

Jöreskog, K. G., & Sörbom, D. (1996). *LISREL 8 user's reference guide.* Chicago: Scientific Software International.

Judge, T. A., Thoresen, C. J., Bono, J. E., & Patton, G. K. (2001). The job satisfaction-job performance relationship: A qualitative and quantitative review. *Psychological Bulletin, 127*(3), 376-407.

Jung, D. I. (2001). Transformational and transactional leadership and their effects on creativity in groups. *Creativity Research Journal, 13,* 185-195.

Jung, D. I., & Avolio, B. J. (2000). Opening the black box: An experimental investigation of the mediating effects of trust and value congruence on transformational and transactional leadership. *Journal of Organizational Behavior, 21*(8), 949-964.

Jung, D. I., Chow, C., & Wu, A. (2003). The role of transformational leadership in enhancing organizational innovation: Hypotheses and some preliminary findings. *The Leadership Quarterly, 14,* 525-544.

Jurkiewicz, C. L., & Brown, R. G. (1998). Gen xers vs. boomers vs. matures: Generational comparisons of public employee motivation. *Review of Public Personnel Administration, 18,* 18-37.

Jurkiewicz, C. L., Massey, T. K., & Brown, R. G. (1998). Motivation in public and private organizations. *Public Productivity and Management Review, 21*(3), 230-250.

Kellough, J. E., & Lu, H. (1993). The paradox of merit pay in the public sector: Persistence of a problematic procedure. *Review of Public Personnel Administration, 13*(2), 45-64.

Kemery, E. R., Bedeian, A. G., Mossholder, K. W., & Touliatos, J. (1985). Outcomes of role stress: A multisample constructive replication. *Academy of Management Journal, 28*(2), 363-375.

Kennedy, J. R., & Anderson, R. D. (2002). Impact of leadership style and emotions on subordinate performance. *The Leadership Quarterly, 13,* 545-559.

Kim, S. (2005). Individual-level factors and organizational performance in government organizations. *Journal of Public Administration Research and Theory, 15*(2), 245-261.

Kline, R. B. (2005). *Principles and practices of structural equation modeling.* New York: Guilford.

Kohn, A. (1993). Punished by rewards: *The trouble with gold stars, inventive plans, A's praise, and other bribes.* Boston: Houghton Mifflin.

Lewis, G. B. (1991). Pay and job satisfaction in the federal civil service. *Review of Public Personnel Administration, 11*(3), 17-31.

Little, R. J. A., & Rubin, D. B. (1987). *Statistical analysis with missing data.* New York: John Wiley.

Lowe, K. B., Kroeck, K. G., & Sivasubramaniam, N. (1996). Effectiveness correlates of transformational and transactional leadership: A meta-analytic review of the literature. *Leadership Quarterly, 7*(3), 385-425.

Lyons, S. T., Duxbury, L. E., & Higgins, C. A. (2006). A comparison of the values and commitment of private sector, public sector, and parapublic sector employees. *Public*

Administration Review, 66(4), 605-618.

Mann, G. A. (2006). A motive to serve: Public service motivation in human resource management and the role of PSM in the nonprofit sector. *Public Personnel Management, 35*(1), 33-48.

Maslach, C. (1983). *Burnout: The cost of caring.* Englewood Cliffs, NJ: Prentice Hall.

McGregor, D. (1960). *The human side of enterprise.* New York: McGraw-Hill.

Miner, J. B. (2005). *Organizational behavior 1: Essential theories of motivation and leadership.* Armonk, NY: M.E. Sharpe, Inc.

Moynihan, D. P., & Ingraham, P. W. (2004). Integrative leadership in the public sector: A model of performance-information use. *Administration and Society, 36,* 427-453.

Moynihan, D. P., & Pandey, S. K. (2007). The role of organizations in fostering public service motivation. *Public Administration Review, 67*(1), 40-53.

Naff, K. C., & Crum, J. (1999). Working for america: Does public service motivation make a difference?. *Review of Public Personnel Administration, 19,* 5-16.

Northouse, P. G. (2004). *Leadership: Theory and practice* (3rd ed.). Thousand Oaks, CA: Sage Publications.

Ostroff, C. (1992). The relationship between satisfaction, attitudes, and performance: An organizational level analysis. *Journal of Applied Psychology, 77,* 963-974.

Park, S. M., & Rainey, H. G. (2007). Antecedents, mediators, and consequences of affective, normative, and continuance commitment: Empirical tests of commitment effects in federal agencies. *Review of Public Personnel Administration, 27*(3), 197-226.

Perry, J. L. (1996). Measuring public service motivation: An assessment of construct reliability and validity. *Journal of Public Administration Research and Theory, 6*(1), 5-22.

Perry, J. L. (1997). Antecedents of public service motivation. *Journal of Public Administration and Research and Theory, 7*(2), 181-197.

Perry, J. L., & Porter, L. W. (1982). Factors affecting the context for motivation in public organizations. *The Academy of Management Review, 7*(1), 89-98.

Perry, J. L., & Wise, L. R. (1990). The motivational bases of public service. *Public Administration Review, 50*(3), 367-373.

Perry, J. L., Mesch, D., & Paarlberg, L. (2006). Motivating employees in a new governance era: The performance paradigm revisited. *Public Administration Review, 66*(4), 505-514.

Petty, M. M., & McGee, G. W., & Cavender, J. W. (1984). A meta-analysis of the relationships between individual job satisfaction and individual performance. *Academy of Management Review*, 9, 712-721.

Podsakoff, P. M., MacKenzie, R., & Bommer, W. (1996). Transformational leader behaviors and substitutes for leadership as determinants of employee satisfaction, commitment, trust, and organizational citizenship behaviors. *Journal of Management, 22,* 259-

298.

Podsakoff, P. M., Todor, W. D., & Skov, R. (1982). Effects of leader contingent satisfaction. *Academy of Management Journal, 25,* 810-821.

Rafferty, A. E., & Griffin, M. A. (2004). Dimensions of transformational leadership: Conceptual and empirical extensions. *The Leadership Quarterly, 15,* 329-354.

Rainey, H. G. (2003). *Understanding and managing public organizations* (3rd ed.). San Francisco, CA: Jossey-Bass.

Romzek, B. (1985). The effects of public service recognition, job security and staff reductions on organizational involvement. *Public Administration Review, 45*(2), 282-291.

Roth, P. L. (1994). Missing data: A conceptual review for applied psychologists. *Personnel Psychology, 47,* 537-560.

Ryan, R. M., & Deci, E. L. (2000). Self-determination theory and the facilitation of intrinsic motivation, social development, and well-being. *American Psychologist, 55*(1), 68-78.

Ryan, R. M., & Connell, J. P. (1989). Perceived locus of causality and internalization. *Journal of Personality and Social Psychology, 57,* 749-761.

Ryan, R. M., & Deci, E. L. (1996). When paradigms clash: Comments on cameron and pierce's claim that rewards do not undermine intrinsic motivation. *Review of Educational Research, 66,* 33-38.

Ryan, R. M., & Deci, E. L. (2002). An overview of self-determination theory. In E. L. Deci & R. M. Ryan (Eds.), *Handbook of self-determination research* (pp. 3-33). Rochester, NY: University of Rochester Press.

Scott, P. G., & Pandey, S. K. (2005). Red tape and public service motivation. *Review of Public Personnel Administration, 25*(2), 155-180.

Sosik, J. J., Kahai, S. S., & Avolio, B. J. (1998). Transformational leadership and dimensions of creativity: Motivating idea generation in computer-mediated groups. *Creativity Research Journal, 11,* 111-121.

Tett, R. P., & Meyer, J. P. (1993). Job satisfaction, organizational commitment, turnover intention, and turnover: Path analyses based on meta-analytic findings. *Personnel Psychology, 46,* 259-293.

Walker, R. M., & Boyne, G. A. (2006). Public management reform and organizational performance: An empirical assessment of the UK labour government's public service improvement strategy. *Journal of Policy Analysis and Management, 25,* 371-394.

Wall, T. B., Michie, J., Patterson, M., Wood, S. J., Sheehan, M., Clegg, C. W., & West, M. (2004). On the validity of subjective measures of company performance. *Personnel Psychology, 57,* 95-118.

Wart, M. V. (2003). Public-sector leadership theory: An assessment. *Public Administration Review, 63,* 214-228.

Waters, L. K., Roach, D., & Waters, C. W. (1976). Estimates of future tenure, satisfaction, and biographical variables as predictors of termination. *Personnel Psychology, 29,*

57-60.

Whittington, J. L., Goodwin, V. L., & Murray, B. (2004). Transformational leadership, goal difficulty, and job design: Independent and interactive effects on employee outcomes. *The Leadership Quarterly, 15,* 593-606.

Wright, B. E. (2007). Public service and motivation: Does mission matter?. *Public Administration Review, 67*(1), 54-64.

Yaeger, S. J., Rabin, J., & Vocino, T. (1982). Professional values of public servants. *American Review of Public Administration, 14,* 4062-4412.

Yukl, G. (2002). *Leadership in organizations* (5th ed.). Englewood Cliffs, NJ: Prentice Hall.

Zacharatos, A., Barling, J., & Kelloway, E. K. (2000). Development and effects of transformational leadership in adolescents. *Leadership Quarterly, 11*(2), 211-226.

Appendix

Selected Representative Survey Items[a] (Merit Principles Survey 2000)

Not all items are presented; the actual number of items is listed in parentheses. A complete listing of items in the indices is available from the authors.

Construction of Indices

1. Leadership and Motivation Variables

Transformation Oriented Leadership (TOL) (six items) (Cronbach's Alpha = 0.935)

a. My supervisor looks out for the personal welfare of members of my work unit (Individualized Consideration).
b. My immediate supervisor encourages my career development (Individualized Consideration).
c. My immediate supervisor promotes high standards of integrity, conduct, and concern for the public interest (Idealized Influence).
d. My immediate supervisor would try to help a poor performer improve (Inspirational Motivation).
e. My supervisor keeps me informed about how well I am doing (Intellectual Stimulation).

Transaction Oriented Leadership (TSOL) (five items) (Cronbach's Alpha = 0.770)

a. My supervisor has let the fear of being charged with discrimination adversely affect the way of work is assigned, performance is evaluated, or awards are given (Active Management by Exception).

b. My supervisor would try to remove an employee who even after coaching was not able to perform satisfactorily (Passive Management by Exception).

c. My supervisor retains employees only on the basis of their job performance (Contingent Reward Management).

Public Service Oriented Motivation (PSOM) as a Motivator (six items) (Cronbach's Alpha = 0.775)

a. I am most motivated to do a good job by my duty as a public employee (Normbased Motives).

b. I am most motivated to do a good job by personal pride or satisfaction in my work (Affective Motives).

c. If I perform better in the job, I will receive a non-pay reward (Intrinsic Rewards).

Extrinsically Oriented Motivation (EOM) as a Hygiene Factor (five items) (Cronbach's Alpha = 0.712)

a. I am most motivated to do a good job by monetary reward (Extrinsic Rewards).

b. I am most motivated to do a good job by increasing my chances for a promotion (Self-interest Motives).

c. I am most motivated to do a good job by good working environment overall (Self-interest Motives).

2. Mediating and Moderating Variables

Team and Employee Empowerment (seven items) (Cronbach's Alpha = 0.812)

a. At the place I work, my opinions seem to count.

b. A spirit of cooperation and teamwork exists in my work unit.

c. Employees participate in developing long-range plans in my work unit.

Procedural Equity Perceptions (six items) (Cronbach's Alpha = 0.845)

In the past 2 years, to what extent do you believe you have been treated fairly regarding the following?

a. Promotions

b. Awards

c. Training

d. Annual performance appraisals

e. Discipline

f. Job Assignment

Goal Clarity (two items) (Cronbach's Alpha = 0.716)

a. Employees participate in developing long-range plans in my work unit (Goal Intensity).
b. My performance standards are clearly linked to my organization's goals and objectives (Goal Clarity).

Objective Performance Appraisal Systems (four items) (Cronbach's Alpha = 0.816)

a. Recognition and rewards are based on merit in my work unit (Judgmental Focuses).
b. The performance appraisal rating system has helped increase communications about my job between my supervisor and me (Developmental Purposes).

Effects of Downsizing (RIF) (two items) (Cronbach's Alpha = 0.785)

a. Downsizing has seriously eroded the institutional memory or knowledge in my work unit.
b. Downsizing has helped make my work unit more efficiently (reversed).

Reliance on Contingent Personnel (two items) (Cronbach's Alpha = 0.705)

a. Does your work unit rely on following types of contingent employees to get the work done?
   - Temporary/Term-limited employees; Contract employees

Managerial Flexibility (three items) (Cronbach's Alpha = 0.725)

a. In the past 2 years, I have been given more flexibility in how I accomplish my work.
b. Since 1993, I have been gained additional flexibilities in taking personal actions (supervisors only).

3. Outcome Variables

Job Satisfaction (six items) (Cronbach's Alpha = 0.779)

a. I am satisfied with the recognition I receive for my work.
b. In general, I am satisfied with my job.
c. Overall, I am satisfied with managers above my immediate supervisor.

Performance: 10 Point Scale (three items) (Cronbach's Alpha = 0.769)

a. On a 10-point scale, how would you rate the overall productivity of yourself?
b. On a 10-point scale, how would you rate the overall productivity of your work unit?
c. On a 10-point scale, how would you rate the overall productivity of your organization?

Quality of Work (four items) (Cronbach's Alpha = 0.773)

a. Overall, how would you rate the quality of work performed by yourself?
b. Overall, how would you rate the quality of work performed by your work unit?

Turnover Intentions (five items) (Cronbach's Alpha = 0.758)

If you plan to look for another job in the coming year, how important is each of the following as a reason for your decision?

a. I plan to retire or look for another job because of job stress (your work).
b. I plan to retire or look for another job because of desire to increase opportunities for advancement (advancement=recognition).
c. I plan to retire or look for another job because of unsatisfactory benefits (compensation=benefits).
d. I plan to retire or look for another job because of problems with customers, high-level supervisors, coworkers, and immediate supervisors (working relationships).
e. I plan to retire or look for another job because of health problems (personal).

[a] All Cronbach's scores are standardized based on the standardized items.

Chapter 6

Toward the Trusted Public Organization

: Untangling the Leadership, Motivation, and Trust Relationship in U.S. Federal Agencies

Summary

The purpose of this study is to probe the main determinants of organizational trust, as identified in the relevant literature: cognition-based (i.e., rational) trust and affect-based (i.e., relational) trust. This study explores the nature of trust among public employees and identifies important antecedents and moderating conditions based on systematic and rigorous empirical research. Using large data sets from Merit Principles Survey (MPS) and Best Places to Work (BPTW), as well as drawing upon the scholarly works from several disciplines, this study develops an antecedent-trust model and analyzes the different types of antecedents of organizational trust in the public sector at a hierarchical and multilevel ordering structure. The focus of the study is empirically testing the effects of vertical and shared leadership behaviors and work motivation attributes on organizational trust within U.S. federal agencies. In addition, the moderating impact of leadership on the relationship between work motivation and organizational trust is examined. This research finds that some of these predictors and moderators (e.g., vertical and shared leadership behaviors) play significant roles in fostering organizational trust directly and indirectly. Based on a discussion of the main findings, research and practical implications for public management theory and practice are provided.

Keyword

- □ Cognitive and Affective Trust
- □ Vertical and Shared Leadership
- □ Intrinsic and Extrinsic Motivation
- □ Public Human Resource Management
- □ U.S. Federal Agencies

Sung Min Park Associate Professor, Sungkyunkwan University

Introduction

Public management reform initiatives usually focus on macro- and institutional-level changes heralded by new programs, policies, and systems. Yet these initiatives tend to ignore the fact that these reforms might not succeed without recruiting, nurturing, and retaining excellent employees and organizational leaders, key assets of public organizations. Public managers who shape reliable interpersonal working relationships built on trust are the microlevel-change levers—the necessary precondition to ensuring effective and accountable government (Newell, Reeher, & Ronayne, 2008). Especially during the New Public Management (NPM) and the Public Management Agenda (PMA) reform period, U.S. federal agencies have undergone substantial organizational changes due to decentralization, privatization, and atomization. These changes are designed to increase flexibility and discretion, as reformers believed that NPM reform drivers would transform public organizations to be more accountable, reliable, and effective. These public management reform movements have moved far beyond the traditional personnel systems (e.g., abolishing the traditional merit system and adopting an at-will employment system), while pursuing more advanced public-private hybrid policies (e.g., public-private partnership initiatives) as well as valuing economic rationality based on rational choice theory and principal–agent approach in operationalizing different types of managerial functions (Park, 2010). Apparently, these reforms can cause a perception of uncertainty and vulnerability among public employees, which might affect work attitudes, dispositions, and behaviors and, hence, influence organizational outcomes in significant ways.

Organizational and managerial trust in the public sector has long been recognized as a principal goal, as well as a necessary strategic means, of effective and productive public sector management (Battaglio & Condrey, 2009; Choudhury, 2008). From a public human resources management and human relations perspectives, interpersonal trust in management is one of the core values in socialpsychological relationships occurring at the lateral and hierarchical levels in the organization. It is also believed that a climate with a high level of trust in an organization is often associated with greater employee loyalty to the organization, enhanced public service motivation, better customer service, higher quality of work, and increased efficiency and effectiveness (Rainey & Steinbauer, 1999). A culture of distrust, on the other hand, promotes secrecy and increases turnover rates and work conflicts among employees in the organization (Reece & Brandt, 1999). In public agencies, trust is increasingly being recognized as a primary factor in sustaining and developing interpersonal relationships and in determining organizational success, organizational stability, and the well-being of employees (Cook & Wall, 1980; Shaw, 1997; Tyler & Kramer, 1996). Especially when "there is objective uncertainty about the future," trust should be regarded as a vital mechanism to align and manage organizational culture and climate (Morris, 1995, p. 52).

Thus, it becomes imperative to explore the nature of trust among public employees as well as to identify important antecedent and moderating conditions based on systematic and rigorous empirical research (Choudhury, 2008; Ladebo, 2006).

Despite the potential importance of research on interpersonal, managerial, and organizational trust, it still remains understudied. In particular, little scholarly work has been conducted in exploring the peculiar and distinctive constructs of public organizational trust. Moreover, few studies have explained and confirmed the key roles that organizational leadership and work motivation play in fostering organizational trust in public sector settings. Whereas generic motivation theories have not yet seriously recognized the significant role of leadership, recent studies in work motivation highlight the need to better investigate the moderating role of organizational leadership in enhancing employee work-related attitudes and behaviors, such as organizational commitment, knowledge sharing, job satisfaction, and trust (see Chua, Ingram, & Morris, 2008; Van et al., 2009; Wu, Tsui, & Kinicki, 2010). For example, Paarlberg and Lavigna (2010) argue that one of the main challenges for research on work motivation is to examine how public managers might shape motivation to achieve better organizational outcomes. Drawing upon transformational leadership and public service motivation (PSM) theories, they propose that through developing specific and effective leadership skills, organizational leaders and managers might increase the power of public employees' motivation. Thus, more robust studies on leadership, motivation, and trust are necessary as leaders in the public sector seek to affect intrinsic and extrinsic motivation "through several mechanisms" (Perry & Hondeghem, 2008, p. 308).

Although trust has usually been viewed from an external-environmental or an interorganizational-social perspective, this empirical research mainly focuses on internal dimensions—organizationa-linterpersonal trust, particularly affective and cognitive trust as critical organizational outcomes in U.S. federal agencies. Given the theoretical and practical significance of organizational trust in bureaucratic theory, a set of normative and empirical research questions about trust in public agencies have previously been raised. Do federal bureaucrats trust their supervisors, managers, and their organization? How do we define and identify different types of organizational trust? What accounts for variations in the level of trust in organizations? To what extent do individual, managerial, or organizational characteristics significantly influence organizational trust in the public sector? Using federal data on a sample of 46 U.S. federal agencies and approximately 74,000 federal employees, this study proceeds with a literature review and a presentation of interrelated research hypotheses based upon theoretical models of trust, leadership, and motivation in the public sector.

This research consists of five sections. First, the study conceptualizes and operationalizes the dimensionality of two referents of organizational trust identified in the literature: cognitive based (rational) trust and affective-based (relational) trust. Second, based on different types of management and applied psychology theories, this study explores and analyzes the antecedents and moderators of organizational trust at a hierarchical and multilevel ordering structure in the federal bureaucracy: work motivation attributes and vertical (i.e., senior and supervisory) and shared (i.e., team- and group-based) leadership behaviors. A conceptual research framework is provided followed by a set of research hypotheses (see Figure 1). This study also controls for demographic and job characteristics as well as work experiences. In the third section, information on the data and the measures used in this study is provided. Fourth, using hierarchical linear modeling (HLM), this study empirically tests the effects of work motivation and organizational leadership on affective and cognitive trust across federal agencies. The moderating impact of leadership on the relationship between motivation and trust is also examined by exploring how different types of leadership affect work motivation. The last section provides a discussion of findings and concludes by drawing research implications for public management theory and practice. It is expected that the set of distinctive but interrelated theoretical lenses as well as state-of-the-art methodological applications can help to differentiate this study from already existing organizational trust scholarship.

Theoretial Frameworks

Organizational Trust in the Public Sector

Organizational trust is shaped, developed, or diminished by different types of reciprocal and social contexts, such as information exchange, interpersonal communications, social interactions, and networks. Social exchange and network theorists focus especially on the patterns of relational influence structure and the relationship as the unit of analysis (Mehra, Dixon, Brass, & Robertson, 2006).[1] Trust exists in an interpersonal, group, or interorganizational relationship when an individual or a party (trustor) sufficiently believes in the integrity or character of the other party (target) and when the employees feel confident that "when faced with an uncertainty or risky situation, the organization's words and behaviors are consistent, and are meant to be helpful" (Matthai, 1989, p. 29). Researchers from different disciplines have defined, assessed, and categorized organizational trust using various concepts and definitions. For example, Robinson (1996) sees trust as embodied in "one's expectations, assumptions or beliefs about the likelihood that another's future actions will be beneficial, favorable, or at least not detrimental to one's interests" (p. 576). Mishra (1996) defines trust as "one party's willingness to be vulnerable to another party based on the belief that the latter party is a) competent, b) open, c) concerned, and d) reliable" (p. 265). Kramer (1996) finds that "the importance of trust and the problems that attend it derive at least partially from the reciprocal vulnerabilities and uncertainties that

Figure 1. A Conceptual Model for the Antecedents-Trust Model

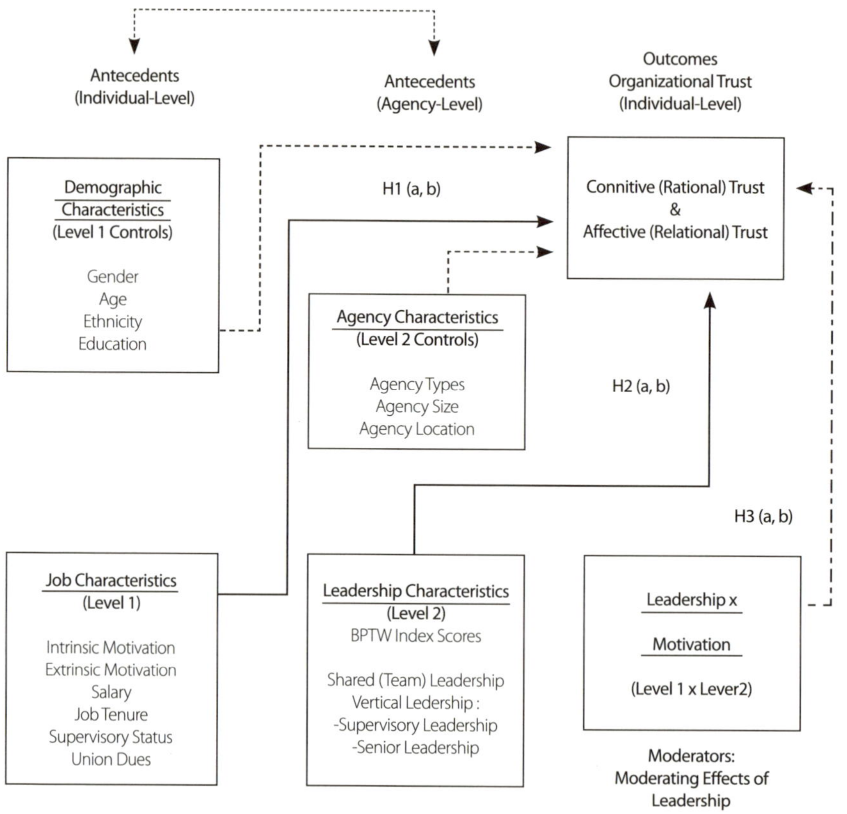

Note: - - - - - Denotes interaction effects; ——— denotes direct effects; .... denotes control effects; and ⇣⇣ denotes nested hierarchical organizational structures.

are inherent in hierarchical relationships" (p. 217). In general, trust represents the level of confidence one has in another to act in a fair, ethical, and predictable manner (Luhmann, 1979), pertaining to "whether or not one individual is able to value what another is up to and demonstrate respect for him or her particularly when the individual's need and those of the person taking the action momentarily compete" (Culbert & McDonough, 1986, p. 175).

In public organizations, evidently most of these social relationships are contingent upon bureaucratic structures, processes, and cultures. "The trust-based paradigm" in the public sector can be supported and harnessed by supportive and effective leadership behaviors, public service-oriented and norm-based motives, unbiased organizational incentive and compensation systems, or streamlined hierarchical and lateral communications and transactions among employees, managers, and supervisors as reported in this research. The trust-based model recommends a change from organizational theories and practice, founded on ensuring control by supervisors over workers, to a new paradigm based on cooperative and communicative working relationships among all employees (Nyhan, 2000). With an emphasis on the reduced need for control, compliance, or obedience in the trusted organization model, it is expected that public employees acknowledge the importance of these organizational values, systems, and practices to reach a higher level of organizational trustworthiness.

Cognition-Based and Affect-Based Trust

A variety of organizational researchers have suggested that trust in organizations is obviously multidimensional, having separate components and constructs (see Johnson & Grayson, 2005; Webber & Klimoski, 2004). For example, Fox (1974) divides organizational trust into interpersonal and institutional trust based on the referents and nature of trust. Although interpersonal trust, which is nurtured by mutual contacts among employees, focuses on a person or a group of people, an organizational entity is the main object of institutional trust, which is assumed to be developed by an organizational culture or through system management (McCauley & Kuhnert, 1992). Especially from sociopsychological and microperspectives, a single important distinction of organizational trust lies in the dichotomy of cognitive versus affective trust. Organizational research on trust values has been defined in affective terms, giving more attention to the role of emotions, internal and normative motives, psychological attachment, and feelings; however, there is also strong evidence that trust can be premised on job-related cognition and rationality (e.g., McAllister, 1995; Weiss, 2002). Cognition-based trust refers to knowledge-based trust grounded in sharing rational and cognitive processes, which provide a basis for understanding the intentions and attitudes of a colleague and for predicting that person's actions and behaviors. This type of trust involves "a calculative and instrumental assessment" based on some criterion of personal evaluation and rational calculation—the assurance that evidence of the other's predictability, competence, information, and reliability under specific circumstances really matters (Atkinson & Butcher, 2003, p. 294; Chua et al., 2008, p. 436). When employees recognize and understand other participants well enough on the basis of shared expectations and cognitions, the level of cognition-based trust will be enhanced. By contrast, affect-based trust is founded on the emotional and psychological attachment to colleagues or organization. Affective trust, which usually involves "empathy, rapport, and self-disclosure processes," can be pronounced, especially when managers and supervisors show a genuine concern for the welfare of employees, commit to intrinsic values, and believe in reciprocal virtue of such relationships (Chua et al., 2008, p. 436). Affect-based trust, hence, can be developed through an emotional, relational, and social identification process within an organization, thereby strengthening employees' cohesiveness and attachment to the organization. Due to these characteristics, affective trust tends to be more intensive, more sustainable, and more generalizable over various situations than is cognition-based trust (Lewicki & Bunker, 1996). Drawing on the previous theoretical and empirical evidence, this study categorizes organizational trust behaviors in the public sector as cognitive-rational trust and affective-relational trust.

Antecedents of Organizational Trust in Public Organizations

As many organizational researchers have suggested, organizational attitudes and perceptions are generated by different types of individual attributes, job characteristics, work experiences, and environments (Hackman & Oldham, 1975, 1976; Moynihan & Pandey, 2007; Perry & Porter, 1982). In the same vein, according to social exchange theory, organizational trust is developed, transformed, diminished, or enhanced by work context and organizational climate. Trust is a differentiated attitude toward different objects of the bureaucracy. Luhmann (1979) suggests that attitudes of trust vary within organizations depending on structural relationships, and an individual's degree of trust varies between supervisors, managers, and the organization as a whole. Considering the typical hierarchical structures of public sector agencies, it is necessary to observe employees' trust perceptions from different personal, bureaucratic, and institutional levels because building trust requires a strategy to find important factors that positively or negatively affect the level of trust within an organization.

It is anticipated that the more employees perceive their job characteristics and work environments positively, the more the employees will tend to trust their supervisors, management, and the organization. This research presents a conceptual framework of a public sector trust model (see Figure 1), identifying different public sector influences on two types of organizational trust, based on the recent scholarly works from several disciplines (see Cardon, Wincent, Singh, & Drnovsek, 2009; De Jong & Elfring, 2010; Dutton, Roberts, & Bednar, 2010; Johnson, Chang, & Yang, 2010; Livengood & Reger, 2010; Puranam & Vanneste, 2009; Van Kleef et al., 2009; Wilson, Sin, & Conlon, 2010; Wong & Boh, 2010; Zhang & Bartol, 2010). Furthermore, drawing upon Hackman and Oldham's (1975) job characteristics model and Perry and Porter's (1982) motivational bases of behavior typology, this study proposes three major categories of predictors while controlling for several critical factors to exclude alternate explanations of organizational trust: (a) demographic characteristics, (b) job characteristics, and (c) organizational characteristics. Specifically, throughout the study, research hypotheses proposed are framed in terms of how cognitive and affective trust attitudes in federal agencies are directly, indirectly, and interactively associated with an individual's work motivation, including intrinsic and extrinsic motivation attributes, and organizational leadership, including vertical and shared leadership characteristics.

Work Motivation Attributes: Intrinsic and Extrinsic Motivation

Most organizational theorists regard motivation and values as separate concepts. Values refer to "conceptions of desirable end-states," whereas motivation refers to "the arousal and direction of effort." Hence, "to have a value is not the same as exerting effort to fulfill it" (Rainey, Koehler, & Jung, 2008, p. 10). People not only have different levels of motivation but also have varied types (or orientation) of motivation because motivation is a multidimensional concept (Ryan & Deci, 2000a-b; Vandenabeele, 2007). The distinction between intrinsic and extrinsic motivation has been popularly introduced in academic disciplines to probe for discrete antecedents or consequences of the two motivations in social psychological processes.[2] The logic of dichotomizing work motivation in the public sector into two separate continua draws on Herzberg's two-factor theory of work motivation (Herzberg, Mausner, & Snyderman, 1959), which suggests that work motivation contains two separate and independent dimensions, which can be called hygiene factors (dissatisfiers) and intrinsic factors (motivators). The hygiene factors as the job context factors, including extrinsic incentives or rewards, indicate issues that give external effects to the job. These factors cause dissatisfaction when they are not present, but because they are external, they are not positively strong enough to motivate employees even when they are present. On the other hand, the intrinsic factor dimensions, the motivators, address values of intrinsic rewards to employees in organizations, for example, recognition or affective and normative motivators. Motivators can strongly and positively motivate employees because of their association with the need for self-actualization, the ultimate intrinsic drive (Tietjen & Myers, 1998). Although hygiene factors can only prevent dissatisfaction, motivators should be critical factors to enhance organizational outcomes (Park & Rainey, 2007; Rainey, 2009; Word & Park, 2009). Based on these theoretical similarities, intrinsic incentives are hypothesized to function as motivators, whereas extrinsic incentives function as hygiene factors in this study.

Motivation-hygiene theory suggests that intrinsically or internally motivated employees are more willing to recognize the social values of streamlined communications, high standards of integrity, equitable treatment, and psychological attachment and, hence, that they are more likely to affectively trust organizational constituents. On the other hand, cognition-based and extrinsically oriented employees are more prone to value and rationally trust specified work conditions, clear formal rules and expectations, and reliable extrinsic reward-based pay, assessment, and feedback systems (Herzberg et al., 1959). In sum, the motivation-hygiene lens implies that two types of trust are differentially related to specific antecedents, such as intrinsic and extrinsic incentives and motivations. For example, many organizational trust researchers empirically revealed that cognitive trust that is calculative and instrumental is significantly related to economic incentives and actions (e.g., financial resources, economic transactions), whereas economic ties have a negative relationship with affective and emotional trust (see Axelrod, 1984; Chua et al., 2008; Hite, 2005; Ingram & Roberts, 2000). Some research has also found that whereas friendship ties, which embrace the values of mutual care and concern, interpersonal and affective attraction, and altruistic behaviors, are likely to develop employees' affect-based trust, task- and resource-oriented ties such as rational information, technical guidance, and monetary rewards are closely related to cognitive trust (see Brass, 1992; Chua et al., 2008; Holste & Fields, 2010). Based on the theoretical and empirical evidence aforementioned, it can be inferred that intrinsic motivators should relate to socioemotional and psychological attributes such as affective-relational trust, whereas extrinsic and monetary hygiene factors should involve rational, calculative, and cognitive behaviors, for example, cognitive-rational trust. First, this study predicts that if public employees positively perceive either of these incentives, they tend to have a higher level of organizational trust in their agencies; that is, while hypothesizing that both types of intrinsic and extrinsic motivation are significantly associated with cognitive and affective trust, this study also predicts that intrinsically motivated employees will trust more affective factors than cognitive ones, whereas extrinsically motivated federal workers will perceive cognition-based factors more positively than affective ones.

Hypothesis 1a: In federal agencies, intrinsic motivation will be positively related to organizational trust. Intrinsic motivation will be more significantly associated with affective trust than cognitive trust.

Hypothesis 1b: In federal agencies, extrinsic motivation will be positively related to organizational trust. Extrinsic motivation will be more significantly associated with cognitive trust than affective trust.

Organizational Leadership: Vertical and Shared Leadership in the Public Sector

Leadership refers to the ability to "influence processes involving determination of the group's or organization's objectives, motivating task behavior in pursuit of these objectives, and influencing group maintenance and culture" (Yukl, 1989, p. 5). Leadership in the public sector is an important aspect of the work environment for employees (e.g., Oldham & Cummings, 1996; Scott & Bruce, 1994). Leadership behaviors are established from both "psychological processes and group dynamics" and "macro-level institutional arrangements" (Rousseau, Sitkin, Burt, & Camerer, 1998, p. 393). Effective public sector leaders possess some major characteristics of value-based leadership styles, that is, directive leadership, transformational and transactional leadership, charismatic and servant leadership, and empowering and integrated leadership (see Bass, 1996; Bass & Riggio, 2006; Burns, 1978; Greenleaf, 1977; Park & Rainey, 2008; Wright & Pandey, 2010). The recent literature also demonstrates that organizational leadership can be analyzed based on a hierarchical spectrum in organizations; that is, leadership behaviors vary among different levels of management and supervisory and managerial status, for example, vertical or top-down leadership and distributed or shared team-based leadership (Pearce & Conger, 2003; Perry & Mankin, 2004).

Vertical leadership constitutes one of the traditional leadership paradigms in the hierarchical structures of public, private, and nonprofit sectors, which have focused on the concept of "leader as commander" and "formal leadership structures" with its emphasis on the relationship between the leader, followers, and the organization (Ensley, Hmieleski, & Pearce, 2006, p. 218). Vertical leadership is more evident in a top-down and bureaucratic decision-making process than in a collaborative and decentralized working environment. Immediate supervisors and senior leaders (e.g., managers and executive appointees) are regarded as principal actors in this spectrum and their visions, inspirations, and long-term values should be the powerful driving forces that create organizational culture that, in turn, promotes organizational performance and effectiveness (Ensley et al., 2006; Reinke, 2003).

Shared or distributed leadership has been defined as "a dynamic, interactive influence process among individuals in groups for which the objective is to lead one another to the achievement of group or organizational goals or both" (Pearce, Manz, & Sims, 2008, p. 354) and "a team property whereby leadership is distributed among team members rather than focused on a single designated leader" (Carson, Tesluk, & Marrone, 2007, p. 1217). The shared leadership dynamics usually empower employees and generate a participative group and team context such as collaborative and bottom-up work processes, which are evident in the team-based culture and structures where the common values of cooperation, delegation, communication, engagement, and knowledge sharing are highly recognized. The leaders in teams allow their constituents to share their dissenting opinions in a way that facilitates "the process of developing shared strategic cognition" (Ensley et al., 2006, p. 221). Those leaders are not official supervisors—they provide employees with day-to-day guidance and advice in work projects but do not usually have supervisory or managerial responsibilities or conduct employee performance evaluations (The Best Places to Work,

2005).

Many organizational researchers have reported that effective leadership yields certain positive organizational outcomes for organizational stakeholders (see Van Wart, 2005; Yukl, 2006). For example, leader–member exchange (LMX) theorists have considered organizational trust one of the core indicators reflecting the quality of the relationship between leaders and employees. Similarly, theories such as transformational leadership and charisma leadership treat organizational trust as a key attribute of successful leaders, emphasizing that trust in leadership increases employees' willingness to accept the leader's activities, goals, and decisions (Dirks, 2000). Those types of leaders have the ability to "create a shared vision, to articulate clear and meaningful goals, to empower employees, and to model ethical and trustworthy behavior" (Paarlberg & Lavigna, 2010, p. 711). These arguments suggest that trust in leaders would positively influence the overall levels of trust in people's behaviors, trust in management norms and systems, and thus, trust in institutions and cultures of the organization.

Regarding the dyadic leadership–trust relationship, especially in public agencies, both vertical and shared leadership should be leading contributors toward organizational trust in public organizations through encouraging social communications, increasing organizational support, and enhancing work motivation and commitment (Albrecht & Travaglione, 2003; Greenleaf, 1977). Senior leaders and supervisors in a hierarchy are expected to involve rational, calculative, and instrumental values with a focus on establishing and managing organizational missions, norms, and institutional goals while having authority and power over various factors such as allocation of resources and promotion. Thus, public employees would be likely to perceive their senior leaders as being more rational and cognitive, and hence, effective vertical leadership is more likely to indicate and affect cognitive organizational trust. On the basis of this rationale, we first hypothesize that vertical leadership is more positively related to rational or cognitive trust than affective or relational trust in federal agencies.

Effective shared leadership, on the other hand, is generated from the routine interactions and informal transactions among peer groups and colleagues, including official as well as unofficial team leaders and managers. Given that interdependency and collaboration is a key process to manage people effectively within a team- and group-based culture, shared leadership could enhance organizational trust by facilitating information sharing/distribution (Zand, 1972) and by aligning individual motivation to interpersonal and collective behaviors (Dirks, 1999). Thus, this research expects that shared leadership entails emotional, affective, and social interactive influence processes within teams or groups, rather than involving cognitive or rational processes, and predicts that trust among employees guided by shared leadership in organizations is likely to be more imperative, reciprocal, and affective (Pearce, 2004). Drawing upon this rationale, we also posit that effective shared leadership will be more positively related to affective organizational trust than cognitive organizational trust.

> **Hypothesis 2a:** In federal agencies, effective vertical leadership will be positively related to organizational trust. Vertical leadership will be more strongly associated with cognitive trust than affective trust.
>
> **Hypothesis 2b:** In federal agencies, effective shared leadership will be positively related to organizational trust. Shared leadership will be more strongly associated with affective trust than cognitive trust.

Moderating Effects of Organizational Leadership on Trust

A great deal of research has been done over the years regarding the association and the interaction between organizational leadership and work motivation (e.g., Kennedy & Anderson, 2002; Moynihan, Pandey, & Wright, 2009; Park & Rainey, 2008). For example, Park and Rainey found that the interaction between transformation-oriented leadership and intrinsic motivation (i.e., public service-oriented motivation) in federal agencies enhances positive outcomes (e.g., perceived performance). The empirical results support the hypothetical argument that specific types of effective leadership are imperative in motivating employees and sustaining that motivation by providing significant moderating impacts on organizational consequences; that is, leaders in public organizations "influence public service motivation (PSM) through several mechanisms, including employees' existing values, infusing jobs with meaning, and highlighting and rewarding public service values" (Moynihan et al., 2009, p. 3).

Self-determination theory (SDT), developed by Deci and Ryan (1985, 2004), illustrates a wellspecified theoretical framework for explaining the interaction between organizational leadership behaviors and individual motivation.[3] SDT suggests that certain types of social or organizational conditions and environments crowd in intrinsic motivation as well as facilitate the internalization process of extrinsic motivation. For example, effective leadership behaviors as key moderators are expected to enhance the effects of intrinsic motivation on organizational outcomes. When public employees are intrinsically motivated, the interactions between intrinsic motivation and organizational leadership will bring about interactive moderating impacts and, hence, will significantly affect organizational trust. In a similar vein, leadership as a critical external factor would develop nonautonomous extrinsic motivation into more autonomous types of extrinsic motivation whose characteristics are similar to intrinsic motivation. Hence, we can still expect that moderating impacts between extrinsic motivation and organizational trust could occur. Drawing on the SDT framework, this study posits that organizational leadership—that is, both vertical and shared leadership—positively moderate the relationships between intrinsic and extrinsic motivation and organizational trust in federal agencies. With higher levels of effective vertical and shared leadership behaviors, the relationship between the two types of motivation and organizational trust is much stronger.

> **Hypothesis 3a:** In federal agencies, vertical and shared leadership will moderate the impact of intrinsic motivation on cognitive and affective trust—with high levels of effective vertical and shared leadership, the relationship between intrinsic motivation and organizational trust would be greater.
> **Hypothesis 3b:** In federal agencies, shared leadership will moderate the impact of extrinsic motivation on cognitive and affective trust—with high levels of effective vertical and shared leadership, the relationship between extrinsic motivation and organizational trust would be greater.

Research Modeling: Hierarchical Linear Model

Federal employees are nested within federal agencies, creating a hierarchical data structure with two levels of random variation: variation among employees within federal agencies (Level 1) and variation among federal agencies (Level 2). As personal attributes, the variables of employees' work motivation and trust are included at Level 1. Based on the assertion that leadership is a group quality where functions and interactions are carried out by a group or organization (see Carson et al., 2007; Holtz & Harold, 2008), not to mention that leadership behaviors are grounded in social exchange (see Blau, 1964), vertical and shared leadership variables are analyzed at Level 2. In the analysis, Level 2 variables were aggregated into agency-based scores. The HLM explicitly explains the nested nature of data and can simultaneously estimate the impact of factors at different levels on individual-level outcomes while maintaining appropriate levels of analysis for predictors (Raudenbush, Bryk, Cheong, & Congdon, 2000). Since the ordinary least squares (OLS) method does not take into account the interdependence of individual-level observations nested within higher-level (i.e., agencylevel) federal agencies, estimates of standard errors may be biased and test statistics may not be valid. To avoid these potential problems caused by hierarchically nested data structures, the ANCOVA and the intercepts- and slopes-as-outcomes models were estimated in this research.

Data and Measures

Data Sources and Sample

This study utilizes two different levels of data sources to operationalize individual (federal employees) at Level 1 and organizational (federal agencies) characteristics at Level 2: the U.S. Merit Systems Protection Board's (MSPB) Merit Principles Survey (U.S. Merit Systems Protection Board, 2005) for individual-level characteristics (e.g., work motivation and cognitive and affective trust) and the Best Places to Work (BPTW) index scores (2005) in the federal government for organization (agency)-level variables (e.g., organizational leadership factors and agency controls). The MSPB used a stratified random sample design to identify and cluster survey respondents—stratifying the sample according to management status and 59 subagency units. A total of 36,926 federal employees completed the survey (a representative sample of the 1.8 million full-time permanent members of the federal workforce) about their attitudes toward their jobs, agencies, and work motivations, rendering a response rate of approximately 50%. The sample of 46 agencies was analyzed, and participants included members of the Senior Executive Service (SES), managers, first-line supervisors, and employees with no supervisory duties.

The BPTW data are the most comprehensive and authoritative rating and analysis of federal employee engagement, commitment, and satisfaction. The data are based on the Federal Human Capital Survey (FHCS), which has been administered by the Office of Personnel Management (OPM) biennially since 2002 (the 2005 rankings were calculated by the FHCS 2004 data, which are composed of the responses of more than 263,000 federal employees). The Partnership for Public Service and the Institute for the Study of Public Policy Implementation developed a statistical model to transform this raw survey data into specific measures of agency-level variables, that is, the Level 2 indicators such as shared and vertical leadership. The unit of analysis is based on the 269 federal agencies, including 32 large agencies and 34 small agencies and their 203 subcomponents (46 federal agencies are included in this study). Agencies and subcomponents are weighted and ranked on an index score of overall employee engagement and satisfaction. In addition, agencies and subcomponents are also scored in 10 workplace environment ("best in class") categories, such as effective leadership, teamwork, strategic management, performance culture, training and development, diversity management, employee skills–mission match, and work–life balance (Best Places to Work, 2005).

For missing data, rather than using the listwise deletion method, this study preserves sample size by employing the expectation-maximization (EM) algorithm method.[4] The survey respondents represented 46 different federal agencies, and we referred to the BPTW agency scores for the Level 2 variables. Each agency was well represented by a number of respondents, with no serious unevenness (i.e., no serious problematic values for skewness or kurtosis) in responses from different agencies. (Details are available from the author.)

Measures of Organizational Trust

First, in order to confirm the construct validity and dimensionality of two types of organizational trust constructs, we determined the subdimension clusters of questions by utilizing confirmatory factor analysis (CFA). Cognitive (nine items) and affective (eight items) trust were developed and operationalized from the MPS 2005 survey instrument (see appendix). The items were measured by a 5-point Likert-type scale from 1 to 5. LISREL was used to generate and obtain factor scores for each subdimension. A second-order CFA model indicates that both of the two latent organizational constructs are significant and distinct. The results show that the factor loadings support the use of these items as indicators of the underlying organizational trust constructs. To find a best-fit model, overall fit indexes and modification indexes (MI) were used. The model of fit statistics was within acceptable levels, and this proposed CFA model of organizational trust is an excellent fit to the data, supporting the face and construct validity of the model. (Details are available from the author.)[5]

Measures of Individual-Level (Level 1) Predictors

Two types of work motivation as main individual-level predictors were included in this study. Motivation variables were measured on a 5-point Likert-type scale in response to specific statements. Respondents were asked to indicate the degree to which the items listed were important in motivating them to do a good job. Sample items included, "Recognition from my coworkers," "My duty as a public employee," "A cash award of US$1,000," or "Desire for a good performance rating." The CFA analysis captures two dimensions of work motivation identified by Ryan and Deci (2000a, 2000b): intrinsic and extrinsic motivation. Based on the CFA, work motivation scales were developed from relevant survey items (see appendix). The results of the CFA indicate that the factor loadings support the use of these items as indicators of the underlying motivational constructs.[6] In addition, eight control variables, such as gender, age, ethnicity, educational level, and union dues, are included as demographic controls at the individual level.

Measures of Agency-Level (Level 2) Predictors

Since a preliminary analysis shows that there is a significant amount of variance in individual characteristics (e.g., intrinsic and extrinsic motivation) among federal agencies, 46 large federal agencies are included as the main unit of analysis at Level 2. Drawing upon the shared vertical leadership behavior continuum, three types of organizational leadership factors, designated as Level 2 predictors in this study, are measured by the BPTW (2005) composite index scores: (1) shared leadership (team managers), (2) supervisory leadership (first-line supervisors), and (3) senior leadership (members of the SES or equivalent; see appendix).[7] Also, agency dummy variables (the Department of Education was left out of the model as a reference group), agency size (large, small, and subcomponents), and agency location (headquarters/field) were added to the model as agency-level controls.

Measures of Moderating Effects (Level 1× Level 2 Predictors)

In order to confirm the interactive moderating effects of shared and vertical leadership (Level 2) on the relationship between motivation and trust variables (Level 1), we measured six interaction terms (i.e., cross-level interaction effects among motivation and leadership in federal agencies), with an expectation that adding interaction variables enables us to incorporate the joint and multiplicative effects of each of the main predictors on outcome variables in this empirical model. The appendix contains the list of questions associated with each scale variable. Table 1 also provides the descriptive statistics of all the variables used in the present study.

Findings and Results

Because federal employees are partially clustered or nested within their leaders and organizations, this study employed the ANCOVA and the intercepts- and slopes-as-outcomes models, which can provide a unique intercept and slope estimate for each federal agency.

The Level 1 (Manager-Level) Model : One-Way ANCOVA Model with Random Effects

In an employee (individual)-level model, a one-way ANCOVA model was employed to incorporate several covariates and to see how these Level 1 predictors would affect outcome variables, cognitive and affective trust.[8] As fixed effects, 10 (including 8 demographic and job characteristics and 2 motivation attributes) covariates were included: (1) gender ($\gamma 10$), (2) age ($\gamma 20$), (3) ethnicity ($\gamma 30$), (4) educational level ($\gamma 40$), (5) salary ($\gamma 50$), (6) job tenure in current position ($\gamma 60$), (7) supervisory status ($\gamma 70$), (8) union dues ($\gamma 80$), (9) intrinsic motivation ($\gamma 90$), and (10) extrinsic motivation ($\gamma 10$). As random effects, Level 1 and Level 2 variances were included.[9] The final Level 1 ANCOVA model is as follows:

Level 1 Model: Yij (Cognitive trust, affective trust) = β0j + β1j (gender) + β2j (age) + β3j (ethnicity) + β4j (educational level) + β5j (salary) + β6j (job tenure) + β7j (supervisory status) + β8j (union dues) + β9j (intrinsic motivation) + β10j (extrinsic motivation) + εij

Table 1. Descriptive Statistics Among Study Variables

Variables	Valid N	M	SD	Minimum	Maximum
Level 1 variables					
Gender (1: male; 2: female)	36,409	1.44	.49	1	2
Age	35,799	48.58	9.21	20	80
Ethnicity (1: minority, 2: White)	36,926	1.66	0.52	1	2
Educational level	36,926	2.67	1.29	1	6
Salary (natural log; in thousands of US$)	35,953	70.23	40.46	0	991
Job tenure: Years with current federal agency (natural log)	36,718	14.58	9.84	0	57
Supervisory status (0: nonsupervisor; 1: supervisor; natural log)	36,926	0.13	0.36	0	1
Union membership dues (1: a member of a union)	36,615	0.17	0.38	0	1
Intrinsic motivation	36,199	3.74	0.64	1	5
Extrinsic motivation	36,035	3.52	0.51	1	5
Level 2 variables					
Shared leadership	46	70.82	4.94	58.50	90.40
Vertical leadership (supervisory leadership)	46	51.52	6.62	25.70	71.00
Vertical leadership (senior leadership)	46	49.45	6.11	22.13	65.99
Agency size	46	16378.33	52134.68	30	611658
Agency location (1: headquarters, 2: field)	46	1.82	0.38	1	2
Outcome variables					
Cognitive trust	36,274	2.32	1.03	1	5
Affective trust	36,410	2.18	1.02	1	5

Note: The expectation-maximization and the Markov Chain Monte Carlo methods were used to deal with missing data at Level 1 and Level 2.

Hypotheses Testing: The Fixed and Random Effects

To test Hypotheses 1a and 1b, we regressed cognitive and affective trust on two types of work motivation attributes, together with eight control variables. First, this study revealed that intrinsic motivation is shown as the most significant predictor of affective trust, such that federal employees' intrinsic motivation is more positively associated with affective trust ($\gamma = .432$, $p < .05$) than cognitive trust ($\gamma = .191$, $p < .05$). Extrinsic motivation, on the other hand, has a more statistically significant relationship with cognitive trust than affective trust ($\gamma = .218$, $p < .05$; $\gamma = .133$, $p < .05$, respectively). The results support the interpretation that intrinsic motivators and hygiene factors are differently related to other outcomes, as Herzberg's two-factory theory suggested. In addition, to test the coefficient difference between intrinsic and extrinsic motivation on organizational trust, this study used an independent sample t-test method by dividing the sample on the basis of the two groups—intrinsic motivation (Group 1) and extrinsic motivation (Group 2). The result of the test showed that the impacts of intrinsic motivation and extrinsic motivation on cognitive and affective trust are statistically different, and the difference is significant overall.

The Level 2 (Agency-Level) Model : Intercepts- and Slopes-as-Outcomes Model

An intercepts- and slopes-as-outcomes (agency-level) model, which assumes that the intercept and slope have random effects, was used.[10] In Step 1, the variables of agency types, agency size, and agency location are included as agency controls. In Step 2, as leadership predictors (at Level 2), the three fixed effects are included: (1) senior leadership ($\gamma04$), (2) supervisory leadership ($\gamma05$), and (3) shared leadership ($\gamma06$). As random effects, Level 1 and Level 2 variances were included. In Step 3, to examine the cross-level interaction effects between work motivation and organizational leadership, six interaction terms were included.[11] We analyzed the effects of interaction terms—the moderating effects of organizational leadership (vertical and shared leadership) on the relationships between work motivation (i.e., intrinsic and extrinsic motivation) and organizational trust (i.e., cognitive and affective trust) variables in federal agencies. Below is the final intercepts- and slopes-as-outcomes model:

Level 2 Model: Intercept: $\beta0 = \gamma00 + \gamma01$ (agency types) + $\gamma02$ (agency size) + $\gamma03$ (agency location) + $\gamma04$ (senior leadership) + $\gamma05$ (supervisory leadership) + $\gamma06$ (shared leadership) + $u0j$

Slope 1: $\beta9j$ (intrinsic motivation) = $\gamma90 + \gamma91$ (agency types) + $\gamma92$ (agency size) + $\gamma93$ (agency location) + $\gamma94$ (senior leadership) + $\gamma95$ (supervisory leadership) + $\gamma96$ (shared leadership) + $u0j$

Slope 2: $\beta9j$ (extrinsic motivation) = $\gamma91 + \gamma92$ (agency types) +

$\gamma 93$ (agency size) + $\gamma 94$ (agency location) + $\gamma 95$ (senior leadership) + $\gamma 96$ (supervisory leadership) + $\gamma 97$ + (shared leadership) + $u0j$

Other slopes: $\beta 1j = \gamma 10$, $\beta 2j = \gamma 20$, $\beta 3j = \gamma 30$, $\beta 4j = \gamma 40$, $\beta 5j = \gamma 50$, $\beta 6j = \gamma 60$, $\beta 7j = \gamma 70$, $\beta 8j = \gamma 80$

Hypotheses Testing: The Fixed and Random Effects

In terms of the Level 2 fixed effects, Level 2 predictors explain well the variation in the grand mean of outcome variables, $\beta 0j$. These Level 2 slope coefficients are the expected change in the outcomes for a one-unit increase in the Level 2 covariates. To test Hypotheses 2a and 2b, which probe the relationship between leadership and trust in federal agencies, we regressed cognitive and affective trust on three types of public sector leadership, together with a set of Level 1 predictors. First, the findings indicate that effective vertical leadership (operationalized by senior and supervisory leadership traits) is significantly and positively associated with both types of organizational trust; for example, effective senior leadership increases the mean levels of cognitive and affective trust (i.e., grand mean of the outcome variables) by .415 and .312, respectively. Furthermore, as hypothesized, this study found that vertical leadership is more strongly associated with cognitive trust than affective trust. Second, the HLM results also confirm that effective shared leadership significantly and positively affects organizational trust—shared leaders are more likely to boost the level of affective trust ($\gamma = .541$, $p < .05$) than cognitive trust ($\gamma = .213$, $p < .05$). These findings suggest that cognition-based trust of federal employees is more actively managed and sustained by hierarchical and focused leadership behaviors, whereas affect-based trust is more influenced by relational, interpersonal, and distributed leadership in federal agencies. The overall results fully supported Hypotheses 2a and 2b.

This study further tested Hypotheses 3a and 3b, which predict the cross-level interaction effects between organizational leadership and work motivation (i.e., the moderating effects of leadership in federal agencies), where the association between Level 1 motivation attributes and the trust outcome variables depends on the effects of Level 2 leadership predictors. The results indicate that, first, the positive relationships between cognitive and affective trust and extrinsic motivation become more pronounced and significant when organizational leaders show effective vertical or shared leadership behaviors. This finding supports and extends previous research that has emphasized the crucial moderating roles of leadership for cultivating employees' interpersonal and institutional attitudes and behaviors in organizations (e.g., Holtz & Harold, 2008; Reinke, 2003; Wright & Pandey, 2010). Whereas federal employees' extrinsic motivation in itself is not significantly associated with affective trust, there arises a significant and positive effect on the relationship between extrinsic motivation and organizational trust only when extrinsic motivation interacts with vertical or shared leadership together, that is, fully internalized into most autonomous motivation.

Second, this study also found that with high levels of effective shared leadership, the relationship between intrinsic motivation and affective and cognitive trust is significant (see Table 2 and 3). The result suggests that intrinsic motivation that has "inherently autonomous" characteristics can be crowded in rather than crowded out through a shared leadership driving factor and that crowding accordingly provides additional positive impact on cognitive and affective trust. The overall results are in partial support of Hypotheses 3a and 3b—with higher levels of effective vertical and shared leadership, the relationship between extrinsic motivation and organizational trust is significantly enhanced. The results are also fairly consistent with the SDT prediction described earlier.

Table 2. Hierarchical Linear Model: Cognitive (Rational) Trust[a]

Cognitive (rational) trust model	1. An employee-level model: One-way ANCOVA model	2. An agency-level model: Intercepts- and slopes-asoutcomes model
Reliability intercept (β_0)	0.387	0.236
Fixed effects		
Intercept (γ00)	2.87**	2.33**
Level 1 slope (individual) model		
Demographic and job characteristics		
Gender (γ10)	0.005 (0.044)	-
Age (γ20)	0.102 (1.448)	-
Ethnicity (γ30)	0.011 (0.279)	-
Educational level (γ40)	0.001 (0.172)	-
Salary (γ50)	0.048 (1.347)	-
Job tenure (γ60)	0.172** (2.288)	-
Supervisory status (γ70)	0.163** (2.636)	-
Union dues (γ80)	0.023 (1.552)	-
Work motivation attributes		
Intrinsic motivation (IM; γ90)	0.191** (2.841)	-
Extrinsic motivation (EM; γ91)	0.218** (3.124)	-
Level 2 intercept (organizational) model		
Agency controls		
Agency types (agency dummy variables; γ01)	-	0.012 (0.024)
Agency size (γ02)	-	0.003 (0.065)

Agency location (headquarter/field; γ03)	-	0.108 (0.121)
Leadership characteristics		
Vertical leadership: Senior leadership(γ04)	-	0.415** (3.232)
Vertical leadership: Supervisory leadership (γ05)	-	0.265** (2.416)
Shared leadership: Teamwork management (γ06)	-	0.213** (2.187)
The interaction (Level 1 × Level 2) model: Leadership × Motivation		
Senior Leadership × IM (γ92)	-	0.003 (0.142)
Senior Leadership × EM (γ93)	-	0.134 (1.227)
Supervisory Leadership × IM (γ94)	-	-0.012 (–0.307)
Supervisory Leadership × EM (γ95)	-	0.188* (2.012)
Shared Leadership × IM (γ96)	-	0.237** (3.351)
Shared Leadership × EM (γ97)	-	0.192** (2.533)
Random effects		
Level 1 effect (r_{ij}) variance	0.093	0.088
Level 2 effects (μ_{0j}) variance	0.007**	0.003**
Interclass correlation (ICC)		
Conditional ICC	28.4%	25.4%
Proportion of the variance in r_{ij} explained by the model (%)	37.43%	43.58%
Proportion of the variance in μ_{0j} explained by the model (%)	25%	33.3%
Deviance	304.44	214.98
Number of parameters	2	2

Note: Critical values are 1.96 for p < .05 and 1.65 for p < .10 (*t* statistics are in parentheses).
a. (1) Individual-level, n = 22,731 federal employees; (2) Organizational level, n = 46 federal agencies.
*p < .10: significant at .10 level. **p < .05: significant at .05 level.

Table 3. Hierarchical Linear Model: Affective (Relational) Trust[a]

Affective (relational) trust model	1. An employee-level model: One-way ANCOVA model	2. An agency-level model: Intercepts- and slopes-as-outcomes model
Reliability intercept (β_0)	0.384	0.331
Fixed effects		
Intercept (γ00)	3.14**	1.33
Level 1 slope (individual) model		
Demographic and job characteristics		
Gender (γ10)	0.034 (0.944)	-

Age (γ20)	0.182* (1.987)	-
Ethnicity (γ30)	0.001 (0.091)	-
Educational level (γ40)	0.001 (0.062)	-
Salary (γ50)	0.008 (0.9812)	-
Job tenure (γ60)	0.157* (1.998)	-
Supervisory status (γ70)	0.113 (1.636)	-
Union dues (γ80)	0.123 (1.652)	-
Work motivation attributes		
Intrinsic motivation (IM; γ90)	0.432** (3.777)	-
Extrinsic motivation (EM; γ91)	0.133** (2.133)	-
Level 2 intercept (organizational) model		
Agency controls		
Agency types (agency dummy variables; γ01)	-	0.001 (0.012)
Agency size (γ02)	-	0.005 (0.044)
Agency location (headquarter/field; γ03)	-	0.101 (0.021)
Leadership characteristics		
Vertical leadership: Senior leadership(γ04)	-	0.312** (2.972)
Vertical leadership: Supervisory leadership (γ05)	-	0.198 (1.816)
Shared leadership: Teamwork management (γ06)	-	0.541** (3.658)
The interaction (Level 1 × Level 2) model: Leadership × Motivation		
Senior Leadership × IM (γ92)	-	−0.001 (0.122)
Senior Leadership × EM (γ93)	-	0.102 (0.927)
Supervisory Leadership × IM (γ94)	-	0.053 (0.878)
Supervisory Leadership × EM (γ95)	-	0.201** (2.444)
Shared Leadership × IM (γ96)	-	0.191** (2.301)
Shared Leadership × EM (γ97)	-	0.292** (3.173)
Random effects		
Level 1 effect (r_{ij}) variance	0.356	0.298
Level 2 effects (μ_{0j}) variance	0.05**	0.038**
Interclass correlation (ICC)		
Conditional ICC	27.2%	27.8%
Proportion of the variance in r_{ij} explained by the model (%)	39.33%	47.23%
Proportion of the variance in μ_{0j} explained by the model (%)	33.3%	100%
Deviance	404.11	232.48
Number of parameters	2	2

Note: Critical values are 1.96 for $p < .05$ and 1.65 for $p < .10$ (t statistics are in parentheses).
a. (1) Individual-level, n = 22,731 federal employees; (2) Organizational level, n = 46 federal agencies.
*$p < .10$: significant at .10 level. **$p < .05$: significant at .05 level.

Discussion

The present study is motivated by four main goals: (1) conceptualize and operationalize the dimensionality and the construct of organizational trust (i.e., cognitive and affective trust) identified in the key literature; (2) test empirically the relationship between individual-level (Level 1) characteristics, such as employees' intrinsic and extrinsic motivation and organizational trust, using a sample from U.S. federal agencies and HLM; (3) investigate the effects of vertical and shared leadership on organizational trust at an agency level (Level 2); and (4) assess leadership as a key moderator of the influence of work motivation on employee trust. This research demonstrates that some antecedent conditions, such as elements of motivational incentives and organizational leadership, are valuable managerial tools to nurture and enhance organizational trust in federal bureaucracy. The overall findings of the analysis suggest that there are meaningful relationships among these organizational characteristics that should be addressed as significant findings of this study.

Theoretical Implications

This study has several theoretical implications for organizational trust research. First, as noted earlier, the results of this study strongly support PSM and SDT research hypotheses that two types of federal employees' motivational constructs responding to organizational incentives, intrinsic and extrinsic motivation, are differently associated with job attitudes, such as affective and cognitive trust. Intrinsically motivated federal employees are more likely to have a high level of affective trust, whereas extrinsically motivated employees are prone to trust cognitively and rationally other organizational constituents. For future research, we need to determine whether and to what extent the association between work motivation (such as PSM or public sector motivation) and trust would vary across different referents of organizational trust (e.g., trust in immediate supervisors, managers, or trust in management systems and institutions) and to explore and identify whether and how the level of public work motivation and trust would be different based on the types of public agencies (Lowi, 1964).

Second, recent organizational research has identified four main types of organizational leadership that can stem from vertical or shared leadership: directive, transactional, transformational, and empowering (Pearce, 2004). The findings of this study confirmed that organizational leadership behavior is a critical intangible asset to public organizational members in increasing the level of trust and that both vertical and shared leadership in federal agencies are positively related to organizational trust. As hypothesized in Hypotheses

2a and 2b, vertical leadership is more strongly associated with cognitive trust than affective trust, whereas shared leadership is shown to be a more strongly positive predictor of affective trust than cognitive trust. These current findings lead to future research questions, such as (a) How can we best develop vertical or shared leadership in the public sector? (b) How can public organization leaders identify a more appropriate model of leadership for developing organizational trust or other important organizational behaviors? (c) How can public organization leaders effectively utilize both vertical and shared leadership to leverage the employees' trust in public sector organizations?

Third, the results of the cross-level interaction effects between vertical and shared leadership and intrinsic and extrinsic motivation illustrate that effective vertical and shared leadership in the public sector should be critical organizational ingredients to modify and then assimilate extrinsically oriented work motivation into forms of intrinsic (or at least forms of autonomous) or nonmonetary work preferences, which significantly increase the level of organizational trust of federal employees. For future research, there is a need to investigate the effects of other particular trust-moderating attributes, including organizational communication or social networks, on the relationship between leadership and trust.

Managerial Implications

The role of trust is crucial to government agencies. It should be noted that, first, citizens' trust in government relies in part on having an effective and accountable government. As highly efficient and accountable public agencies usually have a high level of trust among their members, leaders should develop organizational trust that can motivate their subordinates who are committed to the organizational missions and goals (Dirks & Ferrin, 2002; Newell et al., 2008); that is, interpersonal trust among organization members serves as a foundation for building trust at an organizational level, which in turn helps build public or citizens' trust. Although this research focused on investigating the issue of trust from an internal perspective—that of administrators within federal agencies—both internal trust (trust within government organizations) and external trust (citizens' trust in government and trust among nonprofit and government organizations) are critical to increasing public sector performance, efficiency, and accountability.

Second, as long as we accept that trust is an important factor influencing employee attitudes and behaviors in the workplace, we need to develop and manage trust to secure efficient and productive organizations. Agency executives, managers, and first-level supervisors should constantly develop, customize, and implement effective and acceptable managerial tactics and strategies to bolster trust through participation, empowerment, and feedback systems. Specifically, the MSPB "call to action report" (Merit Systems Protection

Board [MSPB] Report, 2010) reported that many supervisors demonstrate levels of supervisory skill "substantially lower than what is needed to effectively engage employees and manage their performance" (p. 7). The report emphasizes that supervisors and managers should "set the tone for the work relationship by meeting with each employee to become mutually acquainted with each other's goals, concerns, interests, communication preferences, and working styles," as well as "strive to continuously enhance your leadership skills and enlist the help of both your manager and your employees" (p. 13). The overall findings of this report suggest that, as trust in supervisors and managers reflects the employees' overall evaluation of managerial activities, federal agencies should keep building and securing effective supervisory leadership structures and maintaining appropriate monetary incentive systems. Supervisory and managerial accountability also needs to be strengthened. The general findings of this study underscore and confirm the report's recommendations.

Third, from a human capital perspective, human resource development (HRD) issues should be more significantly pronounced, though this has not been popularly discussed in the public sector yet;[12] that is, not many federal employees have received the training and development opportunities they need to achieve the agency's expectations and to manage their work effectively. According to the MSPB's MPS (U.S. Merit Systems Protection Board, 2007) results,

> Less than two-thirds of supervisors said that they received training prior to or during their first year as a supervisor. Of those who received training, almost half (48 percent) received one week or less. Overall, more than three-quarters of new supervisors did not receive training. (p. 89)

Federal agencies need to strategically develop and maintain more effective and comprehensive training and education programs, including technical and formal training, on-the-job learning, job rotations, and job shadowing. Similarly, team leaders and first-line supervisors could devise career development programs, specifically designed to develop leadership skills, facilitate work motivation, and strengthen commitment in their agencies. Effective and reliable mentoring and coaching systems, for example, might be a significant benefit in the process. All the HRD efforts not only can ensure better organizational effectiveness and employee performance but also, more importantly, can provide employees with humanized, democratized, and trustworthy work environments and conditions. To play a more strategic role in the functioning of the public sector organizations, managers and supervisors in agencies should let employees participate directly in strategic management, provide education and training in concepts and methods of strategic management and planning with employees, and provide employee training that is aligned with agencies' goals and strategies (Werner & DeSimone, 2009). Financial support and institutional incentives are also necessary to encourage federal agencies to adopt more state-of-the-art and effective HRD systems.

Fourth, as this study implies, different managerial and incentive practices in federal agencies should be prioritized in cultivating different types of trust (i.e., affective and cognitive trust) at different levels of authority (i.e., shared and vertical leadership) and offering incentives (intrinsic and extrinsic motivation). To gain a higher level of trust, supervisory and senior leaders need to focus on developing calculative, rational, and instrumental assessment tools and designing more cognitive compensation and appraisal systems, whereas shared or team-based leaders need to pay more attention to emotional, relational, and social identification processes in organizations. Through formal coaching activities, for example, employees can learn unit values and norms, establish working relationships, and learn how to function in their jobs. Counseling, on the other hand, helps employees deal with more personal issues such as substance abuse, stress management, family conflicts, smoking cessation, fitness, nutrition, weight management, and so on.

Future Research Directions

It is believed that government agencies usually seek to "produce goods and services of public value that maximize or foster public values and that pursuit of public values, or production of them, might have significant influences on structures, processes, and behaviors in the organizations that do so" (Rainey et al., 2008. p. 2). For example, as an individual attribute, public sector motivation (i.e., intrinsic motivation in public organizations) is usually associated with serving the public good or public interest. Hence, we can speculate that public sector motivation should be more influential and valid in nurturing organizational trust when some specific organizational values (e.g., rational and normative values), behaviors (e.g., prosocial behaviors and institutionally grounded behaviors) and cultures (e.g., group or developmental culture) in public organizations are dominant and pervasive. Further research is necessary to probe the relationship between public sector motivation, values, behaviors, and other organizational characteristics nested in public organizations.

Other relevant issues on trust also require future research. Investigating trust as a prerequisite of improved organizational performance and effectiveness is an example. Also, because employees' attitudes and behaviors might vary within federal organizations depending on structural and cultural relationships, more rigorous and systematic qualitative research is warranted on the basis of in-depth case studies or content analyses, that is, exploring and confirming current idiosyncratic characteristics, such as goals, missions, leadership, organizational culture, and information systems, and political orientation embedded in each federal agency. The importance of managing trust is not confined to the federal government. Rather, the study of trust needs to be replicated in state and local governments. Longitudinal data analyses, such as latent growth curve modeling, could also contribute to a better understanding of organizational trust, for example, whether and how the level of trust shifted during the period under study and at what period the shift occurred. Having an opportunity to observe commonalties and anomalies of specific organizational phenomena, researchers could expand their knowledge of theory and practice in the field of public human resource management.

Notes

1. For example, Blau (1964) defined social exchange as "voluntary actions of individuals that are motivated by the returns they are expected to bring from others" (p. 91). Similarly, Aryee, Budhwar, and Chen (2002) argued that "social exchange is premised on a long-term exchange of favors that precludes accounting and is based on a diffuse obligation to reciprocate" (p, 267).
2. For example, cognitive evaluation theorists have suggested that extrinsic reward systems might be detrimental to an employee's intrinsic motivation and affective commitment; those systems (e.g., a performance-pay system) might reduce and crowd out intrinsic motivations and, hence, might have a negative impact on performance (Moynihan, 2008; Paarlberg, Perry, & Hondeghem, 2008). Instead, these theorists emphasize social and moral reward systems and the power of a feeling of competence, a sense of autonomy, and an internal perceived locus of causality (see Deci & Ryan, 1985). On the other hand, in social learning (cognitive) theory, extrinsic incentives as instrumental values may play a significant and positive role in human learning, self-directiveness, and self-motivation. This approach further suggests that "human behavior is extensively regulated and adapted by its consequences" and the expectations of future outcomes of actions, that is, rewards and punishments (see Bandura, 1986, p. 228; Cameron & Pierce, 2002).
3. SDT introduced the self-determination continuum (from amotivation, to extrinsic motivation, to intrinsic motivation), which explicates the different forms of extrinsic motivation and the contextual influences that either develop or thwart "internalization and integration of the regulation for these behaviors" (Ryan & Deci, 2000b, p. 72). The continuum ranges from controlled to autonomous motivation, each of which could be differently affected by external factors such as leadership, culture, institutions, incentives, and so on.
4. Although listwise deletion (by which cases with a missing score on any variable are excluded from all analyses and the effective sample size includes only cases with complete records) is the most common method for handling missing data, this approach sacrifices a large amount of data by eliminating all cases with any missing data (Kline, 2005; Roth, 1994). The EM algorithm (a) replaces missing values with estimated values, (b) estimates parameters, (c) reestimates the missing values assuming the new parameter estimates are correct, and (d) reestimates parameters, and so on, iterating until convergence. The EM method allows us to obtain an effective sample size and to minimize possible bias in parameter estimates in an HLM analysis. This approach also fully captures the asymptotic properties of the underlying population.
5. One of the major differences between exploratory and confirmatory factor analysis is

that, in the CFA, more aspects of the model can be specified a priori. For example, in the CFA, we can specify (a) which variables load on which factors, (b) which (if any) factors are correlated, (c) which (if any) measurement errors (uniquenesses) are correlated, and (d) how many factors there are. Two first-order factors (each subdimension of the second-order factors) and one second-order factor were analyzed—examining the factor loadings, the measurement error variances, the factor variances, the factor correlations or covariances, and the measurement error correlations (and covariances).

6. Since exploratory factor analysis (EFA) is an atheoretical method that might sometimes result in poor indexing, we employed the CFA method, which is based on SDT, to develop more theory-oriented intrinsic and extrinsic motivation scales in this study. The table with factor loadings of the EFA and the CFA models is available from the authors.
7. The variable of effective shared leadership is measured by the BPTW survey items, asking respondents whether employees and managers "promote communication among different work units (e.g., about projects, goals, and needed resources)" or "encourage employees in work units to share their knowledge with each other" through mutual cooperation among team members. We also measure effective vertical leadership, for example, supervisory leadership and senior leadership, using the BPTW scores based on such survey statements as, "Supervisor and team leaders in my work unit provide employees with the opportunities to demonstrate their leadership skills" (supervisory leadership), and "My organization's senior leaders maintain high standards of honesty and integrity" (senior leadership).
8. In this ANCOVA model, each slope of the covariate is assumed to have the same effect on each level of the factor (i.e., homogeneity of regression). Each predictor (covariate) was sequentially added, and only one variable was retained when it shows that it has reliability greater than .05 and has a statistically significant random effect. Based on the results, 14 predictors were retained at the employee-level.
9. In this model, both the uncentering (for dummy variables) and grand-mean centering methods were used because there is no random effect in the slope (that is, $\beta 1j$ is fixed across agencies). In other words, the Level 1 covariates (X variables) were included to control for their effects on the outcomes, rather than to model between group variance on the slope of these variables. The intercept here is interpreted as the expected value of two outcome variables for each employee with an average score on each of the Level 1 predictors. In this regard, grand-mean centering adjusts the variation in the intercept between agencies to control for differences in the Level 1 predictors across agencies.
10. In the intercepts- and slopes-as-outcomes model, we can include Level 2 predictors. After we have established that significant variation existed between group intercepts and slopes, we then use those parameter estimates as Level 2 outcomes. The Level 2 models are used for the purpose of modeling the associations between Level 2 predictors and the outcomes and to track the degree to which those predictors explain variance

in the Level 2 outcomes. In this model, a grand-mean centering option was used and variables were added one at a time for model building while examining their coefficient for significance (of random effect) and reliability.

11. In the cross-level interaction model, an interaction (moderating effects) is when the association between Level 1 predictors (i.e., employees' work motivation) and the outcome variables depend on the level of Level 2 predictors (i.e., organizational leadership). The cross-level interaction will be between the Level 1 random effect and the Level 2 predictors in the slopes-as-outcomes model.
12. HRD refers to a process for developing and unleashing human expertise through organizational development (which enhances the effectiveness of an organization and its employees through planned interventions), career development (an ongoing process by which individuals progress through a series of stages, each characterized by a relatively unique set of issues, themes, and tasks), personnel training (which provides skills and knowledge to job or task), and personnel development (which prepares for future employment needs) for the purpose of improving performance and job satisfaction (Swanson & Holton, 2001; Werner & DeSimone, 2009).

References

Albrecht, S. L., & Travaglione, A. (2003). Trust in public-sector senior management. *International Journal of Human Resource Management, 14*(1), 76-92.

Aryee, S., Budhwar, P. S., & Chen, Z. X. (2002). Trust as a mediator of the relationship between organizational justice and work outcomes: Test of a social exchange model. *Journal of Organizational Behavior, 23,* 267-285.

Atkinson, S., & Butcher, D. (2003). Trust in managerial relationships. *Journal of Managerial Psychology, 18,* 282-304.

Axelrod, R. (1984). *The evolution of cooperation.* New York, NY: Basic Books.

Bandura, A. (1986). *Social foundations of thought and action: A social cognitive theory.* Upper Saddle River, NJ: Prentice Hall.

Bass, B. M. (1996). *A new paradigm of leadership: An inquiry into transformational leadership.* Alexandria, VA: U.S. Army Research Institute for the Behavioral and Social Sciences.

Bass, B. M., & Riggio, R. E. (2006). *Transformational leadership* (2nd ed.). Mahwah, NJ: Lawrence Erlbaum.

Battaglio, Jr., R. P., & Condrey, S. E. (2009). Reforming public management: Analyzing the impact of public service reform on organizational and managerial trust. *Journal of Public Administration Research & Theory, 19,* 689-707.

Blau, P. M. (1964). *Exchange and power in social life.* New York, NY: John Wiley.

Brass, D. J. (1992). Power in organizations: A social network perspective. In G. Moore & J. A. Whitt (Eds.), *Research in politics and society* (pp. 295-323). Greenwich CT: JAI Press.

Burns, J. M. (1978). *Leadership.* New York, NY: Harper & Row.

Cameron, J., & Pierce, W. D. (2002). *Rewards and intrinsic motivation: Resolving the controversy.* Westport, CT: Bergin & Garvey.

Cardon, M. S., Wincent, J., Singh, J., & Drnovsek, M. (2009). The nature and experience of entrepreneurial passion. *Academy of Management Review, 34,* 511-532.

Carson, J. B., Tesluk, P. E., & Marrone, J. A. (2007). Shared leadership in teams: An investigation of antecedent conditions and performance. *Academy of Management Journal, 50,* 1217-1234.

Choudhury, E. (2008). Trust in administration: An integrative approach to optimal trust. *Administration & Society, 40,* 586-620.

Chua, R. Y. J., Ingram, P., & Morris, M. W. (2008). From the head and the heart: Locating cognition and affect-based trust in managers' professional networks. *Academy of Management Journal, 51,* 436-452.

Cook, J., & Wall, T. (1980). New work attitudes measures of trust, organizational commitment, and personal need non-fulfillment. *Journal of Occupational Psychology, 75,* 39-52.

Culbert, S. A., & McDonough, J. J. (1986). The politics of trust and organizational empowerment. *Public Administration Quarterly, 10,* 171-188.

De Jong, B. A., & Elfring, T. (2010). How does trust affect the performance of ongoing teams? The mediating role of reflexivity, monitoring, and effort. *Academy of Management Journal, 53,* 535-549.

Deci, E. L., & Ryan, R. M. (1985). *Intrinsic motivation and self-determination in human behavior.* New York, NY: Plenum.

Deci, E. L., & Ryan, R. M. (2004). *Handbook of self-determination research.* Rochester, NY: University of Rochester Press.

Dirks, K. T. (1999). The effects of interpersonal trust on work group performance. *Journal of Applied Psychology, 84,* 445-455.

Dirks, K. T. (2000). Trust in leadership and team performance: Evidence from NCAA basketball. *Journal of Applied Psychology, 85,* 1004-1012.

Dirks, K. T., & Ferrin, D. L. (2002). Trust in leadership: Meta-analytic findings and implications for research and practice. *Journal of Applied Psychology, 87,* 611-628.

Dutton, J. E., Roberts, L. M., & Bednar, J. (2010). Pathways for positive identity construction at work: Four types of positive identity and the building of social resources. *Academy of Management Review, 35,* 265-293.

Ensley, M. D., Hmieleski, K. M., & Pearce, C. L. (2006). The importance of vertical and shared leadership within new venture top management teams: Implications for the performance of startups. *Leadership Quarterly, 17,* 217-231.

Fox, A. (1974). *Beyond contract: Work, power, and trust relations.* London, UK: Faber and Faber.

Greenleaf, R. K. (1977). *Servant leadership: A journey into the nature of legitimate power and greatness.* New York, NY: Paulist Press.

Hackman, J. R., & Oldham, G. R. (1975). Development of the job diagnostic survey. *Journal of Applied Psychology, 60,* 159-170.

Hackman, J. R., & Oldham, G. R. (1976). Motivation through the design of work: Test of a theory. *Organizational Behavior and Human Performance, 16,* 250-279.

Herzberg, F., Mausner, B., & Snyderman, B. (1959). *The motivation to work.* New York, NY: John Wiley.

Hite, J. (2005). Evolutionary processes and paths of relationally embedded network ties in emerging entrepreneurial firms. *Entrepreneurship Theory and Practice, 29,* 113-144.

Holste, S., & Fields, D. (2010). Trust and tacit knowledge sharing and use. *Journal of Knowledge Management, 14*(1), 128-140.

Holtz, B. C., & Harold, C. M. (2008). When your boss says no! The effects of leadership style and trust on employee reactions to managerial explanations. *Journal of Occupational and Organizational Psychology, 81,* 777-802.

Ingram, P., & Roberts, P. W. (2000). Friendships among competitors in the Sydney hotel industry. *American Journal of Sociology, 106,* 387-423.

Johnson, D., & Grayson, K. (2005). Cognitive and affective trust in service delivery. *Journal of Business Research, 58,* 500-507.

Johnson, R., Chang, C., & Yang, L. (2010). Commitment and motivation at work: The relevance of employee identity and regulatory focus. *Academy of Management Review, 35,* 226-245.

Kennedy, J. R., & Anderson, R. D. (2002). Impact of leadership style and emotions on subordinate performance. *The Leadership Quarterly, 13,* 545-559.

Kline, R. B. (2005). *Principles and practices of structural equation modeling.* New York, NY: Guilford.

Kramer, R. (1996). Divergent realities and convergent disappointments in the hierarchic relation: Trust and the intuitive auditor at work. In R. M. Kramer & T. R. Tyler (Eds.), *Trust in organizations: Frontiers of theory and research* (pp. 216-245). Thousand Oaks, CA: Sage.

Ladebo, O. J. (2006). Perceptions of trust and employees' attitudes: A look at Nigeria's agricultural extension workers. *Journal of Business and Psychology, 20,* 409-477.

Lewicki, R. J., & Bunker, B. B. (1996). Developing and maintaining trust in work relationships. In R. M. Kramer & T. R. Tyler (Eds.), *Trust in organizations: Frontiers of theory and research* (pp. 114-139). Thousand Oaks, CA: Sage.

Livengood, R. S., & Reger, R. K. (2010). That's our turf! Identity domains and competitive dynamics. *Academy of Management Review, 35*(1), 48-66.

Lowi, T. (1964). American business, public policy, case-studies, and political theory. *World Politics, 16,* 677-715.

Luhmann, N. (1979). *Trust and power.* New York, NY: John Wiley.

Matthai, J. M. (1989). Employee perception of trust, satisfaction, and commitment as predictors of turnover intentions in a mental health setting. *Dissertation Abstracts International, 5*(2).

McAllister, D. J. (1995). Affect- and cognition-based trust as foundations for interpersonal cooperation in organizations. *Academy of Management Journal, 38,* 24-59.

McCauley, D. P., & Kuhnert, K. W. (1992). A theoretical review and empirical investigation of employee trust. *Public Administration Quarterly, 16*(2), 265-285.

Mehra, A., Dixon, A., Brass, D., & Robertson, B. (2006). The social network ties of group leaders: Implications for group performance and leader reputation. *Organization Science, 17*(1), 64-79.

Merit Systems Protection Board (MSPB) Report. (2010). *A call to action: Improving first-level supervision of federal employees.* Washington, DC: Office of Policy and Evaluation.

Mishra, A. (1996). Organizational responses to crisis: The centrality of trust. In R. M. Kramer & T. R. Tyler (Eds.), *Trust in organizations: Frontiers of theory and research* (pp. 261-287). Thousand Oaks, CA: Sage.

Morris, L. (1995). Creating and maintaining trust. *Training & Development, 49,* 52-53.

Moynihan, D. P. (2008). The normative model in decline? Public service motivation in the age of governance. In J. L. Perry & A. Hondeghem (Eds.), *Motivation in public management: The call of public service* (pp. 247-267). Oxford, UK: Oxford University Press.

Moynihan, D. P., & Pandey, S. K. (2007). Finding workable levers over work motivation: Comparing job satisfaction, job involvement, and organizational commitment. *Administration & Society, 39,* 803-832.

Moynihan, D. P., Pandey, S. K., & Wright, B. E. (2009). *Pulling the levers: Leadership, public service motivation and mission valence.* Paper presented at the International Public Service Research Conference, Bloomington, IN.

Newell, T., Reeher, G., & Ronayne, P. (2008). *The trusted leader: Building the relationships that make government work.* Washington, DC: CQ Press.

Nyhan, R. C. (2000). Changing the paradigm: Trust and its role in public sector organizations. *The American Review of Public Administration, 30,* 87-109.

Oldham, G. R., & Cummings, A. (1996). Employee creativity: Personal and contextual factors at work. *Academy of Management Journal, 39,* 607-634.

Paarlberg, L. E., & Lavigna, B. (2010). Transformational leadership and public service motivation: Driving individual and organizational performance. *Public Administration Review, 70,* 710-718.

Paarlberg, L. E., Perry, J. L., & Hondeghem, A. (2008). From theory to practice: Strategies for applying public service motivation. In J. L. Perry & A. Hondeghem (Eds.), *Motivation in public management: The call of public service* (pp. 268-293). Oxford, UK: Oxford University Press.

Park, S. M. (2010). The effects of personnel reform systems on Georgia State employees' attitudes: An empirical analysis from a principal-agent theoretical perspective. *Public Management Review, 12,* 403-437.

Park, S. M., & Rainey, H. G. (2007). Antecedents, mediators, and consequences of affective, normative, and continuance commitment: Empirical tests of commitment effects in federal agencies. *Review of Public Personnel Administration, 27,* 197-226.

Park, S. M., & Rainey, H. G. (2008). Leadership and public service motivation in U.S. federal agencies. *International Public Management Journal, 11*(1), 109-142.

Pearce, C. L. (2004). The future of leadership: Combining vertical and shared leadership to transform knowledge work. *Academy of Management Executive, 18*(1), 47-57.

Pearce, C. L., & Conger, J. A. (2003). All those years ago: The historical underpinnings of shared leadership. In C. L. Pearce & J. A. Conger (Eds.), *Shared leadership: Reframing the hows and whys of leadership* (pp. 1-18). Thousand Oaks, CA: Sage.

Pearce, C. L., Manz, C. C., & Sims, H. P. (2008). The roles of vertical and shared leadership in the enactment of executive corruption: Implications for research and practice. *The Leadership Quarterly, 19,* 353-359.

Perry, J. L., & Hondeghem, A. (2008). Directions for future theory and research. In J. L. Perry & A. Hondeghem (Eds.), *Motivation in public management: The call of public service* (pp. 294-313). Oxford, UK: Oxford University Press.

Perry, J. L., & Porter, L. W. (1982). Factors affecting the context for motivation in public organizations. *Academy of Management Review, 7,* 89-98.

Perry, R. W., & Mankin, L. M. (2004). Understanding employee trust in management. *Public Personnel Management, 33,* 277-290.

Puranam, P., & Vanneste, B. S. (2009). Trust and governance: Untangling a tangled web. *Academy of Management Review, 34*(1), 11-31.

Rainey, H. G. (2009). *Understanding and managing public organizations* (4th ed.). San Francisco: Jossey-Bass.

Rainey, H. G., & Steinbauer, P. (1999). Galloping elephants: Developing elements of a theory of effective government organizations. *Journal of Public Administration Research and Theory, 1,* 1-32.

Rainey, H. G., Koehler, M., & Jung, C. (2008). *Public values and public service motivation: How do public values relate to patterns of public service motivation?.* A paper proposed for the workshop on public values and public interest- normative questions in the evaluation and development of the public sector, The University of Georgia, Athens.

Raudenbush, S. W., Bryk, A. S., Cheong, Y., & Congdon, R. T. (2000). *HLM 5: Hierarchical linear and non-linear modeling.* Chicago: Scientific Software International.

Reece, B., & Brandt, R. (1999). *Effective human relations in organizations* (7th ed.). Boston: Houghton Miffin.

Reinke, S. J. (2003). Does the form really matter? Leadership, trust, and acceptance of the performance appraisal process. *Review of Public Personnel Administration, 23*(1), 23-37.

Robinson, S. L. (1996). Trust and breach of the psychological contract. *Administrative Science Quarterly, 41,* 574-599.

Roth, P. L. (1994). Missing data: A conceptual review for applied psychologists. *Personnel Psychology, 47,* 537-560.

Rousseau, D. M., Sitkin, S. B., Burt, R. S., & Camerer, C. (1998). Not so different after all: A cross-discipline view of trust. *Academy of Management Review, 23,* 393-404.

Ryan, R. M., & Deci, E. L. (2000a). Intrinsic and extrinsic motivations: Classic definitions and new directions. *Contemporary Educational Psychology, 25,* 54-67.

Ryan, R. M., & Deci, E. L. (2000b). Self-determination theory and the facilitation of intrinsic motivation, social development, and well-being. *American Psychologist, 55*(1), 68-78.

Scott, S. G., & Bruce, R. A. (1994). Determinants of innovative behavior: A path model of individual innovation in the workplace. *Academy of Management Journal, 37,* 580-607.

Shaw, R. B. (1997). *Trust in the balance: Building successful organizations on results, integrity and concern.* San Francisco, CA: Jossey-Bass.

Swanson, R. A., & Holton, E. F. (2001). *Foundations of human resource development.* San Francisco: Berrett-Koehler.

The best places to work. (2005). Retrieved from http://bestplacestowork.org/BPTW/about/.

Tietjen, M. A., & Myers, R. M. (1998). Motivation and job satisfaction. *Management Decision, 36,* 226-231.

Tyler, T. R., & Kramer, R. M. (1996). Whither trust? In R. M. Kramer & T. R. Tyler (Eds.), *Trust in organizations: Frontiers of theory and research* (pp. 1-15). Thousand Oaks, CA: Sage.

U.S. Merit Systems Protection Board. (2005). *Merit principles survey 2005.* Washington, DC: Author.

U.S. Merit Systems Protection Board. (2007). *Merit principles survey 2007.* Washington, DC: Author.

Van Kleef, G. A., Homan, A. C., Beersma, B., Van Knippenberg, D., Van Knippenberg, B., & Damen, F. (2009). Searing sentiment or cold calculation? The effects of leader emotional displays on team performance depend on follower epistemic motivation. *Academy of Management Journal, 52*(3), 562-580.

Van Wart, M. (2005). *Dynamics of leadership in public service: Theory and practice.* Armonk,

NY: M. E. Sharpe.

Vandenabeele, W. (2007). Toward a public administration theory of public service motivation. *Public Management Review, 9,* 545-556.

Webber, S. S., & Klimoski, R. J. (2004). Client-project manager engagements, trust, and loyalty. *Journal of Organizational Behavior, 25,* 997-1013.

Weiss, H. M. (2002). Deconstructing job satisfaction: Separating evaluations, beliefs, and affective experiences. *Human Resource Management Review, 12,* 173-194.

Werner, J. M., & DeSimone, R. L. (2009). *Human resource development* (5th ed.). Mason, OH: Cengage/South-Western.

Wilson, K. S., Sin, H., & Conlon, D. E. (2010). What about the leader in leader-member exchange? The impact of resource exchanges and substitutability on the leader. *Academy of Management Review, 35,* 358-372.

Wong, S., & Boh, W. F. (2010). Leveraging the ties of others to build a reputation for trustworthiness among peers. *Academy of Management Journal, 53*(1), 129-148.

Word, J., & Park, S. M. (2009). Working across the divide: Job involvement in the public and nonprofit sectors. *Review of Public Personnel Administration, 29*(2), 103-133.

Wright, B. E., & Pandey, S. K. (2010). Transformational leadership in the public sector: Does structure matter?. *Journal of Public Administration Research and Theory, 20*(1), 75-89.

Wu, J. B., Tsui, A. S., & Kinicki, A. J. (2010). Consequences of differentiated leadership in groups. *The Academy of Management Journal, 53*(1), 90-106.

Yukl, G. A. (1989). *Leadership in organizations* (2nd ed.). Upper Saddle River, NJ: Prentice Hall.

Yukl, G. A. (2006). *Leadership in organizations* (6th ed.). Upper Saddle River, NJ: Prentice Hall.

Zand, D. E. (1972). Trust and managerial problem solving. *Administrative Science Quarterly, 17,* 229-239.

Zhang, X., & Bartol, K. M. (2010). Linking empowering leadership and employee creativity: The influence of psychological empowerment, intrinsic motivation, and creative process engagement. *Academy of Management Journal, 53*(1), 107-128.

Appendix

Selected Representative Survey Items[a] (Best Places to Work, 2005; Merit Principle Survey, 2005), Construction of indices

Level 1 (individual level) and controls: demographic characteristics.

a. Gender: female: 2; male: 1 (a dummy variable)

b. Age: Respondent's age
c. Ethnicity (racial identification): Minority: 1; majority: 2 (a dummy variable)
d. Educational level: Respondent's highest level of formal education
e. Salary
f. Job tenure: Years with current federal agency (natural log)
g. Supervisory status (natural log)
h. Union membership (dues): A member of a union?

Level 1 (individual level) predictors: Work motivation attributes; intrinsic motivation (seven items, standardized coefficient alpha = .761).

How important are each of the following in motivating you to do a good job?

a. Recognition from my coworkers
b. My duty as a public employee
c. Desire to help my work unit meet its goals
d. Personal pride or satisfaction in my work
e. Noncash recognition (e.g., letter of appreciation, plaque)

Extrinsic motivation (five items, standardized coefficient alpha = .764).

How important are each of the following in motivating you to do a good job?

a. A cash award of US$100
b. A cash award of US$1,000
c. Desire for a good performance rating
d. Increased chances for promotion
e. A time off reward of 8 hours

Level 2 (agency-level) controls.

a. Agency types (agency dummy variables)
b. Agency size
c. Agency location: headquarters/field

Level 2 (agency-level) predictors:
Leadership factors. Best Places to Work (2005) index scores.

Shared leadership (teamwork management composite scores): Not official supervisors; those who provide employees with day-to-day guidance in work projects but do not have supervisory responsibilities or conduct performance appraisals.

Vertical Leadership I (supervisory leadership composite scores): First-line supervisors who do not supervise other supervisors, typically those who are responsible for employees' performance appraisals and approval of their leave.

Vertical Leadership II (senior leadership composite scores): The heads of departments/agencies and their immediate leadership team, typically these individuals would be members of SES or equivalent.

Outcome variables: Cognitive and affective trust (A 5-point Likert-type scale); cognition-based (rational) trust (nine items; standardized coefficient alpha = .815).

a. I trust my supervisor to fairly assess my performance and contributions
b. I trust my supervisor to support me in pay and award discussions with upper management
c. I trust my supervisor to apply discipline fairly and only when justified
d. I trust managers above my immediate supervisors to clearly communicate organizational performance expectations
e. I trust managers above my immediate supervisors to apply discipline fairly and only when justified
f. I trust third party investigative or adjudicatory agencies (such as the OSC, EEOC, FLRA, MSPB) to respond appropriately to complaints

Affect-based (relational) trust (eight items, standardized coefficient alpha = .803).

a. I trust my supervisor to listen fairly to my concerns
b. I trust my supervisor to clearly communicate conduct expectations
c. I trust managers above my immediate supervisors to act with integrity
d. I trust managers above my immediate supervisors to refrain from favoritism
e. I am comfortable discussing workplace conflicts with my supervisor

Note. [a] A complete listing of items in the indices is available from the author

Case Study

'Please, Don't Boss Me Around'

Hyun-chae Chung

"My boss persistently persuaded me to join a bicycle club. I even had to buy a new bicycle and I hate myself for being a single and free on weekends."

What juniors won't tell you but want you to know

How many of us are carrying a letter of resignation in our pockets or in our mind? Many workers think about leaving their jobs after having survived cut-throat competitions in today's ever harsher job market and landed their initial dream jobs. The main reason is often their bosses.

According to a survey of 499 workers conducted two weeks ago by job portal site Career, some 80 percent of them said that they have complaints against their bosses. The average score of the respondents' level of satisfaction about their bosses was only 2.2 out of five. What they disliked the most about their managers was the lack of consideration toward them.

The dissatisfaction with bosses is apparently common across the world. "Horrible Bosses," a black comedy film directed by Seth Gordon and released in 2011, showed three exaggerated types of bad bosses — a "psycho," a "man-eater" and a "tool." Moviegoers would have laughed at those blown-up characters, but unfortunately, horrible bosses do exist in real life, which isn't a comedy. They would influence their junior staff not just at work but outside as well.

Through a string of interview with office workers, Business Focus found patterns in bad bosses. They are all real.

Entertainment show producer

A lot of new recruits are required to prepare a talent show. Typically, they have to sing and dance to the latest K-pop songs at a year-end party.

Some oppressive supervisors force them to do so because they already went through the same things at the early stage of their career.

"It would be easy, even fun for people with talents, but for people who are shy like me, it is a drag," said an employee with a surname of Lee at telecommunication firm.

Do-gooder

The long-time bachelor surprised his colleagues by announcing that he is getting married. Everyone heartily congratulated him, and then the boss suddenly gathered employees and suggested holding an event for the broom.

"I am happy for my colleague and deeply congratulated him. But speaking as just a co-worker, I feel like holding a party is overdoing it," Lee said.

Scrooge

Responding to the government's initiative to save electricity, state-owned entities had to keep the temperature at 28 degrees Celsius or above last summer while any privately-held large buildings weren't allowed to be cooler than 26 degrees. That was bearable for the most, but one boss found the office too hot. He proposed to his colleagues to make a group purchase of mini electric fans.

"No one had the guts to say, 'No.' Plenty of mini electric fans were shipped to our office. They had childish cartoon characters printed on them, and definitely did not fit into my desk. I had to bite the bullet and pay for it," said a worker at an insurance company.

Now winter is near, and people are already worried about a suggestion to make a group purchase of mini heaters.

Athlete — professional golfer, mountaineer, swimmer

Bosses in this category lead or join sports clubs in their companies such as hiking, swimming and bicycling clubs.

The healthy lifestyle is something that the junior staff can emulate, but they do not want to be forced by their bosses to participate in those clubs after work or on the weekends. They are already fed up with working with their bosses in weekdays.

"My boss persistently persuaded me to join a bicycle club. I even had to buy a new bicycle and I hate myself for being a single and free on weekends," Lee complained.

For women, playing sports together may be a sensitive issue. Another Lee, who works for a small-size company here, recalled her personal experience, "My boss once told us to go swimming together. We were all women, but it was somehow embarrassing. I would like to protect my own privacy."

For men, however, different kind of difficulty comes along. "When my boss suggests doing sports together, I didn't know how to play. What if I'm really good at it?" Lee said.

Scheduler

Many bosses seem to forget that their subordinates also have their own lives. This type of bosses tends to arrange company dinners fit to their own schedule. Workers are often informed on the day of the event.

"Even though they have a previous engagement, they hardly can say that they cannot make it," all the interviewees said.

Not only for company dinners, but also for short trips, workers have to be ready to adapt their schedule to their bosses'.

"Last winter, my boss notified me a fishing trip abruptly. I was of little mind to go due to my physical condition, but I had to go. We nine people just sat close together in a small boat about three hours catching only one fish in total. I was almost frozen to death," said Park, an employee at a construction material distributor.

How to deal with them

Commonly bosses who aren't married yet suggest doing something together with employees on weekends. If there's a heavy workload, one surely cannot be available. But when employees reject their bosses' suggestions too often, they are afraid of being put into disadvantageous position by their bosses in the future.

In this case, Yeon Jung-hum, a section chief at employment website Saramin, says employees should intimate their schedule to their bosses in both indirect and direct ways.

▪ Place a calendar with red circles on the dates on your desk in ways that they can be clearly shown to the boss.

▪ Keep a diary or a personal scheduler and put it on your desk for everyone passing by your desk to see.

▪ Make a phone call in a loud voice that shows you have plans on certain dates.

▪ In a daily or weekly report, write down your personal schedule. Be careful because depending on the personality of your boss, you might come across as a person who drags on every small detail.

Yeon adds that you should sometimes force yourself to join unappealing events as missing all of them may cause troubles between you and your boss.

He said that you should first ask yourself, "Why does my boss suggest these things to me?" When they offer something, there must be a reason. Try not to grumble all the time and control your mind by understanding the situation.

Source: The Korea Times (2012.11.02)

Questions for Discussion

1. Discuss transformational, transaction, and charismatic leadership styles. Do you think these leadership styles should depend on the social or organizational culture and structure?

2. Many public organizations undergo significant change in priorities after elections. In your opinion, what is the role of a leader in such a situation? Reference any theory or research findings that inform your answer.

3. Describe the characteristics of someone you consider a leader. In what ways might this person rely on his/her personal qualities to influence and motivate? And then, interview the person you described as a leader and ask how his/her personal qualities are used to influence and motivate? Encourage the interviewee to provide examples. Based on your results, write a memo supporting or refuting the position that "management matters" to organizational results.

Section 4

Culture

- Determinants of Positive Job Attitude and Behavior in the Asian Work Context
  : Evidence from Korean Central Government Agencies

- The Roles of Integrative Leadership in Enhancing Organizational Effectiveness in the Chinese Public Sector
  : A Research Note

Section 4

Culture

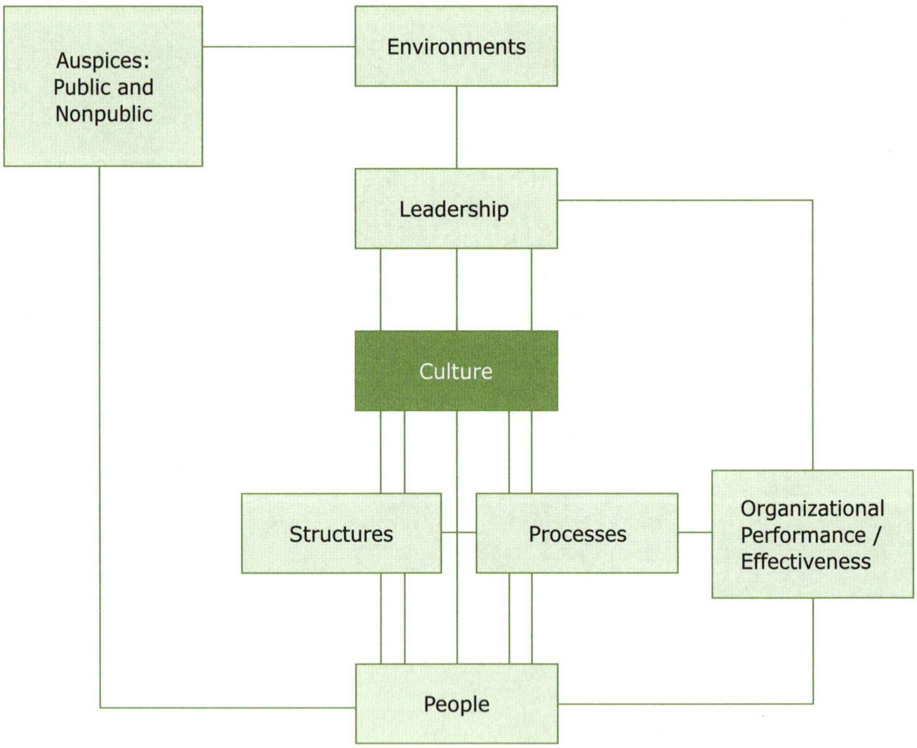

Chapter 7

Determinants of Positive Job Attitude and Behavior in the Asian Work Context
: Evidence from Korean Central Government Agencies

Summary

This study probes and tests the impacts of organizational commitment (OC) and organizational citizenship behaviour (OCB) among public employees in the Asian context. Using a 2010 Korean Central Government Survey of forty Korean central government agencies(totalling 1,122 respondents), an antecedent-outcome model is developed which analyses how different types of interpersonal and organizational characteristics affect OC and OCB using hierarchical and multi-level ordering statistical techniques. The research finds that certain predictors, such as trust in colleagues (TC), formalized structures, and group culture, play significant roles in fostering OC and OCB among employees. In conclusion, suggestions are made for further research, and practical implications for Asian civil servants are considered.

Keyword

- □ Positive Job Attitude and Behavior
- □ Interpersonal Trust
- □ Organizational Structure
- □ Organizational Culture
- □ Korean Public Agencies

Sung Min Park Associate Professor, Sungkyunkwan University
Hyung Jun Park Associate Professor, Sungkyunkwan University
Eun Young Ryu Assistant Professor, Dong-A University

Introduction

Public sector organizations currently operate in turbulent environments driven by changes in managerial, political, and technical arenas as the organizations seek to improve performance, effectiveness, and accountability (Berry, 2007). Government organizations are typified as working under cumbersome and restrictive personnel systems that prevent effective delivery of services (Rainey, 2009). General reforms and reforms in the human resources (HR) departments of public agencies are focused on redirecting mechanistic, bureaucratic rigidities toward flexible and organic systems. For example, decentralization is commonly understood as a way of empowering agencies to make their own staffing decisions and of enabling other actions that loosen the bureaucratic system (Carnevale and Housel, 2001). Characteristically Western prescriptions such as these, however, are somewhat at odds with East Asian bureaucratic structures and cultures. Indeed, the bureaucratic structures and cultures of East Asia are more hierarchical, centralized, and formalized, in addition to being based around Confucian values.

This study explores the nature of Asian public management/administration in relation to dominant Western models and analyzes the most crucial features. More specifically, this study examines whether hierarchical, centralized, and formalized structures associated with Confucian societies are able to nurture positive job attitudes and behaviors of public employees, as anticipated in Western texts. For example, previous studies found that hierarchical, centralized, and formalized structures have significant and typically negative effects on positive job attitudes and behaviors (see, for example, George and Jones, 1997; Lawrence and Lorsch, 1967). Using quantitative methods, this study adds to the existing literature by focusing on central government agencies in Korea. It address the central questions of how and to what extent do individual, cultural, and structural factors in a Confucian-based bureaucracy affect the current job attitudes of public employees and organizational behaviors, as expressed by organizational commitment and organizational civic behaviors.

The study is presented in five parts. The first section briefly overviews Korean civil service systems and reviews existing literature about the two main outcome variables, i.e., organizational commitment (OC) and organizational citizenship behavior (OCB). The second section, drawing on different types of theories of management and applied psychology, as well as testing a number of research hypotheses, explores and analyzes the determinants of OC and OCB in the hierarchical and multi-level structure of the Korean central government bureaucracy. A conceptual research framework is provided, followed by a set of research hypotheses. This is followed by methods, where data and measures are described. Fourth, using hierarchical linear modeling (HLM), this study empirically tests the effects on OC and OCB of demographic, interpersonal, structural, and cultural factors across Korean public agencies. Finally, a discussion of findings draws research implications and assesses the limitations of this study.

An Overview of Korean Civil Service Systems

The Korean career civil service system is intended to attract and retain outstanding young people with a high sense of honor and morality for public office. The modern career civil service system, which is usually based on a merit system, has qualification standards such as knowledge, skills, and abilities that are rigorously evaluated during the recruiting and selection process. Conventional types of career civil service systems typically refer to generalist-driven, rank-in-person-based, closed, and seniority-based career systems. A stable, hierarchical, and merit-based (i.e., rank-in-person) system was developed during a period of Korean military control in 1961-87. Korean bureaucracy, however, has been consistently criticized for "its closeness, rigid structure and culture, lack of flexibility, and lack of global competitiveness" (Kim, 2010, p. 383). In order to renew and innovate outdated personnel systems in pursuit of more efficient, performance-based, and business-like civil service systems, the Korean government has reformed and overhauled the major functions of public sector HR departments, including recruitment, compensation and pension, training and development, and performance evaluation. For example, the Korean government established the Senior Civil Service (SCS) to accomplish an open and proactive recruitment system and a rank-in-job system. In addition, in order to nurture Korean employees as specialists rather than generalists, the Korean training and education systems are redefining organizational and individual capacity, with an emphasis on decentralization, openness, competiveness, performance, and responsibility (World Bank, 2009).

On the other hand, efforts toward devolvement of authority and increasing flexibility for the personnel system of the central government might bring about profound and potentially adverse consequences for Korean "career" civil service systems. In other words, these performance-based civil service reform tasks, which focus on systems and cultures of productivity improvement, reinvention, process re-engineering, entrepreneurial leadership, privatization, and performance measurement, have been argued to undermine the values of equity and fairness that have traditionally been associated with the civil service and with the "public ethos" that provides civil service with a constitutive role in a system of governance (Park and Joaquin, 2012; Thompson, 2001). In addition, it might be true that the reforms have not led to any significant behavioral or institutional changes for employees or organizations. Indeed, certain aspects of current reform initiatives might actually create more problems than they solve. Due to these civil service reform initiatives, current Korean civil service cultures and structures, as well as the overall attitudes of public employees, are constantly changing and transforming.

OC and OCB in the Korean Public Sector

According to both Weberian views, "the source of bureaucracy's dominance over [other forms of] governance lies in its capacity for rationally calculating the most precise and efficient means for the resolution of problems" (Heugens, 2005, p. 551). Indeed, even as diversified, privatized, and decentralized organizational environments are becoming dominant in the public sector, bureaucratic forms and institutions are still shown to yield high organizational efficiency and effectiveness. Although the existing research on bureaucratic organizations indicates both positive and negative implications, the rigidity of bureaucratic environments tends to yield negative reactions from employees regarding their job attitudes and behaviors (e.g., Bhargava and Kelkar, 2000).

Organizational Commitment (OC)

OC is concerned with attitudinal, behavioral, and cultural antecedents among employees (Park and Rainey, 2007). For example, the aspect of "social capital"— found in relationships characterized by high levels of trust and shared cultures— tends to generate higher levels of organizational commitment among employees. In turn, highly committed employees are more likely to retain their jobs long-term. Highly committed employees also show high levels of job satisfaction, quality of work, and job performance. OC can be conceptualized as a multi-layered variable, comprised of three aspects of commitment, including affective, normative, and continuance aspects.[1] A common theme in existing research about organizational commitment is analysis of means to enhance employee commitment and, in turn, how to improve other organizational and social consequences, such as job satisfaction, turnover intentions, organizational performance and accountability, and volunteer activities among employees. For example, Park and Rainey (2007) found that there are three distinctive constructs of OC in U.S. federal agencies, and that certain antecedents such as empowerment, goal clarity, and perceptions of procedural equity have direct and indirect effects on OC. Also, a number of empirical studies indicate that decentralized team structures increase the job satisfaction of Korean public sector employees (Lee and Kim, 2011; Kang, 2006), but that bureaucratic cultures and centralized structures still have strong positive relationships with organizational commitment in Korean police departments (Lee and Park, 2011a; Yoo, 2010).

Organizational Citizenship Behavior (OCB)

OCB has been defined, operationalized, and applied in various ways (e.g., Graham, 1991; Organ, 1988). Basically, OCB includes positive work-related informal behaviors by employees that transcend the rules and regulations formally dictated by organizational policies and job descriptions. According to Meyer and Allen (1997), OCB typically includes things such as "providing extra help to coworkers, volunteering for special work activities, being particularly considerate of coworkers and customers, being on time, and making suggestions when problems arise" (p. 33). Similarly, Organ (1988) defined OCB as "individual behavior that is discretionary, not directly or explicitly recognized by the formal reward system, and that in aggregate promotes the effective functioning of the organization (p. 4). Organ (1988) also proposed a multi-dimensional OCB construct, including aspects of altruism, conscientiousness, sportsmanship, courtesy, and civic virtue. Work by Podsakoff et al. (2003) describes OCB as consisting of seven dimensions, i.e., helping behavior, sportsmanship, organizational loyalty, organizational compliance, individual initiative, civic virtue, and self-development. Previous works report that OCB benefits organizations in general by means of positive employee attitudes toward work or adherence to informal rules to keep order, among other examples.

In Korea, in particular, public bureaucrats tend to have distinctive values, motives, and goals compared to the public employees of other countries (Kim, 2010; Lee and Moon, 2007). Cultural, institutional, and structural environments affect the perceptions and behaviors of Korean public bureaucrats. That is, specific types of idiosyncratic organizational cultures (e.g., either hierarchical or group cultures) that characterize Korean bureaucracy tend to significantly affect certain organizational outcomes. For example, many empirical studies on OCB in Korean bureaucracy suggest that organizational justice and organizational trust are the most critical factors for enhancing OCB among Korean public officials (Bae, 2007; Park and Kim, 2003; Moon and Kim, 2006), and that bureaucratic cultures and hierarchical structures still have strong positive relationships with OCB among street-level bureaucrats in a representative Korean local government (Song and Kim, 2002). Given the fact that Korean personnel management reform initiatives are currently racing in pursuit of procedural changes, process innovations, and technological applications, it is sufficiently worthwhile to evaluate how the structural or interpersonal factors in a changing environment affect OC and OCB among Korean public employees. For the purposes of analyzing the main impacts of interpersonal-bureaucratic cultures and structures in Korean bureaucracy, this study focuses on two outcome variables at the reaction level of public employees, namely, OC and OCB.

Theories and Research Hypotheses

The present study focuses primarily on the roles of trust, structure, and culture as antecedents of OC and OCB. The specific pattern of relationships examined in this study is shown in Figure 1. Even though considerable research has examined the empirical antecedents of OC and OCB, much of the existing work has focused on these outcomes in private business sectors rather than in government organizations, with even fewer studies in Confucian culturebased bureaucracies (e.g., Farh et al., 1997). This study expects that OC and OCB are differently associated with various types of organizational trust, structures, and cultures in Korean central agencies.

Figure 1. Hierarchical Linear Model (HLM): Determinants, Controls, and Outcomes

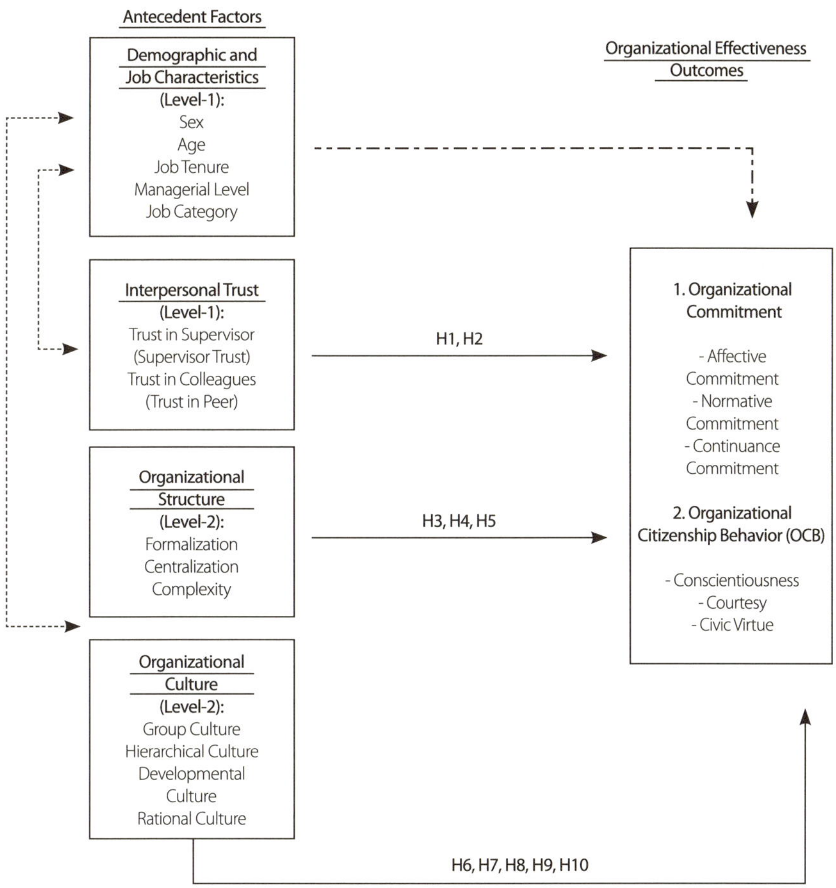

Independent Variables	Outcomes
- Interpersonal Trust - Organizational Structure - Organizational Culture - Demographic Factors	- Organizational Commitment - OCB **Controls: Demographic and Job Factors** Sex Age Job Tenure Managerial Level Job Category

Interpersonal Trust, OC, and OCB

Trust is defined as the optimistic expectation of one party about the behavior of another party, characterized by conditions of vulnerability and dependence, in situations when the party must make a decision about how to act (Hosmer, 1995). Distrust produces excessive monitoring and control costs beyond any necessary standard and subsequently bring outs a defensive attitude by the distrusted party. This type of negative exchange leads to a vicious circle of distrust in organizations (Shapiro, 1987). Therefore, affective and interpersonal management strategies based on trustworthiness have many merits to achieve successful organizational outcomes such as OC and OCB. For example, increasing trust among members of an organization reduces the need to monitor the behaviors of colleagues, minimizes transaction costs (including monitoring and negotiation costs), increases flexibility by reducing unnecessary procedures and regulations, encourages participation, and facilitates informal cooperation among members, thereby enhancing OC and job involvement among employees. Accordingly, trust has the potential to solve the principal-agent problem in an organization and thereby raise the level of managerial accountability and effectiveness of the organization in the long run (Shapiro et al., 1992; Smith et al., 1995). Empirical research has detected the benefits of trust in many contexts. Trust reduces conflict (Zaheer et al., 1998), improves individual performance (McAllister, 1995), promotes inter-organizational cooperation (Ring and Van de Ven, 1994), and increases the commitment of foreign subsidiary managers (Kim and Mauborgne, 1993). At the highest level of analysis, studies have shown empirically that societies with greater levels of trust are actually more economically developed (La Porta et al., 1997).

Empirical research has detected the benefits of trust in many contexts (e.g., Podsakoff et al., 1990). For example, trust between supervisors and subordinates improves the quality of communication (Muchinsky, 1977; Yeager, 1978), overall citizenship behavior (McAllister, 1995), and the problem solving and decision making of employees (Barnes, 1981). Trust in the workplace is a manifestation of a social exchange process. Processes of social exchange, in turn, contribute to OCB by encouraging employees to behave in ways that are not strictly mandated by their employers (Rousseau and Parks, 1993). It follows that employees with higher levels of trust in their organizations are likely to display more OCB, regardless of the type of organization for which they work. A study by Deluga (1994) found that the trust-building behavior of supervisors is closely associated with OCB among employees. As a consequence of social exchange, trust in supervisors by employees is likely to affect the OCB of employees.

While there is evidence of significant positive associations among trust in peers, job satisfaction and commitment among employees in public organizations (e.g., Lehmann-Willenbrock and Kauffeld, 2010), trust researchers have neglected to examine the effects of interpersonal trust among peers in the workplace on organizational outcomes in the public sector (Chattopadhyay and George, 2001; Ferres et al., 2004; Tan and Lim, 2009). As the presence of trust within organizations facilitates cooperative behavior, reduces conflict, and decreases transaction costs at work (Rousseau et al., 1998), we strongly believe that these positive impacts of interpersonal trust will be effective and applicable in the Korean public sector in a similar manner. For example, Kim and Son (2009) found that two types of organizational justice and supervisory trust in the Korean public sector have significant influence on organizational commitment among employees. Empirical research by Bae (2007) also confirms the positive impact of interpersonal trust on the collaborative behavior of employees, while Hong (2010) identified that organizational trust, trust in superiors, and trust in colleagues (as perceived by revenue officers in Korea) provide positive effects on team commitment, and that higher team commitment leads to higher job productivity. Drawing upon these previous findings, the current study hypothesizes that trust in supervisors and trust in colleagues (i.e., trust in peers) is an important predictor of positive organizational outcomes such as OC and OCB (Van Dyne et al., 2000).

Hypothesis 1: In Korean public agencies, as the degree of trust in supervisors increases, the degrees of OC and OCB among employees will increase.
Hypothesis 2: In Korean public agencies, as the degree of trust in colleagues increases, the degrees of OC and OCB among employees will increase.

Organizational Structure, OC, and OCB

From an agency theory perspective, the critical issue of public management seems to be the extent to which an organization requires strict control and close monitoring of employees. According to the principal-agent theory, the actions of managers - acting in the role of principals - are usually dictated by such organizational factors as structure, policies, and culture, and managers are expected to exert these concerns over the actions of their employees. Many public management researchers have investigated whether government bureaucracies have distinctive and peculiar structural and legal characteristics, as well as how and to what extent these characteristics impact organizational performance (Downs, 1967; Brewer and Walker, 2012).[2] While an overall, single measure of organizational structure has not been established, the use of discrete dimensions of organizational structures to evaluate performance includes features of formalization, centralization, and complexity.

Formalization refers to the degree to which organizational information is encapsulated in documentation that is easily accessible to employees. Organizational documentation is one of the extrinsic sources from which employees can seek feedback. Accordingly, in more formalized organizations, we expect more feedback behaviors among employees. In turn, we expect that the employees of more formalized organizations will be more likely to be satisfied and committed to their jobs. The aspect of centralization evaluates where the locus of power to influence decisions resides in the hierarchy of an organization. The higher this locus is located in a hierarchy, the more centralized is the organization. Hage and Aiken (1967) distinguished two types of centralization as involving participation in decision making and hierarchy of authority. The lower the degree of participation in decision-making, and the higher the degree of hierarchy of authority, the more centralized is the organization (Krasman, 2011, pp. 16-17). The complexity of an organization is usually measured by the number of subunits, levels, and specializations (Rainey, 2009). Bureaucratic organizations are characterized by high levels of formalization, specialization, and hierarchy, as well as a lack of flexibility. Several studies have indicated the benefits of such characteristics for organizational efficiency. For example, formalization, a central dimension of bureaucracies, serves to support constitutional order and thereby assist employees in mastering their tasks more efficiently (Lawrence and Lorsch, 1967).

The argument for structure as an antecedent to the organizational outcome of OCB is that organizational contexts either provide opportunities to engage in OCB or impose constraints against these behaviors. A study by George and Jones (1997) further argues that OCB levels should be higher in less structured, organic organizations than in more structured, mechanistic organizations. The implication is that organizational structure may be a predictor, or antecedent, of OCB, and that the degree of OCB among public employees varies significantly depending on the structural variances and idiosyncrasies in different public agencies.

In any centralized Korean HR system, the bureaucratic structure is an influential factor on the behavior and attitudes of employees. This study posits that, while excessively formalized, centralized, and complex organizational structures provide negative impacts on the job attitudes of public employees in general, the levels of OC and OCB among employees could increase (at least marginally) with the influences of formalization and centralization. There are two mechanisms through which structure may enhance OC and OCB. First, this hypothesis is in keeping with the uniquely Asian perspective of paternalistic leadership, Confucian norms, and authoritarian cultures, because Korean public employees recognize the positive impacts of a firmly-structured and well-developed civil service system. In other words, by utilizing structural mechanisms, such as emphasizing organizational loyalty and organizational compliance, different dimensions of structural environments in Korean public agencies (i.e., formalization, centralization, and complexity) will enhance OC and OCB among Korean public employees. For instance, the research of Ryu et al. (2010) confirms that organizational structures are positively associated with affective commitment and normative commitment, and that there is a positive relationship among formalization, complexity, and job satisfaction in employees.

Second, it is believed that the traditional career civil service system in Korea (including a closed and centralized recruitment system, a rank-in-person system, and a tenured and merit system) partially relies on the control and exploitation of the superior. In other words, subordinates tend to show conformity and dependence in order to receive rewards or avoid punishment. Hence, public employees, as self-interested actors and rational utility maximizers with divergent interests and conflicting goals, are expected to engage in OC and OCB through this structure-conformity dyadic mechanism. To this end, we develop the following hypotheses:

> **Hypothesis 3:** In Korean public agencies, as the degree of formalization increases, the degrees of OC and OCB will increase.
> **Hypothesis 4:** In Korean public agencies, as the degree of centralization increases, the degrees of OC and OCB will increase.
> **Hypothesis 5:** In Korean public agencies, as the degree of complexity increases, the degrees of OC and OCB will increase.

Bureaucratic Culture, OC, and OCB

Organizational culture can be defined as a pattern of basic assumptions that are invented, discovered, or developed by a given group as the organization learns to cope with the problems of external adaptation and/or internal integration (Schein, 1992). The framework is built upon two dimensions with two axes, each representing a superordinate continuum. The first dimension is the flexibility-control axis, and the second dimension is the internal-external axis. The combination of these two dimensions results in four quadrants of cultural dimensions, namely group, developmental, hierarchical, and rational cultures.[3] Certain types or styles of organizational cultures have been associated with either positive or negative outcomes for either the effectiveness of the organization or for individual employees within the organization (Schein, 1996). For example, a study by Likert (1967), among many other studies, suggests that the type of positive, employee-focused management practices that are consistent with group culture values are likely to inspire employees to make greater efforts with their work, which should result in higher levels of OC. Organizational culture is also associated with OCB in that the culture provides guidance to behavior in any society of employees, in ways that are both apparent and sometimes unnoticeable. A study by Moorman and Blakely (1995) suggests that individuals from collectivist cultures will exhibit higher levels of OCB than individuals from individualist cultures, based on the assumption that individuals in collectivist cultures will place greater emphasis on harmony and interpersonal cooperation within in-groups than individuals in individualist cultures.

In the Korean context, a study by Kim (2002) examines the impact of organizational culture on organizational effectiveness in local government. Three major findings of this research indicate that (1) some organizational cultures differ significantly across local governments, as well as across units of local governments, (2) the type of organizational culture has an impact on OC and job satisfaction among employees, and (3) strong comprehensive cultures, in contrast to other culture profiles, more significantly impact OC and job satisfaction. Research by Seo and Lee (2006) also presents a model of relationships among organizational cultures, leadership styles, leader trust, OC, and OCB. The results support the indirect effect of leadership style on OCB, showing the mediating effect of leader trust and OC combined between leadership styles and OCB. Han's study (2009) also finds that organizational cultures act as effective antecedents of factors of organization effectiveness, such as OC and OCB. While the Asian cultural traditions of Confucianism, legalism, and hierarchism are widespread in the Korean public sector, the current study hypothesizes that the four quadrants of cultural dimensions characterize Korean central agencies in ways that are not exhaustive, but are still distinctive. That is, some agencies feature more internal, flexible cultures, while other agencies are more likely to be oriented toward external and controlled cultures. These idiosyncratic cultural factors will be differently related to organizational outcomes. Based on previous studies, we test the impacts of organizational culture on OC and OCB. As follows, we hypothesize that, while four types of organizational cultures will provide significant impacts on OC and OCB, internal and flexible cultures more positively affect OC and OCB than external and controlled cultures.

Hypothesis 6: In Korean public agencies, as the degree of group culture increases, the degrees of OC and OCB will increase.
Hypothesis 7: In Korean public agencies, as the degree of developmental culture increases, the degrees of OC and OCB will increase.
Hypothesis 8: In Korean public agencies, as the degree of rational culture increases, the degrees of OC and OCB will increase.
Hypothesis 9: In Korean public agencies, as the degree of hierarchical culture increases, the degrees of OC and OCB will increase.
Hypothesis 10: In Korean public agencies, group and developmental cultures are more strongly associated with OC and OCB than rational and hierarchical cultures.

Research Methods

Data and Measurements

The empirical portion of this study utilizes our primary data, 2010 Korean Central Government Survey data, which includes 40 Korean central government agencies [with a total of 1,122 Korean public employees and a response rate of 93.5 percent (ranging from a low of 76.67 percent to a high of 100 percent)]. In order to ensure the presence of key subgroups within the sample, a stratified random sampling method was used. To obtain a stratified sample of Korean central officials, we divided the entire target population into 40 different subgroups (ministry-level) and then randomly selected 30 public employees (employee-level) from each subgroup.[4] Division managers of the agencies were responsible for internal distribution and collection of surveys. Prior to distributing surveys, the division managers clearly communicated to all participants the purpose of the study, assured their voluntary participation, and ensured that their responses would remain anonymous (see Tables 1 and 2).

Table 1. Characteristics of Respondents in Korean Central Agencies (Number of Agencies = 40; Number of Respondents = 1,122)

Variables		Frequencies	%	Variables		Frequencies	%
Sex	Male	785	70.47	Managerial Level	Level-3 and higher	13	1.19
	Female	329	29.53		Level-4	123	11.29
Age	20's	60	5.48		Level-5	273	25.07
	30's	417	38.08		Level-6	354	32.51
	40's	495	45.21		Level-7	181	16.62
	50's	123	11.23		Level-8	145	13.31
	60s and over	0	0.00	Job Category+	Category 1	726	65.41
Job Tenure (current position)	Less than 5 years	161	14.84		Category 2	142	12.79
	5-10 years	237	21.84		Category 3	68	6.13
	10-20 years	411	37.88		Category 4	122	10.99
	20-30 years	226	20.83		Category 5	18	1.62
	30 years and more	50	4.61		Category 6/ Others	15/19	1.35/1.71

Table 2. Agencies and Response Rate (%)

Agencies		Surveys		Response Rate (%)		Surveys		Response Rate (%)
Ministry-level	Ministry of Strategy and Finance	30	27	90.00	Ministry of Government Legislation	30	30	100.00
	Ministry of Education, Science and Technology	30	30	100.00	Ministry of Patriots & Veterans Affairs	30	30	100.00
	Ministry of Foreign Affairs and Trade	30	30	100.00	National Tax Service	30	29	96.67
	Ministry of Unification	30	26	86.67	Korea Customs Service	30	29	96.67
	Ministry of Justice	30	28	93.33	Public Procurement Service	30	30	100.00
	Ministry of National Defense	30	30	100.00	Statistics Korea	30	30	100.00
	Ministry of Public Administration and Security	30	30	100.00	Supreme Prosecutors' Office	30	30	100.00
	Ministry of Culture, Sports & Tourism	30	23	76.67	Military Manpower Administration	30	28	93.33
	Ministry of Food, Agriculture, Forestry and Fisheries	30	30	100.00	Defense Acquisition Program Administration	30	23	76.67
	Ministry of Knowledge Economy	30	26	86.67	National Police Agency	30	26	86.67
	Ministry of Health & Welfare	30	24	80.00	National Emergency Management Agency	30	23	76.67
	Ministry of Environment	30	30	100.00	Cultural Heritage Administration	30	30	100.00
	Ministry of Employment and Labor Reserved	30	30	100.00	Rural Development Administration	30	30	100.00
	Ministry of Gender Equality & Family Republic of Korea	30	26	86.67	Korea Forest Service	30	27	90.00
	Ministry of Land, Transport and Maritime Affairs	30	27	90.00	Small & Medium Business Administration	30	30	100.00
Commit-tee-level	Korea Communications Commission	30	28	93.33	Korea Intellectual Property Office	30	30	100.00
	Fair Trade Commission	30	28	93.33	Korea Food & Drug Administration	30	26	86.67
	Financial Services Commission	30	29	96.67	Korea Meteorological Administration	30	29	96.67
	Anti-Corruption & Civil Rights Commission	30	27	90.00	Korea Coast Guard	30	30	100.00
	National Human Rights Commission	30	26	86.67	1,121(93.50%)			
Office-level	Prime Minister's Office	30	27	90.00				

First, we measured two dimensions of organizational outcome variables, including OC and OCB. As suggested by a study by Meyer and Allen (1991), organizational commitment is a psychological state among employees that characterizes their relationship with the organization, with implications for employee decisions about whether or not to continue membership in the organization (Wasti, 2003). To measure the OC of public employees in Korea, we included three distinct indicators of sub-dimensions of commitment (i.e., affective, normative, and calculative) (Park and Rainey, 2007). Utilizing Organ's (1988) OCB typology, we also included OCB as an outcome variable. Fifteen relevant survey items were utilized to capture three sub-dimensions of the OCB concept. The sub-dimensions include conscientiousness (e.g., a co-worker in our department is conscientious), courtesy (e.g., a co-worker in our department is always careful in his or her behavioral habits that impact the work of other employees), and civic virtue (e.g., I try to solve problems when they happen, rather than complain and assign blame). Based on these theoretical and heuristic arguments, which propose that there are distinctive and latent factor constructs nested in Korean bureaucracy, this study performed preliminary exploratory factor analyses (EFA) of the main independent and outcome variables. The main EFA results are reported in the Online Appendix.

Secondly, we measured two critical dimensions of organizational trust, i.e., trust in supervisors and trust in colleagues (Nyhan, 2000). Third, we measured three key factors of organizational structures, i.e., complexity, centralization, and formalization (Aiken and Hage, 1968; Robbins, 1987). We anticipate that these three factors are theoretically and empirically distinctive, and that, to different degrees, they influence organizational commitment in the context of Korean bureaucracy. Finally, in order to measure the role of culture, we employed Quinn and Kimberly's (1984) categorization of distinctive values, including group, developmental, hierarchical, and rational cultures. Based on this framework, four distinct variables to represent types of organizational cultures were included in this study. Tables 1, 2, 3, 4, and 5 are shown in the Online Appendix.

Insert Online Appendix Tables 1, 2, 3, 4 and 5

Research Modeling: Hierarchical Linear Modeling (HLM)

Because government bureaucracies have shown an inherent hierarchical structure, with people employed in certain programs and units within public agencies, this research employed hierarchical linear modeling (HLM). HLM explicitly explains the nested nature of data and simultaneously estimates the impacts of factors at different levels on individual-level outcomes while maintaining appropriate levels of analysis for predictors. The basic practical and statistical assumption of the HLM in this study is that Korean public employees are nested within their agencies and subcomponents, creating a hierarchical data structure with two levels of random variation. HLM explicitly explains the nested nature of data and simultaneously estimates the impacts of factors at different levels on individual-level outcomes while maintaining appropriate levels of analysis for predictors.[5] The sample sizes of the level-1 (individual level) and level-2 (agency level) variables were 1,122 and 40, respectively. The survey respondents represented 40 different Korean central agencies, and the level-2 variables were the average scores (i.e., imputation procedure means) for those variables for the respondents from each agency. Each of the 40 agencies was well represented by a number of respondents, with no serious unevenness in responses from different agencies.[6]

Results

Because Korean public employees are partially clustered or nested within their leaders and organizations, this study employed the Analysis of Covariance (ANCOVA) and the intercepts- and slopes-as-outcomes models, which provide unique intercept and slope estimates for each central agency. For example, in the ANCOVA model, each slope of the covariate is assumed to have the same effect on each level of the factor (i.e., homogeneity of regression), while the intercepts- and slopes-as-outcomes model is used for purposes of modeling the associations between level-2 predictors and outcomes, as well as to track the degree to which those predictors explain variance in the level-2 outcomes.

Level-1 (Individual-Level) Model: One-Way ANCOVA Model with Random Effects

In the individual-level model, a one-way ANCOVA model was employed in order to incorporate several covariates and to analyze how these level-1 predictors would affect outcome variables. Eight covariates were included as fixed effects, including 1) sex ($\gamma 10$), 2) age ($\gamma 20$), 3) job tenure in current position ($\gamma 30$), 4) managerial level ($\gamma 40$), and 5) job category ($\gamma 50$). As random effects, level-1 and level-2 variances were included.[7] The final level-1 ANCOVA model is as follows:

Level-1 Model:
Yij (OC, OCB) = β0j + β1j (sex) + β2j (age) + β3j (job tenure) + β4j (managerial level) + β5j (job categories) + β6j (trust in supervisors) + β7j (trust in colleagues) + εij

The results of the six ANCOVA models show that all reliability estimates (β0) are greater than the threshold value of 0.05. For example, the conditional Intraclass Correlation Coeffcient (ICC) indicates that, in the AC model, there is approximately 18.3 percent variation in the AC of Korean public employees across agencies. Similarly, in the models of NC and CC, the proportions of variance across central agencies are approximately 20.5 percent and 16.5 percent, respectively.[8]

Hypotheses Testing: Fixed and Random Effects

The HLM results on OC and OCB are reported in Tables 3 and 4. To test Hypotheses 1 and 2, we regressed OC and OCB on two types of interpersonal trust, together with five control variables.

Table 3. Hierarchical Linear Model (HLM) Results: Organizational Commitment (Affective, Normative, and Continuance)

OC Model	1. Employee-level Model: One-way ANCOVA Model			2. Agency-level Model: Intercepts- and Slopes-as-Outcomes Model		
	Affective	Normative	Continuance	Affective	Normative	Continuance
Reliability Intercept (β0)	.211	.384	.122	.188	.321	.108
Intercept (γ00)	2.96**	3.14**	2.12**	2.26**	2.87**	1.91**
Level-1 Slope (Individual) Model						
1. Demographic Controls, Individual- level						
Sex (γ10)	-.013 (-.262)					
Age (γ20)	-.002 (-.433)					
Job Tenure (γ30)	.003 (.739)					
Managerial Level (γ40)	-.011 (-.630)					
Job Category (γ50)	.041** (2.446)					
2. Interpersonal Trust						
Trust in Supervisor (γ60)	.231** (7.343)	.147** (4.279)	-.067(-1.720)			
Trust in Colleagues (γ70)	.158** (5.225)	.213** (6.419)	-.052(-1.392)			

Level-2 Intercept (Organizational) Model						
1. Organizational Structure						
Formalization (γ01)				**.080**(2.883)**	**.088**(2.916)**	-.025(-.731)
Centralization (γ02)				**.110**(3.838)**	**.102**(3.224)**	.027(.760)
Complexity (γ03)				-.001(-.048)	.028(.969)	**.133**(4.153)**
2. Organizational Culture						
Group Culture (γ04)				**.185**(6.481)**	**.099**(3.155)**	-.052(-1.475)
Hierarchical Culture (γ05)				**-.067** (-2.582)**	-.018(-.621)	**.132**(4.127)**
Developmental Culture (γ06)				**.083**(2.803)**	.029(.882)	-.057(-1.570)
Rational Culture (γ07)				.036(1.373)	.035(1.218)	**.054*(1.688)**
Random Effects						
Level-1 effects (rij) variance	.097			.095		
Level-2 effects (μoj) variance	**.003****			**.003****		
Inter-class correlation (ICC)						
Conditional ICC	18.3%			16.8%		
Proportion of the variance in r_{ij} explained by the model (%)	25.13%			32.53%		
Proportion of the variance in μ_{oj} explained by the model (%)	0%			33.3%		
Deviance	404.25			397.28		
Number of parameters	2			2		

[a] 1) Individual-level N = 1,122 public employees; 2) Organizational-level N = 40 Korean central agencies
•Critical values are 1.96 for P < .05 and 1.65 for P < .10 (t-statistics are in parentheses).
***P* < .05: significant at 0.05-level
**P* < .10: significant at .10-level

Table 4. Hierarchical Linear Model (HLM) Results:
OCB (Conscientiousness, Courtesy, and Civic Virtue)

OC Model	1. Employee-level Model: One-way ANCOVA Model			2. Agency-level Model: Intercepts- and Slopes-as-Outcomes Model		
Reliability Intercept (β0)	Affective	Normative	Continuance	Affective	Normative	Continuance
	.211	.384	.122	.188	.321	.108
Intercept (γ00)	**2.96****	**3.14****	**2.12****	**2.26****	**2.87****	**1.91****
Level-1 Slope (Individual) Model						
1. Demographic Controls, Individual- level						
Sex (γ10)	.038					

Age (γ20)	.003					
Job Tenure (γ30)	-.002					
Managerial Level (γ40)	.014					
Job Category (γ50)	-.029					
2. Interpersonal Trust						
Trust in Supervisor (γ60)	.136**(4.698)	.107** (3.702)	.127** (4.192)			
Trust in Colleagues (γ70)	.128**(4.712)	.096** (3.501)	.092** (3.219)			
Level-2 Intercept (Organizational) Model						
1. Organizational Structure						
Formalization (γ01)				.130** (4.790)	.142** (5.233)	.107** (3.772)
Centralization (γ02)				.039(1.442)	**.087** (3.246)**	.027 (.975)
Complexity (γ03)				.045(1.874)	.029 (1.183)	.038 (1.497)
2. Organizational Culture						
Group Culture (γ04)				.219** (8.103)	.152** (3.155)	.132**(4.663)
Hierarchical Culture (γ05)				-.041** (-1.961)	-.042 (-2.016)	-.015 (-.702)
Developmental Culture (γ06)				.051** (1.968)	.083** (.3.186)	.114 **(4.179)
Rational Culture (γ07)				.061** (2.313)	.033 (1.261)	.050 (1.837)
Random Effects						
Level-1 effects (r_{ij}) variance	.097			.095		
Level-2 effects (μ_{oj}) variance	.003**			.003**		
Inter-class correlation (ICC)						
Conditional ICC	18.3%			16.8%		
Proportion of the variance in rij explained by the model (%)	25.13%			32.53%		
Proportion of the variance in µoj explained by the model (%)	0%			33.3%		
Deviance	404.25			397.28		
Number of parameters	2			2		

[a] 1) Individual-level N = 1,122 public employees; 2) Organizational-level N = 40 Korean central agencies
•Critical values are 1.96 for P < .05 and 1.65 for P < .10 (t-statistics are in parentheses).
***P* < .05: significant at 0.05-level
**P* < .10: significant at .10-level

First, the results of this study reveal that TS is the most significant predictor of AC among employees, to the extent that supervisory trust among Korean public employees is more positively associated with AC (γ = .231, $p < 0.05$) than NC or CC (γ = .147, $p < 0.05$; γ = -.067, $p < 0.05$, respectively). Similarly, TC among employees has a more statistically significant relationship with AC and NC than CC (γ = .158, $p < 0.05$; γ =

.213, $p < 0.05$; $\gamma = -.052$, $p < 0.05$, respectively). Second, with regard to the relationship between interpersonal trust and OCB, the results show that TS enhances all the dimensions of OCB, with particularly positive and significant impacts on behaviors of conscientiousness and civic virtue among Korean public employees ($\gamma = .155$, $p < 0.05$; $\gamma = .126$, $p < 0.05$). Another dimension of trust, TC, is also very positively associated with OCB in a way that most significantly increases conscientiousness behaviors of Korean public employees ($\gamma = .149$, $p < 0.05$). The results confirm that, in Korean public agencies, both types of interpersonal trust are critical to increase the commitment and loyalty of public employees to their organizations and to develop the civic and moral behaviors of public employees in significant and positive ways. While this research does not measure actual performance or productivity outcomes, the findings imply that a high level of interpersonal trust will positively impact individual and organizational performance via OC and OCB mediators.

Additionally, in order to test the coefficient differences between TS and TC on OC and OCB, this study used an independent sample T-test method by dividing the sample into two groups of TS (Group 1) and TC (Group 2). Results of the test show that the impacts of TS and TC on OC and OCB are statistically different, and that the difference is significant overall. Each of six ANCOVA models shows that all reliability estimates (β0) are greater than 0.05. We also measured proportions of level-1 variance as explained by seven level-1 predictors and examined the fixed and random effects [this analysis confirmed hypotheses 1 and 2].

Level-2 (Agency-Level) Model: Intercepts- and Slopes-as-Outcomes Model

An intercepts- and slopes-as-outcomes model (agency-level), which assumes that intercepts and slopes have random effects, was used for further hypotheses testing.[9] Seven fixed effects were included as predictors of organizational structure and culture (at level 2), including 1) formalization (γ01), 2) centralization (γ02), 3) complexity (γ03), 4) group culture (γ04), 5) hierarchical culture (γ05), 6) developmental culture (γ06), and 7) rational culture (γ07). As random effects, level-1 and level-2 variances were included.[10] Below is the final intercepts- and slopes-as-outcomes model:

Level-1 (Individual) Model:

Yij (OC, OCB) = β0j + β1j (sex) + β2j (age) + β3j (job tenure) + β4j (managerial level) + β5j (job categories) + β6j (trust in supervisors) + β7j (trust in colleagues) + εij

Level-2 (Agency) Model:

Intercept: β0 = γ00 + γ01 (formalization) + γ02 (centralization) + γ03 (complexity) + γ04 (group culture) + γ05 (hierarchical culture) + γ06 (developmental culture) + γ07 (rational culture) + u0j

Slope 1: β6j (TS) = γ60 + γ61 (formalization) + γ62 (centralization) + γ63 (complexity) + γ64 (group culture) + γ65 (hierarchical culture) + γ66 (developmental culture) + γ67 (rational culture) + u0j

Slope 2: β7j (TC) = γ70 + γ71 (formalization) + γ72 (centralization) + γ73 (complexity) + γ74 (group culture) + γ75 (hierarchical culture) + γ76 (developmental culture) + γ77 (rational culture) + u0j

Other Slopes: β1j = γ10; β2j = γ20; β3j = γ30; β4j = γ40; β5j = γ50

In the three intercepts- and slopes-as-outcomes models, all reliability estimates are greater than 0.05. For example, the conditional ICC coefficient indicates that, in the OCB conscientiousness model, there is approximately 16.8 percent variation across agencies. Similarly, in the OCB models of courtesy and civic virtue, the proportions of variance across central agencies are approximately 21.4 percent and 22.4 percent, respectively.[11]

Hypotheses Testing: Fixed and Random Effects

This study finds that the level-1 fixed effects of the intercepts- and slopes-as-outcomes models are not different from the level-1 fixed effects of the ANCOVA model (see Tables 8 and 9). First, our findings from tests about structural impacts confirm that, in general, formalized and centralized organizational structures in Korean bureaucracy are positively associated with the AC, NC, and courtesy in OCB of Korean public employees (e.g., centralization coefficients are *B* = .110**, *B* = .102**, and *B* = .087**, respectively). On the contrary, complexity in Korean public agencies does not positively influence the mean levels of AC, NC, and OCB (i.e., the grand mean of the outcome variables) among public employees. Interestingly, this study also finds that the impact of complexity on CC (*B* = .133**) is more significant and positive than the impact of complexity on AC or NC. This finding implies that the more complex is an organization, the less psychological attachment or organizational loyalty exists among public employees in Korea. Consequential to this finding, it is also expected that employees would make career changes and leave their current organizations if certain extrinsic conditions were fulfilled [this analysis partially confirmed hypotheses 3, 4, and 5].

Second, the results indicate that some dimensions (e.g., group and developmental cultures) of organizational cultures significantly and positively affect six different outcomes among Korean public employees. For example, group culture and developmental culture variables are positively and significantly related to AC and conscientiousness in OCB (B = .185**, B = .083**, and B = .242**, respectively), as well as all three OCB sub-constructs. These findings suggest that Korean employees working within group or developmental cultures are more likely to make commitments to their organizations, and that they are more likely to provide extra help to coworkers and to volunteer for special work activities. Third, the results of hierarchical culture impacts on outcome variables suggest that Korean public employees working in hierarchical cultures are less likely to show high levels of OC and OCB, as well as to be generally negative (in cases of AC, conscientiousness and courtesy of OCB, for example, B = -.067**, B = -.053**, and B = -.056**, respectively). On the contrary, CC is positively and significantly associated with hierarchical culture. This finding implies that hierarchical organizations are less likely to achieve high levels of long-term organizational effectiveness and productivity [this analysis partially confirmed hypotheses 6, 7, 8, 9, and 10]. Table 5 presents our ten hypotheses and their results.

Table 5. Summary of the Hypotheses and Results

		HLM Model: Level-1	HLM Model: Level-2
Hypothesis 1	In Korean public agencies, as the degree of trust in supervisors increases, the degrees of OC and OCB among employees will increase.	Confirmed	
Hypothesis 2	In Korean public agencies, as the degree of trust in colleagues increases, the degrees of OC and OCB among employees will increase.	Confirmed	
Hypothesis 3	In Korean public agencies, as the degree of formalization increases, the degrees of OC and OCB will increase.		Confirmed
Hypothesis 4	In Korean public agencies, as the degree of centralization increases, the degrees of OC and OCB will increase.		Confirmed
Hypothesis 5	In Korean public agencies, as the degree of complexity increases, the degrees of OC and OCB will increase.		Partially Confirmed
Hypothesis 6	In Korean public agencies, as the degree of group culture increases, the degrees of OC and OCB will increase.		Confirmed
Hypothesis 7	In Korean public agencies, as the degree of developmental culture increases, the degrees of OC and OCB will increase.		Confirmed
Hypothesis 8	In Korean public agencies, as the degree of rational culture increases, the degrees of OC and OCB will increase.		Partially Confirmed
Hypothesis 9	In Korean public agencies, as the degree of hierarchical culture increases, the degrees of OC and OCB will increase.		Confirmed

Hypothesis 10	In Korean public agencies, group and developmental cultures are more strongly associated with OC and OCB than rational and hierarchical cultures.		Confirmed

Discussion and Conclusion

With regard to the public management profession in Asian countries, there are claims about its distinctiveness compared to the dominant global public management models originating from the major Western nations. Recognizing major diversities in the past and present contextual factors (embedded in the formations of administrative systems) among countries within Asia, this study analyses whether global public management models, theories, and practices can be generalized across countries. By testing and confirming a number of research hypotheses developed within a Korean bureaucratic context, this research at least partially addresses some major issues of both the "uniqueness" and "universality" of Asian public management.

OC and OCB in the public service sector are important organizational characteristics, as it is fair to posit a proximal relationship between the perceived outcomes of OC and OCB and actual performance at both individual and organizational levels. Although considerable research has investigated the antecedents of OC and OCB, much of the existing work has focused on OC and OCB in business sectors, rather than in the major government agencies of Western countries. The research that has examined the job involvement of public employees, while valuable, does not thoroughly assess how interpersonal trust, organizational structure, and the dimensions of workplace cultures influence employees in central government agencies to become more committed and to show more civic-oriented behavior in their work. The aim of this study is to fill the gap in existing public management research by examining how one individual-level factor (i.e., interpersonal trust) and two organizational-level factors (i.e., organizational structure and workplace culture) impact the OC and OCB of public employees in government work settings in Korea. The three main factors, together with the set of control variables included in this research, explain a substantial amount of variance in OC and OCB outcomes in a sample of 1,122 Korean public employees and 40 Korean central government agencies.

First, the HLM results suggest that interpersonal trust plays a critical role in enhancing OC and OCB among Korean public employees. Both types of interpersonal trust (i.e., trust in supervisors and trust in colleagues) increase OC and OCB outcomes among employees of Korean bureaucracies. These findings from the Asian work context are consistent with results found in previous studies about public employees in the U.S. (e.g., Park and Rainey, 2012). This consistency implies that the positive impacts of interpersonal trust on the behaviors of public employees are universal and can be generalized regardless of national or organizational characteristics. From a performance management point of view, even though managers must take an active and positive role in employee performance to ensure that goals are met, managers also need to develop a process that encourages employees to accept responsibility for their own performance, to enable them to achieve and sustain superior performance, and to treat them as partners in working toward organizational goals and effectiveness. To achieve better performance in Korean public agencies through the use of managerial tactics such as mentoring and coaching approaches, HR managers in Korean central agencies need to develop and maintain trust-based mechanisms and processes. These mechanisms and processes can be referred to as organizational trust socialization, through which an individual employee acquires the social knowledge and skills necessary to assume an organizational role and develop high levels of OC and OCB.

Second, this study indicates that organizational structure plays a vital role in enhancing the OC and OCB of Korean employees. From a comparative perspective, the major findings of this study imply that certain aspects of Asian bureaucratic structures and institutional arrangements are key factors in understanding and managing public employees in this region. Specifically, as anticipated, formalization and centralization variables are significantly and positively associated with most of the sub-dimensions of OC and OCB. These results suggest that formalized and centralized organizational structures in Korean bureaucracy bring positive consequences to both employees and organizations and, accordingly, contribute to building and developing individual and organizational capacities. One of the reasons for the positive impact of formalization and centralization in Korean central agencies may be due to rank-in-person HR systems, which are sharply different from the rank-in-job systems of the U.S. and other European countries (Kim, 2010; Lee and Moon, 2007). Centralized and Confucian-based HR systems in Korea tend to cause employees to perceive formalized and/or centralized structures as more acceptable, efficient, and even equitable. This perception ultimately increases the level of positive organizational behaviors among employees. These are important new findings as no previous study about public management in East Asian countries has investigated the role of organizational structures in increasing OC and OCB among employees. We should be cautious, however, in interpreting the results as directly impacting positive organizational outcomes, because this study does not explicitly measure performance or productivity among employees in Korean bureaucracies. Accordingly, future studies need to investigate whether these structural characteristics actually lead to positive performance outcomes.

Third, the results indicate that, as the degree to which Korean public employees recognize their organizational cultures as group or developmental cultures increases, the levels of OC and OCB among employees increase. That is, this study confirms that certain types of organizational cultures in the public service sector are associated with Confucian societies, and that these cultures are able to nurture the positive job attitudes and behaviors of Asian public employees. A group or team-based culture in Korean bureaucracy is the most important characteristic of Asian organizational cultures in predicting the OC and OCB of Korean public employees, followed by a developmental culture, rational culture, and hierarchical culture. These results suggest the workable angles used by Korean public managers for increasing the OC and OCB of public employees. For example, in order to improve employee OC and OCB, managers need to develop, promote, and accommodate characteristics of group and developmental cultures, such as open communication, participation, managerial flexibility, innovative strategies, and continual adaptation to the external environment. Efforts to decentralize and deregulate Korean traditional HR systems are necessary on an ongoing basis. The important contributions of this study should be acknowledged in light of certain limitations. This study relied on a cross-sectional design. Consequently, conclusions regarding causal connections between individual-level and organization-level factors and the OC and OCB of Korean public employees should be made with great caution. Additionally, data for this study was collected from public employees in 40 Korean central agencies. Although each of these central agencies handle diverse public responsibilities, the results reported in this study may have somewhat limited generalizability. Accordingly, additional empirical tests with samples of public employees from a broader range of public organizations in East Asian countries would provide more validity for the framework of our research.[12]

Notes

1. AC refers to the affective or emotional attachment an employee feels toward the organization of which the employee is part, characterized by identification and involvement with the organization, as well as enjoyment in being a member of the organization (Allen and Meyer, 1990; O'Reilly and Chatman, 1986). Normative commitment, which is the extent to which a person feels obligated to stay with an organization, emphasizes a belief about the formal and informal responsibility of an employee to the organization and a perceived duty by the employee to work for the organization and its functions (Wiener, 1982). Continuance or calculative commitment reflects "the extent to which an employee needs to stay with an organization based on the individual's recognition of the costs (or lost opportunities, such as pay or promotion) associated with discontinuing the activity or leaving the organization" (Allen and Meyer, 1990, p. 3).
2. For example, Brewer and Walker (2012) found that personnel system constraints in public organizations (e.g., personnel removal constraints and personnel reward constraints) have varying effects on public service performance, which suggests that the degree of structural efficiency in the public sector plays a crucial role in organizational performance.
3. Group culture emphasizes flexibility and internal organization. Organizations that emphasize group culture consequently promote the development of human resources focusing on openness, participation, cohesiveness, and commitment to membership. Development culture also emphasizes flexibility but with greater focus on the external environment. The orientation of a development culture is toward growth, stimulation of creativity, resource acquisition, innovation, and continual adaptation to the external environment. Likewise, the rational culture is focused on the external environment but is control oriented. It emphasizes productivity, performance, and goal achievement. One of the primary motivating factors of a rational culture is competition. The hierarchical culture is both control oriented and internally oriented. It emphasizes rules and regulations, along with standardization to achieve control and stability (Moynihan and Pandey, 2007).
4. A stratified random sampling technique has a high statistical precision compared to simple random sampling, which does not ensure that subgroups are represented equally or proportionally within the sample because the variability within the subgroups is lower compared to the variations in an entire population.
5. One of the rationales for using the HLM method in this study is that ordinary least squares (OLS) modeling does not take into account the interdependence of individual-level observations nested within higher-level (i.e., agency-level) public agencies. Consequently, estimates of standard errors may be biased, and test statistics may not

be valid. To avoid potential problems caused by hierarchically-nested data structures, both the ANCOVA and the intercepts- and slopes-as-outcomes models are used in this research.

6. To address missing data in this study and in order to preserve sample size, we employed the expectation-maximization (EM) algorithm (level 1) and the Markov Chain Monte Carlo (MCMC) imputation method (level 2). The EM algorithm (a) replaces missing values with estimated values, (b) estimates parameters, (c) re-estimates the missing values assuming the new parameter estimates are correct, and (d) re-estimates parameters, and so forth, iterating until convergence. The EM method allows us to obtain an effective sample size and to minimize possible bias in parameter estimates in an HLM analysis. This approach also fully captures the asymptotic properties of the underlying population.
7. In this model, both the un-centering (for dummy variables) and grand-mean centering methods are used because there is no random effect in the slope (that is, ß1j is fixed across agencies). In other words, the level 1 covariates (X variables) are included to control for their effects on the outcomes rather than to model between group variance on the slopes of these variables. The intercept here is interpreted as the expected value of four outcome variables for each public employee, with an average score on each of the level-1 predictors. In this regard, grand-mean centering adjusts the variation in the intercept between agencies to control for differences in the level-1 predictors across agencies.
8. The results also show that, first, the proportions of level-1 variance explained by the seven level-1 predictors in the three models are 25.13 percent (AC), 23.12 percent (NC), and 24.87 percent (CC). Second, the proportions of level-2 variance explained by the eight level-2 predictors in the three models are 0 percent (AC), 25 percent (NC), and 33.3 percent CC).
9. In the intercepts- and slopes-as-outcomes model, we include level-2 predictors. After establishing that significant variation exists between group intercepts and slopes, we use those parameter estimates as level-2 outcomes. The level-2 models are used for purposes of modeling associations between level-2 predictors and outcomes and to track the degree to which those predictors explain variance in the level-2 outcomes. In this model, a grand-mean centering option is used, and variables are added one at a time for model building, while examining coefficients for significance (of random effects) and reliability.
10. Additionally, to examine the cross-level interaction effects between demographic factors (such as managerial level and job tenure) and organizational characteristics, eight interaction terms are included. In the cross-level interaction model, an interaction is defined when the association between level-1 predictors and the outcome variables depend on the level of level-2 predictors. Cross-level interaction occurs between the

level-1 random effect and the level-2 predictors in the slopes-as-outcomes model.

11. First, proportions of level-1 variance explained by the eight level-1 predictors and level-2 predictors in the three models of OC are 32.57 percent (affective), 33.62 percent (normative), and 28.26 percent (continuance). Second, the proportions of level-2 variance explained by the seven level-2 predictors (including interaction effects) in the three models of OCB are 33.33 percent (conscientiousness), 100 percent (courtesy), and 100 percent (civic virtue). Overall, the proportions of level-1 and level-2 variances explained by the intercepts- and slopes-as-outcomes model are greater than the proportions of variance explained by the ANCOVA model.
12. Similar to all prior studies that have focused on OC and OCB using self-reported data, this study shares the potential problem of a common method bias. A variety of non-statistical procedures were introduced in the design of this study in order to reduce potential common method bias. For instance, the anonymity of responses was assured repeatedly in all correspondence and evidenced in every aspect of data collection. A stratified sample method was used, and surveys were completed at different times and in multiple office locations. Varied response formats were presented. These steps successfully attenuated, if not eliminated, common method bias in the results. Future research should rely on longitudinal designs and multiple data sources to more accurately assess the antecedents and consequences of OC and OCB among employees working in Korean government agencies.

References

Aiken, M., & Hage, J. (1968). Organizational interdependence and intra-organizational structure. *American Sociological Review, 33,* 912-930.

Allen, N. J., & Meyer, J. P. (1990). The measurement and antecedents of affective, continuance, and normative commitment to the organization. *Journal of Occupational Psychology, 63,* 1-18.

Bae, K. W. (2007). A study on the organizational justice and organizational citizenship behaviors. *Korean Public Administration Quarterly, 19*(3), 473-500.

Barnes, L. B. (1981). Managing the paradox of trust. *Harvard Business Review, 59,* 107-116.

Berry, F. S. (2007). Strategic planning as a tool for managing organizational change. *International Journal of Public Administration, 30,* 331-346

Bhargava, S., & Kelkar, A. (2000). Prediction of job involvement, job satisfaction, and empowerment from organizational structure and corporate culture. *Psychological Studies, 45,* 43–50.

Brewer, G. A., & Walker, R. M. (2013). Personnel constraints in public organizations: The impact of reward and punishment on organizational performance. *Public Administration Review, 73*(1), 121-131.

Carnevale, D. G., & Housel, S. W. (2001). Human resource management reform in the staes: Entrepreneurialism and incremental change. In S. E. Condrey & R. Maranto (Eds.), *Radical reform of the civil service.* New York: Lexington Books.

Chattopadhyay, P., & George, E. (2001). Examining the effects of work externalization through the lens of social identity theory. *Journal of Applied Psychology, 86,* 781-788.

Deluga, R. J. (1994). Supervisor trust building, leader-member exchange and organizational citizenship behavior. *Journal of Occupational and Organizational Psychology, 67,* 315-326.

Downs, A. (1967). *Inside Bureaucracy,* Boston: Little Brown.

Farh, J. L., Earley, P. C., & Lin, S. C. (1997). Impetus for extraordinary action: A cultural analysis of justice and organizational citizenship behavior in Chinese society. *Administrative Science Quarterly, 42,* 421-444.

Ferres, N., Connell, J. and Travaglione, A. (2004), Co-worker trust as a social catalyst for constructive employee attitudes. *Journal of Managerial Psychology, 19,* 608-622.

George, J. M., & Jones, G. R. (1997). Organizational spontaneity in context. *Human Performance, 10,* 153-170.

Graham, J. W. (1991). An essay on organizational citizenship behavior. *Employee Responsibilities and Rights Journal, 4,* 249-270.

Hage, J., & Aiken, M. (1967). Relationship of Centralization to Other Structural Properties. *Administrative Science Quarterly, 12,* 72-92.

Han, B. J. (2009). The mediating effect of job satisfaction and organizational commitment on the relationship between organizational culture, leadership styles, and organizational citizenship behaviors. *Korea Journal of Public Administration, 47*(3), 165-199.

Heugens, P. (2005). A neo-weberian theory of the firm. *Organization Studies, 26,* 547-567.

Hong, S. B. (2010). Effects of tax officials' self-leadership on their empowerment and organization commitment. *Journal of Korea Contents Review, 10*(10), 326-333.

Hosmer, L. T. (1995). Trust: The connecting link between organizational theory and philosophical ethics. *The Academy of Management Review, 20,* 379-403.

Kang, J. S. (2006). The relationship between organizational structure and effectiveness of social welfare organization. *Journal of Public Welfare Administration, 16*(2), 287-311.

Kim, H. J. (2002). The effects of organizational culture on organizational commitment and job satisfaction in the public sector. *Korean Public Administration Review, 36*(4): 87-105.

Kim, K. S., & Son, J. Y. (2009). A Study of the effect of organizational interpersonal supervisory trust on organizational commitment. *Business Information Research, 28*(2), 41-67.

Kim, P. S. (2010). Korean civil service system and civil service reform. In P. S. Kim (Ed.), *Civil service system and civil service reform in ASEAN member countries and Korea* (pp. 357-393). Seoul, Korea: Daeyoung Moonhwasa Publishing Company.

Kim, W. C., & Mauborgne, R. A. (1993). Procedural justice, attitudes, and subsidiary top management compliance with multinationals' corporate strategic decisions. *The Academy of Management Journal, 36,* 502-526.

Krasman, J. (2011). Taking feedback-seeking to the next "level": Organizational structure and feedback-seeking behavior. *Journal of Managerial Issues, 13,* 9-30.

La Porta, R., Lopez-de-Silanes, F., Shleifer, A., & Vishny, R. W. (1997). Trust in large organizations. *American Economic Review, 87*(2), 333-338.

Lawrence, P. R., & Lorsch, J. W. (1967). *Organization and environment,* Boston: Harvard Business School.

Lee, C. K., & Moon, M. J. (2007). *Performance management reforms in South Korea. In Public administration in east asia* (pp. 427-449). CRC Press.

Lee, H. B., & Kim, D. K. (2011). Effectiveness for team system related to organizational performance in local government: The case of the Daegu metropolitan city. *Korean Public Administration Quarterly, 23*(3), 693-732.

Lee, H. J., & Park, T. H. (2011). Emotional intelligence and organizational citizenship behavior with the theoretical perspective of emotional competence towards public servants of korean central government. *Korea Journal of Organizational Studies, 8*(2), 67-110.

Lee, J. H., & Park, D. K. (2011). The moderating effect of organizational justice on police organization cultures and job satisfactions. *The Journal of Social Science, 18*(1), 89-122.

Lehmann-Willenbrock, N., & Kauffeld, S. (2010), Development and construct validation of the German workplace trust survey (G-WTS). *European Journal of Psychological Assessment, 26,* 3-10.

Likert, R. (1967). *The Human Organization.* New York: McGraw-Hill.

Mayer, R. C., Davis, J. H., & Schoorman, F. D. (1995). An integrative model of organizational trust. *Academy of Management Review, 20,* 709-734.

McAllister, D. J. (1995). Affect and cognition-based trust as foundations for interpersonal cooperation in organizations. *Academy of Management Journal, 38,* 24-59.

Meyer, J. P., & Allen, N. J. (1991). A three-component conceptualization of organizational commitment. *Human Resource Management Review, 1,* 61-89.

Meyer, J., & Allen, N. (1997). *Commitment in the workplace: Theory, research, and application.* Sage Publications.

Moon, H. K., & Kim, K. S. (2006). Critical essay on Korean OCB researches: Mediating effects on organizational trust and organizational commitment. *Korean Business*

Administration Review, 35(2), 609-43.

Moorman, R. H., & Blakely, G. L. (1995). Individualism-collectivism as an individual difference predictor of organizational citizenship behavior. *Journal of Organizational Behavior, 16,* 127-142.

Moynihan, D. P., & Pandey, S. K. (2007). The role of organizations in fostering public service motivation. *Public Administration Review, 67,* 40-53.

Muchinsky, P. (1977). Organizational communication: Relationships to organizational climate and job satisfaction. *Academy of Management Journal, 20,* 592-607.

Nyhan, R. C. (2000). Changing the paradigm: Trust and its role in public sector organizations. *American Review of Public Administration, 30,* 87-109.

O'Reilly, C., & Chatman, J. (1986). Organizational commitment and psychological attachment: The effects of compliance, identification and internalization on prosocial behavior. *Journal of Applied Psychology, 71,* 492-499.

Organ, D. W. (1988). *Organizational citizenship behavior: The good soldier syndrome.* Lexington, MA: Lexington Books.

Park, C. M., & Kim, D. W. (2003). The effects of organizational justice on supervisory trust and organizational commitment. *Korean Public Administration Review, 37*(4), 125-45

Park, S. M., & Joaquin, M. E. (2012). Of alternating waves and shifting shores: The configuration of reform values in the U.S. federal bureaucracy. *International Review of Administrative Sciences, 78*(3), 514-536.

Park, S. M., & Rainey, H. G. (2007). Antecedents, mediators, and consequences of affective, normative, and continuance commitment: Empirical tests of commitment effects in federal agencies. *Review of Public Personnel Administration, 27,* 197-226.

Park, S. M., & Rainey, H. G. (2012). Work motivation and social communication among public managers. *The International Journal of Human Resource Management, 23*(13), 2630-2660.

Podsakoff, P., MacKenzie, S., Lee, J., & Podsakoff, N. (2003). Common method bias in behavioral research: A critical review of the literature and recommended remedies. *Journal of Applied Psychology, 88,* 879-903.

Podsakoff, P., MacKenzie, S., Moorman, R., & Fetter, R. (1990). Transformational leader behaviors and their effects on followers' trust in leader, satisfaction, and organizational citizenship behaviors. *Leadership Quarterly, 1,* 107-142.

Quinn, R. E., & Kimberly, J. R. (1984). Paradox, planning and perseverance: Guidelines for managerial practice. In J. R. Kimberly & R. E. Quinn (Eds.), *Managing organizational transitions* (pp. 259-313). Homewood, IL: Dow Jones-Irwin.

Rainey, H. G. (2009). *Understanding and managing public organizations.* San Francisco, CA: Jossey-Bass.

Ring, P. S., & Van de Ven, A. H. (1994). Developmental processes of cooperative interorganizational relationships. *Academy of Management Journal, 19,* 90-118.

Robbins, S. P. (1987). *Organization theory: Structure, design, and applications* (2nd ed.). Englewood Cliffs, NJ: Prentice-Hall.

Rousseau, D. M., & Parks, J. M. (1993). The contracts of individuals and organizations. In L. L. Cummings & B. M. Staw (Eds.), *Research in organizational behavior* (Vol. 15, pp. 1-43). Greenwich, CT: JAI Press.

Rousseau, D. M., Sitkin, S. B., Burt, R. S., & Camerer, C. (1998). Not so different after all: A cross-discipline view of trust. *Academy of Management Review, 23,* 393-404.

Ryu, E. Y., Kim, Y. H., Lee, K. H., & Seo, Y. S. (2010). A study on the relationships among organizational structure, organizational commitment and job satisfaction at central government agencies in Korea. *Korean Policy Science Review, 14*(4), 317-341.

Schein, E. H. (1992). *Organizational culture and leadership* (2nd ed.). San Francisco: Jossey-Bass.

Schein, E. H. (1996). Culture: the missing concept in organization studies, *Administrative Science Quarterly, 41,* 229-240.

Seo, I. D., & Lee, W. H. (2006). The mediating effect of leader trust and organizational commitment on the relationship between organizational culture, leader style, and organizational citizenship behaviors. *Journal of Human Resource Management Research, 13*(4), 71-106.

Shapiro, D., Sheppard, B. H., & Cheraskin, L. (1992). Business on a handshake. *Negotiation Journal, 8,* 365-377.

Shapiro, S. P. (1987). The social control of impersonal trust. *American Journal of Sociology, 93*(3), 623-658.

Smith, K. G., Carroll, S. J., & Ashford, S. J. (1995). Intra- and inter-organizational cooperation: Toward a research agenda. *Academy of Management Journal, 38,* 7-23.

Song, W. S., & Kim, J. H. (2002). The influence of job autonomy on the relationship between personal characteristics and organizational citizenship behavior among lower ranking public officials. *Korean Public Administration Review, 36*(1), 117-37.

Tan, H. H., & Lim, A. K. H. (2009). Trust in coworkers and trust in organizations, *Journal of Psychology, 143,* 45-66.

Thompson, J. R. (2001). The civil service under Clinton: The institutional consequences of disaggregation. *Review of Public Personnel Administration, 21,* 87-113.

Van Dyne, L., Vandewalle, D., Kostova, T., Latham, M. E., & Cummings, L. L. (2000). Collectivism, propensity to trust and self-esteem as predictors of organizational citizenship in a non-work setting. *Journal of Organizational Behavior, 21,* 3-23.

Wasti, S. A. (2003). Organizational commitment, turnover intentions and the influence of cultural values. *Journal of Occupational and Organizational Psychology, 76,* 303-321.

Wiener, Y. (1982). Commitment in organizations: A normative view. *Academy of Management Review, 7,* 418-428.

World Bank. (2009). Retrieved December 1, 2009, from http://info.worldbank.org/

governance/wgi/sc_country.asp

Yeager, S. J. (1978). Measurement of independent variables which affect communications: A replication of Roberts & O'Reily. *Psychological Reports, 43,* 1319-1324.

Yoo, Y. H. (2010). Comparison of organizational commitment according to a trust type of maritime police and general police. *The Journal of Social Science, 17*(3), 191-201.

Zaheer, A., McEvily, B., & Perrone, V. (1998). Does trust matter? Exploring the effects of interorganizational and interpersonal trust on performance. *Organization Science, 9,* 141-159.

Chapter 8

The Roles of Integrative Leadership in Enhancing Organizational Effectiveness in the Chinese Public Sector :A Research Note[1]

Summary

The main purpose of this study is threefold: (1) to verify whether three leadership styles (i.e., servant leadership, ethical leadership, and participative leadership) contribute to enhancing organizational trust and commitment, (2) to test the full and partial mediating roles of organizational trust and commitment in the relationship between the three leadership predictors and organizational outcomes (i.e., in-role performance and managerial accountability), and (3) to probe indirect leadership impacts on performance and accountability outcomes. Using the alumni database (for 10 years, from 2001 to 2010) of the department of public administration at Zhejiang University, we constructed a survey (2011) (all items are self-reported: first round: 362 participants; second round: 300 participants; third round: 252 participants; valid sample size: 239 participants) that measured public employees' perceptions and behaviors in public organizations such as regarding leadership, commitment, HR policies, perceived organizational state, OCB, job tension, and trust. We employed exploratory factor analysis (EFA) and confirmatory factor analysis (CFA) to operationalize the variables and confirm the latent constructs from the relevant survey questions. Second, to confirm the total direct and indirect effects, we employed a full structural equation model (SEM) (i.e., a measurement model with a path model) to test the interrelationships among variables and to assess the relative strength of each variable. Based on a discussion of the main findings, research and practical implications for public management theory and practice are provided.

Keyword

□ Servant, Ethical, Participative Leadership □ Guanxi
□ Organizational Commitment □ Organizational Trust □ In-Role Performance
□ Managerial Accountability □ Chinese Organizational Culture □ Public Sector

Sung Min Park Associate Professor, Sungkyunkwan University
Qing Miao Associate Professor, Zhejiang University
Min Young Kim M.P.A., Sungkyunkwan University

Introduction

China's economic reform has led to a massive influx of foreign investment as well as Western management ideas and practices, which have become some of the major factors influencing leadership behavior in the Chinese public sector (Tsui, Wang, Xin, Zhang, & Fu, 2004). Drawing upon these market- and entrepreneurship-oriented reform initiatives, a growing number of public organizations have adopted Western management practices such as human resource management and development practices (He, Chen, & Zhang, 2004; Lewis, 2003; Warner, 1997) and employee participation and empowerment programs (Hua, Chin, Sun, & Xu, 2000; Lee, 2004; Noronha, 2002) in order to increase employees' positive outcomes such as commitment, job satisfaction, and performance. For example, as collaborative and employee-empowered leadership tools have started being labeled as a way of securing employee commitment to organizations in the West (Lashley, 2000; Quinn & Spreitzer, 1997; Shipper & Manz, 1992), theorists and practitioners in China have begun to see the nonhierarchical leadership approach as an effective way to secure employee commitment and loyalty (Scott et al., 2003; Tsui et al., 2004; Wang, 1994), and public managers in China have been encouraged to adopt participative leadership (Chen, 2002; Wang, 1994; Wong et al., 2001).

Increasingly prominent in leadership research are the concepts of servant, ethical, and participative leadership. For example, servant leadership, which can be defined as "a process of leaders and followers partnering together for the purpose of achieving a common vision in which the good of the led are placed over the good of the leaders (Maak, & Pless, 2006:p.110)," has been proved to have positive impacts on the effectiveness of organizations in the attainment of common objectives or goals (Edmondson, Roberto, & Watkins, 2003; Gibson & Vermeulen, 2003; van der Vegt & Janssen, 2003). In a similar vein, some studies have also revealed that a good leader is an ethical and effective leader and that ethical leadership builds trust, brings credibility and respect for both employees and the organization, and creates a good climate within the organization (Ciulla, 1995). A participative or shared leadership style, which takes into consideration the opinions and thoughts of subordinates before decisions are made, is described as "broadly distributed among a set of individuals instead of centralized in the hands of a single individual who acts in the role of a superior" (Pearce & Conger, 2003:p.1).

The main purpose of this study is to investigate the relationships among the three aforementioned types of leadership, (i.e., servant leadership, ethical leadership, and participative leadership), mediators, and organizational outcomes in the Chinese public sector. Drawing on previous literature and relevant theories, we develop a set of research hypotheses to test the relationships among the different leadership characteristics, organizational trust (affective and cognitive trust) and commitment (affective, continuance, and normative commitment), and other effectiveness outcomes such as managerial accountability and in-role performance in the Chinese public sector (shown in Figure 1). Studying and analyzing these predictors, mediators, and outcomes is of significant importance to theory because this research has empirically tested a set of research hypotheses to probe whether the impacts of those variables on in-role performance and managerial accountability within a modern-Confucian bureaucracy would be pronounced and to confirm whether a set of theories of the main variables derived fundamentally from a Western perspective would also be conceptually generalized and empirically validated in the Chinese public sector. This study also lays the groundwork for additional bureaucratic practice in the area by providing a number of practical and managerial implications for Asian civil servants.

Figure 1. Research Modeling

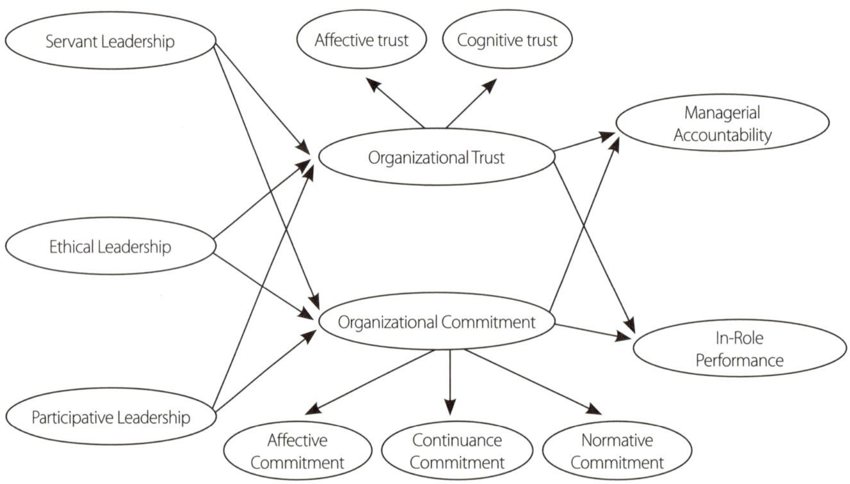

The Coming Wave : Emerging Attributes of Integrative Leadership in the Chinese Public Sector

Servant Leadership

Servant leadership focuses on developing employees to their fullest potential in the areas of task effectiveness, community stewardship, self-motivation, and future leadership capabilities (Greenleaf, 1977). Servant leadership is based on the premise that to bring out the best in their followers, leaders should rely on one-on-one communication to understand the abilities, needs, desires, goals, and potential of those individuals. With knowledge of each follower's unique characteristics and interests, leaders then assist followers in achieving their potential. This encouragement is done through building self-confidence (Lord, Brown, & Freiberg, 1999), serving as role models, inspiring trust, and providing information, feedback, and resources. In this regard, conceptually and practically speaking, servant leadership may conspicuously differ from traditional approaches to leadership in that it stresses personal integrity and focuses on forming strong long-term relationships with employees. It is also unique, effective, and innovative in that it extends outside the organization—servant leaders serve multiple stakeholders, including their communities and society as a whole (Graham, 1991). Servant leadership shows promise as a way to build trust with employees, customers, and communities.

Leadership research over the past few decades has suggested that the relationships that form between leaders and followers are central to servant leadership and that the relationships employees develop with their leaders are critical for understanding the ways in which employees can fulfill their potential and become self-motivated and committed (Manz & Sims, 1987). When leaders nurture self-efficacy and self-motivation and stress community involvement, employees in turn become more committed to organizational values and goals (Shamir, House, & Arthur, 1993) and hence they are more willing to maintain high performance levels (Wayne, Shore, & Liden, 1997) and they are more likely to voluntarily accept their leaders' concern for the community in which the organization operates.

The very concept of servant leadership is based on the values of humility and respect for others. The primary functional elements of servant leadership grow out of proper leadership values. The values of servant leaders not only yield observable attributes but also affect the leaders' organizations. The personal values of leaders, such as honesty and integrity, play a primary role in establishing interpersonal and organizational trust. Trust holds together servant-led organizations. Leaders who show appreciation for others reflect appropriate, unconditional love for their followers. Such leaders incorporate empathy, patience, and encouragement in their relational styles. The empowerment of organizational members also grows out of a trusting environment. Overall, considering this evidence, we conclude that servant leaders are expected to significantly and directly increase the levels of employees' trust and organizational commitment and, furthermore, that servant leaders can enhance the accountability and job performance of their employees indirectly but ultimately.

Ethical Leadership

A key distinction of ethical leadership is its emphasis on an internalized moral perspective, moral person, and moral manager and on idealized influence (see Brown & Treviño, 2006; Walumbwa et al., 2008). Ethical leadership, in its true sense, promotes ethical conduct by practicing as well as consciously managing ethics and holding everyone within the organization accountable for it (Treviño & Brown, 2004). Brown et al. (2005) defined ethical leadership as "the demonstration of normatively appropriate conduct through personal actions and interpersonal relationships, and the promotion of such conduct to followers through two-way communication, reinforcement, and decision-making" (also, see Brown & Treviño, 2002: p.120).

Fundamentally, ethical leadership involves leading in a manner that respects the rights and dignity of others (Ciulla, 2004). Because leaders are by nature in a position of social power, ethical leadership focuses on how leaders use their social power in the decisions they make, the actions they engage in, and the ways they influence others (Gini, 1997). Additionally, leadership is a relational concept in the sense that it is constructed in and through social interactions with followers. Furthermore, being an ethical leader is about being both a moral person as well as a moral manager (Treviño, Hartman, & Brown, 2000). Moral managers consciously attempt to foster their followers' moral behavior by setting clear moral standards and expectations and creating ground rules for moral conduct (Brown & Treviño, 2006; Enderle, 1987; Treviño et al., 2003). That is, leadership is an essential feature of the ethical culture of an organization and it is the leader who is able to place ethics on the organizational agenda (Treviño, Brown, & Hartman, 2003; Treviño et al., 2000).

As noted above, moral managers consciously attempt to foster their followers' moral behavior by setting clear moral standards and expectations and creating ground rules for moral conduct (Brown & Treviño, 2006; Enderle, 1987; Treviño et al., 2003). The notion of the moral manager is founded on three concepts: role modeling through visible action, the use of rewards and discipline, and communicating ethics and values (Treviño et al., 2000, p. 131). From a global perspective, regardless of regions, sectors, or institutions, because ethical leaders might be able to create and develop positive organizational climates and cultures through social interactions with followers, we posit here that ethical leaders in the Chinese public sector are also expected to significantly and directly increase the levels of employees' trust and organizational commitment. In a similar vein, servant leaders could also indirectly enhance the accountability and job performance of their employees.

Participative Leadership

Participative leadership is defined as leadership that involves employees across all levels of the hierarchy in decision-making (Spreitzer, 2007). Participative leaders involve their subordinates in making and implementing decisions. They seek subordinates' input on important decisions and value others' points-of-view. Participatory systems allow employees to use their voices to influence internal and external strategy, protect organizational responsiveness, and hold the managers accountable. Likewise, participative leadership aims to increase the participation of followers by providing them with greater discretion, attention, influence, support, information, and other resources and to share the issue of problem solving with followers by consulting them before making decisions (Bass, 1990; Nystrom, 1990).

Participative leadership is very much a Western management concept in that it embodies joint decision making and shared influence among followers (Koopman &Wierdsma, 1998). Growing evidence from cross-cultural research indicates that intrinsic task motivation may not have favorable impacts on employees in countries with a large power-distance culture, such as China. Some researchers maintain that participative leadership may not work effectively in China not only because the large power-distance culture of China promotes the virtues of submission, humility, tolerance, and hierarchy (Hofstede, 1991, 2001) but also because of the influence of Confucian ideology whereby leaders are expected to act as the parent of the group or organization and to practice authoritarian control (Bond, 1996; Hui & Tan, 1996). Moreover, other researchers have contended that Communist ideologies, which emphasize wholehearted service to the people, loyalty to the Party and the leader, and hard work and self-sacrifice for the collective interest, help to foster a more command-based leadership style, especially in the Chinese public sector (e.g., Tsui et al., 2004).

There is also a growing body of literature on participation and employee empowerment that has discovered that the more participative various aspects of an organization are, the more the visible chances for its effectiveness can be observed (Summers & Hyman, 2005). As is proposed in this study, participative leadership may influence work performance through generating high levels of employees' trust in their immediate supervisors and high levels of commitment to their organizations. Previous studies illustrate that the concepts and theories of these three types of integrative leadership behaviors mainly derive from Western cultures and structures. Hence, from a comparative perspective, it should be valuable to find evidence that there are distinctive and unique constructs among the three styles—servant, ethical, and participative leadership—in the Chinese public sector, as has been similarly shown in Western countries.

The Chinese Cultural Context: Guanxi, Confucianism, and Collectivism

Admittedly, traditional Chinese cultural factors have affected organizational values and systems and even employees' attitudes and behaviors. Although these Chinese cultural values are not conceptually exhaustive, it has been believed that some of these cultural factors, such as guanxi, Confucianism, and collectivism, can be broadly captured (Lin, 2008). We hypothesize that these traditional values have been conflicted, conflated, or complemented with some of the Western managerial values and that this mixed socio-organizational climate will mirror, shape, and modify current Chinese leadership behaviors differently and will influence employees' job attitudes and behaviors accordingly.

First, as collectivists, Chinese people see themselves as part of a larger whole who place high priority on their in-groups, similar to the in-group versus out-group bias in social psychological literature (e.g. Bond & Hwang, 1986; Chan, 1963; Katz & Kahn, 1966; Triandis, 1990; Triandis et al., 1990; Tung, 1991). Those who do not share in-group relationships are walled into a different social network (Hui & Graen, 1997). Guanxi defines who is included in the in-group and who is considered in the out-group, and these connections are thought to very much affect how people are treated. Supervisor–subordinate guanxi is a Chinese term for connections that can make or break business deals, people's fortunes, or even changes in relationships within social or organizational contexts.[2] Guanxi with government officials may act as protection against unstable conditions and may even be a viable alternative to markets (Lovett et al., 1999).

We suppose that supervisor–subordinate guanxi, which is a quality relationship that indicates that managers and employees should be concerned with and considerate of each other even outside of work (Law et al., 2000), may affect leadership behaviors and their impacts on certain organizational outcomes in the Chinese public sector in a way that boosts the effectiveness of particular types of leadership behaviors. That is, Chinese managers are likely to be encouraged to develop guanxi with their subordinates by taking the time to mentor and demonstrate concern for employees in order to secure their loyalty (Cheng et al., 2004), and this process can be continued to the extent that many Chinese employees become allied with specific managers whom they consider their friends (Pearce, 1997). The ability to initiate and maintain supervisor–subordinate guanxi in the Chinese culture may be very important for leaders.

Likewise, Confucianism, one of the most influential social philosophies or managerial ideologies in China, has been transplanted to public organizations as Confucian management practices. Because some of the Confucian managerial values, such as benevolence, sympathy, forgiveness, loyalty, and humility, are closely related to the main components of integrative leadership (e.g., the values of ethics, harmony, righteousness, and trust), we believe that Confucianism could contribute to integrative leadership success in general (Cheung & Chan, 2005) but also that the different impacts of Confucian organizational culture on the relationship between each type of leadership and employees' job attitudes and behaviors can be observed. Additionally, according to the study by House et al. (2004),

Chinese society and organizations are still dominated by collectivistic culture. Drawing upon the individualist- collectivist theoretical dimension of culture and on empirical findings from previous comparative studies, as well as addressing the important aspects of Chinese collectivistic cultural tradition and leadership practices (e.g., see Neubert and Wu, 2006; Walumbwa and Lawler, 2003), we suppose that collectivism is expected to at least indirectly or partially influence the impact of specific types of leadership on positive job attitudes in Chinese organizations.

Therefore, we should admit that Chinese cultural factors such as guanxi-, Confucianism-, or collectivism-based social interactions within an organization are crucial contingencies that surround the configuration of the leadership-mediator-outcome relationship and that, because China and Western countries represent significantly different cultures, the relationship is not the same. To summarize, one may posit that under specific cultural or organizational contexts, particular leadership styles will be more prominently associated with a set of organizational positive outcomes than will others. Against this backdrop, in order to test the impact of leadership on organizational outcomes within peculiar and idiosyncratic Chinese cultural and managerial environments, i.e., guanxi, Confucianism, and collectivism, we include three types of effective integrative leadership practices (servant, ethical, and participative leadership). The common characteristics of these integrative leadership behaviors are distributive, collaborative, empowered, and nonhierarchical, which are very distinctive from the conventional leadership styles. We examine the latent constructs of the three dimensions of integrative leadership in the Chinese public sector and then measure the impacts of each dimension, i.e., servant, ethical, and participative leadership, on two mediators (organizational trust and commitment) and two outcome variables (managerial accountability and in-role performance).

Methods

Samples and Measures

Using the alumni database (for 10 years, from 2001 to 2010) of the department of public administration at Zhejiang University, we constructed a survey (2011) (all items are self-reported; first round: 362 participants; second round: 300 participants; third round: 252 participants; valid sample size: 239 participants) that measured public employees' perceptions of and behaviors in public organizations including the areas of leadership, commitment, HR policies, perceived organizational state, OCB, job tension, and trust.

Research Process

Wave 1		wave 2 (two weeks later)		wave 3(four weeks later)
Zhejiang University alumni database (10 years, 2001 to 2010), 1,800 alumni members received short messages or phone calls to be invited to the survey. Members logged on to the survey website using the random password received from the short message. Members finished the survey online. 362 volunteer participants.	➡	Persons who attended the first wave received a short message or a phone call to be invited to the survey. Members logged on to the survey website using the random password received from the short message. Members finished the survey online. 252 out of 362.	➡	Persons who attended the second wave received a short message or a phone call to be invited to the survey. Members logged on to the survey website using the random password received from the short message. Members finished the survey online. 240 (ultimately valid) out of 252.

* All questionnaires were the same as the ones used in the Western journal with honors (e.g., the JAP), first translated into Chinese and then back to English by two language experts, with the aim of confirming the translation's quality.

Analyses and Findings

First, we employed exploratory factor analysis (EFA) and confirmatory factor analysis (CFA) to operationalize the variables and confirm latent constructs from the relevant survey questions. Second, to confirm the total direct and indirect effects of the main variables, as well as to test the interrelationships among variables and to assess the relative strength of each variable, we adopted a full structural equation model (SEM) (i.e., a measurement model with a path model). Third, making organizational trust (OT) and organizational commitment (OC) the key mediators in the SEM, we hypothesized that OT and OC among Chinese public employees are influenced by the effects of the three types of leadership behaviors. In addition, we proposed that OT and OC increase managerial accountability and in-role performance among Chinese public employees. Moreover, to assess whether OT and OC mediate the effects of a set of antecedents on outcome variables, we used a Sobel's Z statistic test and a bootstrap method. Each indirect path coefficient was calculated to determine whether the indirect effects (mediating effects) were statistically significant. The three antecedent variables of leadership had positive and indirect impacts on both managerial accountability and in-role performance through organizational trust and commitment. As shown in Table 3, some of the coefficients for the indirect paths of the SEM were significant (i.e., the Sobel's Z statistics 5), 6), 11), 12) were statistically significant).

Table 1. Zero-Order Correlations among Antecedents, Mediators, and Consequences

	Servant Leadership	Ethical Leadership	Participative Leadership	Organizational Trust	Organizational Commitment	In-role Performance	Managerial Accountability
1	1						
2	.814**	1					
3	.615**	.641**	1				
4	.807**	.872**	.648**	1			
5	.371**	.438**	.360**	.424**	1		
6	.197**	.252**	.271**	.227**	.269**	1	
7	.133**	.181**	.129**	.167**	.250**	.378**	1

+$p < 0.1$, *$p < 0.05$, **$p < 0.01$, ***$p < 0.001$

Figure 2. Second-Order Three-Factor Model of Integrative Leadership

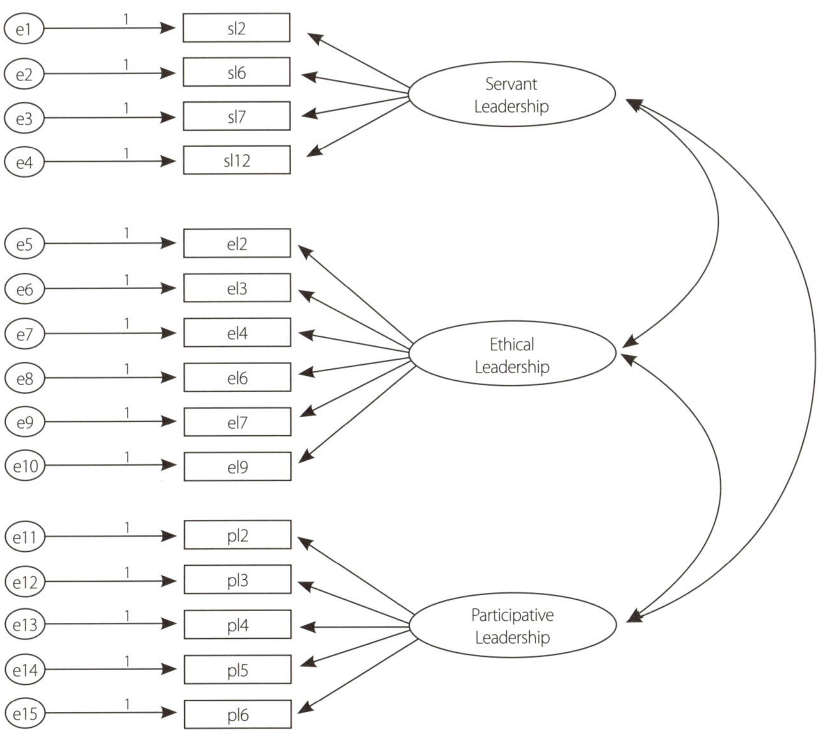

Model	df	X^2	df/ X^2	RFI	NFI	IFI	CFI	RMSEA
Suggested Cutoff Values			<3	>0.90	>0.90	>0.90	>0.90	<0.08
	87	212.419	2.442	.926	.939	.963	.963	.078

All standardized factor loadings are significant at $p<.01$

Sample Items: Measurement of the Three Types of Leadership

Participative leadership(Arnold et al., 2000) (6 items)					
Encourages us to express ideas and suggestions	Listens to our ideas and suggestions	Uses our suggestions to make decisions that affect us	Gives us a chance to voice our opinions	Listens to our ideas when he/she disagrees with us	Makes decisions that are not based only on his/her own ideas
Servant leadership (Ehrhart, 2004; Mitchell, 2008) (14 items)					
Spends the time to form quality relationships	Emphasizes the importance of giving	Creates a sense of community	Decisions are influenced by the department	Tries to reach consensus among the department	Sensitive to department employees' responsibilities
Ethical leadership (Brown et al., 2005) (10 items)					
Disciplines employees who violate	Conducts their own personal lives	Has the best interests	Makes fair and balanced decisions	Listens to what employees say	Discusses business ethics and values

Figure 3. The Full Structural Equation Model (SEM)

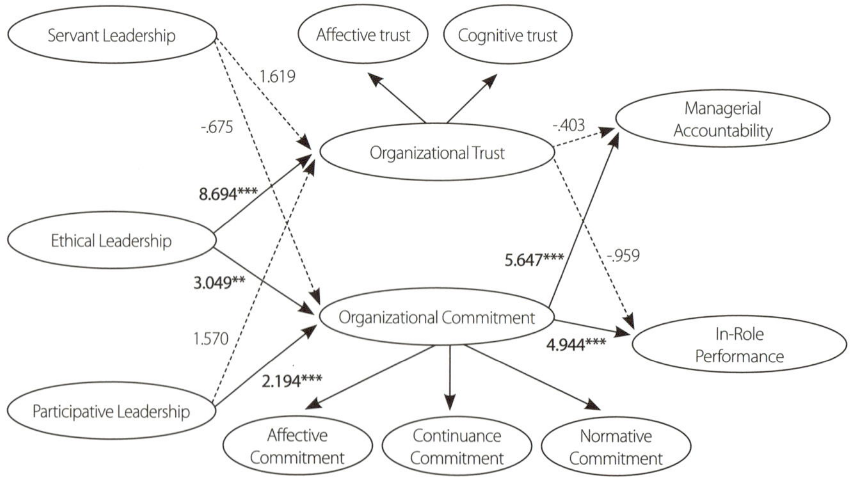

+p < 0.1, *p < 0.05, **p < 0.01, ***p < 0.001

Model	df	X^2	df/ X^2	RFI	NFI	IFI	CFI	RMSEA
Suggested Cutoff Values			<3	>0.90	>0.90	>0.90	>0.90	<0.08
	780	1306.731	1.810	.839	.851	.928	.927	.058

Table 2. Indirect Effects

	Servant Leadership	Ethical Leadership	Participative Leadership	Organizational Trust	Organizational Commitment	In-role Performance	Managerial Accountability
Organizational Trust	.000	.000	.000	.000	.000	.000	.000
Cognitive Trust	.103	.751	.067	.000	.000	.000	.000
Affective Trust	.104	.759	.068	.000	.000	.000	.000
Organizational Commitment	.000	.000	.000	.000	.000	.000	.000
Continuance Commitment	-.010	.051	.023	.000	.000	.000	.000
Normative Commitment	-.086	.432	.194	.000	.000	.000	.000
Affective Commitment	-.069	.348	.157	.000	.000	.000	.000
In-role Performance	-.055	.162	.097	.000	.000	.000	.000
Managerial Accountability	-.060	.252	.123	.000	.000	.000	.000

Table 3. The Results of the Sobel's Test

Path	Test Statistic	p-value ($p < \alpha$=0.05)
1) Servant Leadership → Organizational Trust → Managerial Accountability	-0.3908	0.690>α=0.05
2) Ethical Leadership → Organizational Trust → Managerial Accountability	-0.4102	0.681>α=0.05
3) Participative Leadership → Organizational Trust → Managerial Accountability	-0.3969	0.691>α=0.05
4) Servant Leadership → Organizational Commitment → Managerial Accountability	-0.6740	0.502>α=0.05
5) Ethical Leadership → Organizational Commitment → Managerial Accountability	**2.6536**	**0.007<α=0.05**
6) Participative Leadership → Organizational Commitment → Managerial Accountability	**2.0267**	**0.042<α=0.05**
7) Servant Leadership → Organizational Trust → In-role Performance	-0.8307	0.406>α=0.05
8) Ethical Leadership → Organizational Trust → In-role Performance	-0.9623	0.335>α=0.05

9) Participative Leadership → Organizational Trust → In-role Performance	-0.8210	$0.411 > \alpha = 0.05$
10) Servant Leadership → Organizational Commitment → In-role Performance	-0.6729	$0.501 > \alpha = 0.05$
11) Ethical Leadership → Organizational Commitment → In-role Performance	2.5865	$0.009 < \alpha = 0.05$
12) Participative Leadership → Organizational Commitment → In-role Performance	1.9963	$0.045 < \alpha = 0.05$

Discussion and Conclusion

The several theoretical and practical inquiries of this study were inspired by the notion of which leadership skills and approaches are viable, effective, and fruitful to increase positive job attitudes and job performance. The results of this study indicate that ethical and participative leadership variables play a crucial role in managing and enhancing trust and commitment in the Chinese public sector. This study also shows that organizational commitment is significantly and positively associated with in-role performance. A few findings and implications can be provided.

First, the EFA and CFA results show that the three-factor structure of integrative leadership was confirmed in the Chinese context. The results imply that even when peculiar cultural or institutional factors (e.g., guanxi, Confucianism, or collectivism) that differ from the factors in Western countries might prevail in Chinese public organizations, we can be convinced that these three new types of leadership behaviors and practices are latent but distinct, universal, significant, and effective. In addition, the confirming two-factor structure of organizational trust (i.e., affective and cognitive trust) and the three-factor structure of organizational commitment (i.e., affective, normative, and continuance commitment) provide strong and valid evidence that these theory-based constructs can be generalized in the Chinese context.

Second, we found that ethical leadership in the Chinese public sector is most prevalent and effective. That is, ethical leaders could be outstanding in terms of developing organizational trust, strengthening organizational commitment, and, in indirect ways, increasing employees' accountability and performance in general. Some interpretations can be suggested based on the notion that ethics-based leaders should be more important because certain informal or relational social interactions and communications (e.g., guanxi) or traditional cultural values (e.g., Confucianism and collectivism) prevail in hierarchical structures and cultures within a Chinese context and thus ethical values, affective motives, and trustworthy behaviors can function as invisible but very persuasive norms, rules, and informal regulations for leaders and subordinates. Additional research on the relationship between cultural factors and leadership in the Chinese public sector should be pursued.

Third, from a mediating analysis, our findings revealed that organizational commitment evidently plays a more influential role between ethical leadership and organizational outcomes than does organizational trust is in a way that significantly affects managerial accountability and the in-role performance of Chinese public employees. From a strategic viewpoint, the results might stress the point that under the rubrics of guanxi and the collectivistic culture, Chinese public-sector leaders should be more ethical and should delve into a set of human resource management and development strategies that lead to more-committed people (especially normatively committed employees) within the public sector in order to transform personal guanxi or collectivism behaviors into organizational assets.

Some research limitations can be enumerated. It should be acknowledged that generalizability might be an issue because of the small sample size, some lower numbers below the cutoff criterion in the model fit index, and a mono-method bias coming from using self-reported data. Further research on the leadership-mediator-outcome model is required to overcome these shortcomings by employing panel data and both comparative and time-series research designs and by obtaining more objective performance and effectiveness indicators. More research on the direct impacts of leadership on actual employee performance would be promising because the importance of integrative leadership studies cannot be restricted to the Chinese public sector. With the use of more diverse and advance methodological tools as well as by adopting state-of-the art theoretical approaches, future studies on the effects of integrative leadership on outcomes should be unendingly shaped, replicated, developed, and applied across organizations, sectors, and nations in a globalized world.

Notes

1. Relevant theme tracks of this research:

    1) Key topics in government accountability and government performance management in China. Are they unique or similar to the general performance management literature and why?
    2) Government performance and human resource management
    3) The sociocultural as well as political aspects of government performance management in China, such as Confucianism, a paternalistic leadership style, and guanxi

2. Researchers have elaborated on the meaning and value of guanxi: it is a private channel through which people communicate, interact, and exchange (Hackley & Dong, 2001). Those who have guanxi are granted a high level of trust, respect, and obligation. The closer the guanxi is, the more possible that a misdeed can be forgiven and dismissed as a mistake (Kiong & Kee, 1998).

References

Arnold, J. A., Arad, S., Rhoades, J. A., & Drasgow, F. (2000). The empowering leadership questionnaire: The construction and validation of a new scale for measuring leader behaviors. *Journal of Organizational Behavior, 21,* 249-269.

Bass, B. M. (1990). *Bass and stogdill's handbook of leadership.* New York: Free Press.

Bond, M. H. (1996). *The handbook of Chinese psychology.* New York, NY: Oxford University Press.

Bond, M. H., & Hwang, K. K. (1986). The social psychology of Chinese people. In M. H. Bond (Ed.), *The psychology of the Chinese people* (pp. 213-267). New York: Oxford University Press.

Brown, M. E., & Treviño, L. K. (2002). Conceptualizing and measuring ethical leadership: Development of an instrument. In *Academy of Management Proceedings* (Vol. 2002, No. 1, pp. D1~D6). Academy of Management.

Brown, M. E., & Treviño, L. K. (2006). Ethical leadership: A review and future directions. *The Leadership Quarterly, 17,* 595-616.

Brown, M. E., Treviño, L. K., & Harrison, D. (2005). Ethical leadership: A social learning perspective for construct development and testing. *Organizational Behavior and Human Decision Processes, 97,* 117-134.

Chan, W. T. (1963). *A Sourcebook of Chinese Philosophy.* Princeton University Press.

Chen, X. P. (2002). Leader behavior and employee turnover. In A. S. Tsui & C. M. Lau (Eds.), *The management of enterprises in the People's Republic of China* (pp. 325-346). Boston: Kluwer.

Cheng, B. S., Chou, L. F., Huang, M. P., Wu, T. Y., & Farh, J. L. (2004). Paternalistic leadership and subordinate reverence: Establishing a leadership model in Chinese organizations. *Asian Journal of Social Psychology, 7*, 89-117.

Cheung, C., & Chan, A. C. (2005). Philosophical foundations of eminent Hong Kong Chinese CEO's leadership. *Journal of Business Ethics, 60,* 47-62.

Ciulla, J. (2004) Ethics and leadership effectiveness. In J. Antonakis, A. T. Cianciolo, & R. J. Sternberg (Eds.), *The Nature of Leadership* (pp. 302-327). Thousand Oaks/London/New Dehli: Sage.

Ciulla, J. B. (1995). Leadership ethics: Mapping the territory. *Business Ethics Quarterly. 5*(1), 5-28.

Edmondson, A. C., Roberto, M. A., & Watkins, M. D. (2003). A dynamic model of top management team effectiveness: managing unstructured task streams. *The Leadership Quarterly, 14*(3), 297-325.

Ehrhart, M. G. (2004). Leadership and procedural justice climate as antecedents of unit-level organizational citizenship behavior. *Personnel Psychology, 57*(1), 61-94.

Enderle, G., (1987). *Sicherung des existenzminimums im nationalen und internationalen kontext.* Bern: Eine wirtschaftsethische studie.

Gibson, C., & Vermeulen, F. (2003). A healthy divide: Subgroups as a stimulus for team learning behavior. *Administrative Science Quarterly. 48*(2), 202-239.

Gini, A. (1997). Moral leadership: An overview. Journal of Business Ethics, *16*(3), 323-330.

Graham, J. W. (1991). Servant-leadership in organizations: Inspirational and moral. *Leadership Quarterly, 2*(2), 105-119.

Greenleaf, R. K. (1977), Servant leadership: *A journey into the nature of legitimate power and greatness.* New York, NY: Paulist Press.

Hackley, C. A., & Dong, Q. (2001). America public relations and China's guanxi. *Public Relations Quarterly, 46,* 16-19.

He, W., Chen, C. C., & Zhang, L. H. (2004). Rewards allocation preferences of Chinese employees in the new millennium: Effects of ownership reform, collectivism, and goal priority. *Organization Science, 15,* 221-231.

Hofstede, G. (1991). *Cultures and organizations: software of the mind. London.* UK: McGraw-Hill.

Hofstede, G. (2001). *Culture's consequences, second edition: Comparing values, behaviors, institutions and organizations across nations.* Thousand Oaks, CA: Sage.

House, R. J., Hanges, P., Javidan, R., Dorfman, P., Gupta, V., & GLOBE Associates. (2004).

Leadership, culture and organizations: The GLOBE study of 60 societies. Thousand Oaks, CA: Sage.

Hua, H. M., & Chin, K. S., Sun, H. Y., & Xu, Y. (2000). An empirical study on quality management practices in Shanghai manufacturing industries. *Total Quality Management, 11*(8), 1111-1112.

Hui, C. H., & Tan, C. K. (1996). Employee motivation and attitude in the Chinese workforce. In M. H. Bond (Ed), *The handbook of Chinese psychology* (pp. 364-378). Hong Kong: Oxford University Press.

Hui, C., & Graen, G. (1997). Guanxi and professional leadership in contemporary Sino-American joint ventures in mainland China. *Leadership Quarterly, 8,* 451-465.

Katz, D., & Kahn, R. L. (1966). *The social psychology of organizations.* New York: John Wiley.

Kiong, T. C., & Kee, Y. P. (1998). Guanxi bases, Xinyong and Chinese business networks. *British Journal of Sociology,* 75-96.

Koopman, P. L., & Wierdsma, A. F. M. (1998). Participative management. In P. J. D. Doentu, H. Thierry & C. J. de-Wolf (Eds.), *Personnel psychology: Handbook of work and organizational psychology* (Vol. 3, pp. 297-324). Hove, UK: Psychology Press.

Lashley, C. (2000), Introduction. In C. Lashley & A. Morrison (Eds.), *In search of hospitality: Theoretical perspectives and debates* (pp. 1-17). Oxford: Butterworth-Heinemann.

Law, M., King, G., Rosenbaum, P., Kertoy, M., King, S., Young, N., et al. (2000). *The participation of children with physical disabilities.* Bethesda, MD: National Institutes of Health.

Lee, C. C. (2004). Energy consumption and GDP in developing countries: A cointegrated panel analysis. *Energy Economics, 27*(3), 415-427.

Lewis, S. (2003). The integration of paid work and the rest of life: Is post-industrial work the new leisure?. *Leisure Studies, 22*(4), 343-345.

Lin, C. (2008). Demystifying the chameleonic nature of Chinese leadership. *Journal of Leadership & Organizational Studies, 14*(4), 303-321.

Lord, R. G., Brown, D. J., & Freiberg, S. J. (1999). Understanding the dynamics of leadership: the role of follower self-concepts in the leader/follower relationship. *Organizational Behavior and Human Decision Processes, 78,* 167-203.

Lovett, S., Simmons, L. C., & Kali, R. (1999). Guanxi versus the market: Ethics and efficiency. *Journal of International Business Studies, 30*(2), 231-247.

Maak, T., & Pless, N. M. (2006). Responsible leadership in a stakeholder society-a relational perspective. *Journal of Business Ethics, 66*(1), 99-115.

Manz, C. C., & Sims, jr., H. P. (1987). Leading workers to lead themselves: the external leadership of self-managing work teams. *Administrative Science Quarterly, 32,* 106-129.

Mitchell, T. D. (2008). Traditional vs. critical service-learning: Engaging the literature to differentiate two models. *Michigan Journal of Community Service Learning, 14,* 50-65.

Neubert, M. J., & Wu, J. C. (2006). An investigation of the generalizability of the Houghton and Neck revised self-leadership questionnaire to a Chinese context. *Journal of Managerial Psychology, 21,* 360-373.

Noronha. C. (2002). Chinese cultural values and total quality climate. *Managing Service Quality, 12*(4), 210-223.

Nystrom, H. (1990). Organizational innovation. In M. A. West & J. L. Farr (Eds.), *Innovation and creativity at work* (pp. 143-161). New York: John Wiley & Sons Ltd.

Pearce, C. L. (1997). *The determinants of change management team effectiveness: A longitudinal investigation.* Unpublished doctoral dissertation. University of Maryland, College Park.

Pearce, C. L., & Conger, J. A. (2003). All those years ago: The historical underpinnings of shared leadership. In C. L. Pearce & J. A. Conger (Eds.), *Shared leadership: Reframing the hows and whys of leadership* (pp. 1-18), Thousand Oaks, CA: Sage

Quinn, R. E., & Spreitzer, G. M. (1997). The road to empowerment: Seven questions every leader should consider. *Organizational Dynamics, 26,* 37-49.

Scott, K., Kumar, N., Velusamy, S., Childers, B., Davidson, J., & Soffa, M. (2003). Retargetable and reconfigurable software dynamic translation. In Proceedings of CGO 2003 (pp. 36-47).

Shamir, B., House, R. J., & Arthur, M. B. (1993). The motivational effects of charismatic leadership: A self-concept based theory. *Organization Science. 4*(4), 577-594.

Shipper F., & Manz C. C. (1992) Employee self-management without formally designated teams: An alternative road to empowerment. *Organizational Dynamics, 4,* 48-61.

Spreitzer, G. (2007). Giving peace a chance: Organizational leadership, empowerment, and peace. *Journal of Organizational Behavior, 28*(8), 1077-1095.

Summers, J., & Hyman, J. (2005). *Employee participation and company performance: A review of the literature.* Joseph Rowntree Foundation.

Treviño, L. K., & Brown, M. E. (2004). Managing to be ethical: Debunking five business ethics myths. *Academy of Management Executive, 18,* 69-81.

Treviño, L. K., Brown, M., & Hartman, L. P. (2003). A qualitative investigation of perceived executive ethical leadership: Perceptions from inside and outside the executive suite. *Human Relations, 55,* 5-37.

Treviño, L. K., Hartman, L. P., & Brown, M. (2000). Moral person and moral manager: How executives develop a reputation for ethical leadership. *California Management Review, 42,* 128-142.

Triandis, H. C. (1990). Theoretical concepts of use to practitioners. In R. Brislin (Ed.), *Crosscultural applied psychology* (pp. 34-55). Newbury Park, CA: Sage.

Triandis, H. C., McCusker, C., & Hui, H. C. (1990). Multimethod probes of individualism and collectivism. *Journal of Personality and Social Psychology, 59,* 1006-1020.

Tsui, A. S., Schoonhoven, S. B., Meyer, M. W., Lau, C. M., & Milkovich, G. T. (2004). Organization and management in the midst of societal transformation: The people's republic of china. *Organization Science, 15*(2), 133-144.

Tsui, A. S., Wang, H., Xin, K. R., Zhang, L. H., & Fu, P. P. (2004). Let a thousand flowers bloom: Variation of leadership styles in Chinese Firms. *Organization Dynamics, 33,* 5-20.

Tung, M. (1991). Insight-oriented psychotherapy and the chinese patient. *American Journal of Orthopsychiatry, 6*(2), 196-194.

Van der Vegt, G. S., & Janssen, O. (2003). Joint impact of interdependence and group diversity on innovation. *Journal of Management. 29*(5), 729-751.

Walumbwa, F. O., & Lawler, J. J. (2003). Building effective organizations: Transformational leadership, collectivist orientation, work-related attitudes and withdrawal behaviors in three emerging economies. *International Journal of Human Resource Management, 14,* 1083-1101.

Walumbwa, F. O., Avolio, B. J., & Zhu, W. (2008). How transformational leadership weaves its influence on individual job performance: The role of identification and efficacy beliefs. *Personnel Psychology, 61,* 793-825.

Wang, Z. M. (1994). Organizational decision making and competence utilization among Chinese managers. *Journal of Managerial Psychology, 9,* 17-25.

Warner, M. (1997). China's HRM in transition: Towards relative convergence?. *Asia Pacific Business Review, 3*(4), 19-33.

Wayne, S. J., Shore, L. M., & Liden, R. C. (1997). Perceived organizational support and leader-member exchange: a social exchange perspective. *Academy of Management Journal, 40,* 82-111.

Wong, C. S., Wong, Y. T., Hui, C., & Law, K. S. (2001). The significant role of Chinese employees' organizational commitment: Implications for managing employees in Chinese societies. *Journal of World Business, 36,* 326-340.

Case Study

Corporate Culture Stunts Flexitime

Seung-woo Kang

A group of salaried workers head to a rehearsal after work in Seoul. The number of employees who spend more time on self-improvement thanks to flexible working schedules has been growing of late. However, people say that it is still difficult to do so under Korea's corporate culture.

Cho Su-jin, a worker in the financial industry, usually leaves work at 5 p.m. and heads to a swimming pool.

Thanks to newly-introduced flexible working schedules, her daily life has improved greatly.

"As a woman, it is tough to work in this area for a long time," said the early 30-something Cho, who starts work at 7 a.m.

"After calling it a day earlier, I spend most of my time on self improvement. I go to the pool, take computer programming classes and study to get more certificates.

"I felt some eyebrows were raised over my behavior at first, but now I am used to it," she said.

Overall throughout Korea Inc., employees like Cho are rare, as they are not used to this concept and they fear that they will stand out among the crowds by taking advantage of it.

The discretionary flexible work schedule, in contrast to traditional work arrangements, gives employees a choice over the actual times they work their contracted hours, meaning they can select the beginning of business (BOB) and close of business (COB) in accordance with their circumstances and optimize their off-duty time.

"The system made its debut with much fanfare a month ago, but I think it is in not popular now," said a sales manager of a local financial group on condition of anonymity.

"If someone wants to come in earlier, work eight hours and leave earlier, he needs to be more competent than anyone else. Otherwise, he will definitely be in the hot seat and hear others complain behind his back."

He said that just one out of seven members in his division is currently capitalizing on the system and thanks to his well-earned reputation at work, he has no problem doing so.

In addition, he said that within Korea's corporate culture, the flexible work scheme cannot come to fruition.

"People still take it for granted that employees can't leave the office until after their seniors," he added.

"Therefore, employees seen coming early is a disadvantage because they will have to keep their butts in the seats anyhow."

An employee at a leading major electronics company, also says that hierarchical companies are not the right place to introduce the adjustable working-hour system.

"The top line of the company orders each division to implement the system, but due to the heads of the departments, we cannot willingly take advantage of it," said the salaried worker, who declined to be named.

The public sector appears to be making a more concerted approach toward the implementation of flextime.

The Ministry of Public Administration and Security proposed the plan in May and it will have operated the system on a trial basis until the end of this month before coming up with a finalized one.

Currently, approximate 1,000 public servants from 17 agencies are under this pilot program.

Some say that, if flextime proves to be more productive, more corporations will introduce it. Currently, Korean workers log long hours but compare poorly with workers from other advanced countries in terms of productivity.

According to the OECD, Koreans worked 2,316 hours a year on average in 2007, the longest among OECD member countries. They worked around 1,000 hours more than workers in the Netherlands, and around 500 hours more than the OECD average.

But the nation's productivity is much lower than that of its counterparts, ranking 22nd.

"Korean businesses are still caught in the mentality of the industrialization period. They are working with their bodies not with their brains," said Ahn Byung-wook, a researcher at Samsung Economic Research Institute.

Source: The Korea Times (2010.06.24)

Questions for Discussion

1. Explain in general and then provide examples of how the following organizational characteristics affect the organization's culture:

   a. The design of physical spaces
   b. The absence of formal statements, charters, and creeds
   c. A promotion policy that gives preference to individuals with the most years of service

2. Find an example of a public agency's mission statement or list of priorities. Discuss the connection between the statements within the mission statement and the culture it suggests.

3. Khademian (2002) proposed a cultural roots framework to describe the basic elements of every public agency or program: the public task to be done, the resources available to do it, and the environment in which the agency or program has to operate. Name an organization or department that serves the public in some capacity. Identify and discuss its cultural roots. What are the managerial implications for the culture you describe?

4. What actions can leaders take to change the organizational culture?

Section 5

Structures

- Working Across the Divide
  : Job Involvement in the Public and Nonprofit Sectors

- Research on Accountability in the Korean Central Government Agencies
  : Exploring Antecedent and Moderating Effects of Public Service Motivation, Goal Clarity, and Person–Organization Fit

Section 5

Structures

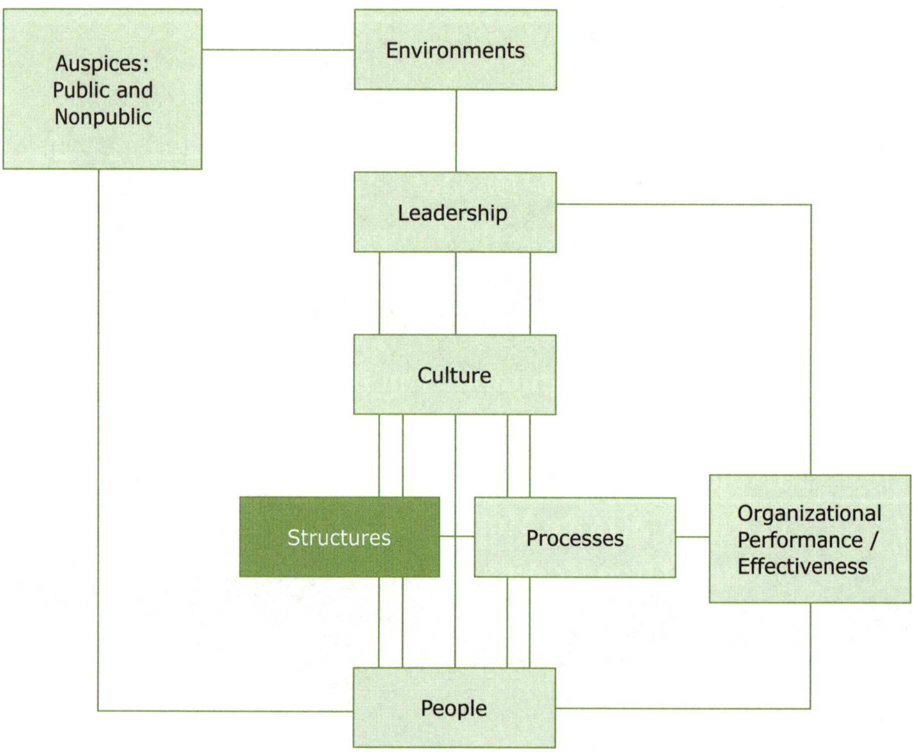

Chapter 9

Working Across the Divide
: Job Involvement in the Public and Nonprofit Sectors

Summary

Job involvement is a principal factor in the lives of most people; employees in the workplace are mentally and emotionally influenced by their degree of involvement in work. Using the data from the National Administrative Studies Project III, this study empirically compares the level of job involvement between managers in the public and nonprofit sectors and explores different aspects including demographic, managerial, and institutional factors that contribute to the apparent differences. The results of the study indicate that the mean level of nonprofit managers' job involvement is significantly greater than for public managers. Each sector had specific variables that significantly and uniquely contributed to job involvement. Overall, the results suggest a need to more fully investigate the various mechanisms and functions of situational and organizational contexts, organizational norms, and culture that were associated with job involvement regardless of sector. Implications and limitations of this research are also discussed.

Keyword

- □ Nonprofit and Public Human Resource management
- □ Job Involvement
- □ Job Design
- □ Motivation
- □ Red Tape

Jessica Word Associate Professor, University of Nevada, Las Vegas
Sung Min Park Associate Professor, Sungkyunkwan University

Introduction

Recent research has shown an increased interest in the role of nonprofit organizations and their management. Increased interest has occurred not only within the field of nonprofit management but also in the area of public administration and management research. The interest of public management and administration scholars in this field stems from increasingly close ties between the public and nonprofit sectors through contracting out of public services (Gazley & Brudney, 2007) and the growth of nonprofit management specializations and degrees in many public administration programs across the country (Mirabella & Wish, 2000). These developments suggest that there are and will continue to be similarities in management between the two sectors.

Theoretical and anecdotal evidence suggests there are both great similarities and great differences between the two sectors. The similarity of serving a public interest has been one of the major forces promoting stronger ties and relationships between the two sectors (Mirabella & Wish, 2000). However, differences in culture and legal structures and the increasing amount of interdependence between the two sectors have created some tensions and negativity toward partnerships, especially on the part of nonprofit executives (Gazley & Brudney, 2007). Differences between operational and employee characteristics between the two sectors might also contribute to tensions. However, little research has been conducted that probes differences between the sectors at the operational level or that examines how these differences affect employees.

The similarities and differences between public and nonprofit organizations are the result of the origins, purpose, history, culture, and legal structures of the two sectors as well as differences between the makeup of each sector' work forces. Just as Rainey and Bozeman (2002) called for a more empirical examination of the differences and similarities in management between the public and private sectors, this article calls for a more empirical examination of the differences and similarities between the public and nonprofit organizations that compares theoretical assertions to empirical observations. This research begins by exploring some of the expected differences and similarities between the two sectors predicted by the literature. The research then uses data from the National Administrative Studies Project III (NASPIII) to empirically compare the level of job involvement between managers in the two sectors and discusses possible reasons for differences, including differing demographic, managerial, and institutional factors. This research is intended to contribute to both the study and practice of public administration and nonprofit management through clarifying theoretical and empirical differences in management between the two sectors.

The Public and Nonprofit Sectors

Development and Origins of the Sectors

Some of the very first observations made about the fledgling government of the United States were made by French philosopher Alexis de Tocqueville in his work Democracy in America, first published in 1835. Similarly, some of the earliest observations about the American voluntary or nonprofit sector were also made by Tocqueville (1835/2000), when he commented on the tendency of individuals in American society to form voluntary and moral associations to address unmet community and individual needs. Tocqueville went on to explain that it is this voluntary spirit and tendency of Americans to form voluntary associations that make American democracy and government work in the face of a culture of individualism. From these early comments, it was clear that from the very outset of our country the fate of the public and nonprofit sectors was intertwined.

The connection between the public and nonprofit sectors in part comes from what is believed to be their origins in society. Economic theory suggests that the governmental and nonprofit sectors have developed in response to the failure of economic markets to meet all of society' needs (Weisbrod, 1975). The failure of markets to meet the needs of society is known as market failure. Market failure occurs because markets fail to provide adequate quantities of collective goods, because there are insufficient profits to be gained from providing these goods because of underspecified property rights (Steinberg, 2006). Non-market-based organizations such as governments and nonprofit organizations are then created to meet these collective needs. If the needs are broad enough to appeal to the majority in a democratic society, then most of these needs can and will be met by governments.

The question then arises, when and why do nonprofit organizations exist, if governments fill in the gaps in the face of market failure? Governments are only partially able to fill the gap between the demands for goods and services and their supply because, in general, a majority of citizens must support a policy or program to create government action (Steinberg, 2006; Weisbrod, 1975). Because of diversity of population in terms of culture, heritage, and economic differences, governments in the United States are often limited in their ability to act because no majority consensus can be reached. The wide heterogeneity of needs and preferences of individuals for goods and services gives rise to an alterative organizational form to provide collective goods, through organizations that are not contained in either the government or the market. The failure of both government and markets is needed to explain the existence and the rise of the nonprofit or third sector.

Alternative theories relating to the origins of the two sectors suggest that inherent qualities shape the two sectors and those within them. Sociological and institutional theorists suggest that nonprofit organizations are not the result of the market but instead result from the combination of religious motivation (Ben-Ner & Van Hoomissen, 1991), public policy (Weisbrod, 1988), the desire to restrain the role of the state in civic life, and public policy and public opinion about the appropriateness of profit in certain areas (Dimaggio & Anheier, 1990). Instead of suggesting that nonprofit and public sector organizations arise because of the market, these theories suggest that the process has more to do with the construction of community values and meaning. This, like the literature surrounding public service motivation, suggests that it is perhaps the nonmarket similarities and differences between the public and nonprofit sectors that shape their place in society.

Similarities Between the Sectors

The theoretical underpinnings of both nonprofit organizations and governments lead us to point out that one of the most substantial similarities between the two is that they both exist, to some extent, to supply collective goods or create some sort of public benefit. In addition, because both are owned and created collectively, neither can distribute excess revenues for individual gains (DiMaggio & Anheier, 1990; Weisbrod, 1998). For this reason, both nonprofits and governments often provide services in areas where the quality is difficult to measure and where markets cannot be trusted to allocate the goods and services because businesses with profit motives will be tempted to cut corners to increase the size of their returns.

Public and nonprofit organizations are also similar in terms of operating in less competitive environments than organization in the for-profit sector (Osbourne & Gaebler, 1992), but competition in some portions of the nonprofit sector can be very high or even place nonprofit enterprises into direct competition with for-profit enterprises. Competition has also increased in the public sector because some forms of privatization have placed agencies and public employees into direct competition to bid for delivery of public services (Martin, 1999).

Both nonprofit and public organizations face similar challenges in terms of management of very complex organizations with multiple goals and difficult-to-measure outcomes (Bailey & Koney, 1996; Brooks, 2002; Kushner & Poole, 1996; Tuckman & Chang, 1991). This, in part, results from the very nature of delivering public goods and services that are difficult to define. In addition, both public and nonprofit organizations face difficulties in defining the criteria that can help them to judge success in delivery of those goods and services. Public agencies with overlapping layers of legislation and multiple stakeholders often find it difficult to define their mission and focus agency activities. Nonprofits, although guided by an underlying mission, face difficulties because of multiple layers of accountability from different funding sources and stakeholders, often making it unclear which goals are the most important (Kim, 2005). Public agencies and nonprofits are also similar in that the outcomes from their efforts are often difficult or impossible to measure directly.

In addition, the growing number of contracts and grants between nonprofits and governments has led to growing similarities in the ways public and nonprofit organizations carry out their missions and employ some management techniques. For example, nonprofit organizations have seen an increase in government funding, which in many cases has come with the requirement that nonprofits comply with governmental accounting standards. In addition, acceptance of government contracts and funding has required more advanced training of managers and the use of outside consultants to meet these standards (DiMaggio & Anheier, 1990; Keating & Frumkin, 2003). Governmental contract requirements and increasing involvement from and sophistication of other funding organizations and donors have required nonprofit organizations to increase their ability to measure outcomes and to account for program results. Overall, these changes have resulted in increased professionalization of the nonprofit sector and a growing push for nonprofit managers to obtain more advanced degrees (Mirabella & Wish, 2000).

Similar changes in operations and sophistication of management have occurred in the public sector, and indeed some of these changes were the result of the same movement, New Public Management (Anheier & Salamon, 2006; Behn, 2001; Morrison & Salipante, 2007; Ospina, Diaz, & O'ullivan, 2002). The movement has led both public and nonprofit managers to establish a similar emphasis on outcomes and the measurement of results. In addition, New Public Management' emphasis on "steering rather than rowing," in part, can be said to be responsible for the transfer of delivery of services from governments to nonprofits. Governments, under New Public Management, are expected to purchase goods rather than produce them directly to gain flexibility and cost savings not available through direct service provision.

Finally, the literature on public service motivation suggests that similarities might exist in the motivation of both public and nonprofit sector employees. Public service motivation can be defined as a "general altruistic motivation to serve the interests of a community of people, a state, a nation or humankind" (Rainey & Steinbauer, 1999, p. 20). Research about the motivations of public sector employees has found that, in general, they are less motivated by monetary incentives and that public employees have a greater interest in altruistic or ideological goals (Rainey, 2003). A survey of nonprofit employees found that they held similar motivations (Light, 2002).

Differences Between the Sectors

Despite the close attention paid to nonprofits in public management and administration literatures, real differences between the two sectors exist and need to be more closely examined to promote greater theoretical understanding about what makes each sector unique. This understanding may aid managers in both sectors to more fully understand the needs and challenges of the other as they work together. Studies of collaboration between the two sectors have documented real difficulties in the relationships between the two sectors (Brooks, 2000; Fosler, 2002; Gazley & Brudney, 2007; O'onnell, 1996; Rainey, 2003) that might be reduced through a better understanding of the distinct challenges, management styles, and techniques used across the sectoral divide.

Public organizations are established by law and publicly funded to carry out mandated activities and policies assigned to them by democratically elected or appointed policy makers. Mandates from higher levels of government increase the number and complexity of restrictions in the areas of personnel and procurement (Rainey & Bozeman, 2002). Restrictions in the area of personnel create difficulties for public managers in the realms of hiring, disciplining, firing, and even rewarding employees (Moynihan & Pandey, 2007b). This contributes to the feeling by the public that government is unresponsive because shortfalls in staffing or changes in the level of demand for services cannot be easily or quickly remedied because of difficulty in hiring or changing the staffing levels in government agencies to meet emerging needs. It also contributes to the frustration of employees and the public because it is often a difficult and time-consuming task to remove unproductive employees.

Nonprofits, in contrast, are often formed by individuals or small groups interested in carrying out a particular mission or filling some unmet need in their community or society (Lohmann, 1989). A recent national survey of nonprofit executives found that a large proportion of the leaders (21%) actually founded the organizations they now operate (Bell, Moyers, & Wolfred, 2006). An additional contrast is that nonprofits largely have control over selecting their own goals and the means by which goals are accomplished. However, to qualify for tax relief granted by the federal government, nonprofit organizations are required to serve some public or collective benefit (Weisbrod, 1988). Further restrictions on operational means are sometimes imposed through the receipt of public contracts or regulations in common areas of nonprofit service delivery, such as health or child care.

A recent study conducted by Feeney and Bozeman (2007) documented that one of the key differences between the two sectors appears to be the number of work hours put in by managers. In their research, they found that managers in nonprofit organizations tend to work longer hours in comparison to public managers. This seemingly minor difference suggests that there are likely many more differences that persist in the personnel and cultural norms between the sectors that could have significant management implications.

In part because of the historical development and culture of nonprofit organizations, substantial differences can also be observed in the characteristics of employees among the public, nonprofit, and private sectors. A telephone survey conducted by the Princeton Survey

Research Associates (Light, 2002) examined characteristics of the nonprofit workforce and found significant differences between their responses when compared to those of public and private workers. In particular, nonprofit employees were much more likely to indicate that they came to work because of the nature of their job and the common good (41%) than were either public (5%) or private (0%) employees. This suggests that nonprofit employees might be even more service oriented than their public sector counterparts. Of nonprofit employees, 75% disagreed that their work was boring, in comparison to 46% of public and 54% of private employees. Nonprofit employees were also less likely to believe that their jobs were a dead end with no future (58%) than were public (47%) and private (54%) sector employees. However, 24% of nonprofit sector employees expressed frustration with a limited ability to advance within their organization.

In addition, using General Social Survey data, Frank and Lewis (2004) found that public sector employees are intrinsically motivated more than are for-profit employees (see also Buelens & Broeck, 2007) and that public employees showed a higher work effort than did private sector employees. Houston (2006) examined the behavioral implications of public service motivation within public, private, and nonprofit sectors and investigated the relationship between public employment and different types of charitable activities. The findings suggest that government employees and nonprofit workers are more prone to engage in charitable activities than are private employees. The differences between the opinions and behaviors of employees across the three sectors suggest that differences in the motivational factors, culture, and structure of organizations are shaping attitudes and creating different incentives to attract individuals to professions in these sectors.

Job Involvement

A review of the literature in organization and management studies reveals that there has been an increasing interest in research about the relationship between job design in organizations and its effect on employee behavior. It is evident that interpreting, analyzing, and conceptualizing the models of work-related attitudes such as job involvement, job satisfaction, organizational commitment, and employee motivation are important and vital areas of research, especially in the area of organizational behavior (e.g., Cherns & Davis, 1975; Moynihan & Pandey, 2007a; Taylor, 1975).

Job involvement is a principal factor in the lives of most people in that employees are mentally and emotionally influenced by their degree of involvement in or alienation from work. The level of job involvement is also of interest to managers and policy makers in general because it eventually plays a role in organizational effectiveness and performance (Argyris, 1964). Job involvement can be characterized as " the degree to which a person identifies with his or her job, actively participates in it, and considers his or her performance important to a sense of worth, self-esteem, or image" (Robbins, 2003, p. 72; also see Moynihan & Pandey, 2007a), as the degree to which it is perceived to be a major source of job satisfaction and salient needs in the workplace (Lawler & Hall, 1970), or as one of the indexes of the quality of work life in organizations. Job involvement is also closely related to the concept of " employee engagement " that is currently in wide use. Drawing on the job design model (e.g., Hackman & Oldham, 1980), the literature on employee engagement has put more emphasis on key elements of engagement such as organizational commitment, teamwork, empowerment, two-way communication, and interpersonal trust (Vance, 2006). More engaged employees are, therefore, expected to achieve higher levels of performance, productivity, and service quality (Erikson, 2004).

According to Kanungo (1982a, 1982b), job and work involvement can be clearly divided because they are differently conceptualized and constructed in the work context and the job context. An employee' involvement in a job is more dependent on the extent to which his or her job satisfies his or her own needs (i.e., more situationally affected). In contrast, involvement with work is assumed to be a more stable psychological characteristic because it is a "normative belief about the value of work in one' life" and is "more a function of one's past cultural conditioning and socialization" (Elloy, Everett, & Flynn, 1991, p. 162). In sum, previous literature has proposed four different constructs of job involvement in organizations: Employees are involved in their job (a) when work to them is a central life interest, (b) when they actively participate in their job, (c) when they perceive performance as central to their self-esteem or sense of worth, and (d) when they perceive performance as consistent with their self-concept (Saleh & Hosek, 1976, pp. 213-214).

Although job involvement may interact with and moderate the relationship among other job attitudes, the construct can be distinguished from job satisfaction or organizational commitments, which are organizational attitudes that are more context specific (Locke, 1976, p. 1300). The subject of job or work involvement may have more important and broader practical and research implications in organizational studies particularly when it is related to such outcome variables as satisfaction, performance, turnover, and absenteeism and to a set of demographic, managerial, and institutional antecedents such as gender, age, intrinsic and extrinsic motivation, and other organizational structural and cultural influences (Park & Rainey, 2008).

A number of significant conceptual and methodological questions regarding job involvement- for example, measures, scales, and relations with other constructs-have been raised and discussed for a long time but are not yet resolved. Furthermore, the generic research on job involvement in private sector organizations (e.g., see Diefendorff, Brown, Kamin, & Lord, 2002; Igbaria, Parasuraman, & Badawy, 1994) leads to another question about the level of job involvement across public, nonprofit, and private sector agencies because of the specific organizational or managerial contexts that might provide differential impacts on the degree of involvement. Hence, as an exploratory research query, this study begins to explore the issues of job involvement in the public and nonprofit sectors. We expect that managers in the nonprofit sector will display a higher level of job involvement than their public sector counterparts will because of the high level of involvement that nonprofit managers have in their organizations. This level of involvement stems, in part, from the fact that many nonprofit managers founded the organizations they now lead (Bell et al., 2006; Chambre & Fatt, 2002). The first research question concerns whether we can observe a significant difference in job involvement across the public and nonprofit sectors.

> **Research Question 1** (job involvement across the sectors): Is there a significant difference in the level of job involvement among public and nonprofit managers?

Antecedents of Job Involvement

The work of Rabinowitz and Hall (1977) revealed there are clear linear relationships between job involvement and three classes of variables: (a) personal and (b) situational characteristics (antecedents) and (c) work outcomes (consequences). Their empirical results indicated that the relationships between job involvement and selected variables from each of the three categories are almost equal in their explanatory power (i.e., r or R^2). That is, " none of the classes of variables show clearly stronger relationships to job involvement than any other" (Rabinowitz & Hall, 1977, p. 284). However, using a 20-item job involvement scale and multivariate analyses of personal and situational correlates of job involvement, Saal (1978) concluded that a larger portion of variance in job involvement was explained by perceived situationaljob characteristics than by personal-demographic variables. Using meta-analyses of 51 pairwise relationships related to job involvement, Brown (1996) reported that job involvement is significantly related to personality and situational variables. The results obtained by Saal, Rabinowitz and Hall, and Brown offer inconsistent explanations of the antecedents on job involvement. In this study, based on the empirical findings of previous research on job involvement, we investigate the relationships among three categories of independent variables (demographic, managerial, and institutional levels) and the outcome variable, job involvement. More specifically, this research analyzes these variables in the public and nonprofit sectors separately to empirically test whether the causal relationships between these antecedents and job involvement would differ across the sectoral contexts within which the variables are embedded.

> **Research Question 2** (antecedents of job involvement across the sectors): What are the main antecedents of public and nonprofit managers' job

involvement?

Demographic (Personal) Factors

Especially when we conceptualize job involvement as an individual difference (i.e., an individual predisposition approach) rather than viewing job involvement as a reaction or an interaction of employees to certain types of job characteristics or work situations (i.e., a situational-job design approach), demographic characteristics could be important determinants that explain the degree of job involvement (Lawler & Hall, 1970). According to Rabinowitz and Hall' (1977) argument, job involvement is influenced significantly by a set of demographic antecedents, including age, gender, ethnicity, and/or education level as well as by several types of job characteristics. The study by Sekaran and Mowday (1981) also suggested that both demographic factors and job characteristics are important antecedents of job involvement. They found that level of education was negatively related to job involvement, whereas age was strongly and positively related to job involvement. However, gender was not a significant predictor. We expect that demographic factors will influence the level of job involvement for managers in both the public and nonprofit sectors.

> **Hypothesis 1** (demographic factors and job involvement): Demographic factors will be jointly and significantly associated with public and nonprofit managers' job involvement.

Managerial (Situational) Factors

Saal (1978) found that job involvement was more highly correlated with managerial-situational characteristics than with personal-demographic variables. In this study, we hypothesize that a group of managerial antecedents such as intrinsic motivation, extrinsic motivation, and managerial power will be significantly related to the job involvement of managers in both the public and nonprofit sectors. We expect managerial factors to be more strongly related to job involvement than to demographic factors.

For example, the survey collected data on intrinsic motivation, which can be defined as " behaviors for which there is no apparent reward except the activity itself " ; or " the doing of an activity for its inherent satisfactions rather than for some separable consequence" (e.g., an inclination for psychological rewards, feelings of accomplishment, or working for public interests; Cameron & Pierce, 2002, p. 12; Lepper & Greene, 1975; Park & Rainey, 2007; Rainey, 2003; Ryan & Deci, 2000, pp. 56-60). Moon (2000) suggested that intrinsic motivation will have a stronger positive relationship with job involvement than will extrinsic motivation (see also Naff & Crum, 1999; Rainey, 2003). In their study of state government agency managers based on NASP-II data, Moynihan and Pandey (2007a) also found that job involvement is significantly related to public service motivation.

In addition, from a behavioral science perspective, we hypothesize that job tenure, managerial power, and hierarchical job authority as managerial factors will be related to a manager's job involvement in different ways (Daft, 2007). We hypothesize that managers in the upper echelons of public and nonprofit agencies (i.e., who have stayed longer and hence who have more managerial power in their agencies) will be more involved in their job because they are likely to have greater job responsibilities and " to some extent they are validating their own performance and entitlement " (Bozeman & Murdock, 2007, p. 300). On the other hand, it is also expected that hierarchical authority in their job (e.g., increased and more intense bureaucratic control and managerial supervision), which tends to create rigid and directive human resource (HR) management systems, will be negatively related to job involvement (Bozeman & Kingsley, 1998). We suspect that some of the managerial factors will differ across the public and nonprofit sectors in terms of their relationship to job involvement of managers.

Hypothesis 2 (managerial factors and job involvement): Managerial factors will be jointly and significantly associated with public and nonprofit managers' job involvement. Managerial factors will be a more important influence than demographic factors will be on public and nonprofit managers' job involvement.

Hypothesis 2a: Intrinsic motivation will be significantly and positively associated with public and nonprofit managers' job involvement.

Hypothesis 2b: Job tenure will be significantly and positively associated with public and nonprofit managers' job involvement.

Hypothesis 2c: Managerial power will be significantly and positively associated with public and nonprofit managers' job involvement.

Hypothesis 2d: Hierarchical job authority will be significantly and negatively associated with public and nonprofit managers' job involvement.

Institutional (Organizational) Factors

Regardless of the types of governing structures, organizations function as informal and formal institutions (or systems) that influence and shape job-related attitudes and administrative behaviors (Moynihan & Pandey, 2007b). Especially in the public and nonprofit sectors, the influence of organizational institutions—for example, culture, norms, rules, regulations, and structure—cannot be overemphasized as key factors in understanding these attitudes and behaviors. In this regard, red tape, hierarchical culture, organization size, and state HR systems were examined in this study to account for the importance of these institutional and contextual characteristics.

Red tape in an organization can be defined as " burdensome administrative rules and excessive procedures that remain in force and that have negative effects on the organization's effectiveness and performance as well as job satisfaction and job involvement" (Rainey, Pandey, & Bozeman, 1995, p. 567; also see Bozeman, 2000, chap. 3). Buchanan (1975) found that red tape in the public sector lowers the level of job involvement on the part of public employees in comparison to their private sector counterparts. Hierarchical culture is another important factor that is associated with a focus on " people, organizational control and structure, rules and regulations, management of information and communication, risk aversion, and organizational stability " (Moynihan & Pandey, 2007b, p. 43; also see Quinn & Kimberly, 1984). High levels of organizational red tape and hierarchical culture may have a negative impact on job involvement.

The relationship between organizational size on HR practices and employee attitudes is well documented, especially in business literature (e.g., see Wagar, 1998). Larger organizations are more likely to display high levels of differentiation, centralization, and formalization (Blau, 1972). Organization size can be a dominant institutional factor that shapes the level of public or nonprofit managers' job involvement, as smaller agencies may more provide family-like or people-oriented work environments and tend to pursue a more affective culture rather than a formal or hierarchical culture. We expect that the increased formality associated with a large organizational size will negatively influence job involvement.

Finally, as institutional antecedents, different political or administrative environments could be important factors influencing organizational attitudes in public and nonprofit agencies. Specifically, in the state-level research context, we examine the extent to which the state's context, such as the state's managerial or HR systems and policies, influence the level of public and nonprofit managers' job involvement.[1] We expect that differences in policy, state law, and reforms will influence the level of managers' job involvement in public sector managers. Although these reforms in state personnel systems and state contexts are probably largely important to the public sector, it is unlikely that state context will be related to the job involvement for nonprofit managers because the laws governing nonprofit organizational structures do not significantly vary by state. Based on these theoretical and practical rationales, we hypothesize that four types of institutional factors will be highly associated with organizational outcomes such as job involvement in the public and nonprofit sector (see Figure 1).

Hypothesis 3 (institutional factors and job involvement): Institutional factors will be jointly and significantly associated with public and nonprofit managers' job involvement.

Hypothesis 3a: Greater levels of organizational red tape will be negatively and significantly related to public and nonprofit managers' job involvement.

Hypothesis 3b: Increased hierarchical culture will be negatively and significantly related to public and nonprofit managers' job involvement.

Hypothesis 3c: Larger organization size will be negatively and significantly related to public and nonprofit managers' job involvement.

Hypothesis 3d: State context will be significantly related to the job involvement of public managers.

Hypothesis 3e: State context will not be significantly related to job involvement of nonprofit managers.

Data and Measures

Data Collection and Sample

This study utilizes data from the NASP-III survey (Feeney, 2005), which collected data from managers working in public (N = 802) and nonprofit (N = 375) agencies in the states of Illinois and Georgia. The sample was a representative sample of state public and nonprofit employees, including 61 public agencies and 305 nonprofit organizations in these two states. The overall response rate was 39.0% (42.5% for the public sector sample and 33.0% from the nonprofit sector sample). Regarding missing data adjustments, rather than using the listwise deletion method, we employed the expectation-maximization algorithm method to preserve effective sample size. This method can increase statistical power of the regression model and reduce possible nonresponse bias in parameter estimates (Roth, 1994).[2] The survey instrument measured the managers' perceptions about various organizational issues such as work motivation, mentoring theories, career histories, hiring practices, and organizational cultures and structures, in addition to investigating numerous individual and organizational characteristics-or example, affiliated agencies, agency mission and goals, gender, ethnicity, education level, salary, and age.[3]

Figure 1. Conceptual Framework for the Job Involvement Model

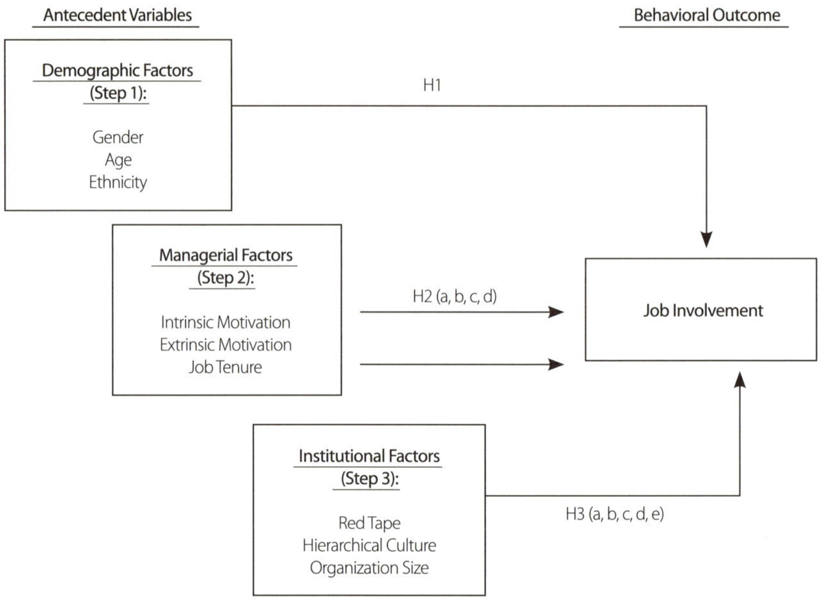

Measures of Job Involvement

This research employed a six-item job involvement scale that originally came from Kanungo' (1982a) 10-item scale. Further details about the items used in scale construction can be found in the appendix. Internal consistency is important in this research because the homogeneity of involvement in other scales makes it critical to accurately measure the respondents' attitudes about the survey items. To assess internal consistency and to ensure reliability of the job involvement scale, Cronbach's alpha reliability test was done, and the job involvement scale showed a high level of internal consistency reliability (Cronbach's α = .715).

Demographic Characteristics

In the job involvement model, four variables were included as demographic antecedent variables that measure personal characteristics of Georgia and Illinois public and nonprofit managers, including gender, age, ethnicity, and level of education. Among these variables, gender (female = 1) and ethnicity (non-White = 1) were coded as dummy variables.

Measures of Managerial Predictors

The managerial or situational factors include five variables: job tenure, managerial power, hierarchical job authority, and two types of work motivation-intrinsic and extrinsic motivation. The motivation variables were measured and developed from the 11 items (4-point scale) as shown in the appendix. To operationalize motivation scales, principal axis factoring analysis, using varimax rotation techniques, and confirmatory factor analysis (CFA) methods were performed to obtain factor extraction. At one eigenvalue, two dimensions resulted. These two dimensions, intrinsic (Factor 1) and extrinsic (Factor 2) motivation, account for 73.53% of the total variance. The results of factor analyses (i.e., exploratory factor analysis and a second-order CFA model) indicate that the factor loadings support the use of these items as indicators of the two underlying motivation constructs (factor loadings range from .598 to .872 and from .608 to .792 for intrinsic motivation and extrinsic motivation, respectively).[4] Such goodness-of-fit indexes as the comparative fit index (.96), normed fit index (.98), relative fit index (.97), root mean square error of approximation (.065), and standardized root mean square residual (.045) in a CFA model also show that the fit of the entire model is within acceptable levels.[5] We also created ordinal-level variables (four categories) for job tenure (year job started) and managerial power (the number of employees supervised in organizations) because responses to these items were highly skewed. The hierarchical job authority variable is measured by asking public and nonprofit managers the following questionnaire item:

> In your current job, do you feel that you have about the right amount of supervision, too little, or not enough? (Answers were coded on a 0 to 10 scale, from 0, not enough supervision, to 10, too much supervision.)

Measures of Institutional Factors

To probe the relationship between institutional factors and job involvement, four institutional variables were included: organizational red tape, hierarchical culture, organization size, and state. First, organizational red tape was measured by asking respondents, " How would you assess the level of red tape in your organization? " : (on a 0 to 10 scale).[6] For the measure of hierarchical culture, we employed five items and created a hierarchical culture scale that is relevant to the issues of organizational rules and procedures (Cronbach's α = .66). To transform the distribution into a more normal form and to reduce the problems with skewness and kurtosis, organizational size is measured by the natural log of the total number of full-time employees for the public and nonprofit organizations. In this case, organizational size distribution was highly skewed, and without the log transformation extreme values would have unduly affected correlations of organizational size with other variables.[7] We also included a dummy-coded variable that controls for state context (Georgia = 1, Illinois = 0). Because the state of Georgia has changed many traditional personnel systems, pursuing more deregulation, decentralization, and market-oriented initiatives through privatization, the inclusion of this variable may empirically contrast and elaborate the role of state context (e.g., the effect of state HR reform systems and policies) on managers' job involvement. Descriptive statistics for each of these antecedent and dependent variables in this research are reported in Tables 1 and 2.

Table 1. Descriptive Statistics: Public Agencies

Variables	Valid N	M	SD	Min	Max
Demographic factors					
Gender (female = 1)	796	0.439	0.497	0.00	1.00
Age	793	49	8.588	23	72
Ethnicity (non-White = 1)	780	0.189	0.391	0.00	1.00
Level of education (1 = less than college, 3 = graduate degree)	796	2.266	0.712	1.00	3.00
Managerial factors					
Intrinsic motivation	779	2.733	0.616	1.00	4.00
Extrinsic motivation	785	3.214	0.561	1.00	4.00
Job tenure (year job started)	771	2.520	1.059	1.00	4.00
Managerial power (the number of employees supervised)	677	2.579	0.957	1.00	4.00
Hierarchical job authority	792	5.430	1.538	0.00	10.00
Institutional factors					
Organizational red tape	786	7.050	2.124	0.00	10.00
Hierarchical culture	795	2.994	0.407	1.40	4.00
Organization size (natural log)	760	3.318	0.657	0.70	4.27
State context (state personnel reform systems and policies proxy; Georgia = 1)	802	0.540	0.499	0.00	1.00
Outcome variable					
Job involvement	792	3.188	0.456	1.29	4.00

Table 2. Descriptive Statistics: Nonprofit Agencies

Variables	Valid N	M	SD	Min	Max
Demographic factors					
Gender (female = 1)	370	0.492	0.501	0.00	1.00
Age	369	50.450	9.404	26	78
Ethnicity (non-White = 1)	353	0.048	0.214	0.00	1.00
Level of education (1 = less than college, 3 = graduate degree)	366	2.430	0.662	1.00	3.00
Managerial factors					
Intrinsic motivation	360	2.840	0.559	1.00	4.00
Extrinsic motivation	357	2.915	0.642	1.00	4.00
Job tenure (year job started)	347	2.297	1.094	1.00	4.00
Managerial power (the number of employees supervised)	341	2.569	0.800	1.00	4.00
Hierarchical job authority	361	5.260	1.143	2.00	10.00
Institutional factors					
Organizational red tape	366	4.130	2.569	0.00	10.00
Hierarchical culture	367	2.372	0.572	1.00	3.80
Organization size (natural log)	344	1.445	0.661	0.00	3.88
State context (state personnel reform systems and policies proxy; Georgia = 1)	375	0.230	0.424	0.00	1.00
Outcome variable					
Job involvement	365	3.460	0.367	1.57	4.00

Statistical Modeling and Results

In this study, to test our research questions and hypotheses, two statistical methods were used. First, as an initial step, we used an independent samples test to test for statistically significant differences between public and nonprofit managers' job involvement level (Phase 1). Second, two multivariate hierarchical regression models were used to test the relationship among four demographic factors (Step 1), five managerial factors (Step 2), four institutional factors (Step 3), and the outcome variable of job involvement (Phase 2).

Phase 1: Independent Samples t Test

To test for statistically significant differences between the two sectors, we used an independent samples t test method by dividing the sample on the basis of the two groups-public (Group 1) and nonprofit (Group 2) sectors. As we can see from Table 3, the result of the test showed that the mean level of job involvement among public and nonprofit managers is statistically significant (t = −10.834, p = .000). That is, the mean level of nonprofit managers' job involvement is greater than that of public managers, and the difference is statistically significant.

Phase 2: Hierarchical Multivariate Regression

In Phase 2, for the purpose of investigating the possible causal relationships between several antecedents and job involvement, a hierarchical multivariate regression analysis was employed. Three different equations (i.e., Steps 1, 2, and 3) were regressed on job involvement to see the changes in total variance influenced by each set of factors (i.e., changes). β represents the standardized regression coefficient that estimates the relative importance of each antecedent variable association with job involvement.[8] The main statistical results of the regression model are reported in Tables 4 and 5.[9]

Table 3. Independent Samples t Test: Job Involvement

		Levene's Test for Quality of Variance		t Test for Equality of Means				
		F	Sig.	t	df	Sig. (two-tailed)	M Difference	SE Difference
Job involvement	Equal variance assumed	17.170	.000	−10.004	1155	.000	−.27214	.02720
	Equal variance not assumed			−10.834	866.032	.000	−.27214	.02512

Note: The job involvement among public managers = Group 1. the job involvement among nonprofit managers = Group 2. mean difference = Group 1 − Group 2.

Table 4. Results of Hierarchical Multivariate Regression Analysis: Public Agencies

Main Antecedent Variables	Job Involvement (Total N = 802)		
	Step 1	Step 2	Step 3
	Standardized Coefficient β (t-statistics)	Standardized Coefficient β (t-statistics)	Standardized Coefficient β (t-statistics)
Step 1: Demographic factors			
Gender (female = 1)	**.080** (1.971)**	**.079** (1.985)**	**.082** (2.043)**
Age	**.131*** (3.176)**	**.124** (2.944)**	**.097** (2.352)**
Ethnicity (non-White = 1)	.026 (0.627)	–.173 (0.863)	–.014 (–0.561)
Level of education	–.057 (–1.388)	–.051 (–1.277)	–.036 (–0.977)
Step 2: Managerial factors			
Intrinsic motivation		**.176*** (3.802)**	**.120*** (2.707)**
Extrinsic motivation		–.071 (–1.545)	–.047 (–1.073)
Job tenure		.042 (1.028)	.001 (0.013)
Managerial power		**.204*** (5.094)**	**.204*** (5.421)**
Hierarchical job authority		**–.168*** (–4.207)**	**–.136*** (–3.504)**
Step 3: Institutional factors			
Organizational red tape			**–.188** (–4.567)**
Hierarchical culture			**–.125** (–3.122)**
Organization size (natural log)			–.048 (–0.376)
State context (state personnel reform systems and policies proxy; Georgia = 1)			**.094** (2.012)**
R^2	.026	.124	.212
Adjusted R^2	.019	.110	.198
ΔR^2	.026	.099	.088
F statistic	3.777***	8.992***	11.355***

Table 5. Results of Hierarchical Multivariate Regression Analysis: Nonprofit Agencies

	Job Involvement (Total N = 375)		
	Step 1	Step 2	Step 3
Main Antecedent Variables	Standardized Coefficient β (t-statistics)	Standardized Coefficient β (t-statistics)	Standardized Coefficient β (t-statistics)
Step 1: Demographic factors			
Gender (female = 1)	.060 (0.957)	.113 (1.761)	.145** (2.320)
Age	.233***(3.810)	.210*** (3.073)	.188*** (3.077)
Ethnicity (non-White = 1)	–.167***(–2.790)	–.160*** (–2.715)	–.152*** (–2.716)
Level of education	.051 (0.828)	.020 (0.330)	.075 (1.292)
Step 2: Managerial factors			
Intrinsic motivation		–.033 (–0.537)	–.062 (–1.038)
Extrinsic motivation		–.006 (–0.082)	.086 (1.347)
Job tenure		–.040 (–0.600)	.000 (0.007)
Managerial power		.154** (2.457)	.180*** (3.063)
Hierarchical job authority		–.178*** (–3.013)	–.131** (–2.312)
Step 3: Institutional factors			
Organizational red tape			–.260** (–3.788)
Hierarchical culture			–.088 (–1.477)
Organization size (natural log)			–.176*** (–2.877)
State context (state personnel reform systems and policies proxy; Georgia = 1)			.035 (0.500)
R^2	.090	.143	.288
Adjusted R^2	.075	.113	.244
ΔR^2	.090	.054	.145
F statistic	6.320***	4.684***	6.899***

Public Organization Model

In the first model (Table 4), we analyzed the relationship between a set of antecedents and job involvement in the context of the public sector. First, demographic (personal) factors were regressed on job involvement in the first step. The four individual characteristics accounted for only approximately 2.6% of the total variance of job involvement ($p < .01$). Gender ($\beta = .080, p < .05$) and age ($\beta = .131, p < .01$) are significantly associated with public managers' job involvement. The results suggest that female and older public managers are more likely to have a higher level of job involvement in their agencies than are male and younger public managers. These findings provide partial support for Hypothesis 1.

In the second step, the addition of the five managerial factors accounted for 12.4% of total variance in job involvement ($p < .01$), which suggests that the managerial variables are the best predictors, at least for managers working in the public sector. As predicted in the aforementioned hypotheses, intrinsic motivation ($\beta = .176, p < .01$) and managerial power ($\beta = .204, p < .01$) are significantly and positively related to the level of job involvement displayed by public managers. Hierarchical job authority, on the other hand, is associated with significantly lower job involvement ($\beta = -.168, p < .01$). Extrinsic motivation and job tenure do not have a statistically significant relationship with job involvement (both $p > .10$). Standardized coefficients indicate that, among managerial factors, managerial power has the strongest influence on job involvement, followed by hierarchical job authority and intrinsic motivation. These findings provide support for Hypotheses 2, 2a, 2c, and 2d.

In the third step, when four institutional or organizational factors were added, the total variance of job involvement accounted for by these factors significantly increased to 21.2% ($p < .01$). As hypothesized, except for organization size, all variables are significantly related to job involvement ($p < .05$), suggesting that the existence of organizational red tape and hierarchical culture negatively influences job involvement. Moreover, the results suggest that public managers in the state of Georgia have a higher level of job involvement compared to Illinois public managers, which might be because of HR reforms in the state. We argue that the Georgia Gain personnel reform program adopted in 1996 has not, at least, been harmful to the job involvement of state managers. Moreover, the reform efforts may have increased state managers' work morale or productivity by enhancing their level of job involvement. As indicated by standardized regression coefficients among institutional factors, organizational red tape has the strongest negative influence on job involvement ($\beta = -.188, p < .05$), followed by hierarchical culture ($\beta = -.125, p < .05$) and state ($\beta = .094, p < .05$). These findings provide support for Hypotheses 3, 3a, 3b, and 3d.

Nonprofit Organization Model

In the nonprofit organization model, we observed patterns similar to the public organization model overall. Four demographic characteristics accounted for approximately 9% of the total variance in job involvement ($p < .01$). Among these variables, the age ($\beta = .233, p < .01$) and ethnicity ($\beta = -.167, p < .01$) variables proved significant. The result shows that non-White ethnic groups in nonprofit agencies are not as involved in their jobs. This finding is somewhat surprising on the surface but may simply reflect cultural differences between different ethnic groups in terms of the value they place on family and work. These findings provide partial support for Hypothesis 1.

In the second step, the five managerial factors in nonprofit agencies accounted for 14.3% of total variance in job involvement ($p < .01$). The most interesting finding was that none of the motivational variables were significant in the nonprofit agency model. That is, unlike public agencies, intrinsic motivation is not a principal or critical factor to increasing the job involvement of nonprofit managers. The results may imply, among several possibilities, that the recent tendency toward marketization in the managerial processes within nonprofit agencies has weakened the relationship between intrinsic motivation and job involvement. Standardized regression coefficients indicate that managerial power in nonprofit agencies had the strongest positive relationship to job involvement ($\beta = .181$, $p < .01$). Managerial power was consistently the most important managerial antecedent of job involvement regardless of sector. These findings provide support for Hypotheses 2, 2c, and 2d.

In the third step, the four institutional factors significantly improved the prediction above and beyond the demographic and managerial characteristics ($R^2 = .288$, adjusted $R^2 = .244$), accounting for an additional 14.5% of the variance in job involvement at a highly significant level ($p < .01$). This result indicates that the most powerful predictors of job involvement in nonprofit organizations are the institutional (organizational) antecedents. Specifically, both organization red tape and organization size significantly but negatively contribute to nonprofit managers' job involvement. We expect that the larger nonprofit agencies with higher levels of organizational red tape discourage managers from being involved in their jobs. From the standardized coefficients among institutional factors, we also confirm that organizational red tape is the most important and significant antecedent variable ($\beta = -.260$, $p < .05$), similar to the public agency model. In contrast to the public sector model, state context did not prove to be significantly related to job involvement of managers in the nonprofit sector because there is little difference in state policy governing organizational structure of nonprofits. These findings provide support for Hypotheses 3, 3a, 3c, and 3e.

Discussion and Implications

The results of the analysis point to several distinctions in both the level of job involvement and the factors associated with job involvement for managers across the public and nonprofit sectors. These differences suggest that there are real and distinct characteristics for each sector in terms of organizational and demographic characteristics and organizational structures. The differences in these characteristics appear to have a relationship with the level of job involvement for managers in the public and nonprofit sectors. These results provide insight into some of those differences and suggest avenues for future research as well as implications for current theory and practice in public and nonprofit management.

The first research question posed was, "Is there a significant difference in the level of job involvement among public and nonprofit managers?" The research found that there was a difference in the level of job involvement between the two sectors. This finding is important because it shows the difference between sectors is a difference not only in name but also in terms of the experiences and motivations of the individuals within these organizations. Nonprofit managers showed a higher level of job involvement than did managers in the public sector. It is possible that the level of the involvement is shaped not only by the institutional and managerial factors of the sector but also by the culture of nonprofit organizations as organizations that exist to serve their communities and civil society in general (Eikenberry & Kluver, 2004).

A second possible explanation for the difference in job involvement might stem from the self-selection of individuals into each sector. Some of the apparent differences may, in fact, be the result of differently motivated individuals choosing a particular career path over another. It has been well documented that those working within public organizations face difficulties because of the public' perception about the quality and motivation of these employees (Bozeman, 2000; Goodsell, 1994; Rainey & Steinbauer, 1999). Because of the negative perception of public employment, some individuals wishing to serve their communities and the common good may choose employment in the nonprofit sector over the public sector, despite differences in pay and benefits. The higher level of job involvement might also stem from self-selection of some individuals into the nonprofit sector because of religious or moral callings (Light, 2002). In addition, service in the nonprofit sector may provide an outlet for those who have a philosophical objection to government involvement in social services and other aspects of communities but want to serve their communities.

One of the more surprising findings of our study was the apparent lack of relationship between intrinsic motivation and job involvement for nonprofit managers, even though intrinsic motivation did prove significant for managers in the public sector. There are two possible explanations for the apparent differences in the importance of intrinsic motivation to job involvement in public and nonprofit organizations. The first possible explanation stems from the increasing "marketization" or adoption of the values and approaches of the private market by the nonprofit sector (Salamon, 1995; Weisbrod, 1998). A second and equally reasonable explanation is that the ways in which intrinsic motivation is measured in this study do not fit the intrinsic motivation of nonprofit managers. This applies most clearly to the inclusion of red tape as an indicator of intrinsic motivation for nonprofit managers. Because nonprofit managers deal with red tape only as external actors to the process of government, the inclusion of this variable in the measurement equations may have led to a decreased efficiency, especially for nonprofit managers. Both possible explanations have implications for theory and future research surrounding differences between the public and nonprofit sectors.

Marketization could explain why job involvement of nonprofit managers was not significantly related to intrinsic motivation because intrinsic motivation is related to the nonmonetary aspects of work that motivate employees to perform. Increasing influence of market-based principles and incentives and recruitment of individuals who align themselves within this philosophical belief system would point to an increasing importance for monetary or extrinsic motivation for those in the nonprofit sector. However, the results of our study indicate that extrinsic motivation was also not significantly related to job involvement of nonprofit managers. This suggests that perhaps marketization is not the cause of the lack of a significant relationship between job involvement and intrinsic motivation for nonprofit managers.

Furthermore, the survey of public, nonprofit, and private sector employees conducted by Light (2002) suggested that nonprofit employees come to work for reasons such as the nature of work and the common good. These reasons seem to be more consistent with intrinsic motivation than with any other factors. Further examination of our study's operationalization of intrinsic motivation reveals that some of these questions may be better suited to values that intrinsically motivate public sector workers but not nonprofit workers. For example, the survey asked respondents if the " desire for less bureaucratic red tape " motivated them to take their job, but red tape is not commonly a characteristic associated with the internal operations of nonprofit organizations. Future research examining intrinsic motivation across the sectors is needed to fully clarify the best possible and most universal method to measure this construct.[10]

In contrast to the nonprofit sector findings, state context proved an important factor in public sector job involvement. Although there is a limitation in interpreting this quantified state effect as an indicator of the personnel reform role in the creation of job involvement, this finding has significant implications when examined in light of the civil service reform movement undertaken in the state-level public sector as of late. Georgia has undertaken significant civil service reforms, which might have altered the state context and contributed to understanding the unique context of the state. However, without additional data, it is not possible to determine what other differences between Georgia and Illinois contribute to the apparent differences.

Among the institutional factors, red tape had the strongest relationship to the level of job involvement of managers in both the public and nonprofit sectors. This finding suggests that red tape has a strong negative impact on managers no matter what the context. Red tape in previous research has been linked to lowered job satisfaction and commitment (DeHart-Davis & Pandey, 2005) and risk aversion (Bozeman & Kingsley, 1998). Our findings suggest that these negative aspects of red tape apply universally and not just to public sector managers.

Red tape is often seen as more prevalent in the public sector, but increasing ties between sectors have caused some transfer of governmental rules and accountability to nonprofit organizations that receive financial support. One of the reasons cited for the desirability of nonprofit organizations as contracting partners for public organizations is their ease in adapting to a changing environment. This flexibility stems, in part, from lower levels of red tape or bureaucracy governing nonprofit organizations. Recent research by Gazley and Brudney (2007) pointed to a strong undercurrent of negativity by nonprofits toward intersectoral partnerships with public agencies. The transfer of red tape through these partnerships to nonprofit organizations might explain differential perceptions by managers of the outcomes of such partnerships. In this regard, how to reduce organizational red tape while maintaining the necessary level of organizational hierarchy and rules (i.e., "green tape" in both of the sectors can be another important query not only for public and nonprofit managers but also for researchers.[11]

Another important aspect of this study is that we confirmed the conclusions drawn by Saal (1978) with empirical findings. That is, as Saal suggested, a larger portion of variance in job involvement was explained by situational-managerial characteristics than by demographic factors. Situational factors such as managerial power and hierarchical job authority were highly correlated with job involvement in both of the sectors. In addition, the results offer new evidence that institutional or organizational factors are much more important antecedents to understanding job involvement in public and nonprofit sectors than are demographic or even situational (e.g., managerial) factors, at least within the public and nonprofit contexts. The result implies that we need more investigation into the various mechanisms and functions of organizational institutions, systems, norms, and culture that are very actively and significantly associated with job involvement, regardless of the sector.

The fact that institutional factors can significantly affect job involvement in both sectors suggests that there are mechanisms or " levers " to change the level of job involvement of both public and nonprofit employees. One significant finding of our research is that red tape, hierarchical job authority, and hierarchical culture all have a negative relationship to job involvement and managerial power has a positive relationship, regardless of sector. This suggests that public organizations need to be mindful about transferring bureaucratic constraints to the nonprofit sector. Often these constraints are transferred in the form of accountability requirements that are overlapping and expensive to implement (Conner-Snibbe, 2006). Although it is important to understand that accountability for performance has an important place in governance, public managers need to take steps to make sure that the accountability does not create too many barriers in the delivery of goods and services. The results suggest that these types of bureaucratic requirements negatively influence the involvement of managers.

In terms of methodological problems, reliance on an employee attitude survey raises concerns about mono-method bias, positive response bias, and subjective measures of the variables, especially the outcome variable. Another methodological concern can be raised on the issue of statistical modeling: Although we confirmed that the model we used here satisfied ordinary least squares regression assumptions, it is necessary to explore whether other advanced techniques such as nonlinear modeling, hierarchical linear modeling, or structural equation modeling are available and acceptable in the future research.[12] We agree that a more rigorous statistical approach would provide more reliability to readers, including practitioners and researchers in our field.

Another limitation of the research is its dependence on legal status to capture sectoral differences. The increasing overlap between the sectors because of contractual relationships, collaboration to solve community issues, and the use of nonprofits to deliver public goods and services has led to a significant blurring of the sectoral lines. Earlier research about the distinctions drawn between public and private entities suggested that legal status might be less important than the " publicness " of a particular agency (Bozeman & Bretschneider, 1994; Lan & Rainey, 1992). The available data limited the ability to fully explore the concept of publicness, but future research would benefit from clarifying the role of this concept in the creation of job involvement in organizations. In addition, more information about the individual missions of both public and nonprofit entities might help sort out some of the differences across sector by allowing for more control over differences in job types that probably also have a significant influence on job involvement.

Notes

1. The state of Georgia, for example, has recently adopted a radical personnel reform system called GeorgiaGain and the Civil Service Reform Law (Act 816), which launched an at-will employment system and a new pay-for-performance system. The purported advantages, such as better customer service, less bureaucracy, employee empowerment, and enhanced motivation and performance, have been expected to result from the reforms in Georgia.
2. According to Little and Rubin (1987), the expectation-maximization algorithm (a) replaces missing values with estimated values, (b) estimates parameters, (c) reestimates the missing values assuming the new parameter estimates are correct, and (d) reestimates parameters, and so forth, iterating until convergence (p. 129).
3. Extensive documentation about the National Administrative Studies Project III (NASP-III) is available at the project Web site, http://www.uga.edu/padp/nasp.html.

   The NASP-III project began as a project in a research design course at the Georgia Institute of Technology taught by Barry Bozeman and Hal Rainey in the spring of 2005. Funding for this project was provided by Barry Bozeman, Hal Rainey, Gordon Kingsley, and Julia Melkers. NASPIII is unique in its attempt to blend the goals of NASP-I and II while addressing a few new themes of its own. NASP-III aims to collect data on public and nonprofit managers. It also expands beyond a single state, surveying managers in Georgia and Illinois, but does not have a national focus. Unlike NASP-II, which focuses on a single functional agency (health and human services), the NASP-III sample includes managers from agencies and organizations of numerous functions. (Feeney, 2005, pp. 3-4)

4. These methods enabled us to extract communalities from different variables and, by doing this, combine different variables into new variables. Because exploratory factor analysis (EFA) is an atheoretical method, we also employed a second-order confirmatory factor analysis (CFA) model to develop more theory-oriented motivation constructs in this study. The results (e.g., factor loadings) of EFA and CFA are fairly consistent. The tables with factor loadings of EFA and CFA models are available from the authors.
5. Fit indexes in CFA are often divided into two basic types: stand-alone fit indexes and incremental fit indexes. Incremental fit indexes evaluate fit by comparing the model to the fit of a null or baseline model. Stand-alone indexes, as the name implies, are not based on any type of model comparison. According to Hu and Bentler (1999), standardized root mean square residual (SRMR) is the most sensitive index to models with misspecified factor covariance. In addition, non-normed fit index (NNFI), incremental fit index (IFI),

relative noncentrality index (RNI), comparative fit index (CFI), and root mean square error of approximation (RMSEA) are the most sensitive to models with misspecified factor loadings. In a CFA model, cutoff values of .95 for NNFI, RNI, IFI, and CFI in combination with a cutoff value of .09 (or .08) for RMSEA and SRMR are recommended.

6. As one of the reviewers pointed out, a single measure of red tape (i.e., a 0 to 10 measurement scale) in this study might be problematic, especially given the recent measurement theory work. For future research, we need to develop an index variable using multiple indicators, which can more accurately measure multifaceted and encompassing red tape constructs.
7. Other than these methodological reasons, the log transformation of organizational size should be based on a theoretical ground. From a theoretical perspective, as Blau (1970) suggested, " Increasing organizational size generates differentiation along various lines at decelerating rates " (p. 204), and hence " organizational structure [variables] may be more sensitive to size differences in smaller organizations than in larger ones " (Maguire, 2003, p. 160). Drawing on these methodological and theoretical justifications, we concluded that the log transformation should be necessary.
8. However, a use of standardized regression coefficients is still controversial in the statistical literature. We acknowledge that future research should provide and compare semipartial correlations (which find the correlation between two variables with the third held constant in one of the variables) to obtain better measures of the concept.
9. We tested main ordinary least squares (OLS) assumptions such as linearity, multicollinearity, normality, or homoscedasticity using a Stata (Version 10) program. We confirmed that the model we used here satisfied all these assumptions.
10. The construct of intrinsic motivation describes " the natural inclination toward assimilation, mastery, spontaneous interest, and exploration that is so essential to cognitive and social development and that represents a principal source of enjoyment and vitality throughout life " (Ryan & Deci, 2000, p. 70). In this regard, future research on universal intrinsic measures across the sectors should emphasize certain attributes such as a sense of duty or achievement (e.g., " Doing my job well gives me the feeling that I have accomplished something worthwhile ", job importance (e.g., " The things I do on my job are important to me ", and organizational loyalty (e.g., " Even if the organization were not doing well financially, I would be reluctant to change to another employer ").
11. Green tape (or white tape) refers to organizational rules and regulations that have positive and beneficial social psychological effects for employees (Bozeman, 1993). According to DeHart-Davis (2008), green tape is characterized by five distinct attributes: (a) written requirements, (b) with valid means–ends relationship, which (c) employ optimal control, (d) are consistently applied, and have (e) purposes understood by stakeholders (p. 2).

12. Structural equation modeling (SEM) can provide a more realistic and flexible approach than OLS regression by allowing for nonrecursive paths and simultaneous tests of the relationships of the variables. For example, using SEM, we can consider the effect that job involvement has on managerial and institutional factors such as intrinsic motivation and red tape. The use of hierarchical linear modeling allows for the inclusion of organization-level influences by accounting for clustering observations, which are often neglected in traditional organizational behavior studies.

References

Anheier, H. K., & Salamon, L. M. (2006). The nonprofit sector in comparative perspective. In W. W. Powell & R. Steinberg (Eds.), *The non-profit sector: A research handbook* (pp. 89-116). New Haven, CT: Yale University Press.

Argyris, C. (1964). *Integrating the individual and the organization.* New York: John Wiley.

Bailey, D., & Koney, K. (1996). Interorganizational community collaboratives: A strategic response to the shape of the social work agenda. *Social Work, 41*(6), 577-596.

Behn, R. D. (2001). *Rethinking democratic accountability.* Washington, DC: Brookings Institution Press.

Bell, J., Moyers, R., & Wolfred, T. (2006). *Daring to lead: A national study of nonprofit executive leadership.* Retrieved September 10, 2008, from http://www.compasspoint.org/assets/194_daringtolead06final.pdf

Ben-Ner, A., & Van Hoomissen, T. (1991). The relative size of the nonprofit sector in the mixed economy: A demand and supply analysis. *Annuals of Public and Comparative Economics, 62,* 519-550.

Blau, P. M. (1970). A formal theory of differentiation in organizations. *American Sociological Review, 35,* 201-218.

Blau, P. M. (1972). Interdependence and hierarchy in organizations. *Social Science Research, 1,* 1-24.

Bozeman, B. (1993). A theory of government red tape. *Journal of Public Administration Research and Theory, 3,* 273-303.

Bozeman, B. (2000). *Bureaucracy and red tape.* Englewood Cliffs, NJ: Prentice Hall.

Bozeman, B., & Bretschneider, S. (1994). The "publicness puzzle" in organizations theory: A test of alternative differences between public and private organizations. *Journal of Public Administration Research and Theory, 4*(2), 197-223.

Bozeman, B., & Kingsley, G. (1998). Risk culture in public and private organizations. *Public Administration Review, 58*(2), 109-118.

Bozeman, B., & Murdock, A. (2007). Public managers' religiosity: Impacts on work attitudes and perceptions of co-workers. *International Public Management Journal, 10*(3), 287-306.

Brooks, A. C. (2000). Is there a dark side to government support for nonprofits?. *Public Administration Review, 60*(3), 211-218.

Brooks, A. C. (2002). Can nonprofit management help answer public management's "big questions"?. *Public Administration Review, 62*(3), 259-266.

Brown, S. P. (1996). A meta-analysis and review of organizational research on job involvement. *Psychological Bulletin, 120*(2), 235-255.

Buchanan, B. (1975). Red tape and the service ethic: Some unexpected difference between public and private managers. *Administration & Society, 6*(4), 423-444.

Buelens, M., & Broeck, H. V. D. (2007). An analysis of differences in work motivation between public and private sector organizations. *Public Administrative Review, 67*(1), 65-74.

Cameron, J., & Pierce, W. D. (2002). *Rewards and intrinsic motivation: Resolving the controversy.* Westport, CT: Bergin & Garvey.

Chambre, S. M., & Fatt, N. (2002). Beyond the liability of newness: Nonprofit organizations in an emerging policy domain. *Nonprofit and Voluntary Sector Quarterly, 31*(4), 502-524.

Cherns, A. B., & Davis, L. E. (1975). Assessment of the state of the art. In L. E. Davis & A. B. Cherns (Eds.), *Quality of working life: Problems, prospects and state of the art* (pp. 12-54). New York: Free Press.

Conner-Snibbe, A. (2006). Drowning in data. *Stanford Social Innovation Review, 4*(3), 38-45.

Daft, R. L. (2007). *Organization theory and design* (9th ed.). Mason, OH: Thomson/ Southwestern.

de Tocqueville, A. (2000). *Democracy in America.* Chicago: University of Chicago Press. (Original work published 1835)

DeHart-Davis, L. (2008). Green tape: A theory of effective organizational rules. *Journal of Public Administration and Theory.* Epub ahead of print February 25, 2008. DOI: 10.1093/jopart/mun004.

DeHart-Davis, L., & Pandey, S. (2005). Red tape and public employees: Does perceived rule dysfunction alienate managers?. *Journal of Public Administration Research and Theory, 5*(1), 153-167.

Diefendorff, J. M., Brown, D. J., Kamin, A. M., & Lord, R. G. (2002). Examining the roles of job involvement and work centrality in predicting organizational citizenship behaviors and job performance. *Journal of Organizational Behavior, 23*(1), 93-108.

DiMaggio, P. J., & Anheier, H. K. (1990). The sociology of nonprofit organizations and sectors. *Annual Review of Sociology, 16*(1), 137-159.

Eikenberry, A. M., & Kluver, J. D. (2004). The marketization of the nonprofit sector: Civil society at risk?. *Public Administration Review, 64*(2), 132-140.

Elloy, D. F., Everett, J. E., & Flynn, W. R. (1991). An examination of the correlates of job involvement. *Group and Organization Studies, 16*(2), 160-177.

Erikson, B. (2004). Nature times nurture: How organizations can optimize their people's contributions. *Journal of Organizational Excellence, 24*(1), 21-30.

Feeney, M. K. (2005). *National administrative studies project III: A survey of managers in public and non-profit organizations in Georgia and Illinois. Summary report.* Athens: University of Georgia, Department of Public Administration and Policy.

Feeney, M. K., & Bozeman, B. (2007, October). *Staying late: Comparing work hours in the public and nonprofit sectors.* Paper presented at the Public Management Research Conference, Tucson, AZ.

Fosler, R. S. (2002). *Working better together: How government, business, and nonprofit organizations can achieve public purposes through cross-sector collaboration, alliances, and partnerships.* Washington, DC: Independent Sector.

Frank, S. A., & Lewis, G. B. (2004). Government employees: Working hard or hardly working?. *American Review of Public Administration, 34*(1), 36-51.

Gazley, B., & Brudney, J. L. (2007). The purpose (and perils) of government-nonprofit partnership. *Nonprofit and Voluntary Sector Quarterly, 36*(3), 389-415.

Goodsell, C. T. (1994). *The case for bureaucracy: A public administration polemic* (3rd ed.). Chatham, NJ: Chatham House.

Hackman, J. R., & Oldham, G. R. (1980). *Work redesign.* Boston: Addison-Wesley.

Houston, D. J. (2006). "Walking the walk" of public service motivation: Public employees and charitable gifts of time, blood, and money. *Journal of Public Administration Research and Theory, 16,* 67-86.

Hu, L., & Bentler, P. M. (1999). Cutoff criteria for fit indexes in covariance structure analysis: Conventional criteria versus new alternatives. *Structural Equation Modeling, 6*(1), 1-55.

Igbaria, M., Parasuraman, S., & Badawy, M. K. (1994). Work experiences, job involvement, and quality of work life among information systems personnel. *MIS Quarterly, 18*(2), 175-201.

Kanungo, R. N. (1982a). Measurement of job and work involvement. *Journal of Applied Psychology, 67*(3), 341-349.

Kanungo, R. N. (1982b). *Work involvement.* New York: Praeger.

Keating, E., & Frumkin, P. (2003). Reengineering nonprofit financial accountability: Toward a more reliable foundation for regulation. *Public Administration Review, 63*(1), 3-15.

Kim, S. E. (2005). Three management challenges in performance improvement in human services agencies: A case study. *International Review of Public Administration, 10*(1), 83-93.

Kushner, R. J., & Poole, P. P. (1996). Exploring structure-effectiveness relationships in nonprofit arts organizations. *Nonprofit Management & Leadership, 7*(2), 119-136.

Lan, Z., & Rainey, H. G. (1992). Goals, rules, and effectiveness in public, private, and hybrid organizations: More evidence on frequent assertions about differences. *Journal of Public Administration Research and Theory, 2*(1), 5-28

Lawler, E. E., III, & Hall, D. T. (1970). Relationship of job characteristics to job involvement, satisfaction, and intrinsic motivation. *Journal of Applied Psychology, 54,* 305-312.

Lepper, M. R., & Greene, D. (1975). Turning play into work: Effects of adult surveillance and extrinsic rewards on children's intrinsic motivation. *Journal of Personality and Social Psychology, 31,* 479-486.

Light, P. C. (2002). The content of their character: The state of the nonprofit workforce. *Nonprofit Quarterly, 9*(3), 6-16.

Little, R. J., & Rubin, D. B. (1987). *Statistical analysis with missing data.* New York: John Wiley.

Locke, E. A. (1976). The nature and causes of job satisfaction. In M. Dunnette (Ed.), *Handbook of industrial and organizational psychology* (pp. 1297-1350). Chicago: Rand McNally.

Lohmann, R. A. (1989). And lettuce is nonanimal: Toward a positive economics of voluntary action. In J. S. Ott (Ed.), *The nature of the nonprofit sector* (pp. 197-204). Boulder, CO: Westview.

Maguire, E. R. (2003). *Organizational structure in American police agencies: Context, complexity, and control.* Albany: State University of New York Press.

Martin, L. L. (1999). Public private competition: An employee alternative to privatization. *Review of Public Personnel Administration, 19*(1), 59-70.

Mirabella, R. M., & Wish, N. B. (2000). The "best place" debate: A comparison of graduate education programs for nonprofit managers. *Public Administration Review, 60*(3), 219-229.

Moon, M. J. (2000). Organizational commitment revisited in the new public management: Motivation, organizational culture, sector, and managerial level. *Public Performance and Management Review, 24*(2), 177-194.

Morrison, J. B., & Salipante, P. (2007). Governance for broadened accountability: Blending deliberate and emergent strategizing. *Nonprofit and Voluntary Sector Quarterly, 36*(2), 195-217.

Moynihan, D. P., & Pandey, S. J. (2007a). Finding workable levers over work motivation: Comparing job satisfaction, job involvement, and organizational commitment. *Administration & Society, 39*(7), 803-832.

Moynihan, D. P., & Pandey, S. J. (2007b). The role of organizations in fostering public service motivation. *Public Administration Review, 67*(1), 40-53.

Naff, K. C., & Crum, J. (1999). Working for America: Does public service motivation make a difference?. *Review of Public Personnel Administration, 19*(5), 5-16.

O'Connell, B. (1996). A major transfer of government responsibility to voluntary organizations? Proceed with caution. *Public Administration Review, 56*(3), 222-225.

Osbourne, D. E., & Gaebler, T. (1992). *Reinventing government: How the entrepreneurial spirit is transforming government.* Reading, MA: Addison-Wesley.

Ospina, S., Diaz, W., & O'Sullivan, J. F. (2002). Negotiating accountability: Managerial lessons from identity-based nonprofit organizations. *Nonprofit and Voluntary Sector Quarterly, 31*(1), 5-31.

Park, S. M., & Rainey, H. G. (2007). Antecedents, mediators, and consequences of affective, normative, and continuance commitment: Empirical tests of commitment effects in federal agencies. *Review of Public Personnel Administration, 27*(3), 197-226.

Park, S. M., & Rainey, H. G. (2008). Leadership and public service motivation in U.S. federal agencies. *International Public Management Journal, 11*(1), 109-142.

Quinn, R. E., & Kimberly, J. R. (1984). Paradox, planning, and perseverance: Guidelines for managerial practice. In J. R. Kimberly & R. E. Quinn (Eds.), *Managing organizational translations* (pp. 295-313). Homewood, IL: Dow Jones-Irwin.

Rabinowitz, S., & Hall, D. T. (1977). Organizational research on job involvement. *Psychological Bulletin, 84*(2), 265-288.

Rainey, H. G. (2003). *Understanding and managing public organizations* (2nd ed.). San Francisco: Jossey-Bass.

Rainey, H. G., & Bozeman, B. (2002). Comparing public and private organizations: Empirical research and the power of the a priori. *Journal of Public Administration Research and Theory, 10*(2), 447-469.

Rainey, H. G., & Steinbauer, P. (1999). Galloping elephants: Developing elements of a theory of effective government organizations. *Journal of Public Administration Research and Theory, 9*(1), 1-32.

Rainey, H. G., Pandey, S. J., & Bozeman, B. (1995). Research note: Public and private managers' perceptions of red tape. *Public Administration Review, 55*(6), 567-574.

Robbins, S. (2003). *Organizational behavior.* Upper Saddle River, NJ: Prentice Hall.

Roth, P. L. (1994). Missing data: A conceptual review for applied psychologists. *Personnel Psychology, 47,* 537-560.

Ryan, R. M., & Deci, E. L. (2000). Intrinsic and extrinsic motivations: Classic definitions and new directions. *Contemporary Educational Psychology, 25*(1), 54-67.

Saal, F. E. (1978). Job involvement: A multivariate approach. *Journal of Applied Psychology, 63*(1), 53-61.

Salamon, L. M. (1995). *Partners in public service: Government-nonprofit relations in the modern welfare state* (pp. 202-242). Baltimore: Johns Hopkins University Press.

Saleh, S. D., & Hosek, J. (1976). Job involvement: Concepts and measurements. *Academy of Management Journal, 19*(2), 213-224.

Sekaran, U., & Mowday, R. (1981). A cross-cultural analysis of the influence of individual and job characteristics on job involvement. *International Review of Applied Psychology,*

30, 51-64.

Steinberg, R. (2006). Economic theories of nonprofit organizations. In W. W. Powell & R. Steinberg (Eds.), *The nonprofit sector: A research handbook* (2nd ed., pp. 89-116). New Haven, CT: Yale University Press.

Taylor, J. C. (1975). *The quality of working life: An annotated bibliography.* Los Angeles: University of California, Center for Organizational Studies.

Tuckman, H. P., & Chang, C. F. (1991). A methodology for measuring financial vulnerability in charitable nonprofit organizations. *Nonprofit and Voluntary Sector Quarterly, 20*(4), 445-460.

Vance, R. (2006). *Employee engagement and commitment: A guide to understanding, measuring and increasing engagement in your organization.* Alexandria, VA: Society for Human Resource Management.

Wagar, T. H. (1998). Determinants of human resource management practices in small firms: Some evidence from Atlantic Canada. *Journal of Small Business Management, 36*(2), 13-23.

Weisbrod, B. A. (1975). Toward a theory of the voluntary non-profit sector in a three-sector economy. In E. S. Phelps (Ed.), *Altruism, morality, and economic theory* (pp. 171-195). New York: Russell Sage.

Weisbrod, B. A. (1988). *The nonprofit economy.* Cambridge, MA: Harvard University Press.

Weisbrod, B. A. (1998). The nonprofit mission and its financing: Growing links between nonprofits and the rest of the economy. In B. A. Weisbrod (Ed.), *To profit or not to profit: The commercial transformation of the nonprofit sector* (pp. 1-24). Cambridge, UK: Cambridge University Press.

Appendix

Construction of Indexes

Job Involvement Scale (six items) (Standardized coefficient alpha: .715)

a. I put forth my best effort to get the job done regardless of the difficulties.
b. Time seems to drag while I am on the job. (reversed)
c. It has been hard for me to get very involved in my current job. (reversed)
d. I do extra work for my job that isn't really expected of me.
e. The most important things that happen to me involve my work.
f. I do not have enough authority to determine how to get my job done. (reversed)

Intrinsic Motivation Scale (five items) (Standardized coefficient alpha: .711)

The factors that motivated managers to accept a job at their current organization:

a. The organization's reputation for opportunities for women and minorities
b. Overall quality and reputation of this organization
c. Desire for less bureaucratic red tape
d. Desire for increased responsibility
e. Ability to serve the public and the public interest

Extrinsic Motivation Scale (six items) (Standardized coefficient alpha: .717)

The factors that motivated managers to accept a job at their current organization:

a. Opportunity for advancement within the organization's hierarchy
b. Job security
c. The organization's pension or retirement plan
d. Benefits (medical, insurance)
e. "Family-friendly" policies (e.g., flexible work hours, parental leave)
f. Salary

Red Tape Scale (0 to 10 scale)

How would you assess the level of red tape in your organization?

Managerial Power Scale (4-point scale)

The number of employees supervised

Hierarchical Culture Scale (five items) (Standardized coefficient alpha: .66)

a. Even if a manager's performance is poor, formal rules make it hard to remove them from the organization.
b. The formal pay structures and rules make it hard to reward a good employee with higher pay here.
c. Employees in this organization are afraid to take risks.
d. Most employees here are clear about the tasks they are expected to perform.
e. Top management in this organization is afraid to take risks.

Note: Not all items and variables are presented here. A complete listing of items and variables in this study is available from the authors.

Chapter 10

Research on Accountability in the Korean Central Government Agencies:

Exploring Antecedent and Moderating Effects of Public Service Motivation, Goal Clarity, and Person–Organization Fit

Summary

Using hierarchical regression analysis, this study tests hypotheses about the antecedent and moderating effects of three dimensions of public service motivation (PSM) (rational, normative, and affective motivation) and two types of goal orientation (goal clarity and goal congruence, i.e., personal–organization [P-O] fit) on two different work dispositions (internal accountability and external accountability) among central government officials employed in Korean public agencies. The results show that goal clarity and goal congruence substantially explain the variations of accountability of Korean public employees. Affective PSM is especially important to the outcomes. Analysis of cross-interaction effects among PSM dimensions, goal clarity, and goal congruence on outcome variables support self-perception theory's prediction that when individuals are more exposed to unstable and ambiguous organizational environments, the relationship between PSM (especially affective and normative) and accountability becomes more pronounced. Theoretical and practical implications and limitations of this research are also discussed.

Keyword

□ Accountability □ PSM □ Goal Clarity □ Goal Congruence □ P-O Fit
□ Human Resource Management □ Public Management

Sung Min Park Associate Professor, Sungkyunkwan University
Min Young Kim M.P.A., Sungkyunkwan University

Introduction

Organizational effectiveness in the public sector can be improved when social capital in an organization is created, accumulated, and developed through individuals' formal and informal relationships with the organization, systems, responsibilities, networks, and standards. In this context, the roles of accountability have been drawing a great deal of attention as factors that influence these exchange activities (Coleman, 1998). In general, an organization in which individuals are highly accountable and responsible is durable and resistant to internal and external influences, with positive effects on organizational productivity and effectiveness, as well. In addition, social capital is perceived in terms of public values and necessities. For example, the concept of accountability is frequently discussed in the public sector as a government official's personal obligation and means to secure legitimacy in a government role. Generally, it is believed that democracy cannot be realized until administrative policy and goal-based administrative control are implemented. However, expansion, specification, and specialization of administrative functions have been observed to lead to limitations in external administrative control. Therefore, internal control in the form of "subjective and voluntary accountability" becomes more important. In fact, they are key elements of a new paradigm in management of administrative organizations, which can support the conventional result- and customer-oriented New Public Management (NPM).

Although the theoretical and practical implications of accountability have become more important in Korea's public sector, there is little research on the improvement of accountability from the perspective of human resources and social capital in a Korean context. Therefore, this study seeks to provide theoretical grounds and feasibility for hypotheses of relationships among the following three concepts: public service motivation (PSM), goal clarity and fit, and accountability. The study is presented in five parts. First, to get a grasp of idiosyncratic values and ideologies nested in Korean public sector, we briefly introduce the main features of the Korean Public Personnel administration, followed by examining the applicability of general theories to Korea's public sector through a review of research on accountability. Second, we conceptualize these ideas as internal accountability, and external accountability. Then, we develop suggestions from studies of PSM, goal clarity, and P-O fit from the Korean perspective through analysis of the factors that enhance accountability in public sector. To achieve this, we define the concepts of PSM (and its subdimensions of rational, norm-based, and affective) and organizational goal clarity and person–organization goal fit, and we employ related theories to conceptualize and analyze causality among these major concepts. Fourth, we also empirically investigate moderating effects on these relationships. We propose hypotheses and a framework for our research models which we have used to investigate the organizational behavior of government employees in Korea's central administrative body, based on empirical data. Finally, we discuss the results of our analyses and provide useful implications for the development of theories and policies for public sector and personnel management in the Asian work context.

Main features of the Korean Public Personnel Administration System

The Korean public personnel administration system is a rank-based combination of the career civil service and position classification systems. Employment, education, performance evaluation, promotion, compensation, welfare, protection of rights and moral responsibility comprise the main features of Korean public personnel administration system. Employees are selected through examinations based on open and performance-related theories. Regular government service is divided into nine levels, while research and education services are divided into two. The Senior Civil Service is intended for public offices over level 3. There are two different types of examinations prior to employment: the open competitive examination and the work experience competitive examination. The open competitive examination is for individuals without prior work experience, while the work experience competitive examination is for professionals or those who do have experience (Civil Service Act Art. 8, Art 31). The open recruitment exams are divided into three types: level 5 (regular service, administration service, technological service, foreign service), level 7 (administration service, technological service) and level 9 (administration service, technological service). The examinations - different for all kinds of jobs ranging from prosecutor affairs to agriculture - are conducted by the minister of Ministry of Public Administration and Security (MOPAS). The minimum age for regular service is twenty for level 7 and higher, and eighteen for technological services or level 8 and below; maximum age is not set. Discrimination based on educational background had been banned in 1973.

Second, all central organizations, related educational organizations, and MOPAS educate and develop public officials. MOPAS establishes basic rules and policies to develop, support, and evaluate their education process. MOPAS is also responsible for commissioning employee education both within and outside of Korea. Each central administrative agency is responsible for educating its own personnel about its policies and other relevant departments. Public office education institutes are responsible for providing basic education of prospective officials and professional education for current workers. There are thirty related central institutes (e.g. Central Officials Training Institute [COTI]), fifteen local training institutes, and six Fire Service Academies.[1]

Third, Korean public officers over level 4 are evaluated by the job performance agreement system for senior civil servants and public officers. Those below level 5 are evaluated by the performance evaluation system for public officers. These results can be used for deciding promotions, bonuses, education, training, placement, etc. (Personnel Office in MOPAS). Fourth, salary is managed by the salary step system. Thirty types of bonuses are given in total. Each employee's salary is made up of family budget bonuses, special service/region bonuses, and overtime payments. However, for public officials over level 4, the annual salary system applies. Officials in political service receive fixed payments, while senior civil service and public officials over level 4 are paid based on their performance. Welfare is also available through the personnel welfare system, which offers sixteen types of welfare support including housing support, education loans, medical expenses, parental expenses and insurance (Performance-related payment Portal of MOPAS). Last but not least, the status of Korean public officials is guaranteed: they may not be dismissed unless they are subjected to legal action. Leaves of absence are granted for up to three years in case of sickness, overseas study, and pregnancy, and the retirement age is sixty (Civil Service Act Art. 71 Art. 72 Art. 74). Employees should remain faithful to work hours and are required to keep all work-related material confidential (Civil Service Act Art. 58 Art. 60). Additionally, Korean public officials may not accept donations or treats, and cannot hold another job (Civil Service Act Art. 61 Art. 64). Finally, the officials must remain politically neutral and refrain from participating in political demonstrations (Civil Service Act Art. 65 & Art.66).

Drawing on these common characteristics in a Korean personnel management system, we posit that the main structures and relations among main variables in this research would be significantly influenced by Korean or Confucian values, norms, and institutions. For example, Confucian ethics and collective cultures, as well as the higher reputable prestige as a public servant in Korean bureaucracy might affect and modify the structures and dimensions of public service motivation (PSM). Consequently, the normative and affect motives of PSM would be more predominant factors than the rational motives, and hence, the antecedent and moderating impacts of each three motives of PSM on organizational outcomes (e.g., goal clarity, P-O fit, and accountability) would differ accordingly (Kim, 2009).

Theoretical Framework and Development of Hypotheses

Accountability: Internal and External

In practical and theoretical aspects, administrative accountability is a fundamental topic of public administration, which should be addressed as an administrative value that can help prevent corporate corruption, given the "publicness" of administrative ethics. In particular, administrative accountability has never been more important, considering the current internal and external circumstances of Korea's public sector, which have become expanded in terms of administrative functions and more specified and complicated in terms of quality, with greater influences on society. Accountability has been defined in various ways and much discussed (Thomas, 2003; Romzek & Ingraham, 2000).[2] For example, Romzek and Dubnick (1998) defined accountability as a "relationship being formed to respond to the performances which occur when an individual or institution is invested with a certain authority," classifying it into legal accountability, administrative accountability, professional accountability, and political accountability, depending on the origin and level of control.[3] Behn (2001) defined accountability as an "explainable and tangible state" and classified it into accountability for finances, accountability for performance, and accountability for fairness. Han (2010) defined accountability in Korea's public sector as an "obligation to i) prove for internal control and ii) accept, receive and adjust the needs and expectations from internal and external interested parties regarding administration" and specified it as political, bureaucratic, market, and managerial accountability.

Based on these diverse discussions on the concept of accountability, this study has defined accountability as having two dimensions: internal accountability (administrative and professional) and external accountability (legal and political), as shown in Table 1, which is in accordance with Romzek et al. (1987, 2000) and Johnston and Romzek (1999).

We address the specific characteristics of accountability as follows. Administrative accountability with low autonomy characterizes a government official's responsibility to observe internal rules and regulations. Professional accountability entails high autonomy and respect for government officials' expertise with the belief that they make their best efforts based on their professional knowledge. Legal accountability (external type) is found in relationships among government officials who enact and execute laws. Finally, political accountability involves external accountability with high discretionary power; it emphasizes responsiveness to interested parties from the outside, such as government employees' proper responses to citizens' and interested parties' needs and demands (Eom, 2009).

Table 1. Types of Accountability

		The position of the person who blames	
		Inside (Internal Control)	Outside (External Control)
Characteristics of "Criteria for Judgment of Accountability"	Low autonomy (High control level)	Administrative accountability: Vertical control, efficiency	Legal accountability: Control legitimacy in consignment and national assembly
	High autonomy (Low control level)	Professional accountability: Autonomous control based on expertise and professional ethics	Political accountability: Control of external interested parties; responsiveness

Source: Romzek & Dubnick (1987) and Johnston & Romzek (1999), reorganized by the current authors.

Public Service Motivation (PSM)

The concept of government employees' motivation has drawn interest, dispute, and academic discussion for a long time. For public personnel management, motivation in a public sector can be viewed as public sector motivation and public service motivation (PSM). Public sector motivation is composed of various motivations to perform public service, and PSM is one type of public sector motivation. Besides PSM, public sector motivation includes other intrinsic motivators and extrinsic motivators (e.g., stable tenure systems, government employee pension systems, and promotion guarantee systems) provided by public sector, public organizations, and pseudo public sector. Although there has been some disagreement on its definition among scholars, public sector motivation can be defined as the "motivation or behavior in a public sector, performed for social good, public interest and others."[4] It has been introduced as a theoretical concept under various names in Korea: public service motivation (Lee, 2005), PSM (Kim, 2009), and public service choice motivation (Kim, 2005). However, it appears appropriate to analyze PSM after dualizing it as i) PSM in a job choice stage and ii) PSM in a duty fulfillment and socialization process stage, under the proposition of conceptual differences between job choice motivation and work motivation (Vandenabeele, 2008; Word & Park, 2009; Park & Rainey, 2012).

From the conventional perspective, Perry and Wise (1990) defined PSM as "an individual's predisposition which uniquely exists in a public sector system or institution." A person with high PSM often tends to select a public organization, and a positive relation has been found between PSM and performance in public sector. Hypotheses have been proposed that higher levels of PSM are less dependent on extrinsic and economic factors. In other conventional literature, PSM has been defined as "altruistic motivation or public service ethics in an interested field such as local community, nation and humankind (public service ethics)" (Rainey & Steinbauer, 1999), "motivation or behavior to form social wellbeing with altruistic attitude" (Perry & Hondeghem, 2008), and "influence on political interests or motivation of individual behavior with trust, value and attitude, exceeding personal or organizational interests" (Vandenabeele, 2007). PSM entails an intrinsic rewards system that occurs prior to extrinsic rewards. It is a prosocial motivation that emphasizes professional ethics (Perry & Wise, 1990; Perry, 1996). Therefore, it has been argued that employees working in the public sector are more interested in norm-based and affective motives that emphasize public interests and intrinsic motivations than in personal-interest-centered, rational, or authority-oriented motivations (Perry & Wise, 1990; Perry, 1996; Brewer, 2003; Kim & Vandenabeele, 2010). Conceptually, PSM can be viewed as consisting of three dimensions: rational, norm-based, and affective. Table 2 provides a public service motivation scale developed by Perry (1996) and based on a study by Perry and Wise (1990). Here, the current authors have reorganized PSM from Perry's[5] six categories to a set of four categories, excluding social justice and civic duty.

Table 2. Components of PSM

Type	Component	Description
Rational motivation	Attraction to public policy-making process	Desire to: - Participate in policy making - Identify important public policy - Support particular interests
Norm-based motivation	Commitment to public interest and civic duty	- Calling to public service - Loyalty and duty toward government - Drive to pursue social equity
Affective motivation	Compassion, self-sacrifice	- Commitment to a policy due to its social importance - Patriotism or benevolence

Source: Perry & Wise (1990) and Perry (1996), reorganized by the current authors.

Rational Motivation

Rational motivations are desires to participate in policy making, identify important public policies, and support particular interests. This motive reflects a sense of personal utility and wanting to do something beneficial for society. It has rational, transactional, and authority- and interest-oriented characteristics. Thus, government employees do not work based only on altruism or public-mindedness, but also on rational efforts to maximize personal utility (Perry & Wise, 1990). This represents government employees' strong desire to maximize power and self-importance by participating in developing public policies (Wright, 2008). In addition, such efforts of government employees to enhance social welfare tend to increase their self-satisfaction and self-esteem. Thus, rational motivation for success of certain public policies can be viewed as a drive for personal success or to provide public services to a particular group and protect its rights.

Norm-based Motivation

Norm-based motivation reflects the desire to improve a public image, carry out public duties to realize public benefits, and fulfill duties as citizens of a community. Public service has been suggested to be a common norm-based motive. Prosocial values of citizens and governments, such as patriotism and loyalty, are expressed in government employees' altruistic behaviors, OCB, and high job performance. Norm-based ethical motivation is applied in the proposal, establishment, execution, and evaluation of diverse public policies. An example is the pursuit of social equity, which is the effort to improve social welfare for politically and economically disadvantaged people through social welfare policies. Government employees can satisfy this norm-based motivation by insisting that public services be provided that enhance social equity with respect to economics (Frederickson, 1971).

Affective Motivation

Affective or humane motives are the desire to devote energy toward functions and policies essential for a society. A government employee's affective commitment to public interest can be understood as both personally and socially self-sacrificing in intention. Frederickson and Hart (1985) described affective motives as reflecting a "patriotism of benevolence," which is to love all citizens in the political territory and protect their basic rights. They argued that self-sacrifice for others occurs through humanity and sympathy.

Organizational Goal Clarity and Person–Organization (P-O) Fit

Goal Clarity

An organization can accomplish its objectives, such as improved efficiency and effectiveness, through setting clear goals. Goal clarity helps people to i) develop goal-oriented plans, ii) concentrate on goal-oriented behavior, iii) make efforts to achieve goals, and iv) continue to pursue goals when faced with obstacles (Seo, et al., 2009). Organizational goals require continued effort and sustained interest. In particular, appropriate goal setting can play a catalytic role that increases individuals' motivation to achieve the goals and improves job attitude (Vancouver & Schmitt, 1991; Wright, 2007; Mento, Steele & Karren, 1987). These positive functions of clear goals have direct effects on organizational performance. According to goal setting theory by Locke (1968), organizational performance is determined by conscious goals and intentions and has a significant effect on personal performance, depending on goal difficulty and specificity (Moorhead & Griffin, 1992).

In conventional studies, goal clarity has been described as a rational entity that enhances work performance (Locke & Latham, 1990). Buchanan (1974) concluded that goals affect organizational commitment, while Wright (2004) described goals' relationship with motivation. In particular, Halachmi and Krogh (2005) explained that employees are highly motivated by clear organizational goals because they make employees aware of what they should do, and they are in positions to make the efforts required. Thus, goal clarity has a positive effect on organizational result variables such as job satisfaction, organizational commitment, and performance (Park & Rainey, 2007). Because a specific goal is indicative of the direction and level of an employee's job, it ultimately can have a negative effect on organizational trust, commitment, and performance unless the goal is clear with job difficulty, accountability, and specificity clearly defined. For example, under "management by objectives" (MBO), the goals of a nonprofit organization are often somewhat unclear, contradictory, and multiplex, compared to a private organization. Therefore, it is difficult to thoroughly measure and manage individual and organizational performance and effectiveness. Additionally, when goals are unrelated with organizational performance, it is more difficult to manage performance in a nonprofit organization.

Person–Organization (P-O) Fit

P-O fit has various aspects, such as person–job, person–organization, and person–environment (P-E) fit. P-E fit refers to congruence between an individual's personality and the work environment. From the P-E fit perspective, organizational performance and personnel management can be understood as a series of processes aimed to match a person's intrinsic values with organizational values through thoughtful recruitment, staffing, and training. P-E fit has been treated seriously in organizational behavior and psychology. The research on P-E fit can be classified as person–organization fit, person–job fit, person–group fit, and person–supervisor fit (Kristof et al., 2005). P-O fit has been defined variously as a "person–organization correspondence which occurs when either person or organization responds to the counterpart's request, or similar basic propensity is shared (Kristof, 1996)," "a level of matching or fit between person and organizational value, goal and characteristics (Lauver & Kristof, 2001)," and "a level of matching between personal characteristics and organizational atmosphere" (Bowen, Ledford & Nathan, 1991; Burke & Deszca, 1982). Person–organization fit has been analyzed in terms of supplementary fit and complementary fit (Kristof, 1996; Muchinsky & Monahan, 1997; Cable & Edwards, 2004). In these aspects, employees recognize how much their characteristics fit with organizational factors (Shin, 2008; Muchinsky & Monahan, 1987). Fit can be achieved when a person and an organization share similar or matched goals and values (supplementary fit) or when the person's and organization's characteristics provide what each wants and the person is satisfied with the resources provided by the organization (complementary fit). This study focuses on supplementary fit, which has been emphasized in Korea's nonprofit organizational culture.

Discussion of Causality in Concepts and Hypotheses

Social exchange theory (Blau, 1964) describes how the members of an organization engage in social exchange relationships based on reciprocal standards or systems; these may include rewards and trade that are affective as well as physical exchanges. Such reciprocal mechanisms can explain the relationships among the current study's concepts of motivation, goal clarity, goal fit, and accountability. In particular, the unique culture of Korea's public sector is based on social exchange, as can be seen in the hierarchical and status-guarantee-based career paths within Korea's civil service system. Social exchange significantly influences government employees' intrinsic motivations, interpersonal relationships, solidarity, and affective connections. This study analyzes reciprocity in Korea's nonprofit organizations based on social exchange theory from the macroscopic perspective, by investigating PSM and goals clarity and fit. In addition, this study demonstrates the influence of reciprocity via causal relationships among study variables of internal and external organizational accountability, affective and cognitive dimensions. Hypotheses regarding causal and modulating effects among variables have been specifically established in this study with consideration of theoretical relevance and practical applicability.

PSM and Accountability

Recently, high external control, such as performance management, has been shown to de-emphasize public values, such as individuals' morality, self-reflection, and organizational norms. Thus, accountability has emerged as an issue in the public sector. PSM is a major variable in public administration, associated with organizational productivity, accountability, government trust, and management technique as well as with motivation (Brewer et al., 2000). It is hard for employees in a public sector, where intrinsic motivation such as PSM is strong, to achieve job satisfaction and organizational commitment unless they are sure of social ripple effects from their work. In addition, the low level of discretionary power in organizational management can lead to depression among those in public service (Perry & Porter, 1982; Buchanan, 1974; 1975).

Theoretical approaches to securing accountability have included agent theory and stewardship theory. Conventional agent theories have emphasized that external control plans (legal and bureaucratic rules and political-monitoring rights such as elections) are not able to secure accountability in a public sector. Therefore, new ways to secure accountability have been suggested from the perspective of stewardship theory. While agent theory focuses on objective accountability, which addresses who is responsible in accordance with organizational regulations, stewardship theory concentrates on psychological dimensions of responsibility and behaviors, such as subjective accountability, identity, and loyalty (Mosher, 1968). Block (1993) argued that unity with public service values in an organization can produce inner accountability, which in turn induces responsible behavior. In stewardship theory, a self-realized person is centered and has a "core value which stipulates human behavior is public service" (Davis et al., 1997). In other words, awareness of public values regarding disadvantaged people and affective and norm-based awareness and motivation in a local community and society are government employees' rights and, at the same time, their obligations. In fact, these are the critical factors that lead to responsible behavior. Based on our theory that stewardship-theory-based, public-interest-oriented, benevolent, norm-based, affective PSM is more effective than rational, transactional, bureaucratic, personal-interest-oriented PSM, this study investigates the relationship between PSM and accountability through the following hypotheses, with the aim of enhancing accountability in public sector.

Hypothesis 1: Affective and norm-based PSMs have strong positive effects on internal and external accountability in Korean public sector.
Hypothesis 2: Rational PSM does not have a strong effect on internal and external accountability in Korean public sector.

Goal Clarity, P-O Fit, and Accountability

Accountability is an individual's subjective experience based on personal work experience. Therefore, it is hard to measure it in theory and in practice. From the perspectives of goal theory and social capital theory, clear organizational goals accelerate the internalization of diverse human resources capital (e.g., personal ability, performance, peer network, and trust). In addition, clear goals transform these inner capabilities into organizational social capital (e.g., collaboration of government with other administrative bodies, citizen participation, cooperation, and social and administrative accountability). Employees in a public sector cannot ignore demands for social and political accountability even when goals are unclear. However, mid- and long-term improvement of organizational culture and structure, goal-oriented leadership, and clear organizational goals are required to achieve diverse accountability in a public organization as well as to enhance performance (Wilson, 1989). Lee et al., (2005) found that, in particular, rational cultures in which organizational goals are clearly set and rationally accomplished are most likely to achieve high accountability. In addition, according to a study on stewardship theory and administrative accountability, commitment to public service values and organizational goals is positively related to inner accountability (Won, 2008).

P-E fit and accountability can greatly influence organizational results (Stephen et al., 2010); for example, it has been shown empirically that interaction effects between accountability and person–work fit affect organizational results such as job satisfaction, commitment, and work stress (Wheeler & Halbesleben, 2009). Additionally, from the supplementary fit perspective, P-E fit increases accountability in an organization. Based on these findings, we developed the following hypotheses:

> **Hypothesis 3:** Goal clarity has a strong positive effect on internal and external accountability in Korean public sector.
> **Hypothesis 4:** P-O fit has a strong positive effect on internal and external accountability in Korean public sector.

Moderating Effects of Goal Clarity and P-O Fit on the Relationships between PSM and Accountability

Employees in a public sector prefer various types of PSMs. Compared to private companies, public organizations tend to have unclear goals and difficulty in interpreting them, which in turn has negative effects on accountability. Because Korean public sector are situated in a hierarchical culture implementing rank-in-person personnel systems, in contrast to the position classification system employed in the U.K. and the United States, it is not easy to increase person–job, person–group, and person–organizational fits without continued investments in training and organizational redesign. Therefore, this study is significant in that it investigates how goals and PSM interact and how goals' clarity and fit moderate PSM's relationships with accountability. This study's hypotheses regarding interaction and moderation effects are based on the following two inferences, using the theoretical background of self-perception theory (Bem, 1972).[6]

First, as stated in hypotheses 1 to 4, we propose that, in addition to independent antecedent effects in relationships among PSM, goal clarity, P-O fit (antecedent variables), and two types of accountability in the public sector, these influence are modified by interactions between PSM and goal clarity and P-O fit. Second, the strength of cause-and-effect relationships can vary depending on the influence of other organizational variables (Choi et al., 2005). For example, under circumstances in which an individual's PSM has a significant effect on accountability (hypotheses 1 and 4), PSM would have a stronger effect if the P-O fit with the organization were low. If the P-O fit became high, in contrast, PSM's influence on accountability would decline (hypothesis 5). This study hypothesizes the effects of interactions of a new conceptualization of PSM, which is that norm-based and affective PSMs play a bigger role when organizational goal clarity and P-O fit are low. These hypotheses regarding the moderating effects of goal clarity and P-O fit on the relationships between PSM and accountability have been developed as follows:

> **Hypothesis 5:** Goal clarity and P-O fit regulate the relationships of norm-based and affective PSMs with accountability in Korean public sector. Specifically, as goal clarity and P-O fit decrease, the relationships of norm-based and affective PSMs with accountability become stronger.

Figure 1. Research Model

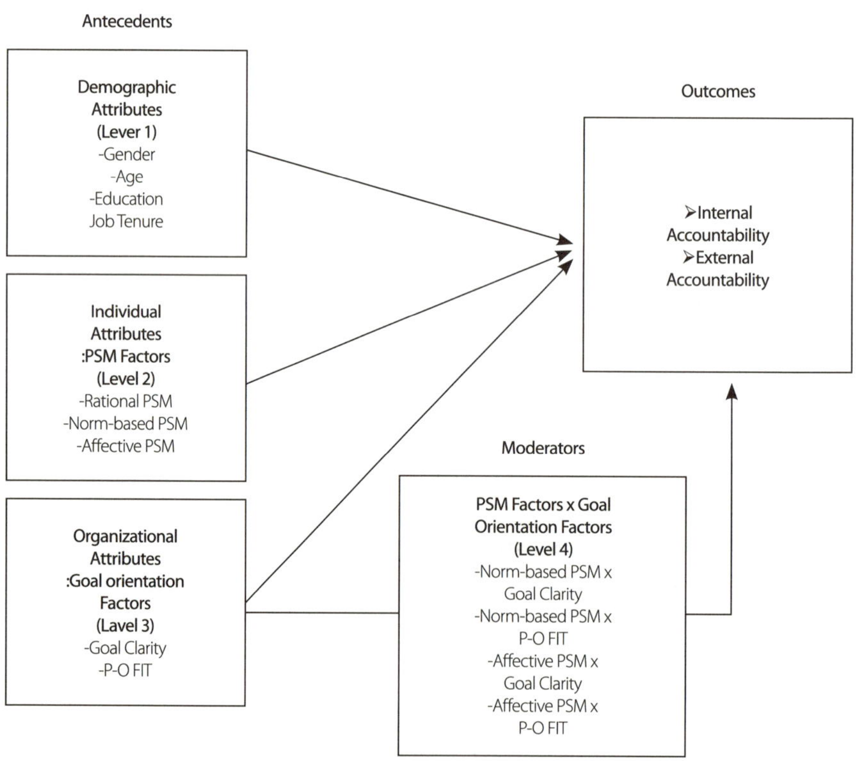

Research Methods

Data Gathering and Sample Characteristics

To analyze the relationships among the variables shown in Figure 1, including government officials' PSM, goal clarity P-O fit, and accountability, a questionnaire survey titled "Government Officials' Accountability and Trust Survey" was used to gather data from government employees who received training at the Central Officials Training Institute (COTI) from October to November in 2011, and related data were also collected. Participants were informed that all information collected would be kept confidential. Out of 350 distributed questionnaires, 255 were collected and used for the study.[7]

The distributions of socio-demographic characteristics of the sample are provided in Table 3. Men and women comprised 86.7% and 10.6% of the sample, respectively. More people were in their "40s" (49.8%) than in any other age category. In terms of education, "Bachelor" was the most common with 52.4%, followed by "Master & Doctorate" (28.3%) and "College Graduates" (9%). In terms of respondents' grade, "Rank 6" was the most frequent (62.4%), followed by "Rank 5" (23.9%) and "Rank 7" (1.2%). In terms of length of employment, "25–30 years" was the most common with 23.5%.

Table 3. Respondents' Characteristics

Factors		Frequency(%)
Gender	Male	221(86.7)
	Female	27(10.6)
	Missing	7(2.7)
Age	21 - 30 years	2(0.8)
	31 - 40 years	12(4.7)
	41 - 50 years	127(49.8)
	Above 51	103(40.4)
	Missing	11(4.3)
Education	High School	19(7.5)
	College	23(9.0)
	Bachelor	129(52.4)
	Master & Doctorate	72(28.3)
	Missing	10(3.8)

Factors		Frequency(%)
Level	Rank 4	1(0.4)
	Rank 5	61(23.9)
	Rank 6	159(62.4)
	Rank 7	3(1.2)
	Rank 8	1(0.4)
	Rank 9	1(0.4)
	Contract Worker	17(7.1)
	Missing	12(4.7)
Years of Experience	Less than 5 years	4(1.6)
	10 ~ 15 years	10(4.0)
	15 ~ 20 years	53(21.2)
	20 ~ 25 years	49(19.6)
	25 ~ 30 years	59(23.5)
	More than 30 years	57(21.4)
	Missing	11(4.3)

Configuration of variables

The questionnaire categories and variables have been developed based on theoretical discussions and empirical research in the domestic and foreign literature. They are configured as follows: 12 PSM variables, 4 goal clarity variables, 4 P-O fit variables, 6 interpersonal trust variables, 6 organizational trust variables, 6 internal accountability variables, and 6 external accountability variables. The questionnaire was composed of single questions that used a 7-point Likert scale with the range of 1 (never) to 4 (maybe) to 7 (very likely).

To measure PSM, we constructed an ordinal scale of three dimensions that includes Perry's (1996) widely used PSM measurement scales (rational, norm-based, and affective motives). Goal clarity was measured with indexes based on those of Wright (2004) and Wright and Pandey (2011). In addition, P-O fit variables were measured based on conventional theories (Lauver & Kristof, 2001) and empirical studies. Finally, accountability variables were classified into internal and external accountability, depending on the origin of control inside or outside of the organization. Based on works by Cavalluzzo and Ittner (2004), Romzek and Dubnick (1987), and Johnston and Romzk (1999), this study classified professional accountability as internal accountability, and legal and political accountability as external accountability.

Table 4. Summary of Measurement Variables

<table>
<tr><th></th><th>Variables</th><th>Items</th><th>Researchers</th></tr>
<tr><td rowspan="6">Independent Variables</td><td rowspan="3">Rational PSM</td><td>Politics is a dirty word.(r)</td><td rowspan="6">Perry, J. L. (1996)</td></tr>
<tr><td>The give and take of publicmaking doesn't appeal to me.(r)</td></tr>
<tr><td>I don't care much for policians.(r)</td></tr>
<tr><td rowspan="3">Norm-based PSM</td><td>I consider public service a civic duty.</td></tr>
<tr><td>I would prefer seeing public officials do what is best for the community, even if it harmed my interests.</td></tr>
<tr><td>Meaningful public service is very important to me.</td></tr>
</table>

<table>
<tr><td rowspan="6"></td><td rowspan="6" colspan="2">Affective PSM</td><td>Most social programs are too vital to do without.</td><td rowspan="6"></td></tr>
<tr><td>It is so difficult for me to contain my feelings when I see people in distress.</td></tr>
<tr><td>I have little compassion for people in need who are unwilling to take the first step to help themselves.(r)</td></tr>
<tr><td>Making a difference in society means more to me than personal achievement.</td></tr>
<tr><td>I feel people should give back to society more than they get from it.</td></tr>
<tr><td>I am prepared to make enormous sacrifices for the good of society.</td></tr>
<tr><td rowspan="8">Independent /Moderator Variables</td><td rowspan="4" colspan="2">Goal Clarity</td><td>I know well my duties and responsibilities.</td><td rowspan="4">Wright (2004), Wright & Pandey (2011)</td></tr>
<tr><td>I was given clear goals and objectives for my job.</td></tr>
<tr><td>I know well how my work relates to the overall objectives of my work unit.</td></tr>
<tr><td>I can expect the results of my work.</td></tr>
<tr><td rowspan="4" colspan="2">P-O Fit</td><td>My values match those of the current employees in this organization.</td><td rowspan="4">Lauver & Kristof (2001)</td></tr>
<tr><td>I am not very comfortable within the culture of my organization.</td></tr>
<tr><td>I feel a strong sense of "belonging" to my organization.</td></tr>
<tr><td>What this organization stands for is important to me.</td></tr>
<tr><td rowspan="12">Dependent Variables</td><td rowspan="6">Internal Accountability</td><td rowspan="4">Hierarchical Accountability</td><td>Executive directors hire, supervise, manage contracts</td><td rowspan="12">Kearns(1994), Cavalluzzo & Ittner(2004) Romzek & Dubnick (1987), Johnston & Romzek (1999)</td></tr>
<tr><td>Following administrative procedures and rules</td></tr>
<tr><td>Obedience to organizational directives</td></tr>
<tr><td>Rules regarding case load limits accepted as part of contract</td></tr>
<tr><td rowspan="2">Professional Accountability</td><td>Achieving professional credentials</td></tr>
<tr><td>Improving quality of services and best practices</td></tr>
<tr><td rowspan="6">External Accountability</td><td rowspan="3">Legal Accountability</td><td>Maintaining annual contract with the government</td></tr>
<tr><td>Fulfilling documentation requirements of the government</td></tr>
<tr><td>Obtaining accreditations from an external auditing agency</td></tr>
<tr><td rowspan="3">Political Accountability</td><td>Responsive to clients' performance expectations</td></tr>
<tr><td>Working with community members in shaping policies</td></tr>
<tr><td>Maintaining a good relationship with the local Media</td></tr>
</table>

*: 'r' refers to reverse coding.

The measured variables were analyzed using SPSS 18.0 for Windows. First, a reliability analysis and a confirmatory factory analysis (CFA) were performed for each of the variables in the study. Then, correlation analysis was conducted to analyze how validity and reliability are correlated with the verified variables. The interaction and moderating effects of the three dimensions of PSM (rational, norm-based, and affective) and the effects of the independent variables of goal clarity and P-O fit on accountability and trust were investigated by performing a 4-stage hierarchical multiple regression (stage I: demographic variables, stage II: adding individual variables, stage III: adding organizational variables, and stage IV: adding goal orientation moderating variables)[8].

Analysis Results

Reliability Analysis

Table 5. Reliability Analysis

Variables	Mean	Std. Dev.	Cronbach's Alpha
Rational PSM	3.596	1.747	.598
Nome-based PSM	5.072	1.171	.842
Affective PSM	4.934	1.277	.722
Goal Clarity	5.770	1.037	.947
P-O Fit	5.456	1.268	.911
Internal Accountability	5.848	.846	.933
External Accountability	5.505	1.065	.859

In this study, Cronbach's alpha was used to test reliability. The values were .70 or above, indicating good reliability, for the constructs: norm-based and affective PSMs, organizational goals parameters, and accountability (Hair et al., 2006). While the value of Cronbach's alpha for rational PSM was slightly below .70, the variable was included in the model as we were convinced that a rational dimension of PSM in the Korean context cannot be ignored either.

Correlation Analysis

In addition to obtaining descriptive statistics, we performed correlation analysis on the variables in the hypotheses. As shown in Table 6, positive correlation was found between age and P-O fit (P<.01). Length of employment was negatively correlated with rational PSM (P<.01). Affective PSM was positively correlated with goal clarity (P<.05) and with P-O fit, and internal accountability (P<.01). Rational PSM was negatively correlated with goal orientation variables (goal clarity and P-O fit) (P<.01) and negatively correlated with both internal accountability (P<.01). In contrast, norm-based and affective PSMs were positively correlated with organizational goal clarity, P-O fit, internal accountability, and external accountability (P<.01). Organizational goal clarity and P-O fit were positively correlated with internal and external accountability (P<.01). Results were used to examine the hypotheses that goal clarity and P-O fit variables moderate the positive relationships between norm-based and affective PSMs and the dependent variables. The moderating effects were analyzed, and methodological validity was determined, as described below.

Table 6. Correlations among PSM, Organizational Goal and Accountability

Variables	Mean	S.D.	1	2	3	4	5	6	7	8	9	10	11
1. Gender	1.10	.31	1										
2. Age	48.06	5.52	-.34**	1									
3. Education	3.20	2.19	-.09	.26**	1								
4. Job Tenure	23.31	7.48	-.26**	.85**	.36**	1							
5. RationalPSM	3.59	.98	-.01	-.10	-.07	-.17**	1						
6. Norm-based PSM	4.98	.94	.01	.04	.06	.08	-.32**	1					
7. Affective PSM	5.00	.77	-.02	.09	.01	.14*	-.42**	.69**	1				
8. Goal Clarity	5.77	.94	.06	.10	.04	.15*	-.17**	.38**	.42**	1			
9. P-O Fit	5.45	1.00	-.05	.18**	.02	.30**	-.16**	.35**	.39**	.74**	1		
10. Interpersonal Accountability	5.81	.79	.09	.05	.07	.17**	-.16**	.46**	.48**	.65**	.57**	1	
11. Organization Accountability	5.21	.91	.05	.01	-.09	.09	-.12	.30**	.34**	.34**	.43**	.58**	1

*:p<.05 ,** : p<.01

Hypothesis Test and Results[9]

Analysis of Influences of PSM and Goal Clarity and P-O Fit on Accountability

For internal accountability, the demographic variables (model 1) explained about 4%

of the variance. For model 2 with PSM variables added, the explained variance of internal accountability was 30.8%. This result confirmed that rational, norm-based, and affective PSMs all tended to increase internal accountability. For model 3 with organizational goal clarity and P-O fit variables added, the explained variation (R^2) of internal accountability increased substantially to 51.8% at a 95% significance level. In model 4 with interaction added between PSM and organizational goal clarity and P-O fit, the standardized regression coefficient (β) was .298 ($p<.05$) for affective PSM, .075 ($p>.01$) for rational PSM, .453 ($p<.01$) for goal clarity, and .222 ($p<.05$) for P-O fit. These results support hypothesis 5 (affective PSM) and hypotheses 6–8. Additionally, model 4 explains 52.3% of variance in internal accountability which, compared to model 3, was a small increase in explained variance (ΔR^2) at a 90% significance level ($\Delta R^2=.005$, $p<.05$). These results confirmed that moderating effects exist between PSM and goal clarity and P-O fit variables. In particular, moderating effects between norm-based PSM and P-O fit (+) and between affective PSM and P-O fit (-) were statistically significant for internal accountability.

For external accountability, model 1 (with demographic variables only) explained 1.3% of variance. Model 2 (with PSM), explained 16.1% of variance in external accountability, confirming that norm-based and affective PSMs increase external accountability. In model 3 (with goal orientation variables), explained variance (R^2) dramatically increased to 21.5% in a 95% significance level. In model 4 (with interaction added between PSM and organizational goal clarity and P-O fit), the standardized regression coefficient (β) became .280 ($p<.05$) for affective PSM, .045 ($p>.01$) for rational PSM, and .366 ($p<.05$) for P-O fit, confirming hypothesis 5 (affective PSM) and hypotheses 6 and 8. Also, Model 4 explained 25.7% of variance in external accountability. Compared to model 3, explained variance was increased in a 90% significance level ($\Delta R^2=.042$, $p<.05$), confirming that moderating effects occur for PSM and goal clarity and P-O fit variables. In particular, P-O fit had a statistically significant moderating effect on the relationship between affective PSM (+) and external accountability.

Table 7. Results of Analysis on Internal Accountability

	Internal Accountability											
	Model 1			Model 2			Model 3			Model 4		
	B	β	t	B	β	t	B	β	t	B	β	t
Step 1 (Demographic Attributes)												
Gender	.244	.090	1.345	.234	.087	1.514	.167	.062	1.268	.158	.058	1.211
Age	-.035	-.224	-1.783*	-.018	-.119	-1.105	.000	.001	.011	.002	.014	.155

Education	.001	.002	.022	.008	.022	.363	.018	.048	.962	.013	.035	.696
Job Tenure	.044	.392	3.058**	.025	.226	2.032**	.003	.028	.291	.002	.016	.158
Step 2 (Individual Attributes: PSM Factors)												
Rational PSM				.089	.108	1.731*	.054	.066	1.264	.062	.075	1.432
Nome-based PSM-A				.308	.341	4.712***	.144	.159	2.513**	.023	.026	.243
Affective PSM-B				.283	.282	3.647***	.152	.152	2.303**	.299	.298	**2.816****
Step 3 (Organizational Attributes: Goal Orientation Factors)												
Goal Clarity-C							.354	.416	5.827***	.385	.453	**4.946*****
P-O FIT-D							.136	.164	2.183**	.185	.222	**2.220****
Step 4 (PSM Factors * Goal Orientation Factors)												
A * C										.223	.751	**1.920***
A * D										-.016	-.053	-.129
B * C										-.243	-.793	**-2.042****
B * D										-.008	-.027	-.068
	adjR^2=.042, F=3.536**			adjR^2=.308, F=15.789***			adjR^2=.518, F=28.858***			adjR^2=.523, F=20.655***		

* p < .10 , ** p < .05, *** p < .01

Table 8. Results of Analysis on External Accountability

	External Accountability											
	Model 1			Model 2			Model 3			Model 4		
	B	β	t	B	β	t	B	β	t	B	β	t
Step 1 (Demographic Attributes)												
Gender	.110	.036	.532	.113	.037	.589	.114	.038	.614	.101	.033	.534
Age	-.017	-.096	-.751	-.002	-.014	-.122	.013	.074	.632	.014	.080	.672
Education	-.061	-.150	-2.137**	-.051	-.125	-1.910*	-.037	-.092	-1.433	-.040	-.099	-1.511
Job Tenure	.029	.234	1.797*	.012	.096	.782	-.007	-.058	-.464	-.008	-.064	-.505
Step 2 (Individual Attributes: PSM Factors)												
Rational PSM				.058	.063	.919	.034	.037	.558	.042	.045	.673

Nome-based PSM-A				.192	.190	2.382**	.094	.093	1.152	.041	.040	.294
Affective PSM-B				.313	.279	3.269**	.239	.213	2.530**	.314	.280	2.050**
Step 3 (Organizational Attributes :Goal Orientation Factors)												
Goal Clarity-C							.019	.020	.219	.009	.009	.076
P-O FIT-D							.264	.283	2.956**	.341	.366	2.837**
Step 4 (PSM Factors * Goal Orientation Factors)												
A * C										.166	.498	.987
A * D										-.063	-.190	-.357
B * C										-.166	-.484	-.965
B * D										.029	.083	2.162*
	$adjR^2$=.013, F=1.794			$adjR^2$=.161, F=7.378***			$adjR^2$=.215, F=8.072***			$adjR^2$=.257, F=5.675***		

* p < .10 , ** p < .05, *** p < .01

Moderating Effects of Goal Clarity and P-O Fit on Relationships between PSM and Accountability

As shown in the tables above, explained variance was increased for each dependent variable modeled by adding the interactions of PSM dimensions with goal clarity and P-O fit variables. To precisely determine the moderating effects of goal clarity and P-O fit on the relationships of (norm-based and affective) PSMs with accountability, these relationships were expressed as regression lines for two conditions of goal variables. Specifically, the relationships between norm-based and affective PSMs and accountability were expressed as regression lines, shown in Figures 2-3, under two conditions: goal clarity and P-O fit are high (one standard deviation above the mean) or low (one standard deviation below the mean) (Aiken & West, 1991).[10]

Figure 2. Moderating Effect of Goal Clarity and P-O Fit on the Relationship between PSM and Internal Accountability

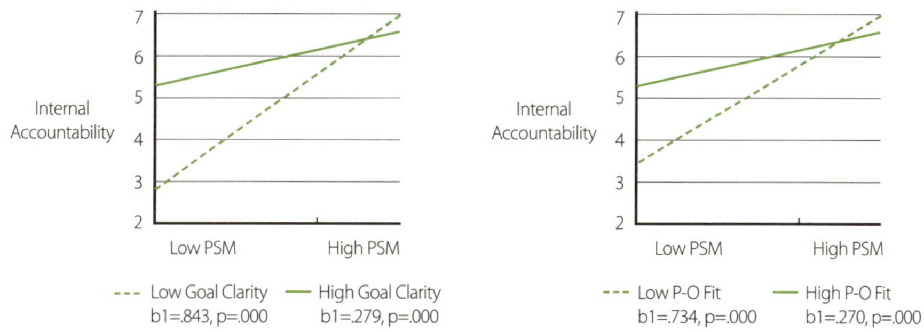

Figure 3. Moderating Effect of Goal Clarity and P-O Fit on the Relationship between PSM and External Accountability

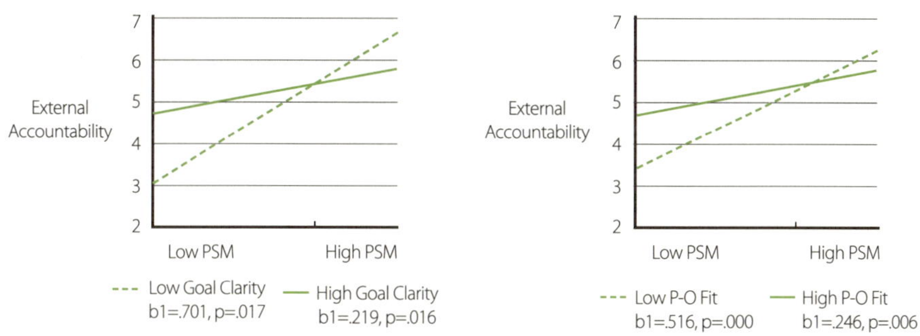

Figures 2 and 3 illustrate hypothesis 5. When the goal clarity and P-O fit levels are low, the relationship between PSM and (internal and external) accountability gets stronger. When high, the relationship weakens (for example, b1 was .843 under low goal clarity and .279 under high goal clarity for internal accountability). This result is similar to the result of the moderating effect on trust variables above. In addition, it supports hypothesis 5.

Conclusions and Suggestions

This study started with the question, what is the meaning and role of accountability as a cognitive dimension in Korean public sector with respect to enhancement of organizational effectiveness. To investigate this question, hypotheses and research models were designed to determine the antecedent and moderating factors (PSM and organizational goal clarity and P-O fit) of accountability from the perspective of social capital theory. To analyze these effects, empirical analysis was carried out using hierarchical regression. Testing of the 5 hypotheses demonstrated strong effects of affective PSM on accountability, which seems to originate from Korea's unique, affective, hierarchical, and relationship-centered organizational culture. Additionally, goal clarity and fit were confirmed to play a critical role by moderating the relationship between PSM and accountability among employees in a central government agency. Based on this study's analysis from the perspectives of public management and personnel management, the theoretical and policy implications can be summarized as follows.

First, while government employees' affective PSM had positive effects on internal and external accountability, no similar effect was found for rational PSM. This result indicates that the conventional PSM theory developed by Perry and Wise (1990), which posits that each of the three dimensions of PSM has a positive effect on organizational effectiveness, is not always true in all public organizations. In particular, Korea's hierarchical public service system rooted in Confucian values differs from the position-classification system of personnel management common in the West. Therefore, Korean government employee's PSMs are likely to differ from those in the West in content and scope. In Korea's hierarchical, group-centered, and relationship-centered culture, for example, the rational motive to participate in policymaking could be seen as a power- and personal-interest-oriented "pseudo rational motive." Based on this study's results for the different effects of the three dimensions of PSM, it is necessary to apply a new perspective for PSM in a Korean context, develop a Korean PSM scale, and model and study with an approach of differentiated PSM.

Second, whereas goal clarity had significant effects only internal accountability, P-O fit was positively related to all dependent variables: internal and external accountability. This result supports goal setting theory which states that goal difficulty and specificity motivate employees to enhance their performance. In addition, it implies that specific organizational goal and vision setting is a strategy to establish and nurture professional accountability in a public sector as well as in a private sector. In particular, when employees' adaptation and acceptance of organizational goals and P-O fit levels are high, employees tend to share organizational values, faith, and culture. This improves organizational performance in the mid- and long-term by promoting extra-role behavior rising from commitment to internal and external accountability. Therefore, personnel-policy-making divisions in a central government body (for example, the System Management Division or Personnel Policy Division in the Ministry of Public Administration and Security) need to make continued efforts to strengthen the MBO evaluation system from the perspective of strategic human resources capital theory and upgrade and promote strategic human resource development (HRD) and strategic HRD systems that encourage employees to share organizational goals, visions, and values.

Third, goal clarity and P-O fit were shown to positively moderate the relationship between affective/norm-based PSMs and accountability. As shown in the figure, for low goal clarity and P-O fit levels, government employees' intrinsic motivations were high. In other words, they show efforts to improve a certain types of accountability (behaviors) by increasing their affective and norm-based PSMs (attitudes). This result supports self-perception theory. Furthermore, the finding of moderating effects supports the fourth hypothesis, as expressed by Perry and Wise (1990): "As uncertainty continues in a public sector, the influence of PSM on organizational effectiveness would increase, which has not been mentioned in the conventional PSM theory."

Although this study provides meaningful suggestions through empirical analysis, it has some limitations. First, the scope of research was limited to a central government administrative body. Therefore, the results of this study may not apply to all administrative organizations in Korea. Future research should broaden the scope to include the motivations, goals, trust, and accountability of employees in local governments, public organizations, and NGOs. Second, because antecedent and consequence variables are measured through the same questionnaire data, common variance effects or mono-method bias can take place. To overcome this problem, future research should include a longitudinal study showing changes over time and introduce a panel survey. Third, the "goal orientation factors" used in this study is an upper-level organizational variable between employees and the organization. If it is conceived at the "person" level, variance bias and atomistic fallacy can occur. To overcome this obstacle, it is necessary to apply a multi-level data-based hierarchical linear model (HLM) that is hierarchically nested in both person and organization dimensions. Finally, because this study employed quantitative research methods through a survey of government employees, future study should expand the findings by performing an in-depth qualitative study on this study's topics. For example, an inductive approach with in-depth interviews and grounded theory methodology should be applied, and scales for Korean PSM, and accountability should be developed.

Notes

1. Education and training takes place both domestically and abroad. Domestic education has several components: long-term training for section chiefs and bureau directors, commissioned education in universities and graduate schools, commissioned foreign language education, and privately commissioned professional education. Long and short-term education abroad may take place in English speaking countries (U.S.A., U.K., Canada, Australia, etc.), non-English speaking countries (Japan, Germany, France, etc.) and other regions (China, Russia, Latin America). Long term education is intended for senior civil servants, while short-term education is for other individuals, teams, and associations (Education and Training of Public Officials Information Center in MOPAS).
2. Accountability appears in legal relations as well, and it is not just a phenomenon that is found only in the public sector. In this study, however, we have focused on government bureaucracy-grounded administrative accountability due to the study's scope of research targets and limitations of analysis models.
3. The origin of control in a public sector refers to control's arising from inside or outside of the organization. Internal control occurs through professional ethics, internal audit, and hierarchical order; and external control is executed by a person with a specific legal authority (i.e., a citizen). High control levels occur for bureaucratic organizations having low autonomy, and low control levels occur with high self-regulation based on professional ethics or citizen responsibility (Romzek & Dubnick, 1987; Romzek & Ingraham, 2000).
4. In various studies, PSM has been defined somewhat differently, depending on the educational system and academic perspective. From a sociological perspective (e.g., Piliavin & Charng, 1990), PSM is interpreted as altruism. Organizational behavior scholars (e.g., Brief & Motowidlo, 1986) view PSM as prosocial behavior. Public administration scholars and political scientists have recently provided extrinsic expansion and multiple interpretations of the concept of PSM as humane and altruistic motivation for the public system, community, network, and social services of a public sector.
5. Perry classified public service motivation among employees from the public sector and the public sector into 6 categories: 1) public policy-making, 2) public interest, 3) social justice, 4) civic duty, 5) compassion, and 6) self-sacrifice (1996; Perry & Wise, 1990).
6. In this study, we assume that the employees of a public sector evaluate their attitudes through their perceptions of their behavior or circumstances, based on self-perception theory. In other words, in negative situations (low goal clarity and incomplete P-O fit), they require a high level of attitude and PSM to improve trust in the organization and individuals and justify behaviors to secure accountability. As a result, as goal clarity and P-O fit decrease, the positive relationships between PSM and trust and between PSM and accountability become stronger.

7. The invited sample (350 employees) was randomly selected with equal probability of selection for all members of the target group, those who received training at the Central Officials Training Institute (COTI), to minimize bias.
8. In hierarchical multiple regression, the order of independent variables is set by the investigator based on theoretical and empirical grounds. This kind of regression is used to test hypotheses on the effects of individual independent variables and the effects of their interactions (Yang, 1998).
9. A test of the moderating effects of moderating variables on relationships between dependent and independent variables is performed in three stages:
   - Stage I: Regression analysis for dependent and independent variables
   - Stage II: Regression analysis for dependent, independent, and moderating variables
   - Stage III: Regression analysis for dependent, moderating, interacting (independent and moderating variables), and dependent variables

   If the amount of explained variance (R^2) significantly increases when interactions between independent and moderating variables are added to the regression equation in stage III, it can be interpreted that a moderating effect exists (Song Ji-joon, 2012). In this study, we analyzed the moderating effects of goal clarity and P-O fit on the relationships of affective and norm-based PSM with trust and accountability.

10. Additional analysis of interaction and possible moderating effects of rational PSM and goal clarity and P-O fit found no significant moderating effect among these variables

References

Allen, N. J., & Meyer, J. P. (1990). The measurement and antecedents of affective, continuance, and normative commitment to the organization. *Journal of Occupational Psychology, 63,* 1-18.

Behn, R. (2001). *Rethinking democratic accountability.* Washington: Brookings Institute.

Bem, D. J. (1972). Self-perception theory. In L. Berkowitz (Ed.), *Advances in experimental social psychology* (Vol, 6, pp. 1~62).

Berry, Frances S. (2007). Strategic planning as a tool for managing organizational change. *International Journal of Public Administration, 30,* 331-346.

Blau, P. M. (1964). *Exchange and power in social life.* New York, Wiley: Basic Books.

Block, P. (1993). *Stewardship: Choosing service over self-interest.* San Francisco: Berrett-Koehler.

Bowen, D. E., Ledford, jr., G. E., & Nathan, B. R. (1991). Hiring for the organization not the job. *Academy of Management Executive, 5,* 35-51.

Bradely, E. W. (2008). Methodological challenges associated with public service motivation research. In J. L. Perrt & A. Hondeghem (Eds.), *Motivation in public management: The call of public service* (pp. 80-98). Oxford: Oxford University Press.

Brewer, G. A. (2003). Building social capital: Civic attitudes and behavior of public servants. *Journal of Public Administration Research and Theory, 73*(1), 121-131.

Brewer, G. A., Selden, S. C. & Facer Ⅱ, R. L. (2000). *Individual conceptions of public service motivation. Public Administration Review, 60*(3), 254-64.

Brief, A. P. & Motowidlo, S. J. (1986). Prosocial Organizational Behaviors. *The Academy of Management Review, 11*(4):710~725.

Buchanan, B. (1974a). Building organizational commitment: The socialization of managers in work organizations. *Administrative Science Quarterly. 19*(4), 533-546.

Buchanan, B. (1974b). Government managers, business executives, and organizational commitment. *Public Administration Review, 35,* 339-347.

Buchanan, B. (1975). Red tape and the service ethic: Some unexpected differences between public and pivate managers. *Administration and Society, 6,* 423-444.

Burke, R. J. & Deszca, E. (1982). Preferred organizational climates of Type A individuals. *Journal of Vocational Behavior, 21,* 50-59.

Cable, D. M., & Edwards, J. R. (2004). Complementary and supplementary fit: A theoretical and empirical integration. *Journal of Applied Psychology, 89*(5), 822-834.

Carnevale, D. G., & Steven W. H. (2001). Human resource management reform in the states: Entrepreneurialism and incremental change. In S. E. Condrey & R. Maranto (Eds.), *Radical reform of the civil service.* New York: Lexington Books.

Cavalluzzoa, K. S., & Ittner, C. D. (2004). Implementing performance measurement innovations: Evidence from government. *Accounting, Organizations and Society, 29*(4), 243-267.

Choi, M. O., & Yoo, T. Y. (2008). The effects of person-organization, person-job, and person-supervisor fit on organization commitment, job satisfaction, and turnover intention: The focus on interaction effects among three types of fit. *Korean Psychology Review. 18*(1): 139-162.

Coleman, J. (1988). Social capital in the creation of human capital. *American Journal of Sociology, 94*(Suppl.), 95-120.

Davis, J. H., Schoorman, F. D. & Donaldson, L. (1997). Toward a stewardship theory of management. *Academy of Management Review, 22*(1), 20-47.

Eom, S. J. (2009). Accountability of Public Administration. *Korean Public Administration Review. 43*(4), 19-45.

Frederickson, H. G. (1971). *Toward a new public administration: The minnowbrook perspective.* Chandler Pub.Co.

Frederickson, H. G., & Hart, D. K. (1985). The public service and the patriotism of benevolence. *Public Administration Review, 45*(3), 547-553.

Halachmi, A., & Krogt, T. V. D. (2005). The role of the manager in employee motivation. In S. E. Condrey (Ed.), *Handbook of human resource management in government* (pp. 469-498). San Francisco: Jossey-Bass.

Han, S. I. (2010). The accountability and the governance structure of the korean public institutions. *Korean Organizational Studies Review. 7*(1), 65-90.

Johnston, J. M., & Romzek, B. S. (1999). Contracting and accountability in state medicaid reform: Rhetoric, theories, and reality. *Public Administration Review, 59*(5), 383-399.

Kim, K. S., & Son. J. Y. (2009). A study of the effect of organizational interpersonal supervisory trust on organizational commitment. *Business Information Research, 28*(2), 41-67.

Kim, S. M. (2005). Public service motivation and public employees's behavior. *Korean Public Administration Review, 14*(2), 297-325.

Kim, S. M. (2009). Testing the structure of public service motivation in Korea: A research note. *Journal of Public Administration Research and Theory, 19*(4), 839-851.

Kim, S. M., & Vandenabeele, W. (2010). A strategy for building public service motivation research internationally. Public Administration Review, *70*(5), 701-709.

Kim, S. Y. (2009). An empirical study of the determinants of public service motivation. *Korean Journal of Public Administration. 47*(2), 181-209.

Kristof, A. L. (1996). Person-organization fit: An integrative review of its conceptualizations, measurement, and implications. *Personnel Psychology, 49,* 1-49.

Kristof, A. L., Zimmerman, R. D., Johnson, E. C., & Henry, B. (2005). Consequences of individuals' fit at work: A meta-analysis of person-job, person-organization, person-group, and person-supervisor fit. *Personnel Psychology, 58*(2), 281-342.

Lanivich, S. E., Brees, J. R., & Hochwarter, W. A. (2010). P-E Fit as moderator of the accountability–employee reactions relationships: Convergent results across two samples. *Journal of Vocational Behavior, 77,* 425-436.

Lauver, K. J., & Kristof-Brown, A. (2001). Distinguishing between employees' perceptions of person-job and person-organization fit. *Journal of Vocational Behavior, 59,* 454-470.

Lee, G. J. (2005). Public service motivation and performance: Empirical evidence in Korea. *Korean Society and Public Administration. 16*(1), 81-104.

Lee, H. B., Kim, T. Y., & Lee, S. C. (2005). The effects of organizational culture on public servant's accountability. *Korean Journal of Public Administration. 43*(3), 29-52.

Locke, E. A. (1968). Toward a theory of task motivation and incentives. *Organizational Behavior and Human Performance, 3,* 157-189.

Locke, E. A., & Latham, G. P. (1990). A theory of goal setting and task performance. Englewood Cliffs, NJ: Prentice Hall.

Mento, A. J., Steele, R. P., & Karren, R. J. (1987). A meta-analytic study of the effects of goal setting on task performance: 1966-1984. *Organizational Behavior and Human Decision Processes, 39,* 52-83.

Meyer, J. & Allen, N. (1997). *Commitment in the workplace: Theory, research, and application.* Sage Publications.

Moorhead, G., & Griffin, R. (1992). *Organizational behavior* (3rd ed.). Boston. MA:Houghton Miffin Co.

Mosher, F. C. (1968). *Democracy and the public service.* New York: Oxford University Press. dsf.

Muchinsky, P. M., & Monahan, C. J. (1987). What is person-environment congruence? Supplementary versus environment models of fit. *Journal of Vacational Behavior, 31,* 268-277.

Park, S. M., & H. G. Rainey. (2007). Antecedents, mediators, and consequences of affective, normative, and continuance commitment empirical tests of commitment effects in federal agencies. *Review of Public Personnel Administration, 27*(3), 197-226.

Park, S. M., & Rainey, H. G. (2012). Work motivation and social communication among public managers. *The International Journal of Human Resource Management, 23*(13). 2630-2660.

Perry, J. L. (1996). Measuring public service motivation: An assessment of construct reliability and validity. *Journal of Public Administration Research and Theory, 6,* 5-22.

Perry, J. L., & Hondeghem, A. (2008). Building theory and empirical evidence about public service motivation. *International Public Management Journal, 11*(1), 3-12.

Perry, J. L., & Porter, L. (1982). Factors affecting the content for motivation in public rrganizations. *Academy of Management Review, 7,* 89-98.

Perry, J. L., & Wise, L. R. (1990). The motivation bases of public service. *Public Administration Review, 50*(3), 367-373.

Piliavin, J. A., & Charng, H. W. (1990). Altruism: A review of recent theory and research. *Annual Review of Sociology, 16,* 27-65.

Rainey, H. G., & Steinbauer, P. (1999). Galloping elephants: Developing elements of a theory of effective government organizations. *Journal of Public Administration Research and Theory, 9,* 1-32.

Robinson, S. L. (1996). Trust and breach of the psychological contract. *Administrative Science Quarterly, 41,* 574-599.

Romzek, B. S., & Dubnick, M. J. (1987). Accountability in the public sector: Lessons from the challenger tragedy. *Public Administration Review, 47*(3), 227-238.

Romzek, B. S., & Dubnick, M. J. (1998). Accountability. In J. M. Shafritz (Ed.), *International encyclopedia of public policy and administration* (Vol. 1, pp. 6-11). Boulder, CO: Westview Press.

Romzek, B. S., & Ingraham, P. W. (2000). Cross pressures of accountability: Initiative, command, and failure in the ron brown plane crash. *Public Administration Review, 60*(3), 240-253.

Seo, I. D., & Lee, W. H. (2006). The mediating effect of leader trust and organizational commitment on the relationship between organizational culture, leader styles, and organizational citizenship behaviors. *Journal of Human Resource Management Research, 13*(4), 71-106.

Seo, J. H., Seol, H. D., Song, S. H., & Lee, H. S. (2008). *Organizational behavior.* Hankyungsa.

Shin, Y. h. (2008). Effects of team-level person-organization and person-job fit on team organizational citizenship behaviors and team efficacy. *Korea Journal of Manageement, 16*(1), 1-35.

Song, J. J. (2012). *Methods of SPSS/AMOS statistical analysis.* 21c book.

Tellefsena, T., & Thomas, G. P. (2005). The antecedents and consequences of organizational and personal commitment in business service relationships. *Industrial Marketing Management, 34*(1), 23-37.

Thomas, P. (2003). Introduction of accountability. In B. Guy Peters & Jon Pierre (Eds.), *Handbook of Public Administration.* London: Sage Publication.

Vancouver, J. B., & Schmitt, N. W. (1991). An exploratory examination of person- organization fit: Organizational goal congruence. *Personnel Psychology, 44,* 333-352.

Vandenabeele, W. (2007). Toword a theory of public service motivation: A institutional apporoach. *Public Management Review, 9*(4), 545-556.

Vandenabeele, W. (2008). Government calling: Public service motivation as an element in selecting government as an employer of choice. *Public Administration. 86*(4), 1089-1105.

Wheeler, A. R., & Halbesleben, J. R. B. (2009). *A conservation of resources view of person-environment fit.* Paper presented at the 3rd Global e-Conference on Fit.

Wilson, J. Q. (1989). *Bureaucracy.* New York, NY: Basic Books.

Won, G. H. (2008). Applications of stewardship theory to local public service accountability. *Korea Association of Public Management Review. 22*(4), 507-529.

Word, J., & Park, S. M. (2009). Working across the divide job involvement in the public and nonprofit sectors. *Review of Public Personnel Administration, 29*(2), 103-133.

Wright, B. E. (2004). The role of work context in work motivation: A public sector application of goal and social cognitive theories. *Journal of Public Administration Research and Theory, 14*(1), 59-78.

Wright, B. E. (2007). Public service and motivation: Does mission matter?. *Public Administration Review, 67*(1), 54-64.

Wright, B. E., & Pandey S. K. (2011). Public organizations and mission valence when does mission matter?. *Administration & Society January, 43*(1), 22-44.

Yang, B. H. (1998). *Understanding and utilization of multivariate data analysis.* Hakjisa.

Case Study

Emphasis on Hierarchy Hampers Globalization

Alan Timblick

Corporate Sector Needs to Rethink 'Punishment Culture' to Make Officials Willing to Take Risks

When Korea began to open its frontiers to foreigners during the latter half of the 19th Century, the office in charge of foreign relations within the Royal Court was the Office of Ritual.

It was an appropriate allocation of responsibility, given the strong Confucian discipline of national governance at the time. But it did lead to some problems in 'interfacing' with the Western world, since the strict protocol requirements concentrated more on issues of who was allowed to communicate with whom, depending on status and rank, rather than on the substance of the proposals being made.

Today's Korea still exhibits a strong respect for status and the "pecking order" of rank. Recently, there was an incident when the head of a foreign firm who was having trouble with rather significant tax claims sent a fax to a Korean minister offering a large donation to a public cause. The minister's juniors advised him to ignore the fax, as not being an appropriate means of communication to someone of his standing.

It is one of the major sources of confusion and misunderstanding between Koreans and Westerners that the hierarchy of relationships is so very important in this country. If I describe someone, for example, as a "friend," and that person happens to be a decade or so younger than me, my Korean counterpart may ask "How can someone so much younger be your friend?"

Also, it can be amusing for a foreigner to watch how the courtesy of yielding the "president's seat" at the right-hand rear of the car is acted out when businessmen share a ride. In the west, the best seat is, if not the driver's seat behind the wheel, then probably the front seat next to the driver, on the grounds that it provides the best views of the passing scenery.

But how appropriate is this behavior in a modern world and does the drive towards globalization mean that Korea has to give up some of this emphasis on hierarchy and rank?

First, let's consider how education is affected by these Confucian values. Placing a high value on education, parents spend huge sums of money, sacrifice their own careers and even family life, in order to improve the chances of their offspring getting into one of the top universities. There is a hierarchy among educational institutions and this has a strong influence on later job prospects. As a result, all possible efforts are made to ensure the child scores well in the examinations.

But increasingly, the use of multiple-choice exam results as a means of judging competence or suitability in a work environment is coming into question. A western journalist coming to the end of her sojourn in Korea wrote recently about Korean education as follows:

"The system rests largely on rote learning and places almost no value on analysis, creative thinking or practical application. High school students who can score 99 per cent in an English test are often unable to hold even a simple conversation, while university students who express a contrary view to their professor simply fail."

If Korea is to succeed in the ranks of global economies, its education system should allow students to debate, to be creative in demonstrating their understanding of the subjects studied, and not to be silenced by the notion that the teacher, being senior in rank, must therefore always be right.

Second, Korean corporate life, which is run with the same discipline as a military organization, placing the same emphasis on hierarchy, status and the following of orders, may be becoming steadily obsolete as a business culture, out of tune with the environment where many Korean firms have to operate as they invest in overseas operations.

Non-Korean employees of Korean companies can be very uncomfortable with the style of management they are faced with. For example, issuing an "order" to a junior staff member could be considered as insulting and demeaning, especially when a simple "request" could have sufficed. Korean managers are not known to walk around their premises and to visit juniors at their desks, on the grounds that it would be beneath their dignity. Juniors, therefore, should be summoned to the boss's office.

The amount of time, energy, internal costs and diversion from customer-oriented activity which goes to make sure a Korean boss is pampered, escorted, satisfied, eulogized and sheltered from criticism is quite extraordinary and would not pass the appraisal of any western management audit process.

In a global corporation, answerable to its shareholders, the luxury of incurring costs such as these would not be tolerated.

Some western observers of Korean corporate culture have described it as a "punishment culture." Indeed, on a job application form there is usually a space where "rewards and punishments" are supposed to be listed. In the West, performance related remuneration is generally the main tool, or carrot, for encouraging good results. In Korea, there is also the negative side of the range — the "disincentive" stick to beat the poor performer.

The implication is that corporate officers tend to be in fear of taking risks, since if things go wrong, they are likely to face punishment. But without being prepared to accept a level of risk, it is difficult to see how entrepreneurship can flourish.

Third, and lastly, there is the issue of ageism. The respect for hierarchy results in the decision-taking process migrating to the top of the ladder. Even if one does not subscribe to 'the Peter Principle' ("in a hierarchy, every employee tends to rise to his level of incompetence") there is evidence to suggest that older people have less energy, less incentive to succeed, and more investment in maintaining the status quo than younger, up-and-coming dynamos. That means that a society run exclusively by those at the top of the age ladder is likely to be more resistant to change, slower to generate new ideas, less flexible and less well equipped to survive in today's rapidly shifting commercial, political and social milieus.

I have to confess that, having achieved a certain age and standing, as well as having become a grandfather, it is rather comfortable to enjoy the luxury and trappings of Confucian respect for seniors and the aged. But at the same time, given that we live in an era of competition between countries and societies, Korea needs to equip itself with the tools of success and survival. I am not sure that Confucianism is any longer the most appropriate instrument in the toolbox for today's conditions.

Suggestions for Better Education, Corporate Sectors

Korea still exhibits a strong respect for status and the pecking order of rank. Hierarchy is too important in this country. Korea has to give up some of this emphasis.

If Korea is to succeed in the ranks of global economies, its education system should allow students to debate, to be creative in demonstrating their understanding of the subjects studied, and not to be silenced by the notion that the teacher, being senior in rank, must therefore always be right.

Korean corporate culture is a "punishment culture." The disincentive stick to beat the poor performer leaves corporate officers in fear of taking risks, since if things go wrong, they are likely to face punishment. But without being prepared to accept a level of risk it is hard to make companies globally competitive.

A society that is run exclusively by those at the top of the age ladder is likely to be more resistant to change, slower to generate new ideas, less flexible and less well equipped to survive in today's rapidly shifting commercial, political and social milieus. In an era of competition between countries and societies, Korea needs to equip itself with the tools of success and survival, not ageism.

Source: The Korea Times (2008.11.24)

Questions for Discussion

1. How do you detect organizational structure, and how do you find out if it is productive?

2. What does research indicate about the structures of public organizations? What do we know about structural differences between public, nonprofit, and private organizations?

3. According to mainstream organization theory, some factors may influence organizational structure more than the private/public status. What are these factors?

Section 6

Processes

- Work Motivation and Social Communication among Public Managers
- The Effects of Personnel Reform Systems on Georgia State Employees' Attitudes

Section 6

Processes

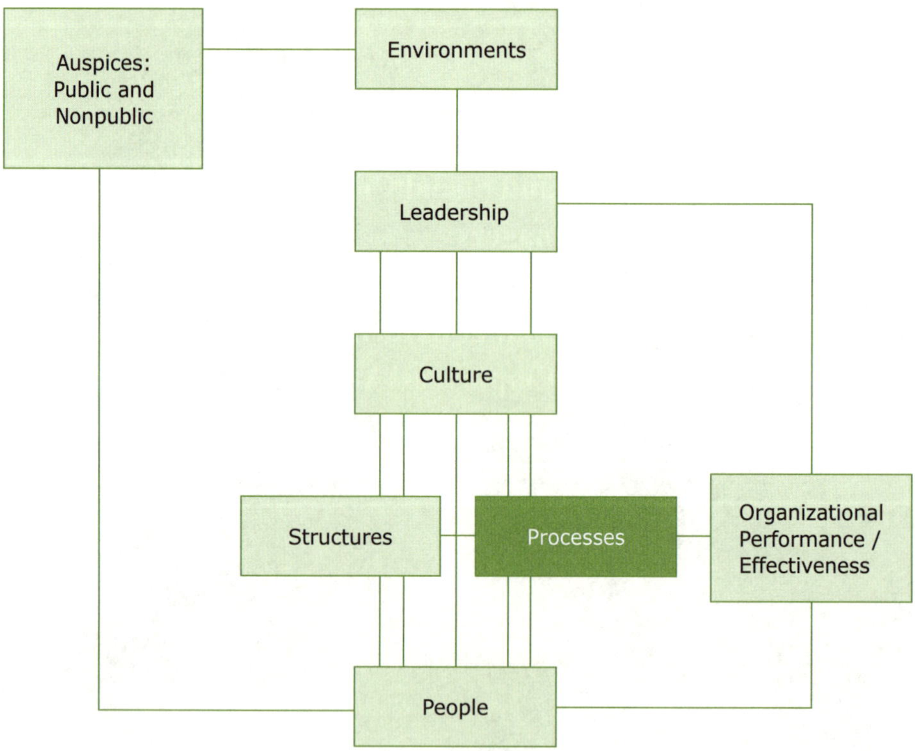

Chapter 11

Work Motivation and Social Communication among Public Managers.[1]

Summary

This article tests hypotheses about the effects of two types of work motivation (i.e. intrinsic motivation and extrinsic motivation) and four types of social communication on three important work dispositions (i.e. job involvement, red tape, and perceived organizational effectiveness) among 790 managers employed in public agencies in the states of Illinois and Georgia. The results show that intrinsic motivation is significantly associated with public managers'' job involvement, perceptions of red tape, and organizational effectiveness. Also, certain types of organizational communication and mentoring socialization are closely related to the outcomes. The results of cross-interaction effects between motivation and communications on outcome variables support the SDT prediction that when public managers are more involved with different types of social communication behaviors, the relationship between extrinsic motivation and three outcome variables becomes more pronounced. That is, communication in public agencies provides more autonomy and discretion for extrinsically motivated public managers, thus leading to more positive organizational dispositions.

Keyword

- □ Job Involvement
- □ Mentoring
- □ Organizational Behavior
- □ Organizational Dispositions
- □ Public Human Resource Management
- □ Red Tape

Sung Min Park Associate Professor, Sungkyunkwan University
Hal G. Rainey Alumni Foundation Distinguished Professor, The University of Georgia

Introduction

Public sector reform initiatives in numerous nations have sought to improve motivation of government employees through pay-for-performance initiatives and other measures. In the USA, the US Office of Personnel Management and the US Merit System Protection Board regularly conduct large sample surveys of federal employees. These developments reflect the widely accepted assumption that government employee motivation is a crucial challenge, and that work attitudes and perceptions play an important role in motivating members of the public workforce.

The analysis reported here contributes to research on motivation and work attitudes by examining relations of government managers' extrinsic and intrinsic motivations for choosing their positions to important work attitudes and perceptions including job involvement, perceived red tape, and perceived organizational effectiveness. While this analysis concentrates on governmental managers, the results are clearly relevant to managers in all sectors. Human motivation refers to 'what energizes a person's behavior, what directs it, and what maintains and sustains it' (Porter and Miles 1974, p. 546). Research on work motivation has distinguished between two types of motives and incentives involved in energizing and directing effort. These include intrinsic incentives that are mediated within the person and focus on the work itself and value associated with it, and extrinsic incentives that are externally mediated, such as salary. The distinction is imperfect, in that the two types can overlap. As described later, however, researchers have developed the distinction in important ways, and while intrinsic incentives play an important role in all work settings, they appear particularly important in government sector. Numerous studies have found that public sector employees, compared to employees of private firms, place lower value on extrinsic rewards such as pay. Public employees and especially those in managerial and professional roles, compared to those in private firms, are more likely to value intrinsic rewards such as the opportunity to help others and to do work that is useful to society and that serves the community and the public interest (Crewson 1997; Houston 2000, 2005; Park and Rainey 2007). Recent developments in research on public service motivation (PSM), an intrinsic form of motivation, emphasize its important role in motivating government employees in numerous nations (Houston 2005; Scott and Pandey 2005; Buelens and Broeck 2007; Moynihan and Pandey 2007; Perry and Hondeghem 2008; Park 2010).

A Theoretical Perspective

A general theoretical perspective guides our analysis of extrinsic and intrinsic motivations, their relations with our dependent variables, and the influence of social communication and mentoring on those relations. This perspective holds that individuals choose their jobs or positions because they have combinations of intrinsic and extrinsic motives - they seek intrinsic and extrinsic rewards. The expectation that they can fulfill or satisfy these motives induces them to seek a particular job. In the language of the expectancy theory of motivation, they perceive a likelihood that they will attain rewards that they value by choosing the job. We will refer to these behaviors as work motivations (i.e. motivation to choose the job). Some individuals place higher value on intrinsic motives to choose a job, while others place more emphasis on extrinsic motives - evidence reported below supports this distinction. Then, the person's experiences in the position will determine whether the expectations are met and the motives fulfilled. Factors influencing these experiences include job design, incentive systems, employee participation and communication, mentoring systems, and others (Perry, Mesch and Paarlberg 2006). When the job fulfills the motives, the individual will express more positive work attitudes and perceptions. When the motives are frustrated or disappointed, the person will express more negative work attitudes. Our theoretical perspective contends that individuals with stronger intrinsic motives will fare better in the public sector than those motivated by extrinsic incentives. Public organizations vary among themselves, of course, but research indicates that public personnel systems, including systems for pay and advancement, tend to be more formalized, structured, and less flexible than those of private firms (Bozeman and Rainey 2000) and of nonprofit organizations (Light 2002; Feeney and Rainey 2009). A person with predominantly extrinsic motivations is more likely to find such conditions disappointing. For example, a person with extrinsic motivations who takes a position in government because it offers higher pay than a previous position will experience frustration in seeking still higher pay over time.

In spite of stereotypes about the public sector (and in spite of some contrary evidence that we describe below), we posit that public sector management jobs offer more opportunities for fulfillment of intrinsic motives than extrinsic ones. Management jobs in government often involve experiences and responsibilities that make the work intrinsically interesting, including opportunities to fulfill intrinsic motives of altruism and public service. Those expressing intrinsic motivations for choosing their position will have a higher probability of maintaining intrinsic motivation over time in the job (as distinguished from intrinsic motivation to choose the job in the first place).

Our dependent variables are chosen in part to analyze these processes. As elaborated below, job involvement can be regarded as an indication of intrinsic motivation in the job (again, as opposed to intrinsic motivation to choose the job). Perceived level of red tape and perceived organizational effectiveness are important organizational perceptions in themselves, but they can also indicate intrinsic motivation in the job. Moynihan and Pandey (2007) report that government managers expressing higher PSM perceive lower levels of red tape, suggesting that PSM overcomes frustrations due to red tape. Perceived effectiveness can also reflect intrinsic motivation because in the public sector, organizational effectiveness would normally include effective altruistic service or service in public and community interests, as opposed to extrinsic gains.

Then, the analysis examines the role of experiences in the organization that can strengthen or weaken a person's sense of control and efficacy, such as social communications and mentoring. Social communication refers to interactive communication with others, as contrasted, for example, with sending out a newsletter or posting a notice in a newspaper. More social communication should strengthen a person's sense of engagement and support from others (Garnett, Marlowe and Pandey 2008). Mentoring will have a similar positive impact on the sense of support and empowerment, and self-determination theory suggests that support and empowerment will enhance and maintain intrinsic motivation and positive job attitudes over time.

As for managers who choose the job due to extrinsic motivation, an important development in the theory of extrinsic and intrinsic motivations, SDT, leads to important research questions about the influence of social communications and mentoring. SDT contends that a person needs a sense of self-control to experience intrinsic motivation (Deci and Ryan 1985). A person cannot enjoy a task for itself because if the person feels that he or she is forced to do it, it fulfills idealistic motives. One needs to feel that one is choosing to engage in the activity, based on internalized motives and values. Deci and Ryan further contend that a person with predominantly extrinsic motivation for a task can move toward intrinsic motivation. If the person experiences more control over the task and her or his actions in relation to it, the person is more likely to internalize the task goals and values. The person will be more likely to experience intrinsic motivation for task performance -- that she or he is doing it for his or her own interests, fulfillment, and values, rather than for money or some other extrinsic incentive. Deci and Ryan contend that even money can enhance intrinsic motivation if the administration of the money is perceived as supportive rather than controlling.

Following this reasoning, social communication and mentoring should enhance intrinsic motivation and positive perceptions for those who chose the job due to intrinsic motivations. Social communication and mentoring should have even greater influence on those who entered government management jobs for extrinsic motivation than on those more intrinsically motivated. As communication and mentoring enhance their sense of control and support, those managers who report that extrinsic motivation determined their job choice will move more toward intrinsic motivation and positive perceptions of the organization.

Following this general theoretical perspective, this study first tests hypotheses about the effects of intrinsic and extrinsic motivations to choose the job on job involvement, red tape, and organizational effectiveness. Second, this study also examines the relationship between four types of social communications - three types of organizational communications and mentoring socialization - with the three dependent variables. Third, the analysis examines interactions between managers' job choice motivations and social communications on the dependent variables, testing propositions based on Deci and Ryan's (1985) SDT. Finally, we discuss the implications for theories of motivation in government, and for the importance of social communication and mentoring in those processes.

Concepts and Hypotheses

Job Involvement, Red Tape, and Organizational Effectiveness

As described earlier, this study used three dependent variables: job involvement, red tape, and organizational effectiveness. Job involvement is 'the degree to which a person identifies with his or her job, actively participates in it, and considers his or her performance important to self-worth' (Robbins 2003, p. 72; Vance 2006). Researchers have treated job involvement as an important work attitude, especially for professional and managerial level employees. As described later, it relates to other important work dispositions (Saleh and Hosek 1976, p. 125).

Red tape involves excessive rules, and regulations that 'do not advance the legitimate purposes the rules were intended to serve' and reduce organizational effectiveness (Bozeman 2000, p. 12; Dehart-Davis and Pandey 2005). Red tape is distinct from formalization, which is 'the extent to which rules, procedures, instructions and communications are written' (Pugh, Hickson, Hinings and Turner 1968, p. 75). Formalization can enhance 'organizational knowledge' and clarify goals, whereas red tape is related to negative organizational impacts (Bozeman 1993; Pandey and Rainey 2006; Dehart-Davis 2009). Another focal variable in this study is effectiveness of public sector organizations - the achievement of formal goals in public agencies. Organizational effectiveness refers to both outcome and output measures. Outputs are 'the immediate results of organization activities' and outcomes are 'measures of the extent that organizations attain their goals or ultimate purposes' (Berman 2006, p. 6). Perceived organizational effectiveness concerns 'whether the agency does well that which it is supposed to do, whether people in the agency work hard and well, whether the actions and procedures of the agency and its members are well suited to achieving its mission, and whether agency actually achieves it mission' (Rainey and Steinbauer 1999, p. 13).

Work Motivation in Public Organizations: Intrinsic and Extrinsic Motivations

Motivation is a value-based concept. People not only have different levels of work motivation, but also have varied types and dimensions of motivation, which have been identified as influencing sector employment choice and human resource management and development in general (Ryan and Deci 2000a; Vandenabeele 2007). Intrinsic motivation refers to 'behaviors for which there is no apparent reward except the activity itself' or 'the doing of an activity for its inherent satisfactions rather than for some separable consequence' whereas extrinsic motivation is defined as 'a construct that pertains whenever an activity is done in order to attain some separable outcome' and 'behaviors in which an external controlling variable can be readily identified' (e.g. an inclination for explicit and tangible rewards, incentive and salary, threat, or surveillance) (Lepper and Greene 1975; Ryan and Deci 2000a, pp. 56-60; Cameron and Pierce 2002, p. 12; Moynihan and Pandey 2007, p. 809). Cognitive evaluation theorists have suggested that extrinsic reward systems (e.g. a performance-pay system) might reduce and crowd out intrinsic motivation (Moynihan 2008; Paarlberg, Perry and Hondeghem 2008). Instead, these theorists emphasize social and moral reward systems and the power of a feeling of competence, a sense of autonomy, and an internal perceived locus of causality (Deci and Ryan 1985).

In the public sector, research indicates that many public administrators have strong motives to perform meaningful public service — that is, PSM (Brewer and Selden 1998; Paarlberg et al. 2008). The literature on PSM indicates that many public employees are characterized by public service and intrinsic motives while private counterparts place more value on extrinsic rewards (Perry and Wise 1990; Crewson 1997; Houston 2000; Brewer 2008). Some research indicates that an overemphasis on extrinsic rewards (e.g. pay and benefits) can be counterproductive, actually making workers less productive if their original motivations are 'primarily intrinsic' or service oriented (Deci 1971, p. 108; Kohn 1993; Crewson 1997).

Motivation and Organizational Outcomes

There exist different categories of antecedents (e.g. organizational and institutional factors) and consequences (e.g. reward preferences, job satisfaction, and effectiveness) of motivation in the public sector (Pandey and Stazyk 2008). Research has suggested that levels of PSM or intrinsic motivation significantly affect important work-related attitudes and behaviors (Houston 2008). Drawing upon the literature on intrinsic and extrinsic motivations as well as PSM (Perry and Wise 1990; Crewson 1997; Rainey and Steinbauer 1999; Wilson 1999; Brewer and Selden 2000; Lewis and Frank 2002; Perry and Hondeghem 2008), this study analyzes how the two types of motivators are differently associated with the three dependent variables in a multilevel and multi-actor organizational setting.

Job involvement has important practical and research implications because it often relates to satisfaction, performance, turnover, absenteeism, and to antecedents such as gender, age, intrinsic motivation, or other organizational structural and cultural influences. As Moon (2000) found, intrinsic motivational factors have more positive effects on job involvement than extrinsic motivational factors (see also Naff and Crum 1999). In their study of state government agency managers, Moynihan and Pandey (2007) found job involvement to be significantly related to PSM, group culture, and advancement opportunities.

Rainey and Steinbauer (1999)'s organizational effectiveness framework suggests that three forms of motivation -- task, mission, and PSM -- increase public agency effectiveness. These are essentially intrinsic forms of motivation, and the framework implies that higher intrinsic motivation should increase perceptions of organizational effectiveness. Perry et al. (2006) found that individual monetary incentive systems are generally ineffective in public sector organizations. Park and Rainey (2008) report evidence that public service--oriented motivation reduces variables that should relate to effectiveness, such as turnover intentions, and indirectly affects perceived performance and quality of work. Thus, perceived organizational effectiveness should be more positively associated with the level of intrinsic work motivation than with extrinsic work motivation (Perry and Wise 1990; Rainey 2003).

Red tape can be affected by antecedents such as hierarchy, goal ambiguity, formalization, and communication processes (Bozeman 2000; Pandey and Welch 2005; Rainey, Pandey and Bozeman 1995). Scott and Pandey (2005) reported that public managers with higher levels of PSM were less likely to perceive high levels of red tape, compared to public managers who have lower levels of PSM (p. 174). This finding suggests that, in state agencies, high levels of PSM and intrinsic factors will play a crucial role in reducing negative perceptions on organizational rules and institutional regulations as being burdensome or unnecessary procedural barriers. That is, intrinsic motivation relates to lower perceived levels of 'red tape', and hence leads to stronger determination to overcome obstacles to delivering public services (Scott and Pandey 2005). These attitudes should enhance the level of job involvement, effectiveness, and performance.

Hypothesis 1 (Intrinsic motivation): Higher levels of public manager' intrinsic motivation to choose their job will be positively associated with the managers' job involvement and perceived organizational effectiveness, while it will be negatively associated with the perception of red tape.

Hypothesis 2 (Extrinsic motivation): Compared with intrinsic motivation effects, increasing levels of public managers' extrinsic motivation will be less positively associated with job involvement and organizational effectiveness, while it will be less negatively associated with the perception of red tape.

Social Communications in Public Organizations: Organizational Communication and Mentoring Socialization

Organizational researchers have paid attention to the importance of organizational social processes, with emphasis on the direct, indirect, or mediating roles of communication and exchange processes among organizational constituents (Downs 1967; Garnett 1992; Putnam 2000; Pandey and Garnett 2006; Garnett et al. 2008). These processes include social communications and coordination of information and ideas, collaborative and networked relationships, and the creation and transfer of knowledge (Kogut and Zander 1996). Especially, the whole entity of the structures and processes of social and organizational communication can be also conceptualized by the social capital theoretical perspectives. Social capital refers to any type of social structure that creates, develops, and facilitates individual actions and decisions, and hence generates autonomous motivational behaviors within that social structure (Coleman 1990; Crossan, Lane, White and Djurfeldt 1995; Seibert, Kraminer and Liden 2001). Organizational social capital increases when organizational constituents communicate in a way that facilitates access to social resources (Coleman 1990).

The impact of social communication within or among work groups has important implications for organizations because they provide organizational constituents with resources and can enhance organizational effectiveness and positive job attitudes (Brass 1984; Balkundi and Harrison 2006). The different forms of social communication develop through interpersonal collaboration and coordination, group interactions, mentoring programs for employees, and participation in voluntary activities (Levinthal and March 1993; Leonard and Sensiper 1998). Social communications can enhance norms of reciprocation and collaboration, rather than opportunism (Putnam 2000). Since social communications in organizations help employees to share information and knowledge, social communications in the public sector should have positive effects on work behaviors and attitudes (Garnett et al. 2008). Social communications are also related to the concept of 'organizational socialization' which is defined as a 'process by which an individual comes to appreciate the values, abilities, expected behaviors, and social knowledge essential for assuming an organizational role and for participating as an organizational member' (Louis 1980, pp. 229 - 230).

The patterns of organizational socialization into public service are pronounced in the formal mentoring programs and informal social interactions in the workplace because mentoring and informal interactions with peers are 'key factor(s) in the transmission of values' (Wilson and Elman 1990; Bozeman and Feeney 2009; Paarlberg et al. 2008, p. 271). As Kram (1985) suggested, mentoring socialization can be described as a developmental and mutual relationship in which 'a less experienced organization member (the protégé) receives help and guidance from a more experienced member (the mentor) whose intent is to provide career and mental support' (Seibert et al. 2001, p. 220) -- that is, support provided through sponsorship, coaching, friendship, developing, and counseling. Mentoring facilitates the protégé socialization to his or her role in the organizational culture in that the mentor--protégé relationship increases 'an individual's social network affiliations' and enhances the level of 'communication and access to additional information' (Bozeman and Feeney 2009, p. 3). Informal social interactions in the public sector also 'provide important cues about organizational values and expectations' (Paarlberg et al. 2008, p. 271). In this regard, recognizing the importance of socialization experiences, it is necessary that public organizations probe any significant impact of socialization process on employee attitudes and organizational effectiveness (Brewer 2008).[2]

Social Communications and Outcomes

Social capital theory posits that successful social exchange and communication should positively influence organizational performance, interpersonal or organizational trust, and other job attitudes (Whitener, Brodt, Korsgaard and Werner 1998; Leana and Pil 2006). The previous research findings confirm that increased access to relevant information and advice through formal or informal social interactions or social communications in organizations would increase psychological empowerment (Spreitzer 1996), enhance the level of job involvement, and positively affect job attitudes (Hackman and Oldha 1980; Spreitzer 1996). Feldman's contingency theory of socialization (1976, 1981) also suggests that different types of socialization processes (e.g. congruence, accommodation, communication, and adjustment to group norms and values) are closely related to several behavioral and affective attitudinal outcomes including job satisfaction and job involvement. Additionally, from Kram's mentoring theory (1985), we may infer that the mentoring program will furnish two principal mentor functions --career development and psychological functions -- and that both the functions are positively associated with career and job attitudes in organizations (Ragins, Cotton and Miller 2000).

We expect that formal and informal communications would positively affect public employees' job attitudes and behaviors since more social interactions and communications with other public and private entities could provide a high level of knowledge and skill resources, could share and disseminate new ideas among participants, could diversify organizational values and norms with new perspectives, and hence could set well-specified goals in a timely manner. In sum, work collaboration with other governmental and private entities is expected to lead to cultural assimilation among employees and change their motivation styles in a more positive way that makes them more adaptive to their work environment.[3]

Recently, Pandey and Garnett (2006) analyzed the relationship between different types of public sector communication performance (i.e. interpersonal, external, and internal communication performance) and a set of independent variables including goal clarity, red tape, culture, and size. Garnett et al. (2008) also investigated communication's mediating and moderating roles between organizational culture and organizational performance. They found that organizational communication in the public sector acts as 'a meta-mechanism for shaping and imparting culture in mission-oriented organizational cultures' (p. 266). Previous research suggests that well-developed social capital and socialization structure in public agencies will enhance such valuable collective resources as knowledge sharing, communications, and intrinsic work motivation in an organization, and should lead to better organizational outcomes. We also expect that better organizational communication will lower the level of public employees' perceptions of red tape because it will clarify the purposes of regulations, making them more acceptable to employees. Within that type of organizational setting, employees are more willing to identify legitimate, consistent, beneficial, and effective rules and procedures (i.e. perceiving green or white tape) and thus less likely to perceive excessive formal and hierarchical administrative rules and procedures (i.e. perceiving red tape as less of a problem) (Adler and Borys 1996; Dehart-Davis 2009).

As Monge, Heiss and Margolin (2008) argue, intra- and interorganizational communication system is a crucial component in establishing organizational structure and culture.At the organizational level, this study probes four types of social communications in state agencies as main predictors: (1) intra-social communication among managers within state agencies, (2) inter-social communication with other government agencies and institutions, (3) inter-social communication with private companies, and (4) a mentoring socialization program. It is hypothesized that social communications and mentoring are positively associated with job involvement and organizational effectiveness while negatively associated with managers' perception of red tape.

> **Hypothesis 3 (Intra-social communications):** Higher levels of social communications within state agencies will be positively associated with job involvement and organizational effectiveness, whereas it will be negatively associated with perceived red tape.
>
> **Hypothesis 4 (Inter-social communications):** Higher levels of social communications with other government agencies will be positively associated with job involvement and organizational effectiveness, whereas it will be negatively associated with perceived red tape.

Hypothesis 5 (Inter-social communications): Higher levels of social communications with private firms will be positively associated with job involvement and organizational effectiveness, whereas it will be negatively associated with perceived red tape.

Hypothesis 6 (Mentoring socialization): Mentoring socialization in state agencies will be positively associated with job involvement and organizational effectiveness, whereas it will be negatively associated with perceived red tape.

Self-Determination Theory: The Logic of the Interactive Behaviors in Organizations

As suggested earlier, the two types of work motivation -- intrinsic motivation and extrinsic motivation -- involve different cognitive processes and contrasting organizational results. The cognitive evaluation theory (CET) framework mainly focuses on intrinsic motivation and suggests that intrinsic motivation is affected by organizational factors such as regulations, autonomy, events, or communications. That is, according to CET, the degree of intrinsic motivation can be facilitated or diminished by different organizational environments (Ryan and Deci 2000b). CET emphasizes that people are intrinsically motivated only when employees can perceive 'activities (that have the appeal of novelty, challenge, or aesthetic value) as intrinsic interest for themselves'.

On the other hand, the major contribution of SDT is to provide a more diversified approach to motivation by investigating social--contextual conditions that hinder or facilitate the processes of self-motivation and psychological development within organizations (Deci and Ryan 1985; Ryan and Deci 2000b). SDT proposes that extrinsic motivation varies in terms of its 'relative autonomy' in intentional behaviors (Heider 1958; Ryan and Connell 1989). Deci and Ryan (1985) introduced the self-determination continuum (from amotivation, to extrinsic motivation, to intrinsic motivation), which explicates the different forms of extrinsic motivation and the contextual influences that either develop or thwart 'internalization and integration of the regulation for these behaviors' (Ryan and Deci 2000b, p. 72). In the continuum, the extrinsically motivated behaviors include four separate regulatory styles (listed here from least autonomous to most autonomous motivation): (1) external regulation, (2) introjected regulation, (3) identified regulation, and (4) and integrated regulation, each of which could be differently affected by external factors.[4]

Motivation, Social Communications, and Outcomes

Drawing on the SDT approach, we expect that the social communication processes (i.e. organizational communication and mentoring socialization) function as important organizational mediators (i.e. intervening to affect the impact of motivations on outcomes) or moderators (i.e. affecting the effect of the mediating) which facilitate the internalization process of extrinsic motivation (Perry et al. 2006). That is, when public employees and managers work within effective communication structures in which an organization is willing to provide organizational constituents highly autonomous, integrated, and self-determined environments, their extrinsic motivation could be easily assimilated into intrinsic motivation (or, at least into the status of integrated regulation), could share characteristics of intrinsic motivation, and could thus obtain more positive organizational outcomes (i.e. positively influencing job involvement and organizational effectiveness while reducing perceptions of red tape), compared with extrinsically motivated people who work within less developed socialization relationships with relatively few organizational interactions and communications (Vallerand 1997). This study hypothesizes that, first, when public managers are intrinsically motivated, the interactions between intrinsic motivation and social communications will have additive moderating impacts and hence significantly affect the three organizational outcomes. Second, when employees are extrinsically motivated, the interactions between extrinsic motivation and social communications will have interactive moderating impacts. That is, those interactions will assimilate extrinsic motivation into more autonomous motivation (i.e. integrated regulation) or inherently autonomous motivation (i.e. intrinsic motivation). The interaction effects will also be significantly associated with organizational dispositions - job involvement, organizational effectiveness, and perceived red tape.

Hypothesis 7 (Intrinsic motivation with social communications): Public managers' intrinsic motivation interacts with social communications to positively affect job involvement and organizational effectiveness, while negatively affecting perceived red tape. Social communications will significantly moderate the relationship between public managers' intrinsic motivation and those three organizational outcomes.

Hypothesis 8 (Extrinsic motivation with social communications): Public managers' extrinsic motivation interacts with social communications to positively affect job involvement and organizational effectiveness, while negatively affecting perceived red tape. Social communications will significantly moderate the relationship between public managers' extrinsic motivation and those three organizational outcomes (Figure 1).

Research Modeling: Hierarchical Linear Models (HLM)

Government bureaucracies have shown an inherent hierarchical structure, with people employed in certain programs and units within public agencies. State employees are nested within state agencies, creating a hierarchical data structure and clustering observations with two levels of random variation: variation among employees within state agencies (level 1) and variation among state agencies within two states, Georgia and Illinois (level 2). Level-2 variables were aggregated into agency-based scores. The hierarchical linear model (HLM) explicitly explains the nested nature of data and can simultaneously estimate the impact of factors at different levels on individual-level outcomes while maintaining appropriate levels of analysis for predictors (Raudenbush, Bryk, Cheong and Congdon 2000). One of the rationales for using the HLM method in this study is that OLS does not take into account the interdependence of individual-level observations nested within higher-level (i.e. agency-level) state agencies; hence, estimates of standard errors may be biased, and test statistics may not be valid. To avoid these potential problems caused by hierarchically nested data structures, the ANCOVA and the intercepts- and slopes-as-outcomes models were estimated in this research.

Data and measures

Data and sample

This study utilized the National Administrative Studies Project (NASP) III survey instrument, which collected data on managers working in public agencies in the states of Illinois (N = 358) and Georgia (N = 432).[5] Respondents were representative of the original random sample of the managers of both states. The survey instrument measured public-sector managers' perceptions about organizational issues such as work motivation, career histories, hiring practices, and organizational cultures and structures. It also asked about numerous individual and organizational characteristics -- for example, affiliated agencies, agency mission and goals, gender, ethnicity, educational level, salary, and age.

In this study, for missing data, to preserve sample size, we employed the expectationmaximization (EM) algorithm (at level 1) and the Markov Chain Monte Carlo (MCMC) imputation method (level 2).[6] The total sample sizes of the level-1 (individual level) and level-2 (agency level) variables were 790 and 61, respectively.[7] The survey respondents represented 61 different state agencies, and the level-2 variables were the average scores (i.e. the mean imputation procedure) for those variables for the respondents from each agency. Each agency was well represented by a number of respondents, with no serious unevenness in responses from different agencies (Details available from the authors) (Table 1).[8]

Figure 1. Hierarchical Linear Model (HLM): Motivation, Communication, Interactions, and Outcomes.

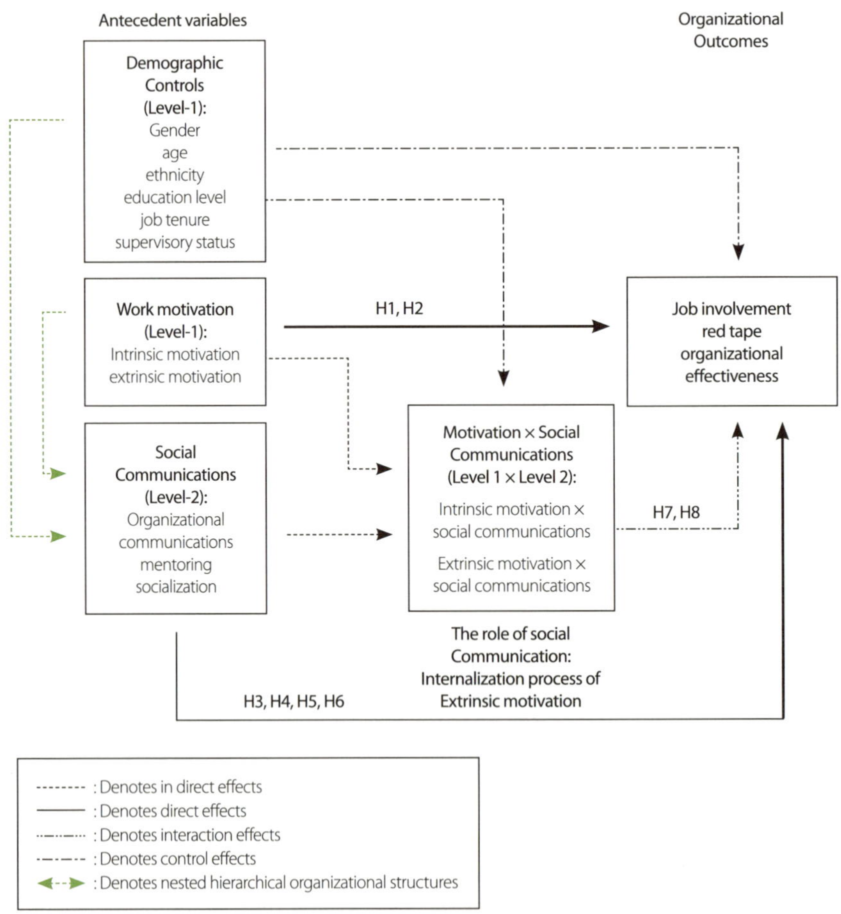

Instrumentation and Measures

Some responses were measured on a four-point Likert scale with specific statements. We employed exploratory factor analysis (EFA) and confirmatory factor analysis (CFA) to operationalize variables as well as to confirm latent constructs of these variables. Based on these empirical tools, intrinsic and extrinsic work motivation scales, a mentoring scale, and job involvement and organizational effectiveness scales were developed from relevant survey items (see Appendix). First, factor extraction (using eigenvalues greater than 1.0) was obtained from EFA, and each of these item scales was converged onto a unitary factor which creates an index variable. To assess internal consistency and to ensure reliability of each scale, we used Cronbach's alpha reliability test (with a 0.7 cutoff value).[9] Second, through a CFA model, we also estimated the latent constructs of intrinsic and extrinsic motivations.[10] A second-order CFA model indicates that both of the two latent motivation constructs are significant and distinct. The model of fit statistics was within acceptable levels and this proposed CFA model of work motivation is an excellent fit to the data, supporting the construct validity of the model.[11]

Table 1. Descriptive Statistics among Study Variables.

Variables	Valid N	Mean	Std. Deviation	Minimum	Maximum
Level-1 variables					
Gender (Female: 0 Male:1)	790	0.58	0.49	0.00	1.00
Age	790	49.02	8.54	25.00	72.00
Ethnicity (non-White: 0 White: 1)	790	0.80	0.40	0.00	1.00
Educational level	790	4.78	1.18	1.00	6.00
Job tenure (natural log)	790	2.446	1.081	1.00	4.00
Supervisory status (natural log)	790	2.5701	0.904	1.00	4.00
Intrinsic motivation	790	2.71	0.62	0.80	4.00
Extrinsic motivation	790	3.20	0.57	1.00	4.00
Level-2 variables					
Intra-social communication (with employees)	61	66.87	15.47	25.00	100.00
Inter-social communication (within government agencies)	61	9.13	4.40	0.00	20.00
Inter-social communication (with private companies)	61	5.92	6.00	0.00	40.00
Mentoring socialization	61	3.33	0.18	2.63	3.75
Outcome variables					

Job involvement	790	2.96	0.32	1.57	3.71
Red tape	790	7.11	2.11	0.00	10.00
Organizational effectiveness	790	3.04	0.66	1.00	4.00

Note: The expectation-maximization (EM) and the Markov Chain Monte Carlo (MCMC) methods were used to deal with missing data at level 1 and level 2.

Measures of Individual (Level-1) Predictors

Eight variables as controls measured the personal and job characteristics of the public managers in the states of Georgia and Illinois: gender, age, ethnicity, educational level, job tenure, and supervisory status, as well as two types of work motivation -- intrinsic and extrinsic motivations.[12] The natural logarithm of job tenure (the total number of years in the job) and supervisory status (the total number of employees supervised) were employed to transform the skewed distributions into more normal forms. The motivation variables were measured and developed from the 11 (four-point scale) items shown in appendix. Researchers have frequently used these items to measure intrinsic and extrinsic motivations. For example, Manolopoulos (2008) used an item about esteem and reputation as a measure of intrinsic motives. To operationalize motivation scales, we used a principal axis factoring (PAF) analysis with varimax rotation to obtain factor extraction. These methods extract communalities from different variables and combine different variables into new variables.[13]

Measures of Social Communications (Level-2) Predictors

The level-2 predictors were measured by the average scores on the variables for the respondents from each agency.[14] While the NASP III data has results for questions about five different categories of organizational communication, we only included three of these items in our analysis. This means that responses to these items have a lot of room to vary among themselves. They are not dependent on each other (i.e. the three social communication variables are neither a linear combination of each other and nor do they necessarily sum to 100%). This is further shown in the correlation matrix in Table 2. The correlations between our communication variables are not strong enough to conclude that the three variables are highly dependent on each other (further information supporting this conclusion is available from the authors).

First, three types of the organizational communication scale were included: (1) intra-social communication (employees within the organization), (2) inter-social communication (with government agencies), and (3) inter-social communication (with private companies).

The intra-social communication variable was measured by asking what percentage of work-related mail, email, and phone calls the state managers sent to persons within this organization. The inter-social communication variables were operationalized by asking what percentage of work-related mail, email, and phone calls the state managers sent to each of the following categories of recipients: (1) government agencies or institutions or (2) private companies (see appendix).[15] Another social communication variable addressed the mentoring socialization process within state agencies. Eight survey items made up the mentoring socialization scale. In the survey, for example, state employees were asked to indicate whether mentors and protégés share similar professional values, whether mentors have a great deal of respect for protégés' ideas, or whether mentors have significantly contributed to protégés' success in the organization (Cronbac's alpha = 0.762; see appendix).

Measures of Interaction Effects (Level-1 X Level-2 Predictors)

In order to confirm the additive and interactive effects between the two types of motivation (level-1) and four types of social communication (level-2) variables, we measured eight interaction terms (i.e. cross-level interaction effects within state agencies). Adding interaction variables enables us to incorporate the joint and multiplicative effects of each of the main antecedents on outcome variables in the empirical model.

Measures of Outcome Variables: Job Involvement, Red Tape, Organizational Effectiveness

The first variable, 'job involvement,' was created by factor analysis, all converged onto one factor (Cronbach's alpha = 0.715). All items were responded on a 4-point scale and measured by a six-item scale with items from Kanungo's (1982a; 1982b; see also Word and Park 2009) 10-item scale (see the Appendix). The second outcome variable, perceived red tape, used the procedure used frequently by Bozeman, Pandey, and other red tape researchers asking, 'How would you assess the level of red tape in your organization?' The response choices were on a 10-point scale, from 0 to 10. For the third outcome variable, 'organizational effectiveness,' a factor analysis included four survey items (asking the levels of the overall quality of work, clients' satisfaction, goal and task clarity, and innovativeness in state agencies) into one factor index (Cronbach's alpha = 0.796). Correlation and HLM analyses examined the statistical relations among these antecedent and outcome variables.

Table 2. Zero-Order Correlations among Antecedents, Moderators, and Consequences in the HLM.

Variables	1	2	3	4	5	6	7	8	9	10	11	12	13	14	15
1. Gender															
2. Age	0.156**														
3. Ethnicity	0.074**	0.019													
4. Educational level	0.083**	0.086**	-0.054												
5. Job tenure	-0.150**	-0.357**	-0.066*	-0.060*											
6. Supervisor status	0.073*	0.069*	0.023	-0.022	0.016										
7. Intrinsic motivation	-0.154**	-0.023	-0.131**	-0.082**	0.050	-0.009	(0.711)								
8. Extrinsic motivation	-0.118**	-0.186**	-0.097**	-0.240**	0.064*	-0.068*	0.399**	(0.727)							
9. Intra-social communication (with employees)	-0.048	-0.089**	-0.031	-0.054	0.120**	0.067*	0.101**	0.139**							
10. Inter-social communication (with government agencies)	0.023	-0.010	-0.009	0.010	0.009	0.001	0.078**	0.008	-0.323**						
11. Inter-social communication (with private companies)	0.109**	0.051	0.052	-0.041	-0.105**	-0.019	-0.015	0.056	-0.403**	0.005					
12. Mentoring socialization	-0.029	-0.011	0.049	0.023	0.034	-0.016	0.186**	0.003	-0.065	-0.063	0.005	(0.762)			
13. Job involvement	-0.007	0.124**	0.018	0.056	-0.051	0.042	0.130**	-0.083**	0.145**	0.021	0.031	0.205**	(0.702)		
14. Red tape	-0.009	-0.116**	-0.047	-0.043	0.100**	-0.006	-0.131**	0.199**	-0.017	0.002	-0.068*	-0.067	-0.359**		
15. Organizational effectiveness	0.021	0.127**	0.000	0.019	-0.099**	0.046	0.201**	-0.052	0.164**	-0.047	0.021	0.146**	0.477**	-0.501**	(0.717)

Note: ** Correlation is significant at the 0.01 level (two-tailed). * Correlation is significant at the 0.05 level (two-tailed). The numbers in parentheses are Cronbach's alpha values.

Results and Findings

The Level-1 (Manager-Level) Model: One-Way ANCOVA Model with Random Effects

In a manager (individual)-level model, a one-way ANCOVA model was employed in order to incorporate several covariates and to see how these level-1 predictors would affect outcome variables.[16] As fixed effects, eight covariates were included: (1) gender ($\gamma 10$), (2) age ($\gamma 20$), (3) ethnicity ($\gamma 30$), (4) educational level ($\gamma 40$), (5) job tenure in current position ($\gamma 50$), (6) managerial power ($\gamma 60$), (7) intrinsic motivation ($\gamma 70$), and (8) extrinsic motivation ($\gamma 80$). As random effects, level-1 and level-2 variances were included.[17] The final level-1 ANCOVA model is as follows:

Level-1 Model:
Y_{ij} (Job involvement, Red tape, Organizational effectiveness) = β_{0j} + β_{1j}(Gender) +
= β_{0j} + β_{1j}(Gender) + β_{2j}(Age) + β_{3j} (Ethnicity) + β_{4j} (Educational level) + β_{5j} (Job tenure) + β_{6j} (Managerial power) + β_{7j} (Intrinsic motivation) + β_{8j} (Extrinsic motivation) + ϵ_{ij}

Reliability and the Conditional ICC Coefficient

In the three ANCOVA models, all reliability estimates (β_0) are greater than 0.05. The conditional ICC indicates that, in the job involvement model, there is approximately 18.3% of variation in state managers' job involvement across agencies. Similarly, in the models of red tape and organizational effectiveness, the proportions of the variances across state agencies are approximately 20.5% and 16.5%, respectively.

Proportion of Variance Explained

First, proportions of level-1 variance explained by the eight predictors at level-1 in three models are 25.13% (job involvement), 23.12% (red tape), and 24.87% (organizational effectiveness). Second, the proportions of level-2 variance explained by the eight predictors at level 2 in three models are 0% (job involvement), 25% (red tape), and 33.3% (organizational effectiveness).

The Fixed and Random Effects

ANCOVA covariates would statistically adjust for the initial advantage. Especially when the covariates are grand mean centered, ANCOVA can control for the influence of the covariate and the variance term on the intercept is adjusted. As shown in Tables 3 - 5, managerial power (β = 0.003**) and intrinsic motivation (β = 0.08**) are statistically significant (p , 0.05) in the job involvement model, whereas intrinsic motivation (20.391**) is significantly and negatively related in the red tape model. In the organizational effectiveness model, age (β = 0.009**), managerial power, (β = 0.001**), and intrinsic motivation (β = 0.195**) are statistically significant. [confirmed Hypotheses 1 and 2]

The level-2 (Organizational-Level) Model: Intercepts- and Slopes-as-Outcomes Model

In an organizational-level model, an intercepts- and slopes-as-outcomes (organizationallevel) model, which assumes that the intercept and slope have random effects, was used.[18] As social communication predictors (at level-2), the four fixed effects were included: (1) intra-social communication (with employees) ($\gamma01$), (2) inter-social communication (with government agencies) ($\gamma02$), (3) inter-social communication (with private companies) ($\gamma03$), and (4) mentoring socialization ($\gamma04$). As random effects, level-1 and level-2 variances were included. Additionally, to examine the cross-level interaction effects between motivation and social communications, eight interaction terms were included.[19] Below is the final intercepts- and slopes-as outcomes model:

Level-1 model:
Y_{ij} (Job involvement, Red tape, Organizational effectiveness) = β_{0j} + β_{1j} (Gender) + β_{2j} (Age) + β_{3j} (Ethnicity) + β_{4j} (Educational level) + β_{5j} (Job tenure) + β_{6j} (Managerial power) + β_{7j} (Intrinsic motivation) + β_{8j} (Extrinsic motivation) + ϵ_{ij}

Level-2 model:
Intercept: β_0 = γ_{00} + γ_{01} (Intra-social communication) + γ_{02} (Inter-social communication1) + γ_{03} (Inter-social communication 2) + γ_{04} (Mentoring socialization) + u_{0j}

Slope 1: β_{7j} (Intrinsic motivation) = γ_{70} + γ_{71} (Intra-social communication) + γ_{72} (Inter-social communication 1) + γ_{73} (Inter-social communication 2) + γ_{74} (Mentoring socialization) + u_{0j}

Slope 2: β_{8j} (Extrinsic motivation) = γ_{80} + γ_{81} (Intra-social communication) + γ_{82} (Inter-social communication 1) + γ_{83} (Inter-social communication 2) + γ_{84} (Mentoring socialization) + u_{0j}

Other slopes: $\beta_{1j} = \gamma_{10}$; $\beta_{2j} = \gamma_{20}$; $\beta_{3j} = \gamma_{30}$; $\beta_{4j} = \gamma_{40}$; $\beta_{5j} = \gamma_{50}$; $\beta_{6j} = \gamma_{60}$

Table 3. Hierarchical Linear Model (HLM) Results for Job Involvement.[a]

1. Job involvement model	1. An employeelevel model: oneway ANCOVA model	2. An agency-level model: intercepts-and slopes-as-outcomes model
Reliability intercept (β_0)	0.211	0.183
Fixed effects Intercept (γ_{00})	**2.96****	**1.41****
Level-1 slope (individual) model		
1. Demographic controls, individual level		
Gender (γ_{10})	-0.002 (-0.094)	-0.001 (-0.091)
Age(γ_{20})	0.003 (1.448)	0.003 (1.422)
Ethnicity (γ_{30})	0.008 (0.279)	0.006 (0.245)
Educational level (γ_{40})	0.0015 (0.172)	0.002 (0.188)
Job tenure (γ_{50})	0.0012 (0.688)	0.001 (0.682)
Supervisory status (γ_{60})	**0.003** (2.636)**	0.001 (1.139)
2. Work motivation		
Manager's intrinsic motivation (γ_{70})	**0.08** (3.18)**	**0.09** (3.22)**
Manager's extrinsic motivation (γ_{80})	-0.02 (-0.681)	0.01 (1.342)
Level-2 intercept (organizational) model : social communications		
1. Organizational communications		
Intra-social communication (with employees) (γ_{01})		**0.032** (3.020)**
Inter-social communication (with government agencies) (γ_{02})		0.001 (0.165)
Inter-social communication (with private companies) (γ_{03})		0.005 (1.209)
2. Mentoring socialization		
Mentoring socialization (γ_{04})		**0.347** (3.036)**
The interaction (level 1 x level 2 interaction terms) model : internalization process		
Intrinsic motivation x Intra-social communication (with employees) (γ_{71})		0.001 (0.149)
Intrinsic motivation x Inter-social communication (with government agencies) (γ_{72})		0.004 (0.427)
Intrinsic motivation x Inter-social communication (with private companies) (γ_{73})		-0.002 (-0.307)
Intrinsic motivation x Mentoring socialization (γ_{74})		0.021 (0.084)
Extrinsic motivation x Intra-social communication (with employees) (γ_{81})		**0.212** (2.850)**

Extrinsic motivation x Inter-social communication (with government agencies) (γ_{82})		**0.190**** (2.564)**
Extrinsic motivation x Inter-social communication (with private companies) (γ_{83})		**0.208**** (2.796)**
Extrinsic motivation x Mentoring socialization (γ_{84})		**0.406**** (2.439)**
Random effects		
Level-1 effect (r_{ij}) variance	0.097	0.095
Level-2 effect (μ_{0j}) variance	**0.003****	**0.003****
Inter-class correlation (ICC)		
Conditional ICC	18.3%	16.8%
Proportion of the variance in r_{ij} explained by the model (%)	25.13%	32.53%
Proportion of the variance in μ_{0j} explained by the model (%)	0%	33.3%
Deviance	404.25	397.28
Number of parameters	2	2

**p < 0.05: significant at 0.05 level. *p < 0.10: significant at 0.10 level. Critical values are 1.96 for p < 0.05 and 1.65 for p < 0.10 (t-statistics are in parentheses).
[a] Individual level N = 637; organizational level N = 61.

Table 4. Hierarchical Linear Model (HLM) Results for Red Tape.[a]

2. Red tape model	**1. An employee-level model: one-way ANCOVA model**	**2. An agency-level model: intercepts- and slopes-as-outcomes model**
Reliability intercept (β_0)	0.492	0.471
Fixed effects Intercept (γ_{00})	**6.61****	**16.07****
Level-1 slope (individual) model		
1. Demographic controls, individual level		
Gender (γ_{10})	0.139 (0.815)	0.137 (0.809)
Age(γ_{20})	-0.014 (-1.503)	-0.011 (-1.502)
Ethnicity (γ_{30})	0.156 (0.788)	0.154 (0.788)
Educational level (γ_{40})	0.006 (0.947)	0.006 (0.933)
Job tenure (γ_{50})	0.012 (0.828)	0.009 (0.788)
Supervisory status (γ_{60})	-0.001 (-1.368)	-0.001 (-1.348)
2. Work motivation		
Manager's intrinsic motivation (γ_{70})	**-0.391**** (-2.458)**	**-0.376**** (- 2.457)**
Manager's extrinsic motivation (γ_{80})	0.193 (1.066)	0.188 (1.014)
Level-2 intercept (organizational) model : social communications		

1. Organizational communications		
Intra-social communication (with employees) (γ_{01})		0.015 (0.926)
Inter-social communication (with government agencies) (γ_{02})		0.041 (0.881)
Inter-social communication (with private companies) (γ_{03})		**-1.532** (- 2.317)**
2. Mentoring socialization		
Mentoring socialization (γ_{04})		**-2.61** (- 2.198)**
The interaction (level 1 x level 2 interaction terms) model		
Intrinsic motivation x Intra-social communication (with employees) (γ_{71})		-0.006 (-0.30)
Intrinsic motivation x Inter-social communication (with government agencies) (γ_{72})		-0.070 (-1.199)
Intrinsic motivation x Inter-social communication (with private companies) (γ_{73})		-0.006 (-0.134)
Intrinsic motivation x Mentoring socialization (γ_{74})		-1.41 (0.847)
Extrinsic motivation x Intra-social communication (with employees) (γ_{81})		**-0.35** (-2.093)**
Extrinsic motivation x Inter-social communication (with government agencies) (γ_{82})		-0.015 (-0.170)
Extrinsic motivation x Inter-social communication (with private companies) (γ_{83})		**-0.24** (-2.326)**
Extrinsic motivation x Mentoring socialization (γ_{84})		-0.330 (-0.183)
Random effects		
Level-1 effect (r_{ij}) variance	3.809	3.837
Level-2 effect (μ_{0j}) variance	**0.724****	**0.654****
Inter-class correlation (ICC)		
Conditional ICC	20.5%	21.4%
Proportion of the variance in r_{ij} explained by the model (%)	23.12%	33.62%
Proportion of the variance in μ_{0j} explained by the model (%)	25%	100%
Deviance	404.25	403.54
Number of parameters	2	2

**p < 0.05: significant at 0.05 level. *p < 0.10: significant at 0.10 level. Critical values are 1.96 for p < 0.05 and 1.65 for p < 0.10 (t-statistics are in parentheses).
[a] Individual level N = 637; organizational level N = 61.

Reliability and the Conditional ICC

In the three intercepts- and slopes-as-outcomes models, all reliability estimates are greater than 0.05. The conditional ICC indicates that, in the job involvement model, there are approximately 16.8% of the variations in state managers' job involvement across agencies.

Similarly, in the models of red tape and organizational effectiveness, the proportions of the variances across state agencies are approximately 21.4% and 22.4%, respectively.

Proportion of Variance Explained

First, proportions of level-1 variance explained by the eight level-1predictors and the level-2 predictors (including interaction effects) in the three models are 32.57% (job involvement), 33.62% (red tape), and 28.26% (organizational effectiveness). Second, the proportions of level-2 variance explained by the eight predictors and the level-2 predictors (including interaction effects) in the three models are 33.33% (job involvement), 100% (red tape), and 100% (organizational effectiveness). Overall, the proportions of level-1 and level-2 variances explained by the intercepts- and slopes-as-outcomes model are greater than those explained by the ANCOVA model.

Table 5. Hierarchical Linear Model (HLM) Results for Organizational Effectiveness.[a]

3. Effectiveness model	1. An employee-level model: one-way ANCOVA model	2. An agency-level model: intercepts- and slopes-as-outcomes model
Reliability intercept (β_0)	0.432	0.394
Fixed effects Intercept (γ_{00})	**3.15****	**1.34**
Level-1 slope (individual) model		
1. Demographic controls, individual level		
Gender (γ_{10})	-0.009 (-0.220)	-0.009 (-0.210)
Age(γ_{20})	**0.009** (3.199)**	**0.008** (3.112)**
Ethnicity (γ_{30})	-0.02 (-0.505)	-0.02 (-0.498)
Educational level (γ_{40})	-0.006 (-0.238)	-0.004 (-0.211)
Job tenure (γ_{50})	-0.001 (-0.151)	-0.001 (-0.144)
Supervisory status (γ_{60})	**0.001** (4.613)**	**0.001** (4.529)**
2. Work motivation		
Manager's intrinsic motivation (γ_{70})	**0.195** (5.219)**	**0.193** (5.117)**
Manager's extrinsic motivation (γ_{80})	0.023 (0.404)	0.022 (0.401)
Level-2 intercept (organizational) model : social communications		
1. Organizational communications		
Intra-social communication (with employees) (γ_{01})		**0.070** (2.023)**
Inter-social communication (with government agencies) (γ_{02})		0.001 (0.115)

Inter-social communication (with private companies) (γ_{03})		0.000 (0.038)
2. Mentoring socialization		
Mentoring socialization (γ_{04})		**0.694** (2.67)**
The interaction (level 1 x level 2 interaction terms) model		
Intrinsic motivation x Intra-social communication (with employees) (γ_{71})		-0.004 (-0.858)
Intrinsic motivation x Inter-social communication (with government agencies) (γ_{72})		0.000 (0.066)
Intrinsic motivation x Inter-social communication (with private companies) (γ_{73})		-0.006 (-0.063)
Intrinsic motivation x Mentoring socialization (γ_{74})		-0.106 (-0.256)
Extrinsic motivation x Intra-social communication (with employees) (γ_{81})		0.134 (1.468)
Extrinsic motivation x Inter-social communication (with government agencies) (γ_{82})		**0.188** (2.414)**
Extrinsic motivation x Inter-social communication (with private companies) (γ_{83})		**0.250** (2.326)**
Extrinsic motivation x Mentoring socialization (γ_{84})		0.895 (1.635)
Random effects		
Level-1 effect (r_{ij}) variance	0.367	0.366
Level-2 effect (μ_{0j}) variance	**0.05****	**0.042****
Inter-class correlation (ICC)		
Conditional ICC	16.5%	22.4%
Proportion of the variance in r_{ij} explained by the model (%)	24.87%	28.26%
Proportion of the variance in μ_{0j} explained by the model (%)	33.3%	100%
Deviance	404.25	398.48
Number of parameters	2	2

**p < 0.05: significant at 0.05 level. *p < 0.10: significant at 0.10 level. Critical values are 1.96 for p < 0.05 and 1.65 for p < 0.10 (t-statistics are in parentheses).
[a] Individual level N = 637; organizational level N = 61.

The Fixed and Random Effects

We found that the level-1 fixed effects are not different from those of the ANCOVA model (see Tables 3 - 5). First, the findings indicate that a mentoring socialization effect is significantly associated with state managers' job involvement, red tape, and organizational effectiveness.[20] Second, the results indicate that some of the social communication behaviors among state managers significantly affect three different outcomes; for example, intra-social communication is positively and significantly related to job involvement and organizational effectiveness (B = 0.032** and 0.070**, respectively), whereas inter-social communication (with private companies) has a negative and significant relationship with the level of perceived red tape in state agencies (B = 21.532**). These findings suggest that certain types of social communications may be much more effective than others to achieve better organizational outcomes. [partially confirmed Hypotheses 3 - 6]

Third, regarding the cross-level interaction effects, where the association between level-1 motivation variables and the outcome variables depends on the level of level-2 social communication predictors, the results indicate that when state managers are more involved with the different types of social communications, the relationship between extrinsic motivation and the three outcome variables becomes more pronounced. For example, while public managers' extrinsic motivation in itself does not significantly affect job involvement, when extrinsic motivation interacts with four types of social communication variables, the effects of extrinsic motivation on job involvement are pronounced and significant (see Table 3). The results are by no means unopposed in the SDT prediction described earlier. On the other hand, although intrinsic motivation in itself is significantly related to the three outcome variables, none of the interaction terms between intrinsic motivation and social communications was significant -- that is, there is no meaningful interaction effect. Instead, only marginally additive or possibly spurious effects between cross-level variables on outcome variables exist. The result suggests that intrinsic motivation already has an "inherently autonomous" characteristic that is not moderated and internalized by interaction with other organizational actors (e.g. social communications). In sum, the findings suggest that certain types of social communications develop and transform state managers' extrinsically oriented motivation into more intrinsically oriented motivation (or, at least into autonomous motivation). The modified motivation characteristics from cross-level interaction effects were positively and significantly associated with job involvement and organizational effectiveness. They also significantly reduce the degree of perceived red tape in state agencies just as intrinsic motivation. [partially confirmed Hypotheses 7 and 8]

Conclusions and Implications

This research addressed two major topics for organizational behavioral studies in the public sector: (1) individual work motivation - that is, intrinsic motivation (as a motivator) and extrinsic motivation (as a hygiene factor) - and (2) social communications - that is, organizational communications and mentoring socialization. The SDT assertion of an underlying control-to-autonomy continuum suggests that the types of extrinsic motivation vary in their degree of self-determination (from controlled motivation to autonomous motivation) and intrinsic motivation is inherently self-determined (Gagne and Deci 2005). The social capital and socialization theories suggest that the effects of organizational communications and the socialization process on organizational outcomes depend on the access to organizational information and interaction, congruence of values, resources, and sponsorship opportunities resulting from social contacts (Feldman 1981; Blau and Alba 1982). Mentoring theory also predicts that mentoring programs, which emphasize developmental contacts and interpersonal relationships, play a pivotal role in actualizing positive organizational outcomes (e.g. promotion, job satisfaction, and job involvement) (Dreher and Ash 1990). Based on these theoretical frameworks and utilizing HLM, this study probed the independent and cross-level effects of motivation (individual level) and social communications (organizational level) on job involvement, red tape, and organizational effectiveness.

First, the results of this study strongly support PSM research hypotheses confirming that two types of incentives, intrinsic motivation and extrinsic motivation, are differently associated with job attitudes. In all three models, as an individual-level predictor, intrinsic motivation significantly increases the level of public managers" job involvement and the level of perceived organizational effectiveness. Also, we found that public managers with a high level of intrinsic motivation perceive less red tape than extrinsically motivated public managers do. These results suggest that a high level of public managers" intrinsic motivation facilitates positive job attitudes and increases perceived organizational effectiveness in public organizations. Second, the results of HLM analysis indicate that some types of social communications are closely related to the outcomes; for example, intra-social communication has a significant relationship with job involvement and organizational effectiveness whereas inter-social communication (with the private sector) reduces the perceptions of red tape significantly. It is also clear that the presence of an effective mentoring program relates to positive outcomes in state agencies.

Third, most importantly, the results of cross-level interaction effects support the SDT prediction that, in more autonomous or self-determined social contexts (provided and indicated by high levels of social communication), extrinsic motivation transforms into the most advanced type of extrinsic motivation called 'integrated extrinsic motivation' or into intrinsic motivation (called inherently autonomous motivation).This study found that when state managers are more engaged in organizational communications and mentoring activities, the relationship between extrinsic motivation and the three outcome variables becomes more pronounced - that is, more communication with others in the organization provides autonomous and discretionary environments for extrinsically motivated public managers. The transformed autonomous motivation, which was operationalized as the interaction effects between extrinsic motivation and social communication variables, has a significant relationship with job involvement, red tape, and organizational effectiveness. From the ANCOVA and intercepts- and slopes-as-outcomes models, we also confirmed that the three outcome variables significantly vary across Georgia and Illinois state agencies. The findings indicate that organizational researchers should take into account the state government context of state agencies more carefully and systematically. At the same time, the main findings hold across two states with different state government contexts. Despite these significant findings, some methodological and data limitations should be acknowledged. A single-source (mono-method) bias is possible, since 'self-reported' and 'perceived' measures were used. Thus, it is plausible that the regression coefficients are inflated. Some authors contend, however, that mono-method bias is not as serious a problem as often assumed (Podsakoff and Organ 1986; Crampton and Wagner 1994).[21]

Even so, the findings have important implications for research on motivation, social communication, organizational socialization, and other job attitudes at the state and the federal level. First, this study employed self-determination, social capital, and mentoring theories to explicate the logic of interactions between motivation, social communications, and mentoring on organizational consequences. Second, other types of contextual factors (moderators) and mediators, such as the nature of the task and human resource policies, that may influence public employees' attitudinal and behavioral outcomes need attention, as do factors such as leadership, trust, and informal or formal networks. These additional research steps are justified by the findings reported here: When they report higher levels of intrinsic motivation for choosing their current job, state government managers show more positive job involvement, red tape (perceiving less red tape), and perceived organizational effectiveness. Effective mentoring also relates strongly to more positive levels of these attitudes. Consistent with SDT, higher levels of social communication interact with extrinsic motivation to increase positive responses about job involvement, red tape, and organizational effectiveness. These findings show the theoretical value of analyzing communication and mentoring processes, and the practical value of investing in such processes in government agencies.

Finally, this study can offer important implications and future directions for the study of public sector employees' dispositions and behaviors in other than the US countries. Although we examined public sector motivation and social communication in the context of US public sector, in future research we need to probe whether the results we found in this study would be consistent with the pattern of findings in a larger body of international studies (e.g. studies of other types of governments in European and East Asian countries). Public sector motivation, for example, is a concept that is relevant in many national contexts such as Belgium (Vandenabeele and Hondeghem 2004), France (Castaing 2006), the Netherlands (Steijn 2006), Germany (Vandenabeele, Scheepers and Hondeghem 2006), Italy (Cerase and Farinella 2006), South Korea (Kim 2005), and Australia (Taylor 2007). Similar to our results, other findings suggest that the effects of intrinsic motivation are distinct from those of extrinsic motivation on organizational effectiveness outcomes (Kim 2005; Cerase and Farinella 2006; Steijn 2006). For example, in Danish society, Andersen

(2009) found that when strong professional norms exist, economic incentives are less important. Ritz (2009) also found that commitment to the public interest has a positive impact on organizational performance in the federal administration of Switzerland. In a similar vein, some findings from the Belgian public sector suggest that individual PSM significantly correlates with performance (Vandenabeele 2009) and that certain institutional factors (e.g. the organizations for which one works, political affiliation, education, and gender) are significantly associated with PSM (Vandenabeele 2011). While the findings from international settings are valuable, international research will face difficulties in measuring and validating dimensions of public sector motivation internationally. More rigorous comparative research designs will be necessary, sampling public agencies that are more heterogeneous in organizational, institutional, and geographical settings (such as organizational environments, culture, structure, leadership, and other HR systems). We expect that the study of motivation can be replicated in other governments in a way that effectively extends the findings from the US public organizations and hence obtains a higher level of generalizability.

Notes

1. An earlier version of this manuscript was presented at the 68th Annual Conference of the Academy of Management (AOM), Anaheim, California, held from 8 to 13 August 2008.
2. As teams, committees, and other groupings make up the overarching structure and culture of organizations, organizational communications travel through various channels and processes (e.g. team-based management and team-based/shared leadership). These different dimensions of communications such as horizontal, bottom-up, or local communications and hierarchical, top-down, or vertical communications occur in organizations. Local and group-based communication activities influence organizational outcomes. The data include no subunit-level data and hence we could not devise a three-level HLM analysis (i.e. including individual level variables, subunit-level variables, and organizational-level variables altogether). However, we emphasize that this study utilized the National Administrative Studies Project (NASP) III survey instrument, which collected data on perceptions and attitudes reported by managers who are working in public agencies in the states of Illinois (N = 358) and Georgia (N 432). That is, the respondents represent the upper-level values, issues, and identities from a manager's perspective.
3. While we put a heavy emphasis on the positive side of organizational communication in this study, we also acknowledge the contrasting findings and arguments that organizational communications, such as mentoring, and other types of communications might impose structural, cultural, or communicative barriers that might have detrimental effects. For example, 'horizontal communications encounter difficulties as a result of conflict, competition, or other differences between subunits and groups' while 'vertical communications encounter difficulties as a result of hierarchical filtering and superior–subordinate relationships, including resistance, inattentiveness, misunderstanding, and reticence or withholding of information by persons at lower levels' (Rainey, p. 367). Lack of feedback, noise in communication, and misuses of language might also lead to ineffective communications and bring difficulties in organizations. Specifically, some authors point out that 'communication distortions' might be frequently observed in the public sector, which include the notions of 'jargon, inflated prose, and the manipulation of information for political or bureaucratic purposes' (Rainey, p. 368).
4. Although integrated regulation (i.e. autonomous motivation) is still regarded as extrinsic motivation, it has a full range of autonomous regulations and an internal locus of causality, characteristics very similar to those of intrinsic motivation (i.e. inherently autonomous motivation). In this stage, extrinsic motivation shares some qualities with intrinsic or autonomous motivation and is characterized as 'internalization of extrinsically motivated activities' with respect to particular behaviors (Gagne and Deci 2005, pp. 335–336).

Intrinsic motivation and integrated extrinsic motivation were identified as the two distinct types of autonomous motivation.

5. The sample actually included some respondents classified as 'professionals', in addition to managers. Professionals often have levels of responsibility comparable to those of managers, and have experience with their agencies' administrative and personnel management systems, obviously. More importantly, various analyses indicate that the distinction between manager and professional does not relate significantly to the findings reported here. Results are available from the authors.
6. Although list-wise deletion (where cases with a missing score on any variable are excluded from all analyses and the effective sample size includes only cases with complete records) is the most common method for handling missing data, this approach sacrifices a large amount of data by eliminating all cases with any missing data (Roth 1994). The EM and the MCMC methods allow us to obtain an effective sample size and to minimize possible bias in parameter estimates in an HLM analysis. These approaches also fully capture the asymptotic properties of the underlying population.
7. A simple random sample of 2000 public managers was selected from original population (1000 from Illinois and 1000 from Georgia). An overall response rate of 42.47% was achieved (790 usable completed surveys out of 1853 in the original sample). Extensive documentation about the NASP-III (e.g. sampling procedures and survey instruments) is available at the project Web site, http://www.uga.edu/padp/nasp.html
8. Skewness can show whether the item's distribution deviates from the symmetry distribution. We can argue that skewness values outside the range of ±2 would be problematic because this is a serious level of skew. Kurtosis measures the degree to which the area in a distribution is in the middle and the tails of a distribution. As a rule of thumb, the range of ±2 is often considered as a significant departure from normality (Pedhazur 1997). In this research, most items show a relatively stable and similar amount of variance. The results of Kolmogorov-Smirnov and Shapiro normality tests suggest that items in this study do differentiate responses fairly well. In terms of individual normality, most items have a high positive kurtosis value, which means that most respondents have selected the same response option. Most variables of skewness or kurtosis are all between $-2 < s(k) < 2$, and we can argue that these variables are approximately normally distributed. Relative multivariate kurtosis ($1.155 < 2.0$) also indicates approximate multivariate normality.
9. The alpha values indicate that the scale content is homogeneous and answers are consistent. Internal consistency is important in this research because the homogeneity of motivation and other scales is critical for measuring the respondents' attitudes about the survey items accurately. Moreover, when the content is consistent, it is also easier to interpret. To assess internal consistency and to ensure reliability of each scale, Cronbach's alpha reliability test was done.

10. Since EFA is an atheoretical method that might sometimes result in poor indexing, we also employed the CFA method, which is based on SDT, to develop more theory-oriented intrinsic and extrinsic motivation scales in this study. The table with factor loadings of EFA and CFA models is available from the authors. We also statistically tested the coefficient difference between intrinsic motivation and extrinsic motivation. In order to test for statistically significant differences between the two coefficients on outcome variables, we used an independent samples t-test method by dividing the sample on the basis of the two groups – intrinsic motivation (group 1) and extrinsic motivation (group 2). The result of the test showed that the effects of intrinsic motivation and extrinsic motivation on three outcome variables are statistically different and the difference is significant.
11. For example, the comparative fit indices (CFI) are more than 0.95 (greater than 0.90 is acceptable), and the root mean square error approximation (RMSEA) is 0.065 (less than 0.08 is acceptable).
12. Among these variables, 'gender' (female = 0) and 'ethnicity' (non-White = 0) were recoded as dummy variables. We also created ordinal-level variables (four categories) for 'job tenure (log)' and 'managerial power (log)' because responses to these items were highly skewed on the right or left side.
13. In measuring these constructs of motivation as well as other ordinal scale variables, 11 noncontinuous ordinal variables (e.g. four-point Likert scale) were used, which might cause potential problems of nonlinearity and non-normality. Both non-normality and nonlinearity will generally result in underestimation of the relationship among variables. In other words, variable communalities, percentage of variance accounted for, and factor loadings will be lower than continuous and normally distributed data. As one solution to this problem, a polychoric-based solution was used in this model and polychoric correlation (PC) matrix, ranging from 21.0 to 1.0, was developed for the measurement.
14. The level-2 variables were measured by the average scores on the variables for the respondents from each agency. That is, we aggregated individual data into level 2. The main rationale to aggregate individual data into level 2 in this research is social communication (i.e. organizational communication and mentoring socialization) usually occur within an organizational context and hence we needed to analyze those behaviors from an organizational (not individual) behavior perspective. In this regard, we examined level-1 and level-2 variables separately (even though all variables are individual level measures) and we aggregated the individual level data in organizational level (level 2).
15. Our measure of the communication variables measures the intensity (a percentage measure) of communication rather than measuring the actual quantity (a count measure) of communication. These communication indicators measure the relative

amount of time that a manager spends communicating internally, relative to externally with business, or externally with government. Future research should use quantity or count measures to examine how 'intensity' of social communication would affect work motivation and organizational effectiveness. Nevertheless, the results in Table 3 indicate that relatively high levels of these three types of communication interact with extrinsic motivation. This supports our conclusions about the joint effects of communication and extrinsic motivation.

16. In this ANCOVA model, each slope of the covariate is assumed to have the same effect on each level of the factor (i.e. homogeneity of regression). Each predictor (covariate) was sequentially added and only one variable was retained when it shows that it has reliability greater than 0.05 and has a statistically significant random effect. Based on the results, eight predictors were retained at the employee level.
17. In this model, both of the un-centering (for dummy variables) and grand-mean centering methods were used because there is no random effect in the slope (that is, b1j is fixed across agencies). In other words, the level-1 covariates (X variables) were included to control for their effects on the outcomes, rather than to model between group variance on the slope of these variables. The intercept here is interpreted as the expected value of four outcome variables for each employee with an average score on each of the level-1 predictors. In this regard, grandmean centering adjusts the variation in the intercept between agencies to control for differences in the level-1 predictors across agencies.
18. In the intercepts- and slopes-as-outcomes model, we can include level-2 predictors. After we have established that significant variation existed between group intercepts and slopes, we then use those parameter estimates as level-2 outcomes. The level-2 models are used for purpose of modeling the associations between level-2 predictors and the outcomes and to track the degree to which those predictors explain variance in the level-2 outcomes, In this model, a grand-mean centering option was used and variables were added by one at a time for model building while examining their coefficient for significance (of random effect) and reliability.
19. In the cross-level interaction model, an interaction is when the association between level-1 predictors and the outcome variables depend on the level of level-2 predictors. The cross-level interaction will be between the level-1 random effect and the level-2 predictors in the slope outcome model.
20. That is, mentoring programs in state agencies positively and significantly increase the mean levels of job involvement and perceived organizational effectiveness (i.e. grand mean of the outcome variables) by 0.347 and 0.694, respectively, whereas mentoring programs significantly lower perceived organizational red tape by 0.261.
21. Before moving forward to the analysis, we conducted a preliminary analysis to test the seriousness of the common method bias. One limitation of this research is that

both independent and dependent variables come from a single data source, the NASP III manager survey. By running a principal component factor analysis for all variables included in the model, Harman's single-factor test indicates the seriousness of the bias: one can claim the bias is serious when only one factor is retained and it explains most of the covariance. The principal component factor analysis indicates that several factors are retained and the biggest factor explains 34% of the covariance, which implies that the bias is not very serious in this case. In addition, in order to minimize the common source bias, we measured the data at the two different levels - individual and organizational levels. For example, demographic controls and motivation variables were measured at the individual level (level 1) and organizational communication and mentoring variables were estimated at the organizational level (level 2). That is, although still using data from a same source, we changed the unit of analysis and tried to minimize the bias using HLM which can take into account the interdependence of individual-level observations nested within higher-level (i.e. agency-level) state agencies; hence, we can correct estimates of standard errors using HLM.

References

Adler, P. S., & Borys, B. (1996). Two types of bureaucracy: Enabling and coercive, *Administrative Science Quarterly, 41,* 61-89.

Andersen, L. B. (2009). What determines the behaviour and performance of health professionals? Public service motivation, professional norms and/or economic iccentives. *International Review of Administrative Sciences, 75*(1). 79-97.

Balkundi, P., & Harrison, D. A. (2006). Ties, leaders, and time in teams: Strong inference about network structure's effects on team viability and performance. *Academy of Management Journal, 49*(1). 49-68.

Berman, E. M. (2006). *Essential statistics for public managers and policy analysts.* Washington, DC: CQ Press.

Blau, J. R., & Alba, R. D. (1982). Empowering nets of participation. *Administrative Science Quarterly, 27,* 363-379.

Bozeman, B. (1993). A theory of government "Red tape". *Journal of Public Administration, 3(3), 273-304.*

Bozeman, B. (2000). *Bureaucracy and red tape.* Upper Saddle River, NJ: Prentice Hall.

Bozeman, B., & Feeney, M. K. (2009). Public management mentoring: What affects outcomes?. *Journal of Public Administration Research and Theory, 19*(2). 427-452.

Bozeman, B., & Rainey, H. G. (2000). Comparing public and private organizations: Empirical research and the power of a priori. *Journal of Public Administration Research and*

Theory, 10(2). 447-469.

Brass, D. J. (1984). Being in the right place: A structural analysis of individual influence in an organization. *Administrative Science Quarterly, 29,* 518-539.

Brewer, G. A. (2008). Employee and organizational performance. In J. L. Perry & A. Hondeghem (Eds.), *Motivation in public management: The call of public service* (pp. 136-155). Oxford: Oxford University Press.

Brewer, G. A., & Selden, S. C. (1998). Whistleblowers in the federal civil service: New evidence of the public service ethic. *Journal of Public Administration Research and Theory, 8*(3), 413-439.

Brewer, G. A., & Selden, S. C. (2000). Why elephants gallop: Assessing and predicting organizational performance in federal agencies. *Journal of Public Administration Research and Theory, 10*(4), 685-711.

Buelens, M., & Broeck, H. (2007). An analysis of differences in work motivation between public and private sector organizations. *Public Administration Review, 67*(1), 65-74.

Cameron, J., & Pierce, W. D. (2002). *Rewards and intrinsic motivation: Resolving the controversy.* Westport, CT: Bergin and Garvey.

Castaing, S. (2006). The effects of psychological contract fulfillment and public service motivation on organizational commitment in the French civil service. *Public Policy and Administration, 21*(1), 84-98.

Cerase, F., & Farinella, D. (2006). *Exploration in public service motivation: The case of the Italian revenue service.* Paper presented at the annual European Group of Public Administration Conference.

Coleman, J. S. (1990). *Foundations of social theory.* Cambridge, MA: Harvard University Press.

Crampton, S. M., & Wagner, J. A. III. (1994). Percept-percept inflation in micro-organizational research: An investigation of prevalence and effect. *Journal of Applied Psychology, 79,* 67-76.

Crewson, P. E. (1997). Public service motivation: Building empirical evidence of incidence and effect. *Journal of Public Administration Research and Theory, 4,* 499-518.

Crossan, M. L., Lane, H., White, R., & Djurfeldt, L. (1995). Organizational learning: dimensions for a theory. *The International Journal of Organizational Analysis, 3*(4), 337-360.

Deci, E. L. (1971). Effects of externally mediated rewards on intrinsic motivation. *Journal of Personality and Social Psychology, 18,* 105-115.

Deci, E. L., & Ryan, R. M. (1985). *Intrinsic motivation and self-determination in human behavior.* New York: Plenum Press.

Dehart-Davis, L. (2009). Green tape: A theory of effective organizational rules. *Journal of Public Administration Research and Theory, 19*(2), 361-384.

Dehart-Davis, L., & Pandey, S. K. (2005). Red tape and public employees: Does perceived rule dysfunction alienate managers?. *Journal of Public Administration Research and Theory, 15,* 133-148.

Downs, A. (1967). *Inside bureaucracy.* Boston: Little, Brown.

Dreher, G. F., & Ash, R. A. (1990). A comparative study of mentoring among men and women in managerial, professional, and technical positions. *Journal of Applied Psychology, 75,* 539-546.

Feeney, M. K., & Rainey, H. G. (2009). *Personnel flexibility and red tape in public and nonprofit organizations.* Working paper, department of public administration, University of Illinois at Chicago.

Feldman, D. C. (1976). A contingency theory of socialization. *Administrative Science Quarterly, 21,* 433-452.

Feldman, D. C. (1981). The multiple socialization of organization members. *Academy of Management Review, 6,* 309-319.

Gagne, M., & Deci, E. L. (2005). Self-determination theory and work motivation. *Journal of Organizational Behavior, 26,* 331-362.

Garnett, J. L. (1992). *Communicating for results in government: A strategic approach for public managers.* San Francisco: Jossey-Bass.

Garnett, J. L., Marlowe, J., & Pandey, S. K. (2008). Penetrating the performance predicament: Communication as a mediator or moderator of organizational culture's impact on public organizational performance. *Public Administration Review, 68*(2), 266-281.

Hackman, J. R., & Oldham, G. R. (1980). *Work redesign.* MA: Addison-Wesley.

Heider, F. (1958). *The psychology of interpersonal relations.* New York: Wiley.

Houston, D. J. (2000). Public-service motivation: A multivariate test. *Journal of Public Administration Research and Theory, 10,* 713-727.

Houston, D. J. (2005). Walking the walk of public service motivation: Public employees and charitable gifts of time, blood, and money. *Journal of Public Administration Research and Theory, 16,* 67-86.

Houston, D. J. (2008). Behavior in the public square. In J. L. Perry & A. Hondeghem (Eds.), *Motivation in public management: The call of public service* (pp. 177-199). Oxford: Oxford University Press.

Kanungo, R. N. (1982a). Measurement of Job and work involvement. *Journal of Applied Psychology, 67,* 341-349.

Kanungo, R. N. (1982b). *Work alienation: An integrative approach.* New York: Praeger.

Kim, S. M. (2005). Individual-level factors and organizational performance in government organizations. *Journal of Public Administration Research and Theory, 15*(2), 245-261.

Kogut, B., & Zander, U. (1996). What do firms do? Coordination, identity, and learning. *Organization Science, 7*(4), 502-518.

Kohn, A. (1993). *Punished by rewards: The trouble with gold stars, inventive plans, A's praise, and other bribes.* Boston: Houghton Mifflin.

Kram, K. E. (1985). *Mentoring at work: Developmental relationships in organizational life.* Glenview, IL: Scott, Foresman.

Leana, C. R., & Pil, F. K. (2006). Social capital and organizational performance: Evidence from urban public schools. *Organization Science, 17*(3), 353-366.

Leonard, D., & Sensiper, S. (1998). The role of tacit knowledge in group innovation. *California Management Review, 40*(3), 112-132.

Lepper, M. R., & Greene, D. (1975). Turning play into work: Effects of adult surveillance and extrinsic rewards on children's intrinsic motivation. *Journal of Personality and Social Psychology, 31,* 479-486.

Levinthal, D. A., and March, J. G. (1993). The myopia of learning. *Strategic Management Journal, 14,* 95-112.

Lewis, G. B., & Frank, S. A. (2002). Who wants to work for the government?. *Public Administration Review, 62*(4), 395-404.

Light, P. C. (2002). The content of their character: The state of the nonprofit workforce, The *Nonprofit Quarterly, 9*(3), 6-16.

Louis, M. R. (1980). Surprise and sense making: What newcomer experience in entering unfamiliar organizational settings. *Administrative Science Quarterly, 25,* 226-251.

Manolopoulos, D. (2008). Work motivation in the hellenic extended public sector: An empirical investigation. *The International Journal of Human Resource Management, 19*(9), 1738-1762.

Monge, P. R., Heiss, B., & Margolin, D. (2008). The ecology of communication networks in organizational communities. *Communication Theory, 18,* 449-477.

Moon, M. J. (2000). Organizational commitment revisited in new public management: Motivation, organizational culture, sector, and managerial level. *Public Performance and Management Review, 24*(2), 177-194.

Moynihan, D. P. (2008). The normative model in decline? Public service motivation in the age of governance. In J. L. Perry & A, Hondeghem (Eds.), *Motivation in Public management: The call of public service* (pp. 247-267). Oxford: Oxford University Press.

Moynihan, D. P., & Pandey, S. J. (2007). Finding workable levers over work motivation: Comparing job satisfaction, job involvement, and organizational commitment. *Administration & Society, 39*(7), 803-832.

Naff, K. C., & Crum, J. (1999). Working for america: Does public service motivation make a difference?. *Review of Public Personnel Administration, 19*(4), 5-16.

Paarlberg, L. E., Perry, J. L., & Hondeghem, A. (2008). From theory to practice: Strategies for applying public service motivation. In J. L. Perry & A, Hondeghem (Eds.), *Motivation in Public management: The call of public service* (pp. 268-293). Oxford:

Oxford University Press.

Pandey, S. K., & Garnett, J. L. (2006). Exploring public sector communication performance: Testing a model and drawing implications. *Public Administration Review, 66*(1), 38-52.

Pandey, S. K., & Rainey, H. G. (2006). Public managers perceptions of organizational goal ambiguity: Analyzing alternative models. *International Public Management Journal, 9,* 85-112.

Pandey, S. K., & Stazyk, E. C. (2008). Antecedents and correlates of public service motivation. In J. L. Perry & A, Hondeghem (Eds.), *Motivation in Public management: The call of public service* (pp. 80-98). Oxford: Oxford University Press.

Pandey, S. K., & Welch, E. (2005). Beyond stereotypes: A multistage model of managerial perceptions of red tape. *Administration and Society, 37,* 542-575.

Park, S. M. (2010). The effects of personnel reform systems on Georgia state employees' attitudes: An empirical analysis from a principal-agent theoretical perspective. *Public Management Review, 12*(3), 403-437.

Park, S. M., & Rainey, H. G. (2007). Antecedents, mediators, and consequences of affective, normative, and continuance commitment: Empirical tests of commitment effects in federal agencies. *Review of Public Personnel Administration, 27*(3), 197-226.

Park, S. M., & Rainey, H. G. (2008). Leadership and public service motivation in U.S. federal agencies. *International Public Management Journal, 11*(1), 109-142.

Pedhazur, E. J. (1997). Multiple regression in behavioral research: Explanation and prediction (3rd ed.). Fort Worth: Harcourt Brace Jovanovich.

Perry, J. L., & Hondeghem, A. (2008). Editors' Introduction. In J. L. Perry & A, Hondeghem (Eds.), *Motivation in Public management: The call of public service* (pp. 268-269). Oxford: Oxford University Press.

Perry, J. L., & Wise, L. R. (1990). The motivational bases of public service, *Public Administration Review, 50*(3), 367-373.

Perry, J. L., Mesch, D., & Paarlberg, L. (2006). Motivating employees in a new governance era: The performance paradigm revisited. *Public Administration Review, 66*(4), 505-514.

Podsakoff, P. M., & Organ, D. W. (1986). Self reports in organizational research: Problems and prospects. *Journal of Management, 12,* 531-544.

Porter, L. W., & Miles, R. E. (1974). Motivation and management. In J. W. McGuire (Ed.),, *Contemporary management: Issues and viewpoints.* Englewood Cliffs,(pp. 545-570) NJ: Prentice-Hall.

Pugh, D. S., Hickson, D. J., Hinings, C. R., & Tuner, C. (1968). Dimensions of organizational structure. *Administrative Science Quarterly, 13*(1), 65-105.

Putnam, R. (2000). Bowling alone: The collapse and revival of american community, New York: Simon and Schuster.

Ragins, B. R., Cotton, J. L., & Miller, J. S. (2000). Marginal mentoring: The effects of type of mentor, quality of relationship, and program design on work and career attitudes. *Academy of Management Journal, 43*(6), 1177-1194

Rainey, H. G. (2003). *Understanding and managing public organizations* (3rd ed.). San Francisco, CA: Jossey-Bass.

Rainey, H. G., and Steinbauer, P. (1999). Galloping elephants: Development elements of a theory of effective government organizations. *Journal of Public Administration Research and Theory, 9*(1), 1-32.

Rainey, H. G., Pandey, S. K., & Bozeman, B. (1995). Research note: Public and private managers' perceptions of red tape,' *Public Administration Review, 55*(6), 567-574.

Raudenbush, S. W., Bryk, A. S., Cheong, Y., & Congdon, R. T. (2000). *HLM 5: Hierarchical linear and non-Linear modeling.* Chicago: Scientific Software International.

Ritz, A. (2009). Public service motivation and organizational performance in Swiss federal government. *International Review of Administrative Sciences, 75*(1), 53-78.

Robbins, S. (2003). *Organizational behavior.* Upper Saddle River, NJ: Prentice Hall.

Roth, P. L. (1994). Missing data: A conceptual review for applied psychologists, *Personnel Psychology, 47,* 537-560.

Ryan, R. M., & Connell, J. P. (1989). Perceived locus of causality and internalization, *Journal of Personality and Social Psychology, 57,* 749-761.

Ryan, R. M., & Deci, E. L. (2000a). Intrinsic and extrinsic motivations: Classic definitions and new directions. *Contemporary Educational Psychology, 25,* 54-67.

Ryan, R. M., & Deci, E. L. (2000b). Self-determination theory and the facilitation of intrinsic motivation, social development, and well-being. *American Psychologist, 55*(1), 68-78.

Saleh, S. D., & Hosek, J. (1976). Job involvement: Concepts and measurements. *Academy of Management Journal, 19,* 213-224.

Scott, P. G., & Pandey, S. K. (2005). Red tape and public service motivation. *Review of Public Personnel Administration, 25*(2), 155-180.

Seibert, S. E., Kraimer, M. L., & Liden, R. C. (2001). A social capital theory of career success. *Academy of Management Journal, 44*(2), 219-237.

Spreitzer, G. M. (1996). Social structural characteristics of psychological empowerment. *Academy of Management Journal, 38,* 1191-1205.

Steijn, A. J. (2006). Carrie´rejager of dienaar van de publieke zaak. *Over ambtenaren en hun motivatie* (2006, september 22). Rotterdam: Erasmus Universiteit. Oratie.

Taylor, J. (2007). The impact of public service motives on work outcomes in Australia: A comparative multi-dimensional analysis. *Public Administration, 85*(4), 931-959.

Vallerand, R. J. (1997). Toward a hierarchical model of intrinsic and extrinsic motivation. In M. P. Zanna (Ed.), *Advances in experimental social psychology* (Vol. 29, pp. 271-363). San Diego, CA: Academic Press.

Vance, R. (2006). *Employee engagement and commitment: A guide to understanding, measuring and increasing engagement in your organization.* Alexandria, VA: Society for Human Resource Management (SHRM Foundation).

Vandenabeele, W. (2007). Toward a public administration theory of public service motivation. *Public Management Review, 9*(4), 545-556.

Vandenabeele, W. (2009). The mediating effect of job satisfaction and organizational commitment on self-reported performance: More robust evidence of the PSM-performance relationship. *International Review of Administrative Sciences, 75*(1), 11-34.

Vandenabeele, W. (2011). Who wants to deliver public service? Do institutional antecedents of public service motivation provide an answer?. *Review of Public Personnel Administration, 31*(1), 87-107.

Vandenabeele, W., Scheepers, S., & Hondeghem, A. (2006). Public service motivation in an international comparative perspective: The UK and Germany. *Public Policy and Administration, 21*(1), 21-33.

Vandenabeele, W.,m & Hondeghem, A. (2004). 'L'appel de la fonction publique: la 'motivation deservice public' (public service motivation) en tant que facteur dcisif d'engagement dans la fonction publique, l're de la nouvelle gestion publique. *Revue Conomique et Social,* (dec). 91-102.

Whitener, E. M., Brodt, S. E., Korsgaard, M. A., & Werner, J. M. (1998). Managers as initiators of trust: An exchange relationship framework for understanding managerial trustworthy behavior. *Academy of Management Review, 23*(3), 513-530.

Wilson, J. A., & Elman, N. S. (1990). Organizational benefits of mentoring. *Academy of Management Executive, 4*(4), 88-94.

Wilson, P. A. (1999). A theory of power and politics and their effects on organizational commitment of senior executive service members. *Administration & Society, 31*(1), 120-141.

Word, J., & Park, S. M. (2009). Working across the divide: Job involvement in the public and nonprofit sectors. *Review of Public Personnel Administration, 29*(2), 103-133.

Chapter 12

The Effects of Personnel Reform Systems on Georgia State Employees' Attitudes

: An Empirical Analysis from a Principal-Agent Theoretical Perspective[1]

Summary

In order to maximize the value of human resources, today' reformers have abandoned traditional merit systems, calling instead for public personnel management systems based on a set of new principles known as managerialism. The study at hand, conceived within a principal-agent theoretical framework and using a confirmatory factor analysis (CFA), a hierarchical regression model and a structural equation model (SEM), probed four personnel reform effects in the state of Georgia: (1) a monetary incentive system (i.e. a merit pay system); (2) a performance monitoring system (i.e. a performance appraisal system); (3) a knowledge incentive system (i.e. a training and development system); and (3) a discretionary controlling system (i.e. an at-will system). The research findings indicate that all four personnel reform systems are directly and indirectly associated with organizational consequences. Among these effects, discretionary controlling and performance monitoring systems are most salient and are most effective at enhancing the level of an agent's work motivation and job satisfaction as well as decreasing their turnover intentions. Implications and limitations of this research are also discussed.

Keyword

- □ Civil Service Reform in the USA
- □ Expectancy Theory
- □ Goal-Setting Theory
- □ Job and Work Attitudes
- □ Managerial Reform
- □ New Public Management (NPM)
- □ Organizational Behavior
- □ Principal-Agent Theory
- □ Public Human Resources Management

Sung Min Park Associate Professor, Sungkyunkwan University

Points for Practitioners

This article suggests several managerial strategies which managers or supervisors in the public sector should consider. First, the use of a well-established merit pay system, which links individual employee performance ratings to annual salary increases and differently rewards higher and lower levels of employees' performance, could encourage poor performers to improve their work productivity in public organizations.

Second, the decentralization of personnel management systems giving the greater discretion to agencies and supervisors (i.e. principals) could be used to create an organizational environment which promotes managerial flexibility in public organizations, thereby effectively dealing with public human resources (i.e. agents). Finally, we can conclude that objective performance appraisal systems directly or indirectly play a critical role in enhancing certain types of job and work attitudes as well as increasing an agent's job performance and organizational effectiveness.

Introduction

In the United States, reform efforts aimed at improving the economy and efficiency of government operations have been made with relative frequency and regularity. The initial event that sparked public human resource management reform was the Pendleton Act of 1883, which depoliticized civil service reform. This Act created a merit system, tenure, examinations, and a neutral administrative structure (Ingraham et al. 2001). The administrative reform proposals generally assume that government administrative structure, culture, and procedures are hierarchical and inflexible, as well as unresponsive to stakeholders and to administrative and political leadership. Public personnel systems and practices are sometimes maligned as inferior to the private ones and are regarded as ineffective for increasing the organizational productivity and performance. While the logic of public personnel reforms has been driven by different philosophical sub-components such as managerial, political, or technical reasons, the main purposes of personnel reform in the government are to enhance the level of public managers' job flexibility, managerial empowerment, and work motivation, as well as to make public agencies more business-like and hence more productive organizations using market-friendly strategies (Kellough & Nigro 2006).

During the past two decades, extensive managerial reforms have challenged public management by relying on private sector innovation, which has long been regarded as more effective, efficient, and accountable in the delivery of public services.[2] Instead of continuing the traditional merit systems, today's public sector reformers seek alternative strategies for maximizing the values of human resources (HR), calling for new public personnel management (NPPM) systems based on selected principles derived from business practices (e.g. privatization and marketization), often requiring managers to be more entrepreneurial with greater freedom from political control and oversight, and newly emphasizing the values of flexibility, discretion, and performance (Pollitt 1993; Terry 1998; Gossett 2002). The focus of the civil service has shifted more toward managerial values, including 'efficiency and cost effectiveness of the personnel system itself and strategic HR management in support of the agency's mission and goals' (Ban & Riccucci 2002: 6). More specifically, reformers have advocated such changes as the substantial decentralization of authority for personnel functions, the contracting out of numerous personnel management tasks, the establishment of a broader band pay system and at-will employment system, the movement of labor–management cooperation and participative decision making, and an increased focus on workforce planning and strategic management (Kellough & Selden 2003).

According to Larry Terry (1998), there are four approaches to the generic management field: quantitative/analytical management; political management; liberation management; and market-driven management. He grouped the latter two managerial styles into a broad category of 'neo-managerialism' (Terry 1998). The 'managerialist reforms' and the reinvention movement approaches are called upon as the most distinguished and pervasive values. Pollitt (1993) also describes managerialism as an ideology with two important components: first, that the goals of government can best be accomplished by 'continuing increases in economically defined productivity'; and second, that 'managers are critical to improving productivity and, therefore, must be given the right to manage' (1993: 2–). In this regard, strengthening the power of line managers to deal with classification and compensation, hiring, affirmative action, and employee grievances is consistent with 'managerialist ideology' (Gossett 2002). Managerialism also assumes that business strategies and processes are easily transferable to government sectors and that it is desirable to bring about such a transfer (West 2002: 83). Hood (1995: 94) argues that New Public Management (NPM) and the National Performance Review (NPR) have moved away from traditional approaches of legitimizing the public bureaucracy, such as procedural rigidity on administrative discretion, in favor of 'trust in the market and private business methods and ideas incumbent in the language of economic rationalism'.

King & Stivers (1998: 57) proposed that one of the results of customer and marketoriented reform in the United States would be as follows: 'Seeing citizens as consumers, taxpayers, and customers, and encouraging them to see themselves that way, leads people to evaluate government according to what each individual receives rather than what the community as a whole receives'. That is, the administrative management paradigm has been regarded as a response to the entrepreneurial or market-oriented management paradigm which identifies private sector innovation strategies as an important means for enhancing quality and accountability of public sector service in the long run (Moe 1991). Moreover, with these managerial ideas, public employees, instead of being controlled by a series of general rules and regulations, are now often employed on individualized contracts with very different expectations and rewards. For example, deregulation -that is, reducing rules and other formal constraints, decentralizing hierarchical authority, and enhancing the discretion of managers -can also be addressed for reform initiatives. With well-developed information technology skills, reformers can begin to delegate greater autonomy to managers, increase the attention to performance and productivity, and incur greater flexibility in human resource management (HRM).

Recent Trends in Civil Service Reform in the USA : The State of Georgia Case

Most of the public management reform cases in the developed and market economy countries (the USA, Western Europe, and New Zealand, for example) were mainly adopted and implemented by a 'top-down' rather than by a 'bottom-up' approach from a 'strategic decision-making' perspective (Pollitt & Bouckaert 2004: 26, 184). This top-down reform strategy allows 'elite decision-makers' to have more discretion and authority in their choices of means and methods for public management reform (Pollitt & Bouckaert 2004: 26). The Georgia civil service reform, for example, was initiated by former Governor Zell Miller and the Georgia General Assembly, who had the strong political will to radically reform the entire Georgia civil service system.[3]

Before implementing dramatic civil service reform, the state of Georgia had a traditional and rigid centralized personnel system, originally designed to secure the values of merit, political responsiveness, and social equity within legal-bureaucratic public administration arrangements (West 2002). In 1996, for the purpose of transforming the entire state human resources management systems and policies, the state of Georgia launched two major reform initiatives of its personnel system: (1) the GeorgiaGain program; and (2) the Civil Service Reform Law (Act 816). The GeorgiaGain program was implemented in 1995-6 and involved such changes as reforming the employee performance evaluation processes, implementing a new wage and salary structure, developing new training and development practices, and designing the current pay-for-performance system (Kellough & Nigro 2002, 2006). Act 816 in 1996 stipulated that all state employees hired or promoted after 1 July 1996, be at-will or unclassified in their positions, which means that those at-will employees have neither property interest in their employment nor a right to due process protections regarding dismissal, grievance, or appeals procedures.

Georgia's 1996 civil service reform, with a focus on reform results (e.g. increasing performance) rather than implementation processes, tried to remove long-standing civil service job protection and procedural due process rights for new job hires; furthermore, to restructure public managerial functions and ultimately to ensure efficient organizational systems, reformers pursued deregulation, decentralization, and market-oriented initiatives through the process of privatization (West 2002). The new goals and objectives in the reform agenda were to create performance- and mission-oriented cultures and privatized organizational systems that emphasize increased managerial flexibility through streamlining HRM processes and reducing red tape, focusing on efficiency and cost effectiveness in the use of human and financial resources in state agencies.

Reformers in Georgia also sought to achieve these goals by enhancing line agency managers' flexibility, streamlining adverse action procedures, decentralizing and simplifying merit system operations, and realigning the role of the central personnel department. For that reason, many substantial functions and roles were required to be decentralized, forcing the role of the Georgia merit system to change from one of regulator to that of agency partner or consultant, instituting 'at-will' or 'unclassified' employment status for new hires to minimize the procedural barriers in terminating unsatisfactory employees. The purported advantages, such as better customer service, less bureaucracy, employee empowerment, and enhanced motivation and performance, have been expected from the reforms in Georgia.

Overall, there are a few key characteristics common among personnel management reform initiatives, especially at the state level in the United States. First, we can observe an abrupt shift among three values –'representativeness, neutral competence, executive leadership –that traditionally have characterized public service practices' (Bowman et al. 2003: 286). The concept of the merit system, which protects employees from political attack, was replaced in several state agencies (e.g. Georgia and Florida civil service positions) with employment at-will, a doctrine that 'allows termination of workers for no reason or any reason not contrary to law' (Muhl 2001; Bowman et al. 2003: 287). Second, a more unbiased and accurate performance monitoring system, which is tied to job-related performance standards, was required to increase employees' job motivation or organizational effectiveness. Third, reformers contended that the states' human resource systems needed to absorb the idea that government should be operated entrepreneurially and that state employees' pay increases should be associated with their performance and productivity. Finally, in order to meet a more competitive and market-oriented working environment, state employees have requested adequate resources and training opportunities for their career development and knowledge advancement.

Based upon these philosophical and practical reform rationales with the administrative, political, and legislative supports from Georgia state government, four distinct personnel reform systems were developed in the state of Georgia: (1) a monetary incentive system (i.e. a merit pay system); (2) a performance monitoring system (i.e. a job performance appraisal system); (3) a knowledge incentive system (i.e. a knowledge management and training system); and (4) a discretionary controlling system (i.e. an at-will employment system). These reform rationales, which borrowed from a principal-agent theoretical approach, mainly intend to deregulate and decentralize the traditional civil service structures and procedures.

A Theoretical Framework: The Principal-Agent Theory

Principals, Agents, and Reform Systems

The principal-agent theory (sometimes called agency theory) can be applied to different organizational or socio-economic contexts such as employer-employee, lawyer-client, buyer-supplier, and other dyadic relationships (Harris & Raviv 1978). Agency theorists describe the structuring of hierarchical economic exchange relationships between two relevant parties that are governed by a formal or informal contract and transaction (Jensen & Meckling 1976; Eisenhardt 1989; Noorderhaven 1992). With respect to theoretical contribution and leverage in the fields of public administration or management, agency theory has explicitly supported the logic of making a distinction between politics and administration while discussing the problems of political control and delegation in organizations. The principal-agent model (or paradigm) is considered one of the traditional theoretical approaches to public personnel management reforms which contributed to 'offering a coherent framework for integrating both the bureaucratic and the political dimensions of administrative performance' (Moe 1984: 772). The principal-agent theory exhibits certain analytical strengths in understanding a variety of social, political, and institutional settings. Theoretically, it can explicate various organizational phenomena using only a relatively small number of concepts, and it can easily be formalized and generalized. From a practitioner's perspective, it offers many useful suggestions and implications because it considers 'ubiquitous compliance problems in various settings and in a dynamic process' (Eisenhardt 1989; Petersen 1993; Kim 1996: 122-3).

In a principal-agent relationship, especially within a political-bureaucratic context, high-level managers and political appointees assume the role of the principals, whereas administrators and subordinate employees are regarded as the agents. Based on the market and rationality approaches, principal–agent theory posits that principals and agents are self-interested actors and rational utility maximizers with divergent interests and conflicting goals. The theory also suggests that two parties have a contractual and mutual relationship among organizational constituents structuring the relationship to secure and maintain their own interests, preferences, and goals.[4] As the agent performs tasks in the interests of the principal, agents generally take on more power and authority to access and hold the information than their principals have regarding the individual and organizational task and environment at hand. This information discrepancy can be called information asymmetry, a source of conflict in the principal–agent relationship. In this situation, agents try to maximize their own discretion, utility, and power by increasing discretionary budgets as well as pursuing rational or self-interests rather than ensuring public and community interests. Accordingly, it is necessary for elected officials to maintain political control over employees so that they do not deviate from elected officials' political intentions, hence ensuring the will of the people and improving political responsiveness (Selden et al. 1999: 126).

Adverse selection refers to the misrepresentation of ability by the agent during the employee selection and hiring process (Eisenhardt 1989). That is, when principals do not know exactly the new employees' ability, skills, and work experience, or when the principal is less informed of the agent's willingness to perform their jobs, adverse selection problems arise. To control and reduce this adverse selection problem, hence, how to minimize information asymmetry of hidden action matters. Even after being hired, given the self-interested or rational nature of an agent, employees may cause moral hazard problems (i.e. agent opportunism) by shirking responsibilities (Eisenhardt 1989). They might not perform in the principal's interest, showing red tape behaviors and bureaucratic inertia as well as neglecting their own performance.

Within the manager–employee dyads, the main concerns of agency theory are as follows: (1) how to select and hire reliable agents without full knowledge of the agents' ability, intentions, and dedication to their jobs and organization; and (2) how to arrange an incentive and compensation design, to monitor and appraise the performance of an agent to minimize agency risk, and to ensure the principal's interest and contract compliance. In this principal–agent personnel system and module, different sets of incentive, reward, and controlling schemes are necessary. That is, in order to change and correct the problems outlined above and to minimize agency risk engendered by a contractual relationship, several remedies are suggested: (1) 'making an agent reveal his ability and knowledge'(known as signaling); (2) 'providing the agent with incentives to reveal his ability and knowledge' (also called screening); and (3) 'making use of the reputation of the agent' (Milgrom & Roberts 1992).

More specifically, according to principal–agent theorists, these problems can be decreased by: (1) controlling and monitoring agent behaviors as well as hiring multiple agents to facilitate mutual competition; (2) establishing an information-sharing culture and a knowledge (information) incentive and management system; or (3) designing and providing agents with monetary incentives and compensation compatible with the interests of the principal (e.g. a merit-pay system). Much of the previous principal–agent theory literature focuses on attempts to investigate the theoretical efficacy and practical applications of such incentive and controlling systems in organizations (see, for example, Eisenhardt 1988, 1989; Conlon & Parks 1990; Harrison & Harrell 1993; Abrahamson & Park 1994). Drawing on these theoretical arguments, this study includes four independent variables: (1) a monetary incentive system; (2) a knowledge incentive system; (3) a controlling system for agents' behaviors and attitudes; and (4) a monitoring and appraisal system for employees' job performance.

Work Motivation, Job Satisfaction, and Turnover Intentions

Work motivation, job satisfaction, and turnover intentions of employees are important individual-level job attitudes that can be highly correlated with organizational performance outcomes in certain ways. Prior research has also focused on identifying the relationships among these characteristics in public agencies (see, for example, Naff & Crum 1999; Bright 2008) while investigating the causal effects of these job attitudes on employee and organizational performance and effectiveness (see, for example, Mann 2006; Park & Rainey 2008). For public managers, it is crucial to create, manage, and develop effective and reliable HR management systems and strategies for the purpose of increasing work motivation and job satisfaction as well as limiting public employees' intentions to quit.

Research evidence suggests that work motivation is a multilateral concept that 'captures the psychological forces that direct, energize, and maintain action' (Grant 2008: 50). Work motivation in public service can be assessed as an outcome of specific management practices and a predictor of certain job attitudes and behaviors such as job satisfaction and turnover intentions (Perry et al. 2008; Word & Park 2009). Job satisfaction and turnover intentions which are distinct from work motivation and job performance represent 'the degree(s) to which employees' salient needs are satisfied by their needs' (Bright 2008: 150) based on 'an interaction between employees and their work environment' (Wright & Kim 2004: 19). Reviews of recent research on organizational behavior (OB) suggest that job satisfaction is negatively associated with turnover and turnover intentions in public organizations (see, for example, Rainey 2003; Miner 2005; Moynihan & Pandey 2007; Park & Rainey 2008).

Personnel Reform Systems and Individual Outcomes

Rainey & Steinbauer's (1999: 27) organizational effectiveness framework suggests that using institutional arrangements in public agencies such as incentive, monitoring, and disciplinary controlling HR systems can lead to a higher level of work motivation and organizational effectiveness 'where organizational and task design produces desirable levels of extrinsic and intrinsic rewards through tasks'. In Georgia state agencies, employees (as bureaucratic agents) and managers and elected leaders (as principals) have different goals, roles, and interests, which may lead to a state of conflict in government.[5] Principal–agent theorists hold that these agent problems can be decreased and, hence, organizational effectiveness will be enhanced by providing and maximizing formal rules, incentives, and controlling and monitoring mechanisms. That is, in the principal–agent reciprocal (and sometimes contractual) relationship, incentive, monitoring, and controlling reform systems which align the agent's preferences with the principal's interests are designed to increase individual motivation and satisfaction as well as to minimize employees' negative job attitudes, for example, turnover intentions.

First, it is hypothesized that monetary incentive structures (e.g. a pay-for-performance system) can be an effective tool to increase work motivation and job satisfaction as well as to decrease turnover intentions of employees, that is, agents. Financial incentives are important motivational tools for public employees and the design of the pay-for-performance systems involves strategic choices for the organization in both structure and process. The strong theoretical support for merit pay is found in goal-setting theory and expectancy theory, which are foundational in virtually all monetary incentive policies. Goal-setting theory suggests that working to achieve high, well-specified, and self-accepted goals leads to high performance, which, in turn, triggers increased financial rewards, greater affective motivation, and stronger intrinsic job satisfaction (Locke & Latham 1990). Thus, monetary reward and incentive systems, which were designed as specific goals for agents, should reinforce goal attainment. In a goal-setting-attainment process, it is expected that providing desirable levels of monetary incentive systems, such as pay-for-performance plans through organizational and task designs, will bring positive job attitudes in public organizations (Rainey & Steinbauer 1999). Expectancy theory also supports pay-for-performance models by recognizing that agents' work efforts depend on how they expect to be compensated and rewarded. That is, combinations of salary increases and other compensation rewards encourage employees to expect that increased performance will ultimately be rewarded (Vroom 1964).

The performance monitoring systems consist of several managerial processes such as establishing performance standards, communicating standards and expectations, measuring the actual performance of agents, comparing with standards, evaluating results and providing feedback, and taking corrective actions based on a principal's decision making. The evaluation criteria typically include agents' activities, behavior, and personality traits which predict task and contextual performance. Performance monitoring systems should directly or indirectly affect several job attitudes. Determining how to establish, implement, and administer a performance evaluation plan is critical to the success of the system, the performance of the agents, and the overall performance of the organization. Building further on goal-setting and expectancy theories, this study hypothesizes that performance monitoring systems within a principal–agent dyad can motivate agents, increase job satisfaction, and decrease turnover intentions, especially when agents trust principals and agents perceive the appraisal rating process as objective and unbiased (i.e. valid and reliable) (Milkovich & Wigdor 1991; Park & Rainey 2007).[6]

Equity theory (Adams 1965) suggests that agent job attitudes and work efforts are affected by their view of how other employees are compensated. That is, they tend to compare their input–outcome ratio with that of colleagues and if they sense a disparity in the ratio, they will try to correct in order to feel rewarded fairly for their contribution. Discretionary controlling systems based on Act 816, which removed civil service job protections and created an at-will employment relationship, are expected to 'attract, select, and retain the best employees based on merit, with incentives in the form of equal opportunities for all which will provide technically competent and loyal personnel to render impartial service to the public; and which will eliminate unnecessary and inefficient performers', thereby reducing employees' perceived inequity (State of Georgia 1996: 684). Based on this perspective, this study hypothesizes that discretionary controlling systems will significantly affect agents' job attitudes, that is, work motivation, job satisfaction, and turnover intentions.

Finally, this study hypothesizes that knowledge incentive systems will be significantly associated with agents' motivation, job satisfaction, and turnover intentions. Knowledge incentive and management systems in the public sector have been popularly used to maximize the capacity of agencies by generating, accumulating, sharing, and communicating collective knowledge, practices, norms, and information.[7] In light of benefits of knowledge management activities within public organizations, knowledge incentive systems offer agents adequate resources and opportunities to enhance their skills and experience by providing employee teaching, training, and coaching programs, sharing principals' and agents' knowledge, thereby improving agents' performance and leading to better career development and to positive job attitudes (Cong & Pandya 2003).

Research Questions and Hypotheses

The main purpose of this study is to examine and test the empirical validity of agency theory in the public sector context (e.g. within US state agencies). Based on the theoretical framework described above, first, in order to probe and test the factor structure of these four personnel management reform systems and to assess the construct validity of the four latent variables - that is, a monetary incentive system, and a performance monitoring system, a discretionary (at-will) controlling system, and a knowledge incentive system –a confirmatory factor analysis (CFA) model was included. Using asymptotically distribution-free (ADF) techniques, the CFA model that comprised a second-order factor was examined.[8] The primary confirmatory research questions are whether principal–agent-based managerial systems could be explained by four first-order factors and one second-order factor, and whether these reform systems are conceptually distinct in the CFA model.

Research Question 1a: In a confirmatory factor analysis (CFA) model, are these four latent constructs of managerial reform systems in the state of Georgia explained by first- and second-order factors?

Research Question 1b: In a CFA model, are these four latent constructs of managerial reform systems in the state of Georgia conceptually distinct?

Second, a hierarchical multivariate regression analysis was employed to: (1) probe the effects of the three predetermined major sets of antecedent variables on three different outcomes - work motivation, job satisfaction, and turnover intentions; and (2) identify the most significant effects (ß) among antecedent variables and uncover the incremental explanatory power (ΔR^2). In the three consecutive steps: (a) personal (individual) characteristics (gender, age, ethnicity, and education level); (b) job characteristics (job tenure, position, and managerial power); and (c) the four managerial reform effects were sequentially included based on theoretical grounds (see, for example, Ting 1997; Steijn 2004; Steijn & Leisink 2006).[9] In the hierarchical regression model, this study suggested two exploratory research questions regarding control variables and five research hypotheses about four managerial reform systems, as outlined below. In sum, all three clusters (i.e. personal, job, and reform levels) will affect three outcome variables and will explain the total variances of these outcomes significantly.

Research Question 2a: Are personal characteristics positively or inversely related to the outcome variables? Do these personal characteristics jointly explain the total variances of these outcome variables significantly?

Research Question 2b: Are job characteristics positively or inversely related to the outcome variables? Do these job characteristics jointly explain the total variances of these outcome variables significantly?

Hypothesis 1a: A performance monitoring system will significantly and positively affect state employees' work motivation and job satisfaction while decreasing their turnover intentions.

Hypothesis 1b: A monetary incentive system will significantly and positively affect state employees'work motivation and job satisfaction while decreasing their turnover intentions.

Hypothesis 1c: A discretionary controlling system will significantly and positively affect state employees' work motivation and job satisfaction while decreasing their turnover intentions.

Hypothesis 1d: A knowledge incentive system will significantly and positively affect state employees' work motivation and job satisfaction while decreasing their turnover intentions.

Hypothesis 1e: Four personnel managerial reform systems will be jointly and significantly associated with outcome variables.

Third, in order to measure the total, direct, indirect, and spurious effects in the Georgia managerial reform model, a full structural equation model (SEM) was employed to examine and test four hypotheses -whether and how these four reform systems (exogenous variables) would directly or indirectly (and also positively or negatively) influence organizational outcomes (endogenous variables), as the SEM analysis allows for non-recursive paths and simultaneous tests of the relationships of the variables (Jöreskog & Sörbom 1996; Byrne 2001).

Hypothesis 2a: In a SEM, the greater the level of the four managerial reform system effects, the greater the likelihood that the level of state employees' work motivation will be enhanced.

Hypothesis 2b: In a SEM, the greater the level of the four managerial reform system effects, the greater the likelihood that the level of state employees' job satisfaction will increase.

Hypothesis 2c: In a SEM, the greater the level of the four managerial reform system effects, the greater the likelihood that the level of state employees' turnover intentions will decrease.

Hypothesis 2d: In a SEM, the greater the level of state employees' work motivation and job satisfaction, the greater the likelihood that the level of state employees' turnover intentions will decrease.

As suggested above, the main objectives of this study are to: (1) revisit the state managerial reform initiatives associated with a contractual framework among principals and agents; and (2) investigate and demonstrate the empirical validity of the theory with systematic and rigorous statistical tools -CFA, hierarchical multivariate regression, and SEM.

Research Methods

Data and Instrumentation

The survey instrument was prepared to measure state employees' perceptions about various aspects of the GeorgiaGain program and the Civil Service Reform Law (Act 816). Responses were measured on a six-point Likert scale ranging from (1) 'strongly disagree' to (6) 'strongly agree' with specific statements. From several relevant survey items, four managerial reform system scales and four organizational consequence scales were developed (see Appendix 1). Exploratory factor analysis (EFA) –that is, a principal axis factoring (PAF) and varimax rotation technique – was used to obtain factor extraction (using eigenvalues greater than 1.0) and composite factor scores of these variables (Wright 2004).[10] These techniques would enable us to extract communalities from different variables and to combine different variables into new variables.[11] To assess internal consistency and to ensure reliability of each scale, Cronbach's alpha reliability test was done. These relatively stable alpha values would indicate that test content is rather homogeneous and answers are consistent.[12]

Description of Data

Multivariate Normality

In this research, most items show a relatively stable and similar amount of variance. This suggests that items in this study do differentiate responses fairly well. In terms of individual normality, most items have a high positive kurtosis value, which means that most respondents have selected the same response option. Most variables of skewness or kurtosis are all between $-2<s(k)<2$, and we can argue that these variables are approximately normally distributed. Relative multivariate kurtosis (1.155<2.0) also indicates approximate multivariate normality.[13]

Missing Value Treatment

The listwise deletion method was used to deal with missing data. The total sample size of this study was 1,948 and the total effective sample size was 1,337. In listwise deletion, cases with a missing score on any variable are excluded from all analyses; thus, in this case, the effective sample size after listwise deletion included only cases with complete records. An advantage of this method was that all analyses were conducted with the same number of cases (Kline 2005).[14]

Measurement of Antecedent (Exogenous) Variables

Managerial Reform Systems (Main Variables)

The four antecedent variables should influence work motivation, job satisfaction, and turnover intentions. First, a monetary incentive system was measured by a four-item scale (Cronbach's alpha = .698) that asked whether state employees' pay was really related to performance and whether high-performing employees were consistently rewarded with pay increases. Second, to measure the degree of knowledge incentive system effects in Georgia state agencies (Cronbach's alpha = .809), a five-item scale (asking whether state employees were benefited by sufficient opportunities and resources for job training, career development, and coaching) was developed. Third, four survey items were operationalized and used to measure a discretionary (at-will) controlling system scale. In the survey, state employees were asked to indicate whether an agency had made good use of the greater discretion and whether an at-will employment system would help hire highly qualified people in a timely manner (Cronbach's alpha = .745). Fourth, a performance monitoring system variable was measured by six items from the survey (Cronbach's alpha = .837), asking whether performance ratings accurately reflected state employees' performance and whether performance appraisal discussions and evaluation feedback helped improve state employees' job performance (see Appendix 1).[15]

Personal and Job Characteristics (Control Variables)

In addition to these four main antecedents, eight variables measuring personal (demographic) and job characteristics of Georgia state employees were included as controls: gender; age; ethnicity; educational level; job tenure (years in the current position and the Georgia agency); position (classified/unclassified); and managerial power.[16] As previous organizational research (e.g. meta-analytic research) has suggested, it is expected that a set of control variables (personal and job characteristics) introduced in this study are associated with organizational outcome variables directly and indirectly (see Hackman & Oldham 1975).

Measurement of Outcome (Endogenous) Variables

In this study, three endogenous variables were developed as organizational consequences in Georgia state agencies: work motivation; job satisfaction; and turnover intentions (see Appendix 1). The first variable, 'work motivation', created by factor scores, included four items, all converged onto one factor (Cronbach's alpha = .702).[17] The second outcome variable, 'job satisfaction', was based on three relevant questions (Cronbach's alpha = .755). The third outcome variable, 'turnover intentions', was also measured by a factor analysis collapsing two questions into one factor index (Cronbach's alpha = .769). In hierarchical multivariate regression and a full structural equation model (SEM), the statistical effects among these antecedents and outcomes were examined with the expectation that there would be significant relationships among them.

Analyses and Results

This research employed three statistical methods. First, to find and confirm latent factor structures of four different reform systems from the survey questions, a confirmatory factor analysis (CFA) was used (Phase 1). Second, in order to find the most important antecedents among a set of clusters (i.e. personal and job characteristics and managerial reform systems) and variables, a multivariate hierarchical regression model was employed using the ordinary least squares (OLS) method (Phase 2). Third, in order to probe the total, direct, and indirect effects from four managerial reform systems, a full structural equation model (SEM) was employed (Phase 3). In this model, PRELIS 2.72 and LISREL 8.72 were used to test interrelationships among variables and assess the relative strength of each variable.

Estimation Methods

While an OLS estimation method was used in a hierarchical regression model, in CFA and SEM models, the maximum likelihood (ML) method was employed to estimate the personnel reform model. From multivariate normality tests, severe non-normality patterns are not observed and we can expect that the ML method in CFA and SEM would be more unbiased, consistent, and efficient, especially when the population distribution for the endogenous variables is multivariate normal (Kline 2005). Also, the covariance matrix was used as input to the LISREL 8.72 version to examine the four-factor measurement model (CFA) and full structural model (SEM).[18]

Phase 1: Testing the Measurement (CFA) Model

Fit Indexes for Four-Factor Measurement Models

In a second-order CFA model, a composite managerial reform system in Georgia was explained by four first-order factors and such fix indices as chi-square, Comparative Fit Index (CFI), Non-Normed Fit Index (NNFI), Normed Fit Index (NFI), Incremental Fit Index (IFI), Relative Fit Index (RFI) (five incremental indexes), as well as Root Mean Square Error of Approximation (RMSEA) and Standardized Root Mean Square Residual (SRMR).[19] The value of chi-square in the CFA model was 2,769.03 ($p<.05$). This value is significant and rejects the null hypothesis; thus, we can conclude that this model is not consistent with the data. Although this result might be viewed as disconfirmatory evidence, Jöreskog (1990) and others (e.g. Maruyama & McGarvey 1980) have warned that since the chisquare statistic is sensitive to sample size, the probability of rejecting a hypothesized model increases as N increases. Consequently, with large samples, virtually all models would be rejected as statistically untenable regardless of a good model fit (James et al. 1982; Kemery et al. 1985). From the results of CFI, NNFI, NFI, IFI, RFI, RMSEA, and SRMR values, these indices suggest that this model can be considered to fit well. Ultimately, in the measurement model, all but one of the fit indices show a good model of fit. RFI value stands as the lone exception. See Figure 1.

Parameter Values for Four-Factor Measurement Models

The results of R^2 values and standardized factor loadings indicate that a discretionary controlling system is most salient among personnel reform effects in Georgia. A personnel management reform which gives more discretion and flexibility to employees and removes the classified status and property interest in their jobs is the most outstanding factor in several personnel reform initiatives. In addition, from the t-tests (the critical value is ±2), we can observe that all indicators (19 items) have significant factor loadings on each of four first-order factors. That is, all factor loadings (parameter values) of these four latent variables are positive and significantly different from 0.

Phase 2: Test of the hierarchical regression model

In Phase 2, a hierarchical multivariate regression analysis was employed to uncover the most important antecedents. Three different equations of the personal, the job, and then the reform characteristics (i.e. steps 1, 2, and 3) were regressed on each of the three outcome variables. The main statistical results are reported in Tables 2 and 3. The main statistical results of correlation and regression models are reported in Tables 1, 2 and 3.

Figure 1. The Measurement Model: A Second-Order Confirmatory Factor Analysis (CFA)[a]

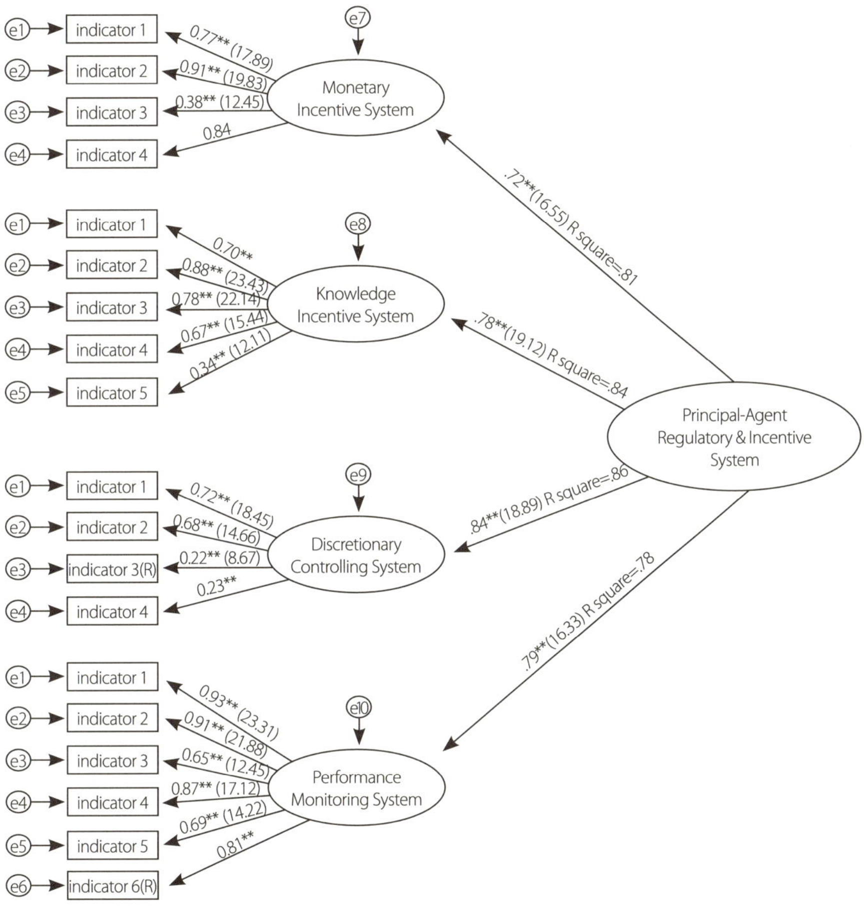

Overall Fit Indexes of the CFA model

Model 1	df	Chi-Square	CFI	NNFI	NFI	IFI	RFI	RMSEA	SRMR
Suggested cut-off values			>.95	>.95	>.95	>.95	>.95	<.08	<.08
A measurement model	436	2769.03	.96	.96	.96	.96	.95	.067	.057

Note: [a]Based on the WLS(ADF) method, all coefficients of the factor loadings (lambda-Ys and gammas) in this CFA model are standardized (t-statistics are in parentheses).

Table 1. Zero-Order Correlations among Antecedent, Control, and Consequent Variables in a Principal–Agent Model

Variables	1	2	3	4	5	6	7	8	9	10	11	12	13	14	15
1. Gender (1=Female)	1														
2. Age	-.035	1													
3. Ethnicity level (1= Minority)	.106**	-.133**	1												
4. Educational level	-.027	.082*	-.077*	1											
5. Job tenure 1 (current position)	-.092**	.331**	-.062	-.067*	1										
6. Job tenure 2 (Georgia agency)	-.010	.500**	-.159**	.054	.562**	1									
7. Position (1=Unclassified)	.053	-.186**	.064*	.123**	-.424**	-.429**	1								
8. Managerial oversight authority (1=More oversight power)	-.147**	.123**	-.062	.117**	-.025	.211**	-.035	1							
9. Discretionary controlling system	.077*	-.041	.150**	-.105**	-.087**	-.146**	.172**	-.057	1						
10. Performance monitoring system	.047	-.074*	.101**	-.022	-.152**	-.142**	.149**	.020	.408**	1					
11. Monetary incentive system	.008	-.004	.082*	-.084*	-.073*	-.040	.117**	.073*	.399**	.501**	1				
12. Knowledge incentive system	-.002	.001	.075*	-.090**	-.048	-.057	.073*	.117**	.447**	.575**	.476**	1			
13. Work motivation	.042	.105**	.009	.048	-.017	.024	.072*	.132**	.350**	.425**	.312**	.390**	1		
14. Job satisfaction	.017	.050	.006	-.088**	-.085**	-.080*	.081*	.072*	.348**	.474**	.388**	.404**	.514**	1	
15. Turnover intentions	-.026	-.196**	.127**	.048	-.137**	-.196**	.065*	-.029	-.166**	-.249**	-.243**	-.211**	-.329**	-.531**	1

**Correlation is significant at the .01 level (two-tailed).
*Correlation is significant at the .05-level (two-tailed).

Table 2. Results of Hierarchical Multivariate Regression Analysis: Work Motivation and Job Satisfaction Model

Variables	Work motivation model (N=1,170)			Job satisfaction model (N=1,184)		
	Step 1 (β)	Step 2 (β)	Step 3 (β)	Step 1 (β)	Step 2 (β)	Step 3 (β)
Step 1: Personal characteristics						
Gender	.052 (1.621)	.069* (2.119)	.047 (1.651)	.024 (.736)	.033 (1.032)	.015 (.536)
Age	.094** (2.889)	.109** (2.952)	.092** (2.862)	.048 (1.492)	.120** (3.257)	.099** (3.138)
Ethnicity (1=Minority)	.027 (.827)	.023 (.708)	-.034 (-1.208)	.013 (.413)	.001 (.043)	-.058* (-2.101)
Education level	.026 (.822)	.001 (.032)	.054 (1.892)	-.098** (-3.061)	-.118** (-3.680)	-.067* (-2.384)
Step 2: Job characteristics						
Job tenure 1 (current position)		.021 (.521)	.031 (.883)		-.037 (-.914)	-.020 (-.574)
Job tenure 2 (Georgia agency)		-.036 (-.802)	.007 (.178)		-.117** (-2.597)	-.079* (-2.018)
Position (0: Classified/1: Unclassified as at-will status)		.094* (2.561)	.024 (.735)		.059 (1.639)	-.010 (-.307)
Managerial oversight authority (1= More power)		.132** (3.910)	.089** (2.976)		.098** (2.936)	.049 (1.678)
Step 3: GA reform systems						
Discretionary controlling system			.180** (5.470)			.128** (4.031)
Performance monitoring system			.263** (7.265)			.289** (8.211)
Monetary incentive system			.046 (1.366)			.127** (3.862)
Knowledge incentive system			.144** (3.925)			.118** (3.335)
R^2	.012	.036	.273	.012	.042	.299
Adjusted R^2	.008	.028	.264	.008	.034	.290
ΔR^2		.024	.236		.030	.257
F statistics (F-ratio)	2.996*	4.535**	29.846**	2.982*	5.322**	34.503**

*p<.05: significant at the .05-level (two-tailed).
**p<.01: significant at the .01-level (two-tailed).

Table 3. Results of Hierarchical Multivariate Regression Analysis: Turnover Intentions Model

Variables	Turnover intentions model (N=1,188)		
	Step 1 (β)	Step 2 (β)	Step 3 (β)
Step 1: Personal characteristics			
Gender	-.046 (-1.460)	-.046 (-1.465)	-.032 (-1.076)
Age	-.189** (-6.028)	-.123** (-3.393)	-.113** (-3.293)
Ethnicity (1=Minority)	.104** (3.290)	.095** (2.999)	.132** (4.374)
Education level	.075* (2.398)	.076* (2.395)	.044 (1.441)
Step 2: Job characteristics			
Job tenure 1 (current position)		-.061 (-1.523)	-.073 (-1.936)
Job tenure 2 (Georgia agency)		-.109* (-2.463)	-.130** (-3.080)
Position (0: Classified/1: Unclassified as at-will status)		-.046 (-1.281)	.002 (.047)
Managerial oversight authority (1= More power)		-.002 (-.060)	.027 (.847)
Step 3: GA reform systems			
Discretionary controlling system			-.076* (-2.190)
Performance monitoring system			-.193** (-5.081)
Monetary incentive system			-.120** (-3.343)
Knowledge incentive system			-.029 (-.770)
R^2	.054	.068	.172
Adjusted R^2	.050	.060	.162
ΔR^2		.014	.104
F statistics (F-ratio)	13.999**	8.914**	16.882**

*p<.05: significant at the .05-level (two-tailed).
**<5.01: significant at the .01-level (two-tailed).

Work Motivation Model

First, regarding the Georgia state employees' work motivation, individual (personal) characteristics were regressed in the first step. The four individual characteristics accounted for about 1.2 percent of the total variance ($p<.05$). In the second step, the addition of the four job characteristic variables explained 3.6 percent of total variance in work motivation ($p<.01$). Most notably, managerial oversight authority (β = .132; $p<.01$) and position (β = .094; $p<.05$) significantly influenced the employees' motivation level. In the third step, when four personnel managerial reform variables were added, the total variance explained was significantly increased to 27.3 percent ($p<.01$). Except for a monetary incentive system, all reform effects are statistically significant ($p<.01$), suggesting the importance of the reform effects in increasing the Georgia state employees' work motivation.

Job Satisfaction Model

In the job satisfaction model, we observe a pattern similar to that of the motivation model. The four individual characteristics accounted for about 1.2 percent of the total variance ($p<.05$). In the second step, the addition of the four job characteristic variables explained 4.2 percent of total variance in work motivation ($p<.01$). In the third step, the four personnel managerial reform variables significantly improved the prediction above and beyond the personal and job characteristics (R^2 = .299, adjusted R^2 = .290), explaining an additional 25.7 percent of variance in job satisfaction at a highly significant level ($p<.01$). While all reform effects significantly contribute to Georgia state employees' job satisfaction ($p<.01$), from the standardized coefficients, we can confirm that a performance monitoring system is the most important and significant antecedent variable (β =.289), followed by a discretionary controlling system (β =.128).

Turnover Intentions Model

In step 3, the results indicate that the addition of the four reform-level variables led to a significant change ($p<.01$) of 10.4 percent in for turnover intentions. A performance monitoring system (β = −.193) appears to be far more important than other system variables, implying that for Georgia state employees the adoption of a well-managed performance monitoring system is the most effective way to reduce employees' desires to leave their jobs. In sum, all of the hierarchical regression model results confirm that, first, the four reform systems jointly and significantly increase the explanatory power of predicting the three outcome variables, suggesting the importance of managerial reform system effects in Georgia state agencies. Second, from the standardized coefficients, the results also clarify that, among these four reform effects, a discretionary controlling system and a performance monitoring system are the most influential and powerful antecedents of the outcome variables. [Confirmed Hypotheses 1a, 1b, 1c, 1d, and 1e]

Phase 3: Test of the full structural model (SEM)

SEM was examined in Phase 3 of the analysis as described in Figure 2. The model fit indexes of CFI (= .962), NNFI (= .98), NFI (= .955), IFI (= .95), RFI (= .96), RMSEA

(= .065), and SRMR (= .073) suggest that the proposed theoretical model does accurately explain the data.

Total Effects

First, in terms of the total effects in the model, the path values of a monetary incentive system (as an exogenous variable) to work motivation (β = 0.19; t = 2.49), to job satisfaction (β = 0.25; t = 3.42), and to turnover intentions (β = -0.16; t =-3.33) are all statistically significant. Second, a discretionary controlling system positively and significantly affects work motivation (β = 0.45; t = 5.87) and job satisfaction (β = 0.43; t= 7.36), whereas this exogenous variable negatively and significantly influences turnover intentions (β =-0.30; t = -0.60). Third, a performance monitoring system positively and significantly affects work motivation (β = 0.35; t = 5.28), job satisfaction (β = 0.28; t = 5.51), whereas this exogenous variable negatively and significantly affects turnover intentions (β = -0.19; t = -5.17). Fourth, a knowledge incentive system has a weak relationship with four endogenous variables; that is, it does not significantly affect work motivation (β = 0.03; t= 0.37), job satisfaction (β = 0.05; t = 1.09), and turnover intentions (β = -0.04; t = -1.09). Fifth, in terms of relationships among endogenous variables, work motivation positively and significantly affects job satisfaction (β = 0.79; t = 6.68), whereas it negatively affects turnover intentions (β = -0.55; t = -6.09). Job satisfaction is also negatively associated with turnover intention (β = -0.72; t = -10.99). Finally, R-squares of the SEM are relatively high: R^2 (Work Motivation) = 0.64, R^2 (Job Satisfaction) = 0.80, and R^2 (Turnover Intentions) = 0.61.

Figure 2. The Full Structural Equation Model (SEM)

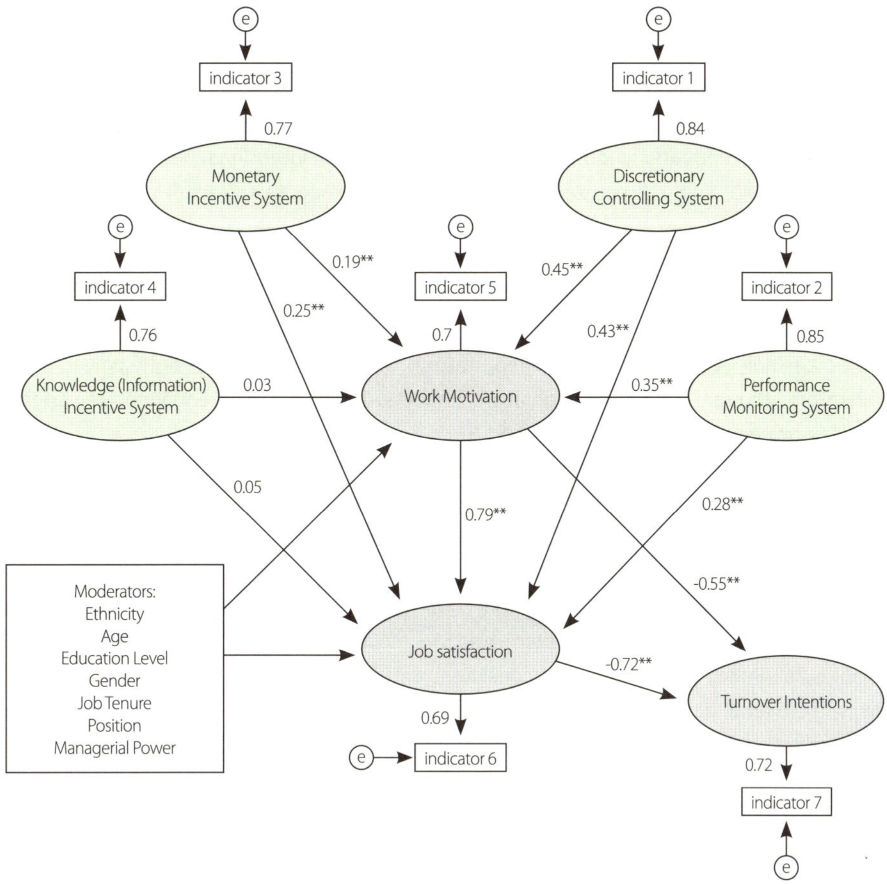

Overall Fit Indexes of the SEM

Model	df	Chi-Square	CFI	NNFI	NFI	IFI	RFI	RMSEA	SRMR
Suggested cut-off values			>.95	>.95	>.95	>.95	>.95	<.08	<.08
A full structural model	447	3731.76	.962	.98	.955	.95	.96	.065	.073

Notes: The structural path estimates are presented as standardized regression weights(β).
The moderating effects are estimated by using eight observable variables.

Indirect, Standardized and Moderating Effects

In terms of indirect effects in this model, first, three exogenous variables (a monetary incentive system, a discretionary controlling system, and a performance monitoring system) indirectly, positively, and significantly affect job satisfaction, whereas these variables indirectly, negatively, and significantly affect turnover intentions. Second, a knowledge incentive system does not show any significant effect on four endogenous variables. From the standardized path values, we can compare the relative power of reform effects on work motivation, job satisfaction, and turnover intentions. As suggested in the standardized total and indirect tables, among the four exogenous variables, a discretionary (at-will) controlling system is shown as the most powerful and significant factor that positively influences motivation and satisfaction but negatively affects turnover intentions. Third, in addition to the four exogenous variables, eight personal and job characteristics were included as moderating variables in SEM: gender; age; ethnicity; education level; job tenure; position (classified/ unclassified status); and managerial oversight power. These moderators, though not having significant impacts, affect the four endogenous variables positively or negatively. See Tables 4 and 5.

Ultimately, this study has identified several important research findings from the SEM analysis. First, except for moderating effects, the path coefficients of the four main exogenous variables are all statistically significant, and in most cases the values of are moderately high in the full structural model (SEM). Second, by comparing the standardized regression weights, we can confirm that a discretionary controlling system and a performance monitoring system are the most influential and powerful exogenous variables, a finding which remains consistent with the results of the regression model. Finally, the overall fit indexes for the SEM indicate that the hypothesized structural equation model achieved a good fit. [Confirmed Hypotheses 2a, 2b, 2c, and 2d]

Table 4. Unstandardized and Standardized Total Effects

			Un-standardized estimate (B)	Standardized estimate (β)	SE	t	R^2
Work Motivation	←	Monetary Incentive System	.19**	.19	.075	2.49	.64
Work Motivation	←	Knowledge Incentive System	.003	.02	.051	.37	
Work Motivation	←	Discretionary Controlling System	.45**	.41	.069	5.87	
Work Motivation	←	Performance Monitoring System	.35**	.31	.059	5.28	
Job Satisfaction	←	Work Motivation	.79**	.78	.12	6.68	.80
Job Satisfaction	←	Monetary Incentive System	.25**	.21	.062	3.42	
Job Satisfaction	←	Knowledge Incentive System	.005	.05	.043	1.09	

Job Satisfaction	←	Discretionary Controlling System	.43**	.38	.052	7.36	
Job Satisfaction	←	Performance Monitoring System	.28**	.25	.045	5.51	
Turnover Intentions	←	Work Motivation	-.55**	-.61	.10	-6.09	.61
Turnover Intentions	←	Job Satisfaction	-.72**	-.78	.071	-10.99	

**Values are significant at p<.05 (one-tailed).

Discussions and Implications

The principal-agent theory suggests a way of designing an organizational structure and culture that minimizes opportunistic behavior. Furthermore, this theoretical approach explains how the goals of the public sector can be achieved within a contractual arrangement (Ferris & Graddy 1998). This study, drawing upon principal-agent theory and others, such as goal-setting theory, expectancy theory, and equity theory, while using different statistical models, probed four personnel reform system effects on work motivation, job satisfaction, and turnover intentions. These reform systems are the state-of-the-art personnel management tools in the state of Georgia, which embraced the concept of managerial flexibility, knowledge management and training, pay for performance, and at-will employment. The results of three statistical models confirmed that the four latent constructs of managerial reform systems are conceptually separate and distinct and that all four personnel reform systems directly and indirectly affect organizational outcome variables. Among these four effects, this study supports the evidence that discretionary controlling and performance monitoring systems can be the most powerful and effective managerial tools to enhance the level of work motivation and job satisfaction as well as to decrease state employees' turnover intentions.

Table 5. Unstandardized and Standardized Indirect Effects

			Un-standardized estimate (B)	Standardized estimate (β)	SE	t	R^2
Job Satisfaction	←	Monetary Incentive System	.14	.14	.06	2.43	.59
Job Satisfaction	←	Knowledge Incentive System	.01	.01	.04	.37	
Job Satisfaction	←	Discretionary Controlling System	.32	.32	.06	5.14	
Job Satisfaction	←	Performance Monitoring System	.24	.24	.05	4.76	
Turnover Intentions	←	Monetary Incentive Systems	-.16	-.16	.05	-3.33	.36
Turnover Intentions	←	Knowledge Incentive System	-.04	-.04	.03	-1.09	
Turnover Intentions	←	Discretionary Controlling System	-.30	-.30	.05	-6.60	

Turnover Intentions ← Performance Monitoring System	-.19	-.19	.04	-5.17	

**Values are significant at p<.05 (one tailed).

The empirical findings in this study suggest several managerial strategies which managers or supervisors (i.e. principals) in the public sector should consider. First, the use of a well-established merit pay system, which links individual performance ratings to annual salary increases and differently rewards higher and lower levels of employee (i.e. agent) performance, could encourage poor performers to improve their work productivity in public organizations (Kellough & Nigro 2002, 2006). It is essential for the organization to establish funding resources for the performance-based pay and a long-term commitment to continued funding to support the extrinsic rewards for public employees that are high performers (Freyss 2004: 79–0). Second, objective and reliable performance monitoring systems should be used to 'build on job-specific criteria and to meet the standard of job-relatedness'; adopting several technical and procedural tools; and focusing a manager's attention solely on the objective, job-related criteria for assessing performance (Daley 2005: 499). The public organization will need to develop clear goals for the organization and clear standards of performance by which it may evaluate employees. As the agent comes to accept the organization's goals and the direction of the organization, the agent's path for success will become clear, ultimately encouraging both cooperation with the organization and innovation for the organization. Finally, the decentralization of personnel management systems giving the greater discretion to agencies and supervisors could be used to create an organizational environment which promotes managerial flexibility and competitiveness in public organizations. In addition, the reduction of merit system protections (e.g. the adoption of an at-will employment system) could be adopted to facilitate the important personnel processes and functions, to successfully remove poor-performers from the workplace, to abolish the inefficient rules and regulations, and to enhance managerial authority over personnel policy in public organizations. In sum, one system alone is not enough to attract and retain the best employees for service to the public, but a system design that takes into account employees' generic work environments and effective compensation, evaluation, and discipline systems with the custom-fit job design component will be necessary.

In the current research, despite several significant findings, some theoretical weaknesses as well as methodological and data limitations suggest that the empirical results of this study should be carefully interpreted. First, as a theoretical downside, the relationship between employees and supervisors is not exactly the same as that suggested by the principal–agent theory, especially in public organizations. That is, there should be multiple agents and principals in the contractual process, who actually have or are willing to develop a multi-dimensional or pooled interdependence relationship rather than a bilateral and reciprocal interaction. In the pooled relationship, we expect that there is little or no formal interaction or coordination among organizational participants, and thus no principal–gent relationship (O'oole & Montjoy 1984).[20] Moreover, in the public sector, not only the agent but the principal would also encounter informational asymmetry problems, leading to a violation of the major assumption of the agency theory. In this regard, agency theory may not fully account for the social dynamics of principal–agent dyads in specific circumstances, for example, in the public sector (Parks & Conlon 1995).

Second, public employees are not always budget or self-interest maximizers as agency theorists posit; they also tend to pursue public service motivation (PSM) and other intrinsic, affective, and normative values beyond extrinsic and continuance interests (Perry & Wise 1990; Park & Rainey 2007). Public employees may work not only to pursue their personal interests and self-interest motives in a formal or contractual relationship, but also to enhance self-esteem and pride, to develop interpersonal trust and cooperation, to fulfill a desire to serve the public interest and social equity, and to achieve team and organizational common goals and missions in a social exchange relationship (Wilson 1989; Park & Rainey 2008). For example, for those agencies whose missions are more akin to nonprofit or social service organizations, controlling and monitoring systems, and monetary incentive systems might not be so valuable in enhancing public agencies' effectiveness nor in increasing employees' positive attitudes regarding their job and organization.[21] Because these social exchange or PSM arguments are not consistent with the empirical findings of this study, additional future research which examines the generalizability of these findings to other organizational settings remains necessary.

Finally, it should be noted that the current reform approach to the state or federal personnel systems and practices might bring about profound adverse consequences regarding issues of 'social equity (i.e., justice as fair treatment), democratization (i.e., citizen and employee empowerment), and humanization (i.e., roles of the state in facilitating a citizen's quest for the good life)' normative values traditionally associated with the civil service and with the 'public ethos' that provides the civil service with a constitutive role in a system of governance (Thompson 2001, 2003; Wise 2002: 558). In this regard, a more careful and comprehensive consideration of reform phenomena in government is needed, keeping in mind that the administrative reform logics of the public sector come not only from pure managerial restructuring necessities but also from symbolic or political rhetoric. In terms of the methodological challenges, a single-source (mono-method) bias should be noted; rather than objectively measured or quantified variables, 'self-reported', and 'perceived' measures were used. In this regard, more objective and unbiased data on organizational performance and effectiveness are required.[22] Second, although the measurement model and the full structural model in this study show a good model of fit, we should be cautious about possible correlated measurement errors which could be caused by model misspecification, incorrect direction of effects, and omitted variables.

Overall, this study attempted to make several theoretical and methodological contributions and advances in the field of public personnel management and civil service reform. Moreover, this study provides some research and practical implications for organizational researchers and public managers. First, for the purpose of understanding the logic of current reform initiatives, development, and consequences, a parsimonious theoretical framework – that is, the principal–agent theory – was offered. This inductive, rational, and market-driven approach can provide a foundation for future research on the effects of public management reform (e.g. NPM-based reform) at the state and the federal level. Thus, it is important that further research should replicate and generalize findings reported here, while addressing the aforementioned theoretical and methodological limitations. Second, more rigorous empirical research on personnel management reform should include other mediators and contextual factors (i.e. moderators) that may influence public employees' attitudinal and behavioral outcomes as well as individual and organizational performance. For example, in addition to individual factors, organizational or institutional characteristics such as the nature of the task, organizational support, job and work design, specific organizational structure and culture, and other types of public personnel management practices should be emphasized. Moreover, many relational factors (e.g. the type and the degree of leadership, commitment, and procedural justice in public organizations) and work experiences variables (e.g. HR policies and procedures) should be incorporated as important antecedents that may also strongly and consistently influence organizational outcomes.

Third, the previous empirical findings that several organizational outcomes significantly vary across state agencies would lead organizational researchers to conclude that we need to investigate state agencies more carefully and systematically. In this regard, we should add (agency- or organization-based) in-depth case studies (e.g. using the qualitative research method) or adopt more advanced quantitative techniques (e.g. hierarchical linear modeling) in order to examine the organizational characteristics embedded in each state agency (e.g. goals, missions, culture, systems, and political orientation), which, ultimately, could positively or negatively influence state employees'job attitudes. Finally, from a comparative or developmental perspective, an emphasis should be placed on the different personnel management reform practices and tools of managing for better performance (e.g. reinventing government and President's Management Agenda initiatives, performance management practices, and strategic public HR management approaches) in a variety of cultural, economic, and political contexts within the United States –at the local, state, and federal levels – as well as in other countries. Thus, future studies are needed to replicate this study in other public agencies that have different personnel systems and cultures from Georgia state agencies. This comparative research approach will enrich our relevant disciplines by illustrating important commonalties and anomalies in contemporary managerial practice and will ultimately broaden our knowledge of the antecedents, interactions, development, and consequences of NPM-oriented personnel management reforms in the public sector.

Notes

1. The original manuscript was presented at the 2006 Southeastern Conference for Public Administration (SECoPA) in Athens, Georgia, USA. This research paper was selected for the Morris W. H. Collins Award (the Best Doctoral Student Conference Paper).
2. However, this way of thinking has made some organizations overlook the many pioneering and groundbreaking ideas fashioned in the public sector. In the United States, it should be noted that several management innovation initiatives have also begun in the public sector with certain key reform programs at the state, local, and federal government levels such as a response to crisis, a focus on prevention, an emphasis on results, and adaptation of technology (for more information, see Walters 2001).
3. In the state of Georgia, the chief official in the executive branch is the Governor who is elected by the voters for a four-year term, with two consecutive terms allowed. The Governor proposes new programs and laws for the state, proposes a state budget for the legislature to consider, vetoes legislation, and appoints members of many of the boards in state government. As of March 2008, there are 126 state agencies in the state of Georgia. Additional information on the Georgia public service is available from www.georgia.gov (Georgia government) or www.spa.ga.gov (Georgia State Personnel Administration).
4. Regarding the conflicts between elected officials and public employees, Selden et al. (1999) proposed five potential sources of conflict between city councils (principals) and city managers (agents). Examples include: (1) the city manager's appointment and removal authority; (2) the city manager's role in formulating the budget; and (3) the city manager's involvement in the political arena (1999: 125).
5. As Wood and Waterman (1994) suggested, the logic of the politics–public administration dichotomy is implicitly or explicitly premised on principal–agent theory. Many theorists (see, for example, Waldo 1948; Lipsky 1980; Wilson 1989), however, criticized this view while emphasizing the political role and power of bureaucracy, bureaucrats' discretionary authority, and their representativeness in government.
6. However, research has noted that there are persistent managerial obstacles for developing and managing objective evaluation systems in the public organizations, and that there are several factors which create ineffective managerial appraisal systems. The primary causes of ineffective performance appraisal systems include the politics of the appraisal process, the lack of objective data for measuring performance, numerous biases and errors, the shortage of well-trained supervisors in evaluating subordinates, unclear performance criteria or ineffective rating instruments, and an ineffective link to reward systems (Kellough & Lu 1993; Longenecker 1997).
7. Davenport & Prusak (1998: 5) defined knowledge as ' a fluid mix of framed experience,

values, contextual information, expert insight and grounded intuition that provides an environment of and framework for evaluating and incorporating new experience and information', whereas Cong & Pandya (2003: 27) suggest that knowledge should be viewed as the 'ability of an organization to use its collective knowledge through a process of knowledge generation, sharing and exploitation enabled by technology to achieve its objectives'.

8. The ADF/WLS method is useful when the sample size is large. ADF produces asymptotically unbiased, consistent, and efficient estimates of the chi-square test, parameter estimates, and standard error, even under conditions of non-normality.
9. The present study used this hierarchical procedure for the purpose of assessing the main effects of personnel management systems and contextual factors, and the mediating effects of task motivation and job satisfaction on organizational effectiveness and turnover intention of employees. F-tests were used to compute the significance of each added variable (or set of variables) to the explanation reflected in R-square.
10. After factor scores and, subsequently, new variables were obtained, the reliability was tested using Cronbach's alpha. Almost all of the scales have an alpha value of .7 or above, so all new variables in this model were considered to exhibit internal consistency.
11. The formula for factor scores is $F_{jk} = \sum W_{ji} Z_{ik}$ (F = individual factor scores; W = weighted values; Z = the standardized variables). There are several advantages for using factor scores in regression. First, we can reduce or eliminate multicollinearity because the variables causing the multicollinearity will combine to form a factor. Second, using a factor index, we can make interval variables instead of ordinal or nominal variables because all ordinal level data can be transformed into interval data that have factor scores rather than six -point Likert scales. Third, we can reduce the number of variables by making new variables. It is expected that this method can provide more statistical reliability and validity that can guarantee a more robust statistical model.
12. Internal consistency is important in this research because the homogeneity of four reform scales is critical for measuring the respondents' attitudes about the scale accurately. Moreover, when the content is consistent, it is also easier to interpret. To assess internal consistency and to ensure the reliability of each scale, Cronbach's alpha reliability test was done. However, high internal consistency is not necessarily an indication of uni-dimensionality. That is, relatively high internal consistency can still be obtained even if a measure is multi-dimensional.
13. Skewness can show whether the item's distribution deviates from the symmetry distribution. We can argue that skewness values outside the range of ±2 would be problematic because this is a serious level of skew. Kurtosis measures the degree to which the area in a distribution is in the middle and the tails of a distribution. As a rule of thumb, the range of ±2 is often considered as a significant departure from normality

(Pedhazur 1997).

14. The missing values raise concern regarding generalizability and validity. To reduce a possible method bias, this study also employed new methods other than listwise deletion, that is, the expectation-maximization (EM) algorithm approach and the pattern-matching method. The results reveal no meaningful differences among these three methods in this case.
15. Since this study does not use time-series or longitudinal data, it is hard to observe any variations or configurations before and after the Georgia reform adoption, especially from an empirical perspective. Instead, this research examined how different employee perceptions on four personnel management reform systems affect certain types of organizational attitudes by operationalizing employee survey items -that is, rather than investigating actual variations in the presence of those systems, this study mainly investigated endogenous causality and perceptual (psychological) paths among antecedents and consequences through regression and SEM approaches.
16. Among these variables, gender (female = 1), ethnicity (minority = 1), position (unclassified at-will status = 1), and managerial power (more oversight power = 1) were dichotomized.
17. Since the task motivation variable was measured by only four items which do not address the intensity (putting forth a considerable effort) and longevity (putting in long hours) of work effort, we may suspect that the motivation construct might lack face and construct validity.
18. In ML estimation, the weight matrix is the inverse of the reproduced covariance matrix. The ML method is generally both scale free and scale invariant. It also assumes multivariate normality and, hence, nonnormality would influence the significant test and the chi-square value.
19. According to Hu & Bentler (1999), SRMR is the most sensitive index to models with misspecified factor covariance. In addition, NNFI, IFI, RNI, CFI, and RMSEA are the most sensitive to models with misspecified factor loadings. In a CFA model, cutoff values of .95 for NNFI, RNI, IFI, and CFI in combination with a cutoff value of .09 (or .08) for SRMR are recommended.
20. In the multi-dimensional network (or coordination) systems in which many private and public sector actors are involved with the delivery of public services, bureaucracies need to face and consider multiple competing principals (e.g. Congress, President, or other political actors) and agents (e.g. different types of private companies and public agency bureaucrats in competition) together, especially in the contracting out and outsourcing process.
21. A social exchange theoretical approach typically 'emphasizes the exchange process, including its development over time, and indicates that successful social exchanges should influence perceptions of risk of non-reciprocation (i.e., opportunism) and trust'

(Whitener et al. 1998: 515).

22. That is, if the antecedent and outcome variables were measured by the same raters or respondents, this could produce confounding results because the assessed overlap between variables may be artifactual (that is, due to common method variance) and may not reflect the true relationship between the underlying constructs.

References

Abrahamson, E., & Park, C. (1994). Concealment of negative organizational outcomes: An agency theory perspective. *Academy of Management Journal, 37*(5), 1302-1334.

Adams, L. S. (1965). *Injustice in social exchanges.* San Diego, CA: Academic Press.

Ban, C., & Riccucci, N. M. (2002). Public personnel management: Where has it been, where is it going?. In C. Ban & N. M. Riccucci (Eds.), *Public personnel management: current concerns, future challenges.* New York: Longman Publishers.

Bowman, J. S., Gertz, M. G., & Gertz, S. C. (2003). Civil service reform in florida state government. *Review of Public Personnel Administration, 23*(4), 286-304.

Bright, L. (2008). Does public service motivation really make a difference on the job satisfaction and turnover intentions of public employees?. *American Review of Public Administration, 38*(2), 149-66.

Byrne, B. M. (2001). *Structural equation modeling with AMOS: Basic concepts, applications, and programming.* New Jersey: Lawrence Erlbaum Associates.

Cong, X., & Pandya, K. V. (2003). Issues of knowledge management in the public sector. *Electronic Journal of Knowledge Management, 1*(2), 25-33.

Conlon, E. J., & Parks, J. M. (1990). Effects of monitoring and tradition on compensation arrangements: An experiment with principal-agent dyads. *Academy of Management Journal, 33*(3), 603-22.

Daley, D. M. (2005). Designing effective performance appraisal systems'. In S. E. Condrey (Ed.), *Handbook of human resource management in government.* San Francisco, CA: Jossey-Bass.

Davenport, T. H., & Prusak, L. (1998). Working knowledge: *How organizations manage what they know.* Boston, MA: Harvard Business School Press.

Eisenhardt, K. M. (1988). Agency and institutional theory explanations: The case of retail sales compensation. *Academy of Management Journal, 31*(3), 488-511.

Eisenhardt, K. M. (1989). Agency theory: An assessment and review. *Academy of Management Review, 14*(1), 57-74.

Ferris, J. M., & Graddy, E. A. (1998). A contractual framework for new public management theory. *International Public Management Journal, 1*(2), 225-240.

Freyss, S. F. (2004). *Human resource management in local government: An essential guide* (2nd ed.), Washington, DC: International City/County Management Organization.

Gossett, C. W. (2002). Civil service reform: The case of Georgia. *Review of Public Personnel Administration, 22*(2), 94-113.

Grant, A. M. (2008). Employees without a cause: The motivational effects of prosocial impact in public service. *International Public Management Journal, 11*(1), 48-66.

Hackman, J. R., & Oldham, G. R. (1975). Development of the job diagnostic survey. *Journal of Applied Psychology, 60*(2), 159-170.

Harris, M., & Raviv, A. (1978). Some results on incentive contracts with application to education and employment, health insurance, and law enforcement. *American Economic Review, 68*(1), 20-30.

Harrison, P. D., & Harrell, A. (1993). Impact of 'adverse selection' on managers' project evaluation decisions. *Academy of Management Journal, 36*(3), 635-643.

Hood, C. (1995) The 'new public management' in the 1980s: Variations on a theme. accounting. *Organizations and Society, 20*(2/3), 93-109.

Hu, L., & Bentler, P. M. (1999). Cutoff criteria for fit indexes in covariance structure analysis: Conventional criteria versus new alternatives. *Structural Equation Modeling, 6*(1), 1-55.

Ingraham, P. W., Jacobson, W., & Seldon, S. C. (2001). Human resource practices in state government: Findings from a national survey. *Public Administration Review, 61*(5), 598-607.

James, L. R., Mulaik, S. A., & Brett, J. M. (1982). *Causal analysis: Assumptions, models, and data,* Beverly Hills, CA: Sage.

Jensen, M. C., Meckling, W. C. (1976). Theory of the firm: Managerial behavior, agency costs, and ownership structure. *Journal of Financial Economics, 3*(4), 305-360.

Jöreskog, K. G. (1990). New development in LISREL: Analysis of ordinal variables ssing polychoric correlations and weighted least squares. *Quality and Quantity, 24*(4), 387-404.

Jöreskog, K. G., & Sörbom, D. (1996). *LISREL 8 user's reference guide,* Chicago, IL: Scientific Software International.

Kellough, J. E., & Lu, H. (1993). The paradox of merit pay in the public sector: Persistence of a problematic procedure. *Review of Public Personnel Administration, 13*(2), 45-64.

Kellough, J. E., & Nigro, L. G. (2002). Pay for performance in Georgia state government: Employee perspectives on GeorgiaGain after 5 Years. *Review of Public Personnel Administration, 22*(2), 146-166.

Kellough, J. E., & Nigro, L. G. (2006). Dramatic reform in the public service: At-will employment and the creation of a new public workforce. *Journal of Public Administration Research and Theory, 16*(3), 447-466.

Kellough, J. E., & Selden, S. E. (2003). The reinvention of public personnel administration:

An analysis of the diffusion of personnel management reforms in the states. *Public Administration Review, 63*(2), 165-176.

Kemery, E. R., Bedeian, A. G., Mossholder, K. W., & Touliatos, J. (1985). Outcomes of role stress: A multisample constructive replication. *Academy of Management Journal, 28*(2), 363-375.

Kim, R. (1996). Aspirations for career advancement in public organizations: The case of south korean bureaucracy. Unpublished doctoral dissertation. University of Southern California.

King, C. S., & Stivers, C. (1998). *Government is us: Public administration in an anti-government era.* Thousand Oaks, CA: Sage Publications.

Kline, R. B. (2005). *Principles and practices of structural equation modeling.* New York: Guilford.

Lipsky, M. (1980). *Street-level bureaucracy.* New York: Russell Sage Foundation.

Locke, E. A., & Latham, G. P. (1990). *A theory of goal setting and task performance, Englewood Cliffs,* NJ:Prentice Hall.

Longenecker, C. O. (1997). Why managerial performance appraisals are ineffective: Causes and lessons. *Career Development International, 2*(5), 212-218.

Mann, G. A. (2006). A motive to serve: Public service motivation in human resource management and the role of PSM in the nonprofit sector. *Public Personnel Management, 35*(1), 33-48.

Maruyama, G., & McGarvey, B. (1980). Evaluating causal models: An application of maximum likelihood analysis of structural equations. *Psychological Bulletin, 87*(3), 502-512.

Milgrom, P. R., & Roberts, J. (1992). *Economics, organization, and management.* Englewood Cliffs, NJ: Prentice-Hall.

Milkovich, G. T., & Wigdor, A. K. (1991). *Pay for performance: Evaluating performance appraisal and merit pay.* Washington, DC: National Academy Press.

Miner, J. B. (2005). *Classics of organizational behavior: Essential theories of motivation and leadership.* Amronk, NY: M. E. Sharpe.

Moe, T. M. (1984). The new economics of organization. *Journal of Law, Economics, and Organization, 28*(4), 739-777.

Moynihan, D. P., & Pandey, S. K. (2007). The role of organizations in fostering public service motivation. *Public Administration Review, 67*(1), 40-53.

Muhl, C. (2001). The employment at-will doctrine: Three major exceptions. *Monthly Labor Review, 124*(1), 3-12.

Naff, K. C., & Crum, J. (1999). Working for america: Does public service motivation make a difference?. *Review of Public Personnel Administration, 19*(4), 5-16.

Noorderhaven, N. G. (1992). The problem of contract enforcement in economic organization theory. *Organization Studies, 13*(2), 229-243.

O'Toole L. J. Jr., & Montjoy, R. S. (1984). Interorganizational policy implementation: A theoretical perspective. *Public Administration Review, 44*(6), 491-503.

Park, S. M., & Rainey, H. G. (2007) Antecedents, mediators, and consequences of affective, normative, and continuance commitment: Empirical tests of commitment effects in federal agencies. *Review of Public Personnel Administration, 27*(3), 197-226.

Park, S. M., & Rainey, H. G. (2008). Leadership and public service motivation in U.S. federal agencies. *International Public Management Journal, 11*(1), 109-142.

Parks, J. M., Conlon, E. J. (1995). Compensation contracts: Do agency theory Assumptions predict negotiated agreement?. *Academy of Management Journal, 38*(3), 821-838.

Pedhazur, E. J. (1997). *Multiple regression in behavioral research: Explanation and prediction* (3rd ed), Fort Worth, TX: Harcourt Brace Jovanovich.

Perry, J. L., & Wise, L. R. (1990). The motivational bases of public service. *Public Administration Review, 50*(3), 367-373.

Perry, J. L., Brudney, J. L., Coursey, D., & Littlepage, L. (2008). What drives morally committed citizens? A study of the antecedents of public service motivation. *Public Administrative Review, 68*(3), 445-458.

Petersen, T. (1993). Recent developments in the economics of organization. *Acta Sociologica, 36*(3), 277-293.

Pollitt, C. (1993). *Managerialism and the public services: Cuts or cultural change in the 1990s?* (2nd ed), Oxford, UK: Basil Blackwell.

Pollitt, C., & Bouckaert, G. (2004). *Public management reform: A comparative analysis* (2nd ed). Oxford & New York: Oxford University Press.

Rainey, H. G. (2003). *Understanding and managing public organizations* (2nd ed.), San Francisco, CA: Jossey-Bass.

Rainey, H. G., & Steinbauer, P. (1999). Galloping elephants: Developing elements of a theory of effective government organizations. *Journal of Public Administration Research and Theory, 9*(1), 1-32.

Selden, S. C., Brewer, G. A., & Brudney, J. L. (1999). The role of city managers: Are they principals, agents, or Both?. *American Review of Public Administration, 29*(2), 124-48.

State of Georgia. (1996). Public officers and employees personnel administration; veterans; unclassified service defined to include all positions filled by new hires; classified service employees to remain in classified service on certain conditions. No. 816 (Senate Bill 635). General Acts and Resolutions 1.

Steijn, B. (2004). Human resource management and job satisfaction in the dutch public sector. *Review of Public Personnel Administration, 24*(4), 291-303.

Steijn, B., & Leisink, P. (2006). Organizational commitment among dutch public sector employees. *International Review of Administrative Sciences, 72*(2), 187-201.

Terry, L. D. (1998). Administrative leadership, neo-managerialism, and the public management movement. *Public Administrative Review, 58*(3), 194-200.

Thompson, F. J. (2001). The civil service under Clinton. *Review of Public Personnel Administration, 21*(2), 87-113.

Thompson, F. J. (2003). *Classics of public personnel policy.* California: Wadsworth.

Ting, Y. (1997). Determinants of job satisfaction of federal government employees. *Public Personnel Management, 26*(3), 313-334.

Vroom, V. (1964). *The motivation to work.* New York: Wiley.

Waldo, D. (1948). *The administrative state.* New York: The Ronald Press Company.

Walters, J. (2001). *Understanding innovation: What inspires it? What makes it successful?.* IBM Center for the Business of Government Report (New Ways to Mange Series). Washington DC.

West, J. P. (2002). Georgia on the mind of radical civil service reformers. *Review of Public Personnel Administration, 22*(2), 79-93.

Whitener, E. M., Brodt, S. E., Korsgaard, M. A., & Werner, J. M. (1998). Managers as initiators of trust: An exchange relationship framework for understanding managerial trustworthy behavior. *Academy of Management Review, 23*(3), 513-530.

Wilson, J. Q. (1989). Bureaucracy: *What government agencies do and why they do It.* New York: Basic Books.

Wise, L. R. (2002). Public management reform: Competing drivers of change. *Public Administration Review, 62*(5), 555-567.

Wood, B. D., & Waterman, R. W. (1994). *Bureaucratic discretion: The role of bureaucracy in a democracy.* Boulder, CO: Westview.

Word, J., & Park, S. M. (2009). Working across the divide: Job involvement in the public and nonprofit sectors. *Review of Public Personnel Administration, 29*(2), 103-133.

Wright, B. E. (2004). The role of work context in work motivation: A public sector application of goal and social cognitive theories. *Journal of Public Administration Research and Theory, 14*(1), 59-78.

Wright, B. E., & Kim, S. (2004). Participation's influence on job satisfaction: The importance of job characteristics. *Review of Public Personnel Administration, 24*(1), 18-40.

Appendix

Construction of indices[a]

Managerial reform variables (a six-point Likert scale)

1. A monetary incentive system effects scale (four items)
(standardized coefficient alpha: .698)

(a) The pay-for-performance system set up by GeorgiaGain is a good way to motivate state employees.
(b) My pay is based on how well I do my job.
(c) Pay raises in my work unit often are not really related to performance(Reversed).
(d) High-performing employees in my work unit consistently are rewarded with pay increases greater than those awarded to average performing employees.

2. A knowledge incentive system effects scale (five items)
(standardized coefficient alpha: .809)
(a) There is a lot of effective teaching, training and coaching of subordinates by my supervisor.
(b) The State offers me enough training to grow and develop.
(c) Adequate resources and opportunities for career development are available to state employees.
(d) Training is identified in performance development plans and is available to employees in my agency.
(e) Training on how to carry out provisions of GeorgiaGain is adequate.

3. A discretionary controlling system effects scale (four items)
(standardized coefficient alpha: .745)
(a) I believe my agency has made good use of the greater discretion it has under the Act 816.
(b) Under authority provided by the Act 816, my agency can hire highly qualified people in a timely manner.
(c) It has been possible to terminate low performers without major procedural delays in my agency.
(d) Supervising workers in unclassified positions is easier than supervising workers in classified positions.

4. A performance monitoring system effects scale (six items)
(standardized coefficient alpha: .837)
(a) Performance appraisal discussions are useful in helping me improve my performance.
(b) My supervisor's evaluation provides feedback that often helps me improve my job performance.
(c) My most recent performance rating accurately reflected my performance.
(d) My supervisor really doesn't know enough about what I am doing to evaluate my performance accurately (reversed).
(e) My immediate supervisor works with me to set performance goals and targets.
(f) My supervisor is able to accurately determine different levels of employee

performance.

Outcome variables (a six-point Likert scale)

1. Work motivation (four items)
(standardized coefficient alpha: .702)
(a) I am doing work that is worthwhile.
(b) Morale is high in my work unit.
(c) I am motivated to be responsive to my customers and clients.
(d) My work group is highly committed to public service.

2. Job satisfaction (three items)
(standardized coefficient alpha: .755)
(a) I like my job.
(b) I would recommend employment with the State of Georgia to family members and friends.
(c) My agency is a good place to work.

3. Turnover intentions (two items)
(standardized coefficient alpha: .769)
(a) Because of dissatisfaction with my job or with state government, I am likely to leave Georgia State government within the next twelve months to take another job.
(b) There is a lot of turnover (retirements, resignations, terminations, etc.) in my work group.

Control variables (personal and job characteristics)

1 **Ethnicity:** What is your race?
2 **Age:** What is your age?
3 **Position:** Your current position is: Classified/Unclassified
4 **Gender:** What is your gender?
5 **Education level:** What is your highest level of education that you have completed?
6 **Job tenure:** How long have you worked in your current position/Georgia agency?
7 **Managerial oversight authority:** Do you supervise other state employees?

Note: [a]Descriptive statistics of main variables are available upon request.
For the empirical study, Kellough and Nigro (2006) designed and administered the survey

data, consulting with the Georgia Merit System (GMS), one of Georgia's central personnel agencies. The survey used a stratified random sampling methodology. Simple random samples of 2,542 non-supervisory personnel and 452 supervisory personnel were drawn from data files maintained by the GMS (Agency N=28). Each of these samples comprised approximately 5 percent of the respective populations. The subsamples were combined to produce a total sample of 2,994 employees. An overall response rate of 65.06 percent was achieved (1,948 usable completed surveys out of 2,994 in the original sample) (see Kellough and Nigro 2002: 149). The author expresses sincere gratitude to J. Edward Kellough for releasing this GMS survey data.

Case Study

Civil Service Reform

The nation's civil service is expected to undergo significant changes beginning next year as the government plans to reform the recruitment system for senior civil servants. For the past six decades, the government has recruited talented officials through the Senior Civil Service Exam, a difficult written test that has served as the gateway to success for government officials. But the government plans to establish a new hiring channel to attract private-sector professionals to the civil service.

On Thursday, the Ministry of Public Administration and Security announced a government plan to fill 30 percent of next year's quota for Grade 5 (junior manager level) officials with specialists from outside the civil service. The selection of this group will be based on the applicants' professional credentials and interviews alone -- without a written test imposed on them. The quota for this professional group is to be gradually raised to 50 percent by 2015.

Another notable aspect of the reform is the renaming of the annual test. As its current Korean name "Haengjeonggoshi" sounds authoritative, it will be simply called the exam for Grade 5 officials. This name change reflects the government's intention to alter the public perception of the examination.

Minister Maeng Hyung-kyu said the reform is aimed to create an atmosphere of open competition in the civil service and to facilitate the hiring of specialists in diverse areas. We share the minister's awareness of the challenges facing the civil service. Few can deny the need for the government to improve its productivity by enhancing competition among officials. It has also been facing a growing need to expand its scope of expertise as demand for public services continually diversifies.

To address these challenges, an overhaul of the current recruitment system for senior civil servants is inevitable. In the past, the Senior Civil Service Exam benefited the nation by attracting competent people to the civil service. It is undeniable that these talented officials had played a central role in Korea's rapid economic growth since the early 1960s.

But the exam has also been the root of serious evils in the officialdom. In the first place, the test's emphasis on legal subjects limits the range of applicants. Students who major in natural sciences are at a disadvantage because they must gain knowledge of law. As a result, the civil service has failed to secure a sufficient number of officials who can deal with technical affairs.

Officials who pass the higher civil service test often lack the incentive to improve their productivity. Since they have an "iron rice bowl," which means life-long job security, they tend to neglect self-development. Furthermore, the traditional rank-in-person system subjects them to frequent position rotation, making it almost impossible for them to become experts in certain fields.

The long dominance of the civil service by this single group of officials has made the administration rigid and inflexible. To address this problem, the government introduced the "open position system" in 1999, requiring each ministry to open up about 20 percent of its Grade 4 or higher positions to talents from both the private and public sectors. This system has failed to attract interest from private-sector specialists due to a lack of job security, a low pay and, above all, the reluctance of public officials to share their posts with private-sector experts.

In promoting its reform plan, the government needs to take lessons from the lackluster outcome of the open position system. Thorough preparations, including an objective performance appraisal system, are necessary to bring on board talented private-sector professionals. Without an injection of new blood, it will be difficult to reshape the civil service into a highly productive and flexible organization.

Source: The Korea Herald (2010.08.15)

Questions for Discussion

1. Work groups are often used in classrooms and in workplace settings to complete projects. Consider a previous group in which you participated and with which you had to complete a project. Discuss the communications channels that you employed. What were the advantages and disadvantages of the communication process? How did the choice of communication channels affect the outcome? Does your experience square with the research on this topic?

2. A recurring theme in this book is the uniqueness of the public sector environment. Are the pressures for organizational change more or less intense for managers of public organizations or for business managers? Explain.

3. What role do leaders play in organizational change and transformation? How might different leadership styles affect approaches to organizational change?

Section 7

People

- Antecedents, Mediators, and Consequences of Affective, Normative, and Continuance Commitment : Empirical Tests of Commitment Effects in Federal Agencies

- Exploring the Antecedents and Consequences of the Acceptance of Performance Appraisal Systems : The U.S. Federal Case

Section 7

People

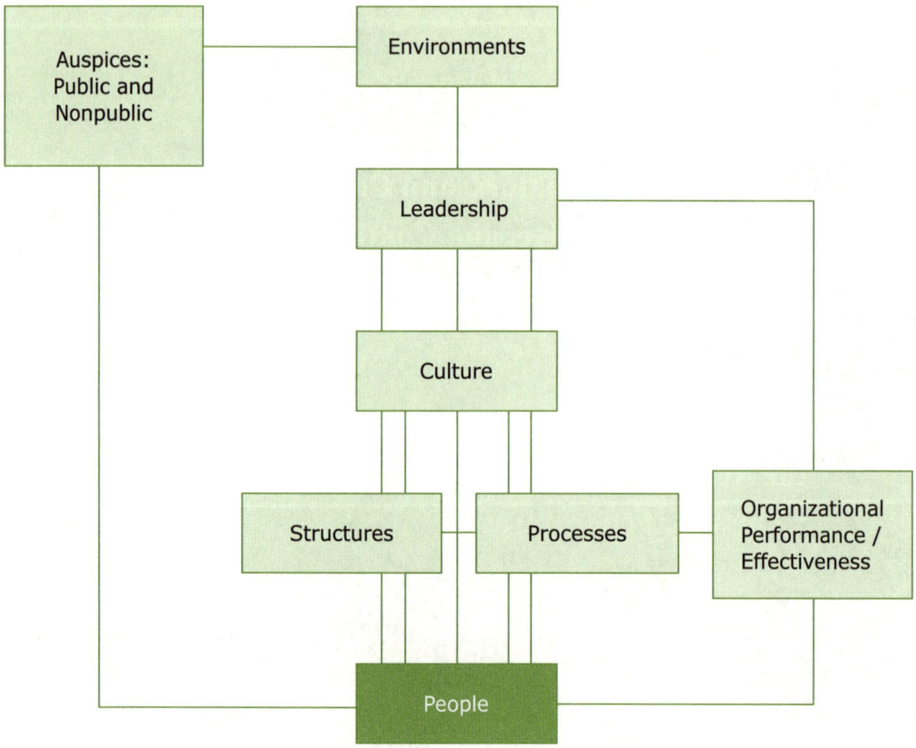

Chapter 13

Antecedents, Mediators, and Consequences of Affective, Normative, and Continuance Commitment
: Empirical Tests of Commitment Effects in Federal Agencies

Summary

This study examines the constructs and the effects of three subdimensions of federal employees' organizational commitment—affective, normative, and continuance. Using the Merit Systems Protection Board (MSPB) 2000 survey instrument and employing an exploratory and confirmatory factor analysis, multivariate regression, and a structural equation model, the authors empirically test and measure (a) the dimensionality of the three commitment constructs, (b) how and to what extent antecedent variables would affect the three different commitment variables—affective, normative, and continuance— and (c) how these three commitment values differently influence several outcome variables. The authors confirm that there are three distinctive constructs of commitment to stay in federal agencies and that transformation-oriented leadership (TOL), empowerment, goal clarity, public service-oriented motivation (PSOM), procedural equity perceptions, and objective appraisal systems have direct and indirect effects on the commitment variables. Affective commitment is most significantly and positively associated with these antecedents, and higher affective commitment also has the most significant effect on organizational consequences.

Keyword

- □ Public Management
- □ Organizational Behavior
- □ Organizational Commitment
- □ Leadership
- □ Job Satisfaction

Sung Min Park Associate Professor, Sungkyunkwan University
Hal G. Rainey Alumni Foundation Distinguished Professor, The University of Georgia

Introduction

In research on organizational behavior, "organizational commitment" has emerged as a principal topic because of its relationship with absenteeism, turnover, burnout, job satisfaction, and individual and organizational performance (Mathieu & Zajac, 1990; Somers, 1993; Tett & Meyer, 1993). These matters are as important in government agencies as in other organizations. One of the organizational goals of public agencies should be the enhancement of each employee' organizational commitment. In the conception and measurement of organizational commitment, various empirical studies have advanced a multidimensional approach (e.g., Allen & Meyer, 1990; Meyer & Allen, 1991, 1997). Even though relatively few studies have seriously dealt with the relationship between commitment and organizational consequences in the public sector, this issue is an urgent one for public sector human resource managers and scholars. By investigating the antecedents and consequences of commitment among federal employees, this study can contribute to finding important factors that increase commitment levels and contribute to organizational effectiveness.

First, this article proposes models for three dimensions of commitment: affective, normative, and continuance. Second, we discuss several antecedents and consequences of commitment to stay in federal agencies, such as transformation-oriented leadership (TOL), public service–oriented motivation (PSOM), empowerment, procedural equity perceptions, job satisfaction, and perceived performance. Third, using an exploratory factor analysis (EFA) and confirmatory factor analysis (CFA), multivariate regression, and a structural equation model (SEM), we test and empirically measure (a) the effects of three dimensions of commitment, (b) how and to what extent the antecedent variables affect three different commitment variables-effective, normative, and continuance-nd (c) how these three forms of commitment have different influences on several outcome variables. That is, this study examines the extent to which such variables as TOL or perceived procedural equity influence commitment variables directly or indirectly, and it also measures the effects of the three dimensions of commitment on work-related outcomes such as job satisfaction and productivity in public agencies. Thus, this study adds to research on organizational commitment in the public sector an analysis of the results of a very large survey of federal employees. It adds analysis of variables, listed above, that have not received attention or have received very little attention in previous research on commitment in the public sector. The analysis employs multiple methods (ordinary least squares-, OLS-regression, CFA, and SEM) in ways that provide more rigorous and reliable empirical results than in many previous studies.

Research on Commitment Roles: Three Dimensional Components of Organizational Commitment

Commitment has been found to be related to many attitudinal and behavioral consequences among employees, such as motivation, leadership, and job satisfaction (Allen & Meyer, 1990; Meyer & Allen, 1997). Highly committed employees are more likely to retain their jobs in the long run; they also show a high level of job satisfaction, quality of work, and job performance. Furthermore, employees who share a high commitment to the organization are more likely to generate the "social capital"-, found in relationships characterized by high levels of trust and shared values-hat prompts "organizational learning"(Robertson, Lo, & Tang, 2003, p. 2).

Meyer and Allen (1991) argued that commitment is a psychological state that characterizes the employee' relationship with the organization and that has implications for decisions to continue or discontinue membership in the organization (Wasti, 2003). In addition, Allen and Meyer (1990) conceptualized and proposed a model of organizational commitment that included three components: affective, normative, and continuance.

Affective commitment refers to emotional attachment to the organization characterized by acceptance of the organization' culture and primary values and by willingness to remain with the organization (Mowday, Porter, & Steers, 1982). This attitudinal dimension can be summarized as "an individual' attitude towards the organization, consisting of a strong belief in, and acceptance of the organization' goals, willingness to exert considerable effort in behalf of the organization, and a strong desire to maintain membership in the organization"(Mowday et al., 1982, p. 27; see also Eby, Freeman, Rush, & Lance, 1999).

Normative commitment, which can be called obligation-based commitment, is distinguished from affective commitment in that rather than emphasizing cohesiveness and attachment to the organization, it is viewed as a belief about the employee' formal and informal responsibility to the organization and a perceived duty to work for the organization and its functions (Wiener, 1982). Wiener (1982) defined commitment as the "totality of internalized normative pressures to act in a way which meets organizational goals and interests"and suggested that employees show certain behaviors solely because "they believe it is the right and moral thing to do"(p. 471). Some other authors have also found that personal norms (defined as a sense of internalized moral obligation) had strong influences on important individual behaviors such as voluntary turnover intentions (Prestholdt, Lane, & Mathews, 1987; Schwartz, 1973).

Continuance or calculative commitment denotes a mutual relationship based on an exchange between the employee and management. This commitment can be developed by "the individual' recognition of the costs (or lost side-bets such as pay or promotion) associated with discontinuing the activity or leaving the organization", (Allen & Meyer, 1990, p. 3). This "cost-induced commitment"(Allen & Meyer, 1990) is closely related to the concept of mutually transactional behaviors, and the cohesiveness would be lessened whenever the perceived material and extrinsic inducements are reduced. These three subcomponents of organizational commitment are not mutually exclusive. Rather, these three commitment variables work together and have common effects on organizational consequences such as job satisfaction, turnover intentions, and performance.

In the public administration literature, the importance of public officials' commitment as the foundation of administrative responsibility has been emphasized for a long time (Friedrich, 1940; Gaus, 1936; Miller, 2000; Robertson et al., 2003, p. 2). According to Miller (2000), the inherent moral hazard problems cannot be solved in public agencies with penalties and incentives alone. He also supports Gaus' (1936) argument that personal "commitment to professional standards"is the ultimate safeguard against "political opportunism"(pp. 39-40). More generally, public employees'& commitment to act in the interests of their organization and the members of the public their organization serves is important to the success of public organizations (Balfour & Wechsler, 1994; Perry & Wise, 1990; Robertson et al., 2003; Romzek, 1990).

These authors have taken conceptual approaches to commitment similar to ours. According to Balfour and Wechsler (1996), public sector commitment can be separated into three forms of commitment—identification commitment, which is based on "the employee' degree of pride"(Rainey, 2003, p. 279); affiliation commitment, which comes from "a sense of belonging to the organization and other members"& (Rainey, 2003, p. 279); and exchange commitment, which refers to the organization' recognition of the member' accomplishments. They found that four factors (i.e., more participation in decision making, lower political penetration, more respectful and supportive supervision, and more opportunity for advancement) influenced commitment (Rainey, 2003).

Robertson and Tang (1995) contrasted two different lenses in the analysis of commitment—he organizational behavior and the rational choice perspectives. From the organizational behavior perspective, ensuring high emotional attachment to organizations (e.g., affective commitment) would be the most important factor for developing collective action systems. On the other hand, rational choice perspectives suggest that establishing high credibility systems (e.g., credible commitments) and structural arrangements would be more effective approaches. Using these two rationales, they compare different mechanisms for cooperative behaviors and organizational culture, different leadership styles, and different roles of commitment in public organizations.

A common theme in the analysis of commitment in the private and public sectors concerns how to enhance commitment and, by doing so, how to improve other organizational consequences such as job satisfaction, turnover intentions, and job and organizational performance. Public sector organizations, however, have distinctive characteristics, and public employees may have distinctive values, motives, and goals. In public organizations, where the organization' goals tend to be ambiguous and diffuse and where organizational reform initiatives (e.g., new public management-NPM-and market-based reinventing-government initiatives and the President' Management Agenda) may affect public employees'motivation and commitment to stay, it is important to analyze organizational commitment and which type of commitment is more strongly related to public employees'job satisfaction and performance.

Until now, as described above, considerable empirical research has focused on finding important antecedent variables and outcomes of commitment in private organizations. In the public sector, however, few studies have been reported that analyze all the relationships that we examine here. We empirically examine how three different forms of commitment influence people in federal agencies using three empirical tools—FA and CFA, multivariate OLS regression, and SEM analysis. Public employees may show different forms of commitment from their private sector counterparts. Moreover, because we used a federal survey focusing on perceptions and behaviors of federal employees, our scales of commitment are somewhat different from the original commitment measurement scales developed by Allen and Meyer (1990) and others. We first need to confirm that the three distinctive dimensions of commitment to stay exist in public organizations. Table 1 presents our 16 hypotheses and their results. (Please see Hypothesis 1 on Table 1.)

Antecedents of Commitment

Several antecedent variables should influence the affective, normative, and continuance commitment variables in different (i.e., direct and indirect) ways. We examine the effects of (a) TOL, (b) PSOM, (c) employees'goal clarity, (d) empowerment, (e) objective performance appraisal systems, and (f) procedural equity perceptions. We use TOL and PSOM to emphasize that our constructs differ from those used by researchers on transformational leadership and public service motivation (PSM), although we have made our constructs as similar to those as possible with the available survey items.[1]

TOL

Regardless of an organization' size, culture, or structure, leaders need to strive to maximize the performance and job satisfaction of their subordinates to achieve organizational goals. In the public sector, the leadership issues could be even more critical because public organizations face political and financial pressures to reform managerial and organizational practices, and the constant waves of reform have potentially negative influences on commitment, which leaders need to prevent (Javidan & Waldman, 2003).

TOL behaviors should enhance commitment. Bass and Avolio (1994) identified transformational leadership as being composed of four unique but interrelated behavioral subdimensions: "Inspirational motivation," "Intellectual stimulation," "Idealized influence," and "Individualized consideration." Transformational leaders empower followers and make them less dependent on the leader, by delegating significant authority to individuals, developing follower skills and self-confidence, creating self-managed teams, providing direct access to sensitive information, eliminating unnecessary control, and building a strong culture to support empowerment (Bass, 1985). In this regard, TOL, which is based on transformational leadership constructs, can be viewed as directly affecting organizational performance and indirectly affecting organizational performance through its effects on subordinates'satisfaction with their leader. It affects performance indirectly through its effects on subordinates'affective commitment (McColl-Kennedy & Anderson, 2002). (Please see Table 1, Hypotheses 2a and 2b.)

Table 1. Summary of the Commitment Hypotheses in Federal Agencies

		Ordinary Least Squares (OLS) Model	Confirmatory Factor Analysis (CFA) or Structural Equation Modeling (SEM) Model
Hypothesis 1	A CFA will confirm that the three latent constructs of commitment to stay in federal agencies are conceptually separate and distinct.		Confirmed
Hypothesis 2a	In federal agencies, transformation-oriented leadership (TOL) will have more positive, direct, and indirect effects on affective commitment than on normative and continuance commitment.	Not confirmed	Confirmed
Hypothesis 2b	In federal agencies, TOL will positively affect organizational variables such as job satisfaction, perceived performance, and quality of work directly and indirectly.	Partially confirmed	Confirmed
Hypothesis 3a	In federal agencies, public service-oriented motivation (PSOM) will have a stronger direct relationship with affective and normative commitment than with calculative (continuance) commitment.	Partially confirmed	Confirmed
Hypothesis 3b	In federal agencies, high levels of PSOM will show strong direct and indirect effects on job satisfaction, performance, and quality of work.	Partially confirmed	Confirmed
Hypothesis 4a	In federal agencies, clearly defined goals for employees will have indirect, direct, and positive effects on affective, normative, and continuance commitment.	Confirmed	Confirmed
Hypothesis 4b	In federal agencies, clearly defined goals for employees will have an indirect and positive relationship with job satisfaction, performance, and quality of work.	Confirmed	Confirmed

Hypothesis 5a	In federal agencies, empowerment will have positive direct and indirect effects on affective, normative, and continuance commitment.	Confirmed	Confirmed
Hypothesis 5b	In federal agencies, empowerment will directly and indirectly influence satisfaction, performance, and quality of work.	Confirmed	Confirmed
Hypothesis 6a	In federal agencies, objective performance appraisal systems will positively influence affective and normative commitment more than calculative commitment in direct or indirect ways.	Partially confirmed	Confirmed
Hypothesis 6b	In federal agencies, objective performance appraisal systems will directly and indirectly increase satisfaction, performance, and quality of work.	Confirmed	Confirmed
Hypothesis 7a	In federal agencies, a high level of procedural equity perceptions will directly and indirectly affect affective, normative, and continuance commitment in a positive way.	Partially confirmed	Confirmed
Hypothesis 7b	In federal agencies, a high level of procedural equity perceptions will directly and indirectly affect job satisfaction, performance, and quality of work in a positive way.	Confirmed	Confirmed
Hypothesis 8	In federal agencies, affective, normative, and continuance commitment will differently influence employees' job satisfaction. Among these, affective and normative commitment will have a more positive and powerful effect on job satisfaction.	Confirmed	Confirmed
Hypothesis 9	In federal agencies, affective, normative, and continuance commitment will differently influence employees' perceived performance. Among these, affective and normative commitment will have a more positive and powerful effect on perceived performance.	Partially confirmed	Confirmed
Hypothesis 10	In federal agencies, affective, normative, and continuance commitment will differently influence employees' perceived quality of work. Among these, affective and normative commitment will have a more positive and powerful effect on perceived quality of work.	Partially confirmed	Confirmed

PSOM

Research evidence suggests that many public employees differ from their private sector counterparts. Public service has been portrayed as a calling, a sense of duty, rather than merely a job (Perry, 1996). Public administrators are often characterized as having an ethic to serve the public and hence motivated by different job characteristics than are private sector employees. In particular, many people in government organizations are motivated by a concern for the community and a desire to serve the public interest (Houston, 2000).

PSOM values include norm-based and affective motives rather than extrinsic rewards and self-interest motives. Perry and Wise (1990) postulated that employees who have higher degrees of PSM would be more positive about working for the government than those with lower PSM. Public employees with high PSOM should show greater commitment to stay in their jobs, a more positive attitude toward government employment, and less of a motive for instrumental incentives, such as pay. PSOM should be more strongly related to affective and normative commitment than to calculative commitment to stay. Moreover, having a higher level of commitment to stay in public agencies, high-PSOM employees should be more satisfied with their jobs and should be better performers. (Please see Table 1, Hypotheses 3a and 3b.)

Goal Clarity

Compared to private organizations, public organizations tend to have diffuse and ambiguous goals. Some scholars further argue that the degree of goal clarity or goal ambiguity influences organizational commitment (Buchanan, 1974) and organizational competencies (Boyatzis, 1982). Locke and Latham (1990) have shown that goal clarity enhances task performance (where goals are challenging but reasonable). Employees show higher levels of motivation when they have clear goals, when what should be done to achieve the goals is clear, and when the individual is in a position to make the necessary effort (Halachmi & Krogt, 2005). With a public sector sample, Wright (2004) has shown that goal specificity relates to higher motivation. The Government Performance and Results Act of 1993 (GPRA) requires all federal agencies in the United States to publicize their goals and performance objectives and to report results to Congress. GPRA is based on the assumption that increased goal clarity will enhance the performance of federal agencies (Chun & Rainey, 2005). Clearly defined goals should be positively related to the three types of commitment in federal agencies, to job satisfaction, and to performance. (Please see Table 1, Hypotheses 4a and 4b.)

Empowerment

Empowerment means giving employees the authority, skills, and self-control to perform their tasks (Hellriegel & Slocum, 2004). Since the 1990s, some managerial reforms in federal and state agencies (e.g., National Performance Review and reinventing-government initiatives) have recommended that public managers give public employees more power and discretionary authority and the opportunity to participate in the organizational decision-making process to enhance motivation, satisfaction, and ultimately job performance. Moreover, empowerment issues are also related to transformational leadership characteristics in that they emphasize "Empowering employees to feel a sense of significance, community, competence, and even fun" (Rainey, 2003, p. 303) rather than hierarchical authority and rule-based bureaucracy. Empowered employees should have higher levels of motivation, commitment, and other positive job attitudes. (Please see Table

1, Hypothesis 5a and 5b.)

Objective Performance Appraisal Systems

The main goals of performance appraisal are twofold: "to create a measure that accurately assesses the level of a person' performance in a job, and to create an evaluation system that will advance one or more operational functions in an organization" (Milkovich & Wigdor, 1991, p. 2). Performance appraisal systems can be used to "build on job-specific criteria and to meet the standard of job-relatedness"; (Daley, 2005, p. 499) to focus a manager' attention on objective, job-related criteria for assessing performance. By doing this, performance appraisal systems can provide the manager with "the means of making appropriate decisions that rationally contribute to the organization' and the individual' effectiveness and performance" (Daley, 2005, p. 501). Performance appraisals can motivate employees and increase organizational commitment when the employees trust the supervisor and perceive the appraisal ratings objective (i.e., unbiased; Milkovich & Wigdor, 1991). Objective performance appraisal systems should directly or indirectly play a critical role in enhancing affective or normative commitment and other job attitudes. (Please see Table 1, Hypotheses 6a and 6b.)

Procedural Equity Perceptions

According to equity theory, employees compare their efforts (inputs) to rewards (outcomes) and then compare their input-outcome ratio with that of colleagues. If they perceive their situation as fair, they are satisfied and perceive that equity prevails; if they sense a disparity in the ratios, they will try to correct it. Equity theory recognizes that "Individuals are concerned not only with the absolute amount of rewards they receive for their efforts, but also with the relationship of this amount to what others receive" (Robbins, 1992, pp. 54-55). Perceived inequity should be harmful to maintaining affective, normative, and continuance commitment to stay, all of which are based on the notion of "motional and norm-based cohesion" or "calculative attachment." (Please see Table 1, Hypotheses 7a and 7b.)

Consequences of Commitment: Job Satisfaction, Perceived performance, and Quality of Work

Researchers on organizational commitment have focused on its influence on other work-related attitudes. For example, Allen and Meyer (1990) found that employees who have a high level of affective commitment tend to show other positive workrelated attitudes about the organization. Mathieu and Zajac (1990) also found that affective commitment is more significantly related than calculative commitment with job involvement, overall job satisfaction, and satisfaction with other employees (Randall & O'riscoll, 1997).

Since the reinventing-government movement of the 1990s, NPM reform proposals have often emphasized results-oriented objectives based on market-oriented values and extrinsic rewards rather than emphasizing a "public service"ethos including such motives as PSM, participation, and social equity. Reforms that heavily emphasize extrinsic rewards might undermine affective and normative bonds to the organization. (Please see Table 1, Hypotheses 8, 9, and 10.)

Research Methods and Measures

We employed EFA and CFA to operationalize variables and to confirm latent constructs from the survey questions. Second, we employed OLS multivariate regression to examine the relationships between sets of independent variables and dependent variables. As a final step, to confirm the total, direct, and indirect effects, we employed a full SEM (i.e., a measurement model with a path model) using PRELIS 2.72 and LISREL 8.72 to test interrelationships among variables and to assess the relative strength of each variable. The full SEM allows for nonrecursive paths and simultaneous tests of the relationships of the variables (Byrne, 2001; Jöreskog & Sörbom, 1996). In addition to the OLS estimation method, the asymptotically distribution free (ADF; weighted least squares) technique and the maximum likelihood (ML) estimation method were employed to obtain more rigorous and unbiased results in this research (R. B. Kline, 2005).[2]

Data and Instrumentation

We analyzed the sample of 23 agencies and more than 6,900 federal employees'; responses to Merit Principles Survey 2000, conducted by the U.S. Merit Systems Protection Board. The survey sample was stratified by agencies (n was 750 surveys per agency).[3] In the survey, one section deals with commitment to stay items, measured by a 5-point Likert-type scale. From these survey constructs, we developed scales for the three kinds of commitment (see the Appendix).[4]

In addition, we used exploratory factor analysis (i.e., principal component analysis) for constructing most of the exogenous variable and outcome variable composite scores.[5] This technique enables us to extract communalities from different variables and to combine different variables into new variables.[6] This method can provide a more robust statistical model. Following this rationale, the commitment model in this study was tested by composite factor scores of the multiple item measures as variables; for factor extraction, we used principal component analysis and the varimax rotation technique (Wright, 2004).[7]

Missing Data Adjustments

Although listwise deletion is the most common method for handling missing observations, this approach sacrifices a large amount of data by eliminating all cases with any missing data (Roth, 1994).[8] Rather than using the listwise deletion method, to preserve sample size, we employed two alternative methods of analyzing the incomplete data: the expectation-maximization (EM) algorithm (in OLS regression) method and the full information maximum likelihood (FIML) approach (in the CFA and SEM models).[9] These approaches allow us to obtain an effective sample size (more than 6,900) in three distinct statistical models. These methods can increase statistical power of the models and minimize possible bias in parameter estimates (Roth, 1994).

Measurement of Organizational Commitment Variables

The CFA model. We used CFA to assess the construct validity of the three latent variables (affective, normative, and continuance commitment). Using ADF techniques, we examined the CFA model that composed a second-order factor.[10] We hypothesized that a composite commitment variable could be explained by three first-order factors (i.e., affective, normative, and continuance commitment) and one second-order factor (composite commitment).[11]

Item analysis of commitment variables. To determine whether the commitment items would be an appropriate scale without bias, we performed item analysis. First, the descriptive statistics show that all items of the three commitment scales are relatively stable and have similar amounts of variance.[12] This means that items in this study do differentiate responses fairly well. From the frequency table of each item, we observed that there is a spread of responses across all the options. We also ensured that the skewness and normality were not big concerns in this model.[13] Second, the high-reliability coefficients that measure internal consistency for the three commitment variables indicate that scale contents are homogeneous (see the Appendix), with consistent subitem structures.[14]

Measurement of Antecedent Variables of Commitment to Stay

The six antecedent variables should influence the three commitment variables: TOL, PSOM, employees'goal clarity and empowerment, objective performance appraisal systems, and procedural equity perceptions (see the Appendix). In addition to these antecedents explained above, we also included demographic variables such as current General Schedule (GS) level, education level, and job tenure (years in the federal government) as controls and moderators.

TOL and PSOM. First, to measure TOL, we sought items in the survey that resembled Bass and colleagues'(e.g., Avolio & Bass, 2002; Bass, 1998) items and represented their leadership dimensions as closely as possible. Our factor solution includes four subcomponents similar to theirs, including (a) idealized influence, (b) individualized consideration, (c) intellectual stimulation, and (d) inspirational motivation (Cronbach' α of this factorial index is .936). Second, we used six survey items to measure PSOM. The survey asked federal employees to indicate the factors that motivate them to do a good job and to express whether they prefer intrinsic rewards (e.g., nonpay and informal recognition) to extrinsic rewards (Cronbach' α = .775).

Goal clarity and empowerment. Goal clarity was measured by two items (Cronbach' α = .617) that ask whether employees can participate in developing long-range plans in their work unit and whether employees'performance standards are clearly linked to the organization' goals and objectives. In addition, to measure the degree of employees'empowerment in federal agencies (Cronbach' α = .814), we developed a six-item empowerment scale (asking whether employees are empowered by sharing information, training, and teamwork).

Objective performance appraisal systems and procedural equity perceptions. Performance appraisals can be employed for two reasons—udgmental and developmental.[15] The variable of objective performance appraisal systems (Cronbach' α = .811) was measured by a four-item scale, which focused on the two purposes mentioned above. Also, to measure procedural equity, we examined the perceived equity of promotions, awards, training, performance appraisal, discipline, and job assignment and made a variable using the factor scores (Cronbach' α = .845).

Measurement of Outcome Variables

We developed three outcome variables: job satisfaction, perceived performance, and perceived quality of work (see the Appendix). The first variable, job satisfaction, created by factor scores, includes six items. All converged onto one factor (Cronbach' α = .782). The second outcome variable, perceived performance, was based on the questions asking for ratings of the overall productivity of (a) yourself, (b) your work unit, and (c) your whole organization (Cronbach' α = .767). The third outcome variable, quality of work, was also developed by a factor analysis collapsing four questions into one factor index. We included the ratings of the quality of work performed by (a) yourself, (b) work unit, (c) larger organization, and (d) federal workforce as a whole in one factor index variable, perceived quality of work (Cronbach' α = .771). In OLS regression and SEM, we examined the statistical effects among several antecedent variables and these consequent variables with the expectation that there would be significant relationships among them.[16]

Findings and Results

CFA Results

Figure 1 shows the results of the second-order CFA. First, the model of fit statistics was within acceptable levels (see the model fit table); for example, the comparative fit indices (CFI) are more than .912 (greater than .90 is acceptable), and the root mean square error approximation (RMSEA) is .068 (less than .08 is acceptable). This proposed model of commitment in federal agencies is an excellent fit to the data, supporting the construct validity of the commitment measurement model.

As we hypothesized, the three subdimensions of commitment are distinct but also correlated with each other, and therefore we constructed a composite value of commitment to stay that includes all three commitment variables. The final model shows that affective and normative commitment are more salient than continuance commitment to stay in federal agencies. Many employees stay in their work because of emotional attachment, intrinsic rewards, and norms or responsibility rather than because of transactional exchange relationships, preferences for extrinsic rewards, or the individual' benefit-cost based calculation.

Correlations and OLS Regression Results

The correlation matrix for all the variables is presented in Table 2. Compared with normative and continuance commitment, all six antecedent variables are more significantly and positively correlated with affective commitment (average r = .355). Normative commitment has higher correlation coefficients (average r = .287) than continuance commitment values (average r = .089) for these antecedent variables.

Second, the correlations between affective commitment and all three consequence variables are also more significant (average r = .487) than those for the normative (average r = .316) or continuance commitment variable (average r = .191). Affectively committed federal employees show more positive job attitudes and perceived performance and quality of work. Although there are also a number of significant correlations among the antecedent and consequence variables themselves, none of these correlations are high enough to warrant concern about multicollinearity in the multiple regressions.[17]

Next, multiple regression results are presented in Tables 3 and 4. In Table 3, we probe the causal relationships between the antecedent variables and the three commitment variables. The F statistics for each of the three regressions are significant at the .01 level. Model 1 (the affective commitment model) shows that the set of antecedent variables accounts for 33.3% of the variance in the affective commitment to stay variable. Goal clarity (β = .131), empowerment (β = .159), and objective performance appraisal systems (β = .062) are statistically significant ($p < .05$). Federal employees who have clear goals, who are highly empowered in their work, or who are working in an objective appraisal culture are much more affectively bonded with their organizations. In addition, job tenure (β = .047) is also positively related to the affective commitment to stay.

In Model 2, in the normative commitment model (R^2 = .249), the variables of TOL (β = .035), PSOM (β = .053), goal clarity (β = .119), empowerment (β = .070), and procedural equity perceptions (β = .030) have a significant and positive effect on normative commitment ($p < .05$). Finally, in the continuance commitment model (R^2 = .125), although R^2 is relatively low, there are also positive and significant effects of goal clarity (β = .062) and objective performance appraisal systems (β = .047) and of three demographic control variables. The negative relationship with procedural equity perceptions (β = −039) implies that more equitable treatment for federal employees would attenuate the degree of continuance commitment and that it would make employees focus more on other types of commitment such as affective or normative commitment in federal agencies.

In Table 4, we also examine the relationships among the three commitment variables and three consequence variables of job satisfaction, perceived performance, and quality of work (F statistics are all significant at the .01 level). First, in the job satisfaction model, the set of antecedent variables and control variables accounts for quite a bit of variance (61.1%). Among the three commitment variables, affective (β = .176) and normative commitment to stay (β = .013) have a statistically significant and positive effect on job satisfaction. This means that compared to calculatively committed employees, affectively and normatively committed persons are more satisfied with their jobs, their work environment, and their

Figure 1. Second-Order Confirmatory Factor Analysis (CFA) for the Composite Commitment Scale

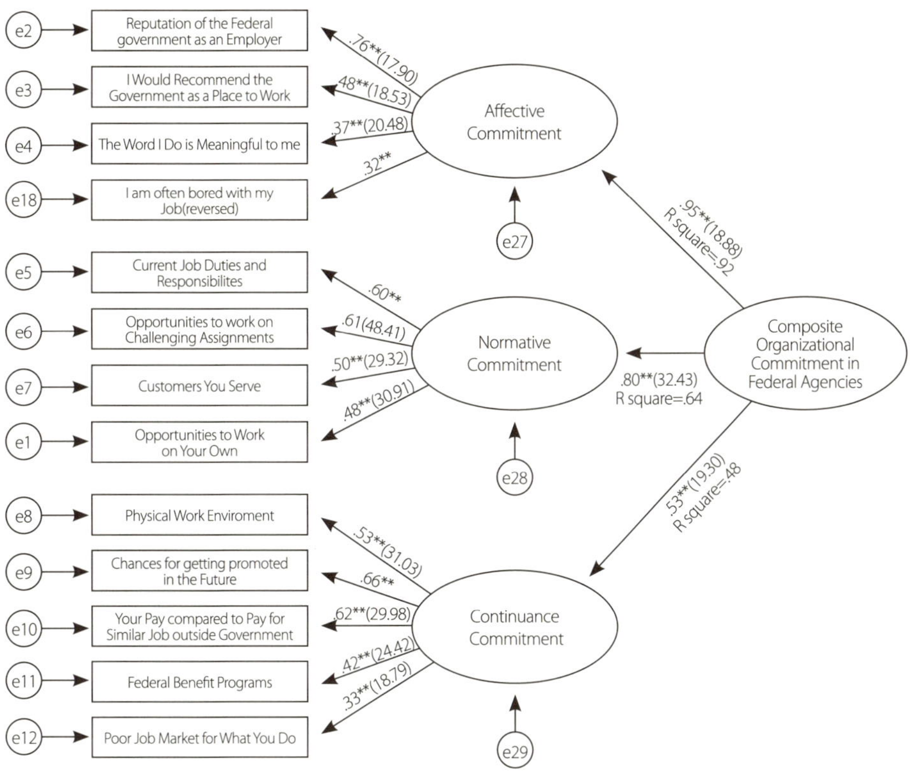

Overall Fit Indices of CFA Model

Model 1	df	χ^2	χ^2/df	RFI	NFI	GFI	CFI	RMSEA	SRMR
Suggested cut-off values			<3	>0.90	>0.90	>0.90	>0.90	< 0.08	< 0.08
Model of commitment in federal agencies	91	210.488	2.313	0.917	0.930	0.931	0.912	0.068	0.061

Note: RFI = relative fit index; NFI = normed fit index; GFI = goodness of fit index; CFI = comparative fit index; RMSEA = root mean square error of approximation; SRMR = standardized root mean residual. Based on the weighted least squares (asymptotically distribution free) method, all coefficients of the factor loadings (lambda Ys and gammas) in this CFA model are standardized (t statistics are in parentheses).

Table 2. Zero-Order Correlations among Antecedent Variables and Consequent Variables in the Commitment Model

Variables	1	2	3	4	5	6	7	8	9	10	11	12	13	14	15
1. Affective commitment	(.719)														
2. Normative commitment	.512**	(.760)													
3. Calculative commitment	.306**	.371**	(.783)												
4. Transformation-oriented leadership (TOL)	.363**	.281**	.104**	(.936)											
5. Goal clarity	.424**	.326**	.139**	.559**	(.617)										
6. Empowerment	.436**	.325**	.091**	.667**	.722**	(.814)									
7. Objective performance appraisal systems	.371**	.264**	.123**	.670**	.628**	.625**	(.811)								
8. Procedural equity perceptions	.296**	.293**	–.015	.608**	.467**	.597**	.553**	(.845)							
9. Public service–oriented motivation (PSOM)	.238**	.231**	.087**	.507**	.400**	.478**	.493**	.485**	(.765)						
Average effects of antecedent variables	.355	.287	.089												
10. Educational level	.048**	–.033*	.209**	–.015	–.008	–.075**	–.036**	–.087**	.012						
11. Job experiences	.141**	.071**	.080**	.002	–.010	–.028*	–.005	.024	.035**	–.116**					
12. Current General Schedule level (GS-1 to SES)	.038*	–.052**	.235**	–.038*	–.048**	–.163**	–.055**	–.185**	–.023	.538**	.192**				
Average effects of demographic control variables	.076	–.00467	.175												
13. Job satisfaction	.610**	.384**	.172**	.710**	.588**	.721**	.683**	.652**	.515**	.018	.046**	–.091**	(.782)		
14. Perceived performance	.419**	.307**	.217**	.382**	.418**	.413**	.354**	.289**	.208**	.106**	–.003	.096**	.405**	(.767)	
15. Perceived quality of work	.431**	.257**	.185**	.396**	.420**	.451**	.415**	.378**	.239**	.050**	–.038**	.026	.449**	.617**	(.771)
Average effects of outcome variables	.487	.316	.191												

Note: The values in parentheses are Cronbach's alpha values.
*Correlation is significant at the 0.05-level (two-tailed). **Correlation is significant at the 0.01 level (two-tailed).

Table 3. Multiple Regression Results: Antecedents of Commitment

Dependent Variables	Model 1: Affective Commitment			Model 2: Normative Commitment			Model 3: Continuance Commitment		
Main Antecedent Variables	Unstandardized Coefficients (B)	t	Standardized Coefficients (β)	Unstandardized Coefficients (B)	t	Standardized Coefficients (β)	Unstandardized Coefficients (B)	t	Standardized Coefficients (β)
Transformation-oriented leadership (TOL)	.001	(0.032)	.001	.041**	(2.530)	.035	–.006	(–0.352)	–.005
Goal clarity	.100**	(7.978)	.131	.090**	(7.038)	.119	.047**	(3.673)	.062
Empowerment	.121**	(9.140)	.159	.053**	(3.894)	.070	.024*	(1.737)	.031
Objective performance appraisal systems	.050**	(4.079)	.062	.005	(0.385)	.006	.038**	(2.979)	.047
Procedural equity perceptions	.007	(0.488)	.006	.030**	(2.193)	.030	–.040**	(–2.864)	-.039
Public service–oriented motivation (PSOM)	.008	(0.831)	.011	.041**	(3.930)	.053	.014	(1.361)	.019
Education level	.002	(0.547)	.008	.000	(0.078)	.001	.050**	(8.070)	.113
Job experiences	.047**	(9.532)	.113	.024**	(4.656)	.057	.023**	(4.412)	.054
Current general schedule level (GS-1 to SES)	.002	(0.547)	.008	–.006*	(–1.655)	-.023	.025**	(6.749)	.096
N		6,957			6,957			6,957	
R^2		.333			.249			.125	
Adjusted R^2		.327			.247			.111	
SE		.691			.710			.713	
Model F (p)		96.457 (.000)			51.150 (.000)			39.330 (.000)	

Note: Critical values are 1.96 for $p < .05$ and 1.65 for $p < .10$. t statistics are in parentheses.
*$p < .10$. **$p < .05$.

Table 4. Multiple Regression Results: Consequences of Commitment

Dependent Variables	Model 1: Job Satisfaction			Model 2: Perceived Performance			Model 3: Perceived Quality of Work		
Main Antecedent Variables	Unstandardized Coefficients (B)	t	Standardized Coefficients (β)	Unstandardized Coefficients (B)	t	Standardized Coefficients (β)	Unstandardized Coefficients (B)	t	Standardized Coefficients (β)
Affective commitment	.231**	(19.558)	.176	.149**	(8.941)	.114	.193**	(12.306)	.156
Normative commitment	.017*	(1.664)	.013	.042**	(2.512)	.032	–.016	(–1.044)	–.013
Continuance commitment	.011	(1.047)	.009	.049**	(3.188)	.037	.050**	(3.449)	.040
Transformation-oriented Leadership (TOL)	.190**	(13.787)	.123	.068**	(3.529)	.044	.024	(1.324)	.017
Goal clarity	.029**	(2.636)	.029	.163**	(10.601)	.164	.107**	(7.385)	.114
Empowerment	.324**	(28.064)	.326	.196**	(12.062)	.197	.176**	(11.443)	.187
Objective performance appraisal systems	.224**	(20.869)	.211	.069**	(4.587)	.066	.121**	(8.472)	.121
Procedural equity perceptions	.166**	(14.255)	.125	.035**	(2.128)	.026	.104**	(6.754)	.083
Public service–oriented motivation (PSOM)	.121**	(13.625)	.120	–.024	(–1.207)	–.024	.029**	(2.427)	.030
Education level	.048**	(9.137)	.082	.037**	(4.986)	.063	.012	(1.647)	.021
Job experiences	.027**	(6.220)	.049	–.035**	(–2.262)	–.068	–.028**	(–4.790)	–.053
Current General Schedule level (GS–1 to SES)	–.020**	(–6.296)	–.058	.031	(7.010)	.091	.019**	(4.579)	.059
N		6,957			6,957			6,957	
R^2		.611			.225			.230	
Adjusted R^2		.610			.224			.228	
SE		.599			.843			.797	
Model F (p)		907.853 (.000)			168.438 (.000)			172.643 (.000)	

Note: Critical values are 1.96 for $p < .05$ and 1.65 for $p < .10$. t statistics are in parentheses.
*$p < .10$. **$p < .05$.

colleagues and leaders. Moreover, all other variables—or example, TOL (β = .123), PSOM (β = .120), and empowerment (β = .326)—ave a significant and positive influence on job satisfaction.

Second, in the performance and quality of work models (R^2 = .225, .230, respectively), in addition to affective and normative commitment, continuance commitment is also significantly and positively related to perceived performance (β = .037) and quality of work (β = .040), although in comparatively weak contributions. This means that transactional or extrinsic reward-based commitment also could increase productivity or quality of work in federal agencies. Moreover, as we hypothesized, several control variables also positively influence these two outcome variables.

SEM Results

From the SEM analysis, we can observe how and to what extent several antecedent and consequence variables would be directly or indirectly related to the set of three commitment variables. The overall fit indices for this path analysis indicate that the hypothesized SEM achieved a good fit (see Figure 2).[18] Of the seven tests, only the ML chi-square test was inconsistent with a good model fit ($\mathcal{X}^2$/df = 38.144, $p < .01$). Although this result might be viewed as disconfirmatory evidence, Jöreskog (1990) and others (e.g., Maruyama & McGarvey, 1980) have warned that because the chi-square statistic is sensitive to sample size, the probability of rejecting a hypothesized model increases as N increases. Consequently, with large samples, virtually all models would be rejected as statistically untenable regardless of a good model fit (James, Mulaik, & Brett, 1982; Kemery, Bedeian, Mossholder, & Touliatos, 1985).

Total and Direct Effects

In Figure 2 and Table 5, we can observe that PSOM and procedural equity perceptions directly, significantly, and positively influence affective (β = .18, β = .23), normative (β = .15, β = .18), and continuance (β = .06, β = .05) commitment to stay. Moreover, as hypothesized, affective commitment is most significantly and positively affected by these two antecedents. So even though PSOM and procedural equity perceptions did not show a significant relation to affective commitment (β = .011, β = .006, respectively) in the OLS model, this result, together with the bivariate correlation (Table 2), supports our hypothesis that PSOM and procedural equity perceptions are more positively related to affective and normative commitment than to continuance commitment. Second, in terms of a consequence variable, affective commitment also more significantly influences job satisfaction (β = .38) than do normative (β = .05) and calculative (β = –002) commitment. These findings also support our hypothesis and are consistent with OLS results. Third, empowerment (β = .38) and procedural equity perceptions (β = .19) are positively and significantly related to PSOM in a direct way, and goal clarity (β = .60) and objective appraisal systems (β = .40), respectively, also significantly affect these two endogenous variables. Finally, it is shown that GS level, educational level, and job tenure are positively and directly related to PSOM.[19]

Figure 2. Commitment to Stay Full Structural Equation Model (SEM)

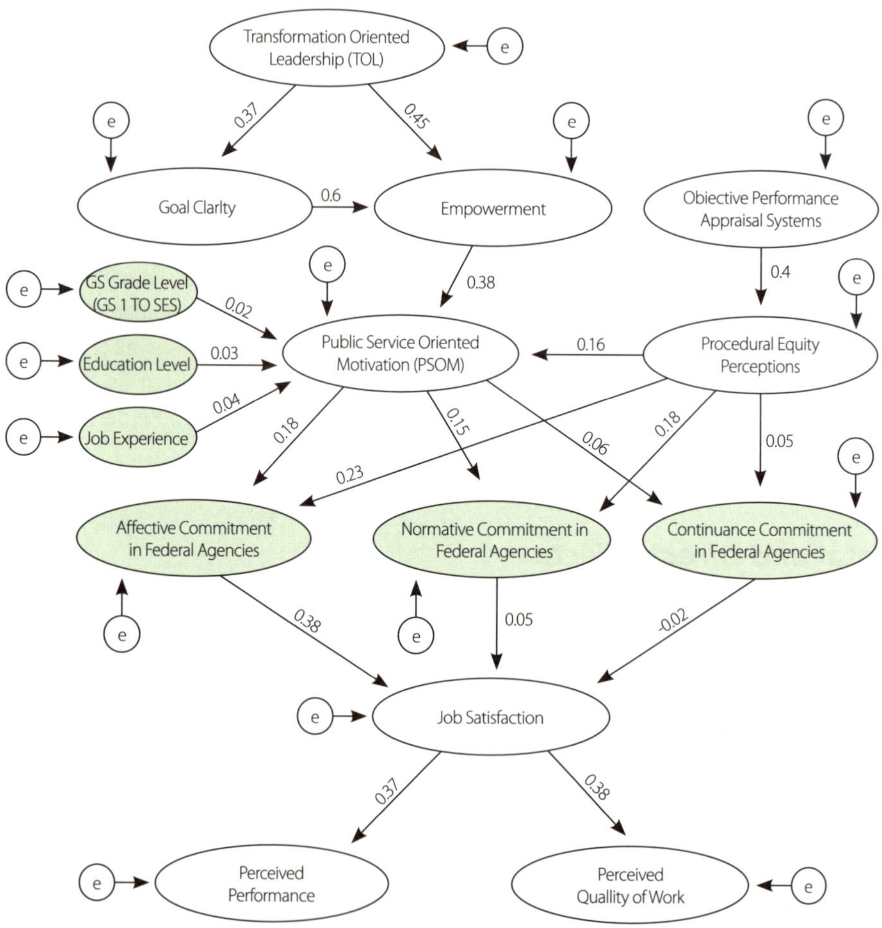

Note: The structural path estimates are presented as standardized regression weights. In this model, all path coefficients (unstandardized) are statistically significant at p < .05 and at p < .01.
Overall Fit Indices of the Commitment to Stay SEM

Overall Fit Indices of the Commitment to Stay SEM

Model	df	χ^2	χ^2/df	RFI	NFI	GFI	CFI	RMSEA	SRMR
Suggested cut-off values			< 3	> 0.90	> 0.90	> 0.90	> 0.90	< 0.08	< 0.08
Model of commitment in federal agencies	184	7018.552	38.144	0.932	0.910	0.910	0.938	0.072	0.068

Note: RFI = relative fit index; NFI = normed fit index; GFI = goodness of fit index; CFI = comparative fit index; RMSEA = root mean square error of approximation; SRMR = standardized root mean residual. Total effective sample size (N) of the SEM model is 6,957 (based on the full information maximum likelihood method).

Table 5. Unstandardized and Standardized Total Effects

	Unstandardized Estimate (B)	Standardized Estimate (β)	SE	t Statis-tic	R^2	p
Goal clarity ← TOL	.58**	.37	.02	33.19	.29	.000
Empowerment ← TOL	.70**	.45	.02	42.24	.51	.000
Empowerment ← goal clarity	.59**	.60	.01	65.95		.000
Procedural equity perceptions ← objective appraisal systems	.33**	.40	.01	36.88	.28	.000
PSOM ← empowerment	.37**	.38	.01	35.63	.20	.000
PSOM ← procedural equity perceptions	.24**	.19	.01	17.81		.000
Affective commitment ← PSOM	.14**	.18	.01	15.11	.17	.000
Normative commitment ← PSOM	.12**	.15	.01	12.63	.14	.000
Continuance commitment ← PSOM	.05**	.06	.01	4.97	.03	.000
Affective commitment ← procedural equity perceptions	.16**	.23	.01	16.23	.22	.00
Normative commitment ← procedural equity perceptions	.12**	.15	.01	12.55	.15	.00
Continuance commitment ← procedural equity perceptions	.05**	.05	.01	5.12	.05	.00
Job satisfaction ← affective commitment	.49**	.38	.01	33.85	.15	.000
Job satisfaction ← normative commitment	.07**	.05	.01	4.78		.000
Job satisfaction ← continuance commitment	–.03**	-.002	.01	–2.09		.000
Perceived performance ← job satisfaction	.37**	.37	.01	33.04	.14	.000
Perceived quality of work ← job satisfaction	.36**	.38	.01	34.49	.15	.000

Note: TOL = transformation-oriented leadership; PSOM = public service-oriented motivation. Total effects can be calculated by summing up direct, indirect,
and spurious effects. Not all total effects were included in this table. Full information about total effects is available from the authors.
**Values are significant at p < .01 and p < .05 (one-tailed).

Indirect Effects

In terms of indirect effects, as hypothesized, the six antecedent variables show positive and indirect impacts on the three commitment variables.[20] However, the effects on the three variables are different; that is, all six antecedent variables most significantly and positively affect the variable of affective commitment, whereas continuance commitment to stay is least influenced by these antecedent variables. These findings are consistent with our hypotheses. The three commitment variables indirectly have a different impact on perceived performance and quality of work; affective commitment has a stronger effect than normative and continuance commitment, whereas the continuance commitment variable has the least (and negative) effect on performance ($\beta = -01$) and quality of work ($\beta = -01$). The results of the indirect effects show that these three commitment variables are sharply contrasted in their relationship with the antecedent and consequence variables.

Discussion and Implications

This study assessed the constructs of three dimensions of commitment in federal agencies and analyzed the antecedents, mediators, and consequences of affective, normative, and continuance commitment. The findings show that there are important differences among the set of work-related attitudes in their relations to the three commitment variables. The SEM confirmed that several antecedents (i.e., TOL, empowerment, goal clarity, PSOM, procedural equity perceptions, and objective appraisal systems) directly and indirectly have significant effects on the commitment variables. More importantly, as predicted, affective commitment is most positively associated with these antecedents, and higher affective commitment also has the most significant effect on job satisfaction, perceived performance, and quality of work. In other words, work attitudes and perceived performance of federal employees whose commitment is affective are very different from people whose commitment is calculative. We need to develop more sophisticated mechanisms to establish affective commitment in federal agencies not only for encouraging employees to stay but also for increasing organizational effectiveness and performance.

A second implication of this commitment study can be related to managerial and civil service reforms in federal agencies. Some recent reform trends have emphasized giving managers more control over employees and market-oriented reforms; some have heavily emphasized extrinsic incentives, as the pay-for-performance reform initiatives around the world have done. These reinventing-government initiatives and the current movement toward privatization of public sector functions often draw on rational choice theory that regards employees as self-interested agents and that emphasizes the contractual relationship with principals (e.g., supervisors). These approaches often emphasize credible commitments or "side bet"conceptions of commitment rather than affective and normative attachment to the organization. Hence, one of the critical issues in reforming federal agencies concerns how to reconcile affectively or normatively committed employees with rationally and calculatively developed managerial systems.

Many reform proposals that focus more on the overall efficiency and instrumental needs of government than on the developmental aspirations and general welfare of employees will be unlikely to achieve high levels of organizational performance or to increase public employees'job commitment. These reform ideas and efforts may have value, but not necessarily, if they work to the detriment of the motives and incentives indicated by the measures of affective and normative commitment in the present study. We should emphasize intrinsic and normative public sector values, such as altruistic service, equity, and participation in public organizations (Wise, 2002).

In addition, some methodological and data limitations suggest that the results should be carefully interpreted. First, a single-source (mono-method) bias could affect the results (Podsakoff & Organ, 1986).[21] Second, we used self-reported, perceived-performance, and quality-of-work variables rather than objectively measured variables. Third, the findings from OLS regression and the SEM analysis are not consistent in some ways. We can assume that the main reason for these different results from these two statistical models is that commitment effects in organizations would have a lot of indirect and unobservable paths (i.e., via several mediating or moderating variables) toward satisfaction or performance rather than having a direct relationship only.[22] In this regard, measuring and interpreting the relationship between antecedents and consequences of commitment should be done more cautiously and rigorously.

Nevertheless, the patterns of the three commitment constructs and effects in federal agencies shown in this study suggest that future research about commitment should be focused on how to manage "human capital" to enhance the performance of people with different kinds of motivation and commitment in federal agencies. It is important to strive for effective design of extrinsic reward systems such as pay systems. The evidence we have presented, from a survey of a large, representative sample of federal employees, indicates the greater importance of finding ways to offer federal employees the incentives and conditions suggested by the measures of affective and normative commitment in this study. These include meaningful, challenging, interesting work and the federal government' reputation as a high-quality employer.

Notes

1. The U.S. Merit Systems Protection Board (MSPB) survey provides important opportunities to analyze federal employee attitudes with a large data set. The survey, however, like other large federal surveys, does not use the same constructs and measures for such concepts as transformational leadership and public service motivation, as researchers who have developed those concepts use (i.e., Bass & Avolio, 1994; Perry & Wise, 1990). This presents us with the challenge of trying to represent those concepts as best we can using the survey items available. To emphasize the distinction between our measures and those more highly developed ones, we refer to our constructs as transformation-oriented leadership (TOL) and public service–riented motivation (PSOM). Although our concepts differ from the more developed ones, they provide valuable evidence about very similar matters from a large sample of federal employees.
2. Some basic assumptions of structural equation modeling (SEM) in this study are (a) the relationship between independent and dependent variables are linear and additive, (b) there is no measurement error in the model, (c) there is no correlation between error terms, and (d) variables are measured by interval or ordinal scales. SEM is particularly sensitive to model specification because failure to include relevant causal variables or inclusion of extraneous variables often substantially affects the path coefficients, which are used to assess the relative importance of various direct and indirect causal paths to the dependent variable.
3. A random sample of 750 full-time, permanent employees was selected from each of the 23 participating agencies. To generalize to the government-wide population, data should be weighted by the STRATWGT variable.
4. We express sincere gratitude to John Ford for releasing the MSPB federal survey data.
5. One of the assumptions of factor analysis is interval data; however, Kim and Muller (1978) suggest that ordinal data can be used if the ordinal categories to the data do not seriously distort the underlying metric scaling.
6. The formula for factor scores is $F_{jk} = \Sigma W_{ji}Z_{ik}$ (F = individual factor scores, W = weighted values, Z = the standardized variables). We gain three advantages by using factor scores in regression. First, we can reduce or eliminate multicollinearity because the variables causing the multicollinearity will combine to form a factor. Second, using factor index, we can use interval-level variables because ordinal-level data can be transformed into interval data that have factor scores. Third, we can reduce the number of variables by making new variables.
7. After getting factor scores and, subsequently, new variables, we assessed reliability (internal consistency), using Cronbach' alpha. Almost all of the scales have an alpha value of .7 or above, so we concluded that all new variables in this model could be

considered as having internal consistency.

8. When we used the listwise deletion method, the total effective sample size (N) of the SEM model was 3,577 out of 6,957; that is, 48.6% of the cases had been dropped from the SEM. To minimize losing data and to keep as much data as possible, we used the expectation-maximization (EM) and the full information maximum likelihood (FIML) methods. There were some differences in the estimated path coefficients and their standard errors.
9. According to Little and Rubin (1987), the EM algorithm (a) replaces missing values with estimated values, (b) estimates parameters, (c) re-estimates the missing values assuming the new parameter estimates are correct, and (d) re-estimates parameters, and so forth, iterating until convergence (p. 129). The FIML method represents a principled method for estimating means and covariances based on incomplete data. In maximum likelihood (ML), parameter estimates are derived such that the likelihood of reproducing the data given the parameter estimates is maximized.
10. The asymptotically distribution free (ADF)/weighted least squares method is useful when the sample size is large. ADF produces asymptotically unbiased, consistent, and efficient estimates of the chisquare test, parameter estimates, and standard error, even under conditions of non-normality.
11. In this study, we used a second-order factor analysis in a confirmatory factor analysis (CFA) model because (a) we wanted to get a more parsimonious CFA model and (b) we found that there were some serious correlated measurement errors in the initial (first order) results.
12. The full information about the descriptive statistics is available from the authors.
13. Skewness can show whether the item' distribution deviates from the symmetrical distribution; kurtosis measures the degree to which the area in a distribution is in the middle or the tails of a distribution. From the descriptive table, we cannot find any serious skewness and normality problem as all values are inside the normal range.
14. However, high internal consistency is not necessarily an indication of unidimensionality. That is, relatively high internal consistency can still be obtained even if a measure is multidimensional. In the composite commitment scale, for example, although there are three subdimensions—ffective, normative, and continuance commitment—e can obtain high internal consistency values.
15. Although both developmental and judgmental appraisals were devised to enhance productivity as their goal, they approach it in two quite distinct ways; that is, judgmental purposes are to assess the management systems, or command-and-control, model of authority, whereas the developmental approach focuses on an individual' potential rather than on his or her current level of skills and capabilities (Daley, 2005).
16. Even though ordinary least squares (OLS) regression is a rigorous and sophistical statistical tool to measure direct casual effects among variables, to examine direct and

indirect effects and to correct for measurement errors, we also employed full SEM, which includes measurement and structural models.

17. All antecedent variables were greater than .20 in tolerance levels and less than 3 in variance inflation factor (VIF), indicating that multivariate multicollinearity was not a great concern in the models.
18. The root mean square error of approximation (RMSEA) was .072, which indicates a relatively good fit for the model (the threshold is .08). Moreover, the values of the relative fit index (RFI), the normed fit index (NFI), the goodness of fit index (GFI), and the comparative fit index (CFI) also point to a good model fit overall, suggesting that the hypothesized commitment to stay model constructed by a path analysis accurately captured the pattern of relationship suggested by the data.
19. Because these three demographic control variables were measured by single indicators, we created three latent variables by assuming reliability values of .8 for each, by setting the factor loading to 1, and by transforming the measurement error variance of these indicators to the appropriate values (e.g., .591).
20. The full information about unstandardized and standardized indirect effects is available from the authors.
21. That is, when the measures of the antecedent and outcome variables come from the same raters or respondents, this can produce confounding results because the assessed overlap between variables may be artifactual (i.e., because of common method variance) and may not reflect the true relationship between the underlying constructs.
22. Concerning the difference between OLS regression and the SEM approach, T. J. B. Kline and Klammer (2001) argue that SEM has some advantages in measuring behavioral and psychological variables more accurately because SEM can provide a more realistic and flexible approach than OLS regression by allowing for nonrecursive paths, by not assuming the variables are measured without error, and by not assuming residuals between the variables are zero (see Pedhazur, 1997).

References

Allen, N. J., & Meyer, J. P. (1990). The measurement and antecedents of affective, continuance and normative commitment to the organization. *Journal of Occupational Psychology, 63,* 1-18.

Avolio, B. J., & Bass, B. M. (2002). *Manual for the multifactor Leadership Questionnaire* (Form 5X). Redwood City, CA: Mindgarden.

Balfour, D. L., & Wechsler, B. (1994). A theory of public sector commitment: Toward a reciprocal model of person and organization. In J. L. Perry (Ed.), *Research in public administration* (pp. 281-314). Greenwich, CT: JAI.

Balfour, D. L., & Wechsler, B. (1996). Organizational commitment: Antecedents and outcomes in public organizations. *Public Productivity and Management Review, 19*(3), 256-277.

Bass, B. M. (1985). *Leadership and performance beyond expectations.* New York: Free Press.

Bass, B. M. (1998). *Transformational leadership: Individual, military, and educational impact.* Mahwah, NJ: Lawrence Erlbaum.

Bass, B. M., & Avolio, B. J. (1994). *Improving organizational effectiveness through transformational leadership.* Thousand Oaks, CA: Sage.

Boyatzis, R. E. (1982). *The competent manager.* New York: John Wiley.

Buchanan, B. (1974). Government managers, business executives, and organizational commitment. *Public Administration Review, 35,* 339-347.

Byrne, B. M. (2001). *Structural equation modeling with AMOS: Basic concepts, applications, and programming.* Mahwah, NJ: Lawrence Erlbaum.

Chun, Y. H., & Rainey, H. G. (2005). Goal ambiguity and organizational performance in U.S. federal agencies. *Journal of Public Administration Research and Theory, 15,* 529-557.

Daley, D. M. (2005). Designing effective performance appraisal systems. In S. E. Condrey (Ed.), *Handbook of human resource management in government* (pp. 499-527). San Francisco: Jossey-Bass.

Eby, L. T., Freeman, D. M., Rush, M. C., & Lance, C. E. (1999). Motivational bases of affective organizational commitment: A partial test of an integrative theoretical model. *Journal of Occupational and Organizational Psychology, 72*(4), 463-483.

Friedrich, C. (1940). Public policy and the nature of administrative responsibility. *Public Policy, 1,* 3-24.

Gaus, J. M. (1936). The responsibility of public administration. In J. M. Gaus (Ed.), *The frontiers of public administration* (pp. 39-40). Chicago: University of Chicago Press.

Halachmi, A., & Krogt, T. V. D. (2005). The role of the manager in employee motivation. In S. E. Condrey (Ed.), *Handbook of human resource management in government* (pp. 469-498). San Francisco: Jossey-Bass.

Hellriegel, D. M., & Slocum, J. W. (2004). *Organizational behavior* (10th ed.). Mason, OH: Thomson/South-Western.

Houston, D. J. (2000). Public-service motivation: A multivariate test. *Journal of Public Administration Research and Theory, 10,* 713-727.

James, L. R., Mulaik, S. A., & Brett, J. M. (1982). *Causal analysis: Assumptions, models, and data.* Beverly Hills, CA: Sage.

Javidan, M., & Waldman, D. A. (2003). Exploring charismatic leadership in the public sector: Measurement and consequences. *Public Administration Review, 63,* 229-242.

Jöreskog, K. G. (1990). New development in LISREL: Analysis of ordinal variables using polychoric correlations and weighted least squares. *Quality and Quantity, 24,* 387-404.

Jöreskog, K. G., & Sörbom, D. (1996). *LISREL 8 user's reference guide.* Chicago: Scientific Software International.

Kemery, E. R., Bedeian, A. G., Mossholder, K. W., & Touliatos, J. (1985). Outcomes of role stress: A multisample constructive replication. *Academy of Management Journal, 28*(2), 363-375.

Kim, J., & Muller, C. E. (1978). *Introduction to factor analysis.* Beverly Hills, CA: Sage.

Kline, R. B. (2005). *Principles and practices of structural equation modeling.* New York: Guilford.

Kline, T. J. B., & Klammer, J. D. (2001). Path model analyzed with ordinary least squares multiple regression versus LISREL. *The Journal of Psychology, 135*(2), 213-225.

Little, R. J., & Rubin, D. B. (1987). *Statistical analysis with missing data.* New York: John Wiley.

Locke, E. A., & Latham, G. P. (1990). *Toward a theory of goal setting and task performance.* Upper Saddle River, NJ: Prentice Hall.

Maruyama, G., & McGarvey, B. (1980). Evaluating causal models: An application of maximum likelihood analysis of structural equations. *Psychological Bulletin, 87,* 502-512.

Mathieu, J., & Zajac, D. (1990). A review and meta-analysis of the antecedents, correlates, and consequences of organizational commitment. *Psychological Bulletin, 108,* 171-194.

McColl-Kennedy, J. R., & Anderson, R. D. (2002). Impact of leadership style and emotions on subordinate performance. *The Leadership Quarterly, 13,* 545-559.

Meyer, J. P., & Allen, N. J. (1991). A three component conceptualization of organizational commitment. *Human Resources Management Review, 1,* 61-89.

Meyer, J. P., & Allen, N. J. (1997). *Commitment in the workplace.* Thousand Oaks, CA: Sage.

Milkovich, G. T., & Wigdor, A. K. (1991). *Pay for Performance: Evaluating performance appraisal and merit pay.* Washington, DC: National Academy Press.

Miller, G. (2000). Above politics: Credible commitment and efficiency in the design of public agencies. *Journal of Public Administration Research and Theory, 10,* 289-327.

Mowday, R. T., Porter, L. W., & Steers, R. M. (1982). *Employee-organization linkages: The psychology of commitment, absenteeism, and turnover.* San Diego, CA: Academic Press.

Pedhazur, E. J. (1997). *Multiple regression in behavioral research: Explanation and prediction* (3rd ed.). Fort Worth, TX: Harcourt Brace Jovanovich.

Perry, J. L. (1996). Measuring public service motivation: An assessment of construct reliability and validity. *Journal of Public Administration Research and Theory, 6*(1), 5-22.

Perry, J. L., & Wise, L. R. (1990). The motivational bases of public service. *Public Administration Review, 50*(3), 367-373.

Podsakoff, P. M., & Organ, D. W. (1986). Self reports in organizational research: Problems and prospects. *Journal of Management, 12,* 531-544.

Prestholdt, P. H., Lane, I. M., & Mathews, R. C. (1987). Nurse turnover as reasoned action: Development of a process model. *Journal of Applied Psychology, 72,* 221-228.

Rainey, H.G. (2003). *Understanding & managing public organizations* (3rd ed.). San Francisco: Jossey-Bass.

Randall, D. M., & O'Driscoll, M. P. (1997). Affective versus calculative commitment: Human resource implications. *The Journal of Social Psychology, 13*(5), 606-617.

Robbins, S. P. (1992). *Essentials of organizational behavior.* Englewood Cliffs, NJ: Prentice Hall.

Robertson, P. J., Lo, C. W., & Tang, S. (2003, October). *Antecedents of commitment among public employees in China.* Paper presented at the Public Management Research Conference, Georgetown University, Washington, DC.

Robertson, P. J., & Tang, S. Y. (1995). The role of commitment in collective action: Comparing the organizational behavior and rational choice perspectives. *Public Administration Review, 55,* 67-80.

Romzek, B. S. (1990). Employee investment and commitment: *The ties that bind. Public Administration Review, 50,* 374-382.

Roth, P. L. (1994). Missing data: A conceptual review for applied psychologists. *Personnel Psychology, 47,* 537-560.

Schwartz, S. H. (1973). Normative explanations of helping behavior: A critique, proposal, and empirical test. *Journal of Experimental Social Psychology, 9,* 349-364.

Somers, M. J. (1993). An examination of the relationship between affective and continuance commitment using non-recursive models. *Journal of Occupational and Organizational Psychology, 66,* 185-192.

Tett, R. P., & Meyer, J. P. (1993). Job satisfaction, organizational commitment, turnover intention, and urnover: Path analyses based on meta-analytic findings. *Personnel Psychology, 46,* 259-293.

Wasti, S. A. (2003). Organizational commitment, turnover, intentions, and the influence of cultural values. *Journal of Occupational and Organizational Psychology, 76,* 303-321.

Wiener,Y. (1982). Commitment in organizations: A normative view. *Academy of Management Review, 7,* 418-428.

Wise, L. R. (2002). Public management reform: Competing drivers of changes. *Public Administration Review, 62,* 555-567.

Wright, B. E. (2004). The role of work context in work motivation: A public sector application of goal and social cognitive theories. *Journal of Public Administration Research and Theory, 14*(1), 59-78.

Appendix

Merit Principles Survey 2000: Selected Representative Survey Items

Antecedent and intermediating variables

Affective commitment (four items) (Cronbach' α = .719)

a. Reputation of the federal government as an employer is important.
b. I would recommend the government as a place to work.
c. The work I do is meaningful to me.

Normative commitment (four items) (Cronbach' α = .760)

a. A reason to stay: Current job duties and responsibilities are important.
b. A reason to stay: Customers you serve are important.
c. A reason to stay: Opportunities to work on my own are important.

Continuance commitment (five items) (Cronbach' α = .783)

a. A reason to stay: Chances for getting promoted in the future are important.
b. A reason to stay: My pay compared to pay for similar jobs outside government.
c. A reason to stay: Poor job market for what you do is important.

Transformation-oriented leadership (TOL; nine items) (Cronbach' α = .936)

a. My supervisor promotes high standards of integrity, conduct, and concern for the public interest (idealized influence).
b. My supervisor looks out for the personal welfare of members of my work unit (individualized consideration).
c. My supervisor would try to help a poor performer improve (inspirational motivation).
d. My supervisor keeps me informed about how well I am doing (intellectual stimulation).

Goal clarity (two items) (Cronbach' α = .617)

a. Employees participate in developing long-range plans in my work unit (measurement of goal intensity).
b. My performance standards are clearly linked to my organization' goals and objectives (measurement of goal clarity).

Empowerment (six items) (Cronbach' α = .814)

a. At the place I work, my opinions seem to count.

b. I am treated with respect in my work unit.

Objective performance appraisal systems (four items) (Cronbach' α = .811)

a. The performance appraisal system motivates me to do a better job (developmental purposes).

b. The standards used to evaluate my performance are fair (judgmental focuses).

Procedural equity perceptions (six items) (Cronbach' α = .845)

In the past 2 years, to what extent do you believe you have been treated fairly regarding the following?

a. Promotions

b. Awards

c. Training

d. Annual performance appraisals

e. Discipline

f. Job assignment

Public service–oriented motivation (PSOM; six items) (Cronbach' α = .765)

a. I am most motivated to do a good job by my duty as a public employee (norm-based motives).

b. I am most motivated to do a good job by personal pride or satisfaction in my work (affective motives).

c. If I perform better in the job, I will receive a non-pay reward (intrinsic rewards).

Outcome variables

Job satisfaction (five items) (Cronbach' α = .782)

a. In general, I am satisfied with my job.

b. Overall, I am satisfied with managers above my immediate supervisor.

Perceived performance: 10-point scale (three items) (Cronbach' α = .767)

a. On a 10-point scale, how would you rate the overall productivity of your organization?

Perceived quality of work (four items) (Cronbach' α = .771)

a. Overall, how would you rate the quality of work performed by the larger organization including your work unit?

Note: All Cronbach scores are standardized based on the standardized items. A complete listing of items in the indices is available from the authors.

Chapter 14

Exploring the Antecedents and Consequences of the Acceptance of Performance Appraisal Systems
: The U.S. Federal Case

Summary

The main purpose of this study is to investigate the antecedents and onsequences of acceptance by employees of performance appraisal systems (APAS) in U.S. federal agencies. Despite the importance of performance appraisal systems (PAS), a relatively small number of studies have explored the topic. Using data collected through a Merit Systems Protection Board (MSPB) survey in U.S. federal agencies, as well as drawing on different types of management theories and a set of testable research hypotheses, this study examines the relationships among antecedents, APAS, and consequences. Placing APAS as a key mediator in a structural equation model, we hypothesize that APAS among employees is influenced by the effects of mission congruency, adequacy of rewards, and organizational justice perceived by employees. In addition, APAS increases job satisfaction and trust in supervisors among employees. The main findings of this research demonstrate that mission congruency, adequacy of rewards, and organizational justice are positively and directly related to APAS. Among these factors, organizational justice is singled out as the most significant factor for APAS. Further, APAS is positively and directly related to job satisfaction and trust in supervisors among employees. Implications of these findings for both public management theory and practice are provided herein.

Keyword

- □ Performance Appraisal Systems
- □ Mission Congruency
- □ Organizational Justice
- □ Job Satisfaction
- □ Organizational Trust

Sung Min Park Associate Professor, Sungkyunkwan University
Byeong il Ahn M.P.A., Sungkyunkwan University

Introduction

Given the material importance of performance appraisal systems (PAS) in an organization, researchers in the fields of human resource management and organizational psychology have long recognized PAS as important factors in the multilateral relationships among a number of work attitudes by employees. In the process of appraising job performance and obtaining feedback, employees ypically gain intrinsic or extrinsic recognition, or receive disciplinary actions, such as salary increases or reductions, compensation, promotions or demotions, transfers, individual training and education, or recommendations for career development (Cleveland, Murphy & Williams, 1989). Studies by Daley (1993), Moussavi and Ashbaugh (1995) have suggested two main purposes of erformance appraisal systems in organizations, which are differentiated by discrete approaches to motivate employees. Two differing types of performance appraisal systems are, 1) developmental approaches to performance appraisal that focus on improving employee performance through organizational support and 2) summative approaches that are explicitly associated with extrinsic rewards, including promotions and increased pay, among other examples of rewards for employees. Drawing on data from the Merit Principles Survey (MPS) 2000, a study by Oh and Lewis (2009) confirmed that extrinsically motivated employees are more likely to have positive views on PAS, implying that performance appraisal systems are able to enhance organizational performance and effectiveness of employees by providing developmental feedback to employees and by linking rewards to individual performance. In addition, by investigating the relationship between the perceptions of PAS and employee intrinsic motivation, Kim and Rubianty (2011) found that public employees' intrinsic motivation or intrinsic reward orientation is significantly and positively associated with perceived procedural fairness of PAS.

Studies associated with performance appraisal are largely focused on finding solutions for the creation and operation of effective and fair performance appraisal management systems. For example, one study by Fedor, Eder, and Buckley (1989) emphasized the credibility of employee raters in terms of job performance. Another study by Longenecker and Gioia (1988) asserted that the acceptability by employees of performance appraisal systems regarding system clarity and achievability of performance standards are what make PAS effective. A study by Rahman (2006) found that even if employees receive low results on their performance appraisals, as long as there is sufficient explanation and proper feedback about the results, then employees report high job satisfaction. In a similar vein, even when receiving lower evaluations, as long as employees feel that they are treated fairly, employees are likely to express more favorable reactions toward PAS in their organizations (Taylor et al., 1995).

These findings reveal that not only performance measurements and results, but also the perceptions or acceptance of PAS among employees, are significant factors for increasing the morale of employees, and consequently, for increasing overall organizational performance. Bowman (1999) noted that the techniques used in a performance appraisal process might be less important than the human and cognitive aspects of the appraisal process. Martin and Bartol (1998) argued that, 1) the quality of the standards used to evaluate employees and 2) employee participation in setting the standards are significant indicators of the effectiveness of a performance appraisal system. A study by Lawler (1967) proposed that perceptions of fairness and acceptability of PAS are influenced by both organizational and individual characteristics.

With respect to the introduction of the pay-for-performance system (PPS), PAS have typically functioned to match levels of individual performance and pay. PPS has been recognized as a type of performance management system that is expected to improve the performance appraisal process in government organizations, and accordingly, to increase organizational effectiveness by helping government employees understand and accept "how their daily performances actually contribute to their overall organizational performance" (Shim et al., 2011, p. 50; GAO, 2003). As Pearce and Perry (1983) suggested, however, in implementing and developing PAS processes for public employees, it is necessary to recognize that public employees might experience some negative or unintentional impacts of a performance- contingent reward system on organizational outcomes within a public organization (Kellough & Lu, 1993). More specifically, in addition to the difficulty of securing and maintaining financial resources and funding in order to adopt PAS in public sectors, public managers typically must consider such fundamental challenges as securing reliable and valid performance appraisal processes, overcoming the weak relationship between pay and motivation in the public sector, and minimizing managerial discretion in the evaluation process. Moreover, organizational goals in the public sector are likely to be more ambiguous, vague, and multidimensional than the organizational goals of private sector agencies. Such multidimensionality makes it more difficult to objectively and accurately measure and evaluate performance or effectiveness of employees in the public sector. A number of empirical studies have provided evidence that a PPS-based performance appraisal system decreases the intrinsic motivation, or public service motivation of government employees, and that public employees in federal and state government agencies show a low level of satisfaction with these new systems (Condrey, 2002; Kellough & Nigro, 2002; Oh & Lewis, 2009; Yang & Kassekert, 2010).

While there are many previous studies on the psychology behind appraisal which investigated the relationship among performance appraisal systems, trust, justice, and important organizational outcomes in the private sector (e.g., see Erdogan, 2002; Greenberg, 1986; Murphy & Cleveland, 1995), there are very few scholarly works that focus on the cognitive and psychological aspects of PAS in a public sector context. That is, while we admit that acceptance of performance appraisal systems (APAS) is the single-most dominant and influential part of performance appraisal processes, in terms of motivating, managing, and compensating public employees, the importance of cognitive processes within PAS is not yet fully emphasized. Moreover, in order to identify the important role of APAS in public organizations, it is necessary to probe other contextual and managerial factors, which possibly affect and mediate the impact of APAS on organizational outcomes. This research utilizes data collected as part of the Merit Principles Survey 2005, conducted by the U. S. Merit Systems Protection Board (MSPB) to identify the nature of APAS in the public sector. First, we present a theoretical framework, which guides our research inquiries into the matter of acceptance by users of performance appraisal systems. Specifically, we probe antecedents and consequences of APAS based on previous research and theoretical arguments. Second, we place APAS as a key variable in the proposed model, and investigate factors that potentially affect the acceptability by employees of performance appraisal systems. Drawing upon previous research and literature about APAS, mission congruency, adequacy of rewards, and organizational justice, this research develops and proposes several research hypotheses. Third, this research tests how APAS is associated with trust in supervisors and job satisfaction among employees, which, for the purposes of this study, are operationalized as organizational consequences. In order to test these hypotheses, this study employs an exploratory factor analysis (EFA), a confirmatory factor analysis (CFA), a multivariate regression analysis, and a structural equation model (SEM) to operationalize and confirm latent constructs, as well as to examine the relationships among variables. Finally, we discuss implications and limitations of our findings for both public management theory and practice.

Performance Appraisal Techniques in the Public Sector

Employee evaluation is a chief activity of management. The selection of an evaluation method depends on the reasons and goals of an organization for evaluating the performance of employees. Within an organizational performance management process, employee appraisal systems are emphasized as crucial personnel management or policy tools that relate the performance goals and achievements of employees to those of the organization and its programs (Nigro et al., 2007). However, in reality, employee evaluation is one of the most difficult and ambiguous personnel functions because "the more appraisal systems are made objective, the more it's evident there is no way to avoid subjectivity" and "although communication of negative information is difficult, not communicating it can be worse" (Berman et al., 2012, pp. 374-375). The most widely used evaluation methods are judgmental approaches which can be categorized as trait-based, behavior-based, and results-based systems.

Traditional Appraisal Systems

Under the rubric of traditional appraisal systems that mainly depend on the ideas of scientific management, merit-based personnel systems, and stipulations of the Civil Service Reform Act (CSRA), the main responsibilities of evaluators were to answer to a set of technical questions which "focus on identifying and ranking job elements, and on how to accurately measure a worker's performance along each of these dimensions" (Nigro et al., 2007, p. 167). Accordingly, the whole evaluation processes in a public organization were not directly related to the core personnel management functions of public agencies such as strategic workforce planning, reward and motivation, program design, and implementation, which causes such three interrelated problems as technical, managerial, and organizational problems that might attenuate the effectiveness and validity of the conventional approaches (Nigro et al., 2007).

New Managerial Approaches

Recently, many public organizations have developed and implemented a hybrid system of MBO, BOS, and BARS techniques. Management by objectives (MBO), which is categorized as a participatory technique, refers to an appraisal process in which exempt employees are partially evaluated on objectives that the employee has co-developed together with his or her supervisor. In participatory reviews, the employee is included in the process of setting performance objectives. While having some disadvantages in public organizations (e.g., MBO processes are more time-consuming than other appraisal methods in terms of setting goals, reviewing employee progress, and completing appraisals), the MBO process is understood to improve organizational communication, clarify expectations for rewards, and increase the commitment of employees to goal attainment (Freyss, 2004). Employees are also evaluated on job-related behaviors associated with specific positions. Such evaluation techniques are relatively common ways of measuring job-related employee performance in the public sector. For example, behavioral observation scales (BOS) ask raters to report the frequency of specific job-related behaviors achieved by employees. In addition, behavioral anchored rating scales (BARS) rely on actual descriptions of important job behaviors that are developed and "anchored" alongside a performance scale for evaluators to select the description of behavior that best matches actual employee behavior for the rating period (Rarick & Baxter, 1986).

Typical barriers to effective performance appraisal include "1) absence of trust in the organization, 2) supervisory training and top management support, 3) rater accountability, 4) overall evaluation of the system itself" and "these can be overcome by nonthreatening feedback, not using numerical rating standards, and ensuring multiple sources of data" (Berman et al., 2012, pp. 401-402). While these performance appraisal techniques are mainly used to provide extrinsic rewards to public employees, it is critical to examine how these techniques and systems are emotionally perceived and affectively accepted by public workers, and further, to investigate which organizational factors might impact the acceptability of PAS in public agencies.[1]

Antecedents of Acceptance of Performance Appraisal Systems

This study proposes a set of antecedent variables that are associated with APAS, job satisfaction, and trust in supervisors among employees in various (i.e., direct and indirect) ways. As a first step, this study examines the effects of (a) mission congruency, (b) adequacy of rewards, and (c) organizational justice on APAS by employees.[2]

Mission Congruency

Mission congruency refers to the level of congruence between the missions held by any person working for an organization and the organization itself, as well as how important the agency's mission is to the employee. The more that employees perceive that they understand the mission of their organization, and perceive that they contribute to the mission of their organization, the more likely that employees have a high level of mission congruency. This situation has been defined as person-organization (P-O) fit (Adkins, Russell & Werbel, 1994). P-O fit is commonly understood in terms of the relative congruence between the values and goals of employees and the resources and culture of an organization (Bright, 2007; Chatman, 1991; Boxx, Odom, and Dunn, 1991), or as the compatibility between person and organization (Kristof, 1996). While the multidimensional nature of P–O fit can be conceptualized into supplementary fit (measured by values congruence and personality congruence) and complimentary fit (measured by work environment congruence), the previous literature suggests that either type of P-O fit has positive impacts on employees' attitudes and behaviors in general (Bretz & Judge, 1994; Bright, 2007). That is, many researchers regard P-O fit as a key predictor, or mediator or moderator, to increase organizational effectiveness due to factors such as employee job satisfaction, commitment, and performance. For example, while Holton (1999) and Cable and Parsons (2001) have proved through longitudinal research that P-O fit has a significant influence on the turnover of newcomers, Bright (2007) showed that P-O fit plays an important role in the relationship between public service motivation (PSM) and job performance among public employees. Because P-O fit is important for understanding how employees will function in their situations, the issue has been much studied in the management literature of many sectors. P-O fit, or mission congruency, has been associated with work-related outcomes such as job satisfaction, turnover intention, and organizational commitment among employees (Fritzsche, Powell, & Hoffman, 1999; Boxx et al., 1991; Cable & Judge, 1996). In a similar vein, Saari and Judge (2004) confirmed that, among many managerial factors, P-O fit is the most important antecedent variable to increasing the job satisfaction of employees. Kristof-Brown, Zimmerman, and Johnson (2005) also found that P-O fit is strongly related to a range of job satisfaction, organizational commitment, and turnover intention. Based on this previous research, we have developed the following hypothesis:

> **Hypothesis 1:** Mission congruency is positively related to job satisfaction. Employees with a high level of mission congruency will have a high level of job satisfaction.

Although not a lot of studies about P-O fit have appeared in performance appraisal system research in particular, a study by Whiting and Kline (2007) found that personal needs and benefits provided by PAS in an organization can significantly influence employee attitudes. That is, this research supports our heuristic proposition that P-O fit or mission congruence affects employee attitudes through its PA system. Whiting et al. (2008) also found that performance appraisal congruency predicted overall system satisfaction, perceived usefulness and fairness. It means that if employees perceive that the performance appraisal system is well congruent with their expectations, then positive outcomes should be guaranteed. Based on these findings, we have posited the following hypothesis:

> **Hypothesis 2:** Mission congruency is positively related to APAS. Employees with a high level of mission congruency will have a high level of APAS.

Adequacy of Rewards

Many previous studies suggest that the fair and acceptable reward systems may lead to the positive views on PAS and hence may enhance the level of performance of an organization. Rewards usually refer to financial rewards, including pay, promotions, and incentives, all of which are supposed to be received from organizations on merit, as a result of individual performance. Recognition means the extent to which employees are appreciated by the organization, as well as how much the outputs of employees are valued (Danish, 2010). The perception or recognition by employees about the adequacy of rewards can be defined as the degree of personal satisfaction brought by the rewards received from an organization, or the degree to which rewards are regarded as a significant factor to intrinsically or extrinsically motivate employees. A motive is an outcome that is desirable, which causes an employee to act in a certain way or do a certain thing. The expectancy theory of motivation explains the process by which outcomes become desirable. A study by Tolman (1938) stated that behavior is directly related to expectations.

From a cognitive theory perspective, the classic expectancy theory proposed by Vroom (1964) attempts to explain how people make decisions (Chiang, Jang, Canter & Prince, 2010). Drawing on three concepts of valence, instrumentality, and expectancy, the theory indicates that individuals will be highly motivated to achieve good performance when they expect that (a) their efforts lead to good performance, (b) good performance leads to valued rewards, and (c) the rewards are valuable to them. The force (F) of an individual's motivation can be expressed in the expectancy equation: $F = V \times I \times E$. That is, if employees elieve that good performance leads to valued rewards within their organizations, then the individuals will be highly motivated to achieve good performance. If a performance appraisal system is operated fairly and effectively, then that system will provide valued rewards to employees as a result of good performance on their part. Within this context, the satisfaction of employees with their rewards implies that they have favorable attitudes toward performance appraisal systems in their organizations. Therefore, when employees experience a high degree of adequacy of rewards, they have a high level of APAS within their organizations. Accordingly, we have developed the following hypothesis:

> **Hypothesis 3:** Adequacy of rewards is positively related to the acceptance of performance appraisal systems among employees. Employees that experience a high degree of adequacy of rewards will have a high level of APAS.

Organizational Justice

Early studies by Adams focused on the psychology of organizational justice among employees (Adams, 1963). Recent academic works have revealed that the perception of employees about organizational justice is a significant predictor of employee attitudes toward work in general (Aree, Budhwar, & Chen, 2002). Organizational justice has been defined as "the individual's and the group's perception of the fairness of treatment received from an organization and their behavioral reaction to such perceptions" (Aryee et al., 2002, p. 269; James, 1993). A meta-analysis study by Cohen-Charash & Spector (2001) found that organizational justice is a multidimensional construct, composed of distributive, procedural, and interpersonal types of justice, which are strongly related to one another but conceptually distinctive. Distributive justice deals with the fairness of outcomes, such as the determination of pay and promotion decisions. Procedural justice is defined as the fairness of the processes by which outcomes are allocated. Interpersonal justice relates to the quality of communication processes with supervisors or managers (Cohen-Charash & Spector, 2001). In contrast to distributive justice, the concepts of procedural and interpersonal justice have been newly developed in recent literature. Researchers have suggested that not only the fair distributive allocations of organizational outcomes, but also procedural fairness, should matter for the overall satisfaction of employees (Greenberg, 1990). In addition, Bies (1986) argued that perceived procedural justice is significantly impacted by the interpersonal skills of supervisors or managers for managing and directing employees.

Adams's equity theory (1965) suggests that individuals tend to compare their rewards and contributions to the rewards and contribution of others. The theory further suggests that the more intense inequity individuals may feel, the stronger the motivation they have to act, or to act out against the inequity. When employees perceive that organizational outcomes are fairly allocated, or when organizational rules and processes are fairly known, employees tend to be satisfied with their positions. Job satisfaction in turn leads to positive attitudes toward their organizations and supervisors. There is much empirical evidence to support the causal relationship between organizational justice and other important organizational outcomes (Choong Kwai Fatt, Edward Wong Sek Khin, & Tioh Ngee Heng, 2010; Whisenant & Smucker, 2009). Research about the relationship between organizational justice and the work attitudes of employees has been conducted in many fields. For example, Using CFA and SEM methods, Colquitt (2001) validated a 4-factor structure to the measure of organizational justice (with distributive, procedural, interpersonal, and informational justice) as distinct dimensions and also found that each dimension of organizational justice provides significant impacts on such organizational outcomes as leader evaluation, rule compliance, commitment, and helping behavior. Among existing research, the relationship between organizational justice and job satisfaction has been a prominent topic (Whisenant & Smucker, 2009). For example, a study by Rubin (2009) found that procedural justice positively affects job satisfaction, as well as trust in managers in the U.S. Department of Defense. A study by Choi (2010) revealed that higher levels of distributive, procedural, and interpersonal justice are positively associated with job satisfaction and trust in management. Based on this theoretical background and previous research, we have posited the following hypothesis:

Hypothesis 4: Organizational justice is positively related to job satisfaction. Employees that experience a high level of organizational justice will have a high level of job satisfaction.

Organizational justice plays an important role in affecting the perceptions of performance appraisal systems among employees. While Gabris & Ihrke (2000) argued that "central to employee acceptance of performance appraisal systems is whether the system deployed is perceived as procedurally fair and valid to recipient employees (p. 42)," both procedural justice in appraisal processes and distributive justice in performance appraisal outcomes should be emphasized and regarded as vital elements that together determine whether employees accept or reject the fairness and effectiveness of performance appraisal systems. Fairness in PAS, for example, is strongly related to organizational justice because fairness will encourage favorable attitudes among employees toward their organizations, and eventually cause a high level of APAS among employees. We have hypothesized that organizational justice (e.g., perceived fairness in PAS, among other measure of perceived justice by employees) significantly influences the acceptance of performance appraisal systems by employees.

Hypothesis 5: Organizational justice is positively related to APAS. Employees that perceive a high level of organizational justice will have a high level of APAS.

Among relationships between organizational justice and work attitudes, the particular relationship of employee trust in supervisors has received considerable attention. Blau's social exchange theory (1964) emphasizes the role of trust in the establishment and preservation of a social exchange relationship. Social exchange refers to the voluntary actions of individuals motivated by the returns the individuals expect to receive. When supervisors or organizations provide fair treatment to employees, the social exchange relationship among the parties is enhanced. In a similar vein, leader-member exchange (LMX) theory also draws on the quality of relationships between supervisors and subordinates, relying on the concept of trustworthy social exchanges (Linden, Sparrowe & Wayne, 1997). Based on these theories, some studies have found that procedural justice plays an important role in fostering employee trust in supervisors (Kim & Mauborgne, 1991; Konovsky & Pugh, 1994). In addition, a few empirical studies have mentioned that distributive justice and interpersonal justice are positively related to employee trust in supervisors (Albrecht & Travaglione, 2003; Aree et al., 2002). Overall, the more that employees perceive that they have been fairly and equitably treated in their organizations (that is, the more that they perceive a clear sense of organizational justice), the more enhanced their level of trust in supervisors will be (Saunders, Mark & Thornhill, 2003).

Hypothesis 6: Organizational justice is positively related to employee trust in supervisors. Employees that perceive a high level of organizational justice will have a high level of trust in 8 supervisors.

Consequences of Acceptabiity of Performance Appraisal Systems

Job Satisfaction

Goal-setting theory has received a great deal of attention in management and employment practices. A study by Locke and Latham (1990) found that goal specificity and goal difficulty significantly influence task performance by employees. That is, when specific and challenging goals are given to employees, the performance of employees is more greatly improved than when goals are vague, numerous, or at cross-purposes with each other. Moreover, when employees participate in goal-setting processes, their commitment to achieving goals and their overall performance within an organization increase (Erez & Arad, 1986).

The process of management by objectives (MBO) employs goal-setting theory and emphasizes "principles and implications" in the workplace as a motivational tool (Drucker, 1974). Some main principles of MBO, such as goal clarity, consistency between the objectives of organizations and the objectives of individuals, participation in decision making, autonomy, and feedback, suggest that employee participation in performance goal setting and periodic feedback from management are critical in making positive impacts on the work attitudes of employees.

The level of individual task performance is affected by active participation in setting goals and standards. Within the context of performance appraisal systems, if these motivational conditions are fully met and employees are willing to accept their performance appraisal systems, then employees will be more satisfied.

Hypothesis 7: APAS is positively related to job satisfaction. Employees that more positively perceive performance appraisal systems will have a high level of job satisfaction.

Trust in Supervisors

Interpersonal and organizational trust can be shaped, developed, or diminished by different types of reciprocal and social interactions, such as information exchange, interpersonal communications, and networks (Park, 2011; Park & Rainey, 2011). Regarding the impact of performance appraisal systems within organizations, the current study asserts that objective and effective performance appraisal systems help organizations foster organizational trust, especially trust in supervisors among employees. A study by Mayer and Davis (1999) suggested that trust can be categorized according to three factors of ability, benevolence, and integrity. In terms of these factors relative to performance appraisal, ability is the extent to which a supervisor has the skills and competencies to properly evaluate employees. Benevolence is the extent to which a supervisor has a sincere interest in employees. Integrity refers to the perception of employees about how effectively their supervisors would measure up to evaluation under the same performance appraisal standards and principles expected of the employees. If these elements of trust are well combined, then the overall level of trust in supervisors by employees will increase. Previous research has confirmed that if performance appraisal systems are more acceptable, then employees show higher levels of trust in supervisors (Cummings, 1983; Mayer & Davis, 1999). Similarly, a study by Mani (2002) found that trust in supervisors is an important predictor in determining the attitudes of employees toward a performance appraisal system.

Hypothesis 8: APAS is positively related to trust in supervisors. Employees that more positively perceive performance appraisal systems have a high level of trust in supervisors.

Trust in Supervisors and Job Satisfaction

According to Herzberg's two-factor theory, in a workplace environment, motivator factors for employees are achievement, recognition, the work itself, responsibility, and advancement. Key hygiene needs include company policy and administration, supervision, salary, interpersonal relationships, and working conditions (Herzberg, Mausner & Snyderman, 1959). Trust, as a key motivator, has been recognized as a vital element to motivate employees and to enhance organizational effectiveness (Argyris, 1973). From an economics perspective, Hill (1990) argued that trust reduces transactional costs and opportunism, and further, that trust facilitates cooperation among organizational constituents. Additionally, McGregor's motivational ideas of Theory X and Theory Y suggest that Theory Y managers tend to believe in, and to empower, employees to work with autonomy and responsibility (McGregor, 1960), implying that trust among employees influences job satisfaction. Previous empirical studies have confirmed these theories by showing that trust in supervisors affects the job satisfaction of employees (Tan & Tan, 2000), and that trust plays an important role in moderating the relationship between individual-job congruence and job satisfaction (Goris, Vaught & Petti Jr., 2003). Each of these previous findings contributes to the following hypothesis:

> **Hypothesis 9:** Trust in supervisors is positively related to job satisfaction. Employees with a high level of trust in supervisors will have a high level of job satisfaction.

Research Methods and Measures

This study first employs exploratory factor analysis (EFA) and confirmatory factor analysis (CFA) to operationalize variables and to confirm latent variables. Second, we employ multivariate regression to examine the relationships among variables. Finally, we develop a structural equation model (SEM) to confirm the total, direct, and indirect effects of variables, and to test interrelationships among variables using AMOS 18.0. We employ the maximum likelihood (ML) estimation method to obtain unbiased results in SEM.

Data

Data utilized in this study is obtained from the Merit Principles Survey 2005, conducted by the U. S. Merit Systems Protection Board (MSPB). The survey aims to investigate the perceptions of federal employees about jobs, work environments, supervisors, and agencies. Twenty-four federal agencies participated in the survey and a total of 36,926 employees completed the survey (U.S. Merit Systems Protection Board, 2008).[3]

Missing Data Adjustments

In handling missing data adjustments, the listwise, or pairwise, deletion method is typically employed. This method sacrifices a number of data, however, due to removing from analysis all cases with missing data. In order to preserve an effective sample size while adjusting for missing data, this study employs the Expectation-Maximization (EM) method. The EM method enhances statistical power of a model and minimizes possible bias in parameter estimates (Roth, 1994).

Measurement of Acceptance of PAS

We have defined acceptance of performance appraisal systems as the perceived acceptability and satisfaction of employees toward performance appraisal systems in agencies. The definition also includes the degree of comprehensive understanding about, and participation in, performance appraisal systems by the employees being evaluated. We use six items (Cronbach's α = .889) to measure employee acceptance of PAS.

Measurement of Antecedent Variables of Acceptance of PAS

We suppose that acceptance of PAS is influenced by three antecedent variables, including mission congruence, adequacy of rewards, and organizational justice. Organizational justice is made up of three components, including distributive, procedural, and interpersonal justice (see Appendix and Figure 1). In addition to these antecedent variables, we include control variables such as gender, age, ethnicity, and education level.

Mission Congruence. We use three items to measure mission congruence. The survey asked employees to evaluate the degree of congruence, meaning that the employees understand their agency's mission and that the agency's mission is important to them (Cronbach's α = .875).

Adequacy of Rewards. Adequacy of rewards is measured by six items (Cronbach's α = .842). Federal employees were asked whether they are satisfied with outcomes provided by their organizations as a result of their performance. Both extrinsic and intrinsic rewards are included in the rewards category in this study.

Organizational Justice. Our study measures distributive justice as the appropriateness and fairness with which employees think they are treated by personnel management (e.g., in terms of opportunities for career advancement, job assignments, and training), and uses four items (Cronbach's α = .786). Procedural justice is the degree of belief of employees that appeal procedures, should employees have occasion to use them, respond appropriately to complaints, and is measured by three items (Cronbach's α = .891). Finally, interpersonal justice represents the quality of communication processes with supervisors or managers, and is measured by five items (Cronbach's α = .862).

Measurement of Outcome Variables

Job Satisfaction and Trust in Supervisors. The two outcome variables utilized in this study are job satisfaction and employee trust in supervisors (see Appendix). The first variable, job satisfaction, includes five items (Cronbach's α = .899). The second outcome variable, trust in supervisors, represents the extent to which employees think that their supervisors exercise authority in a fair and effective manner. This variable is measured by eight items (Cronbach's α = .964). In the following analysis by multiple regression and SEM, we test the statistical effects 13 among antecedent and consequent variables.

Finding and Results

CFA Results

Figure 1 and Table 1 show the results of the second-order confirmatory factor analysis (CFA) for organizational justice. Based on previous studies, we assume that organizational justice is a multi-dimensional construct that includes elements of distributive, procedural, and interpersonal justice, and we confirm these statements by factor analysis. The model fit was within statistically acceptable levels (see the model fit table). Specifically, fit indices, CFI, GFI, NFI, IFI, and RFI, are more than .90 (values greater than 0.90 are acceptable), and RMSEA is .077 (a value less than .08 is acceptable). In addition, CFA outputs reveal that the first-order factor is strongly related to the second-order factor. These results show that the sub-dimensions of organizational justice are strongly related to one another, but also mutually distinct. The model displayed that distributive justice is the most salient factor, followed by interpersonal justice and then procedural justice, in terms of perceptions of organizational justice among employees. The results are consistent with the great deal of attention that distributive justice has traditionally received in existing literature, suggesting that with the fair distribution of the allocation of outcomes, employees perceive justice in their organizations.

Figure 1. Second-Order Confirmatory Factor Analysis (CFA) for Organizational Justice Scale

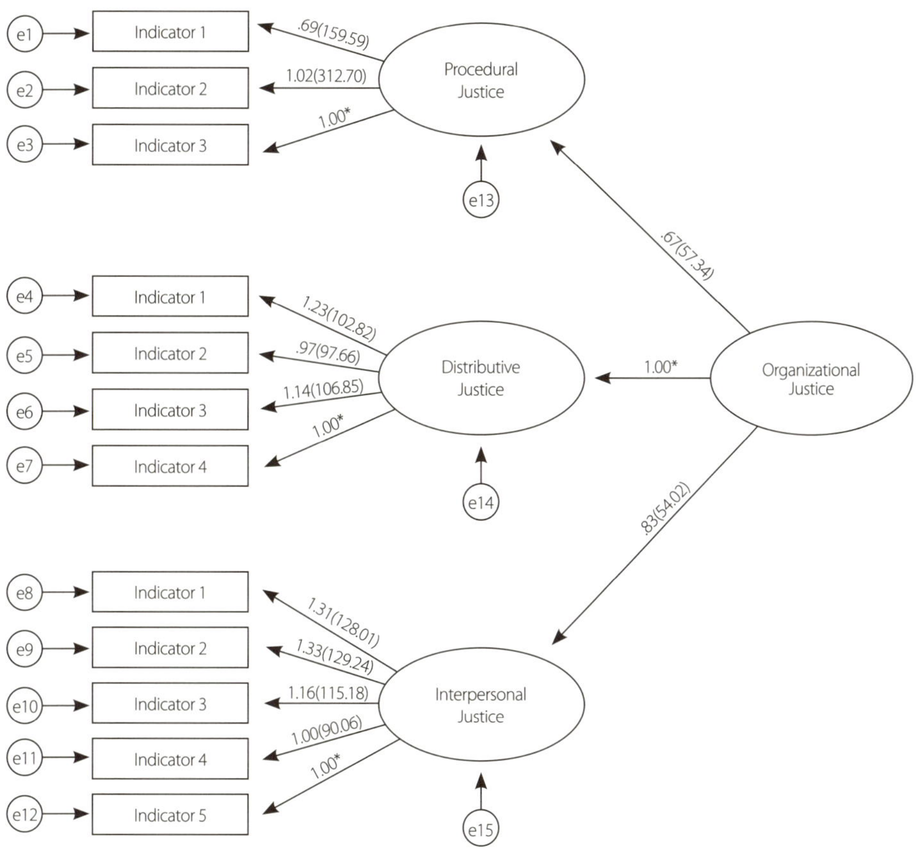

Fit Indices of the CFA Model

Model 1	df	Chi-Square	CFI	GFI	NFI	IFI	RFI	AGFI	RMSEA
Suggested Cut-off Values			>.90	>.90	>.90	>.90	>.90	>.85	<.08
A Measurement Model	51	11162.20	.956	.944	.955	.956	.942	.915	.077

Table 1. Second-Order Confirmatory Factor Analysis (CFA) for Organizational Justice Scale

		Estimate	S. E.	C. R.	p
Procedural Justice	Organizational Justice	.674	.012	57.344	***
Distributive Justice	Organizational Justice	1.000*	-	-	-
Interpersonal Justice	Organizational Justice	.831	.015	54.024	***
Procedural Justice	Indicator 1	.694	.004	159.591	***
	Indicator 2	1.018	.003	312.701	***
	Indicator 3	1.000*	-	-	-
Distributive Justice	Indicator 1	1.228	.012	102.819	***
	Indicator 2	.970	.010	97.663	***
	Indicator 3	1.140	.011	106.854	***
	Indicator 4	1.000*	-	-	-
Interpersonal Justice	Indicator 1	1.309	.010	128.010	***
	Indicator 2	1.334	.010	129.242	***
	Indicator 3	1.157	.010	115.180	***
	Indicator 4	.997	.011	90.056	***
	Indicator 5	1.000*	-	-	-

Note: *The value of 1.0 is assigned for analysis.
***Esimated significantly at .001 level.

Correlations and Multiple Regression Results

The correlations of all the variables are presented in Table 2. First of all, acceptance of PAS is positively correlated with three antecedent variables, including mission congruence, adequacy of rewards, and organizational justice. Among these variables, adequacy of rewards has the highest correlation coefficients (r = .582). Second, the correlations between job satisfaction and other variables are all significant. Not only the main antecedent variables, but also the control variables, are statistically related to job satisfaction. Trust in supervisors has the highest correlation coefficients (r = .656) with job satisfaction, followed by organizational justice (r = .640) and acceptance of PAS (r = .609). Trust in supervisors has similar correlation results to job satisfaction. It is remarkable that organizational justice is the most positively correlated with trust in supervisors.

Any accurate regression analysis of data needs to first resolve the problem of multicollinearity. The significant results of correlation analysis in the current study do not warrant concerns of multicollinearity among antecedent variables. Measures of all antecedent variables were greater than .50 in tolerance levels, and less than 2 in variance inflation factor (VIF). Accordingly, the concern about multicollinearity was not great in the models. The results of multiple regression are presented in Table 3 and Table 4. Table 3 investigates the causal relationships between antecedent variables and the acceptance of PAS among employees.

Table 2. Zero-Order Correlations among Antecedent, Control, and Consequent Variable

Variables	1	2	3	4	5	6	7	8	9	10
Mission Congruence	1									
Adequacy of Rewards	.266***	1								
Organizational Justice	.327***	.593***	1							
Acceptance of PAS	.331***	.582***	.576***	1						
Trust in Supervisors	.278**	.545***	.694***	.607***	1					
Job Satisfaction	.447***	.584***	.640***	.609***	.656***	1				
Gender	.009	.010*	.007	-.017**	.029***	.043***	1			
Age	-.069***	-.046***	.020***	.000	.012*	-.017**	-.104***	1		
Education Level	-.067***	-.062***	-.076***	.001	-.038***	-.034***	-.138***	.049***	1	
Ethnicity	-.030***	-.056***	-.088***	-.012*	-.074***	-.053***	-.119***	.085***	.069***	1

*Correlation is significant at the 0.1 level (two-tailed).
** Correlation is significant at the 0.05 level (two-tailed).
*** Correlation is significant at the 0.01 level (two-tailed).

Table 3. Multiple Regression Results: Antecedents of APAS

Dependent Variables	Acceptance of Performance Appraisal Systems (APAS)		
Antecedent Variables	Unstandardized Coefficients (B)	t	Standardized Coefficients (β)
Mission Congruence	.203**	29.635	.135
Adequacy of Rewards	.345**	67.402	.359
Organizational Justice	.386**	59.862	.326
Control Variables			
Gender	-.021*	-2.671	-.012
Age	.001*	2.796	.012
Education level	.036**	12.139	.052
Ethnicity	.064**	8.180	.035
N	30897		

R^2	.441
Adjusted R^2	.441

*p < .05. **p <. 01

The results show that the set of antecedent variables accounts for 44.1 percent of variance in the acceptance of PAS by employees. Mission congruence (β = .135), adequacy of rewards (β = .359), and organizational justice (β = .326) are statistically significant (p < .01). This finding means that employees that experience congruence of mission between their organizations and themselves, that are satisfied with the rewards for their performance, and that think that their organizations treat them fairly, will have high levels of acceptance of PAS. Accordingly, Hypotheses 2, 3, and 5 are confirmed. Table 4 explores the relationships among antecedent variables and consequent outcome variables, which are job satisfaction and trust in supervisors.

Table 4. Multiple Regression Results: Job Satisfaction & Trust in Supervisor

Dependent Variables	Job Satisfaction			Trust in Supervisor		
Main Antecedent Variables	Unstandardized Coefficients (B)	t	Standardized Coefficients (β)	Unstandardized Coefficients (B)	t	Standardized Coefficients (β)
Mission Congruence	.324**	55.365	.218	.011	1.606	.007
Adequacy of Rewards	.123**	20.960	.130	.113**	20.564	.105
Organizational Justice	.183**	22.473	.166	.626**	91.704	.472
Acceptance of PAS	.173**	34.463	.175	.305**	53.581	.272
Trust in Supervisor	.264**	54.520	.300			
Control Variables						
Gender	.063**	9.425	.035	.060**	7.649	.030
Age	.000	0.542	.002	.001**	3.261	.013
Education level	.014**	5.483	.020	.007*	2.449	.009
Ethnicity	.003	0.518	.002	-.043**	-5.459	-.021
N		30897			30897	
R^2		.588			.554	
Adjusted R^2		.588			.554	

*p < .05. **p < .01

First, in terms of job satisfaction, the set of antecedent variables and control variables accounts for 56.1 percent of variance. All antecedent variables have a statistically significant and positive effect on job satisfaction. Among them, trust in supervisors (β = .300) has the greatest effect on job satisfaction. Mission congruence (β = .218), acceptance of PAS (β = .175), and organizational justice (β = .166) are also statistically significant. That is, employees that trust their supervisors, have congruence of mission between their organizations and themselves, accept the performance appraisal systems within their organizations, and that think that their organizations treat them fairly, will be highly satisfied with their jobs. Accordingly, Hypotheses 1, 4, 7, and 9 are confirmed. Furthermore, the other variables of adequacy of rewards (β = .130), gender (β = .035), and education level (β = .020) have significant and positive effects on job satisfaction for employees.

Second, the set of antecedent variables accounts for 55.4 percent of variance in employee trust in supervisors. With the exception of mission congruence, the rest of the antecedent variables have a statistically significant and positive effect on employee trust in supervisors. Specific results show statistical significance of adequacy of rewards (β = .105), organizational justice (β = .472), and acceptance of PAS (β = .272). In particular (and as hypothesized), organizational justice and acceptance of PAS have a great influence on trust in supervisors by employees. Therefore, Hypotheses 6 and 8 are confirmed.

SEM Results

In the final phase of analysis, we employed a structural equation model (SEM). From SEM analysis, we observe that antecedent and consequent variables are directly and indirectly related to a key variable, namely the acceptance of PAS by employees. The SEM indicated that acceptance of PAS is related to mission congruence, adequacy of rewards, and organizational justice. Acceptance of PAS directly relates to job satisfaction and trust in supervisors, and in turn through trust in supervisors, APAS indirectly influences job satisfaction. Mission congruence relates to job satisfaction directly and by way of acceptance of PAS. Finally, organizational justice has a strong influence on job satisfaction directly and indirectly via employee trust in supervisors. The model fit indices of CFI (= .940), GFI (= .905), NFI (= .939), IFI (= .940), RFI (= .934), AGFI (= .892), and RMSEA (= .502) exceeded the cut-off for acceptable values. Only the result of the chi-square test was not acceptable X^2/df = 99.29). A study by Jöeskog (1990) suggested that the chi-square test is very sensitive to the sample number, and further that the dismissal probability of proposed models increases as sample size increases. Accordingly, even though our proposed model has a good explanatory power, due to the large sample size (n = 36,926), the chi-square value deviated from a good fit.

Figure 2. Structural Equation Model (SEM)

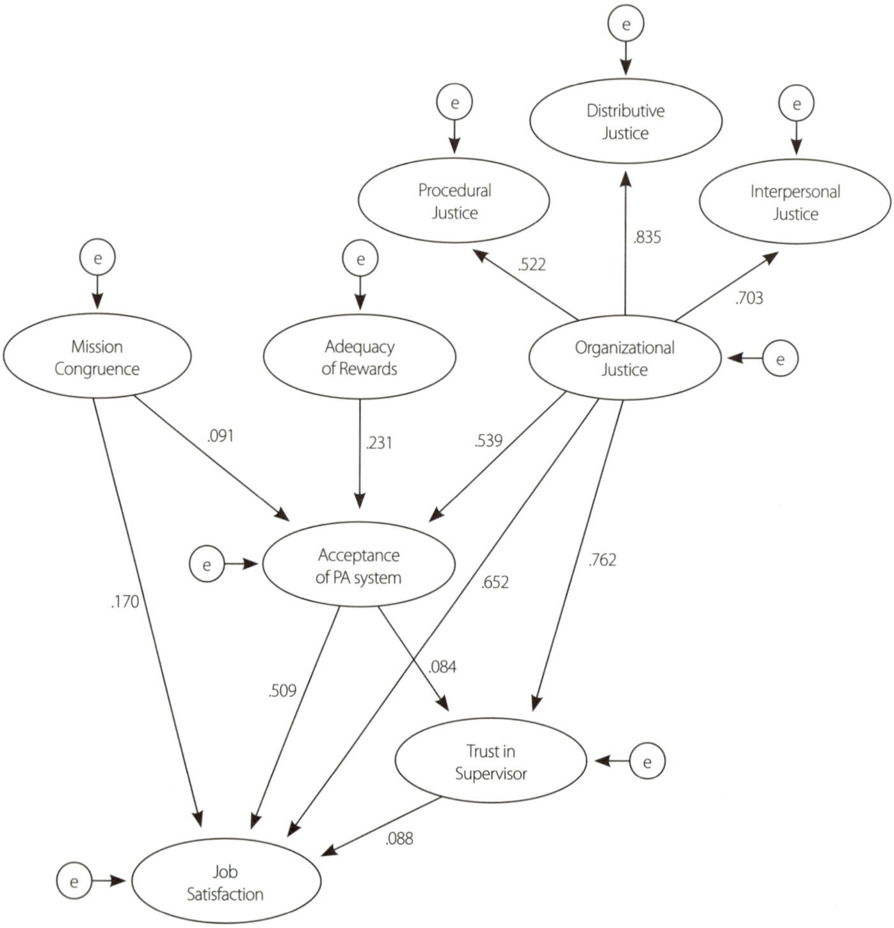

Fit Indices of the SEM

Model 1	df	Chi-Square	CFI	GFI	NFI	IFI	RFI	AGFI	RMSEA
Suggested cut-off values			>.90	>.90	>.90	>.90	>.90	>.85	<.08
Structural equation model /Path model	650	64539.83	.940	.905	.939	.940	.934	.892	.052

Total and Direct Effects

Figure 2 and Table 4 show that mission congruence (β = .091), adequacy of rewards (β = .231), and organizational justice (β = .539) have positive influences on employee acceptance of PAS directly. Second, employee acceptance of PAS significantly influences job satisfaction (β = .509) and trust in supervisors (β = .084) directly. Third, job satisfaction is related to mission congruence (β = .170) and organizational justice (β = .652) in a direct way. Finally, trust in supervisors shows a significant direct relationship to organizational justice (β = .762). These results are consistent with the results of multiple regression analysis, and they support our hypotheses.

Table 5. Unstandardized and Standardized Total Effects

	Un-standardized estimate (B)	Standardized estimate (β)	S. E.	C. R.	p
Acceptance of PAS ← Mission Congruence	.131	.091	.01	17.98	***
Acceptance of PAS ← Adequacy of Rewards	.188	.231	.01	25.30	***
Acceptance of PAS ← Organizational Justice	.979	.539	.02	45.03	***
Trust in Supervisor ← Acceptance of PAS	.098	.084	.01	9.93	***
Job Satisfaction ← Acceptance of PAS	.057	.509	.01	7.57	***
Job Satisfaction ← Mission Congruence	.233	.170	.01	37.58	***
Trust in Supervisor ← Organizational Justice	1.61	.762	.02	66.46	***
Job Satisfaction ← Organizational Justice	1.13	.652	.03	43.38	***
Job Satisfaction ← Trust in Supervisor	.073	.088	.01	9.60	***

Indirect Effects

To assess whether APAS and trust in supervisor mediated the effects of a set of antecedents on outcome variables, we used a Sobel's Z statistic test and a bootstrap method. Each indirect path coefficient was calculated to determine whether the indirect effects (mediating effects) were statistically significant. The three antecedent variables of mission congruence, adequacy of rewards, and organizational justice have positive and indirect impacts on both consequent variables, namely, job satisfaction and trust in supervisors, through the APAS. As shown in Table 6, all the coefficients for the indirect paths of the SEM were significant (all the Sobel's Z statistics are statistically significant). Also, the results of a bootstrap analysis (Table 7) confirm that the mediating effects are shown to be statistically significant ($p < \alpha=0.05$). In particular, organizational justice most significantly affects the job satisfaction and trust in supervisors of employees in an indirect way. In contrast, mission congruence least relates to consequent variables. Job satisfaction is also indirectly influenced by acceptance of PAS through employee trust in supervisors. Analysis of indirect effects clarifies and enriches the relationships among the antecedent and consequent variables.

Table 6. The Results of Sobel's test

Path	Test Statistic	p-value ($p < \alpha=0.05$)
Mission Congruence → APAS → Job Satisfaction	7.15	$0.0 < \alpha=0.05$
Adequacy of Rewards → APAS → Job Satisfaction	7.55	$0.0 < \alpha=0.05$
Organizational Justice → APAS → Job Satisfaction	7.78	$0.0 < \alpha=0.05$
Mission Congruence → APAS → Trust in Supervisor	8.65	$0.0 < \alpha=0.05$
Adequacy of Rewards → APAS → Trust in Supervisor	9.40	$0.0 < \alpha=0.05$
Organizational Justice → APAS → Trust in Supervisor	9.84	$0.0 < \alpha=0.05$
APAS → Trust in Supervisor → Job Satisfaction	6.85	$0.0 < \alpha=0.05$
Organizational Justice → Trust in Supervisor → Job Satisfaction	9.13	$0.0 < \alpha=0.05$

Table 7. The Results of Bootstrap Analysis

Path	p-value ($p < \alpha=0.05$)
Mission Congruence → APAS → Job Satisfaction	$0.007 < \alpha=0.05$
Adequacy of Rewards → APAS → Job Satisfaction	$0.006 < \alpha=0.05$
Organizational Justice → APAS → Job Satisfaction	$0.003 < \alpha=0.05$
Mission Congruence → APAS → Trust in Supervisor	$0.008 < \alpha=0.05$
Adequacy of Rewards → APAS → Trust in Supervisor	$0.007 < \alpha=0.05$
Organizational Justice → APAS → Trust in Supervisor	$0.005 < \alpha=0.05$
APAS → Trust in Supervisor → Job Satisfaction	$0.005 < \alpha=0.05$
Organizational Justice → Trust in Supervisor → Job Satisfaction	$0.003 < \alpha=0.05$

Discussion and Implications

Theoretical Implications

Human resource management (HRM) functions in the public arena, especially under the rubric of new public management (NPM), have seen the radical initiation of results-oriented and market-based reforms in order to respond to cost pressures and increased attention to customer and citizen satisfaction. With emphasis on recruitment, training and development, retention, and performance of employees, these reforms have effectively served to "heighten awareness and scrutiny of the significant role HRM plays in advancing the mission and effectiveness of public agencies" and in responding to "increased competition for talent and changing worker values and expectations in federal agencies" (OPM, 2005, pp. 5-7). The topic of the current research, the acceptability of performance appraisal systems by employees in the public sector, is important because of the essential relationship of APAS with individual and organizational performance. While considerable research has investigated the antecedents and consequences of APAS, much of the existing work has centered on the acceptability of PAS in business sectors rather than in public agencies. The several theoretical and practical inquiries of this study are inspired by the notion that the success of an organization's performance appraisal system may be contingent on how employees perceive the system, and specifically, whether or not employees have positive views about the system (e.g., whether or not employees are willing to accept PAS as fair, effective, and appropriate).

The results of this study indicate that the variable of APAS is an important mediator in federal agencies in terms of increasing the trust in supervisors and job satisfaction of public employees. This study also shows that mission congruence, adequacy of rewards, and organizational justice are significantly and positively associated with APAS, and that these factors indirectly affect perceived and positive outcome variables for employees. Specifically, the confirmatory factor analysis (CFA) model illustrates that, similar to patterns in the business sector, organizational justice in federal agencies is composed of the three distinct constructs of procedural, distributive, and interpersonal justice. Organizational justice plays the most significant role in explaining the APAS of employees in federal agencies. The results suggest that the perceptions of employees about the fairness of decision-making procedures, equity in the allocation and opportunity of job assignments, training, and work-related rewards are the key sources of increasing and facilitating the level of acceptability of performance appraisal systems among employees. These findings extend the findings of previous empirical research about the relationship between organizational justice and positive organizational outcomes in government agencies (Choi, 2011; Kurland & Egan, 1999; Rubin, 2009).

Practical and Managerial Implications

This study draws both practical and managerial implications from the results of analysis. First, in order to secure the acceptance of performance appraisal systems by employees, supervisors or managers in federal agencies must be careful to treat employees fairly and to maintain a highly fair climate and culture in the workplace. This study reveals that organizational justice enhances APAS, job satisfaction, and trust in supervisors among employees. As indicated by the results, federal agencies must make considerable efforts to establish fair organizational decision-making and treatment processes, including distributive, procedural, and interpersonal aspects of justice, in overall human resource management (HRM) systems. In the past, organizations mainly focused on the fair allocation of outcomes based on merit systems. More recently, however, organizations have paid attention to the importance of procedural and interpersonal aspects of justice to improve the perceptions of employees and to enhance the overall job satisfaction of employees. This suggests that employees should be treated as human capital or assets, not as mere personnel resources, and that employees should be more positively recognized as a key aspect of running and developing any organization. A couple of reforms have recently been initiated in the public sector in order to achieve a high level of efficiency and productivity based on the principles of neo-liberalism and new public management (NPM). Some examples include adopting a merit pay system and an at-will employment system, among other systems designed to increase the job satisfaction of employees by way of perceived equity and control. While noting that efficiency is an important principle for organizational systems, we should not overlook such normative values as democratic and social equity values in public organizations.

In 2002, the Chief Human Capital Officers (CHCO) Council was established for the selection, development, training, and management of a high-quality, productive workforce. The strategy aims of the council are to coordinate the human resources systems in OPM, OMB, and other agencies, and to improve the quality of human resources information (Chief Human Capital Officers (CHCO) Council, 2008). The recent administration of President George W. Bush (2001- 2008) carried out a federal management agenda in which the "results-oriented" themes aligned more with NPM than its counterparts such as post-NPM or normative management philosophies. The endless reforms, some of which were the National Public Review, the President's Management Agenda, cutback management, and performance and human capital assessment, prompt us to question the configuration of values in the federal bureaucracy today (Park & Joaquin, 2012). Is there evidence in federal agencies that NPM's strict rationalized bureaucratization values and assumptions of self-interest and market-based values have set in? To what extent is this the case? Can we also find evidence of post-NPM ethic-based management approaches, such as social equity, democratization, and humanization, even though the enforcement of NPM reforms remains? Answers to these questions matter in terms of how NPM systems will be imbedded in positive cultural norms in federal agencies now and going forward.

Second, there should be a close correspondence between the missions of organizations and the missions of the individual employees of organizations. As previous studies have revealed, employees who experience high levels of mission congruence tend to have positive work-related attitudes. Whereas past personnel administration systems have focused on the functions of recruitment, utilization, and maintenance of the workforce, strategic human resource management (SHRM) has attempted to achieve organizational goals through the implementation of strategic workforce planning and successful management strategies in organizations (Wright, & Mcmahan, 1992). This study asserts that SHRM enhances the level of person-organization (P-O) fit, or person-culture fit, and therefore ultimately facilitates the congruence of an individual's beliefs and values with the culture and values of the organization for which the individual works. Under the SHRM rubric, in order to increase the congruence of mission, public managers should ensure that employees are drawn into the process of setting performance objectives. Increased participation in decision-making processes allows employees to accept and contribute to agency missions. For example, processes of management by objectives (MBO) and work planning review (WPR), both of which use participatory and bottom-up techniques, improve social communication, clarify job performance expectations, and enhance the commitment of employees to goal achievement. Also understood is that such strategic and participatory approaches increase the managerial accountability of employees and create horizontal, flexible, and democratic workplace environments.

Third, the results of SEM analysis show that mission congruence and organizational justice are indirectly related to job satisfaction and trust in supervisors through APAS by employees. Originally predicted in a study by Golembiewski (1995), the findings of this study further suggest that, as a key mediator, the importance of the perceptions of employees about performance appraisal systems cannot be diminished. Central to APAS is whether the established system manages to give its employees notions of fairness, clarity, and validity. That is, even though federal agencies may develop and equip the most technically sophisticated and well-designed performance appraisal instruments (especially compared to local and state agencies), if employees perceive that a system is poorly managed, then it is highly likely that the employees will not accept the PAS. Instead the PAS will be rejected as illegitimate and invalid (Gabris & Ihrke, 2000). Certainly, credible leadership enhances the possibility of positively and successfully managing performance appraisal systems in the eyes of employees in the long run.

The contribution of this research should be acknowledged in light of its limitations. Like all previous studies that investigate the relationships among perceived variables using self-reported data, this study shares the potential problems of mono-method bias and positive response bias as well as subjective measures of variables (especially dependent variables). First, the cross-sectional design does not offer clear cause-and-effect relationship examined in the present study and, thus, conclusions regarding causal connections among variables should be made with great caution. We need more qualitative studies to shed light on what happens in the federal agencies. Though we can make a number of observations here based on quantitative data, it would be greatly useful to take a closer look at the causal mechanism to know more about the roles of crucial variables such as organizational justice, APAS, and trust. Second, the individual-level analysis based on self-report data cannot avoid the common method bias. Based on Harman's single-factor test, we found that common method variance is not a huge concern in this study but future researchers must collect panel data from multiple sources, at multiple locations to reduce the potential bias.

Other relevant issues that comprise the full scope of acceptance of performance appraisal systems by employees require future research. Investigating APAS as a prerequisite for improved organizational performance and effectiveness is an example of an issue for continuing study. The varying attitudes and behaviors of employees according to different structural and cultural relationships within federal organizations warrants more rigorous and systematic research on the basis of in-depth case studies or content analyses. hose approaches may contribute to further exploration and confirmation of current idiosyncratic characteristics of discrete federal agencies (e.g., public service motivation, leadership, organizational culture and structure, person-organization fit, pay and appraisal systems, and political orientation of the agencies). The importance of APAS is not confined to the federal government. Rather, the study of APAS needs to be replicated in further research about state and local governments. Some advanced longitudinal data analyses, such as latent growth curve modeling (e.g., which can analyze whether and how the level of APAS has shifted during the period of study, and at what point the shift occurred), would also contribute to a better understanding of APAS. Given the opportunity to observe commonalties and anomalies of specific organizational phenomena, researchers would expand their knowledge of theory and practice in the field of public human resources management.

Notes

1. While there are many firm believers who invite expectancy and equity theories to underpin and justify the logics of the positive impact of perception of a performance-contingent reward system on job satisfaction, we also acknowledged that it is necessary to recognize the negative/unintentional impacts of a performance-contingent reward system (so called a merit-pay system) on organizational outcomes within a public organization (e.g., see Kellough & Lu, 1993). For example, from a practitioner's point of view, we are able to acknowledge the problems of a merit-pay system such as problems with performance appraisal, problems with funding, a weak relationship between pay and motivation.
2. As an overarching theoretical framework which explains the logic of including antecedents, mediators, and outcome variables of this study, we used the job characteristics model, designed by Hackman and Oldham (1976). The job characteristics theory is based on the idea that the task itself is a key to employee job satisfaction. Specifically, it states that there are five core job characteristics (skill variety, task identity, task significance, autonomy, and feedback) which impact three critical psychological states (experienced meaningfulness, experienced responsibility for outcomes, and knowledge of the actual results), in turn influencing work outcomes (job satisfaction, absenteeism, work motivation, etc.). Those theoretical concepts were operationalized into such variables as mission congruence, adequacy of rewards, acceptance of PA system, and trust in supervisor. Also, this study included job satisfaction as a work effectiveness outcome variable.
3. Merit Principles Survey 2005consisted of 69 questions, with 59 to be answered by all employees and 10 to be answered only by supervisory employees. Many of the questions were comprised of multiple subparts. The MPS 2005 specifically explored the performance of the Federal workforce. We analyzed the sample of 24 agencies and the responses of 36,926 Federal employees who completed the mostly online survey as part of a randomly drawn, representative sample of the 1.8 million full-time permanent members of the Federal workforce.). A random sample of 750 full-time, permanent employees was selected from each of the 24 participating agencies.

References

Adams, J. S. (1963). Toward an understanding of inequity. *Journal of Abnormal and Social Psychology*, 67, 422-436.

Adams, J. S. (1965). Inequity in social exchange. In L. Berkowitz (Ed.), *Advances in experimental social psychology:* 267-299. New York, NY: Academic Press.

Adkins, C. L., Russell, C. J., & Werbel, J. D. (1994). Judgments of fit in the selection process: The role of work value congruence. *Personnel Psychology, 47,* 605-623.

Albrecht, S. L.., & Travaglione, T. (2003). Trust in public sector senior management. *International Journal of Human Resource Management, 14,* 1-17.

Aree, s., Budhwar, P. S., & Chen, Z. X. (2002). Trust as a mediator of the relationship between organizational justice and work outcomes: Test of a social exchange model. *Journal of Organizational Behavior, 23,* 267-286.

Aree, s., Budhwar, P. S., & Chen, Z. X. (2002). Trust as a mediator of the relationship between organizational justice and work outcomes: Test of a social exchange model. *Journal of Organizational Behavior, 23,* 267-286.

Argyrsi, C. (1973). *On organizations of the future,* Sage Professional Papers: Administrative and Policy Study Series(Vol. 1, no, 03-006)

Berman, E. M., Bowman, J. S., West, J. P., & Van Wart, M. R. (2012). *Human resource management in public service: Paradoxes, Processes, and Problems.* Thousand Oaks, CA: Sage Publications.

Bies, R. J. (1987). The predicament of injustice: The management of moral outrage. In L. L. Cummings & B. M. Staw (Eds.), *Research in organizational behavior* (pp. 289-319). Greenwich, CT: JAI Press.

Blau, P. (1964). *Exchange and Power in social life.* Wiley: New York.

Bowman, J. S. (1999). Performance appraisal: Verisimilitude trumps veracity. *Public Personnel Management, 28*(4), 557-576.

Boxx, W. R., Odom, R. Y., & Dunn, M. G. (1991). Organizational values and value congruency and their impact on satisfaction, commitment, and cohesion: An empirical examination within the public sector. *Public Personnel Management, 20*(1), 195-205.

Brewer, G. A. (2006). All measures of performance are subjective: More evidence on U.S. federal agencies. In G. A. Boyne, K. J. Meier, L. J. O'Toole, Jr., & R. M. Walker (Eds.), *Public service performance: Perspectives on measurement and management* (pp. 35-54). Cambridge, UK: Cambridge University Press.

Cable, D. M., & Judge, T. A. (1996). Person-organization fit, job choice decisions, and organizational entry. *Organizational Behavior and Human Decision Processes, 67,* 294-311.

Chatman, J. A. (1991). Matching people and organizations: Selection and socialization in public accounting firms. *Administrative Science Quarterly, 36,* 459-484.

Chiang, C. F., Jang, S. C., Canter, D., & Prince, B. (2010). An expectancy theory model for hotel employee motivation: Examining the moderating role of communication satisfaction. *International Journal of Hospitality and Tourism Administration, 9*(4): 327-351.

Chief Human Capital Officers (CHCO) Council. (2008). *Annual Report to Congress FY*

2008.

Choi, S. (2010). Organizational justice and employee work attitudes: The federal case. *The American Review of Public Administration,* Published online before print August 18, 2010, doi: 10.1177/0275074010373275.

Choong Kwai Fatt, Edward Wong Sek Khin, & Tioh Ngee Heng. (2010). The impact of organizational justice on employee's job satisfaction: The Malaysian companies perspectives. *American Journal of Economics and Business Administration. 2*(1), 56-63.

Cleveland, J. N., Murphy, K. R., & Williams, R. E. (1989). Multiple uses of performance appraisal: Prevalence and Correlates. *Journal of Applied Psychology, 74*(1), 130-135.

Cohen-Charash, Y., & Spector, P. E. (2001). The role of justice in organizations: A meta-analysis. *Organizational Behavior and Human Decision Process*, 86, 278-321.

Colquitt (2001). On The Dimensionality of Organizational Justice: A Construct Validation of a Measure. *Journal of Applied Psychology,* 86(3), 386-400.

Condrey, S. E. (2002). Reinventing State Civil Service Systems: The Georgia Experience. *Review of Public Personnel Administration,* 22(2), 114-124.

Cummings, L. L. (1983). Performance-evaluation systems in context of individual trust and commitment. In F. J. Landy, S. Zedrick, & J. Cleveland (Eds.), *Performance measurement and theory:* (pp. 89-93). Hillsdale, NJ: Erlbaum.

Daley, D. M. (1993). Performance appraisal as an aid in personnel decision. *American Review of Public Administration, 23*(3), 201-213.

Danish, R. Q. (2010). Impact on reward and recognition on job satisfaction and motivation: An empirical study from Pakistan. *International Journal of Business and Management, 5*(2), 159-167.

Drucker, P. (1974). *Management: Tasks, responsibilities, practices.* New York: Harper and Row.

Erdogan, B. (1974). Antecedents and consequences of justice perceptions in performance appraisals. *Human Resources Management Review,* 12(4), 555-578.

Erez, M., & Arad, R. (1986). Participative goal setting: Social, motivational, and cognitive factors. *Journal of Applied Psychology, 71*, 591-597.

Fedor, D. B., Eder, R. W., & Buckley, M. R. (1989). The contributory effects of supervisor intentions on subordinate feedback responses. *Journal of Organizational Behavior and Human Decision Processes, 44*, 396-414.

Freyss, S. F. (2004) *Human Resource Management in Local Government: An Essential Guide* (2nd ed), Washington, DC: International City/County Management Organization.

Fritzsche, B. A., Powell, A. B., & Hoffman, R. (1999). Person-environment congruence as a predictor of customer service performance. *Journal of Vocational Behavior, 54,* 59-70.

Gabris, G. T., & Ihrke, D. M. (2000). Improving employee acceptance toward performance appraisal and merit pay systems. *Review of Public Personnel Administration,* 20:

41-53.

Golembiewski, R. T. (1995). *Managing Diversity in Organizations.* Tuscaloosa, AL: University of Alabama Press.

Goris, J. R., Vaught, B. C., & Petti Jr, J. D. (2003). Effects of trust in supervisors and influence of supervisors on the association between individual-job congruence and job performance/satisfaction. *Journal of Business and Psychology. 17*(3), 327-343.

Greenberg. (1986). Determinants of perceived fairness of performance evaluations. *Journal of Applied Psychology, 71*(2), 340-342.

Greenberg, J. (1990). Organizational justice: Yesterday, today, and tomorrow. *Journal of Management, 16,* 399-443.

Hackman, J. R., & Oldham, G. (1976). Motivation through the design of work: Test of a theory. *Organizational Behavior and Human Performance, 16, 250-279*

Herzberg, F., Mausner, B., & Snyderman, B.B. (1959). *The motivation to work.* New York: Wiley.

Hill, C. W. L. (1990). Cooperation, opportunism, and invisible hand: Implications for transactional cost theory. *Academy of Management Review, 15*, 500-513.

James, K. (1993). The social context of organizational justice: Cultural, intergroup and structural effects on justice behaviors and perceptions. In R. Cropanzano (Ed.), *Justice in the workplace: Approaching fairness in human resources management:* 21-50. Hillsdale, CT: Erlbaum.

Kellough, J. E., & Nigro, L. G. (2002). Pay for Performance in Georgia State Government: Employee Perspectives on GeorgiaGain After 5 Years. *Review of Public Personnel Administration, 22*(2), 146-166.

Kim, S. E., & Rubianty, D. (2011). Perceived fairness of performance appraisals in the federal government: Does it matter? *Review of Public Personnel Administration, 31*(4), 329-348.

Kurland, N. B., and T. D. Egan. (1999). Public v. private perceptions of formalization, outcome and justice. *Journal of Public Administration Research and Theory 9*, 437-458.

Jöreskog, K. G. (1990). New development in LISREL: Analysis of ordinal variables using polychoric correlations and weighted least squares. *Quality and Quantity, 24*, 387-404.

Kim, W. C., & Mauborgne, R. A. (1991). Implementing global strategies: The role of procedural justice. *Strategic Management Journal, 12*, 125-143.

Konovsky, M. A., & Pugh, S. D. (1994). Citizenship behavior and social exchange. *Academy of Management Journal, 37*(3), 656-669.

Kristof, A. L. (1996). Person-organization fit: An integrative review of its conceptualizations, measurement, and implications. *Personnel Psychology, 49*(1), 1-49.

Kristof-Browm, A. L., Zimmerman, R. D., & Johnson, E. C. (2005). Consequences of individuals' fit at work: A meta-analysis of person-job, person-organization, person-group, and person-supervisor fit. *Personnel Psychology,* 58: 281-342.

Lawler, E. E. (1967). The multitrait-multirater approach to measuring managerial job performance. *Journal of Applied Psychology, 51,* 369-381.

Linden, R. C., Sparrowe, R. T., Wayne, S. J. (1997). Leader-member exchange theory: the past and potential for the future. *Research in Personnel and Human Resources Management. 15,* 47-119.

Locke, E. A., & Latham, G. P. (1990). *A Theory of goal setting and task performance.* Englewood Cliffs, NJ: Prentice-Hall.

Longenecker, C. O., & Gioia, D. A., (1988). Neglected at the top: Executives talk about executive appraisal. *Sloan Management Review, Winter:* 41-47.

Mani, B. G. (2002). Performance appraisal systems, productivity, and motivation: A case study. *Public Personnel Management, 31*(2), 141-159.

Martin, D. C., & Bartol, K. M. (1998). Performance appraisal: Maintaining system effectiveness. *Public Personnel Management, 27*(2), 223-230.

Mayer, R. C., & Davis, J. H. (1999). The effect of the performance appraisal systems on trust for management: A field quasi-experiment. *Journal of Applied Psychology, 84*(1), 123-136.

McGregor, D. (1960). *The human side of enterprise.* New York: McGraw-Hill.

Moussavi, E., & Ashbaugh, D. L. (1995). Perception effects of participative, goal-oriented performance appraisal: A field study in public agencies. *Journal of Public Administration Research and Theory, 5*(3), 331-344.

Murphy, K. R., & Cleveland, J. (1995). *Understanding Performance Appraisal: Social, Organizational, and Goal-based Perspectives.* Sage Publications.

Nigro, L. G., Nigro, F. A., & Kellough, J. E. (2007). *The new public personnel administration.* Boston: Wadsworth.

Oh, S. S., & Lewis, G. B. (2009). Can performance appraisal systems inspire intrinsically motivated employees?. *Review of Public Personnel Administration, 29*(2), 158-167.

Office of Personnel Management. (2005). *HCAAF Practitioners' Guide.* HCAAF Research Center.

Park, S. M. (2011). Toward the trusted public organization: Untangling the leadership, motivation, and trust relationship in U.S. federal agencies. *The American Review of Public Administration,* DOI: 10.1177/0275074011410417

Park, S. M. & Joaquin, M. E. (2012). Of alternating waves and shifting shores: The configuration of reform values in the U.S. federal bureaucracy. *International Review of Administrative Sciences, 78*(3), 514-536.

Park, S. M., & Rainey, H. G. (2011). Work motivation and social communication among public managers. *The International Journal of Human Resource Management,* DOI: 10.1080/09585192.2011.637060

Pearce, J. L., & Perry, L. J. (1983). Federal merit pay: A longitudinal analysis. *Public Administration Review, 43,* 315-325.

Rahman, S. A. (2006). Attitudes of Malaysian teachers toward a performance-appraisal system. *Journal of Applied Social Psychology, 36*(12), 3031-3042.

Roth, P. L. (1994). Missing data: A conceptual review for applied psychologists. *Personnel Psychology, 47,* 537-560.

Rubin, E. V. (2009). The role of procedural justice in public personnel management: Empirical results from the Department of Defense. *Journal of Public Administration Research and Theory, 19,* 125-143.

Saari, L. M., & Judge, T. A. (2004). Employee attitudes and job satisfaction. *Human Resource Management, 43,* 395-407.

Saunders, Mark N. K., & Thornhill, A. (2003). Organizational justice, trust and the management of change. *Personnel Review, 32*(3), 360-375.

Tan, H. H. & Tan, C. F. (2000). Toward the differentiation of trust in supervisor and trust in organization. *Genetic, Social, and General Psychology Monographs, 126*(2), 241–260.

Taylor, M. S., Tracy, K. B., Renard, M. K., Harrison, J. K., & Carroll, S. J. (1995). Due process in performance appraisal: A quasi-experiment in procedural justice. *Administrative Science Quarterly, 40,* 495-523.

Tolman, E. C. (1938). The determinants of behavior ay a choice point. *Psychological Review, 45,* 1-41.

U.S. Merit Systems Protection Board. (2008). *The power of federal employee engagement.*

Vroom, V. H. (1964). *Work and motivation.* New York: John Wiley.

Walker, R. M. and G. A. Boyne. (2006). Public management reform and organizational performance: An empirical assessment of the UK Labour Government's public service improvement strategy." *Journal of Policy Analysis and Management, 25,* 371–394.

Wall, T. B., Michie, J., Patterson, M., Wood, S. J., Sheenhan, M., Clegg, C. W., & West, M. (2004). On the validity of subjective measures of company performance. *Personnel Psychology, 57,* 95–118.

Whisenant, W. & Smucker, M. (2009). Organizational justice and job satisfaction in coaching. *Public Organizaion Review, 9,* 157-167.

Whiting, H. J., & Kline, T. J. B. (2007). Testing a model of performance appraisal fit on attitudinal outcomes. *The Psychologist-Manager Journal, 10*(2), 127-148.

Whiting, H. J., Kline, T. J. B., & Sulsky, L. M. (2008). The performance appraisal congruency scale: an assessment of person-environment fit. *International Journal of Productivity and Performance Management, 57*(3), 223-236.

Wright, P. M. & Mcmahan, G. C. (1992). Theoretical perspectives for SHRM. *Journal of Management, 18,* 295-320.

Yang, K., & Kassekert, A. (2010). Linking management reform with employee job satisfaction: Evidence from federal agencies. *Journal of Public Administration Research and Theory, 20*(2), 413-436.

Appendix

Construction of Indices

Acceptance of Performance Appraisal Systems (APAS)

Acceptance of Performance Appraisal Systems (six items)
a. The standards used to appraise my performance are appropriate.
b. I understand what I must do to receive a high performance rating.
c. Objective measures are used to evaluate my performance.
d. I understand the basis for my most recent performance rating.
e. I am satisfied with my organization's performance appraisal system.
f. I participate in setting standards and goals used to evaluate my job performance.

Antecedents of APAS

1. Mission Congruency (three items)
a. I understand my agency's mission.
b. My agency's mission is important to me.
c. I understand how I contribute to my agency's mission.

2. Adequacy of Rewards (four items)
a. I am satisfied with the recognition and rewards I receive for my work.
b. If I perform well, it is likely I will receive a cash reward or pay increase.
c. Overall, I am satisfied with my pay.
d. My organization takes steps to ensure that employees are appropriately paid and rewarded.

3. Justice (twelve items)

1) Procedural Justice (three items)
a. I believe that the current employment appeals system, if I had occasion to use it, would be fair.
b. I believe that the current employment grievance system, if I had occasion to use it, would be fair.
c. I trust third party investigative or adjudicatory agencies (such as the OSC, EEOC, FLRA, MSPB) to respond appropriately to complaints.

2) Distributive Justice (four items)

In the past 2 years, to what extent do you believe you have been treated fairly regarding the following?

a. Fairly - Discipline
b. Fairly - Training
c. Fairly - Job assignments
d. Fairly - Career advancement

3) Interpersonal Justice (five items)

To what extent do you think your supervisor (Sup) will exercise each of the following authorities in a fair and effective manner?

a. Sup Fair - Rating the qualifications of applicants for jobs.
b. Sup Fair - Selecting people for vacancies or promotions based on their qualifications.
c. Sup Fair - Determining pay increases and rewards.
d. Sup Fair – Setting the pay of individual employees within broad pay bands.
e. Sup Fair - Taking adverse actions such as suspensions and removals.

Consequences of APAS

1. Job satisfaction (five items)

a. I am able to openly express concerns at work.
b. My opinions count at work.
c. I am treated with respect at work.
d. In general, I am satisfied with my job.
e. I would recommend my agency as a place to work.

2. Trust in supervisor (eight items)

I trust my supervisor (Sup) to:

a. Trust Sup - Fairly assess my performance and contributions.
b. Trust Sup - Support me in pay and reward discussions with upper management.
c. Trust Sup - Listen fairly to my concerns.
d. Trust Sup - Apply discipline fairly and only when justified.
e. Trust Sup - Clearly communicate conduct expectations.
f. Trust Sup - Act with integrity.
g. Trust Sup - Refrain from favoritism.
h. Trust Sup - Keep me informed.

Case Study

Why Bosses Should be Careful When Using Performance-Related Pay

Gray Becker

Of all a firm's inputs, its workers' effort is perhaps the oddest. It is as vital as land, factories or machines, but much harder to control. It is often impossible even to measure. A manager can gauge the firm's output, but not the effort people put in, beyond crude gauges such as the time they spend on the job. Employees have the informational edge, knowing their own effort, output and skill level. This asymmetry makes it hard for managers to distinguish, for instance, between the low-skilled but diligent and the skilled but lazy. Monitoring schemes to reward hard-working employees and punish slackers can boost effort, but they can backfire badly, too.

What should firms do? A good place to start is with the worst kind of behaviour: crime. In a paper published in 1968 Gary Becker, of the University of Chicago, set out the factors which policymakers should consider when deciding on what resources they should devote to detection. In his model criminals calculate the risks and benefits of bad behaviour, taking into account the possible monetary reward, the probability of being caught and the subsequent punishment. To cut crime authorities must increase the probability of being caught, the severity of the punishment, or both. This approach can also be applied to less extreme forms of bad behaviour, such as slow or sloppy work: firms may have to monitor individual workers, and then reward the good and punish the bad.

But a system like this comes with costs. People do not work hard for money alone. They also have other motives, such as doing a good job. In a 1971 paper Edward Deci, of Rochester University, tested the effect that external rewards—cash bonuses or fines—have on such "intrinsic" motivation. Two groups were given a 3D puzzle and asked to create a variety of shapes. Because the puzzle was fun and mentally taxing, intrinsic motivation was high. One group, left to proceed at its own pace, worked hard. A second group was monitored, and given a $1 reward for each shape that was successfully replicated. This payment was later withdrawn, with the result that the second group now put in less effort than the first. Its members switched off, turning instead to Playboy or the New Yorker. Monetary rewards, Mr Deci reasoned, had killed their intrinsic motivation.

Watching workers closely can have other drawbacks. Setting up an incentive scheme for a particular task costs time and money. And it reveals something about the task: that it is important for a firm's success and considered difficult. In a 2003 study Roland Bénabou, of Princeton University, and Jean Tirole, of Toulouse University, showed how this can lead employees to work more slowly. Efforts might simply shift from speed to accuracy.

The effects of monitoring may be even worse if "reciprocity" is taken into account. Matthew Rabin, of the University of California, Berkeley, explored this concept in a paper in 1993. People with a strong sense of fairness like to help those whom they perceive as helpful. But the flip side is that they will punish those they see as being unhelpful. So a monopolist charging rip-off prices may be shunned, even if the shopper really wants the product. Similarly, an unfair boss may be punished with bad work, even if this hurts the worker too.

If monitoring has both benefits and costs, what is the right level? Michèle Belot, of Edinburgh University, and Marina Schröder, of Magdeburg University, have devised a test. They gave volunteers boxes containing €780 ($1,010) in coins and asked them to separate these into different types. The job is trickier than it sounds, because the euro zone has 160 different types of coin: eight values, from one cent to €2, in 20 designs, one for each of the zone's 17 members plus Monaco, San Marino and the Vatican. The task, for which volunteers were paid €20, has some clever properties. First, it can be completed perfectly with effort but not much skill (time pressure was minimal and volunteers were allowed to take the boxes home). Second, bad work can be measured and comes in several forms. The coins could be badly sorted. The box could be returned late. And the coins might be stolen: the boxes contained Vatican coins which are worth more to collectors than their face value. By replacing a 50-cent piece from the Vatican (worth around €3 in online auctions) with a regular 50-cent coin, the volunteer could net €2.50.

High bar or no bar

The researchers tested different configurations of monitoring and rewards. A control group was not supervised at all and paid immediately regardless of performance. Two other groups were watched, and rewarded according to their performance. The first scheme was pretty lax: workers lost just €1 for every ten mistakes. The second was much harsher: the payment was cut by €15 if more than two coins were wrongly identified.

The results suggest that lax monitoring is a bad option: 30% of volunteers made more than ten mistakes—worse than the group with no supervision. On top of this, late returns increased. This means that the resources devoted to monitoring were wasted. The stricter regime, however, did offer some benefits. Accuracy improved, with only 16% of volunteers making more than ten mistakes. But some also shifted their effort, working more slowly and handing the coins in late. Neither system had any effect on theft: in all three groups one in ten volunteers stole coins.

In economics opting for the middle ground is usually best. But in this case the extremes seem to be a better choice: monitor hard, or do not monitor at all. A little bit of monitoring only annoys the good workers, causing them to slacken off. And sometimes the wisest thing is just to let people get on with the job.

Source: The Economist (2013.05.25)

Case Study

No More Sticks and Carrots

Constance Alexander

The art and science of motivating others is one of the world's oldest professions and one of the most misunderstood, but if you take the time to read the work of Daniel Pink, you will discover valuable research on motivation that makes sense in the workplace, the classroom, the community, and even at home.

In his 2009 book, "Drive: The Surprising Truth About What Motivates Us," Pink addresses some of the most common motivational practices and explains why they don't work in situations that demand innovation, critical thinking and rigorous analysis.

Pink cites an MIT study that boggled top economists' minds regarding financial rewards meted out for performance. When the task was mechanical, Pink reports, the carrot-and-stick approach to motivation worked, but if the task required creativity or in-depth thinking, large rewards actually led to poorer outcomes.

In a TED Talk about motivation, Pink declares that our assumptions about motivation, as applied in the carrot-stick construct, are outdated, unexamined, and rooted in folklore. Rather than continuing to follow the well-worn path of reward and punishment, he suggests a new approach, one that is built around intrinsic motivation instead of extrinsic rewards.

Now stay with me here, even if you're a tad skeptical. Just think about it. Intrinsic motivation, which relies on autonomy, mastery and purpose, is desirable when you want people to be engaged in a task and to perform at a high level.

One powerful example is an Australian software company that instituted something they called FEDEX days. That means that once a quarter, in one 24-hour period, engineers are permitted to work on something that interests them, that captures their imagination. The only hitch is that they have to report back in 24 hours on what they came up with or what they did.

A similar concept was applied at Google, and a raft of new products emerged from the process.

Imagine if this approach were applied in the classroom, a place where many of us spent our least engaging hours growing up. Succeeding in that environment typically meant blind compliance, rote memorization, grinding out answers the teacher expected. The reward was an A, a spot on the honor roll, a transcript that would catch the eye of a good college.

That spoon-fed construct works fine as long as you know what the problem is, but connecting information or facts to real world situations demands figuring things out, finding out what the problem actually is before offering solutions.

Source: Murray Ledger & Times (2013.05.23)

Questions for Discussion

1. Are there stereotypes about motivation of public employees? What are they? Do you think they are true? What are some of the assertions about the context for motivation in public organizations? How valid and accurate are these assertions, in your view?

2. Is motivation the only determinant of an individual's performance? What other factors are important? What is the difference between extrinsic and intrinsic incentives? Provide examples of both in the context of your place of work (or your motivation to perform well at school).

3. Herbert Simon made the following statement with regard to incentives: "Everything . . . about economic rewards applies equally to privately owned, nonprofit, and government owned corporations. The opportunity for, limits on, the use of rewards to motivate activities towards organizational goals are precisely the same in all three kinds of organizations" (1995: 283, n. 3). Drawing on key readings and ideas in this chapter and in previous chapters, develop a counter argument. If possible, use examples and/or provide evidentiary support for your position.

4. Interview a person working in a public organization, a private organization, and a non-profit organization to find out what motivated them to seek their jobs. Responses can be compared to research in public service motivation cited in this book.

5. Identify the five core dimensions and three critical psychological states in the Job Characteristics Model and explain the causal path suggested by Hackman and Oldham. How can knowledge of motivation theory help managers who are recruiting employees from diverse cultures?